Frommer's®

Panama

1st Edition

by Kristina Schreck

Wiley Publishing, Inc.

About the Author

Kristina Schreck has traveled extensively throughout Latin America and has lived and worked in Argentina and Chile for 8 years. She is the former managing editor of *Adventure Journal* magazine. Kristina currently resides in Santiago and the Andes, where she works year-round for Ski Portillo.

Published by:

Wiley Publishing, Inc.

111 River St.
Hoboken, NJ 07030-5774

SBN: 978-0-470-04890-0

itor: Matthew Brown
duction Editor: Suzanna R. Thompson
ographer: Andrew Murphy
Editor: Richard Fox
rsary Logo Design: Richard Pacifico
ion by Wiley Indianapolis Composition Services

er photo: Kuna Indian woman, surrounded by colorful textiles and fabrics
photo: Bocas del Toro Islands: Restaurant over the water

ion on our other products and services or to obtain technical support, please
ustomer Care Department within the U.S. at 800/762-2974, outside the
2-3993 or fax 317/572-4002.

shes its books in a variety of electronic formats. Some content that
ay not be available in electronic formats.

e United States of America

Contents

9 Bocas del Toro Archipelago   255

10 Comarca Kuna Yala   282

11 The Darién Province   293

Appendix A: Panama in Depth   300

Appendix B: Glossary of Spanish Terms & Phrases   309

Appendix C: Panamanian Wildlife   313

with assistance from E. Z. Weaver

Index   332

List of Maps

An Invitation to the Reader

In researching this book, we discovered many wonderful places—hotels, restaurants, shops, and more. We're sure you'll find others. Please tell us about them, so we can share the information with your fellow travelers in upcoming editions. If you were disappointed with a recommendation, we'd love to know that, too. Please write to:

Frommer's Panama, 1st Edition
Wiley Publishing, Inc. • 111 River St. • Hoboken, NJ 07030-5774

An Additional Note

Please be advised that travel information is subject to change at any time—and this is especially true of prices. We therefore suggest that you write or call ahead for confirmation when making your travel plans. The authors, editors, and publisher cannot be held responsible for the experiences of readers while traveling. Your safety is important to us, however, so we encourage you to stay alert and be aware of your surroundings. Keep a close eye on cameras, purses, and wallets, all favorite targets of thieves and pickpockets.

Other Great Guides for Your Trip:

Frommer's Costa Rica

Frommer's Costa Rica For Dummies

Frommer's South America

Frommer's Belize

Frommer's Mexico

Frommer's Star Ratings, Icons & Abbreviations

Every hotel, restaurant, and attraction listing in this guide has been ranked for quality, value, service, amenities, and special features using a **star-rating system.** In country, state, and regional guides, we also rate towns and regions to help you narrow down your choices and budget your time accordingly. Hotels and restaurants are rated on a scale of zero (recommended) to three stars (exceptional). Attractions, shopping, nightlife, towns, and regions are rated according to the following scale: zero stars (recommended), one star (highly recommended), two stars (very highly recommended), and three stars (must-see).

In addition to the star-rating system, we also use **seven feature icons** that point you to the great deals, in-the-know advice, and unique experiences that separate travelers from tourists. Throughout the book, look for:

Finds	Special finds—those places only insiders know about
Fun Fact	Fun facts—details that make travelers more informed and their trips more fun
Kids	Best bets for kids and advice for the whole family
Moments	Special moments—those experiences that memories are made of
Overrated	Places or experiences not worth your time or money
Tips	Insider tips—great ways to save time and money
Value	Great values—where to get the best deals

The following **abbreviations** are used for credit cards:

AE	American Express	DISC	Discover	V	Visa
DC	Diners Club	MC	MasterCard		

Frommers.com

Now that you have this guidebook to help you plan a great trip, visit our website at **www.frommers.com** for additional travel information on more than 3,500 destinations. We update features regularly to give you instant access to the most current trip-planning information available. At Frommers.com, you'll find scoops on the best airfares, lodging rates, and car rental bargains. You can even book your travel online through our reliable travel booking partners. Other popular features include:

- Online updates of our most popular guidebooks
- Vacation sweepstakes and contest giveaways
- Newsletters highlighting the hottest travel trends
- Online travel message boards with featured travel discussions

The Best of Panama

For such a thin squiggle of land, Panama offers travelers a surprisingly diverse selection of landscapes, cultures, and experiences. In Panama City alone, modern skyscrapers contrast with 18th-century architecture, and a 10-minute cab ride from downtown puts you deep in rainforest teeming with wildlife. From the cool, fertile highlands in the Chiriquí region to the thick lowland jungle and white-sand beaches of Panama's tropical islands, this tiny nation allows you to pack a lot of fun and adventure into a short period of time. Also, unlike Costa Rica, its more popular neighbor, Panama boasts a rich history and a melting pot of cultures, including seven indigenous groups, many of whom maintain their customs today. Best of all, the country is gloriously free of tourists—but get here soon because Panama is far too attractive to be kept a secret for long.

The following is a list of the best that Panama has to offer, including hotels, natural areas, adventures, restaurants, and more, but expect new places to appear soon as tourism explodes and more travelers discover this fascinating crossroads of the world.

1 The Best of Natural Panama

- **Metropolitan Park** (Panama City): Panama City is the only metropolis that boasts a tropical rainforest within its city limits. Travelers with ample time will want to visit national parks like Soberanía, but there's no denying the appeal of hopping in a cab and, within 10 minutes, exchanging the city streets for a steamy jungle teeming with wildlife. See p. 121.

- **Soberanía National Park** (near Panama City): This national park is very accessible from Panama City—just 40 minutes by car—yet it feels worlds away. The undulating, pristine rainforest that defines Soberanía is protected in part because it acts as a watershed that provides the water to keep the canal in operation. What's unique about the park is that wildlife species from North and South America and migratory birds meet here,

creating a hyper-diverse natural wonderland. A series of nature trails here include the historic Camino de Cruces, which links the two coasts, as well as the famous Pipeline Road, a trail revered by bird-watchers for the more than 500 species of birds that live in the area. See p. 140.

- **Volcán Barú National Park** (Chiriquí Highlands): The rugged, 3,505m (11,500-ft.) Barú Volcano, the highest point in the country, is this national park's centerpiece and a "bioclimatic island." It's home to a wild, dense rainforest packed with bamboo gardens and towering trees dripping with vines and sprouting bromeliads and orchids from their trunks and branches. In higher reaches, an intermittent cloud forest evokes an eerie, prehistoric ambience. The park is very popular with bird-watchers, who come to glimpse the famous resplendent quetzal. One of the most enjoyable full-day hikes in Panama is here along the Quetzal Trail, which links the towns of Guadalupe/Cerro Punta with Boquete, and the crystalline rivers that descend from the volcano provide thrilling white-water rafting. On a clear day, hikers can see both oceans from the summit of the volcano. See p. 230.

- **La Amistad International Park** (Chiriquí Highlands): Like Isla Coiba, UNESCO rated this park a World Heritage Site because it is one of the most biodiverse regions in the Americas. The park is "international" because half of it is in Costa Rica, and it's managed by both nations. Characterized by virgin forests, La Amistad's rugged Talamanca Range is home to more than 400 species of birds and 100 species of mammals, many of them endangered. The park is mostly inaccessible, except near Cerro Punta, where there are several outstanding walking trails suitable for all ability levels, and enjoyable rain or shine. See p. 222.

- **The Darién Wilderness** (Darién Province): This tremendous swath of forest and swampland is considered to be one of the last untouched wilderness regions in the Americas. Even the Darién National Park is largely inaccessible, and the surrounding wilderness is so thick that the "missing link" of the Pan-American Highway, known as the Darién Gap, is here. If you like your nature ruggedly wild and remote, this is your place. The Darién is rated as a world-class bird-watching site for its flocks of colorful macaws, among other showcase species, but you'll need to join a tour and grab a chartered flight to the Cana Field Station. See p. 293.

- **Isla Coiba National Park** (Chiriquí Gulf): Formerly the site of an infamous penal colony for Panama's worst criminals, Isla Coiba is now an untouched paradise for divers, snorkelers, and nature lovers. The national park and UNESCO World Heritage Site protects 38 pristine islands and marine waters so rich in diversity that the area is commonly referred to as the Galápagos Islands of Panama. Isla Coiba boasts the second-largest coral reef in the eastern Pacific, and its waters teem with huge schools of colorful fish, hammerhead and nurse sharks, dolphins, manta rays, tuna, turtles, whales, and other gigantic marine species—even saltwater crocodiles. See p. 248.

- **The Kuna Yala Comarca:** This tropical island paradise, with more than 350 idyllic islands and islets ringed in white sand, coral gardens, and mangrove swamps, is often populated with not much more than slender coconut palms and a few thatch-roofed huts of the Kuna indigenous community. Given the lack of modern development in the region, the views here are not marred by towering hotels and resorts, allowing the natural beauty of the Comarca to shine through. Along the coast, some of Panama's wildest jungle can be explored on hikes arranged by local tour guides, but most visitors come just to soak in the warm breeze and cool turquoise waters. See p. 282.

2 The Best Beaches

In spite of the hundreds of kilometers of coastline on both the Caribbean Sea and Pacific Ocean, Panama's beaches are less than noteworthy. The coastal area surrounding Panama City is mud flats; farther west the sand is dark and the water dirty-green until you reach the pretty beaches at Santa Clara and Farallón. The

Azuero Peninsula and parts of the Caribbean coast are, sadly, receptacles for trash carried by currents from South America and beyond. There are a few exceptions, but to find glorious tropical beaches, you'll need to visit Panama's islands. There are more than 1,000 on the Pacific Side and a little more than half that number on the Caribbean, so you have a lot to choose from. *A word of caution:* Panama is renowned for its riptides. No matter how refreshing the water looks, analyze conditions, stay out of choppy water, or head to a beach known for calm water.

- **Comarca Kuna Yala:** This is *the* premier beach destination in Panama, with 350 islands scattered off the Caribbean coast that offer picture-postcard beaches with powdery white sand, coral reef, piercing turquoise water, and clusters of swaying palm trees. The colorful Kuna indigenous population administers this province, and their fascinating culture is part of the reason to visit the region, too. The glitch is that scuba diving is prohibited, and lodging is mostly Robinson Crusoe rustic, but all you'll want to do here anyway is swim, sun, and swing in a hammock. See p. 282.

- **Isla Bastimentos National Park, Bocas del Toro:** Cayos Zapatillas, or the "Slippers Islands" (so-called because they resemble footprints), not only fulfill the beach lover's fantasy with their soft sand backed by a tangle of jungle; they are also surrounded by a rich display of coral that attracts hordes of fish, providing good snorkeling. The park's main island, Isla Bastimentos, offers terrific beaches with clean sand and blue water, such as **Red Frog Beach, Wizard Beach,** and **Playa Larga,** which can be reached by a short walk or hike, or by boat during the calm-water season from August through October. See p. 275.

- **Santa Clara & Farallón, Pacific Coast:** These two are the most beautiful beaches, and the best for swimming, that lie within a 2-hour drive of Panama City. The beaches' water is bluer and the sand cleaner and whiter that of its neighbors closer to the city. The Decameron Resort produces throngs of beachgoers at Farallón, but for the most part this long stretch of sand sees few crowds outside of weekends. Self-catering cabins, midrange bungalows, and seafood restaurants are abundant. See p. 181.

- **Las Perlas Archipelago:** Despite this Pacific archipelago's proximity to Panama City, its top-notch snorkeling, white-sand beaches, and calm-water swimming conditions, the Pearl Islands are a relatively unsung beach destination. Outside of holidays and the hard-core summer, you won't find crowds here, even during weekends. It's also drier here during the rainy season. **Isla Contadora** offers lodging and day trips for fabulous snorkeling and visits to uninhabited beaches, and there is a luxury lodge, **Hacienda San José,** on Isla San José.

- **Isla Coiba National Park:** Beyond ranking as Panama's number-one diving site, Isla Coiba National Park boasts fine beaches backed by dense jungle. Tiny islands such as **Granito de Oro** are so idyllic that midsize cruise ships make a stop here (which could spoil your day if you're here independently). Even the beach fronting the park station seems too perfect to be true. See p. 248.

- **Las Lajas, Chiriquí Province:** It's not the most beautiful beach in Panama, but the water is the perfect temperature, and produces just the right amount of waves for bodysurfing—though there's little current. All of which means that Las Lajas is ideal for swimming, and since the beach measures more than 13km (8 miles) in length, you can walk forever. Rustic shacks and cheap restaurants are clustered on the beach at the end of the road, but it's best to bring your own snacks. If you're looking for a beach closer to David (and Boquete), try **La Barqueta.** Strong currents at this black-sand beach mean the water is not ideal for swimming, but it is lengthy like Las Lajas and good for walking, and there is a nature reserve here, too. See p. 215.

- **Playa Los Destiladores & Playa Venado, Azuero Peninsula:** Of the multitude of beaches lining the coast of the Azuero Peninsula, these two are the cleanest and the most attractive, and they are within a 20-minute drive from each other. However, given the deforestation in the area, they are less "tropical" than other Panamanian beaches. Currents will occasionally churn up the water along the golden sand at Playa Destiladores, but a protected cove at Playa Venado means it's calm enough for a toddler, and farther east crashing waves have converted the beach into a surfing hot spot. A major bonus here is the nearby picturesque town of Pedasí, and three gorgeous lodges. See p. 203.

3 The Best Adventures

- **White-water Rafting & Kayaking the Chiriquí and Chiriquí Viejo Rivers:** Depending on which section you raft, these two rivers produce serious white-water ranging from technical Class III to Class V, some portions of which are so difficult they've been named "Fear" and "Get Out if You Can." There are plenty of tamer floats on Class II rivers, such as the Esti, for families and beginners. Virtual solitude, beautiful views, and lush surroundings are part of the tour, too. Contact **Chiriquí River Rafting** (© 720-1505; www.panama-rafting.com) in Boquete or, for kayaking, **Panama Rafters** (© 720-2712; www.panamarafters.com). See p. 232.

- **Zipping through the Treetops on a Canopy Adventure:** It's all the rage in Costa Rica, and now Panama has joined in to offer this adrenaline-fueled and exhilarating adventure. Participants climb high to a treetop platform, where they are strapped into a harness and then descend quickly using a pulley attached to a cable. Part of the experience is observing wildlife, mostly birds, from different vantage points in the forest. Both **Canopy Adventure** (© 264-5720; www.canopylodge.com), in El Valle, and **Boquete Tree Trek** (© 720-1635; www.canopypanama.com), in Boquete, offer canopy rides. See p. 184.

- **Surfing Bocas del Toro:** There are plenty of surfing hot spots along the Pacific Coast, especially at Santa Catalina, but Bocas is where surfers find everything from beginner-friendly waves to monster, Hawaii-style waves that reach more than 6m (20 ft.). What's special about Bocas, too, is that the water is clear blue, allowing you to see the reef as you race over it, and there are lots of lodging options, restaurants, and thumping nightlife, unlike in Santa Catalina. Another perk is that the Caribbean tides fluctuate only .9m (3 ft.), whereas the Pacific's fluctuate five times that amount. The waves here are powerful beach breaks, and long, barreling reef point breaks; for organized tours, contact **Panama Surf Tours** (© 6671-7777; www.panamasurftours.com). See p. 253.

- **Diving around Isla Coiba:** This national park only recently opened to the traveling public—a notorious penal colony that closed here in 2004 kept tourists away, and now the park's virgin waters rate as *the* best diving site in Panama. Isla Coiba is often described as the Galápagos Islands of Panama, and although the snorkeling is outstanding, diving gets you close to pelagics such as white-tipped sharks, sailfish, turtles, manta rays, dolphins, and so much more. Coiba is home to one of the largest coral reefs in the Pacific Coast of the Americas. Day excursions involve a minimum of 3 hours round-trip to get here, which is why many multiday excursions include onboard lodging, or at the park ranger's cabins on the island. See p. 246.

- **Trekking the Camino Real:** Centuries before the Panama Canal, the Spanish built a 80km (50-mile) cobblestone path to transport looted gold from the Pacific to galleons waiting in the Caribbean Sea. You can trace their path, much of which still exists in stone, in about 3 days, beginning with a canoe ride up the Chagres River, an overnight in an Emberá Indian Village, and a tramp through earthy jungle full of birds and wildlife to Nombre de Dios, near Portobelo. Lodging is in tents, and the return trip is by railroad to give you an idea of how revolutionary the railroad's construction was to increasing coastal access. **Ancon Expeditions** (© 269-9415; www.anconexpeditions.com) is the company to call. See p. 148.

- **Reeling in a Billfish off the Pacific Coast:** Panama's Pacific Coast is legendary for sport fishing, and anglers can battle monster species such as marlin, sailfish, and tuna in the Gulf of Chiriquí and the Gulf of Panama.

Near Piñas Bay, the **Tropic Star Lodge** has broken more International Game and Fish Association world records than anywhere else on the planet. There are a handful of fishing lodges at Boca Chica, near David, and as many live-aboard fishing operations that use charter yachts or barges as home base. Check out "Fishing" in chapter 4.

- **Kayaking in the Kuna Yala Comarca:** Considering that diving is prohibited in the Kuna Yala, kayaking fills the "sports void," and offers travelers a way to intimately explore the mangrove swamps and the undeveloped beauty of the tiny islands this region is famous for. Along the way, kayakers stop at traditional Kuna communities for cultural tours, land-based hiking, and snorkeling. **Xtrop** (© 317-1279; www.xtrop.com), or "Expediciones Tropicales," is the company to call; they are a well-respected company and the only outfitters with special permission from the Kuna chief to kayak in the Kuna Yala. They employ local guides. See p. 287.

- **Bird-Watching by Dugout Canoe on the Mogue River** (Darién Wilderness): The tour outfitter Ancon Expeditions offers a bird-watching and nature adventure near Punta Patiño that takes travelers up the Mogue River in a motorized dugout canoe, winding past dry forest and ancient mangrove swamps for an absolutely authentic jungle experience. From here, it's off to find the harpy eagle, Panama's national bird, and then spend the night with Emberá Indians in one of their rustic communities. For more information, contact Ancon at (© 269-9415; www.anconexpeditions.com). See p. 297.

4 The Best Day Hikes & Nature Walks

- **The Quetzal Trail** (Volcán Barú National Park): Panama's foremost day hike takes visitors around the northeastern flank of Volcán Barú and through primary and secondary tropical forest and cloud forest that provides a dazzling array of flora and fauna. The trail's namesake resplendent quetzal lives here, too. The trail is mostly downhill from the Cerro Punta side to Boquete, and is the recommended direction unless you really crave a workout. What's unique about this trek is that travelers lodging around Cerro Punta can send their luggage to their next hotel in Boquete, and walk there. See p. 221.

- **Walk to Pirre Mountain** (Darién National Park): This is a serious jungle trail, located in one of the most remote wildernesses in Central America. Pirre Mountain rises above the Cana Field Station in the Darién National Park, and is a moderate-to-difficult trail beloved by nature enthusiasts and bird-watchers for its dense concentration of fauna. Howler monkeys, spider monkeys, sloths, even snakes are easily and frequently spotted, but just as exciting is the wild sensation that comes from the magnificent jungle surrounding you. At the peak's summit, there is a lookout point with sweeping views. See p. 297.

- **Pipeline Road** (Soberanía National Park): As mentioned elsewhere, Pipeline is a bird-watcher's haven, but this trail also provides outstanding opportunities to see wildlife and just to delve into steamy, wild jungle. The farther you walk or bike, the better your chances of seeing monkeys, coatimundis, sloths, and other mammals. The best time to go is early morning, before 9am if possible, when birds and animals are most active. See p. 140.

- **Finca Suiza** (on the road between Almirante and David): The Swiss owners of this tiny ranch-style hostel offer some of the best hiking trails in Panama, both for beauty and because they are so well-maintained and marked. There are three loop trails that connect with one another; all are moderate to difficult but worth the initial climb for the expansive views of the coast and lowlands of the Pacific, and into the peaks of Costa Rica. The trails pass through verdant rainforest, and there are waterfalls with bathing pools for taking a dip. You can visit for the day, or bunk in their simple but attractive rooms (© 6615-3774; www.panama.net. tc). See p. 244.

- **La Amistad International Park** (Chiriquí Highlands): Visitors here can walk a quick 15-minute easy path near the ranger station, or an hourlong (but still easy) path through bamboo gardens and thick jungle, and past clear-water creeks. Another 2-hour hike takes visitors to a series of lookout points with mountain and valley views, and a crashing 49m (160-ft.) waterfall; a detour here to a lookout point offers a view that stretches to the Caribbean. Gung-ho hikers can hack through a narrow trail up to a peak for a coast-to-coast view. Finish it off with a delicious lunch at the local co-op cafe near the ranger station. See p. 222.

5 The Best Bird-Watching

- **Watching Macaws in Flight Over the Forests of Darién National Park:** Few places in the world rival the Darién National Park for bird-watching. The .5 million hectares (1.3 million acres) of rainforest here provide a home for four species of macaws, including blue and gold, red and green, great green, and chestnut-fronted. These noisy and colorful birds sail over the **Cana Field Station,** a converted research facility and bird-watcher's sanctuary run by **Ancon Expeditions** (© 269-9415; www.anconexpeditions.com); they'll take you up Pirre Mountain, where, if you're lucky, you'll glimpse the golden-headed quetzal. Also expect to see a rainbow of tanagers, toucans, oropendolas, and black-tipped cotingas. See p. 297.

- **Looking for More Than 500 Species of Birds Along Pipeline Road in Soberanía National Park:** This is the "celebrity" bird-watching trail for the immense number of species found here. In fact, for several years Pipeline Road has set the world record for 24-hour bird counts. Even non-birders can't help getting caught up in the action with so many colorful show birds fluttering about, such as mot mots, trogons, toucans, antbirds, colorful tanagers, and flycatchers. The farther you walk or bike along the rainforest trail, the better your chances of spotting rare birds. Contact **Advantage Tours** 🐦🐦 (© 6676-2466; www.advantagepanama.com); Guido Berguido can provide you with a bird-watching tour. See p. 66.

- **Catching Sight of the Resplendent Quetzal in the Cloud Forests of the Chiriquí Highlands:** The iridescent green resplendent quetzal is widely considered to be the most beautiful bird in the Americas, and it was revered by the Aztecs and the Mayans. Today bird-watchers are the ones who marvel at a sighting, especially of the male quetzal for his breeding plumage and tail feathers that can reach nearly .6m (2 ft.). Nonbirders, too, can't help getting caught up in the excitement of seeing a quetzal. From December to May, the best place to see a quetzal is in the cloud forests of **Volcán Barú National Park,** but if you want a near guarantee that you'll see one, head to **Finca Lérida** (© 720-2285; www.fincalerida.com) in Boquete and have them book the bird-watching guide **Santiago "Chago" Caballero** (© 6626-2200; santiagochagotours@hotmail.com) or one of his protégés—they're the best in the quetzal-spotting business. See p. 230.

- **Being Taken Aback by the Size of the Harpy Eagle in Punta Patiño Nature Reserve:** The harpy eagle is Panama's national bird and one of the largest eagles in the world, with a wingspan that can reach more than 1.8m (6 ft.). You can't help being struck by this creature's size, though now that they've made the endangered list, they're not the easiest bird to spot. Head to Punta Patiño, and your chances soar. **Ancon Expeditions** (© 269-9415; www.anconexpeditions.com) has a lodge here and organizes bird-watching trips. Short on time? Visit the harpy eagles at **Summit Gardens Park & Zoo** © 232-4850; www.summitpanama.org), near Panama City. See p. 144.

- **Grabbing a Cab to View 200+ Species in the Metropolitan Park:** Panama City's Metropolitan Park is the only protected tropical forest found within the city limits of a major urban area in the Americas—a 10-minute cab ride and you're there, checking out orange-billed sparrows, green honeycreepers, rufous and white wrens, and thrush tanagers, among more than 200 other species. Head to the top of the Cerro Mono Titi hilltop to view canopy birds down the slope, not to mention a pretty spectacular view of the city. See p. 121.

- **Discovering Trogons, Blue Cotingas, and Chestnut-Mandible Toucans on the Little-Known Achiote Road:** The Atlantic Coast village of Achiote, about a 1½-hour drive from Panama City, is quietly revered as a bird-watching mecca by those in the know—the Audubon Society holds their Atlantic Christmas Bird Count here and has counted up to 390 species in a single day. Also fluttering around Achiote are orange-chinned parakeets, barbets, and flocks of swallowtail kites. Check out their website at **www.panamaaudubon.org** to see if they've got any day trips planned to the area. See p. 150.

- **Delving Into the World of Bird-Watching at the Canopy Lodge or Canopy Tower:** These two lodges live and breathe bird-watching, with day trips, viewing platforms, expert guides, and a fully stocked bird-watcher's library. The lodges are located in prime bird-watching spots in Soberanía National Park and the cloud-forest foothills of Valle de Antón (© 264-5720 or 6687-0291; www.canopytower.com). See p. 145.

6 The Best Destinations for Families

- **Panama City:** If you're using Panama City as a base for day excursions to the Canal Zone, the **Country Inn & Suites Causeway** (© 211-4501) is a good bet for families for its safe, quiet location, outdoor pools, bicycle rental, and long walking/jogging shoreline path that connects with the Amador Causeway. On the causeway, visit the **Smithsonian's Marine Exhibit Center** (© 212-8793) to view and touch sea creatures. Kids and adults get a kick out of seeing the colorful **Mercado de Mariscos (Fish Market),** and kids like the **Kuna Cooperative,** where Kuna women affix their traditional beaded bands to the arms and legs of tourists. See p. 124.

- **The Canal Zone:** The Panama Canal, Lake Gatún, and the surrounding rainforest overflow with kid-friendly activities, and parents can either base themselves in Panama City or at **Gamboa Rainforest Resort** (Gamboa; © 877/800-1690), a kid-pleaser for its swimming pools, games center, butterfly farm, reptile displays, and aerial tram. Families can also rent a bicycle for a ride up the Pipeline Road to view wildlife and birds. See p. 145.

- **Jungle Adventure Cruises:** Half-day jungle cruises are fun for families because of wildlife sightings, and also because cruises put participants shockingly close to massive tankers crossing the Panama Canal. Cruises visit Monkey Island, where it is almost guaranteed you'll see four different species; also keep an eye out for capybaras, crocodiles, and sloths. Gamboa Rainforest Resort has their own tour, or try **Ancon Expeditions** (© 269-9415) for their fun guides. See p. 142.

- **Summit Garden & Zoo** (near Panama City; © 232-4850): Wildlife is notorious for shying away from humans, but you can view jaguars, monkeys, tapirs, harpy eagles, and other species endemic to Panama at this zoo. It's not a fancy attraction, but there are extensive lawns and gardens, and the zoo is undergoing a progressive renovation during the next few years. See p. 144.

- **Emberá Villages** (Chagres River, near Panama City): This adventurous trip is fun for kids because it involves traveling a jungle-choked Chagres River by motorized dugout canoe to an Emberá Indian village. Along the way, guides keep an eye out for wildlife. The Emberá's rustic villages, handicrafts, and temporary *jagua*-stain "tattoos" fascinate kids and adults alike. Give **Ecocircuitos** (© 314-1586) a call. See p. 144.

- **Isla Contadora** (Archipiélago de las Perlas): What's special about this island are the dozen beaches that offer calm-water swimming conditions, the best snorkeling in Panama, day excursions to uninhabited islands, fishing trips, and more. The **Hotel Contadora Resort** (© 264-1510), while certainly not the nicest hotel on the island, does front a perfect beach and offers day passes that include lunch and the use of kayaks and other sports equipment; they also have a minizoo with monkeys. See p. 167.

- **El Valle de Antón:** Just 2 hours from Panama City, this mountain village provides families with a host of activities, including horseback riding, hiking, canopy adventures, a serpentarium, and El Nispero Zoo, with its new amphibian center. The most family-friendly hotel here is the **Crater Valley Adventure Spa** (© 983-6167), with a climbing wall, bicycle rental, and kids' activities, as well as an elegant pool and minispa for adults. See p. 186.

- **Bocas del Toro:** Three distinctively different lodges on Isla Bastimentos in Bocas offer family-friendly activities. Go to Bahía Honda to see bat caves, sloths, monkeys, and caimans; snorkel around Cayos Zapatilla, kayak through mangroves or on a Class I inland river, and more. Check out **The Jungle Lodge** (© 6592-5162), **Tranquilo Bay** (© 6620-4179), and **Casa Cayuco** (© 509/996-4178 in the U.S.). See p. 278, p. 279, and p. 280.

- **Chiriquí Highlands:** Many B&Bs in the Chiriquí do not accept kids, so book at the **Manatial Spa & Lodge** (© 771-5126) near Bambito; they have a canopy line, trout fishing, outdoor pools, and kids' activities. A short, kid-friendly trail is in La Amistad International Park. The **Quetzal Trail** offers fairyland rainforest and birds, and is downhill from west to east. If staying in Boquete or Bambito, book a Class II white-water rafting trip with **Chiriquí Rafting** (© 720-1505). See p. 229.

7 The Best Luxury Hotels & Resorts

- **The Panama Marriott Hotel** (Panama City; © 210-9100): Of all the upscale options in Panama City, the Marriott consistently outshines its competitors. The hotel is in excellent shape, chock-full of facilities and amenities; guest rooms are roomy and comfortable, and the staff provides outstanding service. A central location close to restaurants and shops is an added bonus. See p. 94.

- **The Bristol Panama** (Panama City; © 265-7844): It's button-up luxury with conservative textures and hues, English furniture, and carpeted guest rooms, but still the ambience at the Bristol feels cozy rather than stuffy. The Bristol is known for its bend-over-backward service and fine dining at Las Barandas Restaurant, though it doesn't have a pool. See p. 93.

- **Intercontinental Playa Bonita Resort & Spa** (Playa Bonita; ℂ 800/424-6835): If you're looking for a full-scale resort with all the trimmings yet not too far from Panama City, this brand-new destination resort fills the bill. Set on a small inlet on the Pacific Coast, and backed by lush jungle, the Inter-Continental feels more exclusive that other resorts on the Pacific Coast. The beach itself is just a step above mediocre, but the swimming pools, outdoor activities, and sybaritic spa will keep you busy enough. The Intercontinental is so close to Panama City that you can dine there at night; and they offer access to the Tucán Golf Course. See p. 174.

- **Islas Secas** (Isla Secas; ℂ 805/729-2737 in the U.S.): Casual elegance and an eco-conscious design using deluxe, solar-powered yurts for lodging are the hallmarks of this exquisite boutique resort, located on a private island in the blue waters of the Gulf of Chiriquí. Expect outstanding cuisine, impeccable service, access to world-class sport fishing and diving, and the smug feeling of having escaped the crowds. Islas Secas offers a bevy of activities, or they can leave you "stranded" on an uninhabited island for the day or back at home base at their spa. See p. 248.

- **Coral Lodge** (Colón Province; ℂ 317-6754): Spread around a dreamy inlet ringed with white sand and backed by coconut palms and thick jungle, this is a diver's and snorkeler's paradise, and one of the more luxurious and handsome lodges in Panama (it's eco-conscious, too). Lodging is in cozy individual thatched-roof *casitas* with snorkeling just outside your door—and the property is close enough to the Comarca Kuna Yala to tie in a visit there. See p. 159.

- **Hacienda del Mar** (Isla San José; ℂ 866/433-5627): If you're looking for a lodge in a pristine island setting that isn't too far from Panama City, but that offers plenty of outdoor activities—this place fills the bill. Accommodations are in individual bungalows spread across a promontory and offering dynamite views. The overall ambience is intimate and romantic, making it an ideal place for a honeymoon. See p. 169.

- **Villa Camila** (Los Destiladores; ℂ 232-6721): It's one of Panama's finest hotels and one of its most exclusive, tucked away on the wooded shore of the Azuero Peninsula. French architect Gilles Saint-Gilles employed traditional, local woodworking and iron casting techniques to build a gorgeous and sophisticated hybrid of a hacienda and Moroccan villa, with locally produced furniture, individually designed rooms, and a wide veranda with wonderful views out to the sea. Surprisingly, the hotel is little-known, and with so few guests you can expect a high level of intimacy and privacy. Vila Camila prides itself on eco-friendly practices. See p. 207.

- **Tropic Star Lodge** (Piñas Bay, Darién Province; 800/682-3424; www.tropicstar.com): For more than 40 years, the Tropic Star Lodge has drawn VIPs, sports stars, and actors for its world-renowned sport fishing—which is the focus of this lodge. If you're not a VIP, that's okay; this lodge just wants fishing fans, and they openly welcome families to get the kids interested in this high-adrenaline sport. The luxurious Tropic Star is located in the Darién Province on the Pacific Coast, and must be reached by small plane. See p. 299.

8 The Best Ecolodges & Wilderness Resorts

These days, the term "ecolodge" is used so frequently that it has come to mean anything from a converted research station with no electricity to a "sustainable luxury" lodge. Ecolodges, by definition, should employ environmentally sound practices such as proper waste management, and contribute back to the local economy through jobs and an incentive to protect the environment for tourism. Ecolodges should also offer guided nature tours and provide in-depth information. The Gamboa Resort is the least "eco" of the following lodges, but its location, guided tours, and wildlife displays still place it in this category.

- **Canopy Lodge & Canopy Tower** (El Valle de Antón & Soberanía National Park; (C) **264-5720**): Birders flock to these two ecolodges for their focus on our feathered friends and their location in habitats friendly to a wide range of species. The **Canopy Tower,** a remodeled military radar station in thick jungle, is a cross between a stylish B&B and a scientific research center. It's just 25 minutes from Panama City but feels worlds away, and the 360-degree observation deck here provides stunning views and a platform with scopes. The **Canopy Lodge** is more luxurious, with minimalist design that blends into the forested surroundings. Outstanding birding guides, a well-stocked library, day trips, and chats are a part of the stay. See p. 188.

- **Gamboa Rainforest Resort** (Gamboa; (C) **877/800-1690**): They bill themselves as an eco-resort, but the Gamboa is better called a "destination megaresort" that appeals equally to travelers seeking contact with nature to those who just want to be surrounded by nature while kicking back at the pool. Guided nature tours include jungle boat cruises, an aerial tram ride through the rainforest, and a minizoo of reptile, butterfly, and marine species exhibits. There's also a full-service spa. See p. 145.

- **The Jungle Lodge** (Bocas del Toro; (C) **6592-5162**): No other lodge envelops you more in nature than this one—it's like playing Tarzan and Jane for a night. Sleeping in an open-air, thatched-roof bungalow, of course, is not for everyone, but the cabins are stylish, and two sit high in the forest canopy, with sweeping views and wildlife sightings. There are guided nature and cultural visits with Ngöbe-Buglé Indians, organic meals, and an on-site butterfly farm. See p. 279.

- **Cana Field Station** (Darién National Park; (C) **269-9415**): Originally a research facility, this rustic lodge is nestled in the Darién, the wildest and most remote region of Panama and renowned as one of the best birding sites in the world. Ancon Expeditions owns and runs the lodge, but birding specialty tour operators book here, too. Rooms are basic, with shared bathrooms, and meals are shared communally. They include an overnight at the Pirre Tent Camp in the cloud forest. See p. 298.

- **Punta Patiño Lodge** (Darién Province, Gulf of San Miguel; (C) **269-9415**): This hilltop lodge looks out over the Pacific, and though it's rustic, it is a step up in comfort compared to the Cana Field Station, with air-conditioning and private bathrooms. It's also owned by Ancon Expeditions, but international tour outfitters book here, too. The lodge puts travelers close to wetlands, Emberá indigenous communities, sightings of the harpy eagle, and adventurous jungle rides up rivers in dugout canoes. See p. 296.

- **Sierra Llorona Panama Lodge** (Colón Province; ℰ 442-8104): This intimate, family-run lodge is a good bet for birders seeking a less-expensive option than the Canopy Tower. The lodge is nestled in 202 hectares (500 acres) of lush rainforest that is home to more than 150 species of birds, and there are walking trails, a natural bathing pool, and day trips in the surrounding area. Rooms are simple but spotless. See p. 144.

- **Tranquilo Bay** (Bocas del Toro; ℰ 620-4179): Embraced by lush, vibrant jungle and fronted by a thicket of mangroves, this resort, a haven for adventurers, is the most upscale lodging option in Bocas del Toro. The idea here is to provide activities that go where no other tour operator goes, including river kayaking on the mainland, snorkeling in remote areas, jungle hikes, and visits to isolated beaches. The cabins, though simply designed, offer plush interiors with high-quality beds and spacious bathrooms. See p. 280.

- **Trinidad Spa & Lodge** (near Penonomé; ℰ 786/206-0219 in the U.S.; www.posadaecologica.com). The drop-dead views and the fact that this spa and lodge is known to few outside of Panama City make the Trinidad Spa & Lodge a real find. The lodge is nestled in thick, green jungle and dominated by a torlike hill called Cerro La Vieja. Spa services are reasonably priced, and there are walking trails, mule rides, and other outdoor excursions. They serve delicious, organic cuisine, too. See p. 193.

- **Los Quetzales Lodge & Spa** (Guadalupe; ℰ 771-2291): Although the main lodge is in town, there are several rustic wooden cabins set deep in lush rainforest that swarms with colorful birds. The cabins are large enough for groups, and they provide travelers with the wildest independent lodging option in the country. The cabins can be self-catering, or they'll send a chef up to cook for you. Walking trails and horseback-riding trips are options for those who stay here. See p. 225.

9 The Best Small Hotels & B&Bs

- **The Coffee Estate Inn** (Boquete; ℰ 720-2211; www.coffeeestateinn.com): Gorgeous views of Volcán Barú, cozy bungalows with full kitchens, and owner-managed, friendly service tailored to your needs are the hallmarks of The Coffee Estate Inn. The bungalows are enveloped in native forest, fruit trees, and flowers that attract myriad birds. The romantic ambience is ideal for honeymooners. See p. 237.

- **Boquete Garden Inn** (Boquete; ℰ 720-2376; www.boquetegardeninn.com): The price is nice, and the pretty manicured gardens and comfy cabin-style rooms make this B&B an

irresistible deal. The setting, on the outskirts of town, is quiet, save the sound of a babbling creek. The cabins are newly renovated and have kitchenettes. See p. 239.

- **Cielito Sur** (Nueva Suiza; ℰ 771-2038; www.cielitosur.com): The first thing you'll notice at this lovely country inn is the dozens of hummingbirds whizzing around the property. The Cielito is an ideal place for travelers seeking a pastoral setting, snug guest rooms, and easy-to-plan excursions. The inn also has lots of common areas, including a living area with lounge chairs and a well-stocked library. See p. 223.

- **Perla Real Inn** (Isla Contadora; © **250-4095**; www.perlareal.com). This new gem of an inn is owned by a Californian who modeled the decor after Spanish missions from his home state. The Perla is fresh and cool, and a good value, too. Independent travelers can buy their own supplies and book a suite with a kitchenette. The inn looks over a small patio courtyard with a bubbling fountain. See p. 167.
- **Vereda Tropical Hotel** (Isla Taboga; © **250-2154**; www.veredatropical hotel.com): This artfully designed, Mexican-style inn is a welcome addition to an island destination that was formerly starved of decent lodging. Expansive views, an indoor atrium patio, and swirling iron balustrades are key features, and their restaurant, on a breezy veranda, is one of Panama's best spots for a lunch or an afternoon cocktail. See p. 162.
- **La Casa de Lourdes** (El Valle de Antón; © **983-6645**; www.lacasade lourdes.com): Perched on a gently sloping hill and offering picturesque views of the Antón crater, this deluxe boutique hotel is also home to one of Panama's best restaurants. The Tuscan-style hotel recently opened a high-end spa, and they rent bikes and arrange tours. See p. 188.
- **Park Eden Bed & Breakfast** (El Valle de Antón; © **983-6167**; www. parkeden.com): It's the true definition of a B&B: owner-run; lots of charming, country decor; hearty breakfasts; and warm, gracious service. There are doubles and a full house for a group. The storybook setting is amid flowering gardens and forest. See p. 189.
- **Posada los Destiladores** (Playa los Destiladores; © **6675-9715**; www. panamabambu.net). These rustic yet ultrastylish, individual bungalows offer one of the most romantic places to stay on the Pacific Coast of Panama. Secluded among 8.1 hectares (20 acres) of tropical plants and teak trees, the bungalows feature bamboo, thatched roofs, and intricately carved, custom-made furniture using local materials. There is a pool and private access to a beautiful beach. See p. 206.
- **Villa Marina** (© **646/383-7486** in the U.S.; www.playavenado.com). Best described as a family home that happens to rent out rooms, this beachfront B&B is a find, located on the shore of surfing beach Playa Venado. The colonial-style home, set on 89 hectares (220 acres) of private land and boasting beautiful sunsets, is elegantly appointed—but the ambience is easeful, not fussy. Villa Marina is best rented with a group, but individual reservations are accepted, too. See p. 206.

10 The Best Restaurants

- **Manolo Caracol** (Panama City; © **228-4640**): The city's most innovative restaurant features an adventurous and creative daily menu that embraces in-season products and the freshest and most exotic fish of any restaurant in town. Sit back in the colonial, artsy ambience and wait for a "surprise" of 12 courses to be slowly ushered to your table—you never know what you're going to get, but you know it will be good. See p. 106.
- **Limoncillo** (Panama City; © **263-5350**): This little gourmet bistro is headed by a top chef who earned her stripes in New York, and brought that city's dining concept to Panama City: creative taste combinations, chill-out background music, an artsy ambience, and high-end prices. The food

is mostly contemporary Mediterranean and Italian, and the cocktails are divine. See p. 103.

- **Palms** (Panama City; © 265-7256): It's one of the hippest restaurants in Panama City, with a tropical-chic and sleek decor, and delicious, well-conceived dishes that expertly blend Mediterranean, Asian, and Latin American flavors and ingredients. Upstairs is an ultra-modern bar for a nightcap. See p. 104.

- **Las Barandas** (Panama City; © 265-7844): Panama City's best boutique hotel also has one of its best restaurants. At the helm is "Cuquita," nationally famous as the Martha Stewart of Panama, who adapts traditional Panamanian recipes to modern gourmet tastes, and serves her delicious creations in a cozy and sophisticated dining area. They have Sunday brunch, too. See p. 108.

- **Madame Chang** (Panama City; © 269-1313): Few diners are aware that some of the best Chinese food outside of China is here in Panama, and Madame Chang is where you come to savor it. The Peking duck is the restaurant's showcase dish, and they serve potent martinis. The owners have merged Old China with new, both in terms of cuisine and their smart-casual atmosphere. See p. 109.

- **La Casa de Lourdes** (El Valle de Antón; © 983-6450): The cuisine is so to-die-for good that some residents of Panama City endure the 4-hour round-trip to El Valle de Antón just to have Sunday lunch. Ultra-fresh ingredients and exotic fruits are used to create updated takes on Panamanian and Latin American fare. Dining

is alfresco: under the archways of a Tuscan-style manor house, next to an outdoor swimming pool. See p. 190.

- **Restaurant Vista Mar** (Vista Mar; © 215-1111): This brand-new restaurant is run by a renowned French chef, and sports a Moroccan decor that is fresh and chic, plus outdoor dining with ocean views. The Mediterranean-style seafood is well-conceived and bursting with flavor. The restaurant is within the Vista Mar residential community, on the Pacific Coast. See p. 177.

- **Panamonte Inn Restaurant** (Boquete; © 720-1324): This sanctuary of gourmet cuisine is located within the clapboard walls of the oldest hotel in Boquete. The food is inventive and consistently good, and service is attentive and courteous. You can bypass their more formal dining area for a comfy seat in their fireside bar and still order off the main menu. See p. 243.

- **La Ballena** (Bocas del Toro; © 757-9089): A wine bar serving fine Italian food is an incongruous element in the rum-and-beer Caribbean, but that's what makes La Ballena so good. Homemade pastas and thin-crust pizzas; a warm, candlelit ambience; and a pirate's cache of hundreds of wines can be found here. See p. 270.

- **Restaurant Yasinori** (Bocas del Toro; no phone): There's nothing much to this place other than a thatched roof and plastic chairs and tables in the sand, but the simple Panamanian and creole dishes are straight-from-the-sea fresh, and the fruit juices are delicious. Caribbean views also help make this a wonderful spot. See p. 273.

2

Planning Your Trip to Panama

By purchasing this book, you've shown an interest in traveling to Panama, and good for you. Panama is poised to be among the next big travel destinations, but for now the country is deliciously free of crowds—and the country offers the same pristine wilderness and action-packed adventure as its more-popular neighbor, Costa Rica. Panama is but a thin squiggle of a country, but there is a wealth of diversity packed within its borders, from lush rainforests to sultry beaches to craggy mountain peaks— all of which can be reached by a short drive or flight. The Caribbean Sea and Pacific Ocean are so close to each other that you can swim in both in 1 day. If you're a nature lover, consider that Panama is a land bridge between North and South America, and hundreds of wildlife species—more than 900 species of birds alone—meet here at the isthmus, providing a rich environment for eco-travel.

Panama is a safe country, too, and Panamanians are some of the friendliest people in Latin America. So many residents here speak English that it could almost be called Panama's second language. And when compared with Costa Rica's, Panama's infrastructure and capital city are decidedly more modern, and travel budgeting is easier considering that the country's national monetary unit is the U.S. dollar.

So now the question isn't whether you should go, but when? What is the best time to visit, and which destinations should you visit? How can you pre-plan a trip and find cheap deals and other tantalizing offers? These are just a few of the questions that this chapter answers to help you plan an unforgettable vacation.

1 The Regions in Brief

Panama, an S-shaped **isthmus** that measures little more than 77,700 sq. km (30,000 sq. miles), is just slightly smaller than South Carolina—yet there is a huge diversity of landscapes and microclimates within this tiny nation. Costa Rica borders Panama to the west, Colombia to the east; and, in what can be vexing to the traveler with no sense of direction, the Pacific Ocean to the south and the Caribbean Sea to the north. Because Panama City faces southeast, travelers are presented with the uncommon view of the sun rising over the Pacific. At its narrowest point, Panama measures just 50km (31 miles) wide.

Besides the isthmus, Panama is made up of than 1,500 **islands,** many of them uninhabited and cloaked in thick vegetation. These islands are grouped into four regions. In the Caribbean Sea there are the Bocas del Toro and San Blas archipelagos; in the Pacific Ocean, Las Perlas Archipelago in the Gulf of Panama, and Coiba Island and its accompanying tiny islands in the Gulf of Chiriquí.

Panama is home to two **mountain ranges,** the Serranía del Darién in the east, and the Cordillera Central in the west, the latter of which is home to the highest peak in the country, the dormant Volcán Barú, at 3,475m (11,400 ft.). This is the only place in Panama where you are likely to experience brisk temperatures—the rest of the country averages 75°F to 85°F (24°C–29°C) year-round.

Panama is a centralized nation, with about a third of its population of 3 million living in Panama City; in comparison, the population of the second-largest city, Colón, is just under 200,000 residents. The country is divided into nine *provincias,* or provinces, three provincial-level indigenous territories called *comarcas,* and two sub-provincial *comarcas.* For the most part, chapters in this book are divided into general regions rather than provinces. See the map on the inside cover of this book for a visual guide to the regions outlined here.

PANAMA CITY, THE CANAL & SUR-ROUNDINGS Beyond the urban streets of Panama City, the Canal Zone is characterized by a species-rich, dense tropical rainforest, hundreds of rivers, mangrove swamps, the Pacific Ocean coastline, and Las Perlas Archipelago in the Gulf of Panama. Thanks to the Panama Canal and its reliance on the local watershed, the rainforest in this area is protected as a series of national parks and reserves (Chagres, Soberanía, Sherman, and Camino de Cruces, for example). Visitors to Panama City are often surprised how quickly they can reach these parks and surround themselves in steamy jungle, and view a dazzling array of both North and South American birds and other wildlife. Near the city, the shore is consists mostly of mud flats; visitors seeking beaches must head to the islands, or drive about 1 hour southwest (described in chapter 7).

CENTRAL PANAMA Considered the country's cultural heartland, Central Panama in this book covers Panama City beaches, the Coclé Province, and the Azuero Peninsula. In Coclé, city dwellers flock to popular El Valle de Antón, a verdant mountain hideaway located in the crater of an extinct volcano (1,173m/ 3,850 ft. at its highest peak). The area is blessed with a mild climate that is a welcome respite from the humid lowlands. The Pacific Coast southwest of the city is another popular weekend getaway for its beaches and a few all-inclusive resorts. Farther southwest, the Azuero Peninsula has been largely deforested, but it is still a popular destination for its traditional festivals, handicrafts, and Spanish villages whose architecture dates back to the medieval era. The beaches along the peninsula are blissfully uncrowded any time of year.

BOCAS DEL TORO ARCHIPELAGO Bocas del Toro is in the northwest corner of the country, near the border with Costa Rica, and it's one of the more popular and easily accessed Caribbean destinations, with a wide variety of hotels and amenities. The region is characterized by an eclectic mix of indigenous groups, Spanish descendants, Afro-Caribbeans and, more recently, American expats; it is also one of the wettest areas of Panama. Outside of brief dry seasons in September/ October and February/March, the rain is constant, so bring an umbrella or waterproof gear. Although there are a few beautiful beaches here, there are also dangerous riptides, and visitors come more to scuba dive, snorkel, boat, see wildlife, or just soak in the bohemian vibe of Bocas Town, the capital city.

THE WESTERN HIGHLANDS & GULF OF CHIRIQUI The Western Highlands—so-called for the region's location and its Cordillera Central range—is a veritable paradise of fertile peaks and valleys, crystal-clear rivers, mild temperatures, and fresh air. The region is undergoing a palpable growth spurt as hundreds of North Americans continue to buy second and retirement homes here, so expect to hear a lot of English. The region centers around the skirt of Volcán Barú, a dormant volcano capped by a moist cloud forest. Farther south are the humid lowlands, the capital city David, and the wondrous coast and islands of the Gulf of Chiriquí. This is Panama's up-and-coming beach/ocean destination, with its highlight being Coiba National Park, one of the most diverse and pristine islands for scuba diving and snorkeling in the world.

THE DARIEN   The easternmost region of Panama is known as the Darién Province, a swath of impenetrable rainforest and swampland that is undeveloped, save for a handful of tiny villages and indigenous settlements. It is Panama's wildest region and the most difficult to reach: This is the famous "missing link" of the Pan-American Highway that runs from Alaska to Puerto Montt, Chile. The interior of the Darién can be reached only by foot, boat, or small plane—and herein lies the allure of adventure for travelers. Within the province lies the Darién National Park, most of it inaccessible except for the Cana Research Station, an area revered by birders worldwide for the

abundance of endemic and "show-bird" species such as macaws and harpy eagles, the largest predator in the world. Along the Pacific shore is the famous Tropic Star Lodge, but otherwise, lodging in the Darién is in rustic shelters and tents.

THE COMARCA KUNA YALA (THE SAN BLAS ARCHIPELAGO)   Though commonly referred to as the San Blas Archipelago, this semiautonomous region, or *comarca,* is named for the Kuna Yala, perhaps Panama's most well-known indigenous group. The Kuna are recognized for their tightly knit culture, colorful clothing, and handicrafts such as *mola* tapestries. More than 300 lovely, palm-studded islands in turquoise Caribbean waters make up the archipelago in what is truly an unspoiled paradise. The San Blas is a very popular cruise stop. However, staying on the islands requires a sense of adventure because they can be reached only by a small plane or boat. Lodging is alfresco with rustic accommodations and little in the way of activities other than swimming and swaying in a hammock.

2 Visitor Information

The **Panama Tourist Board,** known as the Instituto Panameño de Turismo (IPAT), has a website and toll-free number for North Americans and Canadians (© **800/231-0568;** www.visitpanama.com); English-language brochures are available. The website offers more information

than can be gotten from any IPAT representative on the phone, and also has links to other helpful sites. Make sure to check out **www.panamainfo.com** as well; it's probably the best travel site currently available on Panama.

3 Entry Requirements & Customs

ENTRY REQUIREMENTS
PASSPORTS

The Terrorism Prevention Act of 2004 now requires U.S. citizens traveling to Panama to present a valid passport. (Previously, only a driver's license and copy of your birth certificate were needed to enter Panama.) For information on how to get a passport, go to "Passports" in the "Fast Facts: Panama" section, later in this

chapter—the websites listed provide downloadable passport applications as well as the current fees for processing passport applications. For an up-to-date, country-by-country listing of passport requirements around the world, go to the "Foreign Entry Requirement" Web page of the U.S. State Department at **http:// travel.state.gov**.

Important: Travelers must be able to demonstrate proof of sufficient funds if requested, and they must present an onward or return ticket. Panama charges a departure tax of $20 at the airport (it may already be included in your ticket).

In an effort to prevent international child abduction, many governments require a parent or legal guardian (or someone other than the parent) traveling alone with a child to provide documentary evidence of relationship and travel permission. Having such documentation on hand can facilitate entry/departure if immigration requests it, although it is not always required. Inquire when booking your airline ticket about updated entry/departure procedures for children; many cruise lines require this kind of documentation to board.

VISAS

Citizens of the United States, Canada, Great Britain, and most European nations may visit Panama for a maximum of 90 days. No visa is necessary, but you must have a valid passport and a $5 tourist card, paid when entering by land or at the airline counter before your departure. Carry your passport and tourist card, or better yet, a photocopy, with you at all times.

CUSTOMS
WHAT YOU CAN BRING INTO PANAMA

Visitors to Panama may bring with them personal items such as jewelry, and professional equipment including cameras, computers, and electronics, as well as fishing and diving gear for personal use—all of which are permitted duty-free. Customs officials in Panama seldom check arriving tourists' luggage.

WHAT YOU CAN TAKE HOME FROM PANAMA
U.S. Citizens

Residents and nonresidents may bring home no more than 1 liter of an alcoholic beverage (beer, wine, or liquor) duty-free. Returning U.S. citizens who have been away for at least 48 hours are allowed to bring back once every 30 days $800 worth of merchandise duty-free. You will be charged a flat duty fee for the next $1,000 worth of purchases. Beyond that, any dollar amount is dutiable at whatever rates apply. On mailed gifts, the duty-free limit is $200. Be sure to have your receipts or purchases handy to expedite the declaration process. *Note:* If you owe duty, you are required to pay upon arrival in the United States by cash, personal check, government or traveler's check, or money order, and in some locations, by Visa or Mastercard.

To avoid having to pay duty on foreign-made personal items you owned before you left on your trip, bring along a bill of sale, insurance policy, jeweler's appraisal, or receipt. Or register items that can be readily identified by a permanently affixed serial number or marking—think laptop computers, cameras, and CD players—to avoid problems with Customs. Take the items to the nearest Customs office or register them with Customs at the airport from which you are departing. You will receive, at no cost, a Certificate of Registration, which allows duty-free entry for the life of the item. There is little chance that Customs will seriously question personal items, but better safe than sorry.

For specifics on what you can bring back and the corresponding fees, download the invaluable free pamphlet *Know Before You Go* online at www.cbp.gov. (Click on "Travel," and then click on "Know Before You Go! Online Brochure.") Or contact the **U.S. Customs & Border Protection (CBP),** 1300 Pennsylvania Ave. NW, Washington, DC 20229 (© 877/287-8667) and request the pamphlet.

Canadian Citizens

For a clear summary of Canadian rules, write for the booklet *I Declare,* issued by the **Canada Border Services Agency**

(© 800/461-9999 in Canada, or 204/983-3500; www.cbsa-asfc.gc.ca).

U.K. Citizens

For information, contact **HM Customs & Excise** at © **0845/010-9000** (from outside the U.K., 020/8929-0152), or consult their website at **www.hmce.gov.uk**.

Australian Citizens

A helpful brochure available from Australian consulates or Customs offices is *Know Before You Go.* For more information, call the **Australian Customs Service** at © **1300/363-263,** or log on to **www.customs.gov.au**.

New Zealand Citizens

Most questions are answered in a free pamphlet available at New Zealand consulates and Customs offices: *New Zealand Customs Guide for Travellers, Notice no. 4.* For more information, contact **New Zealand Customs,** The Customhouse, 17–21 Whitmore St., Box 2218, Wellington (© **04/473-6099** or 0800/428-786; www.customs.govt.nz).

4 Money

CURRENCY

The unit of currency in Panama is the U.S. dollar, but the Panamanian balboa, which is pegged to the dollar at a 1:1 ratio, also circulates in denominations of 5¢, 10¢, 25¢, and 50¢ coins. (U.S. coins are in circulation as well.) Balboa coins are sized similarly to their U.S. counterparts, and travelers will have no trouble identifying their value.

EXCHANGING MONEY

Travelers with pounds or euros may exchange money at Banco Nacional, which has branches in the airport and across the nation. To save time, you may want to convert your money into dollars before arriving at Panama.

ATMs

The easiest and best way to get cash away from home is from an ATM (automated teller machine), available throughout Panama in banks and supermarkets, and identifiable by a red SISTEMA CLAVE sign with a white key. ATMs, called *cajeros automáticos,* can be found in larger towns only, so if you're visiting out-of-the-way destinations such as an offshore island, plan to bring extra cash. To find ATM locations in Panama, check out www.sclave.com/english.html.

The **Cirrus** (© **800/424-7787;** www.mastercard.com) and **PLUS** (© **800/** 843-7587; www.visa.com) networks span the globe; look at the back of your bank card to see which network you're on, then call or check online for ATM locations at your destination. Be sure you know your personal identification number (PIN) and daily withdrawal limit before you depart. Some ATMs in Panama limit withdrawals to $200 per day, others to $500. *Note:* Remember that many banks impose a fee every time you use a card at another bank's ATM, and that fee can be higher for international transactions (up to $5 or more) than for domestic ones (where they're rarely more than $2). In addition, the bank from which you withdraw cash may charge its own fee. For international withdrawal fees, ask your bank.

CREDIT CARDS

Credit cards are another safe way to carry money. They also provide a convenient record of all your expenses, and they generally offer relatively good exchange rates. You can withdraw cash advances from your credit cards at banks or ATMs, provided you know your PIN. Keep in mind that you'll pay interest from the moment of your withdrawal, even if you pay your monthly bills on time. Also, note that many banks now assess a 1% to 3% "transaction fee" on **all** charges you incur abroad (whether you're using the local currency or your native currency). Businesses that accept credit cards always accept Visa and Mastercard, and to a lesser extent American Express. Diners Club is not widely accepted.

TRAVELER'S CHECKS

You can buy traveler's checks at most banks. They are offered in denominations of $20, $50, $100, $500, and sometimes $1,000. Generally, you'll pay a service charge ranging from 1% to 4%.

The most popular traveler's checks are offered by **American Express** (© **800/807-6233,** or 800/221-7282 for cardholders—this number accepts collect calls, offers

service in several foreign languages, and exempts Amex gold and platinum cardholders from the 1% fee); **Visa** (© **800/732-1322**)—AAA members can obtain Visa checks for a $9.95 fee (for checks up to $1,500) at most AAA offices or by calling © **866/339-3378;** and **MasterCard** (© **800/223-9920**).

Traveler's checks are readily accepted at major hotels, and less so at budget hotels and restaurants. In fact, beyond major hotels and banks, businesses in Panama seem reluctant to accept traveler's checks. Use an ATM for cash if you can, and bring traveler's checks as a backup in the event of a lost or stolen card.

5 When to Go

Panama lies between 7 degrees and 9 degrees above the Equator, which places it firmly within the Tropics. Accordingly, average year-round temperatures are a balmy 75°F to 85°F (24°C–29°C), varying only with altitude. The average temperature in the Chiriquí Highlands, for example, is 60°F (16°C), and is the only area in Panama where you will likely feel cold.

Humidity is always high in Panama, and rainfall varies noticeably between the Pacific and Caribbean sides of the country, with some areas in the Caribbean receiving almost twice the yearly rainfall of Panama City. The best time to visit Panama is during the summer **dry season** from mid-December to mid-April. This is also **high season,** and some hotels and resorts charge higher rates during this period. Caribbean destinations such as Bocas del Toro have a shorter dry season, usually September/

October and February/March, but really showers can occur on any day.

The Chiriquí Highlands experiences a variety of microclimates that can change drastically, sometimes even within a few miles. In Boquete, high winds and a peculiar misting rain called *bajareque* are common from mid-December to mid-February; January sees the occasional thunderstorm, and March to May are the sunniest months.

If you are unable to visit during the dry season, keep in mind that the early months (Apr–July) are characterized by sudden, heavy thunderstorms in the afternoon that are short in duration, and can happen every few days. Often, the skies are sunny in the morning or afternoon.

For up-to-date information on weather in Panama, go to **www.panama-maps. com** or **www.accuweather.com**.

Average Monthly Temperatures & Rainfall in Panama City

	Jan	Feb	Mar	Apr	May	June	July	Aug	Sept	Oct	Nov	Dec
Temp. (°F)	82	82	82	82	80	80	81	81	81	80	81	82
Temp. (°C)	27	27	27	27	25	25	26	26	26	25	25	27
Days of Rain	4	2	1	6	15	16	15	15	16	18	18	12

PUBLIC HOLIDAYS

There is a saying in Panama that the only thing Panamanians take seriously is their holidays—and it's no joke. Nearly every business, including banks, offices, and many stores and restaurants close, making even Panama City feel like a ghost town. Official holidays that fall on a Saturday or Sunday are usually observed on Mondays, allowing for a long weekend. Transportation services are also greatly reduced. During holidays, most locals head for the beach or other getaway destinations, so if you plan to travel during this time, book lodging well in advance and make certain you have confirmed reservations.

Panama's most revered holiday is Carnaval, the 4 days that precede Ash Wednesday. (Though not officially a holiday, most call in sick to work to recover from Carnaval on Wed.) The largest celebrations take place in Panama City and the Azuero Peninsula, with parades, floats, drinking, costumes, and music. The dates for upcoming Carnavales are: February 16 through 20 (2007), February 2 through 5 (2008), and February 21 through 24 (2009).

Official holidays in Panama include January 1 (New Year's Day), January 9 (Martyr's Day), Good Friday, Easter Sunday, May 1 (Labor Day), August 15 (Founding of Old Panama—observed in Panama City only), October 12 (Hispanic Day), November 2 (All Souls' Day), November 3 (Independence Day), November 4 (Flag Day), November 5 (Colón Day—observed in the city of Colón only), November 10 (First Call for Independence), November 28 (Independence from Spain), December 8 (Mother's Day), December 25 (Christmas Day).

PANAMA CALENDAR OF EVENTS & FESTIVALS

Many of the following listings are annual events whose exact dates vary from year to year, and the majority are local festivals. Call the **IPAT tourism board** at ℂ 800/962-1526, or check out their website at www.visitpanama.com, for more information.

JANUARY

Feria de las Flores y del Café (Flower and Coffee Festival), Boquete. This festival is one of the grandest celebrations of flowers in the world, drawing thousands of people to Boquete for 10 days. Expect lush flower displays, food stands, live music, amusement rides, handicrafts booths, and hotel rooms booked far in advance. Mid-January.

Jazz Festival, Panama City. For one 3-day weekend, Panama City throbs with live jazz performances by outstanding international musicians. Some events are held outdoors and are free; log on to www.panamajazzfestival.com. Late January.

FEBRUARY

Carnaval (Carnival). Panama's largest yearly celebration takes place during the 4 days that precede Ash Wednesday. The largest celebrations are in small towns on the Azuero Peninsula, such as Las Tablas, and Panama City, with parades, music, and dancing. Prepared to get wet by *mojaderos.*

MARCH

Semana Santa. During this week (Holy Week), parades, religious processions, and other special events take place across the country. Palm Sunday through Holy Saturday.

Feria de David. The Chiriquí capital's largest festival draws more than 500 exhibitors from around the world to display industrial products and new technology. During the 10-day event, the city hosts plentiful cultural and folkloric events; www.feriadedavid.com. Mid-March.

APRIL

Feria de Orquídeas (Orchid Festival), Boquete. It's not as grand as the flower festival, but the Orchid Festival is enjoyable because it showcases thousands of varieties of these delicate flowers for public viewing. At the fairgrounds around mid-April.

Feria Internacional del Azuero, La Villa de Los Santos. This multiday festival is something akin to a county fair, with animal displays, food stalls, and lots of drinking. Mid-April.

JUNE

Festival Corpus Christi, La Villa de Los Santos. The town explodes with activity for a 2-week religious festival known for its elaborate dances led by men in devil masks. Forty days after Easter.

JULY

Festival Patronales de La Virgen de Santa Librada, Las Tablas. This festival is famous for its **Festival de la Pollera** on July 22, which showcases the region's most beautiful pollera dresses and elects the "Queen of the Pollera" for that year. July 20 to 22.

SEPTEMBER

Feria Internacional del Mar (International Festival of the Sea), Bocas del Toro. This 5-day event features food stands serving local cuisine, handicrafts booths, exhibits by the Smithsonian Institute and ANAM (the park service), folkloric presentations, and dances. Around the second week of September.

Festival de la Mejorana, Guararé. This nationally famous folkloric festival features hundreds of dancers, musicians, and singers coming together for a week of events and serious partying. Last week of September.

OCTOBER

Festival del Cristo Negro (Black Christ Festival), Portobelo. Thousands of pilgrims come to pay penance and perform other acts of devotion at the Iglesia de San Felipe, home to a wooden black Christ effigy that is paraded around town on this day. October 21.

NOVEMBER

Feria de las Tierras Altas, Volcán. This Highlands Festival is a 5-day celebration of agriculture, local arts, and culture. Around the last week of November.

Independence Days. Panama celebrates three independence days. November 3 and 4 are Independence Day and Flag Day and the largest independence celebrations, featuring parades, fireworks, and other entertainment in Panama City and larger cities like David. November 10th is a holiday for the "First Call for Independence," as is November 28th honoring Independence Day from Spain, with some regional festivities—but nothing matching November 3 and 4.

6 Travel Insurance

Check your existing insurance policies and credit card coverage before you buy travel insurance. There are no major natural disasters such as hurricanes or earthquakes that could upset your plans to visit Panama. Unforeseen costs such as lost luggage and medical expenses are your major concerns. Also, rental-car companies charge a mandatory $12 per day for liability insurance, but you are most likely covered by your credit card for other insurance costs, and therefore you can save a bundle on rental rates. Know what you're covered for before you rent, and what you need in order to make a claim.

The cost of travel insurance varies widely, depending on the cost and length of your trip, your age, your state of health, and the type of trip you're taking, but expect to pay between 5% and 8% of the vacation itself. You can get estimates

Travel in the Age of Bankruptcy

Airlines go bankrupt, so protect yourself by **buying your tickets with a credit card.** The Fair Credit Billing Act guarantees that you can get your money back from the credit card company if a travel supplier goes under (and if you request the refund within 60 days of the bankruptcy). **Travel insurance** can also help, but make sure it covers against "carrier default" for your specific travel provider. And be aware that if a U.S. airline goes bust mid-trip, a 2001 federal law requires other carriers to take you to your destination (albeit on a space-available basis) for a fee of no more than $25, provided you rebook within 60 days of the cancellation.

from various providers through **Insure MyTrip.com**. Enter your trip cost and dates, your age, and other information, for prices from more than a dozen companies.

TRIP-CANCELLATION INSURANCE

Trip-cancellation insurance will help you retrieve your money if you have to back out of a trip or depart early, or if your travel supplier goes bankrupt. Permissible reasons for trip cancellation can range from sickness to natural disaster to the State Department declaring a destination unsafe for travel.

For more information, contact one of the following recommended insurers: **Access America** (© 866/807-3982; www. accessamerica.com); **Travel Guard International** (© 800/826-4919; www.travel guard.com); **Travel Insured International** (© 800/243-3174; www.travel insured.com); and **Travelex Insurance Services** (© 888/457-4602; www.travelex-insurance.com).

MEDICAL INSURANCE

Your medical insurance may or may not offer coverage when traveling overseas, and then it is usually for "reasonable" costs, and not emergency evacuation, which can cost up to $10,000. If you are traveling to a remote or high-risk area, evacuation is something to consider. Also, you must pay upfront for medical services and then seek reimbursement from your

insurance company later. Medicare and Medicaid do not provide coverage outside the U.S.; citizens may wish to contact the AARP for information about foreign medical care coverage with Medicare supplement plans.

As a safety net, you may want to buy travel medical insurance. Try **MEDEX Assistance** (© 410/453-6300; www.medex assist.com) or **Travel Assistance International** (© 800/821-2828; www.travel assistance.com; for general information on services, call the company's Worldwide Assistance Services, Inc., at © **800/ 777-8710**).

LOST-LUGGAGE INSURANCE

On international flights (including U.S. portions of international trips), baggage coverage is limited to approximately $9.07 per pound, up to approximately $635 per checked bag. If you plan to check items more valuable than what's covered by the standard liability, see if your homeowner's policy covers your valuables, get baggage insurance as part of your comprehensive travel-insurance package, or buy Travel Guard's "BagTrak" product.

If your luggage is lost, immediately file a lost-luggage claim at the airport, detailing the luggage contents. Most airlines require that you report delayed, damaged, or lost baggage within 4 hours of arrival. The airlines are required to deliver luggage, once found, directly to your house or destination free of charge.

7 Health & Safety

STAYING HEALTHY

Travelers in Panama should have no problem staying healthy, as standards of hygiene are high, and tap water is safe to drink in most areas. Those with sensitive stomachs will want to drink bottled water when outside major hotels and cities. The most common health problems that affect travelers in Panama are sunburn and mosquito bites. Illnesses that once ravaged humans in the Tropics, such as yellow fever and malaria, are no longer epidemic in Panama. Viral infections and other illnesses are described in "Common Ailments," below. All travelers should be up-to-date on their tetanus immunizations, and receive a Hepatitis A vaccination (see "Dietary Distress," below).

Contact the **International Association for Medical Assistance to Travelers (IAMAT; © 716/754-4883** or, in Canada, 416/652-0137; www.iamat.org) for tips on travel and current information about health concerns in Panama, and for lists of local, English-speaking doctors. The United States **Centers for Disease Control and Prevention** (© **800/311-3435;** www.cdc.gov) provides up-to-date information on health hazards by region or country and offers tips on food safety. The website **www.tripprep.com**, sponsored by a consortium of travel medicine practitioners, may also offer helpful advice on traveling abroad. You can find listings of reliable clinics overseas at the **International Society of Travel Medicine** (www.istm.org).

GENERAL AVAILABILITY OF HEALTHCARE

Hospital quality in Panama City is on a par with that of the United States (most doctors are U.S.-trained), but medical service here is far more economical, and this fact has spawned a curious new "Health Tourism" industry (see "Vacation Goal: A Tan, a Little Sightseeing, a Nose Job," below). Major cities such as David have at least one high-quality hospital, but in small towns, a medical clinic may be the extent of healthcare facilities in the area, and more serious cases must be treated in Panama City. For a list of the best hospitals in Panama City, see "Fast Facts: Panama City," in chapter 5.

English-speaking doctors are very common in Panama—your embassy can provide you with a list if you request one.

COMMON AILMENTS

TROPICAL ILLNESSES Travelers have a low risk of contracting a tropical disease while in Panama. **Yellow fever,** the mosquito-borne disease that decimated canal workers in the late 19th and early 20th century, is no longer epidemic and vaccinations are not required.

Governmental bulletins from the Centers for Disease Control (CDC) recommend that travelers planning to visit Bocas del Toro, Darién, or the San Blas Archipelago be vaccinated against **malaria**—yet cases of malaria are not common and mostly afflict rural citizens who live in remote areas, such as Ngöbe-Buglé Indian tribes. You might consider vaccination against malaria if you plan to spend extended periods in the jungle in the aforementioned areas. Malaria is a parasite that lives in red blood cells and is transmitted by the female anopheles mosquito. The symptoms are cycles of chills, fever, and sweating, sometimes accompanied by headache, backache, and vomiting. Check with your doctor for updated news about malaria outbreaks and what vaccine is best for the region you plan to visit (mosquitoes in the Darién, for example, are resistant to the common vaccine chloroquine).

More common is **dengue fever,** an infectious disease caused by an arbovirus transmitted by daytime mosquitoes. Symptoms of the disease appear suddenly

Vacation Goal: A Tan, a Little Sightseeing, a Nose Job

One of the fastest-growing sectors in worldwide travel is **health and medical tourism,** a term that has begun popping up in countries whose medical care and facilities are comparable to those in the U.S. or Europe, but that offer services at a fraction of the price. Health and medical tourism can apply to simple procedures such as having your teeth fixed or corrective laser eye surgery, or more serious procedures such as gastric bypass surgery, reproduction assistance, or "extreme makeovers" performed by a battery of plastic surgeons and dentists. On average, the cost is about 50% less than in the U.S.— cataract surgery, for example, costs $2,500 in Panama and $6,000 in the U.S. And recuperation in a country that offers a warm climate, a lot of natural beauty, and a high-quality tourism infrastructure is part of the draw.

Interested travelers can check out the new John Hopkins–affiliated state-of-the-art **Hospital Punta Pacifica,** located at Calle 53 in Bellavista (✆ **263-5287**), one of the best facilities in all of Latin America. Or try **Pana-Health,** a consortium of first-rate medical and dental specialists who have teamed up to offer foreigners a central location for information about procedures and easy planning. Most of its members have studied and trained in North American universities and hospitals, and therefore English is widely spoken, and Pana-Health employs the same techniques and technology found in the U.S. Plus Pana-Health can even plan your entire trip for you: As long as you book your own plane ticket, they'll arrange to pick you up from the airport, reserve your hotel room and doctor's appointments, plan city tours, and even book entertainment. For more information, check out their website at www.pana-health.com, or call ✆ **305/675-7306** in the U.S., or 223-6766 in Panama.

and include a high fever, chills, swollen and painful eyes, a headache, and severe aches in the legs and joints—the reason dengue is commonly referred to as "breakbone fever." Symptoms last a week, and though most people recover fully, weakness and fatigue can continue for several weeks. Dengue fever outbreaks have been reported during the past few years in the Bocas del Toro and Colón provinces, mostly affecting locals who live near pools of stagnant water.

The most effective prevention against malaria and dengue fever is to protect yourself against mosquito bites (see "Bugs, Bites & Other Wildlife Concerns," below.)

DIETARY DISTRESS Hepatitis A is a highly contagious viral disease and one of the most common travel-related infections in the developing world. It's transmitted by eating contaminated food, by fecal-oral contact, or by contact with unsanitary conditions. Outbreaks usually occur in poor regions such as the Colón Province, where more than 50 cases were reported in early 2006 due to a contaminated aqueduct and poor food-handling practices. Hepatitis A symptoms range from mild to severe, and can include fever, nausea, and jaundice; cases are normally resolved without complications. The vaccination is safe and effective, and is recommended for anyone traveling to Panama.

Leptospirosis is a disease caused by contact with animals infected with *leptospires,* or by ingesting, or swimming in, water contaminated with animal urine. It causes fever, chills, headache, muscle aches, vomiting, and diarrhea. Travelers become sick from between 2 days to 4 weeks after exposure to the bacteria, the catch being that it can often be misdiagnosed without a blood or urine sample. If you experience the aforementioned symptoms, contact your doctor, who can treat leptospirosis with antibiotics such as penicillin.

The most common illness that affects tourists is TD, or **traveler's diarrhea,** caused by microbes in food and water and typically affecting persons from a country with a high standard of sanitation traveling to an area with a less-advanced system of sanitation. In addition to diarrhea, affected persons may experience nausea and headaches. To prevent TD, avoid foods or beverages from street vendors that look iffy, avoid eating raw or undercooked meat and seafood, and drink bottled water when outside major hotels and restaurants.

BUGS, BITES & OTHER WILDLIFE CONCERNS Panama is replete with bugs that bite, including chiggers, sandflies (also called no-see-ums, or *chitras*), mosquitoes, ticks, and ants. It is very important that you protect yourself against mosquitoes that may or may not carry a disease such as dengue fever. Mosquitoes are endemic, and in mountain ranges they can leave particularly large welts. Ticks are found mostly in the Darién jungle area during March and April.

Chiggers leave a tiny bump that can itch for 2 weeks; but the gross-out factor is that these immature nymphs burrow into your skin—you notice the bite after they've left. *Chitras* live in sand, and are more active during sunrise and sunset—but they can bite at any time of the day.

Panama City is the only area of the country where you won't have to worry too much about getting bitten. Otherwise, spray yourself with insect repellent every day, even if you are just stepping out for dinner at an outdoor cafe. In the jungle, wear long pants (tuck them into your socks) and give your ankle area and all exposed areas a coat of repellent that has at least 30% DEET. Some travelers soak their clothing with the insecticide Permethrin (some companies now sell adventure wear presoaked with Permethrin) to repel bugs. Above all, bring along a bite-soothing, anti-itch product like Sting-eeze.

Panama is home to many poisonous snakes such as the pit viper, the fer-de-lance, and the patoca, but bites are rare. Nevertheless, protect yourself by wearing high boots if you're walking in remote jungle, and keep alert, scanning the trail in front of you. If you're bitten, cutting X-shaped gouges and sucking out the venom is old-fashioned nonsense that won't work; instead, remain calm (panic speeds the venom's diffusion), wash the wound with soap and water if you can, try to identify the species, and seek emergency medical help.

TROPICAL SUN The blistering, equatorial sun can burn your skin faster than you think—even on a cloudy day.

Websites with Health-Related Travel Advice

- **Australia:** www.dfat.gov.au/travel
- **Canada:** www.hc-sc.gc.ca/index_e.html
- **U.K.:** www.dh.gov.uk/PolicyAndGuidance/HealthAdviceForTravellers/fs/en
- **U.S.:** www.cdc.gov/travel

Limit your exposure or apply, liberally, a high-factor sunscreen. The sun is especially strong from 11am to 2pm.

Sunstroke, or heatstroke, can afflict travelers in the Tropics when humidity interferes with the cooling of an overheated body. Sunstroke can be serious, so rest and cool off if you begin to feel dizzy or have a headache. Drink plenty of fluids to keep dehydration at bay.

WHAT TO DO IF YOU GET SICK AWAY FROM HOME

We list **hospitals** and **emergency numbers** under "Fast Facts: Panama," p. 45.

If you suffer from a chronic illness, consult your doctor before your departure. Pack **prescription medications** in your carry-on luggage, and carry them in their original containers, with pharmacy labels—otherwise they won't make it through airport security. Carry the generic name of prescription medicines, in case a local pharmacist is unfamiliar with the brand name.

For travel abroad, you may have to pay all medical costs upfront and be reimbursed later. See "Medical Insurance," under "Travel Insurance," earlier in this chapter.

STAYING SAFE

Panama is one of the safest countries in Latin America, with a few exceptions. The ragged port town of **Colón** is dangerous day and night, except in the Colón 2000 cruise-ship and Zona Libre (Free Zone) areas. The northeastern region of the **Darién Province** near the Caribbean Sea is highly dangerous due to incidents of kidnapping, murder, and drug-running by Colombian guerrilla and paramilitary groups who have crossed the border into Panama. Other regions of the Darién are home to several lodges that are in a no-risk area.

Panama City is safe, with low to moderate crime occurring mostly in neighborhoods such as El Chorrillo and Curundú;

these neighborhoods should be avoided if possible. El Chorrillo surrounds Casco Viejo, to which visitors should take a taxi instead of walking. Panama City is a modern, clean city, yet a very visible poor underclass lives in run-down neighborhoods that feature prominently in the city's west side. As with any urban area, visitors should be alert, exercise caution when taking money out of an ATM, and not walk around with large sums of cash.

Visitors headed for the beach should be extremely cautious when swimming or surfing in both the Pacific and Caribbean oceans, where there are **strong riptides.** Often there are no warning signs; and tour guides rarely advise their clients of dangerous areas. Remember, no matter what happens, stay calm, and swim parallel to the shore and out of the current.

Drugs are easy to buy in Panama, but stiff penalties apply to anyone caught with illegal substances.

For current security information about Panama, check the U.S. Department of State's Travel Advisory website at **http:// travel.state.gov**.

For safety when driving, see p. 39.

DEALING WITH DISCRIMINATION

Panama is a melting pot of races and religions, and in general Panamanians are a tolerant society. Still, Panamanians of African descent and indigenous groups have voiced concerns about racism in the workplace, part of which led to a new antidiscriminatory law put into effect in 2005. For women and for gay and lesbian travelers, see "Specialized Travel Resources," p. 28.

ECOTOURISM

You can find eco-friendly travel tips, statistics, and touring companies and associations—listed by destination under "Travel Choice"—at the TIES website, www.ecotourism.org. **Ecotravel.com** is part online magazine and part ecodirectory that lets you search for touring companies in several categories (water-based, land-based, spiritually oriented, and so on). Also check out **Conservation International** (www.conservation.org)—which, with *National Geographic Traveler,* annually presents **World Legacy Awards** (www.wlaward.org) to those travel tour operators, businesses, organizations, and places that have made a significant contribution to sustainable tourism.

For information about the ethics of swimming with dolphins and other outdoor activities, visit the **Whale and Dolphin Conservation Society** (www.wdcs.org) and **Tread Lightly** (www.tread lightly.org).

8 Specialized Travel Resources

TRAVELERS WITH DISABILITIES

Most disabilities shouldn't stop anyone from traveling. There are more options and resources out there than ever before. Major hotels in Panama City offer wheelchair-accessible guest rooms, and many public bathrooms are accessible to those with limited mobility.

Many travel agencies offer customized tours and itineraries for travelers with disabilities. Among them are **Flying Wheels Travel** (© 507/451-5005; www.flying wheelstravel.com); **Access-Able Travel Source** (© 303/232-2979; www.access-able.com); and **Accessible Journeys** (© 800/846-4537 or 610/521-0339; www.disabilitytravel.com). **Avis Rent a Car** has an "Avis Access" program that offers such services as a dedicated 24-hour toll-free number (© 888/879-4273) for customers with special travel needs; special car features such as swivel seats, spinner knobs, and hand controls; and accessible bus service.

Organizations that offer assistance to travelers with disabilities include **Moss-Rehab** (www.mossresourcenet.org); the **American Foundation for the Blind** (**AFB;** © 800/232-5463; www.afb.org); and **SATH** (Society for Accessible Travel & Hospitality; © 212/447-7284; www.sath.org). **AirAmbulanceCard.com** is now partnered with SATH and allows you to pre-select top-notch hospitals in case of an emergency.

The community website **iCan** (www.icanonline.net/channels/travel) has destination guides and several regular columns on accessible travel. Also check out the quarterly magazine *Emerging Horizons* (www.emerginghorizons.com), and *Open World* magazine, published by SATH.

GAY & LESBIAN TRAVELERS

Panama is more tolerant toward gays and lesbians than other more conservative Latin American societies, but discrimination exists, and displays of public affection are not common. The Catholic Church is the most vociferous anti-gay organization in Panama, rallying against events such as gay participation in Carnaval parades. Panama held its first gay-pride parade in 2005 without incident other than eye-rollings and jokes made by passersby and television reporters. A few hotels in Panama advertise **gay-friendly accommodations;** you can find them at **www.purpleroofs.com**.

The **International Gay and Lesbian Travel Association** (**IGLTA;** © 800/448-8550 or 954/776-2626; www.iglta.org) is the trade association for the gay and lesbian travel industry, and offers an online directory of gay- and lesbian-friendly travel businesses; go to their website and click on "Members."

Many agencies offer tours and travel itineraries specifically for gay and lesbian travelers. Among them are **Above and Beyond Tours** (© 800/397-2681; www.abovebeyondtours.com); **Now, Voyager** (© 800/255-6951; www.nowvoyager.com); and **Olivia Cruises & Resorts** (© 800/631-6277; www.olivia.com).

Gay.com Travel (© 800/929-2268 or 415/644-8044; www.gay.com/travel or www.outandabout.com) is an excellent online successor to the popular *Out & About* print magazine. It provides regularly updated information about gay-owned, gay-oriented, and gay-friendly lodging, dining, sightseeing, nightlife, and shopping establishments at every important destination worldwide.

The following travel guides are available at many bookstores, or you can order them from any online bookseller: *Spartacus International Gay Guide* (Bruno Gmünder Verlag; www.spartacusworld.com/gayguide) and *Odysseus: The International Gay Travel Planner* (Odysseus Enterprises Ltd.); and the *Damron* guides (www.damron.com), with separate, annual books for gay men and lesbians.

SENIOR TRAVEL

Panama is one of the hottest retirement destinations in the world, and most Panama hotels and businesses offer discounts of up to 40% to seniors 60 and older (age varies from business to business). Yet some are reluctant to extend discounts to foreign travelers, and claim the discount is for Panamanian seniors and foreigners with a residential visa only. Nevertheless, it doesn't hurt to request senior rates or discounts when booking. Members of **AARP** (formerly known as the American Association of Retired Persons), 601 E St. NW, Washington, DC 20049 (© 888/687-2277; www.aarp.org), get discounts on hotels, airfares, and car rentals. AARP offers members a wide range of benefits, including *AARP: The Magazine* and a monthly newsletter. Anyone over 50 can join.

Many reliable agencies and organizations target the 50-plus market. **Elderhostel** (© 877/426-8056; www.elderhostel.org) arranges study programs for those aged 55 and over. **ElderTreks** (© 800/741-7956; www.eldertreks.com) offers small-group tours to off-the-beaten-path or adventure-travel locations, restricted to travelers 50 and older. **INTRAV** (© 800/456-8100; www.intrav.com) is a high-end tour operator that caters to the mature, discerning traveler (not specifically seniors), with trips around the world that include guided safaris, polar expeditions, private-jet adventures, and small-boat cruises down jungle rivers.

Recommended publications offering travel resources and discounts for seniors include: the quarterly magazine *Travel 50 & Beyond* (www.travel50andbeyond.com); *Travel Unlimited: Uncommon Adventures for the Mature Traveler* (Avalon); *101 Tips for Mature Travelers*, available from Grand Circle Travel (© 800/221-2610 or 617/350-7500; www.gct.com); and *Unbelievably Good Deals and Great Adventures That You Absolutely Can't Get Unless You're Over 50* (McGraw-Hill), by Joann Rattner Heilman.

FAMILY TRAVEL

Panama is an excellent destination for families, especially those with young children who are easily bored by stuffy museums. Jungle cruises, wildlife sightings, interactive marine museums, and outdoor activities such as snorkeling and kayaking are kid-pleasers. Hotel resorts are generally family-friendly, with children's swimming pools, playgrounds, and even kids' organized activities. A handful of resorts in Panama accept adults only, which is indicated in hotel reviews.

Unfortunately, though many hotels in Panama do not charge for kids under 3, they do charge extra for older kids, usually about $10 to $15 extra per child for a larger "triple" or "quadruple" with additional beds. Other hotels ask that you book a junior suite because a regular double does not have the space for an additional bed. Junior suites and suites have a sofa bed for one to two small children. Major hotels have rooms with connecting doors for two doubles; this can be a costlier option if a hotel doesn't offer a break in price. Ask anyway; you never know what they're willing to offer.

Take special care with the health of your kids. Sunburn, bug bites, and unfamiliar food can take its toll, so review "Health & Safety," earlier in this chapter, before departing. Major hotels offer babysitting service, though it's less common at country-style inns—but ask anyway as they might have a reliable babysitter on hand.

To locate accommodations, restaurants, and attractions that are particularly kid-friendly, refer to the "Kids" icon throughout this guide.

Some tour operators can put together dynamic, activity-rich trips for families, either privately or as part of a larger travel group. Check out "Organized Adventure Trips" on p. 59. **Familyhostel** (© 800/ 733-9753; www.learn.unh.edu/family hostel) specializes in family travel with moderately priced U.S. and international learning vacations. Lectures, field trips, and sightseeing are guided by a team of academics.

Recommended family travel websites include **Family Travel Forum** (www.family travelforum.com); **Family Travel Network** (www.familytravelnetwork.com); **Traveling Internationally with Your Kids** (www. travelwithyourkids.com); and **Family Travel Files** (www.thefamilytravelfiles. com).

WOMEN TRAVELERS

Walking alone at night will probably earn you a couple of catcalls, but women traveling in Panama will not feel overwhelmed by a *macho* presence. The influx of foreigners in Panama has helped, too. The best defense toward an inappropriate comment is to just ignore it and keep walking. In Panama City, women dress up in spite of the heat (meaning no flip-flops and shorts), but skimpier wear is accepted in beach areas.

Check out the award-winning website **Journeywoman** (www.journeywoman. com), a "real life" women's travel-information network where you can sign up for a free e-mail newsletter and get advice on everything from etiquette and dress to safety; or the travel guide *Safety and Security for Women Who Travel* by Sheila Swan and Peter Laufer (Travelers' Tales, Inc.), offering common-sense tips on safe travel.

STUDENT TRAVEL

If you're traveling internationally, you'd be wise to arm yourself with an **International Student Identity Card (ISIC),** which offers substantial savings on rail passes, plane tickets, and entrance fees. It also provides you with basic health and life insurance and a 24-hour help line. The card is available from **STA Travel** (© 800/781-4040 in North America; www.sta.com or www.statravel.com; or www.statravel.co.uk in the U.K.), the biggest student travel agency in the world. If you're no longer a student but are still under 26, you can get an **International Youth Travel Card (IYTC)** from the same people, which entitles you to some discounts (but not on museum admissions). **Travel CUTS** (© 800/667-2887 or 416/614-2887; www.travelcuts. com) offers similar services for both Canadians and U.S. residents. Irish students may prefer to turn to **USIT** (© 01/ 602-1600; www.usitnow.ie), an Ireland-based specialist in student, youth, and independent travel.

SINGLE TRAVELERS

Many hotels offer a "single" rate which is either a smaller room or a standard double at a lower price. Where solo travelers are really hit is with package vacations that add the dreaded "single supplement" to the base price. Still, traveling as part of an organized tour or at a package lodge provides for companions on a journey. For more information, check out Eleanor Berman's latest edition of *Traveling Solo:* *Advice and Ideas for More Than 250 Great Vacations* (Globe Pequot), a guide with advice on traveling alone, either solo or as part of a group tour.

9 Planning Your Trip Online

SURFING FOR AIRFARE

The most popular online travel agencies are **Travelocity** (**www.travelocity.com**, or www.travelocity.co.uk); **Expedia** (**www. expedia.com**, www.expedia.co.uk, or www.expedia.ca); and **Orbitz** (www.orbitz. com).

In addition, most airlines now offer online-only fares that even their phone agents know nothing about. For the websites of airlines that fly to and from your destination, go to "Getting There," p. 33.

Other helpful websites for booking airline tickets online include:

- www.biddingfortravel.com
- www.cheapflights.com
- www.hotwire.com
- www.kayak.com
- www.lastminutetravel.com
- www.opodo.co.uk
- www.priceline.com
- www.sidestep.com
- www.site59.com
- www.smartertravel.com

SURFING FOR HOTELS

Do a little online legwork and check directly with a hotel for special packages and/or Internet rates you might not be aware of. E-mail responses may take several days when contacting remote hotels or lodges. In addition to **Travelocity, Expedia, Orbitz, Priceline,** and **Hotwire** (see above), the following websites will help you with booking hotel rooms online:

- www.hotels.com
- www.quickbook.com
- www.travelaxe.net
- www.travelweb.com
- www.tripadvisor.com

Frommers.com: The Complete Travel Resource

For an excellent travel-planning resource, we highly recommend **Frommers. com** (www.frommers.com), voted Best Travel Site by *PC Magazine*. We're a little biased, of course, but we guarantee that you'll find the travel tips, reviews, monthly vacation giveaways, bookstore, and online-booking capabilities to be thoroughly indispensable. Special features include our popular **Destinations** section, where you can access expert travel tips, hotel and dining recommendations, and advice on the sights to see in more than 3,500 destinations around the globe; the **Frommers.com Newsletter,** with the latest deals, travel trends, and money-saving secrets; and our **Travel Talk** area featuring **Message Boards,** where Frommer's readers post queries and share advice, and where our authors sometimes show up to answer questions. Once you finish your research, the **Book a Trip** area can lead you to Frommer's preferred online partners' websites, where you can book your vacation at affordable prices.

It's a good idea to get a **confirmation number** and make a **printout** of any online booking transaction.

SURFING FOR RENTAL CARS

For booking rental cars online, the best deals are usually found at rental-car company websites, although all the major online travel agencies also offer rental-car reservations services. Priceline and Hotwire work well for rental cars, too; the only "mystery" is which major rental company you get, but for most travelers the difference between Hertz, Avis, and Budget is negligible. Note that inexpensive subcompact vehicles can range from a new Toyota Yaris to a 5-year-old, manual Nissan Sentra.

TRAVEL BLOGS & TRAVELOGUES

The following blogs offer tips, information, and travel stories written by everyday travelers who've been to Panama and want to share their experience. Check out the following:

- www.gridskipper.com
- www.salon.com/wanderlust
- www.travelblog.com
- www.travelblog.org
- www.worldhum.com
- www.writtenroad.com

10 The 21st-Century Traveler

INTERNET ACCESS AWAY FROM HOME
WITHOUT YOUR OWN COMPUTER

To find cybercafes in your destination, check **www.cybercaptive.com** and **www.cybercafe.com**. A hotel without a computer and Internet connection is the rare exception, not the rule. The hourly rate is expensive—you'd do better at a cybercafe—and more isolated hotels can charge up to $10 an hour.

WITH YOUR OWN COMPUTER

More and more hotels, cafes, and retailers are signing on as Wi-Fi (wireless fidelity) "hot spots." Mac owners have their own networking technology: Apple AirPort. To locate other hot spots that provide **free wireless networks** in cities around the world, go to **www.personaltelco.net/index.cgi/WirelessCommunities**.

For dial-up access, most hotels offer dataports for laptop modems, and high-speed connection in their business centers. A few upscale hotels have stepped up to wireless connection in guest rooms, but at costs of $10 to $20 per day. Rates vary wildly from hotel to hotel (some even offer free service), so factor the price into your nightly stay if you're bringing your work with you and need prolonged access to the Internet.

Major Internet Service Providers (ISPs) have **local access numbers** around the world, allowing you to go online by placing a local call. The **iPass** network also has dial-up numbers around the world. You'll have to sign up with an iPass provider, who will then tell you how to set up your computer for your destination(s). For a list of iPass providers, go to www.ipass.com and click on "Individuals Buy Now." One solid provider is **i2roam** (© **866/811-6209** or 920/235-0475; www.i2roam.com).

Wherever you go, bring a **connection kit** of the right power, and phone adapters, a spare phone cord, and a spare Ethernet network cable—or find out whether your hotel supplies them to guests. See "Fast Facts: Panama," later in this chapter, for information about electric current and adaptors.

CELLPHONE USE

The three letters that define much of the world's **wireless capabilities** are GSM (Global System for Mobiles), a big, seamless network that makes for easy cross-border

Online Traveler's Toolbox

- **Airplane Food** (www.airlinemeals.net)
- **Airplane Seating** (www.seatguru.com or www.airlinequality.com)
- **Foreign Languages for Travelers** (www.travlang.com)
- **Maps** (www.mapquest.com)
- **Subway Navigator** (www.subwaynavigator.com)
- **Time and Date** (www.timeanddate.com)
- **Travel Warnings** (http://travel.state.gov, www.fco.gov.uk/travel, www.voyage.gc.ca, or www.dfat.gov.au/consular/advice)
- **Universal Currency Converter** (www.xe.com/ucc)
- **Visa ATM Locator** (www.visa.com); **MasterCard ATM Locator** (www.mastercard.com)
- **Weather** (www.intellicast.com or www.weather.com)

cellphone use throughout Europe and dozens of other countries worldwide. In the U.S., T-Mobile, AT&T Wireless, and Cingular use this quasi-universal system; in Canada, Microcell and some Rogers customers are GSM; and all Europeans and most Australians use GSM. If your cellphone is on a GSM system, and you have a world-capable multiband phone such as many Sony Ericsson, Motorola, or Samsung models, you can make and receive calls around the globe. Just call your wireless operator and ask for "international roaming" activation on your account. Be forewarned, however, that exorbitant charges are applied to making and even receiving calls, from $2 to $3 per minute.

There are no phone-rental kiosks in the Panama City airport, and travelers who need to make a lot of local calls and receive international calls are better off **buying a phone** in Panama. Cellphones that accept prepaid phone cards are as cheap as $30 in electronics stores in Panama City (and come with a bonus of $20 in calls), and phone-card companies have nonstop promotions that double or triple the value of phone cards. Local calls are as low as 10¢ per minute, and incoming calls are free.

Wilderness adventurers headed to remote destinations or cruisers might consider renting a **satellite phone ("satphone")**. It's different from a cellphone in that it connects to satellites and works where there's no cellular signal or ground-based tower. You can rent satellite phones from **RoadPost** (✆ **888/290-1606** or 905/272-5665; ww.roadpost.com) or from **InTouch USA** (✆ **800/872-7626**), which offers a wider range of satphones but at higher rates. Per-minute call charges are comparable to roaming charges with a regular cellphone, but the phone rental is $90 or more per week. As of this writing, purchasing a satphone is prohibitively expensive.

11 Getting There

BY PLANE

All international flights land at the newly expanded **Tocumen International Airport** (PTY; ✆ **238-2600**). Air Panama flights from Costa Rica to Panama City land at the **Marcos A. Gelabert Airport** (PAC), which is more commonly referred to as **Albrook Airport** (✆ **315-0241**).

There is also direct service from San José, Costa Rica, to the David and Bocas del Toro airports (see chapters 8 and 9, respectively). Taca Airlines (see below) has service from Costa Rica, arriving at Tocumen.

The following airlines serve Panama City from the United States, using the gateway cities listed. **American Airlines** (© 800/433-7300 in the U.S., or 269-6022 in Panama; www.aa.com) has two daily flights from Miami; **Copa Airlines** (© 800/359-2672 in the U.S., or 227-0116 in Panama; www.copaair.com) has two daily flights from Miami, and one daily flight from Orlando, New York, and Los Angeles. **Delta Airlines** (© 800/241-4141 in the U.S., or 214-8118 in Panama; www.delta.com) offers one daily flight from Atlanta; **Taca** (© 800/400-8222 in the U.S., or 360-2093 in Panama; www.taca.com) has one daily flight from all major U.S. hubs, but with a stopover in El Salvador or Costa Rica. **Mexicana** (© 800/531-7921 in the U.S., or 264-9855 in Panama; www.mexicana.com) offers daily flights from Miami, Dallas, and Los Angeles; however, they connect with Copa Air in Mexico City, so you're better off with a direct flight with Copa. From Canada, flights to Panama City are available through American Airlines, with a connection in Miami.

From London, **Iberia** (© 0870/609-0500 in the U.K., or 227-3966 in Panama; www.iberia.com) has daily flights to Panama City that connect in either Madrid or Costa Rica; **American Airlines** and **British Airways** have daily flights that connect in Miami; **Continental Airlines** has daily flights that connect in Orlando or Houston; **Delta** has a daily flight that connects in Atlanta.

From Australia, **Qantas** (© 9691-3636; www.qantasair.com) has daily flights in conjunction with Copa Air from Sydney, connecting in Honolulu or Los Angeles; **Air New Zealand** (© 507-264-8756 in

---

(Tips) Getting through the Airport

- Arrive at the airport 1 hour before a domestic flight and 2 hours before an international flight; if you show up late, tell an airline employee and he or she will probably whisk you to the front of the line.

- Beat the ticket-counter lines by using airport electronic kiosks or even online check-in from your home computer, from where you can print out boarding passes in advance. Curbside check-in is also a good way to avoid lines.

- Bring a current, government-issued photo ID such as a driver's license or passport. Children under 18 do not need government-issued photo IDs for flights within the U.S., but they do for international flights to most countries.

- Speed up security by removing your jacket and shoes before you're screened. In addition, remove metal objects such as big belt buckles. If you've got metallic body parts, a note from your doctor can prevent a long chat with the security screeners.

- Use a TSA-approved lock for your checked luggage. Look for Travel Sentry certified locks at luggage or travel shops and Brookstone stores (or online at www.brookstone.com).

New Zealand; www.airnewzealand.com) also works in conjunction with Copa Air with one daily flight from Auckland, connecting in Los Angeles.

For information about getting into town from the airport, see chapter 5.

FLYING FOR LESS: TIPS FOR GETTING THE BEST AIRFARE

- Passengers who can book their ticket either **long in advance or at the last minute,** or who **fly midweek** or **at less-trafficked hours,** may pay a fraction of the full fare. If your schedule is flexible, say so, and ask if you can secure a cheaper fare by changing your flight plans.
- Search the **Internet** for cheap fares (see "Planning Your Trip Online," earlier in this chapter).
- Keep an eye on local newspapers for **promotional specials** or **fare wars,** when airlines lower prices on their most popular routes. You rarely see fare wars offered for peak travel times, but if you can travel in the off-months, you may snag a bargain.
- Try to book a ticket **in its country of origin.** If you're planning a one-way flight from Johannesburg to Bombay, a South Africa–based travel agent will probably have the lowest fares. For multi-leg trips, book in the country of the first leg; for example, book New York–London–Amsterdam–Rome–New York in the U.S.
- **Consolidators,** also known as bucket shops, are great sources for international tickets, although they usually can't beat Internet fares within North

America. Start by looking in Sunday newspaper travel sections; U.S. travelers should focus on the *New York Times, Los Angeles Times,* and *Miami Herald.* U.K. travelers should search in the *Independent, The Guardian,* or *The Observer.* For less-developed destinations, small travel agents who cater to immigrant communities in large cities often have the best deals. *Beware:* Bucket-shop tickets are usually nonrefundable or rigged with stiff cancellation penalties, often as high as 50% to 75% of the ticket price, and some put you on charter airlines, which may leave at inconvenient times and experience delays. Several reliable consolidators are worldwide and available online. **STA Travel** has been the world's lead consolidator for students since purchasing Council Travel, but their fares are competitive for travelers of all ages. **Intratours** (© 800/334-8069; www.intratours.com) is a consolidator that specializes in Latin America, offering competitive prices and spring and summer deals. **ELTExpress** (Flights.com; © 800/TRAV-800; www.eltexpress.com) has excellent fares worldwide. **FlyCheap** (© 800/FLY-CHEAP; www.1800 flycheap.com), owned by package-holiday megalith MyTravel, has good fares to sunny destinations. **Air Tickets Direct** (© 800/778-3447; www. airticketsdirect.com) is based in Montreal and leverages the currently weak Canadian dollar for low fares;

Flying with Film & Video

Never pack film—exposed or unexposed—in checked bags, because the new, more powerful scanners in U.S. airports can fog film. The film you carry with you can be damaged by scanners as well. X-ray damage is cumulative; the faster the film, and the more times you put it through a scanner, the more likely the damage. Film under 800 ASA is usually safe for up to five scans. If you're taking your film through additional scans, U.S. regulations permit you to demand hand inspections. In international airports, you're at the mercy of airport officials. On international flights, store your film in transparent baggies, so you can remove it easily before you go through scanners. Keep in mind that airports are not the only places where your camera may be scanned: Highly trafficked attractions are X-raying visitors' bags with increasing frequency.

Most photo supply stores sell protective pouches designed to block damaging X-rays. The pouches fit both film and loaded cameras. They should protect your film in checked baggage, but they also may raise alarms and result in a hand inspection.

You'll have little to worry about if you are traveling with **digital cameras.** Unlike film, which is sensitive to light, the digital camera and storage cards are not affected by airport X-rays, according to Nikon.

Carry-on scanners will not damage **videotape** in video cameras, but the magnetic fields emitted by the walk-through security gateways and hand-held inspection wands will. Always place your loaded camcorder on the screening conveyor belt or have it hand-inspected. Be sure your batteries are charged, as you may be required to turn the device on to ensure that it's what it appears to be.

they also book trips to places that U.S. travel agents won't touch, such as Cuba. (Panama is a popular gateway to Cuba.)

- Join **frequent-flier clubs.** Frequent-flier membership doesn't cost a cent, but it does entitle you to better seats, faster response to phone inquiries, and prompter service if your luggage is stolen, your flight is canceled or delayed, or you want to change your seat. And you don't have to fly to earn points; **frequent-flier credit cards** can earn you thousands of miles for doing your everyday shopping. With more than 70 mileage awards pro-

grams on the market, consumers have never had more options. Investigate the program details of your favorite airlines before you sink points into any one. Consider which airlines have hubs in the airport nearest you, and, of those carriers, which have the most advantageous alliances, given your most common routes. To play the frequent-flier game to your best advantage, consult Randy Petersen's **Inside Flyer** (www.insideflyer.com). Petersen and friends review all the programs in detail and post regular updates on changes in policies and trends.

LONG-HAUL FLIGHTS: HOW TO STAY COMFORTABLE

- Your choice of airline and airplane will definitely affect your legroom. Find more details about U.S. airlines at **www.seatguru.com**. For international airlines, the research firm Skytrax has posted a list of average seat pitches at **www.airlinequality.com**.
- Emergency-exit seats and bulkhead seats typically have the most legroom. Emergency-exit seats are usually left unassigned until the day of a flight (to ensure that the able-bodied fill the seats); it's worth getting to the ticket counter early to snag one of these spots for a long flight. Many passengers find that bulkhead seating (the row facing the wall at the front of the cabin) offers more legroom, but keep in mind that bulkheads are where airlines often put baby bassinets, so you may be sitting next to an infant.
- To have two seats for yourself in a three-seat row, try for an aisle seat in a center section toward the back of coach. If you're traveling with a companion, book an aisle and a window seat. Middle seats are usually booked last, so chances are good you'll end up with three seats to yourselves.
- Ask about entertainment options. Many airlines offer seatback video systems where you get to choose your movies or play video games—but only on some of their planes. (Boeing 777s are your best bet.)
- To sleep, avoid the last row of any section or the row in front of an emergency exit, as these seats are the least likely to recline. Avoid seats near highly trafficked toilet areas. Avoid seats at the backs of many jets—these can be narrower than those in the rest of coach. You may want to reserve a window seat so you can rest your head and avoid being bumped in the aisle.
- Get up, walk around, and stretch every 60 to 90 minutes to keep your blood flowing.
- Drink water before, during, and after your flight to combat the lack of humidity in airplane cabins. Avoid alcohol, which will dehydrate you.
- If you're flying with kids, don't forget to carry on toys, books, pacifiers, and chewing gum to help them relieve ear pressure buildup during ascent and descent.

12 Packages for the Independent Traveler

Package tours are simply a way to buy the airfare, accommodations, and other elements of your trip (such as car rentals, airport transfers, and sometimes even activities) at the same time and often at discounted prices.

One good source of package deals is the airlines themselves. Most major airlines offer air/land packages, including **American Airlines Vacations** (© 800/321-2121; www.aavacations.com), **Delta Vacations** (© 800/221-6666; www.delta vacations.com), and **Copa Airlines Vacations** (© 800/FLY-COPA; www.copaair. com). Several big **online travel agencies**—Expedia, Travelocity, Orbitz, Site59, and Lastminute.com—also do a brisk business in packages.

Travel packages are also listed in the travel section of your local Sunday newspaper. Or check ads in the national travel magazines such as *Arthur Frommer's Budget Travel Magazine, Travel + Leisure, National Geographic Traveler,* and *Condé Nast Traveler.*

> **Tips   Ask before You Go**
>
> Before you invest in a package deal or an escorted tour:
>
> - Always ask about the **cancellation policy.** Can you get your money back? Is a deposit required?
> - Ask about the **accommodations choices and prices** for each. Then look up the hotels' reviews in a Frommer's guide and check their rates online for your specific dates of travel. Also find out what types of rooms are offered.
> - Request a complete **schedule** (escorted tours only).
> - Ask about the **size** and demographics of the group (escorted tours only).
> - Discuss what is included in the **price** (transportation, meals, tips, airport transfers, and so on—escorted tours only).
> - Finally, look for **hidden expenses.** Ask whether airport departure fees and taxes, for example, are included in the total cost—they rarely are.

13 Escorted General-Interest Tours

Escorted tours are structured group tours, with a group leader. The price usually includes everything from airfare to hotels, meals, tours, admission costs, and local transportation.

Despite the fact that escorted tours require big deposits and predetermined hotels, restaurants, and itineraries, many people derive security and peace of mind from the structure they offer. Escorted tours—whether they're navigated by bus, motorcoach, train, or boat—let travelers sit back and enjoy the trip without having to drive or worry about details. They take you to the maximum number of sights in the minimum amount of time with the least amount of hassle. They're particularly convenient for people with limited mobility and they can be a great way to make new friends.

On the downside, you'll have little opportunity for serendipitous interactions with locals. The tours can be jam-packed with activities, leaving little room for individual sightseeing, whim, or adventure—plus they often focus on the heavily touristed sites, so you miss out on many a lesser-known gem.

14 Getting Around Panama

BY PLANE

Travelers with a tight schedule or little patience for long hours in a bus can fly cheaply and conveniently via one of two national airlines, **Air Panama** (© 316-9000; www.flyairpanama.com) and **Aeroperlas** (© 315-7500; www.aeroperlas.com). Both companies have daily scheduled flights to most major destinations in Panama, and both have similar levels of service and quality of planes. If you are arriving in Panama City and plan to head straight out on a national flight to another destination, keep in mind that you must transfer from the Tocumen Airport to the Albrook Airport, about 45 minutes away.

More remote destinations in Panama can be reached by scheduled or charter flights aboard a small plane, which touches down on a dirt airstrip. Airlines charge a 5% tax on all flights. Most problematic on domestic flights are **weight restrictions,** which are **25 pounds** for checked baggage and **6 pounds** for hand-held luggage. Overweight baggage is charged 1% of the flight cost per pound, and sometimes extra baggage may need to be sent on another flight if the total allowable excess weight of the plane has been exceeded.

BY CAR

Renting a car while visiting Panama City is unnecessary, and braving the chaotic city streets is only for the adventurous. A few visitors opt to rent a vehicle for the freedom to visit attractions around the city; moreover, renting a car is a lot cheaper than the cost of a private tour. In the interior regions, a car is an excellent way to see the sights at your own pace. The biggest headaches for drivers are poorly maintained side roads and lack of signage. If you're planning on traveling along country or secondary roads, or during wet, muddy conditions, consider a 4WD vehicle with high clearance, and book ahead since these vehicles sell out fast. **Thrifty** rents significantly cheaper 4WD vehicles than any other rental company in Panama.

Before driving off, you'll be asked to inspect the vehicle's exterior for any scrapes or dents. Be thorough with the inspection because rental agencies are often not scrupulous when it comes to noting pre-existing damages on your contract—then you're stuck with the bill when you return the car. Also, if you are in an accident, check your bill to make sure the rental agency hasn't charged you more than your deductible.

To rent a car, you'll need a driver's license from your country of residence, your passport, and a major credit card. Drivers must by law be 23 years old to rent; however, most agencies require drivers to be 25 years or older.

Note: It is always cheaper to reserve a vehicle online or from your own country than to book a vehicle upon arrival in Panama.

Among the agencies operating in Panama are: **Avis** (✆ 800/230-4898 in the U.S., or 278-9444; www.avis.com); **Budget** (✆ 800/527-0700 in the U.S., or 263-8777; www.budgetpanama.com); **Hertz** (✆ 800/654-3131 in the U.S., or 260-2111; www.hertz.com); **National** (✆ 800/227-7368 in the U.S., or 265-2222; www.nationalpanama.com); **Payless** (✆ 800/582-7432 in the U.S., or 222-1881; www.payless.com.pa); **Thrifty** (✆ 800/847-4389 in the U.S., or 264-2613; www.thrifty.com). For more listings of Panamanian car-rental agencies, see "By Car" under "Getting Around," in chapter 5.

ROAD CONDITIONS   The Carretera Panamericana (Pan-American Highway) runs from Costa Rica at the Paso Canoa border to the end of the line at Yaviza, in the Darién. This highway is four lanes around major population areas and two lanes in other areas—and for the most part it's in good shape. Major road improvements and maintenance on secondary roads are usually politically motivated, not to mention erratic; rain and tropical sun also play their parts in the quick deterioration of roads. On secondary roads, prepare yourself for lots of crunchy gravel and potholes. Also keep an eye out for livestock grazing along the shoulder.

RENTER'S INSURANCE   Before leaving home, check to see if your own car-insurance policy covers you when abroad, and if this coverage extends to other persons driving the vehicle, if your policy covers liability to injured outside parties, and whether the *type* of vehicle you're renting is covered. Rental agencies charge $12 a day for liability insurance.

Your credit card, if used when renting, may protect you from damages—but not liability. Call your credit card company for details, but usually your credit card will cover you for damages or theft of the vehicle, or cover the deductible if you already hold car insurance.

MAPS   Detailed, reliable maps are hard to come by in Panama. Bookstores, some hotel gift shops, and travel agencies sell **Kevin Healey's "Panama Travel Reference Map"** (ITMB Publishing), the best route map currently available. It's not widely available in Panama, so it's best to order before you leave (www.itmb.com). Distances on maps can be deceiving, considering how much the roads curve and pass over hills; also, poor road conditions will cause you to slow down frequently.

The most frustrating aspect of driving in the country is the almost total lack of signs. You'll want to pay special attention to kilometer distances listed on maps to make sure you're turning off at the correct exit. If you choose to drive at night on country lanes, you'll doubtless get lost as tiny, nameless villages ghost by. Therefore, it's recommended that you drive during the day.

BY BUS

Bus travel is the cheapest form of transportation in Panama, and service is available to all distant corners of the country. Buses are not large coaches but rather "maxivans" that seat around 10 to 25 people, so expect a reasonable level of comfort but nothing as fancy as reclining seats. All buses that head to the interior leave from Panama City's Albrook Terminal, which is about a $2 taxi ride from downtown. Buses to major towns such as David or Valle de Antón leave more or less on the hour or half-hour throughout the day. Excepting buses headed to Costa Rica, bus service operates on a first-come, first-served basis.

Two companies offer service to and from Costa Rica: **Tica Bus** (© **314-6385;** www.ticabus.com) and **Panaline** (© **227-8648**). Both companies have large, air-conditioned coaches. Tica Bus leaves for San José at 11am, Panaline leaves at 12:30pm; the cost is $50 round-trip. *Tip:* Remember that the border-control authorities in both Costa Rica and Panama require proof of onward travel—if you don't have it, you'll be required to buy a round-trip ticket even if you don't plan to use the return portion. It is a good idea to buy your ticket to Costa Rica in advance, especially around holidays.

15 Tips on Accommodations

High season in Panama is the dry season, roughly **early December to late April.** Hotels in Panama City do not generally adhere to high- and low-season rates, but some hotels in popular tourist areas do. Price ranges listed in hotel reviews reflect a range encompassing low and high season; for example, $50 to $75 for a double would mean $50 from May to November and $75 from December to April. Precise start and end dates for high season may vary from hotel to hotel. A few of the more remote lodges may close entirely from April to October. Check with individual properties for details about rates.

ROOM RATES

The hotels listed in this book are categorized broadly by price: **Very Expensive,** $150 and up; **Expensive,** $100 to $150; **Moderate,** $50 to $100; and **Inexpensive,** under $50 for a double. *Rates in this book do not include a government-mandated 10% hotel tax, unless otherwise specified.* This tax could add considerably to the cost of your stay, especially at expensive hotels.

Hotels may include **breakfast** in the price, either continental or a full breakfast or breakfast buffet. If your hotel offers an all-inclusive package that includes meals, compare the package price against the room cost alone paired with ordering meals from their restaurant's menu—some hotels inexplicably gouge travelers when it comes to meals in all-inclusive packages. Also inquire as to whether a hotel includes round-trip transportation from the airport. If not, hotels can usually organize transportation for about $20 one-way.

SAVING ON YOUR HOTEL ROOM

The **rack rate** is the maximum rate that a hotel charges for a room. Small to midsize hotels normally list their true nightly rates, while chains and megaresorts publish rack rates. Hardly anybody pays rack rates, however, except in high season or on holidays. To lower the cost of your room:

- **Ask about special rates or other discounts.** Panamanian hotels commonly offer sizeable discounts to **seniors** who qualify. (Age may vary from hotel to hotel, but generally those 60 and up are considered seniors.) Unfortunately, some hotels extend senior discounts only to Panamanian residents. Hotels in Panama City offer **corporate rates** seemingly to anyone who asks for them, so do not hesitate to do so. At the very most, a hotel may ask you for the name of the company you work for, but rarely is proof of travel for business required.
- **Dial direct.** When booking a room in a chain hotel, you'll often get a better deal by calling the individual hotel's reservation desk rather than the chain's main number.
- **Book online.** Many hotels offer Internet-only discounts, or supply rooms to Priceline, Hotwire, or Expedia at rates much lower than the ones you can get through the hotel itself.
- **Remember the law of supply and demand.** Resort hotels are most crowded and therefore most expensive on weekends, so discounts are usually available for midweek stays. Business hotels in downtown locations are busiest during the week, so you can expect big discounts over the weekend. Many hotels have high-season and low-season prices, and booking even 1 day after high season ends can mean big discounts.
- **Look into group or long-stay discounts.** If you come as part of a large group, you should be able to negotiate a bargain rate. Likewise, if you're planning a long stay (at least 5 days), you might qualify for a discount. As a general rule, expect 1 night free after a 7-night stay.
- **Avoid excess charges and hidden costs.** Buy or rent a cellphone, use pay phones, or use prepaid phone cards instead of dialing direct from hotel phones, which usually have exorbitant rates. Don't be tempted by the room's minibar offerings. Prices for cocktails, beverages, and snacks at more remote lodges can be very high, so bring your own if trying to keep costs down.
- Consider the pros and cons of **all-inclusive** resorts and hotels. The term "all-inclusive" means different things at different hotels. Many all-inclusive hotels will include three meals daily, sports equipment, spa entry, and other amenities; others may include all or most drinks. In general, you'll save money going the "all-inclusive" way—as long as you use the facilities provided. The downside is that your choices are limited and you're stuck eating and playing in one place for the duration of your vacation.
- **Book an efficiency.** A room with a kitchenette allows you to shop for groceries and cook your own meals. This is a big money saver, especially for families on long stays. In most of

Panama, hotels with kitchenettes are referred to as **"aparthotels,"** an amalgam of apartment and hotel. Kitchenettes can be anything from a hot plate and microwave to a full-scale kitchen.

- **Consider enrolling in hotel "frequent-stay" programs,** which are upping the ante lately to win the loyalty of repeat customers. Frequent guests can now accumulate points or credits to earn free hotel nights, airline miles, in-room amenities, and merchandise. Perks are awarded by many chain hotels and motels. Many chain hotels partner with other hotel chains, car-rental firms, airlines, and credit card companies to give consumers additional incentive to do repeat business.

HOTEL OPTIONS

Travelers of every budget and taste will find lodging that meets their needs throughout Panama, including all-inclusive luxury resorts, rustic lodges, intimate bed-and-breakfasts, and pared-down, midrange hotels for those who simply want a cheap place to sleep. In fact, Panama's strong suit is its **moderately priced hotels** in the $50 to $100 range. Hotels from $40 to $65 are lean on style, and mattresses are not orthopedic and fitted with high-thread-count sheets, but more budget-minded or bohemian travelers won't mind. These hotels usually have air-conditioning and TV, too. In the $65 to $100 per night range, you'll find outstanding hotels, ecolodges, and B&Bs that include all amenities and are usually located in beautiful surroundings. Few remote lodges have in-room amenities such as television, telephones, or hair dryers, and some solar-power-generated hotels may have electricity for a few hours only, or no electricity at all. Remote lodges usually have ceiling fans or cross-ventilation instead of air-conditioning.

Panama is a world-class eco-tourism destination, and therefore there are many nature-oriented **ecolodges** throughout the country. These lodges are found in natural settings and frequently offer opportunities to see sloths, monkeys, and a host of birds, sometimes even from your bedroom window. Ecolodges are so-called for their commitment to sustainable tourism, or because they are centered around activities that involve learning about tropical forests or bird-watching. They range from spartan facilities in converted scientific research stations to luxury accommodations. Ecolodges can be quite expensive if you throw in the cost of a chartered plane, guided excursions, and meals. Also, consider the elements you'll be forced to put up with, including biting insects, heat and humidity, strenuous hikes, or rugged transportation to see wildlife.

Tip: When surfing the Internet for a hotel room, keep in mind that some hotels, in an effort to boost occupancy, often make claims about the property that are at best exaggerated and at worst outrageous. Photos can be taken at such an angle as to hide an unattractive element of the hotel (which could be the neighborhood surrounding it), and photos never show the nicks and scrapes that general use leaves behind. Some hotels blow their budget on their website and do little in the way of property upkeep. Use this guide to help make the right lodging decision when booking.

LANDING THE BEST ROOM

Somebody has to get the best room in the house. It might as well be you. You can start by joining the hotel's frequent-guest program, which may make you eligible for upgrades. A hotel-branded credit card usually gives its owner "silver" or "gold" status in frequent-guest programs for free. Always ask about a corner room. They're often larger and quieter, with more windows and light, and they often cost the

> **Tips Dial E for Easy**
>
> For quick directions on how to call Panama, see the "Telephones" listing in the "Fast Facts: Panama" section at the end of this chapter.

same as standard rooms. When you make your reservation, ask if the hotel is renovating; if it is, request a room away from the construction. Ask about nonsmoking rooms; rooms with views; rooms with twin, queen-, or king-size beds. If you're a light sleeper, request a quiet room away from elevators, restaurants, bars, and discos. Ask for a room that has been most recently renovated or redecorated.

If you aren't happy with your room when you arrive, ask for another one. Most lodgings will be willing to accommodate you.

In resort areas, particularly in warm climates, ask the following questions before you book a room:

- What's the view like? Cost-conscious travelers may be willing to pay less for a back room facing the parking lot, especially if they don't plan to spend much time in their room.
- Does the room have air-conditioning or ceiling fans? Do the windows open? If they do, and the nighttime entertainment takes place alfresco, you may want to find out when showtime is over.
- What's included in the price? Your room may be moderately priced, but if you're charged for beach chairs, towels, sports equipment, and other amenities, you could end up spending more than you bargained for.

16 Tips on Dining

Panama is a melting pot of cultures and ethnic groups, and the dining scene here reflects this, especially in Panama City. International restaurants such as Italian, Swiss, Chinese, Middle Eastern, and creative, fusion-style eateries please more sophisticated palates and are plentiful. There are a lot of solid choices for cheap dining, too, and the usual fast-food chains abound.

Tourist-friendly destinations such as Boquete are home to several outstanding restaurants. Outside of major cities and tourist destinations, travelers will find mostly traditional **Panamanian food** that is heavy on seafood—primarily *pargo* (red snapper), *corvina* (sea bass), *langostina* (jumbo shrimp), calamari, and *pulpo* (octopus). Panamanian fare is quite good, though there isn't much diversity, and meat and seafood are always paired with the ubiquitous coconut rice and

beans, a small cabbage salad, and *patacones* (fried green plantains).

If you've booked at a remote lodge or an all-inclusive resort, chances are the only place to dine is within the hotel's own restaurant. Most ecolodges do not beckon romantics with a candlelit table for two—meals are normally served family-style, with a buffet and common dining table that fosters conversation with other guests. This can be a good or bad thing, depending on who the other guests are. Ecolodge meals range from insipid to inspired—some chefs have mastered the art of quality meals in spite of the remote location, others fall back on fried foods and rice and beans.

For inexpensive dining, Panama has dinerlike *cafeterías* that serve a set meal called *comida corriente,* which consists of an appetizer or soup, main course, and usually a beverage; these generally cost from $3 to $5. *Panaderías* are bakeries and a good bet for a modest breakfast of a pastry and coffee; some even have tables.

Restaurants in Panama typically begin serving breakfast between 7 and 8am; lunch runs from noon to 3pm, and dinner from 6 to 10pm. In Panama City, some restaurants stay open until 11pm or midnight. Lodges that cater to early-to-rise, early-to-bed bird-watchers serve breakfast at 6am, and dinner at 7pm. In provincial towns dinner is early, starting at 6 or 7pm, and often the kitchen is closed by 9pm—so plan on early dining.

Restaurants accept **reservations** but they are really only necessary for Panama City's finer establishments or at intimate eateries with just a few tables. And even if you just show up, you usually have to wait only a bit at the bar for a table, or you'll luck out and be ushered to a table right away.

Tipping is a customary 10% of the total bill. *Note:* Avoid overtipping and check the breakdown of charges on your bill, because many restaurants automatically charge a 10% service fee as a tip. The tax on restaurant bills is 5%.

Grocery stores around the country are well-stocked with local and imported products; some towns even boast an organic or gourmet supermarket. The national chain El Rey opens early and closes late, and in some major towns and cities the supermarket is open 24 hours.

Restaurant listings in this book are divided into three price categories, based on the average price of a meal, excluding beverages and tip: **Expensive,** more than $20; **Moderate,** $10 to $20; and **Inexpensive,** less than $10.

For more information about food and drink, see "Panamanian Food & Drink," in appendix A.

17 Recommended Books, Films & Music

For a guide to English-language bookstores in Panama City, see "Fast Facts: Panama City," in chapter 5. For literature concerning the natural habitat of Panama, its forests, birds, insects, and wildlife, head straight to the **Corotu Bookstore** at the Smithsonian in Panama City on Roosevelt Avenue in Ancon (© **212-8000**); you won't find a better selection anywhere. Many of the books listed here can be ordered from a Web-based book dealer such as Amazon.

GENERAL INTEREST & HISTORY *Emperors in the Jungle,* by John Lindsay-Poland (Duke University Press, 2003), digs deep into the history of U.S. military involvement in Panama during the past century. *Panama,* by Kevin Buckley (Touchstone, 1992), is a gripping read by a former *Newsweek* correspondent who vividly describes the events leading to the overthrow of Manuel Noriega. Another probing insight into the

failure of U.S. policy that led to the rise of Noriega and the invasion is *The Noriega Mess: The Drugs, the Canal, and Why America Invaded,* by Luis E. Murillo (Video Books, 1995), but prepare yourself for 900 pages.

CULTURAL *A People Who Would Not Kneel: Panama, the United States and the San Blas Kuna,* by James Howe (Smithsonian Books, 1998), tells of the powerful resistance by the Kuna Indians to set their own terms against invading Europeans and a Panamanian government intent on flattening their culture and relegating them to inferior social status. *The Art of Being Kuna: Layers and Meaning Among the Kuna of Panama,* by Mari Lynn Salvador (University of Washington Press, 1997), is a beautifully illustrated guide to the arts and culture of the Kuna.

THE PANAMA CANAL *Path Between the Seas: The Creation of the Panama*

Canal, 1870–1914, by David McCullough (Simon & Schuster, 1978), brings the epic history of the building of the canal to life with McCullough's meticulously researched book—but at 704 pages, it's a tremendously long read and a heavy book to carry. *How Wall Street Created a Nation: J.P. Morgan, Teddy Roosevelt, and the Panama Canal,* by Ovidio Díaz Espinoso (Four Walls Eight Windows, 2001), is a page-turning account of the intrigue and back-door dealings between a group of Wall Street bankers and lawyers who paved the way for the construction of the Panama Canal.

NATURAL HISTORY   *A Guide to the Birds of Panama,* by Robert S. Ridgley and John A. Gwynne (Princeton University Press, 1992), is the layman's bible to identifying the many birds you'll see during your visit, and includes tips on where you're most likely to see them. Most guides and nature lodges have a copy of this book on hand. *Tropical Nature: Life and Death in the Rainforests of Central and South America,* by Adrian Forsyth and Ken Miyata (Touchstone Books, 1987), is a passionate, lucid exploration of the inter-relationships of flora and fauna in the tropical rainforest. *The Neotropical Companion,* by John C. Kricher (Princeton University Press, 1999), is tremendously popular with field guides, giving a lively and readable overview of ecological processes at work in the neotropics. Juan Carlos Navarro, the mayor of Panama City, is the author of a glossy coffee-table book, *Parques Nacionales de Panamá* (Balboa Ediciones, 2001), featuring gorgeous photos of national parks in Panama and the flora and fauna found within (in English and Spanish). *The Tapir's Morning Bath,* by Elizabeth Royte (Mariner Books, 2002), is an engaging account of the joys and frustrations of scientific fieldwork by biologists at the canal's Barro Colorado Island.

FAST FACTS: Panama

American Express American Express Travel Services has an office on Avenida Balboa (℃ **207-1100,** or for 24-hour service in the United States, 800/111-0006). This office issues traveler's checks and replacement cards, along with other standard services. To report lost or stolen traveler's checks within Panama, call the numbers above, or try ℃ 207-1111.

Area Codes There are no area codes in Panama.

ATM Networks See "Money," p. 19.

Business Hours Hours for service-oriented businesses in Panama are generally 8am to 1:30pm and 3 to 5pm on weekdays, and 8am to noon on Saturdays. Shops open at 9 or 10am and close at 6 or 7pm; shopping malls close around 8pm. Grocery stores are open 24 hours or 8am to 8pm.

Car Rentals See "Getting Around Panama," p. 38.

Cashpoints See "ATM Networks," above.

Currency See "Money," p. 19.

Driving Rules See "Getting Around Panama," p. 38.

Drugstores Called *farmacias* in Spanish, drugstores are plentiful in Panama City. For 24-hour service, visit a branch of **El Rey supermarket,** the most central of which is on Vía España.

Electricity Electrical plugs are the same as in the U.S., as is Panama's voltage, 110 AC.

Embassies & Consulates The **United States Embassy** is located at Avenida Balboa and Calle 38 Este (© 207-7030). The **Canadian Embassy** is at 53 Este and Nicanor de Obarrio (© 264-7115). The **British Embassy** is at Calle 53 Este and Nicanor de Obarrio (© 269-0866). **Australia** and **New Zealand** do not have an embassy or consulate in Panama; however, the British Embassy can provide consular assistance to citizens of those countries.

Emergencies For fire, dial © **103**; for an ambulance, dial **Seguro Social** at © **229-1133**, or **Cruz Roja** at © **228-2187**.

Etiquette & Customs **Appropriate Attire:** Denizens of Panama City dress well in spite of the heat, meaning no flip-flops, shorts, or tank tops—so bring at least one nice outfit with you. Many better restaurants will not serve patrons in shorts, women included. In resort or beach areas, and in smaller towns with a large expat presence like Boquete, casual wear is okay.

Eating & Drinking: See "Tips on Dining," above.

Greetings & Personal Customs: Panamanians usually greet each other with a light kiss on the right cheek, but they are accustomed to North American habits and most likely will greet you with a handshake if they know you're a gringo or if you are in a business environment. Punctuality is appreciated in business settings, but don't be surprised if your Panamanian guest shows up 30 or 45 minutes late for a dinner party. Many Panamanians do not like to be bothered on Sunday, so reconsider if calling on this day. In business settings, always begin a conversation with light talk before getting to the point. In contrast to North America, the do-it-yourself spirit is not very esteemed in Panama; rather, your ability to hire help to do it for you is what people value. Live-in and daily maids are very common in Panama, meaning as a guest you are not expected to make your bed or help out around the house. When entering a room, you are expected to greet everyone either individually or as a group.

Photography: In the San Blas Islands, Kuna Indians frequently request money to have their photo taken.

Holidays For more information on holidays, see "Panama Calendar of Events & Festivals," earlier in this chapter.

Hospitals Many Panamanian doctors receive their medical degrees in the U.S., and therefore many speak English. The best hospitals in Panama City are: **Centro Medico Paitilla,** at Calle 53 and Avenida Balboa (© 265-8800); **Clínica Hospital San Fernando,** at Vía España (© 278-6364), **Hospital Nacional,** at Avenida Cuba between Calles 38 and 39 (© 207-8100 or 207-8102), and **Hospital Punta Pacífica,** at Calle 53 in Bellavista (© 263-5287). Punta Pacífica is the newest and most advanced hospital in the country and is affiliated with the Johns Hopkins hospital.

Internet Access Internet access is plentiful in Panama, except in more remote areas. Nearly every hotel has at least one computer with Internet access; some have dataports or Wi-Fi (usually in the hotel lobby or business center). Most Internet cafes charge between $2 and $3 per hour. See "The 21st-Century Traveler," earlier in this chapter, for more information.

Language Spanish is the official language in Panama, though English is widely spoken in the tourism industry, and many hotel owners are native English-speakers themselves. Panama's seven indigenous groups speak their own languages in their communities, and in some isolated areas indigenous groups do not speak Spanish fluently. On the Caribbean coast, creoles speak a patois called Guari-Guari or Wari-Wari, a mix of English, Spanish, and Ngöbe-Buglé.

Laundromats Hotel laundry services are very expensive. Laundry (both coin-operated and serviced) and dry-cleaning businesses can be found throughout Panama City; in smaller towns, there is at least one laundromat available.

Liquor Laws Panama's legal drinking age is 18, though it is rarely enforced. Beer, wine, and liquor can be purchased at any supermarket or liquor store, although only until 11pm.

Lost & Found Be sure to tell all of your credit card companies the minute you discover your wallet has been lost or stolen, and file a report at the nearest police precinct. Your credit card company or insurer may require a police-report number or record of the loss. Most credit card companies have an emergency toll-free number to call if your card is lost or stolen; they may be able to wire you a cash advance immediately or deliver an emergency credit card in a day or two. **Visa**'s emergency number is © **800/847-2911** toll-free in the U.S., or call 410/902-8022 collect from Panama. American Express cardholders and traveler's check holders should call © **207-1100** in Panama, or their 24-hour service in the United States at 800/111-0006. MasterCard holders should call © **800/307-7309,** or make a collect call to 636/722-7111.

If you need emergency cash over the weekend when all banks and American Express offices are closed, you can have money wired to you via **Western Union** (© **800/325-6000;** www.westernunion.com).

Mail The central post office (Correos y Telégrafos) is open Monday to Friday 8am to 4pm, and Saturday 8am to 1pm, and is located on Avenida Central in front of the Mercado de Mariscos (© **212-7680**); Panama has no stamp vending machines or post boxes, so you'll have to head to the post office to send a postcard, or ask your hotel if they can do it for you. A letter sent regular mail to the U.S. will arrive in 5 to 10 days; the cost, at press time, is 35¢ for a letter and 25¢ for a postcard. For quick service, send a package via a courier; see "Fast Facts: Panama City," in chapter 5.

Measurements See the chart on the inside front cover of this book for details on converting metric measurements to nonmetric equivalents.

Newspapers & Magazines Panama's principal daily newspaper is *La Prensa;* the five other dailies include *La Panamá América, Crítica Libre, El Universal,* and *La Estrella. La Prensa* publishes a weekend guide supplement on Thursdays, and is the best paper for event listings. The English-language *Panama News,* once available in print, is available online at www.thepanamanews.com. *The Panama Visitor* is in Spanish and English and is a free, bimonthly publication for tourists. You can find copies of the *Miami Herald* in English at supermarkets and at the Gran Morrison chain.

Passports Allow plenty of time before your trip to apply for a passport; processing normally takes 3 weeks but can take longer during busy periods (especially spring). And keep in mind that if you need a passport in a hurry, you'll pay a higher processing fee.

For Residents of Australia: You can pick up an application from your local post office or any branch of Passports Australia, but you must schedule an interview at the passport office to present your application materials. Call the **Australian Passport Information Service** at ℂ **131-232,** or visit the government website at www.passports.gov.au.

For Residents of Canada: Passport applications are available at travel agencies throughout Canada or from the central **Passport Office,** Department of Foreign Affairs and International Trade, Ottawa, ON K1A 0G3 (ℂ **800/567-6868;** www.ppt.gc.ca).

For Residents of Ireland: You can apply for a 10-year passport at the **Passport Office,** Setanta Centre, Molesworth Street, Dublin 2 (ℂ **01/671-1633;** www.irl gov.ie/iveagh). Those under 18 and over 65 must apply for a €12 3-year passport. You can also apply at 1A South Mall, Cork (ℂ **021/272-525**) or at most main post offices.

For Residents of New Zealand: You can pick up a passport application at any New Zealand Passports Office or download it from their website. Contact the **Passports Office** at ℂ **0800/225-050** in New Zealand or 04/474-8100, or log on to www.passports.govt.nz.

For Residents of the United Kingdom: To pick up an application for a standard 10-year passport (5-year passport for children under 16), visit your nearest passport office, major post office, or travel agency, or contact the **United Kingdom Passport Service** at ℂ **0870/521-0410.** Or search its website at www.ukpa.gov.uk.

For Residents of the United States: Whether you're applying in person or by mail, you can download passport applications from the U.S. State Department website at **http://travel.state.gov**. To find your regional passport office, either check the U.S. State Department website or call the **National Passport Information Center** toll-free number (ℂ **877/487-2778**) for automated information.

Police For police, dial ℂ **104** or ℂ **316-0080.**

Restrooms It's rare to find a public restroom in Panama—you'll generally have to rely on hotel lobbies or restaurants. For the most part, they are clean, with modern septic systems. In some remote areas or beach locations, an outhouse-style restroom or a toilet that requires flushing with a bucket of water is more the norm. Restrooms are called *baños,* and are marked *hombres* or *caballeros* for men, and *damas* or *mujeres* for women.

Safety See "Health & Safety," earlier in this chapter.

Smoking Most Panama City restaurants have smoking and nonsmoking areas. However, the trend is moving toward banning smoking altogether for indoor dining. The warm climate means many restaurants have outdoor seating, where smoking is allowed. Smoking laws vary from province to province, and some towns such as Boquete have banned indoor smoking altogether in restaurants and bars. In beach areas with public restaurants and bars with cross ventilation, smoking is allowed.

Taxes All hotels charge 10% tax. Restaurants charge 5% on the total cost of the bill, and often sneak in an automatic 10% for service—check your bill carefully to avoid overtipping.

Telephones Panama has a seven-digit phone numbering system, and there are no city or area codes. The country code for Panama is 507, which you use only when dialing from outside the country. Cellphones are prefixed by 6; in this book, telephone numbers include this prefix because most businesses' published phone numbers include the prefix.

The cheapest way to phone is to use a prepaid phone card, available in kiosks, supermarkets, and pharmacies in quantities of $5, $10, and $20—however, these cards have a life span of 15 to 30 days. **ClaroCOM** has the best rates with 5¢ per minute for national and international calls to the U.S. and the U.K., and 35¢ per minute to cellular phones. Cable & Wireless **Telechip** cards are less value at 15¢ per minute for national calls and 25¢ per minute for international calls. The cards have an access phone number and a scratch-off code, as well as bilingual service. Remember that hotels charge a connection fee even if the connection number is a toll-free number.

For directory assistance: For a number within Panama, dial © **102.** For assistance with finding an international number, dial © **106** for an operator who can connect you with international directory assistance.

For operator assistance: If you need operator assistance when making a call, dial © **106.** For an international operator in the U.S., dial © **109** (AT&T), **108** (MCI), or **115** (Sprint).

To call Panama from outside the country: First dial the international access code—**011** from the U.S.; **00** from the U.K., Ireland, or New Zealand; or **0011** from Australia. Then dial the country code **(507)** followed by the number.

To make international calls from within Panama: First dial **00** and then the country code (U.S. or Canada 1, U.K. 44, Ireland 353, Australia 61, and New Zealand 64). Next dial the area code and number. For example, if you want to call the British Embassy in Washington, D.C., dial © 00-1-202-588-7800.

Toll-free numbers: In Panama, numbers beginning with 800 are toll-free, but calling an "800" number in the States from Panama is not toll-free. In fact, it costs the same as an overseas call.

Time Zone Panama is 5 hours behind Greenwich Mean Time (GMT), and 1 hour ahead of Costa Rica. Panama does not observe daylight saving, so from the last Sunday in October to the first Sunday in April, the time in Panama is the same as that in the U.S. Eastern Time Zone (New York, Miami, and others); from April to October, it's the same as that in U.S. Central Time Zone (Chicago, Houston, and others).

Tipping Tipping in Panama at restaurants is 10% (see "Taxes," above). Taxi drivers do not expect tips, but you might consider it if you've rented a taxi for the day. Porters and bellhops should be tipped $2 to $5 depending on the caliber of the hotel.

Useful Phone Numbers **U.S. Dept. of State Travel Advisory:** © 202/647-5225 (staffed 24 hr.); **U.S. Passport Agency:** © 202/647-0518; **U.S. Centers for Disease Control International Traveler's Hot Line:** © 404/332-4559.

Water The water in most of Panama's major cities and tourist destinations is safe to drink, except in Bocas del Toro. Many travelers' stomachs react adversely to water in foreign countries, however, so it might be a good idea to drink bottled water outside of major hotels and restaurants.

3

Suggested Panama Itineraries

Panama is home to a staggering array of natural landscapes, each beautiful in its own way, and each offering attractions and excursions that appeal to different kinds of people. Scuba-diving fanatics or anglers seeking to reel in boatloads of billfish, for example, might plan their entire journey to Panama around their sport. Multisport resorts have been popping up around the country, too, providing guests with a home base and roster of activities as varied as kayaking, hiking, scuba diving, and mountain biking. These range from pricey, boutique-style lodges boasting "rustic elegance" to destination megaresorts, with 300 or more guest rooms.

Whatever your passion or desire, Panama has it all: a thriving metropolis; endless stretches of pristine, hyper-diverse rainforest; legendary sport fishing; scuba diving in the Caribbean and Pacific (even diving both oceans in 1 day, if you wish); white-water rafting and trekking through rugged mountain highlands; cultural encounters with one of the country's seven indigenous groups; a round of golf on a world-class course; a river cruise on a dugout canoe; or boating the Panama Canal. Of course, there are also plenty of relaxing spots for travelers who just want to kick back on a chaise longue or spend their afternoons taking walks along the beach.

Flying is the best way to get around the country. It's fast, inexpensive, and very convenient; Panama has two national airlines with multiple daily flights from the capital to destinations like David or Bocas

del Toro. Few travelers use Panama City as a transfer hub. There's just too much to do and see within the city limits and around the Canal Zone, which is why most travelers want to spend 2 or 3 days here. Also, keep in mind that the Albrook Airport is on the other side of town, about a half-hour to 45-minute drive from Tocumen Airport, so international travelers can't arrive and make immediate connections. (See "Orientation," in chapter 5, for more information on the two airports.) Certain destinations, such as the Comarca Kuna Yala, the Darién, Bocas del Toro, the Pearl Islands, and other offshore islands, cannot be reached by roads, making planes and boats the only feasible methods of arriving.

Driving is a reasonable option for travelers who have enough time and prefer to take the slow road to get to their final destination. El Valle de Antón, the Pacific beaches near Panama City, and the Azuero Peninsula are destinations where travelers are usually better off having rented a car, allowing them to stop along the way at food stands, take photos, and visit those attractions that interest them most. The drive from Panama City to David is approximately 6 hours, so continuing on to Boquete would constitute a full-day's journey (including stops). The most problematic factor when driving is the condition of side roads off the modern Pan-American Highway (also called the Interamericana), which are unpaved and often in poor shape. Some are so rutted and slick that it's impossible to drive without a 4WD. Roads are not properly signed, either. See "By Car" under "Getting Around Panama," in chapter 2, for more information about driving in Panama.

The following itineraries are specific blueprints for memorable vacations that can be adhered to explicitly, or modified according to your desires and likes, or even expanded if you're lucky enough to have an extended vacation.

1 Panama in 1 Week

Given Panama's compact size, and the short flights that quickly connect you to other destinations, travelers can pack a lot into a week here—but the timing is tight. This itinerary includes a 2-day visit to Bocas del Toro, but you might opt instead to spend 2 nights in Boca Chica, near David, and visit Isla Coiba the first day (a long day trip, but worth it), then head out to the Gulf of Chiriquí National Marine Park the next day for sport fishing or lounging on the beach of an uninhabited island.

Day ❶: Getting to Know the City

Arrive and get settled in **Panama City.** If your flight arrives early, visit **Panama Viejo** (p. 113) to get your historical bearings, then head across town for a walking tour of **Casco Viejo** (p. 115). Travelers with little time will want to head straight to Casco Viejo. Dine on Panamanian food at **Las Tinajas** (p. 110) or **Las Barandas** (p. 108).

Day ❷: Getting Deep in the Jungle

One of Panama's top parks for birding, hiking, and just immersing yourself in the earthy, steamy environs of thick rainforest is only 45 minutes from Panama City: **Soberanía National Park** (p. 140). Leave early and bring your binoculars to view hundreds of birds on a walk or mountain-bike ride along **Pipeline Road;** join a **jungle cruise** to see monkeys, crocodiles, and transiting ships on the Panama Canal (p. 142); ride a dugout canoe up the **Chagres River** to visit an Emberá village (p. 144). In the afternoon, pay a visit to the country's star attraction, the **Panama Canal,** at the **Miraflores Locks,** where you can have lunch and tour their visitor center. Head back to Panama City and cool off with a stroll or bike ride along the **Amador Causeway.**

Days ❸ & ❹: To the Highlands

Fly to David and grab a taxi or rent a car for the 45-minute drive to **Boquete.** Settle into your hotel and spend the afternoon getting to know town on foot or by bike, visiting the town's public gardens and other sights. Another option is to dive into an adventurous afternoon activity such as a canopy ride on the **Boquete Tree Trek** (p. 233) or a low-key booked visit to the **Kotowa coffee farm** (p. 234). The following day, hike the **Quetzal Trail** (p. 221), or spend the day **rafting** on a Class II to Class V river. You can also book a bird-watching tour that includes **Finca Lérida** (p. 234) and **Volcán Barú National Park** (p. 230).

Days ❺ & ❻: From the Highlands to the Lowlands

Catch an early-morning flight from David to Bocas del Toro, and settle in to a hotel in Bocas Town, on Isla Colón. Preplan an afternoon tour with your hotel or an outfitter to visit **Swan's Cay** and **Boca del Drago** beach (p. 261), or rent a bicycle and pedal out to Bluff Beach, or take any other hop over to Isla Bastimentos, and then walk the 10 minutes to beautiful **Red Frog Beach** (p. 277). The next day, head out with **Starfleet Scuba** (p. 264), which can put together a

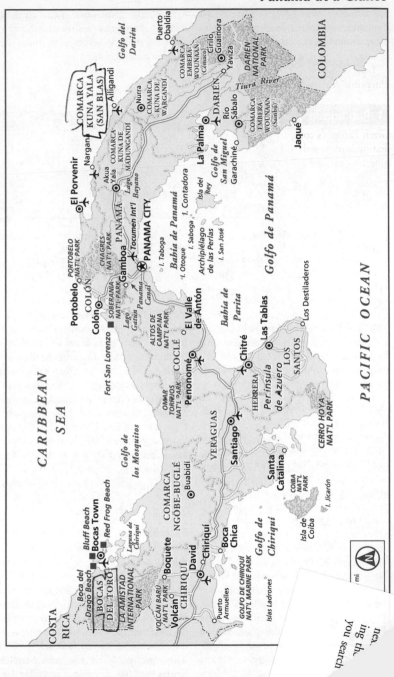

snorkeling or diving trip to the region's top underwater playgrounds, and a cruise through mangrove swamps.

Day ⑦: Leaving Bocas del Toro
Spend the morning wandering around town and soaking up the Caribbean vibe, architecture, and culture. There are quite a few **souvenir shops** in Bocas where you can pick up gifts before your flight back to Panama City.

2 Panama in 2 Weeks

Travelers with 2 weeks will be able to see all of Panama's highlights without feeling as if they're on a tight schedule. This itinerary gives travelers an option of visiting the funky, laid-back region of **Bocas del Toro,** or of experiencing the rustic, indigenous culture of the **Comarca Kuna Yala** and its gorgeous islands. They are two very different island destinations that appeal to different kinds of people.

Days ① & ②: Panama City & Environs
Follow **Days 1** and **2** in the above "Panama in 1 Week" itinerary, but skip the Emberá village trip because you'll visit one in the Darién.

Day ③: Pirates, Ruins & Gold
Ride the **train** (p. 137) along the historical trans-isthmus route to Colón, but skip the city and head out to visit the ruins of **Fuerte San Lorenzo** and **Portobelo** to learn about pirate raids and the historic gold trade (p. 150). Dine on fresh seafood while gazing out over the sea at **Los Cañones** (p. 156), near Portobelo. Drive across the canal and visit the **Gatún Locks** (p. 149) and **Gatún Dam** (p. 149). You can even plan a 1-day Caribbean **scuba-diving** adventure from Panama City, with a tour around Portobelo, by calling **Panama Divers** (p. 154).

Days ④ to ⑥: Wild Darién & Emberá Villages
Join **Ancon Expeditions** for their "Coastal Darién Explorer" that offers a taste of Central America's last great wilderness area (p. 296). You'll get there by small plane to La Palma, and fill the next 3 days with activities such as traveling the **Tuira River** by dugout canoe as you look for dolphins and a wealth of birds, visiting an **Emberá indigenous village,** and trekking through dense and diverse tropical forest. Nights are spent in their simple but comfortable lodge overlooking the Pacific Ocean.

Day ⑦: Off to the Islands
On this day you'll board an early flight from La Palma to **Panama City.** The next destination is the **Caribbean,** and here travelers have two options: Visit **Bocas del Toro** (p. 255) or the **Comarca Kuna Yala** (p. 282) and its gorgeous islands. Travelers to Bocas del Toro can grab a flight out on the same day (Day 7), and lodge anywhere of their choosing. Travelers to the Comarca will need a 6:30am flight out the next day (Day 8). In this case, do a little souvenir shopping and catch the Panama City sights you missed on your first days there.

Days ⑧ to ⑩: Caribbean Fun
Now for a little fun in the Caribbean sun. Book a sailing cruise with **San Blas Sailing** (p. 287), or stay in one of the Comarca's all-inclusive lodges such as **Sapibenega** (p. 292). Visit traditional **Kuna villages,** and spend the rest of your days swimming, snorkeling, or just swaying in a hammock. In Bocas, organize a scuba-diving and/or snorkeling trip to **Crawl Cay** (p. 277) or **Zapatillas Cay**

(p. 263). Hike through jungle on **Isla Bastimentos** and end at a long, empty beach. Visit the **Bahía Honda bat caves** (p. 277). You can also **sea kayak** or take a **surf lesson.** Or just take it easy; you deserve it.

Days ⑪ to ⑭: To the Highlands
Fly from Bocas to **David,** or from the Comarca to Panama City, and then to David. Grab a taxi or rent a car for the 45-minute drive to **Boquete.** Settle into your hotel and spend the afternoon getting to know town by foot or bike, visiting the town's public gardens and other

sights. Aside from the region's trademark coffee tours at farms like **Kotowa** (p. 234), you'll be able to hike through cloud forest on the **Quetzal Trail** (p. 221), bird-watch at **Finca Lérida** (p. 234), zip through the trees on a canopy ride with **Boquete Tree Trek** (p. 233), or spend the day **rafting** on a Class II to Class V river. You can even see both oceans, clouds willing, from the summit of **Volcán Barú National Park** (p. 230), or plan a **sport-fishing** trip leaving from Boca Chica, on the Pacific Coast.

The final day you'll head back to Panama City from David.

3 Panama for Families in 10 Days

Panama is not an overall kid-friendly destination, but then it isn't particularly unfriendly either. A large share of B&Bs, luxury resorts, and boutique hotels do not accept children under 10 to 12 years of age, and discounts for children are not common, either. Also, few hotels outside of destination resorts offer activities specifically tailored to kids and teens—though on the other hand it is easy to book day excursions like snorkeling, jungle treks, or rafting trips, all of which are kid pleasers. If you're not up to planning your own trip, check out chapter 4 for the names of tour operators who can put together a family-oriented vacation for you. Conveniently, a wealth of kid-friendly activities can be found just outside of Panama City. If you have a few more days, add on a trip to the mountain highlands of **Boquete,** where you can white-water raft, ride a canopy zip line, and hike. Kids love swimming pools, so make sure your hotel has one. The following itinerary is best completed in 8 days, with an extra day in Bocas del Toro.

Day ❶: Arrival in Panama City
Head to the **Gamboa Rainforest Resort** (p. 145), near the Panama Canal, a 45-minute to 1-hour drive from the Tocumen International Airport. Gamboa has a games center, tours, a butterfly farm, and an aerial tram. If you want to stay in Panama City, book your family at the **Country Inn & Suites—Panama Canal** (p. 98), an oceanfront hotel with bike path and pool located near the Amador Causeway.

Day ❷: Jungle Cruises & the Canal Zone
Join an early-morning **jungle cruise** on Lake Gatún to visit "Monkey Island"

(p. 142), and view other wildlife like crocodiles, capybaras, and sloths, and motor past huge tankers transiting the canal. Alternatively, ride a dugout canoe up the jungle-shrouded **Chagres River** to visit an Emberá indigenous community and get painted with *jagua* juice. At the Gamboa, take a **bike ride** to Pipeline Road in the afternoon, or visit the resort's serpentarium and butterfly exhibits, and take a ride on their aerial tram. In Panama City, take a bike ride along the **Causeway** and stop at the **Punta Culebra Marine Exhibition Center** (p. 122). Feel free to adapt the following days' suggestions accordingly.

Days ❸ to ❺: From Lowlands to Highlands

Visit the harpy eagle exhibition and see tapirs, ocelots, jaguars, and more at the **Summit Gardens Park & Zoo** (p. 144). Afterward, stop at the Panama Canal's **Miraflores Locks** (p. 136), tour the visitor center, and have an early lunch at their restaurant looking out over ships transiting the locks. After lunch, transfer to El Valle de Antón, 2 hours from the city, and stay at the **Crater Valley Adventure Spa** (p. 186). Relax, bike ride, or let the hotel-activities staff teach your kids to ascend their climbing wall or obstacles course while you have a massage. The following day, book a ride on the **Canopy Adventure** (p. 184) for a thrilling zip-line ride through the forest. Later, families can organize an easygoing horseback ride, bike ride on country lanes, walk to a waterfall, or explore the amphibian exhibit and minizoo at **El Nispero** (p. 186). Spend your last day wandering through the **handicrafts fair** for souvenirs and gifts to take home.

Day ❻: Descent to the Beach

In the morning, transfer back to Panama City for an afternoon flight to the Pearl Islands from Albrook Airport. Settle into your hotel on **Isla Contadora,** or book an all-inclusive stay at the upscale **Hacienda del Mar** (p. 169) on Isla San José. On Contadora, kids get a kick out of renting an ATV or golf cart to zip around the island. Lodge at the **Punta Galeón** (p. 168) for its central location and swimming pool.

Days ❼ & ❽: Sun & Fun in the Pacific Ocean

Your first or second day, book an all-day tour to sail around the idyllic Pearl Islands for the outstanding **snorkeling** and **fishing.** Teens can join a day class to learn the basics of **scuba diving.** For young kids, book a ride in a **glass-bottom boat** to view the underwater world without getting wet. Lounge on one of the island's dozen beaches, especially on the calm-water **Playa Larga Beach** (p. 164), where families can buy a day pass for kids to use the hotel's kayaks, snorkeling gear, swimming pool, and other watersports equipment.

Day ❾: Flight to Panama City

Depending on your departing flight home, leave early or in the afternoon to make your connection. Remember that Albrook Airport is 45 minutes to 1 hour from Tocumen, so plan accordingly.

4 A High-Octane Week of Adventures

Panama can hold its own against adventure-travel heavyweights like Costa Rica, giving you the opportunity to pack a lot of active and adrenaline-fueled excursions into a single week. This is simply an outline, which you should tailor to your interests: Sport fishermen will need to either plan a trip around fishing, or head out for the day from Boca Chica, near David, or from Isla Contadora. If mountain biking is your priority, substitute that for hiking.

Day ❶: Arrive in Panama City

Arrive and get settled in Panama City. If your flight arrives early enough, head to the **Miraflores Locks** (p. 136) at the Panama Canal, tour the museum, and have lunch here while watching massive tankers pass through the locks. In the late afternoon, tour and photograph the picturesque streets of **Casco Viejo** (p. 115), planning your stroll late enough so that you end at **Manolo Caracol** (p. 106) for an adventurous, gourmet meal.

Day ❷: Rumble in the Jungle

Join an adrenaline-charged trip deep into the rainforest of Chagres National Park with **Adventures in Panama** (p. 63). The trip kicks off with a ride in a dugout canoe followed by trekking along narrow trails through wild jungle, **rappelling** a rock face, and taking a cool dip in a creek. Finish with a hot lunch at an **Emberá Indian village** before heading home. At night, check out live jazz music at **Bar Platea** (p. 130) or **Las Bóvedas** (p. 107).

Day ❸: Get Wet & Wild

Grab an early-morning flight from Panama City to David, where **Chiriquí River Rafting** (p. 232) can pick you up on their way to the put-in site at the **Chiriquí Viejo River;** here you'll raft wild Class III to Class V white-water rapids. Afterward, sit back and enjoy the scenery on the ride back to **Boquete,** where you'll settle into your hotel and later get out and stroll around town.

Day ❹: Explore Volcán Barú

Go climb or 4WD to the top of **Volcán Barú,** the highest peak in Panama, for electrifying views spanning from the Caribbean to the Pacific (p. 221). It's a gung-ho and rocky, slippery trail that leaves at sunrise or earlier, and must be planned with a guide or a driver. Or walk the **Quetzal Trail** (p. 221) through emerald rainforest, trekking uphill from Boquete or downhill from Cerro Punta. See if you can spot a **quetzal.** Book a

massage at the **Panamonte Inn & Spa** (p. 238) in the late afternoon to recover from your day of adventure.

Day ❺: Canopy Tour & Biking

Contact **Boquete Tree Trek** to plan a thrilling canopy zip-line ride through the rainforest (p. 233). Arrive early to witness the region's bounty of birds when they are most active. In the afternoon, join the company for a **mountain-bike tour** and downhill ride through the highlands of Boquete; or rent a bike and head out on your own, exploring backcountry roads.

Day ❻: Explore the Underwater World

Wake up early and drive a little over an hour to the Pacific Coast and Boca Chica, where you'll set off with **Exploration Panama** (p. 246) for a scuba-diving, snorkeling, or sport-fishing adventure around the idyllic waters and rocky outcrops of the **Chiriquí Gulf National Marine Park** (p. 245). Have lunch on a deserted island ringed with white sand and turquoise water.

Day ❼: Take a Break & Head Home

Book a flight from David to **Panama City** for your flight home, but remember that you'll need extra time to travel from Albrook to Tocumen Airport. If you can, squeeze in a low-key visit to **Kotowa coffee farms** (p. 234) to see how coffee is produced and head home with a few bags of some of Panama's best beans.

5 Panama City in 3 Days

Panama City is a vibrant metropolis whose proximity to two national parks and the famous canal and its environs makes it an ideal base for travelers who seek to pack in a lot of adventure and sightseeing, but who'd like to finish the day with gourmet dining, comfortable accommodations, and city nightlife.

Day ❶: Getting to Know the City

Start your day at **Panama Viejo** (p. 113), to get your historical bearings and learn about Panama in the handsome visitor

center. Browse the extensive handicrafts market here. Head to **Casco Viejo** for lunch at **Manolo Caracol** (p. 106), then walk it off with a tour around this picturesque neighborhood. Buy a *raspado* at the **Plaza Francia** and enjoy the sea breeze. Check with your hotel for live music and other nighttime events, or drop by a casino at the **Caesar Park Panama** (p. 94) or **Veneto Hotel** (p. 97).

Day ❷: Getting Deep in the Jungle

See Day 2 of "Panama in 1 Week," earlier in this chapter.

Day ❸: Pirates, Ruins & Gold

See Day 3 of "Panama in 2 Weeks," above.

¡BUEN PROVECHO!
Sample Panamanian food at **Las Tinajas,** Calle 51 in El Cangrejo (𝄫 269-3840; p. 110) and be entertained by a folkloric dance show. Or go upscale with gourmet Panamanian fare at **Las Barandas,** Aquilino de la Guardia at Obarrio (𝄫 265-7844; p. 108).

DINNER & ALL THAT JAZZ
Dine on fabulous Peking duck at **Madame Chang,** Av. 5A and Calle Uruguay (𝄫 269-1313; p. 109), or soak up the tropical ambience at the restaurant **La Posta,** Calle 49 at Calle Uruguay (𝄫 269-1076; p. 105). Finish with an evening of jazz at **Las Bóvedas** (p. 107) or **Bar Platea** (p. 130) in Casco Viejo.

4

The Active Vacation Planner

When it comes to active travel, Panama has always taken a back seat to its neighbor Costa Rica, a country that has done much to promote itself as an adventure-travel mecca. Yet Panama is a tropical paradise for adventure-travel enthusiasts, too, offering the same outdoor activities and landscapes as Costa Rica—but with far fewer tourists. Yes, maybe Panama's western neighbor boasts a more developed infrastructure for active travel, but really any kind of sport or outdoor activity in Panama has at least one or two responsible and experienced tour operators that can put together an adventurous trip. A full 30% of Panama's natural habitat is protected, including the wildest jungle in all of Central America, the Darién. There are high peaks with misty cloud forests, primeval rainforest, the best bird-watching in North and Central America, white-water rivers, powdery beaches, and an underwater world packed with sea life.

Plus, unlike Costa Rica, Panama is home to seven Indian groups, as well as Afro-Caribbeans and West African descendants, which provides visitors with fascinating and memorable cultural encounters.

Adventure- and active-travel journeys can be pieced together as day excursions, or your trip can be planned from start to finish by a tour operator. There are a handful of all-inclusive resorts and lodges around the country, too, which plan daily excursions that are either included in the daily rate or are an additional cost. Some of these resorts have bird-watching guides and scuba-diving pros as part of their staff; others subcontract a local outfit. When booking a vacation at an all-inclusive resort, confirm the professional certification of the resort's guides—if you're a fastidious bird-watcher who's come all the way to Panama to see a quetzal, you'll want the finest guide available, not just a guy who likes birds.

1 Organized Adventure Trips

The advantages of traveling with an organized group are plentiful, especially for those who have limited time and resources. Tour operators take the headache out of planning a trip, and they iron out the wrinkles that invariably pop up along the way. The language barrier is less of an issue when you have a guide to translate for you, and a guide can interpret the culture and history of Panama and the natural surroundings of your destination. Most tours include guides, ground transportation, accommodations, meals, and gear. Independent travelers tend to view organized tours as antithetical to the joy of discovery, but leaving the details to someone else does free up substantial time to concentrate on something else. Besides, your traveling companions are likely to be kindred spirits with similar interests.

The best tours limit group size to 10 to 15 people, which allows for personal attention and a bit of breathing room—this is appreciated after a week on the road together. Ask about difficulty levels when you're choosing a tour. Most are focused on "soft" adventure, with light excursions that are suitable even for couch potatoes; be honest with yourself when considering more difficult journeys. A multiday adventure that includes trekking through virgin jungle might look great on paper, but are you physically up to it? Tour operators are responsible for their clients' well-being and safety, but that doesn't let you off the hook. Inquire about your guide's experience, safety record, and insurance policy. Remember, no adventure trip is 100% risk-free.

NORTH AMERICAN–BASED TOUR OPERATORS

These agencies and operators specialize in well-organized, 7- to 15-day tours that allow travelers to pack in a lot of action and diversity in a short period of time. Do a little price comparison when shopping for a tour, as many U.S.-based operators subcontract Panamanian tour operators who can be reached directly. Also, some operators offer trips that are duplicitous in that they plan journeys around all-inclusive lodges that already provide guides and transportation. In other words, the operator is simply booking your reservations and providing a minder-guide to solve any glitches from one stop to the next. A few of the operators include luxury accommodations and gourmet dining as part of the travel itinerary, and are therefore *very* expensive. Remember, the tours shown below do not include airfare! Solo travelers in most cases will be charged the dreaded single supplement that can run an additional $500 to $1,500.

A few tour operators offer custom-made journeys for travelers who wish to craft their itinerary according to their own tastes and interests. Depending on the destination, this option can be reasonably priced or very expensive (less so if you are traveling with a group of friends and meet minimum group size requirements). For more specific activity-oriented tour operators such as those focused on bird-watching, see "Activities A to Z," below. Destination-specific chapters list local guiding services or tour operators.

Abercrombie & Kent (℃ 800/550-7016; www.abercrombiekent.com), an award-winning tour operator that caters to the luxury market, has a new, guided 10-day "Highlights of Panama" tour for $3,835 per person, not including internal airfare. Upscale accommodations and gourmet dining are a feature of this low-key, culturally oriented trip.

Adventure Life Journeys (℃ 800/344-6118; www.adventure-life.com) is a Montana-based operator specializing in travel to Central and South America. Groups are limited to 8 to 12 people, and they only utilize locally run hotels and native guides (prices run $1,270–$1,465 per person). Their weeklong journeys include a trip that combines Panama with Costa Rica; they also offer a 16-day trip ($3,285 per person) with six destinations.

Bike Hike Adventures (℃ 888/805-0061; www.bikehike.com) is a Toronto-based company specializing in multisport adventures for travelers who are in at least moderate shape. Their 9-day "Rumble in the Jungle" includes river rafting, mountain biking, hiking, snorkeling, and canopy rides; as well as visiting the Caribbean Sea, the Pacific Ocean, and the Chiriquí Highlands.

Country Walkers (℃ 800/464-9255; www.countrywalkers.com) focuses on easy to moderate, 3.2 to 9.7km (2- to 6-mile) day hikes through Soberanía National Park, Isla Bastimientos in Bocas del Toro, and the Quetzal Trail in the Chiriquí Highlands, plus a few add-ons like a city tour and a boat cruise in the canal. Lodging is in upscale hotels. Their "Tropical Jewel" trip is 8 days and costs $2,798 per person.

International Expeditions (℃ 800/633-4734; www.ietravel.com) offers a 9-day journey that focuses solely on the Panama Canal region (including boat passage

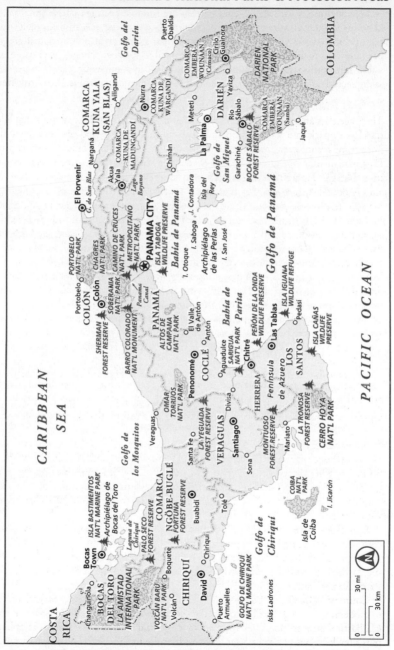

through the canal), with nature and culture excursions in Soberanía National Park, visits to Emberá indigenous villages, and sights along the Caribbean area in the Colón Province; the cost is $2,398 per person. They can add on trips to the San Blas and Bocas del Toro islands.

Wildland Adventures (© 800/345-4453; www.wildland.com) is a well-respected tour operator, offering five journeys from 8 to 14 days that are focused on exploring nature as well as cultural interactions with indigenous groups. The exciting, well-organized trips cover a lot of ground. Wildland Adventures is one of the few U.S. companies to offer trips to the wild Darién jungle. Wildland also offers a 10-day "Family Adventure" with kid-friendly hikes and activities. Prices run $1,850 to $2,450 (adults) and $1,050 (kids under 11).

U.K.-BASED TOUR OPERATORS

Journey Latin America ☆ (© 020/8747-3108; www.journeylatinamerica.co.uk) is the U.K.'s largest tour operator that specializes in Latin American travel. They currently offer tailor-made itineraries and an organized trip, called Tinamou, that includes visits to Canal Zone national parks, the cloud forest of the Chiriquí Highlands, and beaches of Bocas del Toro; the tour lasts 13 days and costs $2,778 per person.

Reef and Rainforest Tours (© 018/0386-6965; www.reefandrainforest.co.uk) specializes in just that, providing small-scale, nature-oriented trips to the Caribbean Sea and the rainforest of the Darién Province (via small plane). The company has an excellent track record, and their trips, though not specifically oriented toward families, are kid-friendly. Their Multiple Wonders of Panama and Panama Wildlife Adventure trips (each lasts 14 days) start at $3,844 per person.

PANAMANIAN TOUR OPERATORS

Foreign tour operators usually subcontract a portion—or 100%—of their tours to established Panamanian companies. Some book their clients on prescheduled trips with other travelers who are not part of the client's tour, while others plan exclusive itineraries but rely on local guides and logistics planners to do the ground work for them. Contacting a local tour operator directly, and thereby cutting out the "middleman," may result in a small price savings.

There are few tour operators in Panama despite the burgeoning tourism industry and the potential that exists here. But the operations that do exist are tried-and-true companies with a staff of full-time, qualified guides, drivers, and customer service reps. Trips can be tailor-made, or operate on predetermined dates, and most offer **day excursions** and **short adventures** that last just a few days. Hotel tour desks can put together a day excursion, but the quality of service can vary dramatically, so it's best to book ahead with one of the companies listed below. Also, if you have a specific activity in mind, it pays to plan ahead because some tours leave only on preset dates or when they have a large enough group. All the companies below have a bilingual staff.

Ancon Expeditions (© 269-9415; www.anconexpeditions.com) is the foremost tour operator in Panama, with a full-time staff of degreed naturalists and bird-watching experts, a handful of remote lodges, and offerings of day excursions and preset and custom-planned journeys to all corners of Panama. Ancon Expeditions began as the travel arm of the Asociación Nacional para la Conservación de la Naturaleza (ANCON), an NGO devoted to the preservation of natural resources and biodiversity; but the two are no longer related. Trips with preset dates can be guaranteed with just two to four people. A few of the more unique offerings are a trek across the isthmus

---

Tips **Getting the Hotel You Want**

Many boutique-style hotels and inns have complained recently that tour operators who receive a hefty commission from a particular hotel tend to steer clients toward that hotel—even if a client has requested different accommodations or is not a good match for the operator's choice of lodging. If a travel operator or agency tells you that a hotel is sold out, and you had your heart set on staying there, do your own investigation and see if this is indeed true.

---

following the old Spanish Camino Real; and Ancon's short adventures (1–5 nights) visiting the San Blas Archipelago, Bocas del Toro, or the Chiriquí Highlands. A few of their trips are based around their own lodges. Ancon specializes in trips that take adventurers deep into the heart of the Darién jungle; they have more trips to this region than any other operator. Day excursions such as a "Panama Canal Rainforest Boat Adventure" are highly recommended, especially for kids.

Ecocircuitos (© 314-1586; www.ecocircuitos.com) is run by a young, dynamic group of travel professionals who specialize in small groups (minimum four and maximum eight people), and who focus heavily on sustainable tourism with a low impact on the environment. They offer everything from a city tour through Casco Viejo to an 11-day bird-watching, trekking, and cultural journey through the San Blas Islands, the Chiriquí Highlands, and Bocas del Toro. Ecocircuitos also has a unique 4-day trip to the Darién that involves trekking through old-growth forest and tent lodging in a traditional Emberá Indian village. Tours are either tailor-made or have a preset itinerary. They recently opened an office in Boquete on Avenida Central (© 720-1506), which offers short adventures in the Chiriquí area.

Adventures in Panama (© 877/726-6222 in the U.S., or 236-8146; www.adventures inpanama.com), whose slogan is "No Tours, Just Adventures," is the operator to go to for active sports such as kayaking, mountain biking, and rock climbing around Panama, and day adventures around Panama City. Tamer adventures, like city tours and cultural encounters with Emberá Indians, are also available and can be combined with sports. One of the company's specialties is the San Blas region—they offer guided tours or can book difficult-to-contact hotels and hostels there. Adventures in Panama focuses on private trips with either a preset itinerary or a tailored adventure to suit your tastes; rates vary according to the size of your party.

Pesantez Tours (© 263-8771 or 223-5374; www.pesantez-tours.com) is an established company that can do all your booking for you, if you're not looking to join a set tour. They focus more on traditional tours of Panama City, trips to El Valle de Antón, the canal, and Portobelo, and they even offer a half-day shopping tour.

2 Activities A to Z

This section is divided by activity, with listings of the prime destinations in Panama for doing each as well as the tour operators and outfitters who tailor trips to the specific activities. Tour operators have local knowledge and, more importantly, they provide guides and in most cases equipment. If you are planning to focus your trip to Panama around one sport or activity, these tour operators and outfitters are your best bet.

Adventure travel carries risks, and travelers should be well aware of dangers before participating in any tour. The operators mentioned in this chapter have been chosen for their safety records and reputations, but ask questions on your own. For example, if your adventure involves boating, what kind of vessel will they use? Dugout canoe *pangas* are common and a colorful way to get around, but for long journeys they're uncomfortable, wet, and dangerous in choppy water; also, few local boat drivers carry radios or safety equipment.

BIKING

Mountain biking is relatively new in Panama. There are few places suitable for riding other than well-established paved and dirt roads, but many of these roads can be dangerous if there is a lot of vehicle traffic. Roads in Panama are curvy, often with hairpin turns, and do not have bike lanes or a proper road shoulder, so keep alert for speeding vehicles coming around a bend. If you just feel like getting out and pedaling around town, you'll find bicycle rentals in more touristy areas that rent for an average of $10 a day. Bicycle-rental shops are listed in regional chapters within this book. There are no tour companies (yet) that offer multiday packages that focus entirely on biking; however, the operators listed below can custom-build a trip for you.

In **Panama City,** the most popular and safest bike-riding area is the Amador Causeway, which is flat and has bike lanes—and a pretty spectacular view to boot. Outside the city, the Gamboa Resort rents bicycles for touring around; from here it's a couple of kilometers to the Pipeline Road Trail, a dirt-and-mud road that is flanked by tropical jungle. **El Valle de Antón** was made for bike riding: Vehicle traffic is light, roads are flat and paved, and a few steep, technical dirt roads offer a good workout. **Boquete,** too, has picturesque, winding roads that provide moderate terrain and pastoral views. Note that rental bicycles around Panama are not top-of-the-line models with shocks and other deluxe fixtures.

Adventures in Panama (see above) offers two bike day trips around Panama City. Their day excursion to the Pipeline Road Trail gives cyclists a chance to get (a little) dirty and ride through jungle at one of the best bird-watching sites in Panama. Across the isthmus, they offer a day tour that begins with a bike ride across the Gatún Locks, connecting with a 6.4km (4-mile) dirt road to Fort San Lorenzo, a road known for birds and wildlife. The company **Bike Hike Adventures** (see above) combines biking on the Amador Causeway and near Fort San Lorenzo as part of their multisport package trips.

BIRD-WATCHING

Panama ranks as one of the world's top bird-watching sites, with more than 950 registered species of resident and migrant birds—more than the U.S. and Canada combined. Because Panama is a land bridge connecting two continents, birders are privy to viewing species from both North and South America. Many of the birds found here are "showcase" birds such as toucans, macaws, and the resplendent quetzal, which delight even non-birders. Keen birders often return home having seen dozens of "life birds," or their first sighting of a bird species. If you head out with a qualified birding guide, expect to see upwards of 100 or more in a single day.

Lodges with the best bird-watching include **Canopy Tower** (p. 145) in Soberanía National Park, and its sister property **Canopy Lodge** (p. 186) in El Valle de Antón; **Sierra Llorona Panama Lodge** (p. 146) southeast of Colón and near Portobelo National Park; **Cana Field Station** (p. 296) in Darién National Park; **Punta Patiño Lodge** (p. 296) in Darién Province near the Gulf of San Miguel; **Los Quetzales Lodge & Spa** (p. 225) on the edge of International Amistad and Volcán Barú national parks. Note that these lodges provide professional bird-watching guides either as part of an all-inclusive package or ordered a la carte. Tour operators listed below center their trips around these all-inclusive lodges, so really what you're getting is a 24-hour professional who is both problem-solver and educational guide.

Bird-watching hot spots include the **Darién Highlands** for macaws, large toucans, colorful tanagers, and endemics such as Pirre Warblers; the **Darién Lowlands,** especially known for harpy eagles; the **Nusagandi** region for speckled antshrikes and sapayoas; **Soberanía National Park** and Pipeline Road, home to more than 525 species including trogons, antbirds, blue cotingas, and other canopy dwellers; **Achiote Road,** near Fort San Lorenzo and Colón, for diurnal raptors and spot-crowned barbets, oropendolas, and pied puffbirds; **El Valle** for North American breeding warblers and black-crowned antpittas; and the neighboring national parks **International Amistad** and **Volcán Barú** (Chiriquí Highlands) for the resplendent quetzal, three-wattled bellbirds, trogons, long-tailed silky flycatchers, tapaculos, and Andean pygmy owls. Two popular birding areas here include **Finca Hartmann** and **Finca Lérida,** both coffee plantations with endemic and migratory species. Seabirds such as magnificent frigate birds nest on **Isla Iguana** in the Azuero; they also nest on **Swan's Cay** in Bocas, along with brown boobies and red-billed tropic birds.

U.S.-BASED TOUR OPERATORS

Caligo Ventures ✛ (© 800/426-7781; www.caligoventures.com) specializes in bird-watching tours, with set itineraries for 9-day tours January through March to the Darién ($2,095), and a combo of Soberanía National Park and the Chiriquí Highlands ($2,560). Caligo uses local, expert birding guides. They also offer 9-day trips for independent travelers for $1,895 from May to November; and $2,095 from December to April.

Field Guides ✛✛ (© 800/728-4953 or 512/263-7295; www.fieldguides.com) is a specialty bird-watching travel operator, with highly esteemed and friendly guides. They offer four all-inclusive 10-day programs from December to March. Their "Wild Darien" visits the Cana Field Station; "Western Panama" focuses on the Chiriquí Highlands; the "Canopy Tower" sticks around Soberanía National Park; and "Wild Panama" visits the San Blas mountain range. Tours cost an average of $2,795 to $3,145, and group size is limited to eight people.

Victor Emanuel Nature Tours ✛✛ (© 800/328-8368 or 512/328-5221; www.ventbird.com) is a well-respected tour operator and the largest company in the world specializing in bird tours. VENT offers not just December-to-March tours, but tours year-round either with one of their own guides or a local guide (or combination). Group limit is 10 people; tours average 7 nights and base around one destination (mostly the Canopy Tower) with optional add-on trips. Prices range from $1,645 to $2,695 for 7 nights.

PANAMANIAN BIRDING COMPANIES

For local independent guides, see the regional chapters in this book. These tour operators provide travelers with multiple-day journeys, but more importantly, they are the companies to contact for shorter day excursions, especially around Panama City. In addition to these operators, the **Panama Audubon Society** (© 232-5977; www.panamaaudubon.org) offers a bird-watching trip around Panama City once a month for nonmembers ($5 per person); and other trips and activities for members. Check their website for dates.

Ancon Expeditions (see above) has the largest staff of professional birding guides, many of whom are contracted by international companies, and they own and run both the Cana Field Station and the Punta Patiño Lodge in the Darién.

Advantage Tours ✦✦ (© 6676-2466; www.advantagepanama.com), which runs the Soberanía Research Lodge in Gamboa, are the travel organizers and outfitters for the international Audubon Society. Their secret asset is Guido Berguido, a degreed bird-watching guide who is one of the friendliest and enthusiastic guides anywhere. Their year-round "Birdwatchers Paradise" combines Soberanía and Achiote Road with Volcán Barú.

CRUISING

It goes without saying that Panama is a major destination for cruise ships drawn by the opportunity to transit the famous Panama Canal. Some cruise ships that focus on the Caribbean simply dock at the Colón 2000 port on the Atlantic side, with passengers taking a day tour on the Panama Railway, visiting Portobelo or an Emberá Indian village, and carrying on to their next port of call—without ever entering the canal.

As a cruise-ship passenger you won't spend a lot of time getting to know Panama, but there is something to be said for experiencing the engineering marvel that is the Panama Canal. Passing through the 80km (50-mile) canal takes about 8 hours from start to finish. Cruise programs that transit the canal are on average 10 to 14 nights long, and visit a handful of Caribbean, Central American, and Mexican ports along the way. Popular stops in Panama include the San Blas Islands, Coiba Island, and Panama City. The company **Aventuras 2000** has the monopoly on shore excursions around the canal.

MAINSTREAM CRUISE LINES   These cruise lines offer something for everyone: **Celebrity Cruises** (© 800/722-5941; www.celebritycruises.com); **Disney Cruise Line** (© 800/951-3532; www.disneycruise.com); **Holland America** (© 877/932-4259; www.hollandamerica.com); **Norwegian Cruise Lines** (© 800/327-7030; www.ncl.com); **Oceania Cruises** (© 800/531-5619; www.oceaniacruises.com); **Orient Lines** (© 800/333-7300; www.orientlines.com); **Princess Cruises** (© 800/421-0522; www.princess.com); and **Royal Caribbean** (© 800/398-9819; www.rccl.com).

LUXURY LINERS   **Crystal Cruises** (© 800/804-1500; www.crystalcruises.com); **Regent Seven Seas Cruises** (formerly Radisson; © 877/505-5370; www.rssc.com); **Seabourn Cruise Line** (© 800/929-9391; www.seabourn.com); and **Windstar Cruises** (© 800/258-7245; www.windstarcruises.com).

SPECIALITY CRUISES   **Lindblad Expeditions** (© 800/397-3348; www.lindblad expeditions.com) has educational cruises that focus on culture and the environment.

Travel agencies and tour operators that specialize in cruises buy in bulk and are often capable of offering lower rates than those advertised by cruise lines, and they stay on top of special deals and promotions. Try **The Cruise Company** (© 800/289-5505; www.thecruisecompany.com); or **World Wide Cruises** (© 800/882-9000; www.wwcruises.com).

DIVING & SNORKELING

Isla Coiba in the Chiriquí Gulf of the Pacific Ocean, is simply *the* best diving site in Panama, often described as a cross between the Cocos Islands in Costa Rica and the Galápagos Islands of Ecuador. Isla Coiba was the site of a notorious penitentiary until 2005, which kept visitors away, and therefore the surrounding waters are untouched.

The snorkeling here is outstanding, too, but diving puts you close to pelagics such as white-tipped sharks, sailfish, manta rays, and dolphins. Coiba is also surrounded by one of the largest coral reefs on the Pacific Coast of the Americas. Other islands such as **Islas Secas,** and the islands within the **National Marine Park** in the Chiriquí Gulf, also provide outstanding diving.

On the Caribbean coast, **Bocas del Toro** is where you want to go to view some of the best and most colorful hard and soft coral in the world. In the Caribbean, visibility is best from March to May, and during September and October. The reef at **Baja Escribano,** between the San Blas and Colón, is the new talked-about dive site for its clear waters and colorful sponges.

Some of the best snorkeling in all of Panama is in the waters surrounding the **Pearl Islands,** for the abundance of marine life found here. Expect multitudinous schools of tropical fish and large pelagics such as white-tipped sharks. Bocas is billed as a top snorkeling site, but you'll need to get away from the standard tours to find the good stuff. **Isla Iguanas,** off the coast of Pedasí in the Pacific Ocean, is excellent for snorkeling, too.

DIVING OUTFITTERS & OPERATORS

The outfitters listed below offer diving trips around Panama, including multi-destination trips. For local dive operations, check the listings in regional chapters. The resort **Islas Secas** in the Chiriquí Gulf and the **Coral Lodge** in the Caribbean are two lodges with on-site dive shops and personalized tours for guests only. For diving in Bocas del Toro, see that chapter.

Panama Divers (© 314-0817 or 6613-4405; www.panamadivers.com) is the premiere dive operation in Panama, based in Panama City and Portobelo. The company plans to open a marina and dive center next to the Coral Lodge, in the Kuna Yala, in 2007. Panama Divers, which is fully insured, has decades of experience and an attentive staff, and they plan trips to Coiba, Escribano, and Portobelo, where they have a dive center and PADI instruction facility.

Exploration Panama (© 720-2470; www.explorationpanama.com) has multiday scuba-diving excursions around the Chiriquí Gulf and Isla Coiba (see "Fishing," below), with a chartered live-aboard ship for six passengers. It's run by a friendly American who has lived in this area intermittently for more than 25 years, and he knows the area well.

Scuba Panama (© 261-3841; www.scubapanama.com) has a bicoastal dive that starts in the Caribbean Sea—visiting a sunken B-45 plane—and then goes to the Pacific Ocean for a dive there. They also have a unique (and spooky) dive in the Panama Canal, and dives around Portobelo and Isla Grande.

FISHING

Panama is a world-class fishing destination known for its fast and furious reeling-in of monster species such as blue, black, and striped marlin; yellowfin tuna; and wahoo and swordfish. Fishing takes place year-round; however, marlin and tuna are more abundant from January to April. The Pacific Ocean is where the best fishing is—there's also fishing in the Caribbean, but the infrastructure (marinas and such) isn't well developed. Anglers looking for a sure bet can't beat Lake Gatún for peacock bass—throw your line in and within minutes you'll snag one, guaranteed, making this a good excursion for kids (see chapter 6). In addition to the information provided below for Lake Gatún, **Gamboa Rainforest Resort** offers fishing trips for guests and even for visitors not lodging at the resort.

Fishing charters are available for day and multiday excursions, either as part of a trip organized by a competent operator, or by simply hiring a local boatman to take you out on the water. Custom sport-fishing tours head to the Pearl Islands, the Gulf of Chiriquí (around Coiba Island), and Piñas Bay—the latter is home to the Tropic Star Lodge (see below), and when they're sold out, a fishing charter is a good second option. Charters typically include transportation, meals, fishing gear, and bilingual or native-English-speaking guides.

FISHING CHARTERS

Exploration Panama (ⓒ 720-2470; www.explorationpanama.com), an American-run company based out of Boca Chica, in the Chiriquí Gulf near David, operates a 15m (50-ft.) refashioned U.S. Coast Guard vessel with a capacity for six overnight guests. Their all-inclusive day excursion around the Gulf of Chiriquí costs, per person, $225; their 1-night, 1-day excursion is $275; and their Coiba Island 2-night, 3-day fishing excursion is $950; they can custom-build a trip to the Darién area, too. Exploration Panama also offers scuba diving and snorkeling during fishing trips. They have land-based lodging at their **Wahoo Willy's** hotel and restaurant at Boca Chica.

Pesca Panama (ⓒ 800/946-3474 in the U.S.; www.pescapanama.com) is a U.S.-based company that offers inshore and offshore sport fishing in the Gulf of Chiriquí, around Coiba and Hannibal Bank. Pesca guests stay aboard their "floating lodge," a 21 by 9.1m (70- by 30-ft.) barge with a maximum capacity of 12 guests (four beds per room). Rates range from $2,795 to $3,895 per person for 5 nights, and dates are set, not customized.

Panama Fishing & Catching (ⓒ 6622-0212; www.panamafishingandcatching. com) has custom charters with prices that vary according to group size and desires, but on average they charge $400 for two for a day tour leaving from Panama City, and $850 to $1,850 for multiday offshore fishing charters (price runs from bare bones to all-inclusive).

Panama Yacht Tours (see contact info in "Yachting & Sailing," later in this chapter) is a more luxurious, and more expensive, option for fishing charters, and they have capacity for small or large groups aboard one of their 11 to 37m (36- to 122-ft.) yachts. This company focuses on the Chiriquí Gulf, the Pearl Islands, and Piña Bay.

Cahill Fishing (ⓒ 877/800-1690 in the U.S., 314-9000; www.gamboaresort.com) offers fishing excursions on Lake Gatún.

FISHING LODGES

Tropic Star Lodge ✸✸✸ (Bahía Piña, Darién; ⓒ 800/682-3424 in the U.S.; www. tropicstar.com). This prestigious fishing lodge is considered the best saltwater fishing resort in the world for its monster black and blue marlin, sailfish, and more. American-run, the lodge has been around since the early 1960s, and is located on the remote shore of Piñas Bay, in the Darién Province. The lodge draws famous VIPs, but is homey enough for families with kids. See p. 299 for a complete review.

Islas Secas ✸✸✸ (Gulf of Chiriquí; ⓒ 805/729-2737; www.islassecas.com) is not a fishing lodge per se, but sport fishing and spear fishing for marlin, billfish, and tuna are among the most popular activities at this elegant ecolodge, situated on 16 private islands in the Pacific. See p. 248 for more information.

Gone Fishing ✦✦ (Boca Chica; ℂ **6573-0151;** www.gonefishing.com) is a new fishing lodge with comfortable, ranch-style accommodations on the shore of Boca Chica, and friendly American owners. The focus is on fishing around the Gulf of Chiriquí, aboard one of their two 9.4m (31-ft.) open boats, and other activities for non-fishing guests. See p. 246 for a complete review.

Panama Big Game Sportfishing Club ✦✦ (Boca Chica; ℂ **866/281-1225** in the U.S.; www.panama-sportfishing.com), like the aforementioned lodges, is American-owned, in this case by two retired charter-boat skippers from Miami. The club is located near the Gone Fishing Lodge in Boca Chica, and they have four upscale teak cabins perched high on a hill, offering lovely views. The lodge has four fishing boats to accommodate all guests. See p. 247 for a complete review.

GOLF

Panama provides golfers with a variety of championship courses, some of which are open for public day use, others as part of an all-inclusive resort. Close to Panama City, **Summit Golf & Resort** (ℂ **232-4653;** www.summitgolfpanama.com) is the ideal venue for those staying in the capital; it's located on the east bank of the Panama Canal on the Gaillard Highway, and is accessible by taxi from the city for about $15 one-way. There is no hotel here, but there are swimming pools, a restaurant, and a pro shop. Designed by noted architect Jeffery Myers, the course is spread across rolling hills, with sweeping views of the Gaillard Cut of the Panama Canal. It's very classy, and there is a traditional 18-hole course as well as a 6-hole course for juniors and beginners. Rates Monday through Friday are $90 per person; Saturday and Sunday $100 per person, which includes a golf cart; and clubs are available for an additional $15. The course is open every day from 6am to 6pm; call ahead to book a tee time.

The **Coronado Golf & Beach Resort** (ℂ **240-4444;** www.coronadoresort.com) is a long-standing, premiere golf resort located on the Pacific Coast, about an hour from Panama City. Designed by Tom Fazio, this is the only seaside 18-hole course in the country; players can come for the day from Panama City, but the resort specializes in packages with lodging included. For more information, see the "Pacific Beaches" section of chapter 7, "Central Panama."

Costa Blanca Golf & Villas (ℂ **986-1915;** www.costablanca.com.pa) is located next to the Decameron Resort on the Pacific Coast, about 1½ hours from Panama City. It has an 18-hole course that, because of its lights, you can play both day and night. The cost is closer to a bargain than other resorts: Monday through Friday it's $30 per person, with an additional $22 for a cart; weekends $72 per person (including cart). The course is within a residential development, and there are a clubhouse and restaurant.

HORSEBACK RIDING

Horseback-riding outfits are sparsely distributed throughout the country, and there is no single lodge that focuses solely on riding with the exception of **Hacienda del Toro** (ℂ **757-9158;** www.haciendadeltoro.com), which offers short rides only, not full-day excursions. Still, it's a solid operation with high-quality horses (p. 280). One of the best places to ride is in **El Valle** with **Mitzila** (ℂ **6646-5813**); she and her team charge $4 per hour and operate daily. Trails here wind through thick forest, offering some wide-open panoramas. They have guides, but speak limited English. In **Boquete,** horses can be rented from **Eduardo Cano** (ℂ **270-1750**) for $5 an hour for tours around the surrounding countryside. Horseback riding here takes place along mountain paths that provide riders with sweeping vistas of the Boquete valley. Eduardo speaks Spanish only, so depending on your own facility with *el español,* have your hotel make arrangements.

KAYAKING & WHITE-WATER RAFTING

Surprisingly, Panama has some of the most thrilling white-water rafting and kayaking in the Americas. The translucent rivers that pour down the Talamanca Mountain Range in the Chiriquí Highlands provide wild Class III and IV kayaking and rafting, principally on the **Chiriquí River** east of Volcán Barú, and the **Chiriquí Viejo River** west of the volcano, near the border with Costa Rica. Unfortunately, the Chiriquí Viejo is being threatened by a series of dams for a hydroelectric project, but for now it's a pristine river and a lot of fun to ride. There are tamer floats, too, such as the **Esti River,** a Class II, that is perfect for younger rafters, families, and beginners. What's special about the Chiriquí area is that relatively few paddlers have discovered it, so rafters and kayakers have the river, and lush mountain scenery full of birds and wildlife, all to themselves. There are two local rafting companies in Boquete with years of experience and expert knowledge of the region; an option is to book with a tour operator that can put together multiday, multi-destination, or instructional trips.

On the other side of the Talamanca, the Guarumo River has family-friendly Class I and II rapids that descend into the Caribbean Sea at Bocas del Toro; only two lodges offer this excursion, **Tranquilo Bay** (p. 280) and **Casa Cayuco** (p. 278).

Closer to Panama City, there is rafting on the Class II and Class III **Chagres River** with **Aventuras Panama** (see below), a 5-hour float through rainforest and past Emberá Indian villages (p. 144).

You'll find kayaks at many hotels and resorts that are located near the ocean, but multiday sea kayak trips have yet to take off in Panama except for in the San Blas Archipelago (Kuna Yala), and even here it is a nascent industry considering that each company that operates here must be granted permission by Kuna Indian chiefs.

Chiriquí River Rafting ⊕ (© 720-1505; www.panama-rafting.com) is owned and operated by Hector Sánchez, who has been rafting this region for more than 25 years. Hector and his professional crew offer year-round, half- and full-day rafting excursions around the Chiriquí, both for die-hards and families seeking an easy, fun float. Packages include lodging at their rustic bunkhouse or at the owner's private home and B&B.

Panama Rafters (© 720-2712; www.panamarafters.com) is a young, American-owned company with rafting and kayaking on the many rivers in the Chiriquí Highlands. They also teach beginning and intermediate kayaking. This company is especially good for rafters and kayakers seeking a wilder ride on the river.

Nantahala Outdoor Center (© 888/905-7238; www.noc.com) is a highly esteemed, North Carolina–based paddling school that offers a weeklong course for intermediate and advanced kayakers around Volcán Barú, tackling just about every rapid in the area including the Chiriquí Viejo, the Caison, and the Macho de Monte rivers. The course takes place in late October/early November for advanced paddlers (when the rivers are at their fullest); and early November for intermediates.

Xtrop (© 317-1279; www.xtrop.com), or "Expediciones Tropicales," is a well-respected company staffed by conservationists who use local, indigenous guides for their kayak adventures, focusing on multiday kayak trips to the San Blas Archipelago (camping or upscale lodging), as well as a sunset kayak trip around the mouth of the Panama Canal near the city.

Aventuras Panama (© 260-0044; www.aventuraspanama.com), is one of Panama's top rafting and kayaking tour companies, offering rafting trips close to Panama City at the Chagres River and the Mamoni River (Class II–Class IV), as well as multiday trips to the Chiriquí Highlands, and 5-day sea kayaking trips in the San Blas.

Seakunga Adventures (© 800/781-2269 in the U.S. and Canada; www.seakunga. com) is a Canadian company with years of experience in Central America. They specialize in sea kayaking in the San Blas Archipelago, often working in conjunction with Aventuras (above) for their 8-day tour, including 3 nights in the San Blas and an overnight in an Emberá Indian village, with rafting on the Chagres.

MOTORCYCLING

Motorcyclists with their own bikes should know that the lion's share of Panama roads are twisty-curvy, with the exception of the Pan-American Highway. Also, most roads off this highway are peppered with potholes, and it is common to see farm animals blocking or sharing the road. The company **ACS Motorcycle Tours** (© 727/787-6278 in the U.S., or 236-7232 in Panama; www.acs-panama.com) offers 10-, 14 , and 21-day Panama–Costa Rica motorcycle tours with a support vehicle, and can include other Central American countries. Tours happen from September to January, and cost $2,850 (rider) and $1,550 (passenger), which includes everything except the flight to Panama.

SPAS

There are no "destination" spas in Panama, but most resorts and a couple of upscale hotels have a top-of-the-line spa, or at the very least provide services such as massage, a gym, a sauna, and sometimes a steam room. I don't foresee a huge boom in this market, in spite of its rapid growth worldwide, but a few hotel owners are slowly catching on to this hot trend. At the time of publication, **La Casa de Lourdes** (© 983-6450; www.lacasadelourdes.com), an exclusive boutique hotel in the relaxed, pastoral setting of El Valle de Antón, was breaking ground on what promises to be a deluxe spa facility for guests and the general public, slated for opening in 2007. Treatments will include stone therapy, massage, and body wraps, and they have a whirlpool and outdoor pool. Instead of a gym, they send guests out on biking and hiking excursions to work their muscles and "feel the energy of the valley."

Inter-Continental Playa Bonita Resort & Spa ✵✵ (© 211-8600; www.ichotels group.com) is brand-new and located on the Pacific, just a 30-minute drive from Panama City. The plush beach resort has a sybaritic spa facility with all the trimmings; services are booked individually, or as part of a package that combines fruit- and chocolate-infused skin treatments, massage, aromatherapy, and body wraps.

Decapolis Radisson ✵✵ (© 215-5000; www.radisson.com), a sleek, trendy hotel, has the Aqua Spa, the top spa in Panama City in terms of service and hip decor, and you don't have to be a guest to book an appointment. They offer a full range of treatments and a stylish beauty parlor for one-stop makeovers.

Veneto Hotel & Casino ✵✵ (© 340-8888; www.venetocasino.com) has a building facade that screams Las Vegas, but inside it's as elegant as can be, and their Bamboo Sea Spa & Gym is a calm oasis that opens out onto a rooftop swimming pool. This is the spa with the widest range of treatments (Vichy-style), including hot stone massage, mud baths, aromatherapy, hydrotherapy and facials, and more.

Gamboa Rainforest Resort ☆ (© **314-9000;** www.gamboaresort.com) is the best-known spa in Panama, and although the service here has always been top-notch, the facilities were clunky and drab—but they're reportedly renovating the spa in late 2006. Expect traditional massages, body scrubs, and facials. If you're not staying at the resort, you can visit the spa anyway, and combine it with a bike ride and lunch.

Panamonte Inn & Spa ☆ (© **720-1324;** www.panamonteinnandspa.com) is the place to go in Boquete to be pampered. It's a country-cozy-style spa and is very complete, with shiatsu, Swedish and sports massage, a sauna and steam room, skin and spa treatments using Natura Bisse products, body scrubs, and mud treatments. Their facials are especially noteworthy.

Los Quetzales Lodge & Spa (© **771-2291;** www.losquetzales.com) is a slight misnomer—there is a "spa" building here but it is small and services are not up to snuff. Massage rooms are shared, for example, unless you throw down extra cash for a private room. There is a sauna, and the spa center is backed by forest and a rushing river, but the center is more a lodge amenity than a spa destination.

SURFING

The powerful swells and hollow reef breaks off the Pacific and Caribbean coasts make Panama *the* destination for a surfin' safari. The water's warm, the waves are uncrowded, and surfing here is consistent year-round, with the largest swells between April and October in the Pacific, and December to March in the Caribbean. If you're a beginner or need tips on technique, a couple of camps specialize in surfing instruction.

Bocas del Toro is often compared to Tahiti or Hawaii for its huge swells—from December to March, and June and July—and monster waves such as **Dumpers** and **Silverbacks,** the latter a right-hand, reef-bottom point break comparable to Backdoor Pipeline in Oahu. Waves in Bocas range between 1.2 to 7.6m (4–25 ft.), and can be powerful beach breaks, big waves, reef point breaks, and spitting tubes. **Isla Grande** has powerful reef breaks and is a good bet if you want to surf the Caribbean but don't want to go as far as Bocas.

In the Chiriquí Gulf, the surf meccas are at **Morro Negrito** (see below), and **Santa Catalina,** internationally renowned among surfers and located straight across the bay from Isla Coiba, in the Pacific. Santa Catalina is a scruffy town, but the surfing is epic, with a consistent easy-to-line-up, rock-bottom point break that averages 1.5 to 6.1m (5–20 ft.). Farther east on the Azuero Peninsula is **Cambutal, Punta Negra, Dinosaurios,** and **Horcones,** other reliable spots for consistent breaks, including beach, point, and reef-bottom breaks that are sometimes even better than at Santa Catalina, and less crowded. The up-and-coming **Playa Venado,** near Pedasí, is a long beach break with lefts and rights and swells that can be as little as 1.5m (5 ft.) or as high as 4.6m (15 ft.). The Pacific beaches that lie between 1 and 2 hours from Panama City are beach breaks and point breaks.

If you just don't want to waste time planning your surf trip, or if you want a local's insider information on the best breaks, check **Panama Surf Tours** (© **6671-7777;** www.panamasurftours.com), a respected company with flexible 5- to 8-day tours that run from economical to luxury. There's also **Panama Surf Expeditions** (© **6582-0402;** www.panamasurfexpeditions.com), run by a group of Santa Catalina locals who build custom surf tours for travelers.

Morro Negrito Surf Camp (© **760/632-8014** in the U.S.; www.surferparadise.com) is located in an out-of-the-way region of the Chiriquí Gulf, about halfway between

Santiago and David, on an island 3.2km (2 miles) off the coast. Guests are limited to 25, and with 10 different breaks (averaging 1.2–2.4m/4–8 ft.), you've pretty much got the whole wave to yourself here. Accommodations are one step above camping—the focus here is on waves, not luxury lodging. The camp has surf guides and lessons.

Río Mar Surf Camp (© 240-9128; www.riomarsurf.com) is just 1½ hours from Panama City, near San Carlos on the Pacific Coast. The camp has simple rooms (two have air-conditioning) that can accommodate three guests, and surf lessons can be booked on an hourly basis. It's a good spot at which to brush up on your technique when you don't have much time in Panama.

Casablanca Surf Resort (© 226-3786; no website) is one of the oldest surf camps in Panama, founded by a Panamanian surf pioneer who has been riding Central American waves since the 1960s. The camp is on a bluff overlooking the ocean, with basic rooms in lovely surroundings, and they have classes and can arrange surf excursions. Unfortunately, their lack of website and e-mail address makes them difficult to contact.

YACHTING & SAILING

Panama Yacht Tours (© 263-5044; www.panamayachttours.com) is a Panama City–based operation with multiple-day charters to Coiba Island, Bocas del Toro, the Pearl Islands, and the San Blas Islands, as well as private charter rental for partial transit of the Panama Canal.

The Panama Yacht Club (© 6616-2408; www.panamayachtclub.com), based out of Fort Amador Marina in Panama City, specializes in private excursions to the Pearl Islands, with a day excursion for $800, and a 4-night, 5-day journey for six passengers for $5,000, aboard their luxury catamaran. The price is for the boat only; contact them for additional prices such as food and beverages.

San Blas Sailing (© 232-7598; www.sanblassailing.com), a French company, has a fleet of sailboats based in the San Blas Archipelago, offering 4- to 14-night all-inclusive adventures sailing around the islands, snorkeling, kayaking, and visiting Kuna villages.

3 Panama's Top Parks & Reserves

Panama boasts one of the most complex ecosystems on the planet, its territory incorporating ancient rainforests, virgin beaches, islands, rugged peaks shrouded in cloud forests, and an underwater world replete with coral reefs and marine life. To protect all this wealth, the Panamanian government has designated 30% of the country's national parks, reserves, or wildlife refuges—about 2 million hectares (5 million acres) all told. The Autoridad Nacional de Ambiente (ANAM) administers Panama's parks and reserves, charging $3 to $10 for entrance fees (less for Panamanian residents). If camping is permitted, the fee is $5. ANAM is under-funded, however, and although park entrances have a token ranger station and maybe even a few bunks for rent, they do not provide visitors with a lot of information, nor do they give out trail maps.

What's interesting is how accessible some of Panama's parks and reserves are—there are five national parks located between 30 minutes and 2 hours of Panama City. And yet some parks are virtually inaccessible, such as the Darién, with its impenetrable jungle, or the north-facing rainforest of La Amistad International Park. Many wildlife refuges are off-limits to protect a breeding ground for birds or animals.

The following is a selective guide to Panama's national parks and reserves—the best in terms of accessibility or interest, or because of a particular sport (scuba diving in

Monkey Business

No trip to Panama would be complete without at least one monkey sighting. Home to five distinct species of primates, Panama offers the opportunity for one of the world's most gratifying wildlife-viewing experiences. Just listen for the deep guttural call of a howler or the rustling of leaves overhead—telltale signs that monkeys are in your vicinity.

A commonly spotted monkey is the **white-faced capuchin,** which you might recognize as the infamous culprit from the film *Outbreak.* Contrary to that film's plot, however, these monkeys are native to the New World tropics and do not exist in Africa. Capuchins are agile, medium-size monkeys that make good use of their long, prehensile tails. They live in a diverse collection of habitats, ranging from high-altitude cloud forests to tropical rainforest at sea level. It's almost impossible not to spot a capuchin at Monkey Island in Lake Gatún, in the Canal Zone, which you can view from a jungle cruise boat ride (see "Jungle Cruises" in chapter 6). Capuchins are also on Isla Bastimentos in Bocas del Toro, and throughout the forest of the Darién.

Howler monkeys are named for their guttural, eerie call. Large and mostly black, these monkeys sometimes seem ferocious because of their physical appearance and deep, resonant howls that can carry for more than a mile, even in dense rainforest. Biologists believe that male howlers mark their territory with these deep, guttural sounds. In the presence of humans, however, howlers are actually a little timid and tend to stay higher up in the canopy than their white-faced cousins. Again, howlers are guaranteed to be seen at Monkey Island, and are fairly common in the Darién and in Soberanía National Park (see chapter 6).

More elusive are **spider monkeys** and **night monkeys.** Spider monkeys have long, slender bodies that range from dark brown to black, and they

Coiba, for example). Detailed information about dining, lodging, activities, and more can be found in the regional chapters that follow.

THE CANAL BASIN

SOBERANIA NATIONAL PARK   Spanning 19,425 hectares (48,000 acres) of undulating, pristine tropical rainforest, this is one of the most accessible, species-rich parks in the Americas—and it's just 40 minutes from Panama City. Wildlife from both continents converges here to create a hyper-diverse region that's home to an estimated 525 bird species and 105 mammal species. Expect to see coatimundi, three-toed sloths, howler monkeys, and Geoffrey's tamarins, which are tiny primates. Soberanía is home to Pipeline Road, the world-famous bird-watching trail, as well as to hiking trails such as the historic Camino de Cruces used by the Spanish to transport gold from the Pacific in the 16th century. **Location:** 25km (15 miles) north of Panama City, on the eastern shore of the canal. For more information, see "Soberanía National Park" in chapter 6.

prefer the high canopies of primary rainforests. Spiders are very adept with their prehensile tails but actually travel through the canopy with a hand-over-hand motion frequently imitated by their less graceful human cousins on playground monkey bars around the world. Spider monkeys are commonly sighted in the Darién and in forest along the Caribbean coast. Apropos of their name, night monkeys are the only true nocturnal monkey, meaning your chances of seeing one are slim, unless you happen to be with a guide who is adept at spotting this elusive creature.

The pint-size **Geoffrey's tamarin** lives in groups of 10 to 15 and spends most of its time on high branches looking for fruits and flowers to eat. It's a hyperactive little primate that likes to bounce from branch to branch and jerk its head around in what seems to be panic. The first response to seeing a Geoffrey's tamarin is usually, "How cute!" because of their size—a trait that makes them hard to spot in the first place.

For a guaranteed sighting of the monkeys mentioned above (except the night monkey), visit Monkey Island by boat on a jungle cruise, or the Summit Gardens Park & Zoo (see chapter 6). The Darién area is home to many primates that can be seen fairly easily, as are the Soberanía National Park and Isla Bastimentos. The alert traveler can usually see Geoffrey's tamarins in Panama City's Metropolitan Park as well (see chapter 5). *Remember:* Monkeys have specific diets and should never be fed human victuals, especially junk food, no matter how fun it may seem to do so. Boycott any tour that attracts monkeys with food, and let your fellow travelers and tour guide know that this is not acceptable practice if you see someone feeding a monkey.

ALTOS DE CAMPANA NATIONAL PARK   In 1966, this became Panama's first national park, covering an area of 4,925 hectares (12,170 acres) of igneous landscape created by the extinct El Valle de Antón volcano. Altos de Campana is characterized by rugged peaks that are almost completely deforested on the Pacific side, and sloping rainforest on the Atlantic side, and there are high cliffs here that provide lookout points with dramatic views of the Canal Basin and Chame Bay. For bird-watching, the park is home to exotic species that can be difficult to view elsewhere, such as violet hummingbirds, white-tipped sicklebills, and orange-bellied trogons. **Location:** 90km (56 miles) west of Panama City. For more information, see "Altos de Campana National Park" in chapter 7.

OCEANS & ISLANDS

COIBA NATIONAL PARK   Panama's largest national park is a gem that covers an astounding 270,128 hectares (667,500 acres) of mostly marine park, as well as Coiba Island. The park owes its pristine state to a notorious penal colony that was located here until 2005, which kept visitors away and the region virtually untouched by development.

Coiba has been called the Galápagos of Central America, providing world-class diving and snorkeling around its coral reef and white-sand beaches. In addition to saltwater crocodiles, turtles, humpback whales, and howler monkeys, this is one of the few places where it is still possible to see a scarlet macaw in the wild. **Location:** Gulf of Chiriquí, 1½ hours by boat from Santa Catalina. For more information, see "Isla Coiba" in chapter 8.

GOLFO DE CHIRIQUI NATIONAL MARINE PARK   This park incorporates two dozen hilly islands and outcrops, but mostly it protects the surrounding ocean area and its rich marine life and coral reefs. Few people visit here, which is surprising given its beauty and proximity to Boquete. A couple of upstart operations offer diving and snorkeling, as well as visits to uninhabited beaches with perfect white-sand beaches; there are two fishing lodges based here, too. **Location:** Just off the southern shore of Boca Chica, in the Gulf of Chiriquí. For more information, see p. 245.

ISLA BASTIMENTOS NATIONAL MARINE PARK   This national park is the reason to come to Bocas del Toro, for its virgin rainforest, turquoise sea replete with preserved hard and soft corals, and the idyllic Cayos Zapatillas, two castaway-type islands with white sand and outstanding snorkeling opportunities. The park also protects the largest area of Caribbean mangrove swamp in the country, and important turtle-nesting sites. About 90% of the park is marine area and home to lots of colorful tropical fish, and there is decent bird-watching on the island, with 68 species. For more information, see "Isla Bastimentos" in chapter 9.

ISLA IGUANA WILDLIFE REFUGE   Only 55 hectares (136 acres), this refuge is surrounded with coral reef and clear blue sea ideal for snorkeling. As the name implies, it's also home to many green iguanas. From June to November, humpback whales breed in the area and are commonly seen by boat. The white-sand beach here is the best in the Azuero area, but unfortunately this region gets hit by currents that carry trash thrown overboard by boats all over the Pacific. **Location:** 3km (2 miles) from the shore near Pedasí, in the Pacific Ocean. For more information, see "Pedasí" in chapter 7.

BARRO COLORADO NATIONAL MONUMENT   A former hilltop, this island was created by the flooding of Lake Gatún during the construction of the Panama Canal. It is now home to one of the most important—and oldest—biological research stations in the world, administered by the Smithsonian Tropical Research Institute (STRI). The monument actually comprises more than 55 hectares (136 acres) of land, including five surrounding mainland peninsulas, but the spotlight is on Barro Colorado Island for its "captive" biodiversity that provides an opportunity for scientists to conduct studies without being encroached upon by outside forces. The island can be visited as a day tour. **Location:** Lake Gatún, in the Canal Zone. For more information, see "Lago Gatún" in chapter 6.

THE HIGHLANDS

LA AMISTAD INTERNATIONAL PARK   Popularly known as PILA, this is one of the more unique parks in Panama because it is shared with neighboring Costa Rica. Unfortunately, the park is not as easily accessed on the Panamanian side, but there are a couple of trails at the administration area near Cerro Punta, in the Chiriquí Highlands, that put you deep in primeval rainforest. The UNESCO Heritage Site comprises 207,000 hectares (511,508 acres) of land spread across the Cordillera Central mountain range, with dramatic peaks, cliffs, and valleys. It's one of the wettest regions in the country, so bring your waterproof gear. **Location:** The park straddles the Costa Rica–Panama border, in the Chiriquí Highlands. For more information, see "What to See & Do in the Northwestern Highlands" in chapter 8.

VOLCAN BARU NATIONAL PARK   This mountainous park is 87,451 hectares (35,390 acres) spread around the Barú Volcano, and it is home to the best short-haul day hike in Panama. The volcano's altitude and fertile soil provide for a bioclimatic "island" that is home to many endemic plants not seen anywhere else around Panama. From the top of the Barú Volcano, you can see the Pacific and Atlantic oceans, but a cloud forest usually blocks the view. More than 250 bird species have been recorded here, making this prime bird-watching territory, especially for the resplendent quetzal and the endemic black-cheeked warbler. **Location:** Barú Volcano in the Chiriquí Highlands, accessible from Boquete or Cerro Punta. For more information, see p. 230.

EASTERN PANAMA

DARIEN NATIONAL PARK   The Darién is mostly impenetrable wilderness that runs the length of the border with Colombia, in eastern Panama. It is the largest, and wildest, national park in Central America, and designated a UNESCO Biosphere Reserve, but it's the least-visited park because of travel logistics and lack of accessibility. The most popular (and really only) destination here is Cana, which draws nature lovers of all kinds, but the Darién is revered mostly by bird-watchers who come to view the outstanding array of 450-plus bird species, including showcase birds such as blue macaws, toucans, and harpy eagles. **Location:** Eastern end of the Darién Province, along the Panama–Colombia border. For more information, see chapter 11.

PUNTA PATIÑO NATURE RESERVE   This reserve is managed by the conservation group ANCON, and because it is on the Gulf of San Miguel and surrounded by dense jungle, the only way to get here is by boat. Birders like Punta Patiño because it offers the best chance to spot harpy eagles, and visits here usually center around Emberá Indian villages and Punta Alegre, home to descendants of West African slaves. There are also hikes and canoe rides. **Location:** Darién Province, on the Gulf of San Miguel. For more information, see chapter 11.

CENTRAL PANAMA

SARIGUA NATIONAL PARK   It's the only "desert" in Panama, but it's not here as a result of natural forces. This park features a lunar landscape of eroded land, fissures, and fossil-like stumps, but more than anything the park provides a vivid example of the ecological ruin that occurs with heavy deforestation caused by man. Along the shore are mangrove swamps and pockets of the dry forest that once covered the nearly 8,094 hectares (20,000 acres) that make up the park. Also, archaeologists have recently been discovering artifacts here left by the oldest known indigenous group in Panama. **Location:** In the Herrera Province on Azuero Peninsula's Parita Bay. For more information, see p. 198.

4 Tips on Etiquette & Safety in the Wilderness

Adventure travel is inherently riskier than travel by cruise ship or on a tour bus, and you should prepare yourself not only physically; you should also double-check your medical coverage and insurance policies. For specific information about diseases and illnesses that can afflict you while trudging through the jungles of Panama, see "Health & Safety" in chapter 2.

It's hot in Panama day and night. However, higher up in the Chiriquí Highlands it gets chilly in the evening, especially if you're in the rainforest and have gotten wet. Even during the summer, the cloud forest here (as well as the Caribbean Coast in general) is damp throughout the year, so bring rain gear and a couple of extra layers of dry clothing if you plan to be outdoors all day.

On the other hand, the equatorial sun is very strong and you can burn fast, so liberally apply a high-factor sunscreen. Bug bites are so common that I recommend you buy a pleasant-smelling but powerful repellent and apply it every day if you are visiting any area outside of Panama City. The beaches in Panama are lovely, but lurking in the sand are *chitras,* or no-see-ums, that leave an irritating welt. Deep in the jungle, chiggers burrow into your skin and leave an itching welt that lasts for 2 weeks. Bring along cortisone or Benadryl cream to soothe itching, and try not to scratch your bites, which can lead to sores and infections; also, the welt goes away faster if you leave it alone.

Tips for Seeing Wildlife

Seasoned bird-watchers and wildlife lovers know that the animal world is most active at sunrise and, to a lesser extent, at sunset. Birds are easier to spot in open areas and secondary forests than in primary forests. I recommend that you hire a guide if you're planning on trekking through the rainforest. A guide's local knowledge, and his or her ability not only to identify flora and fauna but to actually point it out, is invaluable.

Here are a few helpful hints on spotting wildlife:

- **Stay quiet.** Noise scares off animals and birds, so keep chatting to a minimum.
- **Listen.** Guides spot birds by listening to their call, and animals by listening to the sound of rustling leaves or anything else that indicates an animal is in the vicinity.
- **Bring binoculars.** Choose a quality pair with a long range, and learn how to use them before you get on the trail.
- **Be patient and don't try too hard.** Once you relax and soften your focus, you'll see animals and birds more readily.
- **Dress appropriately.** Wear comfortable clothing and good shoes or boots—neutral tones are recommended for blending in with your environment. The better camouflaged you are, the better your chances for spotting wildlife. Also, wear long pants and a long-sleeve shirt, and repellent.
- **Read up.** Familiarize yourself with your surroundings and with the animals and birds you're mostly likely to see. Ecolodges that focus on bird-watching have libraries—some better than others—with field guides and birding books. The best book on the market is *A Guide to the Birds of Panama* by Robert S. Ridgely and John A. Gwynne (Princeton University Press, 1992). The Smithsonian Corotu bookstore (see "Fast Facts: Panama City" on p. 88) has laminated, portable triptychs with color illustrations of common birds, reptiles, and mammals in Panama.

Panama is home to some of the most frightening snakes on the planet, such as boa constrictors and fer-de-lances, though on the whole, snake bites are rare. Still, don't go poking under rocks or fallen branches, and always scan the trail in front of you for any slithering menace. If you encounter a snake, don't panic or make any sudden movements, and don't try to handle the snake. Also, avoid swimming in rivers unless you know it is safe or are with a guide who can vouch for the river's safety. Caimans and crocodiles hide along shorelines, especially in mangrove swamps and river mouths.

Responsible travel tips: Always tread lightly and pack everything out with you when in the wilderness—this means everything, including toilet paper. Do not uproot plants or take flowers, especially wild orchids. Do not buy anything that is made of animal skin or shells, and do not eat seafood such as lobster during mating season from March to July. Be wary of hotels or outfits that call themselves "eco-anything," as the term here has yet to be properly defined or regulated. I've seen hotels that call themselves "eco" for no other reason than that they are located in the forest. Some small-scale hotels in Panama are blazing the trail for sustainable tourism and have been quite successful at it, but unfortunately, others cling to wasteful and damaging practices.

5 Ecologically Oriented Volunteer & Study Programs

The following are a few institutions and nonprofit groups that work on sustainable development or other environmental or social projects in Panama.

Global Vision International (© 800/776-0188; www.earthwatch.org) is a U.K.-based organization that provides support and services to charities, NGOs, and governmental agencies for conservation and humanitarian projects. In Panama, they offer a 2-week volunteer program at two turtle-nesting sites in Bocas del Toro. Volunteers tag, measure, and monitor turtles—and pay $1,525 to do so, sleeping in rustic huts. The program runs from March to mid-June.

Habitat for Humanity International (© 202/628-9171 in the U.S., or 263-3035; www.habitat.org) is a nonprofit, nondenominational Christian volunteer organization that builds homes around the world for needy people. Habitat began two housing projects in 2003 in Panama at Altos de la Colina and Chilibre. They accept volunteer workers; however, volunteers are expected to pay for all living costs including food and housing, as well as the flight to Panama.

Summit Garden & Zoo (© 232-4850; www.summitpanama.org) has volunteer programs working in animal care or environmental education, as well as in their botanical garden, providing opportunities to learn about Panamanian flora and fauna and conservation issues, pick up new skills, and generally help the park through its renovation that began in 2006.

5

Panama City

Long overshadowed by the Panama Canal and a reputation as a hub for drug-running, Panama City is not only reinventing itself as the thriving commercial and financial hub of the Americas, it is asserting itself as a burgeoning tourist destination. Panama City (commonly referred to simply as "Panama") is one of those rare Latin American capitals that has it all: a high standard of living, a seemingly endless supply of investment from abroad, a surplus of natural beauty, and a rich cultural brew of ethnicities and religions. It has been called the new Hong Kong and Miami—a sleek and modern city proud of its role as host to the world.

Signs of Panama City's reinvention are everywhere. The Amador Causeway, formerly a U.S. military base, is ground zero for several multimillion-dollar condominium and commercial-center developments, which include a new Biodiversity Museum designed by famed architect Frank Gehry. The run-down 19th-century buildings of Casco Viejo have been revitalized with private and public funds and declared a World Heritage Site by UNESCO. Along the coast, swiftly rising skyscrapers, spurred by an irresistible 20-year tax exemption, portend a megalopolis in the making: By 2009, 5 of the 10 tallest buildings in Latin America will be here in Panama City, including the tallest, at 104 floors. Even the dirty Panama Bay is undergoing a $360-million cleanup.

But Panama City's visitors need not venture far from their air-conditioned hotels to immerse themselves in the wild tropical jungle that is characteristic of this region. Even the city's Metropolitan Park is the protected home of more than 200 species of birds, mammals, and reptiles. Dozens of remarkable destinations outside the city limits can be reached in less than 2 hours, meaning travelers can spend the day exploring but head back to the city and be well fed and rested for the next day's adventure. For more on the area's day-trip offerings, see chapter 6.

Panama City is the oldest Spanish settlement on the mainland of the Americas, founded in 1519 by Pedro Arias Dávila (Pedrarias the Cruel). The settlement was used as a base for stealing Peruvian gold and silver and transporting it back to Spain via a treacherous road that linked Panama City with the Caribbean Sea. The immense wealth that passed across the isthmus proved irresistible to treasure-thirsty pirates and buccaneers, who conducted raids throughout the region during the 16th and 17th centuries. In 1671, the Welsh buccaneer Henry Morgan sacked Panama City, and the settlement burned to the ground. The ruins of Panama Viejo, or Old Panama, can be toured today. (See "What to See & Do," later in this chapter.)

By 1673, Panama City had been rebuilt in what is now known as Casco Viejo; it was heavily fortified and the city was never taken again. However, raids on the Caribbean coast mounted, and the Spanish, defeated, returned to sailing around Cape Horn in 1746. Panama declared its independence from Spain in

1821, but declined in importance until the Gold Rush of the mid–19th century, when thousands of forty-niners used the isthmus as a shortcut from the East Coast of the U.S. to California. Later, when Panama seceded from Colombia in 1903, Panama City was designated the capital. With the opening of the canal in 1914, Panama City became the most important center of trade and commerce in the Americas.

Panama City's modern history was marred by the rise of strongman dictator Manuel Noriega and by the 1989 U.S.-led invasion to overthrow him, which left hundreds dead, most of whom lived in the poor Chorillo neighborhood. But today, Panama City is one of Latin America's safest cities, and nearly every tourist will feel secure walking the streets day or night.

1 Orientation

GETTING THERE & DEPARTING
BY PLANE

All international flights, except those from Costa Rica, land at the newly expanded **Tocumen International Airport** (PTY), located 21km (13 miles) from Panama City (© 238-2600). Flights from Costa Rica to Panama City land at Albrook Airport (see below), and there is direct service from San José to David and Bocas del Toro airports. (See chapters 8 and 9, respectively.) See chapter 2 for airlines that service Panama City.

There are **IPAT visitors' kiosks** inside Tocumen's arrival terminal (one in baggage claim and another through the Customs gate), with information about Panama City and some brochures; it's recommended, though, that travelers research accommodations and make reservations before their arrival because hotels are often booked.

The unit of currency in Panama is the U.S. dollar, so for those coming from the United States there is no need to exchange money. Euros can be exchanged at the **Banco Nacional** (© 238-4161; Mon–Fri 8am–5pm and Sat 10am–3pm) in the arrival terminal; this bank also has ATMs in the airport terminal.

A licensed taxi to Panama City costs $25, plus toll fees for a total of about $30. Many hotels offer free scheduled pickup and drop-off service, or you can arrange transportation for a cheaper price—inquire when booking at your hotel. Your best bet for taxis is with **Easy Travel Panama** (© 617-4122; www.easytravelpanama.net). They offer high-quality vehicles and bilingual drivers, and cost about the same as regular taxis ($30 for one person, $35 for two, tolls included), but you must reserve ahead of time. Easy Travel offers personalized ground transportation anywhere; contact them for prices for long-distance destinations (the beaches outside of Panama City, for example).

All rental-car agencies have desks in the arrival terminal and are open 24 hours a day. See "Getting Around," below, for more information.

Domestic flights, flights to Costa Rica, and charter flights to the 150 or so airstrips located on Panama's islands and remote jungle areas leave from **Marcos A. Gelabert Airport** (PAC), which is more commonly referred to as **Albrook Airport** (© 315-0241). Albrook is located northwest of Cerro Ancón (Ancón Hill) off Avenue Omar Torrijos Herrera, near the canal. Rental-car agencies here are generally open from 8am to 6:30pm. Each company offers a key drop-box for customers who need to return a vehicle when rental desks aren't open.

Tip: Travelers who arrive at Tocumen Airport and plan to head directly to another destination in Panama via a domestic flight must transfer to Albrook Airport, about a 45-minute drive (or longer during rush hour) from Tocumen. A taxi costs about $30.

Panama City

To Colón
To Gamboa
To El Dorado

Calle 7
Calle 6
Calle 5
Calle 4
Calle 3
Calle 2
Calle 1

Av. Diógenes De La Rosa

Albrook
(Marcos Gelabert)
Airport

Albrook
Mall

ALTOS DE
CURUNDÚ

METROPOLITAN
NATIONAL
PARK

Ferrocarril
de Panamá

Corredor Norte

BALBOA

Avenida Ascanio Villalaz

LA
CREST

Mercado de
Abastos

Av. Juan D. Arosemena

Avenida Frangipani

Avenida Simón Bolívar - Transístm

CURUNDÚ

Cerro
Ancón

Avenida Nacional

National
Archives

Av. Central   España

Parque
Porras

Av. Cuba

ANCÓN

Museo Antropológico
Reina Torres de Araúz

Museo de
Ciencias Naturales

CALIDONIA

To Amador
Causeway

Avenida de los Mártires

Museo
Afroantillano

C. del Estudiante

EL CHORRILLO

Avenida Balboa

Balboa
Monument

Parque
Anayansi

Parqu
Urrac

Marin
Miram

SANTA
ANA

Bahía de Panamá

Casco Viejo

Presidential
Palace

Teatro
Nacional

CASCO VIEJO
(SAN FELIPE)

See "Casco Viejo"
inset map

Museo de
Historia

Plaza de la
Independencia

Museo del
Canal de Panamá

Plaza
Bolívar

Iglesia
San Francisco
de Asis

Iglesia de
Santo Domingo
(Arco Chato)

Teatro
Nacional

Bahía de
Panama

CASCO VIEJO
(SAN FELIPE)

Plaza
de Francia

Paseo de
Las Bóvedas

0   50 m
0   50 yds

CASCO VIEJO

ACCOMMODATIONS ■
Casa Mar Alta **4**

DINING ◆
Ego **7**
Las Bóvedas **1**
Macarena **2**
Manolo Caracol **6**
Mostaza **5**
S'cena **3**

BY BUS

If arriving by bus, you'll be dropped off at the Albrook bus terminal near the Albrook airport and shopping center. A taxi to town costs $2 to $3 and takes 10 to 15 minutes. A taxi to the Gamboa area costs $15 and takes 30 minutes.

BY CAR

Travelers arriving to Panama City by car will do so via the Pan-American Highway from the west, first crossing the canal on the Puente de las Américas (Bridge of the Americas) and arriving in the Balboa district of the city. Follow signs to Avenida Balboa to reach downtown. Drivers headed to Panama City from the west may also use the new Puente Centenario (Centennial Bridge), which crosses the canal near Paraíso, and avoid traffic congestion on the Bridge of the Americas. The road that crosses this bridge is also known as Vía Benedicto XVI, named after Pope Benedict XVI.

The Pan-American Highway continues east toward Colombia and ends in Yaviza, in the Darién Region. It is not possible to reach Colombia by car, and at this book's publication there were no ferries for vehicles to Colombia, although there is talk that this service might be reinstated soon.

VISITOR INFORMATION

The **Instituto Panameño de Turismo (IPAT)** main office is inside the Atlapa Convention Center on Vía Israel, in the San Francisco neighborhood, but although open to the public, it does not have a proper information center (© **226-7000;** www.visit panama.com). IPAT has three visitor centers, located at Vía España and Ricardo Arias (© **269-8011**); in Old Panama on Vía Cincuentenario (© **226-4419**); and in Casco Viejo at Avenida Central and Calle 3 (© **211-1959**).

Where the #@&!%$ Is It?

Ah, the aggravation of finding an address in Panama City. Just like in the U2 song, this is "Where the Streets Have No Name"—most of the residential streets, anyway. And of the streets that do have an appellation, they are either not signed or are referred to by two or three different names. Some say the reason is that Panama City has never had a postal delivery system (the postman only comes if you slip him some cash). Residents have post office boxes, called *apartados,* which is abbreviated as Apdo. or A.P.

Unbelievably, even taxi drivers are clueless when it comes to city street names beyond major avenues, even if they're labeled on a map. With taxi drivers, it is important that you give as much **detailed information** as possible such as the **cross street,** the **closest major intersection,** or better yet, a **recognizable landmark**—the Marriott Hotel, for example. When asking for directions, get as much information as possible. And, if you're nuts enough to drive through Panama City, never do so without a map in your vehicle. Here you'll have double trouble because even major avenue and thoroughfare turnoffs are poorly marked. You'll most likely need to pull over periodically to see if you're still on track. Avenida Balboa runs from Casco Viejo to Panama Viejo and along the coast, and is the least-confusing route across town.

CITY LAYOUT

Panama City lies on the eastern shore of the Panama Canal, and is bordered by the Pacific Ocean to the southeast, which can disorient first-time visitors unaccustomed to seeing the sun rise over the Pacific Ocean. Throw in a mesh of looping avenues and streets with two different names, or no name at all, and prepare to feel hopelessly lost during your first few days in Panama City. Visitors rely on taxis, which are safe and cheap ($1–$2).

In very general terms, Panama can be divided into **four areas:** Old Panama (the ruins of the first settlement here); Casco Viejo, the city center during the late 19th and early 20th centuries; the former Canal Zone; and modern Panama, with its wide boulevards, glittering skyscrapers, and impoverished slums.

At the southwest end of the city lie the Amador Causeway, Casco Viejo, Cerro Ancón (Ancón Hill), and the former Canal Zone. From here, three principal avenues branch out across the city. Avenida Central, which begins in Casco Viejo as a thriving shopping center hawking cheap, imported goods, changes its name to Avenida Central España as it passes through Calidonia, and then becomes Vía España as it runs through the commercial area and financial district of El Cangrejo. Avenida Balboa extends the length of the coast, then forks into Vía Israel, later called Cincuentenario as it heads out to Old Panama. Corredor Sur, a fast-moving toll expressway, connects the city with Tocumen Airport. Avenida Simón Bolivar (also known as Avenida 2da. Norte Transístmica) heads north to Colón; however, a new toll expressway, called the Corredor Norte, provides a faster route to Colón, eventually connecting with the Transístmica around Chilibre.

There are no beaches in the immediate area of the city—only mud flats—and visitors will need to travel northeast to the Caribbean or southwest to the Pacific beaches, about a 1- to 1½-hour drive from the city. The following Panama City neighborhoods run from west to east.

THE NEIGHBORHOODS IN BRIEF

Amador Causeway This man-made peninsula on the south end of town is a popular recreation and dining area that provides sweeping views of the city skyline, and a reliable breeze that is a cool tonic on a hot Panamanian day. It is also the future site of several monstrous condominium and marina developments, as well as a new Frank Gehry museum dedicated to biodiversity.

Casco Viejo/San Felipe Panama's loveliest neighborhood was once a collection of homes built during the late 1800s and early 1900s, before it became fashionable to live elsewhere in the city. The historical barrio, now revitalized with public and private funds, is undergoing a thorough renovation that prompted UNESCO to designate it a World Heritage Site. If you have time to visit just one neighborhood in Panama City, make it this one.

Balboa/Cerro Ancón/Albrook These are three quiet residential neighborhoods located within the former Canal Zone. The domestic airport Albrook is here, occupying what once was the U.S. Air Force base, and many young professionals have moved into the "reverted area" for its trademark, sturdy wooden houses with wide verandas and lush foliage. Cerro Ancón hill is the most salient landmark here, offering a 360-degree view of the city and the canal from the lookout point up high.

The neighborhoods El Chorrillo, Santa Ana, and Chinatown, on the eastern side of Cerro Ancón, are dangerous and not safe to visit, especially at night.

Calidonia/La Exposición The shoreline that fronts these two neighborhoods is the future site of many of Panama City's most ambitious high-rise developments. There are many budget (and downright scary) lodging options here, but low-cost lodging can also be found in better neighborhoods like El Cangrejo. Avenida Balboa, which hugs the shore, is an excellent place for an afternoon stroll.

The Coastline: Marbella/Punta Paitilla/Punta Pacífica Residential towers and shopping malls are the identifying characteristics of this area, where there's a confluence of Panama's newly moneyed, illegally moneyed, and recently retired residents living in glitz-and-glass high-rises overlooking the sea.

El Cangrejo/Area Bancaria/Bella Vista These three neighborhoods border each other, but they are so compact that they could be considered part of the "upscale zone." Older El Cangrejo has a "lived-in" look and hilly streets that lend this neighborhood charm. Just to the south, the Area Bancaria (Financial District), in addition to El Cangrejo, is where most travelers feel happiest lodging, as everything is within walking distance: top restaurants, shopping, and nightlife. Dozens of trendy eateries are concentrated in Bella Vista east of Avenida Frederico Boyd—the reason why Bella Vista is sometimes referred to as the Zona Rosa.

Panama Viejo On the eastern edge of the city are the ruins of Panama Viejo, the first settlement in Panama that later burned to the ground. Many visit as part of a guided tour, but the area also has a pleasant walking/jogging path along the shore and a self-guided interpretive trail that winds through the ruins.

2 Getting Around

BY TAXI

Taxis are inexpensive, safe, and plentiful—except when it is raining during rush hour and it seems that every worker heading to, or leaving, work is trying to flag one down. Every so often a taxi will stop for another passenger if he or she is headed in your general direction, but the driver will deliver you to your destination first. Taxis charge $1 to $2 for most destinations within Panama City, but confirm the price beforehand as the "zones" that taxi drivers use for price reference are vague. *Tip:* Some taxis work directly for a hotel, and rip off guests by charging up to three times the going fare. These are the taxis that await guests directly at the front door. Simply walk out to the street and flag a taxi down for cheaper fare.

ON FOOT

Panama City is not easy to navigate on foot because of its interweaving streets, streets that are not signed, and lack of recognizable landmarks for visitors. To get around without a fuss, take a cab.

On the other hand, the best (really only) way to see **Casco Viejo** is on foot so that you can savor the neighborhood's colonial architecture, visit a museum, and stop for lunch. For a walking tour, see p. 116. Avenida Balboa has a long seafront walkway that starts near Punta Paitilla and ends at the Mercado de Marisco (the fish market). The Calzada de Amador (Amador Causeway) was designed for walking, jogging, and bicycling, with some 6.5km (4 miles) of landscaped pedestrian trails.

Tips for Drivers in Panama City

If for some reason you must drive through town, or are feeling bold on the road, consider the following advice.

- Prepare for abrupt stops when cars turn into or cross your lane, especially on wide avenues such as Balboa. You as a driver should be aggressive in this sense, too, and nose your way into oncoming traffic when making a left turn or merging into traffic—other cars will slow down for you, but this is a maneuver that is best learned from watching other drivers.
- Many streets are unsigned or not named, and often a one-way street is only advertised by the fact that all parked cars face one direction. First-time drivers in Panama City make a lot of U-turns and last-minute decisions, so don't lose patience.
- Keep cool under pressure and don't panic if an unexpected turn takes you into a spooky neighborhood. Have an open map at hand, keep your doors locked, and pull over if you need to find a route to get you headed in the right direction again.
- Do not leave anything inside a parked vehicle.
- On some busy streets, a raggedy, self-styled "parking guard" might ask to watch your car. Pay him or her around 50¢. Some parking guards will demand payment of $1 or $2 before you leave your car in neighborhoods such as Casco Viejo or Bella Vista.

BY BUS

The traveler in Panama City will feel more comfortable getting around by taxi than by bus. There are no printed bus routes, but the name of the bus's destination appears on a sign in the front window. Panama City is currently overhauling its public transportation system, and beginning in 2007 the city's famous "Red Devils" will be replaced by a modern fleet of coaches. Red Devils are retired U.S. school buses that drivers individualize with electric graffiti art, flashing lights, and other knickknacks, and they are driven until the wheels fall off. It's a bittersweet adieu to the Red Devils because they are so emblematic of the funky, vibrant culture that makes Panama what it is. Because the phase-out process will happen slowly, there is a good chance that visitors will still be able to see a Red Devil or two throughout 2007.

BY CAR

You do not need or want a rental car while visiting just Panama City, considering how economical taxis are. Admittedly, there are a lot of destinations and attractions outside the city, and independent travelers who desire a vehicle to see the sights on their own will have better luck renting at one of the airport terminals and heading straight out of the city on a well-signed thoroughfare. Pay attention to every sign on the road because some road signs are small and easy to miss; other times there is no "official" sign for a turnoff, but a couple of commercial signs with the town name, giving you only a vague idea of where you are. Travelers who have a basic command of Spanish and who can ask for directions will have the easiest time. Bring a good map and ask the rental agency exactly how to get to your destination. See "Tips for Drivers in Panama City," above.

There are car rental kiosks at both the Tocumen and Albrook airports (car rental agencies at Tocumen are open 24 hr.; Albrook rental agencies are open 8am–6:30pm), and each agency has a few locations in town. If you are renting a car to visit outlying areas such as the canal, Portobelo, or the Panamanian interior, have your rental agency show you, in detail, the quickest and most efficient route to your destination.

Rental-car agencies in Panama City include **Alamo** (© 236-5777; www.alamo panama.com), **Avis** (© 278-9444; www.avis.com), **Budget** (© 263-8777; www. budgetpanama.com), **Dollar** (© 270-0355; www.dollar.com), **Hertz** (© 260-2111; www.hertz.com), **National** (© 265-2222; www.nationalpanama.com), and **Thrifty** (© 264-2613; www.thrifty.com).

FAST FACTS: Panama City

American Express American Express Travel Services has an office on Avenida Balboa (© **207-1100,** or 800/111-0006 for 24-hr. service in the United States). This office provides traveler's checks and replacement cards, along with other standard services. To report lost or stolen traveler's checks within Panama, call the numbers above, or try 207-1111.

Bookstores **Exedra Books,** on the corner of Vía Brasil and Vía España (© **264-4252;** www.exedrabooks.com; Mon–Fri 10am–9pm, Sat 10am–8pm, and Sun noon–7pm) is the top resource for English-language books, with dozens of titles, a cafe, a reading area, a children's corner, and Internet access. If you're spending extended time in Panama, you may order books on Exedra's website and have them delivered for free for orders over $25. The Smithsonian's small but excellent **Corotu Bookstore,** at the Earl S. Tupper Research and Conference Center on Roosevelt Avenue in Ancón (© 212-8000; www.stri.org; Mon–Fri 10am–4:30pm) offers a comprehensive collection of books about Panama's flora, fauna, history, and culture, including large-format photo books, maps, and gifts. **El Hombre de la Mancha** (www.bookshombredelamancha.com) is a bookstore cafe with a small selection of English-language fiction and the best Panama City map in town. They have locations in the Multiplaza and Multicentro malls, and in Albrook Airport; or try Calle 59, no. 20, at Vía Israel (© 223-1504); or Calle 52 at Avenida Federico Boyd (© 263-6218). The **Gran Morrison** chain (Vía España at Calle 51 Este: © 269-2211; Punta Paitilla: © 264-5266) has a limited English-language book section and a variety of U.S. magazines such as *People* and *Time.*

Camera Repair **Electrónica Caribe,** located at Vía España in front of the Bon Bini cafe (© 223-0205 or 264-7451).

Car Rentals See "Getting Around," above.

Dentists & Doctors Panama City has no shortage of English-speaking dentists or doctors, most of whom trained in the U.S. For a list of dentists or doctors, contact your embassy, or see "Hospitals," below.

Drugstores Called *farmacias* in Spanish, drugstores are plentiful in Panama City. For 24-hour service, visit a branch of **El Rey** supermarket, the most central of which is on Vía España (© 223-1243). Another reliable pharmacy is **Farmacias Arrocha** (© 360-4000), with locations at Vía España in front of El Panama Hotel, Vía Argentina, and Punta Paitilla.

Embassies & Consulates See "Fast Facts: Panama," in chapter 2.

Emergencies For fire, dial © **103;** for an ambulance, dial **Seguro Social** at © **229-1133,** or **Cruz Roja** at © **228-2187.**

Express Mail Services Many international courier and express-mail services have offices in Panama City, including **UPS** (© 269-9222) in Obarrio (near El Cangrejo) at Calle 53 E in the Edificio Torre Swiss Bank; **Fed Ex** (© 800-1122) on Calle 3 in Costa del Oeste; **Mail Boxes Etc,** a one-stop service with locations on Avenida Balboa in Paitilla in the Marisol Building, no. 1, next to McDonald's (© 264-7038), on Vía España, next to Niko's Café in the Financial District (© 214-4620), and in the Multiplaza Mall (© 302-4162).

Eyeglasses Eyeglass shops are referred to as *ópticas.* **Optica López,** in Plaza Paitilla (© 269-0358), and **Natural Vision,** in the Multicentro Mall (© 208-2648), are dependable chains with other locations throughout the city. Both eyeglass shops offer repairs, exams, and name-brand eyewear.

Hospitals Many Panamanian doctors receive their medical degrees in the U.S.; therefore, many speak English. The best hospitals in Panama City are: **Centro Médico Paitilla,** at Calle 53 and Avenida Balboa (© 265-8800); **Clínica Hospital San Fernando,** at Avenida Central España (© 278-6364); **Hospital Nacional,** at Avenida Cuba between Calle 38 and Calle 39 (© 207-8100 or 207-8102); and **Hospital Punta Pacífica,** at Calle 53 in Bella Vista (© 263-5287). Punta Pacífica is the newest and most advanced hospital in the country and is affiliated with Johns Hopkins University.

Internet Access All hotels recommended in this chapter have at least one computer with an Internet connection; some have wireless service in their lobby. Service in guest rooms is usually at an additional, and often expensive, price. Or try the best Internet cafe in town, **ClaroCOM,** at Avenida Eusebio A. Morales and Avenida Vía Veneto (© 200-0015; Mon–Sat 8am–10:30pm and Sun 9am–8:30pm), with **free wireless** service if you have a laptop, no matter how long you need to be connected, as well as plentiful computers. Or try **Esc@pate Internet cafe,** on Vía Argentina close to Avenida España (© 263-0616).

Laundry & Dry Cleaning **Lavandería Diamond Dry Cleaners Plus** (© 213-2216; closed Sun) is at Calle J in El Cangrejo. **Lavandería Flash** (© 213-8092) is at Vía Argentina. **SU-PERC-KLIN** is in Bella Vista next to Supermercado Riba-Smith (© 225-7869), and in El Cangrejo in front of the Einstein statue at Calle F and Calle L -1 (© 223-5666).

Maps IPAT's information desk at the Tocumen Airport offers a general map of Panama City, but the best available is **Mapi,** produced by bookstore El Hombre de la Mancha and available at their stores or at the Gran Morrison stores (see "Bookstores," above). This map is also available at gift shops in major hotels. The tourism publication *Focus* has a fold-out map that is accurate but does not show all street names; this publication can be found at hotels and other tourism-oriented shops and restaurants.

Newspapers & Magazines You'll find the international English version of the *Miami Herald* at drugstores such as Gran Morrison and at supermarkets such as El Rey. Most sell English-language publications like *People, Time,* and *Newsweek* (for additional locations, see "Bookstores," above).

Photographic Needs Few photo shops develop slides—really, you'd do better waiting until you return home to process slides. **Kodak** can be found inside El Rey supermarkets or at Calle San Francisco between Calles 74 and 75 (© **270-3333**). You can also try **FotoDigital** at Calle 50 (© **263-3000**), or in the Multi-plaza Mall (© **302-1100**).

Police Dial © **104** or 316-0080.

Post Office Postal service is scarce in Panama City; your best bet is to ask your hotel to mail something for you, or try Mail Boxes Etc (see "Express Mail Services" above). The central post office (Correos y Telégrafos) is open Monday to Friday 8am to 4pm and Saturday 8am to 1pm, and is located on Avenida Central in front of the Mercado de Mariscos (© **212-7680**).

Restrooms Restrooms, called *baños,* are marked *hombres* or *caballeros* for men, and *damas* or *mujeres* for women. There are few public restrooms in Panama City; your best bet is a hotel lobby or fast-food restaurant.

Safety Panama law requires that foreigners carry their passport with them at all times, but play it safe and carry a photocopy of only the opening pages and entrance stamp or tourist card. Leave all valuables and extra cash in your hotel. As Latin American cities go, Panama City is very safe for foreign travelers who stay out of bad neighborhoods such as Calidonia, Curundú, El Chorrillo, and Santa Ana. Chinatown is dangerous day and night. As in any major urban area, use common sense when it comes to safekeeping valuables—for example, don't put your wallet in your back pocket. Money and other valuables are best carried in hard-to-reach places, like deep pockets or a money belt, but purses are fine for women. Keep an eye out for suspicious characters who linger too close or follow too closely. Also, consider taking money out of ATMs during the day to avoid stepping out from a brightly lit cashpoint into darkness. Scams are not common here; muggings and purse-snatchings happen, but not frequently. If you park a car on the street, do not leave any valuables inside that could attract a thief, even if you park in a guarded parking lot.

Taxes All hotels charge a 10% accommodations tax, which may or may not already be included in the published rate. Restaurants charge 5% tax on all consumption, and they often sneak in a 10% service charge for a tip—check your bill carefully before paying. A tourist card costs $5, and is purchased when checking in for your flight or when crossing the border.

Taxis See "Getting Around," above.

Telephones See "Telephones" in "Fast Facts: Panama" in chapter 2. There are no city or area codes to dial from within Panama; use the country code, 507, only when dialing a Panama City number from outside Panama. Cellphone numbers begin with 6. All cellphone numbers listed in this guide already include the 6 prefix.

Time Zone Panama is on Eastern Standard Time (the same as New York or Montreal), and 5 hours behind Greenwich Mean Time. Panama does not change the hour for daylight saving time, during which the time in Panama coincides with that of the Central Time Zone in the States. *Note:* Panama is 1 hour ahead of Costa Rica and the rest of Central America.

Useful Telephone Numbers For national directory assistance, dial © 102; to reach an international operator, dial © 106; for the time, dial © 105.

Water The water in Panama City is perfectly safe to drink. Nonetheless, travelers with highly sensitive digestive tracts might want to stick to bottled water.

Weather The year-round temperature in Panama City is 85°F to 90°F (29°C–32 °C) during the day, and around 70°F (21°C) at night. The rainy season is from April to December, with torrential rain showers—however, rain occurs during the afternoon, and mornings are generally clear and sunny.

3 Where to Stay

Panama City is relatively small when compared with other major Latin American cities, and walking distances and cab rides, which cost just $1 to $2, are short. Most hotels are concentrated in **El Cangrejo** and the **Area Bancaria (Financial District),** home to banking institutions, commercial services, shopping malls, and many of the city's best restaurants. For charm, you can't beat the cobblestone streets and renovated antique homes in **Casco Viejo,** which has apartment-style lodging units with kitchens. Cab-hailing, however, can be arduous in this neighborhood at night, when raining, or during holidays, and walking to El Cangrejo or Bella Vista from here is out of the question. If you're staying in Casco Viejo, have your hotel provide you with the number of a radio taxi.

Elsewhere, there are excellent hotels scattered about the city in the **Marbella/ Coastal** area, on the slope of leafy **Cerro Ancón** hill, and near the **Amador Causeway** (specific information about these neighborhoods can be found in each lodging description). The neighborhoods **La Exposición** and **Calidonia** are home to mostly anonymous, divey hotels that seem better suited for a criminal hiding out from the feds than for a tourist seeing the sights. There are also quite a few "push-buttons" (see "Push-Buttons & the Pit Stop," below). I've stayed at cheap hotels here (Hotel Montreal and Hotel Marparaíso come to mind), and I do not feel confident recommending these properties when there are solid, inexpensive lodging options available in better neighborhoods.

Lodging Tip: When booking a reservation at a local hotel (meaning not a chain hotel), always ask for the **corporate rate,** even if you're not on corporate business. A hotel may ask for the name of the company you work for, but most do not require any other identification or proof. Corporate rates are $20 to $30 cheaper than rack rates. Also, hotels listed below as "expensive" offer much cheaper rates for travelers booking through their websites. All hotels have free parking.

APARTHOTELS

Visitors on business, travelers on an extended stay in Panama City, or families with kids might consider renting an **aparthotel,** a self-catering unit with a kitchen that is

Push-Buttons & the Pit Stop

Rent-by-the-hour hotels in Latin America are ubiquitous and largely patronized by young adults who still live with their parents, as well as by those carrying on the usual clandestine affairs. In Panama they're called "push-buttons." To admit to having patronized a push-button carries far less stigma here in Panama than it would in the U.S., but still, no one wants to be caught *in flagrante delicto,* and therein lies the origin of the name. Push-buttons are commonly found on the outskirts of towns and are clearly identifiable with cheesy names like "Lagoon of Love." Without getting out of the vehicle, a driver/client pushes an intercom button, and the gate opens. Each room has its own enclosed parking area and private entrance, and a small sliding partition that opens to the hallway means you can pay or order drinks without having to see or talk with anyone. Push-buttons come with all the romantic bells and whistles: heart-shaped tubs, mirrored ceilings, minibars—the works. To leave, the process is reversed, only the intercom button and exit area are called the "pit stop"—as the gate opens, the driver revs his engine, hits the gas, and quickly races to get out and avoid being seen.

rented nightly, weekly, or monthly (with rates based on length of stay). Aparthotels are high on function but low on style (they boast "luxury," but it's a stretch). A few have perks like gyms, swimming pools, and in-room laundry, but unfortunately, they charge up to $10 per day for an in-room Wi-Fi connection (it's sometimes cheaper to use their business center). The following aparthotels are located in El Cangrejo. Remember to ask for the corporate rate when booking, which could be cheaper than rack rates listed here.

Coral Suites Aparthotel ✿   Tile floors, firm beds, and well-maintained rooms make this aparthotel a favorite. The rooms here are the most modern and spacious of the rooms in the aparthotels listed; and the couches double as sofa beds. Their rooftop pool is also the best of the lot, and their gym is small but complete. Their Coral Bay suites have terraces. Breakfast is included (but served in a cold, formal dining room).

Calle D at Vía Veneto. ✆ 269-3898. www.coralsuites.net. 63 suites. $65 single suite; $70 junior suite; $95 Coral Bay suite. AE, MC, V. **Amenities:** Outdoor pool; gym; business center; coin-operated laundry. *In room:* A/C, TV, dataport, full kitchen.

Las Vegas Hotel Suites   It's a shame the owners of the Las Vegas are blind to the retro-cool potential of this early-1970s building, having recently "renovated" with cheap furnishings and zero eye for style. Still, the suites have terraces, and the hotel rises high above the Caffè Pomodoro restaurant and the Wine Bar—convenient if you don't feel like walking far for a meal. This is the cheapest of the area's aparthotels, and service here is the friendliest. Some rooms have old, battered kitchens, others have just a hot plate and minifridge. Ask to see a few rooms—quality varies from one to the next, *especially* the quality of mattresses.

Av. Eusebio A. Morales at Vía Veneto. ✆ 269-0722. www.lasvegaspanama.com. 85 units. $55 studio; $70 suite. AE, MC, V. **Amenities:** Small gym; business center; coin-operated laundry. *In room:* A/C, TV, dataport, kitchenette.

Sevilla Suites   Slightly older but very clean with average beds, this aparthotel has modern kitchenettes and a pool with a view. Suites have two double beds or one queen-size and a separate living area; the junior suite is one open room. Rooms facing the street have the best views. The teensy gym has just a few machines. A continental breakfast is included and served in the ground-floor cafe.

Av. Eusebio A. Morales at Vía Veneto. ⓒ 213-0016. www.sevillasuites.com. 44 suites. $70 junior suite, $85 executive suite. AE, MC, V. Amenities: Outdoor pool; small gym; business center; coin-operated laundry. In room: A/C, TV, dataport, full kitchen, safe.

Suites Ambassador   Located next door to Coral Suites, the Ambassador's rooms are darker owing to its location sandwiched between two buildings; ask for a room facing the back of the hotel. Rooms and bathrooms are clean but starting to show wear and tear. The principal difference between a studio and a suite is, in the latter, a dividing wall between the bedroom and living room (and a king-size versus a queen-size bed). The outdoor pool is uncomfortably close to the top flats of a nearby apartment, but breakfast is included, and the lobby-level breakfast nook is the coziest of all the aparthotels.

Calle D at Vía Veneto. ⓒ 263-7274. www.suitesambassador.com.pa. 39 units. $85 studio; $100 suite. AE, MC, V. Amenities: Snack bar; outdoor pool; business center; cellphone rental; in-room massage; babysitting; coin-operated laundry. In room: A/C, TV, iron.

Torres del Alba ⓖ   This place is clean and comfortable but feels more like a college dorm room than a business hotel. Still, Torres has a plant-filled rooftop patio and pool, and washers and dryers inside each apartment's spacious kitchen. Rooms come with a king-size or two double beds. Its location in El Cangrejo fronts several restaurants, the Veneto Casino, and Internet cafes. Ask for a quiet room—those overlooking the main street can be noisy both day and night. The aparthotel offers $57 a night promotion for seniors. Buffet breakfast costs $3.50.

49 B. Oeste at Av. Eusebio A. Morales. ⓒ 300-7131. www.torresdealba.com.pa. 104 suites. $95 suite. AE, MC, V. Amenities: Outdoor pool; fitness center; 24-hr. business center. In room: A/C, TV, dataport, full kitchen, hair dryer, safe, washer and dryer.

EL CANGREJO/AREA BANCARIA (FINANCIAL DISTRICT)
VERY EXPENSIVE
The Bristol Panama ⓖⓖⓖ   This boutique hotel is an excellent choice for business travelers and those seeking quiet, centrally located accommodations. The decor, uncharacteristic of tropical Panama City, is done in conservative, richly textured hues with mahogany furnishings—very English in style, and guest rooms have carpeted floors. The beds are divine, with deluxe bedding (fluffy down comforters and pillows), and double-paned windows allow a good night's sleep. Luxury bathrooms with spacious Italian-marble countertops, potted orchids, and a big bathtub add even more comfort to the guest rooms. You'll be lured into staying in and ordering room service—and coincidentally, the on-site restaurant is one of the best in town (see "Where to Dine," below). The eager-to-please staff can accommodate any need, including pressing a shirt or arranging a tour, and they issue all guests a set of business cards printed with their name and the hotel's info. The downsides: There's no pool, and the lobby is tiny (though the cozy bar serves 72 kinds of rum).

Aquilino de la Guardia at Obarrio. ⓒ 265-7844. www.thebristol.com. 56 units. $210 double; $250 junior suite. AE, DC, MC, V. Amenities: Restaurant; bar; fitness center; complimentary butler; concierge; limited room service; free meeting room rental; laundry service. In room: A/C, TV, Wi-Fi, minibar, hair dryer, safe, CD player.

Hotel DeVille ⭐⭐   For travelers whose taste runs toward the more refined, and who demand a full range of amenities without giving up intimacy for a grand hotel, the DeVille fills the bill. Centrally located on a leafy street close to the Financial District, the DeVille is a European-style, all-suites boutique hotel that boasts personalized service for a home-away-from-home feeling not provided by most chain hotels. The decor here is conservative, executive style, with historic canal-era photos and richly colored wallpaper. It could be said that the hotel lacks a bit of soul and vibrancy—you can literally hear a pin drop in their small, hushed lobby. Rooms are not carpeted, and their grand suites are two-story affairs that aren't suitable for families with small children. Luxurious bathrooms contain marble countertops and walk-in showers, and orthopedic beds have Egyptian-cotton sheets. Best of all, a full breakfast is included—and can be served to you in bed. The DeVille has an excellent on-site restaurant, the Ten Bistro. On the downside, there is no pool or gym at the hotel. Call for discounted rates.

Calle 50 at Beatriz M. de Cabal. ① **206-3100** or 263-0303. www.devillehotel.com.pa. 33 units. $155 junior suite; $195 luxury suite. AE, DC, MC, V. **Amenities:** Restaurant; bar; concierge; 24-hr. business center; 24-hr. room service; laundry and dry-cleaning service (2 complimentary pressed garments). *In room:* A/C, TV, minibar, CD player, hair dryer.

The Panama Marriott Hotel ⭐⭐⭐   Though I normally find the Marriott chain overpriced for what you get, The Panama Marriott is the overall best grand hotel in the city. First, it's within walking distance of top restaurants and Internet cafes, and taxi drivers always know where it is. (This is saying something in a city without many street names.) Their high-tech fitness center is enormous, and the spa is extensive and reasonably priced. There are amenities galore, including Copa Air, Hertz, and travel-agency desks, and the staff provides courteous, helpful service. The handsome, over-size lobby is generously appointed with huge bouquets of fresh flowers, and an ample, comfortable lounge is the perfect spot for reading the paper, holding an informal meeting, or ordering a snack from the bar or the grab-and-go cafe. The guest rooms are spacious and attractive; standard doubles have a couch and large bathroom. Executive rooms are higher up and nearly identical to standard rooms, but come with upgraded amenities such as a private lounge on the 19th floor with a dynamite view. The Marriott also has a casino, opened in 2005, for a little gaming action and disco nightlife, but one big word of caution: Rooms that end in even numbers suffer from the pounding of DJ music and partying on weekends.

Calle 52 at Ricardo Arias. ① **210-9100**, or toll-free from the U.S. or Canada 800/228-9290. www.marriott.com/PTYPA. 295 units. $170 double; $205 executive. AE, DC, MC, V. **Amenities:** Restaurant; deli; sports bar; casino; outdoor pool; spa and 24-hr. fitness center w/whirlpool, steam room, and sauna; concierge; Hertz and Copa Air desks; travel agency; business center; cellphone rental; 24-hr. room service; babysitting; laundry and dry-cleaning service. *In room:* A/C, TV, minibar, coffeemaker, hair dryer, iron, safe.

EXPENSIVE

Caesar Park Panama ⭐⭐   A perennial favorite with tourists and business travelers for its self-contained, resort-in-the-city feel and comfortable accommodations, Caesar Park Panama is near the Atlapa Convention Center and a 5- to 10-minute cab ride from most sights and restaurants. Designed in a mock Spanish colonial style, with indoor fountains and arched doorways, the hotel has a lush, inviting outdoor pool fringed with palms; its upper-floor rooms have excellent city and ocean views, and there are plenty of restaurants and shops on the premises. The Caesar bills itself as a five-star hotel, but, though well rounded, it's not luxurious, and therefore would be four stars anywhere else. The service here can range from attentive (mostly the front desk) to practically nonexistent (the poolside bar). The concierge desk, presumably accustomed to shuttling out passengers in cabs because of the hotel's distance from downtown, can accommodate any request for transportation or tours. The restaurants are excellent, making this a perfect hotel to head back to, after a long day of play or work, for a breather and a "night in." Management is cagey about plans to "refocus" the Caesar's image; what this means is anyone's guess. Ask for discounts during low season; they have a lot of rooms to fill and if no convention is in town the staff seems eager to make a deal.

Vía Israel at Calle 77. © 270-0477. www.caesarparkpanama.com. 361 units. $145 double; $190 junior suite. AE, MC, V. **Amenities:** 3 restaurants; 2 bars; outdoor pool; spa and fitness center w/whirlpool, steam room, and sauna; concierge; tour desk; business center; cellphone rental; 24-hr. room service; in-room massage; babysitting; laundry service. *In room:* A/C, TV, minibar, coffeemaker, hair dryer, iron, safe.

Courtyard Panama Real Hotel ⊛   The Courtyard's location adjacent to the Multiplaza Mall is ultraconvenient in that shops, services, cinemas, and a food court are just steps away—yet it's precisely this proximity to the mall that gives the Courtyard a cookie-cutter feel. Nevertheless, this brand-new hotel is surprisingly stylish, with potted palms and chrome-and-wood furnishings, and its guest rooms have a complete range of amenities. Like most Courtyard Marriott chains, its rooms are simply furnished yet cozy, with sparkling bathrooms and comfortable beds. Service is prompt and pleasant, except in the restaurant, where service can be slow and prices are quite high for what you get. (Take a cab to a better restaurant.) The busy road that loops around the hotel and mall cuts off walking access, so you'll always need a taxi. There is no pool here, either.

Multiplaza Mall in Punta Pacifica. © 301-0101. http://cymarriott-panama.gruporeal.com. 120 units. $110 double; $130 junior suite (executive king room). AE, DC, MC, V. **Amenities:** Restaurant; bar; 24-hr. gym; business center; limited room service; laundry service. *In room:* A/C, TV, dataport, minifridge, coffeemaker, hair dryer, iron, safe.

Crowne Plaza Panama ⊛⊛   Formerly the Holiday Inn, the owners of this hotel, part of the conglomeration that runs the Intercontinental Hotel and Gamboa Rainforest Resort, slapped on some paint, put the staff in new uniforms, and updated the guest rooms, relaunching in 2005 as the Crowne Plaza. It is now an elegant hotel catering to business travelers seeking high-end accommodations. This is where to go when you absolutely, positively need a good night's sleep: Rooms have double-paned windows, ergonomic beds with high-thread-count linens, and a basket of goodies such as eye masks and relaxation CDs. Plus the hotel has "Silence Zones," where there are no children or large groups. Though the Crowne Plaza is only a 10-minute walk from restaurants in El Cangrejo, it's located on a busy road adjacent to an abandoned building. Also, the staff could stand to smile more, but otherwise this is a very comfortable lodging choice, and website reservations made at least 2 weeks in advance can get you a double for $96 a night. Junior suites (called "executive rooms") have nice kitchenettes with full-size refrigerators and a bar counter, and cost just $15 more; likewise, some suites have balconies for $5 to $10 more, so inquire when booking. Price includes free airport shuttle.

Av. Manuel Espinosa Batista (at Eusebio A. Morales). © 206-5555. www.cppanama.com. 150 units. $140 double; $155 executive room (junior suite). AE, DC, MC, V. **Amenities:** Restaurant; sports bar; outdoor pool; fitness center; tour desk; business center; gift shop; 24-hr. room service; laundry service; heliport. *In room:* A/C, TV, minibar, CD player, coffeemaker, hair dryer, iron, safe.

El Panama   The older, Spanish-owned El Panama has a central location, a casino, and a breezy, tropical ambience with lots of open-air spaces. This latter feature, however, does not work in favor of the hotel; in fact, El Panama feels as if it should be shrunk down by a third because its vast hallways and lobbies, with minimal decoration and furniture, hint of abandonment. Indeed, it seems as though the hotel is on its last legs, slowly giving in to competition. The hotel is popular with Europeans and Latin Americans, and hosts many local and international conventioneers. Although the service is very friendly, most staff don't speak English. Overall, the hotel has a more Panamanian feel than most chain hotels. Guest rooms in the main building are spotlessly clean and quite large, with glossy, tiled floors and stuffy chintz decoration. There are also *cabañas:* double rooms with small terraces that face a large, hourglass-shaped pool with a swim-up bar. The ground-floor *cabañas* have direct access to the pool—to get there from the second floor you have to walk down a hall and a flight of stairs. The landscaping around the pool, and the public area in general, could use a little TLC. However, there's no denying the hotel's good location, and there are lots of on-site shops.

Vía España 111. (℃) 215-9000. www.elpanama.com. 345 units. $125 double; $190 junior suite. AE, MC, V. Amenities: 2 restaurants; bar; casino; fitness center; business center; gift shops; cellphone rental; 24-hr. room service; laundry. In room: A/C, TV, minibar, CD player, coffeemaker, hair dryer, iron.

Four Points by Sheraton ⚐

The Four Points can be found in the heart of the Financial District, next to the World Trade Center, in a more antiseptic area of the city. The hotel is a bit nicer than the usual chain franchise, with spacious rooms, especially the suites, that come with two rooms, two bathrooms, and two televisions, making this a good bet for families. The decor consists of floral-chintz bedspreads, gauzy drapes, and purpose-built furniture—not very "wow," but nevertheless very comfortable. There is a range of amenities, too, including a nicely designed outdoor pool and icy-cold air-conditioning. I don't recommend the Sheraton's restaurant or bar, which are not particularly pleasant spots to hang out. Also, one drawback for business travelers is that Internet service is pricey. Check their website for deals.

Calle 53 at Av. 5A B Sur. (℃) 832-0239. www.fourpoints.com/panamacity. 120 units. $110 double; $199 suite. AE, DC, MC, V. Amenities: Restaurant; bar; gym w/steam room; 24-hr. room service; concierge; business center; massage; laundry service. In room: A/C, TV, dataport, minibar, coffeemaker, hair dryer, safe.

Radisson Decapolis Hotel ⚐⚐⚐

Trendy 30-somethings will find their home at the deliciously fresh and fun Decapolis Radisson, a newer hotel and a benchmark in style and modernity in Panama City. Think glass and steel, a sleek martini-and-sushi bar, stark decoration, and hallways filled with a rainbow of ambient light. This is not a five-star hotel, but it provides excellent value with its fashionable decor and wide range of amenities, including one of the city's best spas; full business services such as cellphone rental; chic restaurants; and a casino and shopping mall connected by a walkway. Bright, spacious guest rooms (with walk-in closets and big bathrooms) are mostly white with wood-grain paneling and touches of whimsical lime, orange, and leopard print. Their large, blown-up photos portray Panama's various ethnic groups; some of these photos, of semi-nude Emberá Indian women, have bothered certain buttoned-up types—but this is not a hotel that appeals to that sort of traveler, anyway. On weekends, there is a throbbing party atmosphere in the lobby-level lounge and fourth-floor pool, which draws the young glitterati of Panama City. If you're looking for quiet (and a view), book anything from the 10th floor up, or consider a different hotel. Check the website for deals.

Av. Balboa at the Multicentro Mall. (℃) 215-5000, or 888/201-1718 in the U.S. www.radisson.com. 240 units. $130 double standard; $150 executive double; $180 executive suite. AE, MC, V. Amenities: Restaurant; martini/sushi bar and pub-style bar; full-service spa; fitness center; concierge; tour desk; business center; cellphone rental; salon; limited room service; in-room massage; babysitting; coin-operated laundry. *In room:* A/C, TV, dataport, minibar, coffeemaker, CD player, hair dryer, safe.

Riande Continental Hotel ⚜ The Continental caters predominately to Panamanians and other Latin American travelers. Located on busy Vía España, and convenient for shops and dining, the Riande has been well maintained since its opening in 1972, and the premises are spotless. The hotel rises high around a small, tropical-style outdoor pool fringed by lounge chairs. Rooms are spacious, but with run-of-the-mill decor on par with that of midrange American chain hotels. Rooms have small balconies, but access is blocked, management says, to avoid accidents. When booking, ask for a room in the back to escape late-night traffic noise from Vía España. One caveat about the hotel: The air-conditioning system is centrally controlled and therefore impossible to adjust; it's also a little loud. The Riande has a casino and a full list of amenities found at five-star hotels; however, this hotel is firmly within the four-star category. Book online for savings of as much as 50% off the rack rate.

Vía España at Ricardo Arías. ⓒ 265-5114. www.hotelesriande.com. 363 units. $160 double, $180 superior. AE, DC, MC, V. **Amenities:** 2 restaurants; bar; outdoor pool; gym; whirlpool; concierge; travel agency; business center; gift shop; newsstand; 24-hr. room service; laundry service; disco; casino. *In room:* A/C, TV, minibar, coffeemaker, safe, Wi-Fi (extra charge).

Veneto Hotel & Casino ⚜⚜ Opened in 2005, this gala hotel and casino is for travelers seeking a little more razzle-dazzle in their stay. There are a lot of amenities on offer here for the price, which makes it a value if you're looking for a hotel with several on-site restaurants and built-in nightlife. The Veneto likens itself to a Las Vegas–style hotel/casino, and from the garish exterior it's easy to see why—but step inside the wide, low-slung lobby and enter a hotel with a lot of style. During the day, their elegant casino on the mezzanine level is hardly noticeable unless you head up the escalator and pay a visit; but at night, the music pumps and the lobby takes on a very festive atmosphere. Strangely, the rooms here are all business, with conservative furniture and cool tones of blue; the beds are ultra-comfortable with crisp linens, duvets, and orthopedic beds, and there are luxurious marble-inlaid bathrooms. The Veneto bills itself as a five-star hotel, but everywhere there are slight defects—some hardly noticeable, others hard to miss. During my stay, there was a foul odor in the hallway, but this wasn't the case on every floor. The bathroom has poor lighting, and there's no cable TV. During conventions, you must walk partially through the convention to get to the outdoor pool and gym. On the other hand, the pool here hints at resort glamour, and their spa is one of the most complete in Panama, plus the service is courteous and accommodating. Top-floor rooms are executive suites with access to a private lounge. Some doubles are an odd rectangular shape and feel a little claustrophobic; they vary in size so you might ask to see more than one.

Av. Eusebio A. Morales at Vía Veneto. ⓒ 340-8888, or 877/531-2034 in the U.S. www.venetocasino.com. 301 units. $100 double; $170 junior suite. AE, DC, MC, V. **Amenities:** 3 restaurants; pool bar and 24-hr. sports bar; outdoor pool; state-of-the-art spa and fitness center w/whirlpool, steam, and sauna; concierge; business center; cellphone rental; gift shop; 24-hr. room service; babysitting; laundry service. *In room:* A/C, TV, dataport, minibar, coffeemaker, iron, safe.

MODERATE
Executive Hotel ⚜ This place is like a time warp back to the 1970s—even the doorman is still dressed in a natty guayabera suit that looks like an original. The Executive was undoubtedly the hotel of choice for discerning travelers when it opened; but

35 years later, the rooms are a tad worn and the beds could stand to be replaced, even though on the whole the hotel has been well maintained. The best things about this spot are its location, in the heart of El Cangrejo; its 24-hour coffee shop, which is great for travelers arriving at odd hours; and some pretty stunning views from the tiny balconies attached to the rooms. (Incidentally, the fifth floor and above are definitely not for those who suffer from vertigo.) Guest rooms are spaced out motel-like in that they are joined by an outdoor walkway. There are a tiny gym with a big view, an outdoor pool at street level that is unfortunately shaded most of the day, and air-conditioning that could use a little more oomph. Service is very friendly here.

Aquilino de la Guardia at Calle 52 E. © 265-8011. www.executivehotel-panama.com. 96 units. $65–$72 double. AE, MC, V. **Amenities:** Restaurant; bar; outdoor pool; fitness center; concierge; business center; 24-hr. room service; laundry service. *In room:* A/C, TV, dataport, minifridge, coffeemaker, CD player, hair dryer.

Las Huacas Hotel and Suites ⚐ (Kids)   This small Best Western franchise hotel, a converted apartment building, is centrally located and features a playful, Panamanian-folklore decor and guest rooms with kitchenettes. It's not luxurious in any sense; indeed, you'll feel as if you're subletting someone's kooky apartment. Las Huacas probably most appeals to a young teen who thinks that the leopard-print-and-bamboo tropical style is cool, as well as to someone seeking a venue for a margarita-fueled bachelor party. On the other hand, this hotel doesn't have the mass-produced feel of chains, and the accommodations are spacious, the service friendly. When choosing a room, keep in mind that the lower floors facing the street can be noisy, and that those accommodations abutting the next-door apartment put you uncomfortably face-to-face with your neighbors.

49 A. Oeste, near Av. Eusebio Morales. © 213-2222. www.lashuacas.com. 33 units. $82 junior suite; $93–$105 suite. AE, DC, MC, V. **Amenities:** Restaurant; fitness center; limited room service; laundry service. *In room:* A/C, TV, dataport, minibar, kitchenette, coffeemaker, safe.

INEXPENSIVE

Casa de Carmen ⚐ (Finds)   Tucked away on a residential street 1 block from Vía España, this eight-room guesthouse is a delightful find for budget travelers seeking a homey atmosphere and personalized attention. The Casa de Carmen is in a converted home and therefore rooms vary in size (and price); one room has bunk beds for backpack travelers, and another is an apartment with kitchen facilities for longer-term renters. Other rooms are doubles with private or shared bathrooms. A perk here is the tranquil, plant-filled backyard patio, with lounge chairs, hammocks, and a small dining area for the free continental breakfast. Casa de Carmen is infused with color and art, and even the rooms are themed "Lilac," "Brown," "Green," and so on, but they are no-frills rooms—adequately comfortable but not deluxe. The guesthouse is located in the neighborhood El Carmen, which is an easy walk or quick taxi ride to restaurants in El Cangrejo.

Calle 1a between Vía Porras and Vía Brasil, El Carmen. © 263-4366. Doubles average $30. No credit cards. **Amenities:** Self-service kitchen; outdoor patio; TV room; library; free Internet; self-service laundry. *In room:* A/C, safe, no phone.

Hotel Marbella ⚐   Because of its price and location, the Marbella is a popular hotel with budget travelers. It offers clean rooms that are in good shape if a bit on the small side—all are fitted with a double and twin bed that take up most of the space. Also, because there is no pool, this is an ideal hotel for travelers who plan to spend their days out and about, and simply need a comfortable place to sleep at night. The bathrooms are on the small side, too, but have large walk-in showers. The front desk staff is courteous and bilingual; there is a (slightly pricey) restaurant for breakfast. If you're staying for a few nights, ask for one of the small refrigerators in storage.

Calle D at Eusebio A. Morales. © **263-2220.** hmarbella@cableonda.net. 84 units. $40 double. MC, V. **Amenities:** Restaurant; business center; limited room service; laundry service. *In room:* A/C, TV, safe.

Hotel Milan ⚘ *Value*   This is a no-frills hotel, but it's brand-new and therefore everything is fresh and works properly. For the price, you'd have a hard time finding a better deal when looking for a downtown hotel close to restaurants and shops. It's a cheap-feeling spot, with frilly bedspreads and aqua-blue guest-room walls, but the manager runs a tight ship and doesn't allow parties, visitors in rooms, or anything else that would undermine the professionalism of the hotel. It's simply a safe and inexpensive place to sleep. The "suite" is a large double with a whirlpool bath (situated incongruously in a room behind a small bar). The lighting in guest rooms is awfully dim, so order a proper nightstand lamp from the front desk. Economic doubles are slightly smaller versions of doubles.

Av. Eusebio A. Morales 31. © **263-7723.** hotelmilan@cwpanama.net. 53 units. $25 economy double; $30 double; $40 suite. AE, MC, V. **Amenities:** Restaurant; limited room service; laundry service; computer for Internet access. *In room:* A/C, TV, minifridge (in suites), Internet service (in some rooms).

CERRO ANCON/BALBOA
EXPENSIVE
Country Inn & Suites—Panama Canal ⚘ *Kids*   Located on the edge of the city, near the Amador Causeway and fronting the ocean, this hotel lacks soul but is worth considering if you have kids, seek quiet accommodations and/or want plenty of space to walk, jog, or ride a bike. The Country Inn & Suites is a little slice of Americana—for example, room service is provided by an adjoining T.G.I. Friday's. So if you're looking for a "Panamanian" experience, or if you want to feel the pulse of the city, this is not your place. The hotel has a view that sweeps from the Bridge of the Americas to the Causeway, overlooking bobbing sailboats and ships awaiting the canal crossing. The decor is country-style and guest rooms look like any cookie-cutter hotel room, but with tile flooring. They all have terraces and kitchenettes, though, and there is an irresistible outdoor pool and a 3.2km (2-mile) walkway along the coast. You'll need a taxi to get anywhere ($3–$5—if you can flag a regular taxi on the periphery of the hotel rather than take the hotel's taxi), or you can rent a bike and pedal out to the Amador Causeway for a meal. Insist on an ocean-view room—it only costs $10 more, and the sparkling nighttime view of the bridge is the unique perk of this hotel.

Av. Amador at Av. Pelícano, Balboa. © **211-4501,** or 800/456-4000 in the U.S. www.panamacanalcountry.com/ amador. 98 units. $104 deluxe standard; $113 junior suite. AE, MC, V. **Amenities:** Restaurant; bar; outdoor pool; tennis courts; gym; spa; bike rental; children's play area; tour and travel agency; business center; newsstand and gift shop; limited room service; laundry service. *In room:* A/C, TV, minifridge, coffeemaker.

INEXPENSIVE
La Estancia ⚘⚘ *Value*   Travelers with an eye for style and a thin wallet will find this bed-and-breakfast to be an outstanding value. Located on the forested slope of Cerro Ancón, in a renovated 1960s Canal Zone home, La Estancia is a quiet refuge from the hustle and bustle of Panama City. The B&B has spotless, bright accommodations and personalized service that includes an on-site, reputable travel agency. There's nothing within walking distance, except the winding road up to the top of the hill (a real plus

for those who enjoy a morning walk capped off with a commanding view of the city), so you'll need a cab for sightseeing or dining out. Doubles are either en suite, or have a bathroom just outside the door. (Choose the latter—the bathroom is for your use only, and these rooms have terraces.) The two suites are enormous, and have sleek kitchens and long outdoor terraces. They are one of Panama City's best options for long-term visitors and families. The intimacy of La Estancia encourages socializing among guests—those seeking absolute privacy will be happiest in a suite or a second-floor room, which has its own common area.

Quarry Heights, Cerro Ancón. © 314-1417. www.bedandbreakfastpanama.com. 10 units. $45 double; $75 suite. MC, V. Parking. **Amenities:** Snack bar; tour desk; Internet access (Wi-Fi); self-service laundry. *In room:* Iron and hair dryer (upon request).

CASCO VIEJO

At press time, because of poor quality and safety concerns, I cannot recommend any standard hotels in Casco Viejo. If you spot a hotel here, beware of pretty facades that belie grim accommodations within, as often happens in this colonial-era neighborhood.

What Casco Viejo does offer travelers are lovingly restored apartments that can be rented nightly or weekly by **Arco Properties,** Calle 2A Oeste, Galería San Felipe (© **211-2548;** www.arcoproperties.com). Rental properties are on a space-available basis (most owners live outside Panama City and visit for short periods during the year), and they feature daily maid service but limited parking. The cost for a one- to two-bedroom apartment ranges, per night, from $85 to $125 May to November, and $100 to $200 December to April. Check out the Arco Properties website for photos (some rentals are fancier than others), or e-mail for availability at info@arcoproperties.com.

Casa Mar Alta ★★★ *Finds* A visitor would be hard-pressed to find a more unique lodging option in Panama City than the Casa Mar Alta. Located on a quiet cobblestone street in one of the most lovingly restored sections of Casco Viejo, the Casa Mar Alta is a gorgeous colonial mansion with all the 19th-century trimmings: intricate ceiling moldings, French doors and windows, a glass cupola, marble countertops, and original hand-painted floor tiles. It's tastefully yet eclectically decorated with Moroccan lamps and Latin American art, and has a terrace that runs the length of the building, on both sides, surrounding the visitor with the sounds of fluttering birds, colorful local music, and conversation that wafts up from the street. This is a B&B whose intimacy, style, and overall experience could define your stay in Panama, but it must be emphasized that this is not a full-service hotel. The manager, Vielka, does pop in occasionally to serve up scrambled eggs (breakfast is included) and can take care of most whims or needs, such as an ironed shirt or a driver for a day tour, but at night, you're on your own.

Casa Mar Alta has two options. The second floor has two en-suite bedrooms; a shared living room, dining room, and kitchen; and a rooftop terrace with lounge chairs and a view. This setup is ideal for two couples or friends traveling together; a single traveler or couple seeking absolute privacy might not find this setup appealing. The second option is the first-floor apartment for two (one bedroom, and a sofa bed for a third person if needed), which has been totally renovated with an eye toward modernity and clean lines. The style is simple and chic, but it isn't as spacious as the upstairs unit, nor does it feature a terrace with a view.

Calle 2A Oeste. © **211-3427,** or 212/517-1706 in the U.S. www.casamaralta.com. 3 units. $125–$150 double. MC, V. **Amenities:** Kitchen; laundry; Wi-Fi (and computer). *In room:* A/C, TV.

THE COAST/MARBELLA
EXPENSIVE
Intercontinental Miramar ⊛   Towering 25 floors over the shore of Panama City, the Intercontinental has a breathtaking five-star view. But other components of the hotel's five-star rating could use some spit and polish—there are frequent complaints about lackluster service and inconsistency in maintenance of guest rooms. All in all, it is an elegant hotel with full amenities, and it's popular with executives, especially conventioneers who travel in groups. (Because of this it seems like a constant battle to get up and down one of the two elevators.) The Intercontinental is also popular with VIPs who travel frequently to Panama City. Standard guest rooms are spacious and have king-size beds and sofas, but the best accommodations here are on one of the five Club Floors because of their exclusive access to a glitzy rooftop pool and plush executive lounge. The shore-level deluxe outdoor pool receives high marks, especially from kids, and the state-of-the-art gym is one of the few in the area to offer yoga classes. The lobby, however, is simply too tiny for a hotel of this caliber.

Av. Balboa near Av. Frederico Boyd. ⓒ **206-8888.** www.miramarpanama.com. 206 units. $185 double, AE, DC, MC, V. **Amenities:** 2 restaurants; bar; outdoor pool; tennis court; spa and fitness center w/whirlpool, steam, and sauna; concierge; car-rental desk; business center; salon; 24-hr. room service; laundry service; cellphone rental; heliport; marina. *In room:* A/C, TV, dataport, minibar, coffeemaker, hair dryer, iron, safe.

The Mayor of Panama City: "A Few of My Favorite Things"

Panama City Mayor Juan Carlos Navarro is one of Latin America's rising political stars, and was the youngest person ever elected to the mayor's office, in 1999, when he was 37 years old. Navarro's passion for Panama City is infectious, as is his dedication to the environment, having founded the country's leading environmental organization, ANCON. "This is Panama City's decade," he says, referring to his multimillion dollar modernization plan. "And we've just begun." Here are a few of Navarro's favorite things about Panama City:

- Octopus **ceviche** at the Fish Market.
- **The Jazz Festival** in late January "is a well-kept secret—it's one of the best in the world, and it's free." The weeklong series has ticketed indoor events but hosts one free full-day show in Plaza Catedral in Casco Viejo. Bring your own chairs, picnic lunch, cold beers, and sunscreen for this unparalleled event (see www.panamajazzfestival.com for updated information).
- Jogging at 6am on the **Amador Causeway.** "Do your workout as the sun rises over the city—it's one of the most beautiful views in the world."
- The *raspados* at Las Bóvedas (Plaza Francia in Casco Viejo). *Raspados* are Sno-cones made from ice shavings, fruit syrup, and a dollop of condensed milk—delicious and very addictive. The vendors, old timers with hand carts, are famous in Panama City and have been around for an eternity.
- The restaurant **Chimborazo,** famous for its *parihuela*, a seafood stew that "gets you walking again" after a hard night out on the town.

INEXPENSIVE

Plaza Paitilla Inn *Value*   This hair-curler-shaped hotel is located in the high-rise residential community of Punta Paitilla—yet it is still only blocks from a few convenience shops and the Multicentro Mall. The best feature of the Plaza Paitilla is its striking view from floor-to-ceiling windows in each guest room. (Book a room with a city or ocean view; otherwise you'll look out onto a neighboring condo.) The staff claims that the hotel, built in the 1970s and another former Holiday Inn, is steadily maintained, but really it's hard to tell if this is true because many of the rooms have furniture that looks to have been scavenged or bought at a discount outlet sale. The staff is friendly enough but is not trained to provide top-notch service. The beds are firm and comfortable, and there is a nice swimming pool fronting the bay, though like the hotel as a whole, it is a little worn on the edges. But, hey, at $50 a night, who can complain?

Vía Italia, Punta Paitilla. *C* **208-0600.** www.plazapaitillainn.com. 252 units. $50 double. AE, MC, V. **Amenities:** Restaurant; bar; outdoor pool; small gym; concierge; business center; limited room service; laundry service. *In room:* A/C, TV, dataport, minibar, safe.

4 Where to Dine

Like any port city worth its salt, Panama City has a gastronomic scene influenced by a melting pot of immigrants from around the world, and by its regional neighbors Colombia, Mexico, and Peru. Foodies will be overjoyed by what's on offer in this metropolitan city: Chinese food ranked by gourmets as the some of the best on this side of the Pacific, fine European cuisine, Middle Eastern eateries, Argentine steakhouses, English-style pubs, and, of course, Panamanian restaurants influenced by Afro-Caribbeans, indigenous groups, and Spanish descendants. Panamanian food is tasty, but a lot of it is fried—especially breakfast items like empanadas, *hojaldras* (fried bread), and tortillas. Most main courses are accompanied by a rice-beans-plantain combo that can become repetitive. In other words, if you're planning to visit other destinations in Panama, I say sample the rich variety of international and fusion-style restaurants here and savor Panamanian fare later.

Restaurant reviews here are divided by their individual neighborhood. The El Cangrejo district represents the area northwest of Vía España. The Financial District southeast of Vía España is included with the area "Bella Vista," which is south of Vía España and also referred to as Calle Uruguay (or Calle 48 Este, just to make it more confusing). Bella Vista is essentially a compact barrio of restaurants, shops and bars.

Don't overlook hotel restaurants. The Hotel Deville's trendy **Ten Bistro** serves contemporary, French-influenced food where each main course costs—you guessed it—$10. **Monsoon,** the Caesar Park Panama's Asian restaurant, has been honored almost with international culinary awards. Monsoon offers a sushi night on Tuesdays, and shellfish specials on Fridays. The Decapolis Radisson's **Fusion** restaurant and its hip sushi lounge is the trendiest see-and-be-seen venue in town for dining. Fusion has a reasonably priced menu and often features a fixed-price buffet lunch for around $15. The **Hotel Executive** serves breakfast 24 hours a day, and an all-you-can-eat breakfast buffet. See below for a review of The Bristol Panama's restaurant, **Las Barandas;** it offers the best Panamanian food in the city and is overseen by Panama's most famous chef.

For cheap Panamanian food you can't beat the 24-hour chain **Niko's Café,** which, in addition to basic sandwiches, serves 100 snacks and items, such as a tamale or fried egg, for less than 90¢ each. Niko's can be found at Vía España and Calle Gerardo

Ortega (Calle 51B Este, near the Continental Hotel), at the Albrook Bus Terminal, or on Calle 50 (Nicanor Obarrio). There are many hole-in-the-walls and cafeterias that serve what's called *comida corriente,* or the cheap daily special that might include a beverage. American fast-food chains, such as Dunkin' Donuts, Bennigan's, McDonald's, T.G.I. Friday's, and Subway, are everywhere. Fast-food chains are clustered next to the Veneto Hotel and the Multicentro Mall.

GROCERY & SPECIALITY STORES   The supermarket chain **El Rey** is Panama's largest, and most branches are open 24 hours a day. You can find national products plus a large selection of imported brands from the U.S. The most convenient location is on Vía España, near El Panama Hotel; there is another in the Albrook area, on Avenida Omar Torrijos on the way to Gamboa. The premier wine store **Felipe Motta,** in Marbella on Calle 53(© 302-5555), is the most complete in Central America, and their prices are reasonable. For organic groceries and health products, try **Orgánica** in Marbella, at the Plaza Paitilla mall on Ramón H. Jurado (© 215-2400; Mon–Fri 10am–5pm).

CULINARY TOURS   If you're a foodie, contact Melissa DeLeon at the **Panama Gourmet** for culinary tours in Panama City (© 225-3511; www.panama-gourmet. com). Melissa, a food writer, chef, and caterer, offers tours designed by local chefs, with bilingual guides and visits to markets and restaurants. Panama Gourmet also has cooking courses.

BELLA VISTA/AREA BANCARIA (FINANCIAL DISTRICT)
EXPENSIVE
Eurasia ✦✦✦ FUSION   One of Panama City's tonier restaurants, Eurasia is not the belle of the restaurant scene that it was several years ago. But the top-notch cuisine and sharp service endure. As the name implies, Eurasia's dishes are European with dashes of Asian flavors, stylishly presented. Daring and delicious, the food truly reflects the immigrant melting pot that is Panama City. The ambience is elegant, with papaya-colored walls, lavish art, heavy Spanish ironwork, and checkered marble floors, and there is a slightly more casual dining area near the bar. Waiters in starched white shirts and shiny cummerbunds provide some of the best service in all of Panama. The menu is lopsided in terms of pricing; some dishes are better—and cheaper—than others. At press time Eurasia was retooling its menu, but expect to find dishes such as jumbo shrimp in tropical tamarind sauce with coconut milk, or filet mignon in a gingery sauce.

Calle 48, Bella Vista. © 264-7859. eurasia_restaurant@hotmail.com. Reservations recommended. Main courses $7–$29. AE, MC, V. Mon–Fri noon–3pm and 7–10:30pm; Sat 7–11pm.

Limoncillo ✦✦✦ CONTEMPORARY MEDITERRANEAN/ITALIAN   I love this little gourmet bistro, and always find it difficult to make up my mind about what to order—everything is so tantalizingly good. Limoncillo, or the "little lemon," is the brainchild of Clara Icaza (one of Latin America's top chefs) and restaurateur Jennifer Spector, both of whom earned their stripes in upscale Manhattan restaurants before bringing New York–style dining—creative taste combinations, chill-out background music, an arty ambience, and high-end prices—to Panama City. Opening in 1999 with little fanfare, Limoncillo has quietly grown in popularity with well-heeled and fashionable Panamanians. Now the restaurant is typically the first place locals recommend to foreign visitors seeking a special place to dine. The food is mostly Mediterranean and Italian, but thoroughly contemporary. Your meal starts with a basket of freshly baked bread. Order the starter Portobella Napoleon with goat cheese and pesto, or a *paratha* (East Indian whole wheat flatbread) with yellow pea purée, and follow it with grilled sea bass with white bean purée and a zesty lemon preserve. Or try one of their creamy risottos with jumbo prawns or the beef tenderloin stuffed with basil and chipotle. Limoncillo has only a dozen or so tables, so it's wise to make a reservation, especially on weekends. If you have to wait, order one of their well-made cocktails.

Calle 47 and Calle Uruguay. ⓒ 263-5350. limoncillo@cwp.net. Reservations recommended. Main courses $14–$22. AE, MC, V. Mon–Fri noon–3pm and 7–10:30pm (until 11pm Fri); Sat 7–11pm.

Palms ✦✦✦ *(Finds)* FUSION   Many Panamanians have yet to hear of it, but Palms is Panama City's hippest restaurant, an avant-garde and tropical-chic homage to great style and innovative cuisine. The menu is divided into "collections," as in the appetizer "collection" and the dessert "collection," displayed on a kitschy menu. But this isn't a flash-in-the-pan eatery that puts looking cool over delivering the goods: The kitchen turns out consistently delicious and well-conceived dishes that expertly blend Mediterranean, Asian, and Latin American flavors and ingredients. I love their clam chowder with smoked pork, the tuna tartar, pumpkin ravioli with sage butter, and sautéed prawns with a garlic and corn risotto. Grilled steaks and fresh fish are also offered. Their simple crème brûleé and chocolate pecan tart with coffee sauce satisfies your sweet tooth without being overwhelming. The dining area is polished and sophisticated, with a rear atrium full of leafy vegetation and separated from the dining area by a floor-to-ceiling glass wall. (There is no outdoor seating.) The atmosphere is relaxed, but it's a good idea to dress smartly for Palms. After dinner, head up to their ultra-modern, all-white bar/lounge, Urbano, on the second floor, which features DJ music and a full cocktail bar.

Calle 48 and Calle Uruguay. ⓒ 265-7256. palmsrestaurant@cableonda.net. Reservations accepted. Main courses $12–$20. AE, MC, V. Mon–Fri noon–3pm and 7–11pm; Sat 7–11pm.

MODERATE

Café Balear ✦✦ SPANISH/STEAKHOUSE   The bulk of the menu at this Spanish-owned restaurant is, fittingly, Spanish—however, not everyone knows that Café Balear is also one of the best steakhouses in the city. Chef Pedro Masoliver runs a tight ship here, and the service and quality of the food, especially his tender cuts of beef, are consistent—which is not true of most steakhouses in Panama City. The restaurant is in a converted chalet-style home and is neither formal nor casual, rather somewhere in between. Try the rib-eye with mushrooms, filet with anchovy sauce, a traditional paella (a Catalan-style seafood risotto), grilled octopus, or fresh tuna steak in peppercorn. Café Balear has a well-chosen wine list, too, with mostly Spanish (along with a few Chilean and Californian) varieties.

Calle Colombia at Rogelio Alfaro. ⓒ 269-2415. Reservations accepted. Main courses $13–$30. AE, MC, V. Mon–Sat noon–3pm and 7–11pm.

El Patio Mexicano ✦ MEXICAN   Panama City's top Mexican restaurant seems more Mexican than Mexico itself. The owners, the Uribe family from Guadalajara, have draped the colorful walls and festooned every nook and cranny with gads of Mexican folk art, historic photos of Mexico, and hand-painted crockery, and fitted the dining area with traditional leather furniture. The food here is authentic Mexican more than Tex-Mex. Don't miss the spicy chicken mole poblano, the "divorced" enchiladas (a red and green enchilada with gooey cheese separated down the middle by a couple of chips), or the *puerco pibil* (a citrus pork dish from Mérida). Wash it down with one of the good, frosty margaritas.

Calle Guatemala, close to Vía España. © 263-5684. Reservations accepted. Main courses $10–$25. AE, MC, V. Tues–Fri 11:30am–3pm and 6–11:30pm; Sat 11:30am–11:30pm; Sun noon–9pm.

La Posta ★★ *Finds* INTERNATIONAL   The crazy popularity of this newer restaurant with the Panamanian jet-set derives more from the lively, 1950s Havana-style ambience than from the cuisine. La Posta has a gorgeous tropical decor, with whirling wicker ceiling fans and a plantation-style architecture, and although elegant, the restaurant does not feel pretentious. During the day, floor-to-ceiling windows separate the dining area from an outdoor patio (with outdoor seating), filled with vegetation, which provides for a bright and cheerful lunchtime setting.

Although La Posta is inexpensive for such a lovely atmosphere, the food is uneven, ranging from five-star to adequate. Stick with the seafood; the meat dishes—especially the chicken—are lackluster in presentation and concept. A good bet? Try the starters (there are more than a dozen, so you might consider ordering an assortment of these rather than an entree): yellowfin-tuna ceviche with capers; *mero* (a high-quality sea bass) carpaccio; or fried polenta with Gorgonzola and portobello mushrooms. The thin-crust pizzas are delicious, as are the risottos. Seafood dishes are tasty but simple, such as jumbo prawns with passion fruit and rice pilaf.

Calle 49 at Calle Uruguay. © 269-1076. mail@lapostapanama.com. Reservations necessary. Main courses $9.75–$14; pizzas $6.50–$9. AE, MC, V. Mon–Sat noon–2:30pm and 7–10:30pm.

Sushi Itto ★ SUSHI   Despite Sushi Itto's being a chain franchise from Mexico, this is the best sushi spot in the city, and their ingredients are always fresh and high-quality. The restaurant is modern though not as flashy as the Decapolis's sushi bar; but Sushi Itto is cheaper, there's more variety, and they deliver. There are dozens of fanciful rolls, with sweet and spicy sauces, that go far beyond the classic California roll and fresh sashimi. They also serve teppanyaki, udon, and yakisoba noodles with meat and shellfish.

Calle Samuel Lewis at Calle 56 Este. © 265-1222. Sushi rolls $6–$8.50. AE, MC, V. Daily noon–1am.

INEXPENSIVE

Crepes & Waffles CONTINENTAL   Like the name says, this casual eatery specializes in crepes and waffles. It's best for lunch or a light meal in the early evening; they even offer a "menú light" during lunch that includes a beverage and crepe for $4.75. There are pre-designed crepes, or you can build your own from a long list of ingredients and sauces, including lots of vegetarian items. Crepes & Waffles also serves huge salads, soups, and sandwiches. They recently opened another restaurant in the Flamenco area of the Amador Causeway.

Calle 47 at Calle Aquilino de la Guardia. © 269-1574. Crepes $3–$9. MC, V. Tues–Sun noon–11pm.

Greenhouse ★ INTERNATIONAL   Like its name implies, this restaurant is full of lush vegetation and surrounded by glass walls—it tries to be a little hipper than it really is, but Greenhouse is contemporary and fresh, and cooled by a good air-conditioning system. It's better to stop here for lunch or an afternoon snack than for dinner; the place is very casual, and the sandwiches, wraps, and appetizers are better than the main courses. Greenhouse has more than a dozen hot and cold wraps—fresh tuna, smoked salmon, and falafel, among others; sandwiches are hearty and include a delicious portobello mushroom sandwich, and probably the only veggie burger available in

Panama City. Fresh salads, shish kabobs, hummus and antipasto platters, plus a couple of heavier fish and meat dishes round out the menu. There is a happy hour with half-off drinks from 5 to 8pm.

In Bella Vista, Calle Uruguay at Calle 47. ℂ **264-6846**. (2nd location in El Cangrejo, on Vía Argentina at Calle Arturo Motta; ℂ **214-7475**.) Main courses $9.25–$15; sandwiches $6.50–$8. AE, MC, V. Daily noon–midnight.

CASCO VIEJO

For a coffee and muffin, sandwich, or sweet dessert (Internet access, too), try **Brooklyn Café** at Calle Primera, near the French Embassy (ℂ **211-0961**).

EXPENSIVE

Manolo Caracol ★★★ *Finds* INTERNATIONAL   Manolo Caracol is my favorite restaurant in Panama City, hands down, but this artistic eatery may not appeal to every diner. I say give it a try. Manolo, the Spanish chef, professes "cooking with love," and an adventurous and creative daily menu embraces fresh, in-season products he finds every morning in the local market. (He's the only chef in town who personally trolls the fish market seeking the best and most exotic seafood.) There's no ordering here: Customers pay $17 for lunch or dinner (drinks excluded), and sit back and wait for a vibrantly composed parade of up to 12 courses to be slowly ushered to their table. A day's menu might include sole carpaccio, green mango ceviche, pork loin with pineapple, and gingery prawns. There is also an $8 three-course lunch for smaller appetites. The dining area is within an antique colonial building, and is casually elegant and warm, with wood tables, white stucco walls, and local art.

Calle 3 at Av. Central Sur (in front of the National Theater). ℂ **228-4640** or 228-9479. www.manolocaracol.net. Reservations recommended for dinner. Fixed-price lunch or dinner $17 per person, drinks additional. AE, MC, V. Mon–Sat noon–3pm and 7–10:30pm.

Mostaza ★★ INTERNATIONAL   Featuring a cozy dining area with thick white tablecloths, candles, exposed brick walls, and cuisine so tasty even President Trujillo pops over occasionally for lunch from his offices 3 blocks away, this is another excellent eatery in Casco Viejo. Like any good Argentine, co-owner Jose Forestier knows his beef, and even imports cuts like rib-eye and filet mignon from the U.S. Mostaza serves pasta, fresh grilled fish, and a few chef's specialties such as *bacalao, osobuco Corleone,* and pork chops with passion fruit or guayaba sauce.

Av. A at Calle 3. ℂ **228-3341**. Reservations for dinner recommended. Main courses $9–$18. AE, MC, V. Tues–Fri noon–midnight; Sat–Sun 5pm–midnight.

S'cena ★★★ INTERNATIONAL   This sexy, sophisticated jazz club/upscale restaurant is the perfect spot for an all-in-one night out. The jazz club, Platea, is on the first floor, the restaurant on the second. The bar in Platea is a good place to start or end a meal, and they serve appetizers for less-hungry patrons. Upstairs, S'cena is casual elegance, with a New York vibe, with white table linens and exposed brick walls. The cuisine is very good and Mediterranean-influenced, crafted by a talented young chef on loan from Spain. The meal begins with a complimentary *amuse-bouche,* a tiny appetizer to pique the taste buds. Order a bottle of wine from the well-chosen, and reasonably priced, wine list, and follow it with shellfish sautéed in Pernod or octopus caramelized in white wine. Main courses include fish and meat dishes, and a few pasta highlights such as "Grandmother's Catalan Cannellonis."

In front of old Club Union. ℂ **228-4011**. Reservations recommended. Main courses $9–$18. AE, MC, V. Tues–Sun noon–4pm and 7:30–11pm (bar until 1am on weekends).

MODERATE

Ego ⊛ TAPAS   The new kid on the block, Ego is a cosmopolitan bar/cafe, on a quiet corner of Plaza Bolívar, that serves tapas. Make a meal out of hot chile ceviche; a salad of arugula, fig, and Camembert cheese; and cilantro beef skewers. Nicely mixed cocktails, a long swooshing bar, and outdoor seating are a few of Ergo's perks. (There's air-conditioned seating indoors.) Large, cold pitchers of sangria are also a treat.

Calle Antonio J. de Sucre, on the corner of Plaza Bolívar. ℂ **262-2045**. Tapas $4–$8.50. AE, DC, MC, V. Mon–Sat 5–11:30pm.

Las Bóvedas ⊛ *(Finds)* FRENCH   Ever dined in a 17th-century Spanish dungeon? Here's your chance. Built in the historic fortress inside a defensive seawall, Las Bóvedas (The Vaults) was later used as torture chamber whose victims were chained and left to watch the waters rise around them at high tide. Today it's been converted into a stylish eatery, with highly arched stone ceilings and low candlelight. The food is better at the restaurants mentioned above, but the ambience here makes up for this. Expect French-influenced salads, shellfish appetizers, grilled seafood, and meats. A bar makes a good spot for a cocktail and light meal, and features live jazz on Fridays and Saturdays from 9pm to 1am.

Plaza Francia. ℂ **228-8068**. Reservations accepted. Main courses $7–$14. AE, MC, V. Mon–Sat 5:30pm–1am.

Macarena ⊛⊛ SPANISH   This cozy little restaurant is an ideal spot for a couple because most items on the menu are prepared for two. In the dining area of wood floors and brick walls, the Macarena's Spanish owner serves food typical of his homeland, including tapas that make an excellent light meal. The bulk of the menu consists of rice and seafood-based dishes including jumbo shrimp stew and more than five kinds of paella, as well as fresh tuna and gazpacho. The restaurant's chic bar features live music on Fridays and Saturdays.

Calle 1a. ℂ **228-0572**. Reservations accepted. Main courses $11–$14; paellas $20–$28 (for 2); tapas $3–$4.50. AE, MC, V. Daily noon–3pm and 6:30–10:30pm (until 11:30pm Fri–Sat).

CALDONIA
INEXPENSIVE

Boulevard Café PANAMANIAN DINER   This casual diner is a throwback to the 1950s; even the waitresses look as if they've been here that long. Locals, including politicians (you won't see any other tourists here), love this joint for its simple, cheap meals and sandwiches made with toasted, spongy bread and roasted meats. Main courses include the usual Panamanian fare: fried snapper, sancocho (a chicken stew), and steak with onion and fries. No matter how complicated the order or how large the group, your waitress will never write it down—and will forget nothing. It's a good lunch stop if you're strolling Avenida Balboa.

Av. Balboa at Calle 32 Este. ℂ **225-0914**. Main courses $4–$12; sandwiches $4–$5. AE, MC, V. Mon–Sat 7am–1am.

Restaurant Mercado del Marisco ⊛⊛ *(Kids)* SEAFOOD   To find the freshest seafood in Panama City, you have to visit the Mercado del Marisco (Fish Market) and its unassuming little eatery on the second floor. This market restaurant serves quite possibly the best ceviche in town, perhaps because the owner is Peruvian and lends his special flavor to such an emblematic Latin American dish. The portions are hearty, the price reasonable and, best of all, you can see below in the market what your catch looked like before it got to your plate. Come before 1pm or after 2pm because this place gets packed during the lunch hour. *Tip:* If the restaurant is full or you are on the run, buy a $1 ceviche from Sheila at her booth; when you walk in the main door, she's just straight ahead. (You can identify her by her gold tooth.)

Av. Balboa (inside the Fish Market) (📞 212-3898. Reservations not accepted. Main courses $3–$8.50. Credit cards not accepted. Daily 11am–7pm.

EL CANGREJO
EXPENSIVE

Las Barandas ★★★ CONTEMPORARY PANAMANIAN   Cuquita, the chef at Las Barandas, is nationally famous as the Martha Stewart of Panama, producing her own line of culinary magazines in addition to a weekly cooking show. At Las Barandas, Cuquita is the creator of the restaurant's gourmet Panamanian food and oversees the kitchen staff. The restaurant, located inside The Bristol Panama, is a sleek and chic dining area with not too many tables—so book ahead. At Las Barandas, traditional recipes are updated to appeal to modern gourmet tastes, with dishes such as maize soup, plantain won tons, grouper in ginger, sea bass in tamarind, and chicken breast roasted with pumpkin seeds, all bursting with flavor yet not too over-the-top so as to appeal to more conservative tastes. In addition to an extensive menu, there is a special "South Beach" menu for dieters watching their waistlines. Of special note is Las Barandas's Sunday brunch from 10am to 3pm.

Aquilino de la Guardia at Obarrio. (📞 265-7844. Reservations recommended. Main courses $12–$25. AE, MC, V. Daily 6–10am breakfast; noon–3pm lunch; 6:30–11pm dinner.

Restaurante Jimmy GREEK   Restaurante Jimmy has a sister restaurant near the Caesar Park Panama hotel, but this branch is a 24-hour, cafeteria-like restaurant with a long list of sandwiches, pastas, seafood, and meat, served mostly to businesspeople who come for their economical fixed-price lunch on weekdays. If you're out late and hungry, this is one of the few places in Panama City where you can grab a bite during the early hours. The owner of Restaurante Jimmy is Greek, and accordingly they serve a list of rather good Greek dishes such as moussaka and tzatziki.

Calle Manuel María Icaza, next to the Transatlantic Bank. (📞 223-1523. Reservations not accepted. Main courses $4–$10. MC, V. Daily 24 hr.

Restaurante 1985 & Rincón Suizo ★★★ FRENCH/SWISS   These are nationally famous chef Willy Diggelmann's two flagship restaurants, both of which are reviewed here since they are located in the same building, a rather incongruous Swiss-alpine-style chalet. Restaurante 1985, widely regarded as one of the best, and most expensive, in the city, is where Panamanians go for a special meal. The fare is predominantly French, with classic dishes such as pâté, escargot, and coquilles St.-Jacques, but there are also German touches such as Wiener schnitzle. The standout at 1985 is the tender veal cutlet in morel mushroom sauce, but the fresh catch of the day, lobster, calamari and scallop stew, and filet mignon in red-wine sauce are divine, too. There is also an extensive gourmet vegetarian menu. For a splurge, order the fixed-price dinner menu for $26. There is lighter fare, but you'll be tempted by many of the creamier, calorie-packed meals, which make up nearly half the menu. For dessert, don't miss the *guanábana* mousse. The ambience is country French, with a cheerier area in the non-smoking section.

Upstairs is the Rincón Suizo, a slightly less-expensive place that pays homage to Switzerland; its waitresses wear dirndls and there's a cozy ambience with checkered tablecloths and soft light. Traditional dishes such as raclette, fondue, goulash, and bratwurst are the mainstays here, as well as rabbit in red wine and *cordon bleu*. Like

1985, Rincón Suizo is heavy on sauces, but there are also fresh salads and diet-friendly grilled fish. It's worth noting that both restaurants feature an outstanding selection of wine, which is difficult to find in Panama.

Eusebio A. Morales and Calle 49B Oeste, in front of Sevilla Suites. ⓒ **263-8571** or 263-8310. www.1985.com. Reservations recommended for dinner. Main courses $12–$33. AE, MC, V. Mon–Fri 11am–midnight; Sat–Sun 5:30pm–midnight.

MODERATE

Beirut ⓖ LEBANESE   This is an excellent spot for a couple or a larger group because it serves reasonably priced combo plates and appetizer platters. Combos come with dozens of little dishes and finger foods such as hummus, labre, baba ghanouj, fried kibbe, almond rice, and so on, offering a filling meal and varied sample of flavors. There are also salads, falafel and other sandwiches, and kabobs. I like Beirut, too, because of its low ceilings, molded banquet seating, and exotic decor, which makes you feel as if you've actually stepped into Lebanon. Additionally, the food is light and fresh, and powerful air-conditioning provides a refreshing escape from the hot Panama City streets. The chef, a Lebanese immigrant, patrols the dining room for quality control, sometimes refilling the occasional guest's hookah pipe, which is de rigueur in this establishment. A Lebanese Table, with a selection of dishes, for four guests is $58; a special combo large enough to feed two is just $10.

Ricardo Arias at Calle 52, near the Marriott Hotel. ⓒ **214-3815.** Main courses $6.50–$15. MC, V. Daily 11am–2pm.

Madame Chang ⓖⓖⓖ CHINESE   Some of the best Chinese food found outside China is here in Panama, and Madame Chang is where you come to savor it. Few restaurants serve a more delectable Peking duck, but there are also the jumbo shrimp a la sal, the gingery San Blas crab, the prawn rolls, and clams in black-bean sauce—really, everything on the menu is worth recommending, so you'll have to go with whatever seems appealing. The proprietor, Siu Mee Chang, and her daughter Yolanda have merged the old with the new: The elegant ambience is more smart-casual than button-up conservative, and the cuisine blends traditional recipes from all Chinese provinces, but with a contemporary touch. Madame Chang also shakes up killer martinis.

Av. 5A and Calle Uruguay. ⓒ **269-1313.** Reservations recommended. Main courses $8–$22. AE, MC, V. Daily noon–3pm and 6–11pm.

Martín Fierro ⓖⓖ STEAKHOUSE   Named after Argentina's epic literary hero, a gaucho who wandered the pampa, this restaurant, accordingly, serves thick slabs of beef and other meats that would satisfy a gaucho or any weary traveler who's had a hard day and longs for a hearty, satisfying meal. Martín Fierro features meats cut Argentine-style, but the price differs between domestic meat and that imported from the U.S. You'll find pastas and fish on the menu, but if you're not a carnivore there's really no reason to eat here. (They boast about their salad bar, but it's insubstantial and won't do much more than decorate your plate.) Martín Fierro strives to be an elegant eating establishment, but bright lights and decor that runs on the casual side make this definitely not a coat-and-tie place.

Eusebio Morales, in front of Bonavel. ⓒ **264-1927.** Reservations accepted. Main courses $8–$25. AE, MC, V. Mon–Sat noon–3pm and 6–11pm; Sun noon–9:30pm.

INEXPENSIVE

Cafetería Manolo's PANAMANIAN   This neighborhood standby is a plain-as-Jane diner with uniformed waitresses and a long list of Panamanian dishes of varying quality. It's the kind of place you go for a quick, no-frills meal, or to kill time with a cold beer while sitting on the outdoor terrace. It therefore draws as many locals as tourists who can't be bothered with a serious sit-down restaurant. Manolo's sandwiches are your best bet here, but there are also quick-fry steaks, grilled fish, and local dishes such as sancocho soup. Try the sugary *churros* (a cornmeal pastry with gooey filling) for dessert. Breakfast can be simple eggs or a Panamanian breakfast with eggs and tortillas. There are two locations, but I like the Vía Veneto diner the best.

Calle 49B Oeste, in front of the Veneto Hotel. ☎ 269-4514. (Another location at Vía Argentina and Av. 2B Norte; ☎ 264-3965.) Reservations not accepted. Main courses $6–$9; sandwiches $2.50–$4.50. No credit cards. Both locations daily 6am–1am.

Caffè Pomodoro ☆ ITALIAN   Star chef Willy Diggelmann's third restaurant is a toned-down and moderately priced venue for a casual, tasty meal. The seating is outdoors, under umbrellas, but the dining area is completely enclosed by soaring buildings (and the Las Vegas Suites hotel), blocking the sun for the better part of the day and keeping temperatures down. The pasta here is fresh, homemade, and hearty, and you can build your own pasta dish by choosing from capellini, spaghetti, fettuccine, and so on, and pairing it with one of 15 sauces. I like the cannelloni with spinach, and the lasagna Bolognese, and there's also a fresh fish of the day and meats. Some of the vegetable dishes, like pasta primavera, are cooked so long that they resemble ragout; if you're looking for vegetables, stick with a fresh salad, of which there are many flavorful varieties such as fresh tomato with basil and mozzarella. At night, patrons can dine in the adjoining Wine Bar and order off Pomodoro's menu.

Calle Eusebio A. Morales and Calle 49B Oeste. ☎ 269-5836. Reservations accepted. Main courses $7–$15. AE, MC, V. Daily 7am–midnight.

El Trapiche ☆☆ PANAMANIAN   Ask anyone in Panama City where to savor great Panamanian food, and chances are the first place they say is El Trapiche. There's nothing palatial about it, but you can cool off in the air-conditioned dining room or people-watch from the outdoor sidewalk cafe. Newcomers to Panama should not miss the house specialty, the "Panamanian Fiesta" combination plate, which offers a taste of eight different local dishes. This is also where you'll want to try the hefty Panamanian breakfast—order *tasajo entomatado* (beef jerky) with eggs and fried-bread *hojaldras*. The old-world sugar-mill decor comes from the name, El Trapiche, which refers to a press used to extract juice from sugar cane. Main courses, such as broiled sea bass or smoked pork chops with rice, beans, and fried plantains, are hearty and satisfy big appetites. Their fresh fruit smoothies are refreshing on a hot day.

Vía Argentina at Av. 2a B Norte. ☎ 269-4353. Main courses $3–$11. AE, MC, V. Sun–Thurs 7am–11pm; Fri–Sat 7am–midnight.

Las Tinajas ☆☆ *Finds* PANAMANIAN   Combining a taste of Panamanian flavors and folklore, Las Tinajas is certainly one of the more touristy restaurants in town, yet it shouldn't be pooh-poohed by those searching for authentic regional cuisine. Las Tinajas features costumed folkloric performances which are enjoyable, not hokey. They take place while diners go about tucking into some of the best Panamanian food in the city. It's no surprise, therefore, that Las Tinajas ranks high on many visitors' itineraries, so make reservations. Classic fare such as *ropa vieja* (spicy, shredded beef over rice), *carimañolas* (yuca rolls stuffed with meat stuffing), ceviche, and creole-style sea bass highlight the extensive menu. Performances begin at 9pm on Tuesday, Thursday, Friday, and Saturday, and there is a $5 cover charge for the show as well as a minimum $10 consumption charge. An on-site gift shop sells handicrafts.

Calle 51. © **269-3840** or 263-7890. www.panamainfo.com/tinajas. Reservations recommended. Main courses $6–$14. AE, MC, V. Mon–Sat 11am–11pm.

AMADOR CAUSEWAY
EXPENSIVE

Bucanero ⓖ SEAFOOD   Of all the restaurants in the Flamenco shopping area, Bucanero, with its kitschy maritime decor, serves the best food. The restaurant is seriously overpriced, but the portions are hearty and the cuisine is a step above that of its neighbors. There are meats on the menu (including *parrilladas,* or barbecue meat platters), but the specialty is seafood. Start with a tangy ceviche, and then have the stuffed sea bass, a rich Parmesan-cheese crab gratin, or jumbo shrimp in a vodka sauce. There are shared platters for groups. Dining is on a breezy veranda overlooking a parking lot and the Flamenco Shopping Plaza. Because the cruise-ship dock is nearby, some passengers stop at the Bucanero for meals. One caveat here has to do with the waiters, who are attentive but try to rip off guests by suggesting a higher quality seafood (jumbo shrimp, for example, as opposed to shrimp), thereby doubling the cost of the dish without warning the diner. Alas, the Flamenco area is a tourist trap anyway. Live jazz is featured on Wednesday, and salsa music on Thursday and Friday.

Flamenco Shopping area (end of the Amador Causeway). © **314-1774.** Reservations accepted. Main courses $14–$26. AE, MC, V. Daily 11.30am–midnight.

MODERATE

Alberto's Pizza & Pasta ⓖ ITALIAN   This restaurant would have the best views on the Amador Causeway if only it didn't front a docking area for monster yachts. As it is, diners are treated only to a peek here and there of the city skyline in the distance. Nevertheless, Alberto's is always packed with tourists, and Panamanians head here for lunch alfresco—there is a lovely, cool breeze and ample outdoor seating. The menu is ridiculously long, with six pages of meats, pastas, pizzas, and seafood (the best bet is the pastas), but then again, Alberto's does offer something for everyone, and there's even a kids' menu. Peckish diners should try the Alberto's Bandeja, with an assortment of seafood and meat goodies. Despite the abundance of waiters in jaunty striped shirts, service can be erratic, even just plain bad. But most diners don't seem to care because no one here is in a rush to get in and out. There is an indoor dining room, but it's always empty.

Inside the Flamenco shopping area, facing the pier. © **314-1132.** Reservations accepted. Main courses $11–$20; pizzas $4–$8; pastas $5.50–$14. AE, MC, V. Daily noon–midnight.

Al Tambor de la Alegría ⓖⓖ *(Finds* PANAMANIAN   Giving Las Tinajas (see above) a run for its money, the new Al Tambor de la Alegría (Drum of Happiness) also offers a 1-hour folkloric dance presentation and good traditional cuisine. Indigenous Panamanians and women in traditional polleras provide a razzle-dazzle show that spans the history of the country, from the arrival of the Spanish to the construction of the canal. The menu features dishes named after the different regions of Panama, such as the Volcán Barú (a sample platter with *carimiñolas,* tortillas, and other local delicacies), a Best of Boquete salad with fresh tomatoes and onions, and the Coiba Island octopus, among other themed dishes with seafood and meats. The show is an additional $10, without a minimum consumption, and takes place at 9pm Monday through Saturday.

Brisas de Amador. © **314-3380.** Reservations recommended. Main courses $7–$15. AE, MC, V. Mon–Sat 6pm–midnight; Sun 9am–11am, noon–3pm, and 6pm–midnight.

INEXPENSIVE

Mi Ranchito ⭐ PANAMANIAN   This is certainly not the best Panamanian food in the city (El Trapiche, Las Barandas, and Tinajas fill that bill), but nevertheless Mi Ranchito is a very popular restaurant for its views of the Panama City skyline, and for the almost constant cool breeze that blows through here. The restaurant is open-air and under a massive thatched-roof *bohío* on Isla Naos, near the Smithsonian Museum. You'll find typical Panamanian dishes here such as grilled meat, prawns, sea bass, and snapper served in a garlic or tomato-and-onion sauce and paired with coconut rice and fried plantains. Mi Ranchito has an appetizer mix of Panamanian specialties such as empanadas, *patacones,* and *carimiñolas,* but they are so deep-fried they almost all look and taste the same. Stick with the fresh fish and shellfish dishes, and an ice-cold beer. After lunch, you can rent a bike next door and go burn off all those calories.

Isla Naos. 𝄢 **228-4909.** Reservations not accepted. Main courses $7–$10. MC, V. Mon–Sat 9:30am–12:30am; Sun 9:30am–11pm.

OTHER AREAS AROUND PANAMA CITY
MODERATE

Palacio Lung Fung ⭐⭐ (Value) CHINESE   It's a little out-of-the-way, but this is Panama City's local favorite for, surprisingly, dim-sum breakfast. Most think of dim sum for lunch or dinner, but traditionally the Chinese dine on these delicacies for breakfast. There are more than 40 varieties of dim sum here; order a half-dozen and you won't pay more than $10. (Incidentally, there is no better hangover cure than a Lung Fung breakfast, so take a cab here the morning after a long night of partying.) After noon, Lung Fung shuts down their dim-sum production line and switches to heartier dishes such as chop suey, chow mein, Pekín duck, and sweet-and-sour jumbo prawns. There are two seating areas, a fast-food area on the ground floor and a more ornate, scarlet-and-gold dining space on the second floor with tablecloths and table service.

Vía Simón Bolívar (Transístmica) and Calle 62 C. Oeste. 𝄢 **260-4011.** Reservations not accepted. Main courses $3.75–$11; dim sum 50¢–$2. AE, MC, V. Daily breakfast 6am–noon; daily lunch and dinner noon–1am.

Parrillada Jimmy BARBECUE   There are two Jimmys, each quite different from the other. This is their flagship restaurant and *parrillada* (barbecue) close to the Caesar Park Panama hotel. Many locals will tell you that this is *the* place for barbecued meats—and, more notably, for their fire-grilled octopus—but the food doesn't live up to its reputation, and it's a little pricey for what you get. The restaurant is hacienda-style with lots of wrought iron and ceramic tile, and there is a pleasant and spacious open-air dining area and indoor air-conditioned eating area. Bustling waiters in bow ties serve mostly grilled tenderloin, New York and T-bone steaks, as well as seafood; the meal comes with an iceberg-lettuce salad and baked potato. Pastas are available. If you're staying at the Caesar Park, you might consider dining here, but if you're downtown I don't recommend going out of your way to dine here.

Vía Cincentenario and Manuel de Jesús Quijano. 𝄢 **226-1096.** MC, V. Reservations not accepted. Main courses $5–$15. Daily 11:30am–11:30pm.

Restaurante Chimborazo ⭐⭐ PERUVIAN/PANAMANIAN   If you treasure discovering those little-known and unpretentious local eateries with tasty, home-cooked food, then head over to Chimborazo. This Peruvian family establishment offers a lengthy menu of traditional Peruvian and Panamanian cuisine, and is most famous for its hearty stews such as *sopa parihuela,* a spicy seafood and tuber soup usually eaten to recover from excessive drinking the night before; and *sopa de levantamuertos,* a cilantro-infused seafood stew that translates as "soup to wake the dead." There are also fresh fish dishes with garlicky and spicy sauces, and meat dishes. Chimborazo has a lively "locals" atmosphere with tables that have their own thatched roofs. There are two locations: the Vía Porras one, closest to downtown; and near the Hipódromo, on the way out to the Tocumen airport.

Vía Porras at Calle Belén, San Francisco; or Vía José Agustin Arango, Juan Díaz. © 266-1349. Reservations not accepted. Main courses $5–$10. MC, V. Daily 11am–11pm.

5 What to See & Do

Few cities in the Americas can compete with Panama City when it comes to things to see and do. Some travelers spend their entire visit in and around Panama City, touring sights such as the historical ruins of Panama Viejo, walking the enchanting streets of Casco Viejo, visiting Metropolitan Park, or strolling along the Amador Causeway. Visitors can also head outside the city limits for day excursions such as boating in the canal, bird-watching and trekking in Soberanía National Park, and visiting Emberá Indian villages. Excursions outside the city limits are highlighted in chapter 6, "Around Panama City."

It is recommended that travelers book a city tour; transportation is included, and the experience is enriched by interpretative background provided by a bilingual guide. Half-day city tours include a morning visit to Old Panama and Casco Viejo; full-day tours head to the Miraflores Locks at the canal in the afternoon. For city tours, refer to "Panamanian Tour Operators" in chapter 4. If you want to see Panama City on your own, taxi drivers charge between $15 and $25 per hour. Every hotel has a personal recommendation for a private cab and can arrange the details.

PANAMA VIEJO ✿✿✿

Panama Viejo, or Old Panama, comprises the ruins of the oldest capital in the Americas, and is a proud emblem—not to mention the most popular tourist attraction—in this historic city. The ruin site covers 23 hectares (57 acres) on the city's eastern edge, where visitors will find crumbling buildings sprinkled about and connected by paths with interpretive signs in both Spanish and English. The good view from this part of the city sweeps east to the Casco Viejo peninsula, and beyond Panama Viejo's significance as a culturally unique attraction it is also a pleasant park and recreation area that provides visitors with a chance to get out and stretch their legs. Some people come here for a sunrise jog along Panama Viejo's path, which hugs the seafront.

In 1519, Pedrarias Dávila arrived with his Spanish expedition; he found a village, which was called Panamá by the *cueva*-speaking indigenous group that lived here. Historians agree that Panama means "abundance," but whether it is abundance of fish, butterflies, or some other plentiful flora or fauna is still open to debate. Not much is known about the *cueva* except that their language was spoken among different indigenous groups all the way to the Darién (near the present-day border with Colombia). In 1521, the Spanish king, Ferdinand of Aragon, bestowed Panama with formal city status in an effort to secure the mainland of the Americas, then called Tierra Firme. Within 40 years, the *cueva* were wiped out. To this day, not much is known about them but recent archaeological digs have unearthed artifacts shedding light on this ancient culture.

It is not clear why the Spaniards chose to build atop this swampy area with no clean drinking water—perhaps it was because the *cueva* represented an available labor force.

Spanish-Language Programs

If you're moving to Panama, or if you plan to stay for an extended time, you'll need to pick up the local lingo. The two top language-institute options offer very different programs for different kinds of people. Classes are either one-on-one or in groups—obviously the keen traveler with time restraints will want private classes.

Spanish Panama is a Canadian-directed school with certified bilingual professors, offering crash courses; private classes either at the school or in your hotel, residence, or business; and a monthlong program that includes excursions around town to place yourself in real-life situations where Spanish is necessary. They also have cultural excursions and Latin dance classes. The Spanish Panama school classrooms are divided units within an old apartment building, and the ambience is folksy and very friendly. They offer three housing options that are suitable for all types. First, there are homestays with Panamanian families. Second, their **Carmen's Realty** finds furnished apartments in the area (basic, at $500 a month, to luxury, at $1,300 a month) that can be rented weekly and monthly. Finally, **Anita's Inn** hostel, on the second floor above the school, has shared rooms for $10, and a few private rooms for $15 to $30 per night; most have shared bathrooms. The hostel hosts fun but mature guests who are serious about learning. Their "Just the Classes" one-on-one program is 16 hours per week for $199, and you decide when and where. Their monthlong program costs $775, with around a total of 50 hours of instruction. Spanish Panama is centrally located on Calle 2a Norte, off Vía Argentina (© **213-3121;** www.spanish panama.com).

Your second option is **ILISA Language School,** with offices in the more austere environment of the so-called "City of Knowledge," the old U.S. Army base in Clayton, which is being renovated as a center for academic organizations. ILISA is a Costa Rican company and a newcomer to Panama; they have group and private classes in a more polished, corporate-style classroom. Their four-person classes are the most popular, and run from 8am to noon, with afternoon activities like coffee chats and excursions; their four-person "Plus" course is the same but with an additional 2-hour private tutoring session in the afternoon. Private, 4-hour lessons cost $655 for 5 days; $885 for 6 hours a day. Groups of four cost $430 per person for 20 hours of instruction per week. ILISA offers homestays, furnished apartment rentals, and two nearby guesthouses with shared rooms starting at $14 a night, and private double rooms for $45. The school is at Calle Gonzalo Crance 8 (© **317-1011,** or 800/454-7248 in the U.S. and Canada; www.ilisa.com).

The Spaniards first erected huts, followed by stone buildings around the end of the 16th century—these are the ruins you see today. In 1671, the famous buccaneer Henry Morgan sacked the city, and it burned to the ground. Panama City was then moved to what is now known as Casco Viejo, on the western side of the city.

This is the best-funded archaeological site in all of Panama and, accordingly, you'll find here a superb **Panama Viejo Visitors' Center & Museum** ✰✰✰ (© 226-8915; Tues–Sun 9am–5pm; $6 adults, $5 seniors, and $3 students; entrance fee includes admission to both the museum and the Cathedral Tower ruin site). The two-story museum offers a thorough historical account, but is the right size so as not to overwhelm visitors with too much information (exhibits are in English and Spanish). There are handsomely displayed pre-Columbian artifacts dating from 700 to 500 years before the Spanish arrival, a model of the city in its 17th-century heyday, interactive video displays of what archaeologists imagine the buildings' interiors to have looked like, and colonial furnishings, clothing, pottery, and more. The visitor center plans to have ready by late 2006 a new interpretive map for visitors to the ruin site who do not have an arranged guide. The best way to see the ruin site is to begin at the center, visit the museum, then walk the to the Cathedral Tower. The visitor center and museum are located about 6.5km (4 miles) east of downtown Panama City, on Vía Israel. To get here, take a taxi from downtown for $2. Another transportation option is the blue minibuses that leave on the hour from the Albrook bus terminal and that cost 25¢.

After 5 years of labor, the renovation of the site's most important relic, **Torre de la Catedral (Cathedral Tower)** is now complete, with a steel interior staircase that visitors can climb for the first time in 335 years; at the top are expansive city views. The tower is too fragile to bear the weight of a replica of the old bell that rang out across the city during colonial times, so a speaker, which chimes at 6:30am, 12:30pm, and 6:30pm, has been installed. *Tip:* Visit the tower in the afternoon, when the morning tour buses have gone. Otherwise, you might find yourself waiting up to 20 minutes to enter. There are Spanish-speaking guides who offer free tours of the tower. If you skip the museum, the cost to get in the area around the tower is $4 for adults, $3 for seniors, and $2 for students; it's open Tuesday to Sunday, 8:30am to 6pm. The cathedral is a good 15-minute walk from the museum.

One of the city's best **handicrafts markets** is at Panama Viejo, and has recently been relocated to the visitor center (no phone; call the visitor center for information; daily 8am–5 or 6pm). *Note:* Even though the Cathedral Tower and museum are closed on Monday, you can still visit the ruins and walking paths.

CASCO VIEJO ✰✰✰

Casco Viejo, the Old Quarter, is also referred to as Casco Antiguo or by its original and formal name, San Felipe. No trip to Panama City would be complete without a visit to this quintessentially charming neighborhood, with its narrow streets; its turn-of-the-19th-century Spanish-, Italian-, and French-influenced architecture; its bougainvillea-filled plazas, and its breezy promenade that juts out into the sea. Visitors often compare Casco Viejo to Havana or Cartagena. The neighborhood's historical importance and antique beauty spurred UNESCO, in 1997, to declare it a World Heritage Site. Because Casco Viejo provides such an ideal place to wander around and lose yourself in the antique splendor of the city streets, I've included a walking tour (see below). Within the walking tour are dozens of points of interest, and you can really begin and end wherever it suits you. Museums mentioned in the following itinerary are reviewed beginning on p. 122.

For the past century, Casco Viejo was nothing more than a run-down neighborhood whose antique mansions were left to rot after wealthy residents moved to other parts of Panama City. With the drop in land value, squatters and low-income families moved in, many of whom continue to live here but are being pushed out by a public and privately funded large-scale gentrification project. This is most evident along the southeastern tip of the neighborhood, where lovingly restored mansions line the streets; elsewhere renovation isn't happening as fast as was hoped when the project began more than 10 years ago. To combat the housing shortage, the government is offering funds to help resettle poor residents. Foundations such as the Oficina Casco Antiguo are working on a plan, slated for completion in 2009, that will invest heavily in tourism, expanding services and even reinstalling the old street car that once ran along the city streets.

Safety Note: In spite of Casco Viejo's renovation projects and the fact that both the mayor *and* the president's offices are located here, tourists should say alert and protect themselves from theft. Generally speaking, the peninsula of Casco Viejo, starting at Calle 11 Este and heading east and away from the Santa Ana neighborhood, is safe. There are two principal entryways into Casco Viejo but both pass through poor ghettos, so always take a **taxi** to get here. Taxis for a trip out of Casco Viejo can usually be found around the Plaza de la Independencia, or if you are dining here, have the restaurant call one for you. Once, during a holiday, I could not find a cab for love nor money, and so I visited the Estación de Policía de Turismo (Tourism Police Station) and an officer shuttled me in a little scooter-car to a busier thoroughfare, where he waited with me until I got in a cab. Of course, I wouldn't do this unless you're in a pinch, but the tourism police are very polite and helpful, and they do a good job of patrolling the streets of Casco Viejo. The station is on Avenida Central at Calle 3a Este (© 211-2410); the office is open 24 hours, and from Monday to Friday, 8am to 5pm, there is an English-speaking attendant.

Most important in this area is to tone down the "gringo look" if possible, meaning no shorts or ostentatious clothing like Hawaiian shirts. Also, do not wear flashy jewelry or walk the streets brandishing your top-of-the-line camera.

WALKING TOUR   HISTORIC CASCO VIEJO

Start:	At Plaza Independencia.
Finish:	At Iglesia de San José (a 2-block walk from Plaza Independencia).
Time:	Approximately 1 to 2 hours.
Best Times:	The streets are quieter on Sundays, and churches are most active. Some restaurants and museums are closed either Sunday or Monday.

---

❶ Plaza de la Independencia

Take a taxi to Plaza de la Independencia and begin your tour. This plaza is where Panama declared its independence from Colombia on November 3, 1903. There are several important landmarks here, notably the **Catedral Metropolitana (Metropolitan Cathedral),** easily recognizable by its contrasting gray, ashlar-stone facade flanked by two white neoclassical bell towers inlaid with mother-of-pearl. The cathedral took more than 100 years to build, and is one of the largest in Central America. On the south side of the plaza is the must-see **Museo del Canal Interoceánico** (p. 124). The neoclassical building was built in 1875 as the Gran Hotel, and converted into Canal Headquarters by the French in 1881; later it was used as offices for the U.S. canal commission. It is considered to be the finest example of French architecture in Casco Viejo. Next door, on the second floor of the Palacio Municipal, is

PANAMA CITY ★

Panama Canal

Area of detail

Bahía de Panamá

CASCO VIEJO (SAN FELIPE)

Iglesia de San José (Altar de Oro)

Plaza Herrera 9

Iglesia de la Merced 8

Catedral Metropolitana

Plaza de la Independencia 1

Palacio Presidencial 2

Museo de Historia

Plaza Bolívar 3

Casa Góngora 7

Iglesia San Francisco de Asis & Salón Bolívar

Museo del Canal de Panamá

Teatro Nacional 4

Iglesia de Santo Domingo (Arco Cható) 6

Museo de Arte Religioso

Bahía de Panama

French Embassy

Paseo de Las Bóvedas

Plaza de Francia 5

0   100 meters
0   100 yards

1   Plaza de la Independencia
2   Palacio Presidencial (Presidential Palace)
3   Plaza Bolívar
4   Teatro Nacional (National Theater)
5   Plaza de Francia
6   Iglesia de Santo Domingo & the Museo de Arte Religioso Colonial
7   Casa Góngora
8   Iglesia de la Merced
9   Plaza Herrera
10   Iglesia de San José

the **Museo de la Historia de Panamá,** a ho-hum display of exhibits charting the history of the Panamanian republic. The **Hotel Central,** on the east side of the plaza, was once among the most luxurious hotels in the Americas, built in 1880. Today it sits abandoned while its two owners bicker about its fate.

Walk north on Calle 6a Este (from the middle of the plaza, toward the city skyline of Panama City) to Av. Alfaro, and turn right.

❷ Palacio Presidencial (Presidential Palace)

Calle 6a Este leads to the Presidential Palace, but you'll have to show your passport (or a copy) to the security guards on the street before they'll let you pass. This is the White House of Panama, the offices of Panama's President Torrijos, and it is a

gorgeous Spanish mansion with a Moorish interior patio and fountain (you can't enter, but you can take a peek from the outside). Two African herons—whose Spanish name, *garza,* is the reason the palace is also called the Palacio de las Garzas—glide back and forth across the front patio. The city skyline views of Panama City's high-rises from this street are outstanding.

Turn right on Calle 5a Este, and head south 1 block, then turn left on Av. B. Walk 1 block until you reach Parque Bolívar.

❸ Plaza Bolívar

One of Casco Viejo's prettiest spots, Plaza Bolívar and the buildings that surround it have undergone a face-lift over the past few years, and there are several cafes here for those who feel like stopping for a coffee or snack. The plaza originally was called Plaza de San Francisco, but was renamed in 1883 in honor of Simon Bolívar, widely considered in Latin America to be the hero of independence from Spain. There is a commemorative monument to Bolívar in the center of the plaza. The grand **Palacio Bolívar** (now the offices of the Ministry of Foreign Relations), on the northeast edge of the plaza, was built on the grounds of a former Franciscan monastery that succumbed to various fires. Of interest here is the totally restored **Salón Bolívar** ✦✦ (© 228-9594; Tues–Sat 9am–4pm, Sun 1–5pm; $1 adults, 25¢ students), site of the famous 1826 congress organized by Bolívar to discuss the unification of Colombia, Mexico, and Central America. The historical importance of this salon prompted UNESCO to declare Casco Viejo a World Heritage Site. During office hours (Mon–Fri 9am–3pm), it is possible to visit the courtyard inside the Palacio and admire the building's lovely architecture and tile work. Next to the Palacio is the **Iglesia y Convento de San Francisco de Asís (Church and Convent of St. Francis of Assisi)**, one of the original structures from Casco Viejo but nearly totally destroyed by fires in 1737 and 1756. It has most recently been restored in 1998.

Across the plaza, on Avenida B and Calle 4 Este (you'll pass it when arriving at the plaza), is the **Iglesia San Felipe de Neri,** one of the first churches built in Casco Viejo (1684–88). Though damaged by fires, the church has recently been restored and is worth checking out.

Turn left on the south end of the plaza onto Av. B to visit the:

❹ Teatro Nacional (National Theater)

Built between 1905 and 1908, on the grounds of the old Concepción Monastery, the lovely Teatro Nacional hosts theater and classical-music and ballet performances; unfortunately, they do not have a website and their show calendar is available only by calling © 262-3525, or by visiting www.thepanamanews.com and clicking on "Calendar." The theater opened in 1908 with a presentation of Verdi's *Aida,* and it is perhaps best known for the frescoes rendered by Panama's most famous painter, Roberto Lewis. Recent renovations have preserved both the frescoes and the baroque decor (scarlet and gilded tiered balconies, and a grand chandelier). The cost to enter and poke around is $1 per person. It's open Monday to Friday 8am to 4pm and sometimes on the weekends (but with no set schedule). Following Avenida B, behind the National Theater, is the **Ministerio de Gobierno y Justicia,** a building initially designed as a presidential building in 1908 and built, in a neoclassical design, in tandem with the National Theater by the Italian architect Genaro Ruggieri.

Continue along Av. B (the street bends and changes names for 1 block to Calle 2da) until it ends at Av. Central. Turn left on Av. Central (Calle 1a) and follow until arriving at the stairs to the Esteban Huertas walkway. Walk up and circle the:

❺ Plaza de Francia

The Plaza de Francia (French Plaza) is a Casco Viejo highlight, a historically important site and a delightful place to stroll around and crunch on a flavored Sno-cone from one of the several vendors. There is also a wonderful fresh breeze here. When you head down Calle 1a, the road turns into an inviting and lovely walkway called **Paseo Esteban Huertas,** which is partially covered by pretty bougainvillea. You're walking atop *las bóvedas,* or "the vaults," which originally functioned as a Spanish dungeon and later as a jail, storehouse, and offices. Now, *las bóvedas* is home to a French restaurant (see "Where to Dine," above), and **Oficina Casco Antiguo** (© 228-3664; boveda1@cwpanama.net), which offers free Saturday tours (in Spanish), leaving from its offices at 9:30am.

This walkway also runs along the old defensive wall that once protected the city. From this vantage point you can see the Bridge of the Americas and ships lining up for their turn to enter the canal. Continue along the walkway and down to the French Plaza. Originally the main plaza (Plaza de Armas) of Panama City, it is now a commemorative monument to the failed French canal effort. Also here at the plaza is **INAC,** the National Institute of Culture (which has an art gallery next to the restaurant in *las bóvedas;* Mon–Fri 8am–5pm) and the French Embassy.

Head back to Av. A and walk west until reaching Calle 3ra. Here you'll find the:

❻ Iglesia de Santo Domingo & Museo de Arte Religioso Colonial

Only ruins remain of Iglesia de Santo Domingo, built in 1678 but victim of several fires including one in 1781, from which time it was never rebuilt. The church kept its fame, however, through the building's unusual supporting arch made of stone, which survived the fire. The arch, called Arco Chato, was unusual in that it was long and not very arching, seemingly defying gravity. When U.S. senators debated whether to build a canal in Panama or Nicaragua, they took the arch's longevity to mean that little earthquake activity made Panama a safer place to build. Next to the ruin site is the **Museo de Arte Religioso Colonial** (p. 123).

Continue 1 more block to Calle 4ta, turn right and walk 1 block to Av. Central. Here on the east corner is:

❼ Casa Góngora

This structure is the best preserved example of a Spanish colonial home in Casco Viejo. The house, built in 1760 by a wealthy merchant, was renovated with city funds, and much of its original woodwork, including ceiling beams, has been maintained. The Casa is also now home to the **Casa de la Cultura y del Artista Panameño** (✆ 212-0388), a cultural center for local artists, with occasional live jazz music, folkloric presentations, fashion shows, and changing art exhibitions. Drop by to see what's happening or check out the newspaper's calendar listings for shows.

Head up Av. Central, crossing the Plaza de la Independencia (where you started). Continue on to Calle 9a to:

❽ Iglesia de la Merced

Built in 1680, this church was transferred, stone by stone, from its Old Panama site. The facade is still an excellent example of one of Casco Viejo's oldest buildings.

Walk south down Calle 9a until you come to:

❾ Plaza Herrera

The lively Plaza Herrera is dedicated to General Tomás Herrera, in honor of his battle for independence when Panama was still part of Colombia. Park benches here are good for people-watching or just for resting.

Walk 1 block east on Av. A to Calle 8a. You'll come to:

❿ Iglesia de San José

Your last stop is at the most famous of Casco Viejo's churches, the Iglesia de San José, and its baroque golden altar. The story goes that when pirate Henry Morgan raided Old Panama, a priest had the altar painted black to hide it from looters, later moving the altar to Casco Viejo. However, studies place the altar's stylistic details in the 18th century, casting doubt on this legend. It's a gorgeous work of art nevertheless, and worth a stop. From here you can head back to Plaza Independencia by walking 1 more block east on Avenida A, turning left on Calle 7, and walking 1 block.

Tips **Money Matters in Casco Viejo**

There is only one cash machine here in Casco Viejo, and it's located within the National Theater (enter through the door on Calle 3A, not through the theater's main entrance). There is a restroom here as well. If the door to the ATM is locked or closed (Sun), enter through the Ministro de Gobierno y Justicia on the back side of the theater on Avenida Central, and ask the security guard to let you use the cash machine.

CERRO ANCON 🐾🐾

This conspicuous forested hill that rises 198m (650 ft.) above the city is another "reverted" property from the canal days that is now open to the public. The hill is bordered in the north by Heights and Culebra streets, and avenidas Arías and de los Mártires in the south. At the entrance to the office of the environmental organization ANCON, at Calle Quarry Heights, a winding, pedestrian-only road provides for a brisk uphill walk to a **lookout point** 🐾🐾🐾, with 360-degree views of the city center, Casco Viejo, and the canal. The hill is home to tiny Geoffrey's tamarins, *ñeques* (agoutis), and migratory birds. Cerro Ancón is currently the focus of a controversial proposal by developers who want to raze the hilltop for a restaurant and parking lots, and install a cable car to transport visitors. Stiff resistance—even the mayor has jumped into the fray, voicing his disapproval—means this is not likely to happen anytime soon, if ever. The **Museo de Arte Contemporáneo** is here (see "Museums," later in this chapter).

Mi Pueblito   Located at the southeastern foot of Cerro Ancón, Mi Pueblito is a mock village depicting three Panamanian cultures: Afro-Caribbean, the interior region, and indigenous groups. At the main entrance is a colonial Spanish hacienda-style building with displays of polleras, both antique and new, plus roped-off interiors with various and sundry antique household items placed to give visitors an idea of life during the 19th century. Here, at the entrance, one of several guides will approach you and offer to explain the historical and cultural significance of each display. Across the street are a few typical Caribbean-style homes, as well as the thatched-roof huts of Kuna and Emberá Indians. Altogether Mi Pueblito is a touristy, uninspiring attraction whose purpose seems less to educate travelers and more to hawk clothing and crafts at high prices. However, travelers who only plan to visit Panama City and are in the Cerro Ancón area might find it interesting to view the sharply contrasting cultural fabric of Panama displayed in the architectural design of the center's buildings.

Entrance at Cerro Ancón from Av. de los Mártires. 🕻 **228-9785.** Admission $2 adults, free for kids under 12. Tues–Sun 9am–6pm. Reached by tour or taxi.

Panama Canal Murals 🐾   Located high on a grassy slope, the **Canal Administration Building,** built by the U.S. in 1914, houses the offices of the Autoridad del Canal de Panamá (Panama Canal Authority). At the bottom of the slope is the formidable Goethals Monument, dedicated to the chief canal engineer, George W. Goethals, who initiated construction of the Canal Building. Entering the building, visitors are taken aback by the beauty of the glass cupola, the focal point of the lobby. The cupola is encircled with handsome murals that narrate the heroism and relentless struggle to build the canal. The murals were done by William B. Van Ingen, a painter

THE TRAVELOCITY GUARANTEE

...THAT SAYS EVERYTHING YOU BOOK WILL BE RIGHT, OR WE'LL WORK WITH OUR TRAVEL PARTNERS TO MAKE IT RIGHT, RIGHT AWAY.

*To drive home the point,
we're going to use the word "right" in every single sentence.*

Let's get right to it. Right to the meat! Only Travelocity guarantees everything about your booking will be right, or we'll work with our travel partners to make it right, right away. Right on!

Here's a picture taken smack dab right in the middle of Antigua, where the Guarantee also covers you.

The Guarantee covers all but one of the items pictured to the right.

For example, what if the ocean view you booked actually looks out at a downright ugly parking lot? You'd be right to call – we're there for you. And no one in their right mind would be pleased to learn the rental car place has closed and left them stranded. Call Travelocity and we'll help get you back on the right track.

Now, you may be thinking, "Yeah, right, I'm so sure." That's OK; you have the right to remain skeptical. That is until we mention help is always right around the corner. Call us right off the bat, knowing our customer service reps are there for you 24/7. Righting wrongs. Left and right.

Now if you're guessing there are some things we can't control, like the weather, well you're right. But we can help you with most things – to get all the details in righting,* visit travelocity.com/guarantee.

*Sorry, spelling things right is one of the few things not covered under the Guarantee.

I'd give my right arm for a guarantee like this, although I'm glad I don't have to.

travelocity
You'll never roam alone.

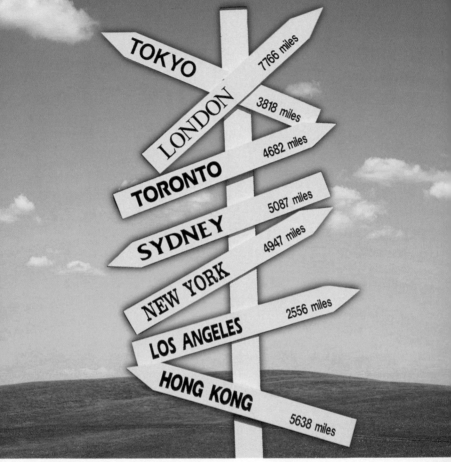

from New York who also did murals for the Library of Congress in Washington and the U.S. Mint in Philadelphia. There are four murals here. The first depicts the excavation of the Gaillard Cut; the second shows the construction of the Gatún Dam; the third the construction of the Gatún Locks; and, finally, the last is an impressive depiction of the building of the Miraflores Locks. Visitors may only visit this wing of the building, and entrance is free.

To put the Canal Zone in perspective, head out to the back of the building, facing the Goethals Monument. The flag pole here once displayed ensigns from both Panama and the United States, but today the only flag proudly flapping in the wind is Panamanian. There is a broad view of the Balboa neighborhood and the Bridge of the Americas beyond it. This area was a residential zone for American canal employees before the handover. Today, the buildings have been converted into residences for Panamanians, most of whom have no connection to the canal.

You may wish to visit the Canal Building before heading up to the top of Cerro Ancón because the road (via Quarry Heights) leads up from here.

PARQUE NATURAL METROPOLITANO ✸✸✸

The Metropolitan Park is the only protected tropical forest within the city limits of a major urban area in the Americas. In other words, one 5- to 10-minute taxi ride and you can delve into the earthy environs of thick jungle with a surprising array of fauna, more than 200 species of birds, and 40 species of mammals. Expect to see mostly birds and the occasional blue Morpho butterfly fluttering by. The park, roughly 265 hectares (655 acres), is located on the northern edge of Panama City, hemmed in by a few rather busy roads including the new and noisy Corredor Norte, which runs the eastern flank of the park. The park is overseen by the Smithsonian Tropical Research Institute, which carries out scientific studies here, and by the city, which maintains an administration center with maps, educational exhibits, and a bookstore. If you're planning to visit any regional national parks such as Soberanía, skip this attraction; if your visit to the country is limited to Panama City, this park is a must-see.

Three short trails give visitors a chance to get out and stretch their legs. **Los Momótides** trail is the shortest (30 min.) and therefore the most appropriate trail for young children and visitors in a hurry. It begins at the administration center, but you must cross busy Avenida Juan Pablo II, so be careful. **Mono Tití Road** heads up to Cedro Hill and a lookout point with sweeping views of the city; alert hikers occasionally catch sight of Geoffrey's tamarins, a pint-size primate, along this trail. The most difficult trail, and the longest at 2 hours round-trip, is **Cienequita Trail,** which begins just up the road from the center. It is possible to connect with Mono Tití Road after reaching the lookout point.

The park is open daily from 6am to 6pm; the visitor center is open Monday to Friday 8am to 4pm and Saturday 8am to 1pm. A trail guide is available for 50¢, and the park offers guided trips in English for $6 with a reservation made at least 24 hours in advance (© **232-5516** or 232-5552).

CALZADA DE AMADOR (AMADOR CAUSEWAY) ✸✸

The Amador Causeway is a series of three small islands—Naos, Perico, and Flamenco—connected by a road and pedestrian walkway that projects out into the Panama Bay, offering spectacular views of the glittering city skyline and a consistent breeze. The islands, once the haunt of pirates, were connected in the early 1900s with rock and dirt excavated from the Culebra Cut in the Panama Canal to form a breakwater for a protective harbor for ships waiting to enter the canal, and to prevent the buildup of sediment. Later, the United States militarized the promontory and fortified it with ordnance for protection during the two world wars. The causeway remained off-limits to Panamanians until 1999, when the canal handover opened this prime spot of real estate, much to the delight of walkers, joggers, bike riders, and diners. There is nothing like jogging or walking along the causeway early in the morning with the sun rising over the Pacific and casting its pastel hues on the glittering high-rises of downtown Panama City. The causeway is packed on Sundays.

Large-scale, multimillion dollar real-estate projects are on the horizon for the causeway, including a grand hotel, a casino, condo development, and new marinas. By any measure, Panamanians are most excited about the **Bridge of Life Biodiversity Museum,** designed by renowned architect Frank Gehry (who is married to a Panamanian), which will feature high-concept exhibitions about the relationship between nature and man. The museum is scheduled to open sometime in 2007; check the website, **www.biomuseopanama.org**, for more information. Once opened, this will be a don't-miss attraction for any visitor.

Punta Culebra Marine Exhibition Center ★★ (Kids   Spread across a patch of dry forest on the tiny island of Naos, a former U.S. defense site during the two world wars, Punta Culebra is a kid-friendly attraction run by the Smithsonian Tropical Research Institute. It's a well-designed but small exhibition, with a short path that offers sweeping views and mounted telescopes that you can use to scan the horizon and get up-close views of ships waiting to transit the canal. The center will take a backseat to the Biodiversity Museum (once it opens). Really, if you're an adult without kids and you're having lunch at Mi Ranchito or riding a bike around, it makes sense to swing through here quickly—otherwise don't go out of your way to visit the center when there are so many other attractions in and around Panama City.

Within the center's grounds are a "touching pool" that allows kids to handle and closely examine aquatic life such as sea cucumbers, sea urchins, and starfish; an aquarium with tropical fish and a comparison between coral reefs of the Pacific and Atlantic; and an information center with videos. An interpretive trail winds through dry forest, which long ago was common up and down the Central American Pacific Coast; if you're lucky, you will catch sight of a sloth or an iguana. Call ahead for a guided tour. You'll see the Marine Exhibitions Center sign just before Mi Ranchito.

Isla Naos. (© 212-8793. www.stri.org. Admission $2 adults, 50¢ kids under 12, $1 seniors. Tues–Fri 1–6pm; Sat–Sun 10am–6pm. Around late Dec to Mar, the center opens for summer vacation daily 10am–6pm, but call ahead to confirm.

BICYCLE RENTAL

Bikes & More, located just past the Figali Convention Center (© **314-0103;** daily 9am–9pm) rents bicycles for $2.50 to $3.75 per hour, and motor scooters for $20 an hour. **Bikes Moses,** farther up the causeway (© **211-8579;** Mon–Fri 8:30am–9pm and Sat–Sun 7am–9pm), rents bikes for $2.50 to $3.50 an hour, and kids' bikes at $1.50. Both rental agencies also have "family bikes," pedal-operated carts for four, which cost $8 an hour.

MUSEUMS

Museums across Panama are under-funded and poorly staffed, and the story here in the capital isn't any different just because it's a metropolitan city. Things could change with the reopening of the Araúz Anthropology Museum in late 2006, which will have a far better location and promises to update its somewhat lackluster exhibition. The

Canal Museum in Casco Viejo has modernized its tours, with bilingual interpretive signs and guides.

Beyond this, most museums in Panama City are worth visiting only if you happen to already be in the neighborhood. Perhaps local indifference to the city's museums arises from the fact that many are closed on Saturday, Sunday, and holidays—the very time when most locals are able to visit. Volunteers and nonprofit organizations are the ones who keep the museums hanging in there, sometimes only by a thread.

Museo Afroantillano 🆁 A small museum housed in the 1910-era Iglesia de la Misión Cristiana, the Museo Afroantillano (Afro-Antillian Museum) pays tribute to the more than 30,000 West Indians who represented 85% of all foreign laborers during the building of the canal. Afro-Antillians were relegated to the most menial and treacherous of all work, and many lost their lives in the process. Within the museum are reconstructed examples of their poor living quarters, and there are old photos and other antiques from the early 1900s. It takes about 20 minutes to see everything; which is good because the neighborhood here is awfully sketchy, and doesn't induce you to linger or wander around. Take a cab directly to and from here.

Calle 24 Este and Av. Justo Arosemena (Av. 3 Sur). 🄯 **262-5348.** Admission $1 adults, 25¢ seniors and children under 12. Tues–Sat 8:30am–3:30pm; closed holidays.

Museo Antropológico Reina Torres de Araúz 🆁🆁 This is Panama's best anthropology museum, with more than 15,000 pre-Columbian pieces, including artifacts from the Barriles tribe, the earliest residents of Panama until 700 B.C. There is also an interesting collection of gold *huacas,* the tiny ceremonial figures that were buried with indigenous VIPs, as well as more modern pollera dresses and antique household items and farm tools.

Unfortunately, I cannot tell you how this museum will eventually look because bureaucratic bungling delayed its move from the Cinco de Mayo Plaza to its new home in the old Museo Tucán, which is a far prettier location on the edge of the Metropolitan Park. By the time you read this, the museum will—fingers crossed—be open and will feature a fresh design and extra funding. Considering that it's the pet project of the president's wife, Vivian, this might not be too far-fetched a wish. Please note that the hours of operation below could change.

Av. Ascanio Villalaz, Metropolitan Park. 🄯 **262-8338.** Admission $1 adults, $2 tourists, 50¢ seniors, 25¢ students. Mon–Fri 9am–4pm; closed holidays.

Museo de Arte Contemporáneo 🆁 The city's Contemporary Art Museum has improved over the years, but it is still erratic when it comes to the quality of temporary exhibitions. Their permanent collection features a selection of mostly watercolor and oil paintings by well-known and up-and-coming Panamanians and other Latin Americans. It's a well-organized museum, operating a cultural center with painting classes for kids and adults and other art activities such as film nights. Check out their website for upcoming shows, or just pop in to see what's on when you're in the Cerro Ancón area.

Av. de los Mártires at Calle San Blas. 🄯 **262-8012.** www.macpanama.org. Admission $1 adults, 50¢ seniors and children. Tues–Sun 9am–5pm; closed holidays.

Museo de Arte Religioso Colonial 🆁 This small but vivid collection of 220 religious art pieces is housed in the old Santo Domingo convent, famous for the Arco Chato (see "Walking Tour: Historic Casco Viejo" on p. 116). The religious pieces are the last vestiges from the height of colonial baroque art in the Americas. Within this irregular but beautiful collection the visitor can find delicate wooden polychromatic sculptures, oil paintings on metal and leather, chalices, and church bells sent from as far away as Sevilla, Lima, and Mexico. Just like the ruins of the church, the pieces here date from the late 17th century to early 18th century. It is worth noting that the colonial baroque altar at the back of the museum was bathed in gold in the 1930s by an anonymous devotee. You'll need about 20 minutes or less to see everything here.

Av. A at Calle 3a, Casco Viejo. ℂ 228-2897. Admission $1 adults, 75¢ seniors, 25¢ students and children. Tues–Sat 8am–4pm; Sun 1–5pm; closed holidays.

Museo de Ciencias Naturales 🌴 🄺🄸🄳🄼   The permanent exhibition of the Museum of Natural Sciences is oriented toward kids and teens, and is reminiscent of the 1970s, with local stuffed animals in glass-enclosed displays of their "natural habitat," large plaster renditions of prehistoric sloths and mastodons, cardboard representations, and so forth. More unusual is the International Specimen Salon, an almost ironic, and sinister, display of donated hunting trophies—to enter you must pass beneath two gigantic elephant tusks. Mounted on the walls are dozens upon dozens of African, Asian, and American animal heads including leopards, elephants, grizzly bears, buffalos, and wolves. There is also a reptile and insect display of specimens found in Panama, and a library.

Av. Cuba between Calle 29 and Calle 30. ℂ 225-0645. Admission $1 adults, 75¢ seniors, 25¢ children. Mon–Fri 8am–3:30pm; closed holidays.

Museo del Canal Interoceánico de Panamá 🌴🌴🌴   Housed in a fine antique building that was once the Gran Hotel and later the French canal headquarters, this is the best museum in Panama City and an obligatory stop for every traveler. The museum is a study of the Panama isthmus—from pre-Columbian times, to the arrival of the Spanish, to the French and the American canal-building efforts, through the present day. The museum gives you a good understanding of the isthmus as the center of world trade; it also provides (somewhat subjectively) an explanation of the effect of the isthmus and the canal on the Panamanian identity. Historical documents here include the 1977 Carter-Torrijos treaty that turned over control of the canal to Panama in 2000, multimedia and interactive exhibits, mock-household exhibits of everyday life during the history of the canal, a register of the U.S. Senate votes approving the canal, and a floor of old coins and stamps, including the famous Nicaragua stamp with an erupting volcano that was sent to senators to sway them from choosing that country to build a canal. This is an impeccable museum, with interpretive information in Spanish and English, and there are on-site guides who give bilingual tours. There are also an excellent library and a small cafe and bookstore, and the museum is wheelchair accessible. You could easily spend a full hour here.

Av. Central at Plaza Independencia. ℂ 228-6231. www.sinfo.net/pcmuseum. Admission $2 adults; 75¢ seniors, students, and children. Mon–Fri 8am–4pm; closed holidays.

6 Spectator Sports & Recreation

Soccer never cast its spell over Panama as it has with the rest of Latin America—here baseball is king, yet stadium crowds and big-league games are not common. Games are mostly by national and local teams vying for regional championships. For spectator sports, check out the horse races (below) for a lively show and lots of colorful Panamanian characters. Walking and bicycling are best on the Amador Causeway, especially early in the morning with the sunrise.

BIRD-WATCHING   Serious birders will want to visit renowned sites such as Pipeline Road. This and other spots are highlighted in chapter 6. Within the city limits, **Metropolitan Park** (p. 121) is a fine spot for glimpsing some of the more than 200 species found here. Check the Panama Audubon Society's website, **www.panama audobon.org**, for upcoming field trips to the park and other destinations around the city.

HORSE RACING   The **Hipódromo Presidente Remón** (© 217-6060; www. hipodromo.com) inaugurated more than a half-century ago, is a prestigious venue and a fun place to spend an afternoon. Races are held on Thursdays, Saturdays, Sundays, and holidays. To get here, take a taxi to Vía José Agustín Arango, on the way out to the airport. The Hipódromo can be reached via the Corredor Sur or by following Vía España until it turns into Vía Arango.

HOTEL SPAS & WORKOUT FACILITIES   Nearly every moderate to high-end hotel has a fitness center, and major hotels have full-service spas, which are the best in the city. Especially noteworthy are the spas at the **Veneto, Decapolis Radisson,** and **Marriott.** These hotels allow you to book a session even if you're not lodging there.

7 Shopping

You'll hear a lot of talk about duty-free shopping in Panama, but it is exaggerated. Really, the only place you can duty-free shop is at the plethora of stores at the Tocumen Airport. Shopping complexes such as the **Flamingo Center** on the Amador Causeway limit duty-free purchases to cruisers landing at their port. Even the duty-free zone in Colón is overrated, as most wholesalers do not sell to independent travelers. The major shopping malls here offer excellent quality and national and international brands, though prices are comparable to those in the United States. A principal shopping avenue is **Vía España,** where both high- and low-end shops vie for business, as well as grocery stores and pharmacies. Designer stores are located around Calle 53 in Marbella and in the nearby World Trade Center's Centro de Comercio. Also try Plaza Paitilla in the Paitilla neighborhood. You'll find electronics shops around Vía Estronga, in the Financial District.

MODERN SHOPPING MALLS

Globalization and the rising demand for high-quality products have shifted the shopping scene to spacious megamalls that house international brands, cinemas, and a food court. **Multiplaza Pacific** (© 302-5380) offers the most in terms of selection and quality, yet it is the most expensive in town. Colombian-owned **Multicentro** (© 208-2500), conveniently located across from the Radisson on Avenida Balboa, has a number of Latin-diva-style boutiques; there's also a cinema and a casino. **Albrook Mall** (© 303-6333) is an air-conditioned shrine to low-cost outlet shopping, but you'll have to do a lot of digging around to find a gem. Because it is next to the bus terminal, it is busy with families who arrive from the interior of Panama, ready to shop. There is a cinema at Albrook Mall, too.

MARKETS

The **Mercado de Mariscos** ✿✿✿, located on Avenida Balboa and Calle 15 Este, is distribution headquarters for fresh seafood pulled from the Pacific and Caribbean. It's a vibrant market with lots of action as fishmongers shout while they deftly fillet corvina, tuna, octopus, and more. You can dine here at their upstairs restaurant. Several

Wildlife Contraband: Don't Destroy What You've Come Seeking

International laws prohibit the trade of endangered plants or animals, or products made from endangered wildlife. Yet many travelers to Panama who purchase such goods rarely realize that what they are doing is illegal, nor do they understand the consequences of their purchase. Illegal trade destroys the very wildlife and habitat that travelers come here to enjoy. You could also set yourself up for being issued a heavy fine by law-enforcement officials upon your return. To help with wildlife conservation, ask yourself, Do I know what this product is made of? Do I know where this product came from? Do I need a special permit to bring this product home?

The World Wildlife Fund's trade monitoring network, TRAFFIC, and the U.S. Fish and Wildlife Service have a series of "Buyer Beware" brochures, including one aimed at travelers in the Caribbean, that you can download from their site at **www.worldwildlife.org/buyerbeware**. When in Panama, you should avoid purchasing:

- Products made from turtle shell (including jewelry)
- Leather products made from reptile skins
- Live birds including parrots, macaws, and toucans
- Live monkeys
- Certain coral products
- Orchids (except those grown commercially)

food stands sell seafood snacks like ceviche. Next door is the brand-new **Mercado Público** 𝒢𝒢, the covered farmer's market of Panama City with exotic fruits and vegetables, meats, dried spices and nuts, and a food court of *fondas,* or cheap food stands serving Panamanian fare. The old market, demolished in 2006, had a touch more character but was filthy—this new market is clean and bright. Don't forget to bring your camera.

Artesanía, or indigenous handicrafts, are the number-one buy here in Panama (with the exception of real estate). *Molas,* the reversed appliqué panels made by Kuna Indian women, rank high on the list of popularity for souvenirs and gifts, either sewn onto a beach bag, as a shirt, or sold individually for you to frame or stitch onto anything you'd like (pillowcases are an ideally sized canvas). Other popular handicrafts, such as *tagua* nuts or vegetable ivory carved into tiny figurines, Ngöbe-Buglé dresses, and Emberá Indian baskets and masks, can be found at the following markets. These markets do not have phones, and all are open daily with the general hours 8 or 9am to 5 or 6pm (until about 2pm Sun). The **Mercado Nacional de Artesanías** 𝒢𝒢𝒢, in Panama Viejo next to the visitor center, is expansive and sells handicrafts from around the country. In Balboa, on Avenida Arnulfo Arias Madrid and Amador, is a small **YMCA Handicrafts Market** 𝒢, with mostly Kuna and Emberá indigenous arts and crafts, and clothing. A little farther east and up Avenida Arnulfo Arias Madrid is the **Kuna Cooperative** 𝒢𝒢, featuring Kuna handicrafts. This market is fun for kids because Kuna women offer to affix their traditional beaded bands onto the arms and legs of tourists, just as they themselves wear them.

For the more adventurous traveler seeking an "authentic" shopping experience, you can't beat **Avenida Central** ✿✿, a pedestrian street and market that stretches from where Justo Arosemena meets Vía España to the Santa Ana Plaza, and that is near Casco Viejo. It's a scrappy, run-down neighborhood, with cheap stores, outdoor fruit and vegetable markets, and a bustling fusion of ethnic groups shopping for a bargain. Visually, it's the most colorful neighborhood in town. Apart from $1-and-under kind of shops, vendors lining the streets hawk clothing, accessories, plastic gizmos, and knickknacks. Shopkeepers like to blare music or announce their deals through megaphones to pull buyers in. It's a slice of everyday Panama, but it's also street theater and people-watching as fascinating as catching sight of Kuna Indian women lining up at McDonald's. Don't wander too far off Avenida Central, and keep an eye on your personal belongings. This area is patrolled by police and is generally safe during the day.

The brand-new **Flamenco Shopping Plaza** is on the Amador Causeway (© **314-0908;** hours are variable but generally noon–11pm; www.fuerteamador.com). It caters predominantly to cruisers docking here, but shops are open to the general public (except the duty-free shop). The Plaza is a high-end, one-stop shopping area for souvenirs, jewelry, and upscale handicrafts. Come prepared: Visit their website and print out their discount coupons worth a savings of 10% to 15%, depending on the store.

SHOPPING A TO Z
ART GALLERIES

The following art galleries showcase Panamanian contemporary artists and other well-known Latin American artists. Check www.thepanamanews.com and its Calendar listing for upcoming shows and special events. **Galería Bernheim,** at Calle 50 and Calle Alquilino in the Financial District (© **223-0012**), has a lengthy roster of paintings and other artwork for sale, as well as antique maps and delicately carved *tagua* nuts. **Imagen Galería de Arte,** located at Calle 50 and Calle 77 (© **226-2649**), displays mostly paintings and sculpture by local artists, and offers professional framing. **Galería y Enmarcado Habitante,** at Calle 47 and Uruguay, has a small collection and

---

(*Fun Fact* **Panama Hats: Not Very Panamanian, After All**

Despite the name, Panama hats did not originate in Panama but in Ecuador, and were traditionally made by the Ecuadorian indigenous group from the Manabí Province using fibers from the *toquilla* palm. The hat was first popularized by Ferdinand de Lesseps during the French canal effort, and later during the canal building by the U.S., when thousands were imported from Ecuador and given to workers for protection from the blistering tropical sun. Hence, the name "Panama hat" stuck. The hat became fashionable not only in the U.S. but also among the English haberdashery and European royalty. Really, you'd have the best luck ordering a high-quality hat over the Internet from a reputable importer, though Panama does its own version called the *sombrero pintado* (see chapter 7), in the Penonomé region. You'll find a range of hats at the stands at Plaza Cinco de Mayo, as well as a limited selection at the YMCA Handicrafts Market in Balboa.

is worth stopping at only if you're in the Bella Vista neighborhood; they also offer framing. As the name states, **Arts & Antiques** (© 264-8121) sells antiques and art antiques representing Spanish colonial, Art Deco, Victorian, and other epochs. The store is located in the Balboa Plaza on Avenida Balboa at Calle Anastacio Ruiz.

HANDICRAFTS

The widest selection of handicrafts in Panama City can be found at one of several markets (see above). Otherwise, an outstanding selection of *molas* can be found at **Flory Saltzman Molas,** located at Calle 49 B Oeste (© 223-6963; www.florymolas.com). Flory also sells bedspreads made of sewn-together molas, but the laborious work required for such an extensive, intricate piece of work means you'll pay top dollar. Another "designer" handicraft boutique is **Breebaart,** at Calle 50 and Calle 39 (© 264-5937), owned by one Hélène Breebaart, who came to Panama as a representative of Christian Dior 30 years ago and stayed on. Breebaart creates designer fashion and accessories that incorporate contemporary looks with Kuna art (she has a crew of Kuna seamstresses on-site), mostly for Panama's rich and prominent women. There are some things for sale here, but Breebaart's specialty is custom-made pieces that take about a week to make.

The **Gran Morrison** variety/department store chain, located at Vía España and Calle 51 Este (© 269-2211), and in Punta Paitilla (© 264-5266), has a selection of handicrafts. In Casco Viejo, two stores sell indigenous crafts and other Panama-themed souvenirs: **Galería de Arte Indígena,** at 844 Calle 1a (© 6634-7064; daily 9am–8pm), sells high-quality indigenous arts and crafts, and features folkloric dancing on Friday and Saturday nights from 6 to 8pm. Down the road from the Galería, on Calle 1era in Casco Viejo, is the shop **La Ronda** (© 211-1001; daily 9am–7pm), with an outstanding selection of high-quality arts and crafts, hats, and paintings. There are shops at the **Mi Pueblito** cultural center (see "Cerro Ancón," under "What to See & Do," earlier in this chapter), but the selection is better elsewhere.

JEWELRY

During the centuries before the arrival of the Spanish, indigenous groups produced decorative gold pieces called *huacas,* which they laid to rest with the dead to protect their souls in the afterlife. The word comes from the Incas, meaning something that is revered, such as an ancestor or a god. Spurred by the theft of *huacas* from the national anthropology museum, an American living in Panama during the 1970s set up Reprosa, located at Avenida Samuel Lewis (© 269-0457; daily 9am–6pm), which makes elaborate and stunning jewelry casts using the "lost wax" process of the ancient indigenous groups. If you're searching for a one-of-a-kind, luxury gift for someone special, come here. Reprosa has several more demure collections that include orchids, treasures from the sea, and so forth.

Reprosa also offers a popular factory tour to demonstrate the casting and assembly process. The factory can be found just off the Costa del Este exit near Panama Vieja, and just after turning left on the first street next to the Felipe Motta shop. English-language tours cost $10 per person and must be booked at least 1 day in advance; call Monica at © 271-0033.

OUTDOOR GEAR & CLOTHING

It's best to buy your outdoor gear and equipment before your trip—there isn't a wide selection of outdoor products in Panama. The chain store **Outdoors** (© 302-4828 or

208-2647) represents the brands Columbia and Caterpillar, and their stores carry clothing and footwear, sleeping bags, and accessories for biking, fishing, bird-watching, and other adventure sports. Outdoors has stores in the Multicentro, Multiplaza, and a low-cost outlet store in the Albrook Mall.

8 Panama After Dark

You don't have to experience 5 days of Carnaval to know that Panamanians are party-loving people. When the sun goes down, Panama City lights up with a vibrant scene that caters to all ages, interests, and levels of stamina. Nightspots are concentrated in four neighborhoods: Bella Vista (also called Calle Uruguay), the Amador Causeway, Marbella (Calle 53 Este), and Casco Viejo, but underground dance clubs pop up across town like mushrooms, and can be best found by asking your concierge or checking out the Weekend supplement in Thursday's *La Prensa* newspaper. *La Prensa* has a daily section called Vivir +, which lists nightly events, but in Spanish only. Also try the Calendar at **www.thepanamanews.com**.

Visitors should be aware that Panamanians are more open-minded about sex than Americans. Prostitution is legal in Panama, and therefore it is common to see prostitutes not just on seedier streets and in brothels but in the nicer parts of town such as El Cangrejo. They're also often at hotel-lobby bars, or employed by one of the many "anything-goes" massage parlors across town. Government authorities demand a weekly health check for all prostitutes, among other regulations, but cases of AIDS and other sexually transmitted diseases are swiftly multiplying in Panama.

THE PERFORMING ARTS
THEATER, BALLET & CLASSICAL MUSIC
Theater tickets can be purchased by calling the theater directly, or you can buy tickets at **Blockbuster** locations and at the bookstore **El Hombre de la Mancha** or **Exedra Books** (see "Bookstores" in "Fast Facts: Panama City" on p. 88). All theater productions are in Spanish, with the exception of the **Ancón Theater Guild** (© 212-0060; www.tga-panama.com; admission donation around $10). The well-respected guild has been around for more than a half-century, first opening its doors in Colón to provide entertainment to U.S. troops during World War II. The guild normally produces contemporary dramas and comedy with a mix of native English speakers and Panamanian actors trained in English-language schools.

Classical music productions, plays, and ballet take place at Panama City's turn-of-the-20th-century **National Theater,** on Avenida B in Casco Viejo (see "Walking Tour: Historic Casco Viejo" on p. 116). The best Spanish-language theater productions can be found at **Teatro la Quadra,** on Calle D in El Cangrejo (© 214-3695; www.teatro quadra.com; tickets average $10). This cultural center was founded to promote and develop the art of theater in Panama, and they receive acclaim for their nightly performances of well-known plays and children's theater. **Teatro ABA** at Avenida Simon Bolívar (Transístmica), near Avenida de los Periodistas in front of the Riba Smith supermarket (© 260-6316; tickets cost an average of $5), produces half its own shows and rents out its 200-person theater to independent groups; productions are mostly comedy, drama, and well-established plays. Check www.prensa.com for theater listings here. **Teatro en Círculo,** on Avenida 6C Norte at Vía Brasil (© 261-5375), is an esteemed playhouse with original Panamanian productions and classic international productions. The historic **Teatro Anita Villalaz** (© 211-4020; tickets average

$10), on Plaza Francia in Casco Viejo, is administered by the National Cultural Institute (INAC); the intimate theater is home to folkloric productions, concerts, and plays, some of which are produced by the University of Panama students.

THE CLUB & MUSIC SCENE

The nightclubs listed below open at 10pm but don't really get going until midnight or later; during the first hours of operation, however, nightclubs typically offer drink specials. Ladies' night specials are a bargain for women, giving them free drinks and entry. Otherwise, expect to pay between $7 and $10 for a cover charge, more if there is live music. Nightclub partyers tend to dress smart for the occasion, so don your slinkiest or sharpest outfit or risk being refused entry (or just feeling out of place). For folkloric presentations in a less-trendy environment, try **Las Tinajas** or **Al Tambor a la Alegría;** for jazz in a one-of-a-kind environment (a stylishly renovated dungeon), don't pass up **Las Bóvedas** (p. 107). Large stadium bands play at the **Figali Convention Center,** on the Amador Causeway (© 314-1414), or at the **Atlapa Convention Center,** on the east side of town (© 226-7000). For schedules, call or check *La Prensa*'s weekend supplement.

Bar Platea   Jazz is alive and well at this new sophisticated bar/club, located on the ground floor of a colonial town house in Casco Viejo. The club shares the building with its partner **S'cena** restaurant (p. 106). Platea is cozy and classy, and appeals to an older crowd more so than most of the city's dance clubs. Doors open at 7pm, except on Mondays, and live music begins at 10pm on Thursdays, Fridays, and Saturdays. Often, Platea hosts hot salsa bands. In front of old Club Union, Casco Viejo. © **228-4011.**

Liquid   Lots of steel and neon tube lighting accent a dark ambience at this popular dance club. It's chic and cool but laid-back, catering to a well-heeled crowd but without the velvet-rope attitude of big-city clubs. Liquid is the place to go for dancing, featuring one of the largest dance floors in the city. The music here ranges from thumping beats to rock. Calle 50 at Calle José de la Cruz, in front of the World Trade Center, Marbella. © **265-3210.**

Moods   This very happening club has weekday no-cover nights with free entry and an older crowd (late 20s to 40s), mostly the collared-shirt and tight-jeans-with-heels partyers who sweat to primarily reggae and Latin music—on Saturdays, the reggae is often live. If you arrive late, expect to wait and be given the once-over by bouncers. Calle 48 and Calle Uruguay, Bella Vista. © **263-4923.**

Next   It's the biggest dance club in Panama—some say in all of Central America—and it's everything you'd expect in a full-scale, throbbing *discoteca:* spacious dance floor, electronic house music, and a full bar and lounge. Thursday is "crossover" night with more musical variety. The *discoteca* offers drink specials until midnight. Av. Balboa, Marbella. © **265-8746.**

Oz Bar and Lounge   Oz draws Panama City's elite 20-somethings for its chic decor, live DJ music (mostly house and chill-out), and popular Tuesday karaoke nights. On Friday from 9 to 11pm it's ladies' night with free shots, and Saturday "Cocktail" Night means free sangria for women until midnight. Calle 53 Este, Marbella. © **265-2805.**

Wasabi Sushi Lounge   Located behind Liquid (see above) in Bella Vista, Wasabi is '60s pop-retro, with low-to-the-ground white tulip chairs, mosaic walls, and orange transparent acrylic furniture. It's trendy and lively, especially on Wednesdays, when women drink free sangria until midnight and snack on sushi. There are several different salons, each with individual music. DJs spin house music and reggae. Look for a green W outside the door. Calle 54 at Calle 50, Marbella. © 264-1863.

BARS

Differentiating between a bar and a nightclub can be difficult these days in Panama City because so many bars have live DJ music, occasional live music, and maybe even a small dance floor and chill-out lounge. Popular hotel bars include the Decapolis (see below), the Peach Monkeys Lounge at the Caesar Park Panama, and the Veneto Hotel's lobby bar. See "Casinos," below, for more information about hotel bars. Happy hours are the norm here. Office workers spill into bars after work for their 5- to-7pm happy hours; the best deals, however, are at bars that cater to late-night revelers: To reel people in before the late crowd, these bars offer happy hours from 10pm to midnight, and even 100% free drinks (usually for women).

The Amador Causeway is an up-and-coming nightlife spot, with new bars and restaurants opening monthly. As a nightspot, the area tends to draw groups of friends, and an upscale, older crowd. The **Wine Bar** (see below) cut the ribbon on their new locale in 2006, with the same offerings as their El Cangrejo location, but with a better view (located at the Brisas del Amador area). At the end of the Causeway, within the Flamenco Shopping Plaza, are a handful of bars, dance spots, and live-music venues such as **Traffic Island,** with Latin music and cocktails, and a windswept veranda with city views; or try **Bar Baviera,** the **Ancla Sport Bar,** or **Karnak.** These nightspots are all next to each other in an American-style minimall—you could head here and stroll around until you find something to your liking. Closer to the city and the Figali Convention Center is **Las Pencas,** with live music on weekends and folkloric presentations every Wednesday at 8pm.

Anemos   Late in the evening, Anemos picks up the tempo with live DJ music and a jabbering crowd (a mix of office workers and university students), but before the clock strikes midnight, this modern, stylish bar can seem relatively empty—and so they offer unbelievable free-drink specials and cheap happy hours early on. It's a wonder they make any money at all, especially considering there never is a cover charge. Thursday night has "orgasmic" cocktails, recommended only for the brave. Calle 47, next to the Limoncillo restaurant, Bella Vista. © 214-6038.

Blu Room Martini Lounge   Panama City is undergoing a love affair with cool lounges, cocktails, and ambient DJ music, and the Blu Room was one of the first to kick-start this trend. It's actually a rather small bar, dark and intimate, with monster martinis and other vodka-mixed drinks. If you're looking to get soused in a more elegant environment, this is your place. You'll hear Latin house music and hip-hop during the week, and house during the weekends. Calle 1, Casco Viejo. © 228-9059.

Decapolis Radisson Sushi Bar & Martini Lounge   This is *the* place to see and be seen on Friday and Saturday nights, located on the lobby level of the Decapolis Hotel. The ultra-chic ambience draws an upscale crowd that spans a range of ages, making this a good bet for travelers seeking a refined, hip bar without the post-teen crowd. Live DJ music, and a second, poolside bar keep the party going well into the night. The scene gets started a little earlier here than in other city bars and nightclubs. Av. Balboa at the Multicentro Mall. © 215-5000.

El Pavo Real The "Peacock" is a traditional British pub with pints of lager and Guinness, pub grub, dart boards and pool, and lots of dark wood. It's a local hangout for the English-speaking expat crowd in Panama, so expect to hear a lot of it here. The atmosphere is laid-back, but things pick up on weekends when live music starts at 11pm. Calle 51 and Calle 50, around the corner from the Marriott. ℭ 262-2448.

Istmo Brew Pub Panama City's first brewpub has a following, though it would be hard to pinpoint who it is because the crowd here varies from night to night (foreign residents, Panamanians, tourists). Opened in 2005, the pleasant, wood-hewn pub has outdoor seating on picnic tables and a limited menu of simple meat dishes and sandwiches. There is ice-cold bottled beer, and a good dark Cócle brew. The mellow ambience is a nice departure from the usual pickup scene. Av. Eusebio A. Morales and Vía Veneto. ℭ 265-5077.

La Casona de las Brujas An arty cultural center–cum–bar located on Plaza Herrera, La Casona is one of the new hip venues popping up around Casco Viejo. Out back, a cement open area and a makeshift stage provide space for the bar's live music on weekends; you'll also find art exhibitions and other cultural goings-on. The scene here is mellow, and they're open during the day. The crowd depends on what kind of entertainment is scheduled that night. Saturdays often feature jazz. Plaza Herrera, Casco Viejo. ℭ 211-0740.

Urbano Located above the Palms restaurant, Urbano is totally white retro-mod, and bathed in red ambient light. It's not much more than a hole-in-the-wall, but there are curvy banquettes and an elevated seating area in the center like an elongated pod. Urbano has DJ music, mostly chill-out and electronica, and well-made martinis. For whatever reason, Urbano is popular on Monday nights. Calle 48 and Calle Uruguay. ℭ 265-7256.

Wine Bar Catering to wine lovers, this spot serves more than 200 varieties from Europe, Chile, and California. It's mostly midrange wine, but there are a few gems on the menu. The Wine Bar is like an Italian tavern, with vine-and-trellis ceilings and trattoria tables. The mood picks up with their live music, usually a one-man act. There is an appetizer menu with cheese platters, but you can order off the menu from the Wine Bar's partner restaurant, Caffè Pomodoro, next door. C Eusebio A. Morales, next to the Las Vegas Suites. ℭ 225-0914.

THE GAY & LESBIAN SCENE

Panama is a mostly Catholic country and although the gay and lesbian scene here is not underground, it is discreet. There are a couple of clubs in the city that operate without much fanfare, and attacks, raids, harassment, and so on are thankfully not very common. For a calendar of gay and lesbian events, check out **www.farra urbana.com**. There are few, if any, venues or events directed at the lesbian-only scene, yet lesbians are welcome at gay venues. Clubs are open at 10pm Wednesday through Sunday; weeknight cover charges are around $3 to $5, $8 to $10 on weekends. Early arrivals can take advantage of happy-hour drink specials (sometimes free drinks).

The most established gay clubs are **BLG,** at Calle 49 and Calle Uruguay (ℭ 265-1624), with dancing to top DJ music Thursday to Saturday, and other special events like Gay Pride Nights on weekdays; **Lips** (no phone) at Avenida Manuel Espinoza Batista, next to Café Duran, has nightly drag shows on weeknights and dancing on Fridays and Saturdays. The largest gay dance club, Box, is now called **Glam: The Club** (ℭ 265-1624), and focus has shifted to nightly drag shows, concerts, fashion shows, and more, followed by late-night dancing until dawn (the best nights are Fri and Sat). To get here, you need a taxi; the club is at Tumba Muerto (in the Urb. Industrial La Esperanza neighborhood) on Vía Ricardo J. Alfaro. **Punta G,** at Calle D in El Cangrejo (next to Ginza Teppanyaki; © **265-1624),** has barmen in spandex, DJ music, and a dance floor.

CASINOS

Gambling is legal in Panama, and virtually every major hotel in the city has an adjoining casino. You'll find slot machines, video poker, gaming tables, sports betting, and special shows and parties. The hottest casino at the moment is at the **Veneto Hotel & Casino.** The Veneto has a sophisticated gaming area and often hosts over-the-top parties such as E! Entertainment's *Wild On.* There is a sushi bar here, too. **El Panama Hotel** has one of the newer centrally located casinos, which offers cheap drink specials for women. The **Caesar Park Panama** hotel has a large, elegant casino, but its out-of-the-way location means it's really only visited by guests. The bar here, though, is popular with young Panamanians.

6

Around Panama City

This chapter incorporates a sizeable region around Panama City, including the **Panama Canal, Canal Zone, Central Caribbean Coast** (including Colón and its surroundings), and **Gulf of Panama.** At first glance, it seems like a lot of ground to cover, but these destinations can be reached by a short drive, a puddle-jump flight, or a boat ride from the city, and some attractions are even close enough to visit by taxi. With its high level of services and amenities, Panama City is an ideal base from which to explore this region, and many travelers, especially those with limited time, plan their entire trips around this area, owing to its surprisingly diverse range of attractions.

The Canal Zone dry season is December to April, while the Caribbean coast sees substantially more rain; showers can occur during the so-called dry season at any time.

Temperatures in the islands off the Pacific Coast are consistently a few degrees cooler than those in Panama City, and less rain falls there.

EXPLORING THE REGION A trip to Panama wouldn't be the same without visiting one of the engineering marvels of the world, the **Panama Canal.** There are several ways to do this: at the viewing platform in Miraflores, on a jungle cruise or partial canal transit, or at the Gatún Locks near Colón. Along the Canal Zone corridor, the national park **Soberanía** puts you in a thick rainforest teeming with birds and wildlife, and you can visit an Emberá Indian village nearby or raft the Chagres River. Near Colón, **Portobelo** pays homage to the Spanish colonial era with its forts and ruins, as well as **Fort San Lorenzo,** on the canal's western side. Around the area, there are a couple of cool ecolodges and resorts that offer accommodations in natural surroundings yet are still close to Panama City—a tantalizing option for travelers deciding where to stay. This chapter also covers the **Archipelago de las Perlas (Pearl Islands)** and **Isla Taboga,** which are located in the Pacific, off the coast of Panama City.

1 The Panama Canal

77km (48 miles) long from Panama City to Colón

The construction of the Panama Canal was one of the grandest engineering feats in the history of the world, an epic tale of ingenuity and courage but marked by episodes of tragedy. When it was finally completed in 1914, the canal cut travel distances by more than half for ships that previously had had to round South America's Cape Horn. Today, the canal is one of the most traveled waterways, annually handling around 13,000 ships that represent 5% of global trade.

The history of the canal dates back to the 16th century, when Vasco Núñez de Balboa discovered that Panama was just a narrow strip of land separating the Caribbean from the Pacific. In 1539, King Charles I of Spain dispatched a survey team to study

---

Tips Keeping the Kids Happy

The area surrounding Panama City is packed with a lot of fun and exciting attractions that are ideal for families with kids. From the Summit Garden & Zoo, to canoe trips on the Chagres River, jungle cruises on Lake Gatún, rainforest expeditions, and beach sports, you can keep your kids busy learning or having fun for at least a week. The most kid-friendly hotel in the area is **Gamboa Rainforest Resort,** which has a huge pool and game center—but even better, the resort has an **aerial tram** that sails passengers through the rainforest to a high lookout platform. Also featured are a butterfly farm, reptile and aquatic life display, bike rental, and more—and these facilities can be used even by non-guests for the day. If you're lodging here, it's easy to plan trips with the company's on-site tour desk. If you're not staying here but would like someone to put together a couple of days or a week's worth of family activities, even using Panama City as a base, check out one of the Panama City tour operators listed in chapter 4.

---

the feasibility of building a waterway connecting the two oceans, but the team deemed such a pursuit impossible.

The first real attempt to construct a canal was begun by the French in 1880, led by Ferdinand de Lesseps, the charismatic architect of the Suez Canal. The Gallic endeavor failed miserably, however, as few had anticipated the enormous challenge presented by the Panamanian jungle, with its mucky swamps, torrential downpours, landslides, floods, and, most debilitating of all, mosquito-borne diseases such as malaria and yellow fever. In the end, more than 20,000 perished.

In 1903, the United States bought out the French and backed Panama in its secession from Colombia in exchange for control of the Canal Zone. For the next 10 years, the U.S., having essentially eradicated tropical disease, pulled off what seemed impossible in terms of engineering: It carved out a 14km (9-mile) path through the Continental Divide and constructed an elevated canal system and a series of locks to lift ships from sea level up to 26m (85 ft.) at Lake Gatún. The lake, created after construction crews dammed the Chagres River near the Gatún Locks, was at the time the largest man-made lake in the world.

In 1977, U.S. President Jimmy Carter and President Omar Torrijos of Panama signed a treaty that would relinquish control of the canal to the Panamanians on December 31, 1999. It was a controversial move because most Americans did not believe that Panama was up to the task—but those concerns have proved to be unfounded. As an autonomous corporation, the Panama Canal Authority has reduced safety problems and improved maintenance and productivity to the point where the canal basically runs itself.

It takes between 8 and 10 hours to transit the entire canal. There are three locks, the **Miraflores, Pedro Miguel,** and **Gatún,** whose maximum size is 320m (1,050 ft.) in length and 34m (110 ft.) in width. Ships built to fit through these locks are referred to as **Panamax** ships, which set the size standard until the 1990s, with the building of post-Panamax ships (mostly oil tankers) that are up to 49m (160 ft.) wide. The Panama Canal Authority now seeks to avoid becoming obsolete, and is debating a multibillion-dollar plan to widen the canal and build two new three-chamber locks to increase traffic. A national referendum in late 2006 will decide the fate of this expensive canal overhaul.

SEEING THE PANAMA CANAL IN ACTION

For information about visiting the canal at the Gatún Locks, see "Colón," later in this chapter. There is no viewing area at the Pedro Miguel Locks.

MIRAFLORES LOCKS ✸✸✸

The best land-based platform from which to see the Panama Canal at work is at **Miraflores Visitors Center** (© 276-8325; www.pancanal.com), located about a 15-minute drive from the heart of the city. The center is an absorbing attraction for both kids and adults, with four floors of exhibitions and interactive displays—and a theater—providing information about the canal's history and its impact on world trade, plus explanations of how the region's natural environment is crucial to the function of the canal. Ships can also be viewed from an observation deck. *Tip:* You'll have better luck catching sight of enormous Panamax ships in the afternoon around 2 or 3pm.

As you view ships in the locks, a monologue (in Spanish and English) piped through a loudspeaker, indicates what a ship is carrying, where it is registered, where it is going, and how much it paid; the speaker is cheerleader-like and tends to qualify the experience by saying such things as, "Can you *believe* they spent $200,000 to transit the canal, man?" There are also a snack bar and gift shop. The center is open daily from 9am to 5pm (ticket office closes at 4pm). Admission to the center's exhibitions and observation terrace is $8 adults, $5 children, and free for children under 5; or $5 adults, $3 children to visit only the restaurant and gift shop.

Best of all, there is the **Miraflores Visitors Center Restaurant** ✸✸✸ (daily 11am–11pm; main courses $7–$20), where you can dine while watching colossal ships transit the locks just a hundred feet away. Lunch is the most popular time to eat here, so arrive early or make a reservation, and try to get a table as close to the railing as possible. At night, the locks are well-lit and provide clear views of the ships. The food is not bad either, but what you're really here for is the one-of-a-kind view.

GETTING THERE & DEPARTING   City tours of Panama usually include a stop at Miraflores, or you can take a taxi for $15 to $20 round-trip for a 45-minute to 1-hour visit. Agree on a price with the driver beforehand. For buses, see "Getting There & Departing," below, under "Gamboa & the Canal Zone."

TRANSITING THE PANAMA CANAL ✸✸✸

Visitors to Panama who are not part of a long-haul cruise can still transit the canal by boat on a journey from Panama City to Colón, or they can do a partial transit from Gamboa to the Pacific or vice versa. Beyond the thrill of transiting locks is the opportunity to get close to colossal Panamax-size ships en route from one ocean to the other. Partial tours are by far the most popular because they pass through the Pedro Miguel and Miraflores locks, and sail under the grand span of the Bridge of the Americas, which is enough for most visitors. Transiting a lock can take up to 2 hours, which can grow tiresome on full-day journeys.

Panama Marine Adventures (© 226-8917; www.pmatours.net) offers partial canal transit with a shuttle leaving from the Flamenco Resort and Marina on the Amador Causeway at 10am and going to their *Pacific Queen*, docked at Gamboa. Trips leave every Saturday year-round, and every Thursday from January to April. The company offers full transit of the canal one Saturday every month (check the website for dates) leaving at 7:30am, first passing through the Miraflores locks and finishing at the Gatún Locks; the company provides transportation by vehicle back to Panama City. Partial transit costs $105 for adults and $55 for kids under 12; full transit costs $155 for adults and $65 kids under 12. The price includes all transportation, a bilingual guide, and lunch and soft drinks. The *Pacific Queen* has a capacity of 275 passengers.

Canal & Bay Tours (© 314-1349; www.canalandbaytours.com) is a pioneer in canal tourism, offering transit aboard one of two boats, the refurbished *Isla Morada,* a wooden boat with a capacity of 100 guests, or the *Fantasía del Mar,* a steel boat with a capacity of 500 passengers. The company offers full-day transit of the canal the first Saturday of every month for $149 adults, $45 children under 12; and partial transit every Saturday for $99 adults, $45 children under 12. Canal & Bay has full transit and partial transit (you pick) the third Tuesday of every month from January to April. Tours leave at 7:30am from the Flamenco Marina, docking in Gamboa or Gatún, depending on the tour. They also offer Saturday-evening **"Rumba in the Bay"** tours of the Bay of Panama, leaving at 9:30pm from their pier, with live music and an open bar.

Panama Yacht Tours (© 263-5044; www.panamayachtours.com) specializes in partial and full transit aboard one of their luxury yachts—however, their niche is private trips, usually corporate and school groups. The company owns five yachts ranging from 18 to 37m (58–122 ft.) for 1 to 100 people, with prices starting at $3,500, not including food, beverages, and dock fees. Clearly, this is an expensive option, best for groups seeking to escape the "cattle call" sort of trip. If the price is too rich for you, check with the company anyway because they often open their "private" Balboa–Gamboa transit, meaning once they drop private guests off at Gamboa, they must make the return trip to Panama City, and they sell this journey on a per-person basis ($99 adults, $45 children); call or check their website for dates. Private transits leave early from Gamboa and transit southbound, arriving at the Flamenco Marina at 4:30pm; the other leaves from Pier 19 in Balboa at 7:30am for the northbound journey to Gamboa (travelers return to Panama City via land). Private transits require at least a week to 2 weeks' advance notice.

THE PANAMA CANAL RAILWAY 𝒢𝒢

The **Panama Canal Railway** (© 317-6070; www.panarail.com) is the most picturesque mode of travel between Panama City and Colón. It gives passengers a chance to relive the experience of the California Gold Rush. The railway was first built in 1855 to meet the demands of forty-niners seeking quick passage from the east coast of the U.S. to the west. It later was rebuilt along more or less the same lines to transport workers and equipment during the building and maintenance of the canal. The train was relaunched in 2001, and features executive and tourist service and renovated coaches modeled after their 19th-century counterparts, with carpeted floors, wood paneling, and blinds. The trains have air-conditioning, and there are open-air viewing platforms. The journey lasts about an hour and borders the canal, racing through lush rainforest, past canal locks, and along slender causeways across Gatún Lake. Round-trip fare is $38 adults, $19 children; one-way fare is $22 adults, $11 children. The Corozal Train Station in Panama City is located in Albrook, and is a $2 taxi ride from downtown Panama. The trip takes 1 hour.

See "Tour Operators," below, for organized trips that include a ride on the train. The major issue for do-it-yourself travelers is departure times. From Panama City, the train leaves at 7:15am, with the return trip leaving Colón at 5:15pm—meaning round-trip travelers need to hire a taxi at the Colón station to get to attractions like

Portobelo, which can be expensive. Killing an afternoon in the city of **Colón** (p. 147) is out of the question. Consider riding the train one-way at the beginning or end of a journey to or from the Caribbean (in other words, after staying at the Meliá Panamá Canal or at a Portobelo hotel). Cruisers docking in Colón are offered this journey, but the ships charter an entire train for their passengers.

2 Gamboa & The Canal Zone

Gamboa is 20km (13 miles) from the Miraflores Locks

This is one of the most exciting natural areas to explore in Panama, if not in the Americas, and most of it is less than an hour's drive from the city. North America meets South America here in a confluence of hyper-diversity and, accordingly, the birdwatching is epic and easy to access in places like Soberanía National Park. There are also a birder's ecolodge, a recreational park and zoo, spots for white-water rafting, and opportunities to visit with Emberá Indian tribes. Gamboa, formerly an American Canal Zone residential area for workers in the canal's dredging division, is also the name for a full-scale resort here. It sits on the shore of Gatún Lake, home to the Smithsonian's Barro Colorado Nature Monument, where visitors can learn about the rich biodiversity of this area. Travelers either lodge here or simply visit the region's highlights by tour, taxi, or rental vehicle.

ESSENTIALS

GETTING THERE & DEPARTING By Taxi or Tour The Gamboa Resort and Canopy Tower offers transportation to and from its property. Nearly every visitor to the Canal Zone is part of a planned tour with a guide, or visitors can hire a taxi for a full- or half-day tour for around $15 to $25 an hour, depending on the number of passengers and the deal you're able to strike with your driver. The road to Gamboa ends at that town, and is about a 40-minute drive from the Cerro Ancón/Balboa area of Panama City.

By Bus Buses headed to Gamboa leave from the SACA station at the Palacio Legislativo at Plaza Cinco de Mayo, near Avenida Central, not from the main terminal in Albrook. The cost is 65¢ adults, 35¢ children. This bus drops passengers off at stops along the Gaillard Highway and Gamboa Road, including at the Miraflores Locks. However, the stop for Miraflores is an 8- to 10-minute walk from the visitor center. Buses leave weekdays at 5am, 5:45am, 6:30am, 8am, 10am, noon, 1pm, 2pm, 3pm, 4:30pm, 6:30pm, 8pm, and 10:30pm; on Saturday and Sunday buses leave at 6am, 7am, 8am, 10am, noon, 2pm, 4:30pm, 6:30pm, 8pm, and 10:30pm.

By Car To get to Gamboa and the Canal Zone, head out of Panama City toward Albrook to the Gaillard Highway, which runs along the canal and passes the Miraflores Locks. The road continues on past the Pedro Miguel locks and the Summit Golf Course until it forks at the ANAM ranger station just after you pass under a railway bridge. To get to Gamboa, the Gamboa Resort, Barro Colorado Island, the Canopy Tower, El Charco Trail, or Pipeline Road, take a left here on Gamboa Road. To get to the Camino de Cruces trail, continue straight on a lovely, jungle-fringed road that cuts through Soberanía National Park and eventually connects with the road to Colón. The sign for the Cruces trail is clearly marked at an off-road picnic site.

The Canal Zone

WHAT TO SEE & DO

Travelers to the Canal Zone have two options: Visit on **day excursions** and lodge in Panama City, where you'll be closer to shops and services; or base yourself at one of the **resorts** or **hostels** (highlighted below) and take part in their in-house tours. (If they don't offer the tour themselves, they can book an outside tour for you.)

TOUR OPERATORS   It makes sense to hire a guide or join a day tour. Transportation, a bilingual nature guide, equipment (if necessary), and often lunch are included in the price.

For contact information about **tour companies** mentioned here, see "Panamanian Tour Operators," on p. 62.

SOBERANIA NATIONAL PARK ✦✦✦

Soberanía National Park comprises 19,425 hectares (48,000 acres) of undulating, pristine tropical rainforest on the eastern shore of the Panama Canal. It is undoubtedly Panama's most important national park in terms of tourism and economics: Not only is Soberanía one of the most accessible, species-rich parks in the Americas, it is also part of the watershed that provides hundreds of millions of gallons of water to keep the Panama Canal in operation and the cogs of international commerce greased and moving. The park is just 40 minutes from Panama City, but it feels worlds away.

Wildlife from North and South America, including migratory birds, meets here in Soberanía, creating a hyper-diverse natural wonderland. The park has 105 species of mammals and a staggering number of bird species—525 at last count. There are jaguars, yes, and collared peccaries and night monkeys, too, but you're more likely to catch sight of a coatimundi, three-toed sloth, or diminutive tamarin monkey. Bring binoculars even if you're not an avid birder.

There are several ways to see the park. ANAM, the park ranger service, has several excellent hiking trails for day excursions that range from easy to difficult; there are a full-scale resort, a birder's ecolodge, a recreational park and zoo, and the Pipeline Road, a site revered for its abundant diversity of birds. Soberanía National Park is open daily from 6am to 5pm, and costs $3 per person to enter (free for kids under 12). Paying is tricky; they ask that you stop at the ranger station to pay because there isn't anyone to collect money at the trail head—but it's unlikely that every visitor does this. Play it safe, though, and stop to pay; the pass permits you to use any trails within the space of a day.

The park can be accessed by rental vehicle or taxi, or by joining a tour. If you take a taxi, plan a time for the driver to pick you up or have the driver wait. For more information, call the park's office at ✆ 232-4192; the website, www.anam.gob.pa, has limited park info in Spanish. The park office is open from 7am to 7pm daily, but if no one is inside, check around out back.

HIKING & BIRD-WATCHING TRAILS   **Sendero El Plantación (Plantation Trail),** located at the turnoff for the Canopy Tower lodge on the road to Gamboa, is a moderate, 6.4m (4-mile) trail that ends at the intersection for the Camino de Cruces trail. This is not a loop trail, so hikers will either need to return via the same trail or, with a little pre-planning, arrange to be dropped off at the Camino de Cruces trail on the road to Colón, hike northwest and connect with the Plantation Trail, and finish near the Canopy Tower, or vice versa (see Camino de Cruces, below). The Plantation Trail follows a road built in the 1910s by La Cascadas Plantation, the largest in the old Canal Zone during that period, producing cacao, coffee, and rubber. Alert hikers will spot remnants of these crops, especially the cacao plant. This trail is popular with birdwatchers, but mammals such as tamarins are frequently seen, too.

Continuing on the road to Gamboa, and to the right, is the trail head for **Sendero Charco (Pond Trail),** an ultra-easy, 20-minute loop that follows the Sardinilla River. The trail gives even the most reluctant walkers a brilliant opportunity to immerse themselves in thick tropical rainforest.

A little more than a mile past the bridge and turnoff to Gamboa Resort is **Camino de Oleoducto,** better known as **Pipeline Road,** the celebrity trail for bird-watching in Panama, renowned worldwide as a record-setting site for 24-hour bird counts. Even non-birders can't help getting caught up in the action with so many colorful show birds fluttering about, such as mot mots, trogons, toucans, antbirds, a rainbow of tanagers, and flycatchers. Bird-watching starts at the crack of dawn, when the avian world is at its busiest, so try to make it here at least before 9am, if not earlier. In spite of the name, the Pipeline Road is not drivable. More than half the bird-watchers who visit here walk only a mile or so, but if you like to hike or mountain bike (see below), push on because the chances of spotting rare birds and wildlife increase the farther you go. To get here by vehicle, pass the Gamboa Resort turnoff, and continue until you reach a fork. Turn left here onto a gravel road and continue until you see the Pipeline Road sign.

Soberanía's other prime attraction is historic **Camino de Cruces (Las Cruces Trail).** Before the railway and the canal existed, the only path from the Caribbean to the Pacific was the Chagres River to what's now called Venta de Cruces, followed by a treacherous walk along Las Cruces Trail. The Spanish used this route during the 16th century to transport looted treasure to the Caribbean and onward to Spain. In some areas, the cobblestone remains of the trail still exist or have been restored, and can be seen even if you walk just 10 or 20 minutes from the picnic area and trail head off Madden Road. The trail is moderate to difficult, and is about 9.7km (6 miles) to its terminus at Venta de Cruces. From here, a local boat can pick you up and drop you off at the Gamboa resort, but you'll need a guide (a tour or your hotel can arrange this for you). Also, hikers may lose their way because the trail becomes somewhat indecipherable the closer you get to Venta las Cruces, another reason to have a guide. Backpackers can camp along the trail, but must pay a $5 fee at the park-ranger station beforehand. If this trail really piques your interest, check out Ancon Expeditions' 8-day **"Camino Real Tour,"** which gives travelers a taste of what it was like to cross the isthmus by foot during the Gold Rush era, and includes tent lodging in the rainforest and at an Emberá Indian village. See p. 148.

The second alternative is to hike the trail and turn into the Plantation Trail, which finishes near Canopy Tower and the road to Gamboa. This hike takes around 5 hours to complete and is a moderately difficult trek. To get to the trail head, continue straight at the fork in the road to Gamboa on what's known as Madden Road (but not signed as such). The road presents a lovely drive through the park along a road flanked with towering rainforest canopy. About 6km (3¾ miles) past the fork there are covered picnic tables and the trail head.

MOUNTAIN BIKING   The tour company **Adventures in Panama** offers a unique half-day mountain-bike trip on the Pipeline Road, leaving Panama City at 8am and returning at 1:30pm (cost averages $95 per person, and includes transportation, equipment, and a box lunch). The bike terrain is sand, pavement, packed dirt, and mud, and is classified as moderate to difficult. Your group can bike up to 29km (18 miles) round-trip or less depending on your appetite for riding. The minimum age for this bike trip is 8 years old.

LAGO GATUN

Engineers understood that the only feasible way to build the Panama Canal was to employ a system of locks to lift ships up and over higher altitudes on the isthmus, and central to this was the creation of Gatún Lake. The lake was formed in 1913 with the completion of the Gatún Dam, which staunched the powerful Chagres River—a tremendous feat considering that Gatún Dam and Gatún Lake were the largest earth dam and largest man-made lake of their time. The lake flooded roughly 425 sq. km (164 sq. miles), an area slightly larger than Detroit, creating islands out of hilltops and submerging entire forests and villages.

The thick rainforest that cloaks the shoreline provides water for Gatún Lake, which in turn provides water for the canal locks, and therefore the Canal Authority is keen to keep deforestation at bay. This is good news for eco-travelers—wildlife sightings are common. Ships traverse 38km (24 miles) across the lake from the Gatún Locks to the Gaillard Cut, and travelers can take part in this experience with a partial canal transit (see "Transiting the Panama Canal," above), or take part in a jungle cruise on the lake. There is also fishing, or you can visit Barro Colorado Island (see "Learn about the Rainforest with the Smithsonian Institute," below). Getting on the lake provides a more intimate view of the canal than a visit to the Miraflores Locks does.

JUNGLE CRUISES 🌴🌴🌴 *Kids*   Half-day jungle cruises in Lake Gatún are mini-adventures that are as fun for kids as for adults, and they are dependable ways to catch sight of monkeys such as white-faced capuchins, howler monkeys, and Geoffrey's tamarins up-close and in their natural habitat. Expect also to see sloths, crocodiles, caimans, turtles, and even *capybaras,* the world's largest rodent. The boat ride also allows passengers to get unusually close to monster tankers and ships transiting the canal. The **Gamboa Resort** offers a jungle cruise as part of their in-house excursions; others leave from the Gamboa pier and provide land transportation to and from Panama City. Guides provide passengers with an entertaining account of the history of the canal, the mechanisms that operate the canal, and fun anecdotes, while ducking in and out of island passageways searching for birds and wildlife. **Ancon Expeditions** (see "Panamanian Tour Operators," in chapter 4) has the best guides and service, not to mention the most experience in the area. Their Panama Canal Boat Rainforest Adventure leaves early from Panama City and returns in the late afternoon; the cost is $99 adults, $50 kids 12 and under, which includes lunch and all transportation.

Jungle Land Explorers, part of Panama City Tours (© **263-8198;** www.Gatún explorer.com), offers an interesting motorboat tour of Gatún Lake and a stop at their anchored, double-decker *Gatún Explorer* houseboat, where guests have lunch and kick back in the middle of the jungle; kayaking and fishing are also options. They have a library with educational videos and books, too. The tour leaves from La Represa dock on the west side of the canal; however, round-trip transportation from Panama City is included, leaving at 8am and returning at 4:30pm. Note that the *Gatún Explorer* works with cruise ship excursionists, and therefore they offer their jungle cruise on **Sundays** only, whereas Ancon can usually plan something any day of the week.

FISHING 🌴🌴🌴   I give this three stars because in Gatún Lake you're guaranteed a fish—or your money back. The lake is packed with peacock bass, and all you need to do is just casually throw a line in and you'll easily snag one, sometimes within minutes. Fishermen tell stories of catching not dozens but hundreds of peacock bass and tarpon, which also reside here. Also, like a jungle cruise, you can get relatively close to ships on the canal and enjoy wild surroundings. **Cahill's Fishing** (© **264-3333** or 6678-2653; www.panama.canalfishing.com) has a 5.5m (18-ft.) Fun Deck with a 115-horsepower motor, live bait box, and fishing rods, and he charges $250 a day for four people, including snacks and beer. The operation is run by Richard Cahill, a Panamanian-American who knows the lake inside and out. If you're looking for something cheaper, he can put you in touch with a local boat operator who will charge $80 a day for a 4.9m (16-ft.) boat, but rods and food are extra (and local guides speak limited English).

Learn about the Rainforest with the Smithsonian Institute

The **Barro Colorado Nature Monument** is home to one of the most important—and oldest—biological research stations in the world, administered by the Smithsonian Tropical Research Institute (STRI). It contains more than 5,261 hectares (13,000 acres) of land, including five surrounding mainland peninsulas, but the spotlight is on Barro Colorado Island in Gatún Lake, a short boat ride away from Gamboa. The forested island is the largest in the lake, and it was once a hill called West Hill that became a 16-sq.-km (6-sq.-mile) island after the surrounding area was flooded during the creation of Gatún Lake. The island is essentially a capsule of biodiversity that provides an opportunity for scientists to monitor population changes and test diversity theories about the rainforest without having their studies encroached upon by loggers, developers, poachers, or farmers. Each year, between 200 and 400 international scientists visit Barro Colorado, making this one of the most well-studied forests in the world. Scientists have so far discovered 1,200 plants, 120 mammals, and innumerable insects on the island, but really the chances of your spotting wildlife here are the same as at any rainforest in Panama (but count on seeing howler monkeys at Barro Colorado).

What's unique here is that the average layman can visit the island and see what's going on in the world of tropical science. It's an outstanding tour—part boat ride, part hike, part learning experience—and the price includes a delicious buffet lunch and access to the visitor center and Espavé bookstore. The only downside to the tour is that it is expensive ($70 adults, $40 students) and nonrefundable—don't even think about showing up late for the boat ride or you'll be left behind. Reservations should be made more than 2 weeks in advance, but you can always call and see if there is a last-minute cancellation. If you're short on time or not up to giving tropical rainforests more than a cursory glance, this is probably not the best tour for you.

The tour leaves at 7:15am on weekdays and 8am on weekends from STRI's dock located just past the turnoff to the Gamboa Resort (heading left at the fork and onto a gravel road). The boat ride to the island takes 45 minutes. Once there, a guided tour takes visitors on a 2- to 3-hour hike along a sometimes steep trail through forest, ending at the visitor center for lunch, followed by a Q and A session. At 3:40pm on weekdays and 2:30pm on weekends (you can see that a weekday tour is longer), the boat takes visitors back to the pier. They do not provide transportation to/from the pier, so you'll need a taxi ($15–$20 each way from Panama City), or a bus to Gamboa (see "Getting There & Departing," above). Bring proper walking shoes, bug repellent, your passport, and your confirmation letter from STRI, and wear long pants, not shorts. Complete information is available from STRI (📞 **202/633-4014** in the U.S., or 212-8000 in Panama; www.stri.org). You can reserve and pay by credit card on their site.

RIO CHAGRES & EMBERA VILLAGES

The Chagres River flows from the San Blas Cordillera down into Gatún Lake near Gamboa—on the other side of the lake, the river is blocked by the Gatún Dam, which created its namesake lake. Travelers visit this river for two reasons: cultural tours of Emberá Indian villages, or intermediate-level white-water rafting. Along the way, the jungle-draped riverbanks teem with birds, animals, and fluttering butterflies, providing an exciting sense of adventure without having to invest a lot of time or money.

EMBERA INDIANS VILLAGE TOUR ★★ (Kids)   Emberá Indians are native to the Darién Province, but many groups have resettled here on the banks of the Chagres River. For the most part, they continue to live life much as they have for centuries, traveling by dugout canoe, wearing nothing more than a skirt or sheath, and sleeping under thatched-roof huts. To earn income, the Emberá villages Parara Puru, Emberá Puru, and Emberá Drua, which are close to the mouth of the Chagres River, have opened to tourism, allowing visitors to share in their culture and see how they live. In the true sense, the villages are not pristine examples of Emberá life, but the chance to travel by dugout canoe, interact with this fascinating culture and, yes, buy a few of their intricately woven baskets and other handicrafts is an informative and delightful experience. For a few bucks, you can have an Emberá hand paint a traditional "tattoo" with *jagua* vegetable dye on a part of your body (kids love this), but keep in mind that it takes 10 to 14 days for the stain to go away! Part of the tour includes a typical Emberá lunch and watching a folkloric dance show; like most folkloric shows, these are demonstrations of rituals long gone, but the music and dancing are still entertaining. Bring your swimsuit because tours include a walk to a cascade for a dip in cool water. All Panamanian tour operators offer this Emberá trip.

RAFTING ★★   The tour company **Aventuras Panama** (© 260-0044; www.aventuras panama.com) specializes in what it calls the "Chagres Challenge," with a hiking and rafting trip down the Class II and III river. It's a long float but technically not difficult, and it starts early, leaving Panama City at 5am by 4WD and going to the village San Cristóbal. From here you hike for more than an hour to the put-in site on the Chagres. The rafting portion lasts about 5 hours, but included in that along the way is a picnic lunch on the river. Travelers pass by Emberá villages but do not spend much time there. Expect to arrive back in Panama City around 7pm. The cost is $125 per person, and includes transportation, breakfast, and lunch, and all equipment. You must be between the ages of 12 and 70 to participate.

SUMMIT GARDENS PARK & ZOO ★★

There's a lot of wildlife in the jungles of Panama, but almost all species shy from the public and are close to impossible to spot in their natural environment. If you're in Panama for the first time, or if you don't have much time here, **Summit Gardens Park & Zoo** is a good introduction to the flora and fauna native to the country. For kids, there's a lot of wide, grassy areas on which to run around, and enough animals on view to delight all ages. It isn't a fancy, state-of-the-art zoo by U.S. standards, however Summit recently hired a new director to refocus and revamp the zoo and gardens and to create a cohesive exhibition that illustrates biodiveristy using animals, birds, and reptile displays. The Houston Zoo is assisting Summit with this project, which may well have already begun by the time you read this.

The zoo has a wonderful display of "showcase" wildlife, including tapirs, white-faced capuchins and spider monkeys, ocelots, a jaguar, puma, collared peccaries, and more, some of which have been rescued from unscrupulous wildlife poachers (the young tapir "Lucia" was saved during a sting operation that nabbed two Panamanians trying to sell her on the Internet). But without a doubt the **harpy eagle** takes center stage here with its own interpretive center. The harpy is Panama's national bird and the largest eagle in the world, about half the size of an average human—it really is worth a visit just to see the size of this regal bird.

Summit began as a botanical garden in 1923, created by the U.S. in an effort to reproduce and distribute tropical plants from around the world. It is now home to the world's leading collection of palms, among other exotic species. Because Panama City has few green spaces for a picnic or a chance to let the kids run free, Summit is popular with families on weekends. The grassy picnic area and park are free, or you can pay $8 for a covered eating area and barbecue pit. The zoo costs $1 for adults and teens, kids 12 and under get in free, and it's open daily from 9am to 5pm. Call © **232-4850** for more information, or check out their site at www.summitpanama.org.

WHERE TO STAY & DINE

Canopy Tower ☆☆ *(Moments)*   Canopy Tower is an ex-U.S.-military radar station that has been converted into a fantasy lodge for bird-watchers—something like a cross between a stylish B&B and a scientific research center. The lodge is a cylindrical, galvanized steel structure topped with a sunflower-yellow geotangent dome (which looks like a gargantuan soccer ball), poking out above the dense canopy of the Soberanía National Park rainforest. It's just 25 minutes from Panama City, giving guests the sensation of having gotten away from it all without having traveled very far. There is a 360-degree observation deck that provides stunning views and a platform for observing the 200-plus species of birds that flutter in the area, and a comfy social lounge with wraparound windows that are flush with the trees. In the morning, the spooky roar of howler monkeys serves as a wake-up call. The hotel, by design, is not wheelchair accessible and there is no elevator. The best room here is the Blue Cotinga Suite, one of two "suites," which are really large doubles with a hammock and private bathroom. Doubles on the second floor are comfortably spaced; however, the pie-slice single rooms are tiny and noisy in the morning (starting at 5:30am), and they do not have curtains. Bird-watchers are the majority of guests here, so it's early to bed and up at sunrise—if you're not as keen as your fellow guests, this will be an issue for you considering the price. Also, there is no air-conditioning, but ceiling fans do the trick in keeping temperatures down. Single rooms have shared bathrooms. The price includes meals, which are not gourmet but very tasty nonetheless, and served buffet-style; tours, with the exception of bird-watching around the lodge, are an additional cost.

Road to Gamboa. © **264-5720** or 6687-0291. www.canopytower.com. $100–$130 single; $125–$175 per person double; $145–$200 per person suite. AE, MC, V. **Amenities:** Restaurant; bar; library; tours.

Gamboa Rainforest Resort ☆☆ *(Kids)*   Sprawled along the shore of the Chagres River in Soberanía National Park, the Gamboa bills itself as an ecolodge but is really more of a destination megaresort that appeals equally to nature-seeking travelers and to those who just want to nurse a cocktail at the swim-up bar and work on their tan. It is an ideal destination for families with kids, given the resort's jungle boat cruises, aerial tram ride through the rainforest, and minizoo of reptile, butterfly, and marine species exhibits. Travelers seeking intimate accommodations with personalized service are advised to look for lodging elsewhere. Every amenity under the tropical sun is offered here, such as a full-service spa, guided tours, and five restaurants; especially recommended is their **Los Largatos Restaurant** on the river, where you can dine while watching ships pass through the canal. The Gamboa's lobby is lofty and vast, with high arching glass windows that look out toward the river, vigorously whirling ceiling fans, and a large, indoor fountain, all of which exude a sense of tropical splendor. However, it is important to note that this is not a luxury lodge. You won't find the architectural uniqueness or level of service provided by five-star hotels—the staff is friendly enough but wear the jaded grin of having seen too many changing faces, and the tour-desk staff is overwhelmed in the morning. Very spacious double rooms have garden or river views (with private balconies) and a pleasant yet anonymous chainlike decor; attractive suites have Indonesian furniture and large living areas. The bathrooms are elegant and spacious.

The resort is located on the old living quarters of canal VIPs; the hotel looks over the manicured lawns of what once was a 9-hole golf course, and the 1930s-era clapboard homes at the resort's entrance have one- and two-bedroom apartments with kitchenettes. The apartments are quite appealing in a historical sense, with their hardwood floors and wicker furniture, but they are the cheapest lodging options because they do not have a view and are a short walk or minivan transfer from the main hotel. If an apartment interests you, book one of the newly renovated units in no. 253, 255, 256, or 258.

Gamboa. (C) **314-9000,** or 877/800-1690 in the U.S. www.gamboaresort.com. 107 units. $175–$250 double with garden view; $195–$285 double with river view; $275–$350 junior suite; $135–$175 1-bedroom apartment. AE, MC, V. **Amenities:** 5 restaurants; 2 bars; outdoor pool; tennis courts; kayak rental; bicycle rental spa and fitness center w/whirlpool, steam, and massage; concierge; tour desk; business center; 24-hr. room service; laundry service; aerial tram; natural exhibits. *In room:* A/C, TV, minibar, robes, coffeemaker, hair dryer, safe.

Soberanía Research Station Hostel   *Value*

The tour operator **Advantage Panama,** which specializes in bird-watching trips, operates a hostel on a residential street in Gamboa, in a two-story converted canal home. It backs a tangle of forest that's home to their resident toucan, who often hangs about with more than 100 birds they've seen around their property. The hostel is divided into two parts: One side is for scientists on long-term study projects with the Smithsonian Institute, the other for regular guests. The obvious perk of staying here is being able to chat with scientists during their downtime (that is, if they're up to talking). The hostel has a room for two with a double bed, and rooms with bunks for three to six people. If they're not too busy, two can book a room intended for three to six guests for the price of a double. They gave the hostel's interiors a new coat of paint and polished the floors, but it's still pretty rustic, and most bathrooms are shared. A taxi here costs $20 to $25 from Panama City; or you can take a bus to Gamboa and the end of the line, and walk a couple of blocks. Contact Advantage for information about packages that include tours. Rates include breakfast.

Gamboa. (C) **6676-2466.** www.advantagepanama.com/soberania.html. 10 units. $35 double. No credit cards. **Amenities:** Cafeteria; tours. *In room:* No phone.

A NATURE LODGE ON THE WAY TO COLON

Sierra Llorona Panama Lodge

If the Canopy Tower is too expensive for your budget but you want accommodations that are more intimate than the Gamboa's, you might want to check out this nature lodge. Sierra Llorona, which means "crying mountain," is a converted home nestled in a gorgeous setting of 202 hectares (500 acres) of private rainforest. It's located just before Sabanitas, about 7.2km (4½ miles) from the Transístmica Highway, on a dirt road. The lush rainforest that surrounds the property is home to more than 150 bird species, and is therefore ideal for traveling bird-watchers. But Sierra Llorona really appeals to any traveler looking for a peaceful place to commune with nature, or to simply unwind. The lodge is family-run and family-style, with very friendly, personalized service and group meals. Guest rooms, like the lodge as a whole, are simply furnished but attractive and neat as a pin. The three "singles" are rooms with two twin beds, and they're located in the main house along with the lodge's sole suite. There is a separate building with four doubles, which have two double beds each. Rooms have forest views; there's no air-conditioning, but you don't really need it here considering that the lodge almost always receives a fresh breeze. A pleasant and spacious, semi-enclosed veranda is great for quiet reflection and relaxing.

Off the main area, along Nance's Trail, is a camping space with a covered dining table and fire pit, but you'll need to bring your own gear. What's nice about this lodge is that there are walking trails that lead out from the lodge, including La Poza Trail, which leads to a clear-water pool where you can take a dip. It rains a lot here, so don't forget your waterproof duds. Room rates include lodging, meals, and a walk around the area with a local guide; but they have lodging-only rates also that include just breakfast. Bird-watching trips to outside destinations, cultural trips, and other day excursions will cost you extra. The staff can arrange transportation to the lodge for $80 for two from Panama City ($25 for each extra person). If you're driving a rental vehicle, you'll need a 4WD because the road is often muddy.

Road to Santa Rita Arriba, near Sabanitas. ✆ 442-8104 or 6614-8191. www.sierrallorona.com. 1 suite, 4 doubles, 3 twin units. $80 double, $98 suite; all-inclusive packages, based on double occupancy, $69 per person per night for a double room, $79 for a suite. AE, MC, V. **Amenities:** Restaurant; bar; walking trails; excursions. *In room:* No phone.

3 Colón

76km (47 miles) NW of Panama City

Spread across a square peninsula at the mouth of the northern canal gateway is **Colón,** capital of the larger Colón Province that runs along Panama's Central Caribbean Coast. Most residents here are Afro-Caribbean descendants of canal workers who arrived around the turn of the 20th century. In spite of its status as the largest **duty-free zone** in the Americas with billions in annual sales, its profits do not trickle down to locals, and the city is rife with poverty and crime. A splashy $45-million cruise-ship port, called **Colón 2000,** has also failed to alleviate mass unemployment or improve living conditions. At the risk of sounding too reactionary, avoid Colón if you can unless you are part of a tour or accompanied by a local guide—and even then you're taking your safety into your own hands. Muggings and purse-snatchings are so common that even Colón's own residents are known to approach tourists on the street and issue a warning. A drive through the city streets provokes shock, sadness, or just a very uncomfortable feeling at how impoverished Colón's residents are.

But don't let Colón scare you from visiting some of Panama's most important historical attractions that lie within a 30-minute to 1-hour drive from the city, such as **Portobelo** and **Fort San Lorenzo,** as well as the impressive **Gatún Locks** and **Gatún Dam** (see "The Panama Canal," earlier in this chapter). The translucent Caribbean Sea also beguiles visitors with outstanding **diving** and **snorkeling** opportunities, and the province is home to several oceanfront hotels and resorts that are popular weekend getaways for Panama City residents.

Colón was founded in 1850 during the California Gold Rush. At the time, crossing the United States from coast to coast was dangerous and time-consuming; a far better option was to take a ship to Panama, cross the isthmus via the Panama Railroad, and board a ship for California. Economically, the city flourished with businesses and hotels catering to travelers until 1869, with the completion of the transcontinental railway in the U.S. The arrival of the French, and later the U.S., around the turn of the 20th century, brought new prosperity to the city, and much of the architecture here dates from that era. Most of these buildings today are dilapidated shells of their former glory, the city having fallen on hard times when the focus turned to Panama City.

ESSENTIALS

GETTING THERE & DEPARTING   By Plane   Aeroperlas (© **315-2700;** www. aeroperlas.com) flies to the Enrique Adolfo Jiménez Airport in Colón from Panama City at 8:30am Monday through Friday. From Colón to Panama City the flight leaves at 5:50pm Monday through Thursday, and at 3:05pm Fridays. The trip takes 15 minutes and costs $26 one-way.

By Bus   The Colón bus terminal is located at Calle Terminal and Avenida Bolívar. There is daily service to and from the Albrook Terminal in Panama City leaving every 20 minutes from 6am to 10pm; the trip is just under 2 hours and costs $2 one-way. Buses headed to Portobelo leave every 15 minutes from 6:30am to 8:45pm; the ride is 1 hour and costs $1.50. To reach Portobelo from Panama City, it is not necessary to transfer in Colón; instead, take a bus to Sabanitas and transfer to a bus headed to Portobelo (on the corner at the El Rey supermarket). The fare is $3.

By Train   By far the most picturesque journey to Colón is aboard the **Panama Canal Railroad** (see "What to See & Do" in "The Panama Canal," earlier in this chapter).

By Car   Driving here can be a little tricky because most streets are not signed. There are two ways to Colón from Panama City: The easiest is via the Corredor Norte, which connects to the Boyd-Roosevelt Highway, also known as the Transístmica Highway, at Chilibre. The other, more scenic route is to go through Soberanía National Park and then connect to the Boyd-Roosevelt highway—follow the Omar-Torrijos Avenue to the Gaillard Highway toward Gamboa, but continue straight rather than turning left at the park ranger's office and the sign for Gamboa and Summit Gardens.

GETTING AROUND   If you are not part of a tour and do not have a vehicle, a taxi (that fits up to four people) is your best bet. Taxis are not metered—expect a driver to set a flat fee for visits to multiple destinations in the area. The Colón 2000 port has set rates for taxis, and even though you may be hiring one from the bus or train terminal, drivers like to adhere to these general rates for all tourists. Average rates are $60 to $80 for Portobelo (3 hr.) and $120 for the Gatún Locks and Portobelo. Negotiate and you might get a better price. Most taxi drivers speak little English and are not tour guides. Considering this, you might want to stick with a bilingual tour.

GENERAL TOUR OPERATORS

The tour operators listed in chapter 4 can put together custom day and multiple-day tours in the central Caribbean region. Typical day tours begin with a ride on the Panama Railroad to Colón, and are followed by minivan transportation to the Gatún Locks and Fort San Lorenzo, a historical tour of Portobelo, and finally return ground transportation to Panama City. **Ancon Expeditions** offers a unique, 7-night "Camino Real Tour" following the old Spanish-built cobblestone trail across the isthmus. The tour involves several days of moderate trekking and overnights in tents and hotels. **Ecocircuitos** has a 7-night "Caribbean Escapade" with hiking in Portobelo National Park, snorkeling and kayaking, and overnights in Bananas Resort. **Adventures in Panama** has tours in the area with add-on extension trips to the San Blas Islands.

WHAT TO SEE & DO

There are two principal attractions here in Colón. The **Colón Free Zone** (www.colon freezone.com; no central phone) is a walled-in, city-within-a-city located on the southeastern edge of town. There are 1,600 showrooms here for wholesalers and retailers in Central and South America who travel here to buy consumer products at cost. The Free Zone is open to the public, but most showrooms sell to wholesalers only, and others only reluctantly sell to individual tourists. Really, you can't buy anything here that isn't available in an airport duty-free store, and legally, any purchase here must be sent by the retailer to the airport for pickup, which is another hassle. To visit, you'll need to sign in and show your passport at the Free Zone office, located at the right of the Free Zone entrance at Calle 13 near Avenida Roosevelt.

Running the length of the city's eastern shore is the modern cruise-ship port, **Colón 2000,** with two restaurants, a dozen shops selling duty-free electronics, jewelry, and other handicrafts. There's really nothing interesting enough to keep you here, and the port is more of a jumping-off point to explore the area outside Colón. Excursions for cruise ships are provided by the port-owned **Aventuras 2000** tour agency.

Tip: ATMs in the central Caribbean region are scarce. Major hotels and most restaurants accept credit cards, but your best (and safest) bet is to use the ATM inside the grocery store in the Colón 2000 cruise-ship port; there is also an HSBC cash machine at the Gatún Locks, next to the entrance at the visitor center; or bring enough cash to cover your visit.

WHERE TO STAY

New Washington Hotel   I only recommend you stay at this hotel if you absolutely, positively need to spend a night in Colón—otherwise head out to the Meliá Panama Canal hotel (see below) or elsewhere. The New Washington is a hotel grande dame, built in 1913 and considered five-star lodging during its time. Over the years, the hotel has been renovated and well-maintained; rooms are clean but bland, but the foyer is elegant and polished. The hotel is tucked back near the sea on a large, fenced-in lot in the least dangerous part of the city. A casino and a disco are located here, too, as is an outdoor pool, but the hotel almost always seems empty. For the price, it's a bargain, but you can't escape the feeling that the New Washington is living off the vapors of its glory days, and the city's too dangerous to encourage you to wander off the premises.

Calle 2. ⓒ 441-7133. www.newwashingtonhotel.com. $40 double. AE, MC, V. **Amenities:** Restaurant; bar; outdoor pool; business center; limited room service; casino; disco. *In room:* A/C, TV.

WEST OF COLON
GATUN LOCKS & DAM ✦✦✦

The Gatún Locks, located at the Caribbean entrance of the canal about 10km (6 miles), or a 20-minute drive, from Colón, are the canal's busiest because there is just one set of locks here instead of the two at Miraflores—meaning you have a better chance of seeing Panamax ships backed up here and waiting their turn to enter the canal. These locks are also the most impressive because they lift ships and tankers up

26m (85 ft.) to the level of Lake Gatún in three steps (taking about 1½ hr. to complete), where they continue for 37km (23 miles) before reaching the Pedro Miguel Locks. The neat thing here is that you can **drive over the canal** at near water level on your way out to Fort San Lorenzo (see "Colón," above). The **Gatún Locks Visitors Pavilion** (daily 9am–4pm; free admission) has a viewing platform, reached by a long flight of stairs, that offers a high perch for excellent photo opportunities. Apart from a model of the canal and a bilingual brochure, there are no other tourist facilities here. The visitor center is not well signed; to get here, head left just at the canal vehicle bridge until you see a parking lot to your right (pass around traffic if there is a line waiting to cross the canal bridge).

About 2km (1¼ miles) from the Gatún Locks is **Gatún Dam,** a tremendous earthen dam across Chagres River that was, at its completion, the largest in the world and one of the finest engineering achievements in history. The dam was built to create the artificial Lake Gatún crossed by ships to reach Pedro Miguel Locks. During the rainy season from April to December, you'll want to visit when the spillway is open, but there are no regular hours so ask at the visitor center at the Gatún Locks.

The majority of visitors here are on shore excursions from the cruise-ship port at Colón or are staying at the Meliá Panama Canal hotel. If you're coming from Colón or the train station (in Panama City), a round-trip taxi ride will cost between $15 and $20 for an hour, or $35 to $40 for 2 hours (to see both the dam and the locks).

FORT SAN LORENZO & ACHIOTE ROAD 🐦🐦

Continuing past the Gatún Locks, the road hugs the edge of the Sherman Forest Reserve until reaching the old U.S. military base Fort Sherman, a part of which was torn down to make way for a new Decameron Resort that never happened. If you're driving your own vehicle, the police guard at the gate may ask to see your passport. Continue for 8.9km (5½ miles) on a paved/unpaved road shrouded in tropical greenery, until the road ends and the view opens onto the Caribbean Sea and the mouth of the Chagres River. The Chagres has been called the "world's most valuable river," for it is was here that the Spanish transported staggering quantities of Incan gold, later followed by forty-niners passing through with millions of dollars of mined treasure, and now the river's immense value is derived by the fact that the Chagres provides the necessary water to keep the Panama Canal in operation. Most intriguing here is **Fort San Lorenzo,** a Spanish defensive fort first built in 1595 but subsequently sacked and burned three times and finally rebuilt in 1761—the version you see today. It was later used as a prison and, for a brief period, a campground for forty-niners during the Gold Rush. Fort San Lorenzo is a UNESCO World Heritage Site, and with its well-preserved state—rusty cannons pointed at enemies long gone, walls made of thick coral and rock, and a grassy moat—it's a worthwhile detour. However, if you're short on time and already planning to visit the forts at Portobelo, you might skip San Lorenzo because of the 1½-hour drive from Colón (unless you're a bird-watcher—see below). The fort is open daily 9am to 4pm, and you must be back out of the police guard station by 6pm. The cost is $3 per person; for more information, see **www.sanlorenzo.org**.

The village of **Achiote** lies midway between Piña and Escobal on the Achiote Road, quietly revered as a bird-watching mecca by those in the know—the Audubon Society holds their Atlantic Christmas Bird Count here and has counted up to 390 species in 1 day, including the black-throated trogon, bare-crowned antbirds, white hawks, blue cotingas, and chestnut-mandible toucans. The area is just now developing as an eco-tourism site as a way to support the small local community, and there is a new

Centro El Tucán (no phone; Mon–Fri 8am–4pm) in Achiote with interpretive exhibits. The best way to visit is with a birding guide who can arrange transportation; try **Advantage Panama** or **Ancon Expeditions,** or check the Audubon Society's site, **www.panamaaudubon.org,** to see if they've got any day trips planned to the area.

WHERE TO STAY & DINE

Meliá Panama Canal 🌟🌟 *Kids*   One of two resorts in the canal area (Gamboa Rainforest Resort is the other), the Meliá, a Spanish-owned chain, is housed in the old quarters of the Escuela de las Americas, the notorious military school that spawned Manuel Noriega. You wouldn't know it today, gazing at this lovely, hacienda-style resort on the shore of Gatún Lake. The resort is popular with families from Panama City, international executives on business in the Free Trade Zone, package tourists, and RCI timeshare association members. Though it is billed as a five-star resort, it is more akin to a five-star hotel, with a few activities thrown in. For the most part, people spend their time poolside, but there are kayaks for paddling around, a canopy-style zip line, day excursions offered to Portobelo and Fort San Lorenzo, and a fairly empty casino—but not much more. The soaring lobby is staffed by attentive, friendly personnel, and decorated with Spanish colonial art reproductions, heavy wood furniture, and colorful ceramics. The Meliá's ambience is more intimate than Gamboa's, and the decor is slightly better. I've noticed, too, that the lobby and rooms *smell* so good, owing to fresh-cut flowers and scented candles. The rooms have king-size beds and marble bathrooms, and suites are very spacious, with a marginally frumpy, classic decor. Across from the hotel are two other buildings with rooms with kitchenettes (popular with businesspeople) as well as overflow rooms typically booked by timeshare members. The hotel is centered around two fabulous, resort-style pools, with a swim-up bar, lounge chairs, and an activity center.

Despite the beauty of the resort's immediate surroundings, the general location is less than desirable—more than a few visitors have said they were put off by having to drive through Colón to get here. The Meliá is located in the reverted residential area of the old canal and military zone, but today the homes are more unkempt than in earlier years. It's hard to fathom how the owners of the hotel's owners chose this site for a resort—perhaps they were overestimating business from the Free Trade Zone. Still, 1 or 2 nights here, combined with a day tour or scuba-diving trip in Portobelo, is enjoyable, but if you're not happy just hanging by the pool, more than 2 nights might be too much. The food here is quite good, but there is only one restaurant. The resort sells packages that include meals, but do a price comparison because their nightly rate (which includes breakfast) coupled with ordering meals a la carte can be substantially cheaper. Also, skip the Duty Free Trade Zone shopping tour, which is overrated.

Gatún Lake, Colón. ✆ **470-1100,** or 888/956-3542 in the U.S. www.solmelia.com. 310 units. $90 double; $140 suite. AE, MC, V. **Amenities:** Restaurant; 2 bars; outdoor pool; fitness center; sports equipment; kayaks; tours; canopy zip line; kids' activities; concierge; business center; 24-hr. room service; massage; babysitting; laundry service. *In room:* A/C, TV, dataport, minibar, hair dryer, safe.

4 Portobelo 🌟🌟

99km (62 miles) from Panama City; 43km (27 miles) from Colón

Portobelo is a modest seaside village made of clapboard homes built around and among the ruins of what was one of Spain's richest and liveliest ports from the mid–16th to

---

Fun Fact **The London–Panama Connection**

Portobelo was named "Puerto Bello" (Beautiful Port) by Christopher Columbus on his first visit here in 1502, a name that gradually became known as Portobelo. Known for its 3-month-long, grand and lively trade fairs and the hordes of gold and silver that flowed through here, Portobelo was irresistible to pirates. But it's a battle led by British Adm. Edward Vernon in 1739 for which the town is most remembered. Vernon attacked Portobelo during the War of Jenkins' Ear, a 9-year British war against the Spanish, and his victory resulted in the placement of "Portobello" as a commemorative name for a well-known farm in what is now the Notting Hill neighborhood of London. The road leading to the farm was called Portobello Road—today this road is itself internationally famous for its own lively market. Vernon is also associated with the term "grog," which was his moniker and therefore the name his sailors gave to the watered-down rum he served them to avoid drunkenness.

---

early 18th century. The village, squeezed tightly between thick jungle and the blue Caribbean Sea, is less than an hour from Colón, and it's a very popular destination on the Central Caribbean Coast for day excursions. You wouldn't know it today, but this historical site was once the scene of the famous Portobelo fairs that took place for 2 centuries, when Spain's plundered gold and silver from South America passed through here. Around Portobelo are well-preserved forts that are splendid examples of 17th- and 18th-century military architecture, as well as a recently restored Customs House. The ruins, along with Fort San Lorenzo (see above), were named World Heritage Sites by UNESCO in 1980.

Portobelo's residents call themselves *congos,* and are descendants of African slaves brought here during the Spanish colonial era; they are culturally different from the Afro-Caribbeans in Colón. The *congos* possess a rich folkloric expression that arose from slavery and African traditions and religion fused with Catholicism, and which is now best expressed by their colorful costumes and devil masks that they don during festivals such as Carnaval and the famous **Black Christ Festival** on October 21 (see "Iglesia de San Felipe & the Black Christ," below).

Sailors and yachties like to anchor in the calm Portobelo bay, and you'll see lots of boats bobbing in the turquoise sea. There is decent scuba diving and snorkeling around here, too. Portobelo is not exceedingly dangerous, but it is an economically depressed town with run-down homes and a worn-out central plaza, and there's always a lot of people hanging around without much to do. If you use common sense and don't flash expensive equipment or money, you shouldn't have any problems.

ESSENTIALS

GETTING THERE & DEPARTING   By Car   Drivers from Panama City should take the Corredor Norte, a modern toll road that ends at Chilibre; from here head right then turn left on the Transístmica Highway and drive about 40km (25 miles) to the town of Sabanitas. Keep your eyes open for El Rey supermarket and turn right on the road just past it. Follow the signs for Portobelo, located about 33km (20 miles) from Sabanitas.

By Bus   Buses from Panama City leave from the Albrook Terminal. You'll want a bus to Sabanitas, or a bus to Colón that stops in Sabanitas (verify this with the driver; the cost is $2), and to transfer at the El Rey supermarket on the highway for a bus to Portobelo ($1.25). To get back to Panama City, you'll need to get a bus to Sabanitas, cross the highway, and flag down a bus headed to Panama City. Buses to and from Colón leave every half-hour.

By Taxi   Taxis from Colón to Portobelo average $20 to $25 for the one-way trip, and $20 per hour thereafter (in the event that you'd like the driver to wait while you tour the ruins).

VISITOR INFORMATION   There is an IPAT visitor center located a half-block from the plaza and in front of the Municipal office (© 448-2200; daily 8:30am–4:30pm). Besides a small display of Congo festival costumes and paintings, there is little information on hand, and the staff speaks limited English. Pick up a copy of the free "Costa Arriba y Conjunto Monumental de Portobelo" map here (also available at the Customs House museum).

See "Colón," earlier in this chapter, for tour operators.

WHAT TO SEE & DO
FORT RUINS & THE CUSTOMS HOUSE ☆☆

If you're a history buff, plan on spending about 2 hours touring the ruins and the Custom House—more if you take a water taxi to the ruins at Fuerte San Fernando across the bay. You'll only need an hour if you plan to just walk around a bit and snap a few photos. Portobelo is tiny enough to see all sites on foot.

Entering town, the first site you'll encounter on your left-hand side is the **Batería Santiago,** a defensive fort built after the famous raid on Portobelo by the British Admiral Edward Vernon in 1739. The fort is remarkably well preserved, with rusty cannons, ramps, and a sentry box. Across the road is a short uphill path to **Casa Fuerte Santiago,** which overlooked the bay and acted as a depository for ammunition.

Farther into town is **Castillo Santiago de la Gloria,** built in 1600 but destroyed after an attack by Henry Morgan, before he sacked Panama City. The fort was rebuilt, but attacked again by Vernon; after this the fort was left in ruins and abandoned. From here you can take a water taxi at the pier ($2.50) to **Fuerte San Fernando,** which really isn't much of a fort any longer because much of the fort's stone was taken and used for construction of the canal by the U.S. Leading up from the Castillo is another short, uphill hike to **Mirador el Perú,** a lookout offering a lofty view of the Portobelo bay.

The **Real Aduana de Portobelo (Customs House),** located in front of the *parque* (plaza) in the center of town, is a highlight here in Portobelo. There is also a small museum here (no phone; daily 8am–4pm). This fine old building is the restored version of what was known as the "counting house" during the Spanish colonial days, so-named for the gold and silver that was counted, registered, and distributed here. For 1 century, a third of all the gold in the world passed through this spot. The Spanish built the Customs House in 1630, but it was damaged in both 1744 (by a cannon) and 1882 (by an earthquake). The museum will hold your attention for about 15 minutes—there's really nothing much to see in the main section except a jumbled collection of clipped articles about Portobelo, cannonballs, coin collections, and other items that are not very representative of the Spanish colonial days. A free map of Portobelo is available here, however. The museum has a short informational video, in Spanish and English, for $1 per person. On the second floor is a Spanish-only folkloric display.

The best-preserved fort in town is **Fuerte San Jerónimo,** next to the Customs House. Like the other forts of Portobelo, this one, originally built in 1664, was attacked by Vernon and rebuilt using a more streamlined design.

IGLESIA DE SAN FELIPE ⨍ & THE BLACK CHRIST

One of the most curious churches in Panama is **Iglesia de San Felipe,** home to the famous "Black Christ" statue and the source of Portobelo's largest yearly festival, on October 21. Legend has it that a ship headed to Cartagena, Colombia, left the statue behind in Portobelo either to lighten its load or because the crew believed that the statue was causing them bad luck. Later, Portobelo residents prayed to the statue to spare them from a cholera epidemic—and indeed they were spared. Praying to the statue has become so widespread that every year pilgrims don ornate purple robes and walk to San Felipe Church, sometimes from as far away as Sabanitas and beyond, either to give thanks or pray for something they need in their lives. It's a spectacle, and not always as religious as you might suspect, with music and drinking thrown into the mix. The best way to see this festival is with a guided tour, because parking is impossible and you might need someone to get you out after a long day.

Behind San Felipe Church is **Iglesia de San Juan,** the original hospital of Portobelo that eventually became a church. Now it holds a small **museum** that displays dozens of the purple robes used by pilgrims during the Black Christ Festival. It's open daily from 8:30am to about 3:30pm.

ADVENTURE ACTIVITIES
SCUBA DIVING & SNORKELING

The waters off Portobelo do not provide divers with the rich diversity of marine life found in places such as Coiba in the Chiriquí Gulf, but diving is one of the main draws to this area beyond touring the ruins in town. One of the most well-respected dive operators, **Panama Divers** (② 314-0817 or 6613-4405; www.panamadivers.com), has a base next to the Coco Plum Cabañas for day trips, multiday trips, and PADI instruction courses. The good news about diving off the Central Caribbean Coast is that it is surprisingly accessible, even if you're lodging in Panama City; the bad news is that visibility is poor when the sea gets churned up (Dec–Feb), or when it rains. On a good day, expect visibility depths of about 40m (131 ft.). Popular dive spots include Drake's Island, with sponges in a rainbow of colors, Buffet Reef, and Iron Castle. Divers can also visit a submerged plane. Panama Divers is a competent, fully licensed, and insured operation with professional guides and travel assistance.

Farther away from Portobelo, heading east toward the San Blas Archipelago, is the relatively undiscovered island **Escribano,** with superb diving opportunities—"Discovery Channel" stuff, as they like to say. Dives in this region require lodging at the Coral Lodge (see "Isla Grande," below), or at Panama Divers' soon-to-be-constructed marina next to the Coral Lodge, which is slated for opening in late 2007. Contact them for more information, or for custom packages. Panama Divers includes a tour of the ruins at Portobelo as part of their scuba excursions. For snorkeling, the best place in the area is Playa Blanca, reached by a 20-minute boat ride from the pier.

If you're just looking to rent snorkeling or diving equipment, try **Scubaportobelo** (② 261-3841; www.scubapanama.com), located before Coco Plum. It's an a la carte operation whereby equipment and boat rides are charged individually. Prices are cheaper than nearby Panama Divers, with snorkel rental for $10 a day and diving-gear rental for about $30 per day. Tank refills are $4. They have a cafe here and a couple of basic cabins, too, for $35 to $50 a night.

BEACHES & BOAT TOURS

Local boatmen operate at the pier near the Castillo Santiago de la Gloria, ferrying passengers to the empty **Playa Blanca,** located on the coast north of Portobelo. It's one of the best beaches in the area—if you're looking for a little beach time, this is your place. The cost to get there is $10, with a two-person minimum.

LAND-BASED ACTIVITIES

An upstart tour company run by a couple of friendly locals, called **Selvaventuras** (© **442-1042** or 6625-7305; wwwgeocities.com/selvaventuras), takes visitors on hiking trips through the rainforest in neighboring Portobelo National Park, visiting the waterfall at Río Piedra, among others. They can even put together a horseback-riding trip, or any custom itinerary, but they speak limited English. A half-day trip averages $15 per person.

WHERE TO STAY & DINE

During the high season (Dec–Apr), restaurants in Portobelo are open according to the times listed in each review. Outside of high season, and sometimes even during high season when tourism is sluggish, restaurants will shut their doors around 5pm. There is only one decent place to stay here—otherwise Playa Blanca or Isla Grande are your best options.

Coco Plum Cabañas ⚔   The Coco Plum Cabañas are a congenial slice of Caribbean tranquillity tucked away on the seashore, about a 5-minute drive from Portobelo. Though independently owned, many guests who book here take part in snorkeling and diving trips with Panama Divers (see above), which has an office and a dock here. All said, it's a cute little place painted in bold, primary colors, with a hammock strung common building and an on site restaurant, Las Anclas (see below). The *"cabañas"* are simple, connecting rooms decorated with marine-themed knickknacks and stenciled art; though clean and cozy, most rooms are dark. Also, there is no hot water in the showers, and the showerhead is just a spigot jutting out of a wall. It's not luxury, but it's not a backpackers' haven, either. There are rooms for two, three, and five guests.

About 5km (3 miles) before Portobelo. © 448-2102. www.cocoplum-panama.com. 12 units. $39 single, $59 single with meals included; $50 double, $90 for double with meals included. No credit cards. **Amenities:** Restaurant; dock; on-site dive shop. *In room:* A/C, TV, no hot water.

Tesoro del Caribe ⚔⚔   This American-owned secluded lodge is about 20 minutes by boat from Portobelo, tucked away in an idyllic cove and facing a sandy beach at Playa Blanca. You won't have the convenience of being in town, but the hotel will take you there or to visit the ruins if you'd like. It's so relaxing here that you probably won't want to go anywhere, though. The perk here is direct access to a fine beach, where you can swim or snorkel around a fair amount of coral not too far from shore. There's no road to get here, which lends a sense of exclusivity to the place. However, the feel of the Tesoro del Caribe is tropical-beach casual: simple guest rooms with beds draped with mosquito nets, a pleasant open-air common area strung with hammocks, and solar-powered ceiling fans. There are seven rooms, three of which are in their own building, away from the common area, with views and a kitchen. A couple would be happy here, but it's a better choice for a group of friends because meals are served family-style, and there isn't an overall sense of absolute privacy. You can bring your own food and cook, or book a room that includes meals, which are fresh and very good. Rates include snorkeling, and use of their canoes and Sunfish sailboats, as well as all beverages and round-trip transportation from Portobelo.

Playa Blanca. ℭ 6613-1558 or 6613-5749. www.tesorodelcaribe.com. 7 units. $125 per person with meals included; $75 per person without meals. No credit cards. **Amenities:** Restaurant; kitchen; canoes; Sunfish sailboats; free snorkeling gear; tours. *In room:* No phone.

Restaurante Los Cañones ☞☞ SEAFOOD   This is the best restaurant in the area for seafood. It's located a little under 6km (3½ miles) from Portobelo on the left side of the road. The restaurant sits over the water, facing a pretty cove, so guests dine while gazing out onto the sea. The highlights here are *cambombia* (conch) in coconut milk, and octopus—a very common dish in the area. Their fried snapper, or whatever's fresh on the menu and fried, is good, but not, of course, for dieters.

About 6km (3¾ miles) from Portobelo. ℭ 448-2980. Main courses $5–$10. No credit cards. Daily 11am–6pm.

Restaurant Las Anclas ☞ PANAMANIAN   Las Anclas is located on the left side of the road just before Portobelo, next to the Coco Plum Cabañas. The fun ambience comes with a cluttered, marine-kitsch decor, and they have an extensive menu. Just plan for enough time because busy or slow, it takes 20 minutes or more to be served once you order. Expect seafood stew in coconut milk, squid in pineapple and ginger, tangy ceviche, meats, and the usual dishes prepared with garlic, breaded and fried or done creole-style. Their bargain lunch is a fixed-price "tourist menu" with fried snapper, coconut rice, fried plantain *patacones,* and a salad and soft drink for $7. Las Anclas serves full breakfasts, too.

Next to the Coco Plum, about 5km (3 miles) before town. ℭ 448-2102. Main courses $5–$10. No credit cards. Daily 7:30am–7:30pm, sometimes until 8:30pm on Fri–Sat.

Restaurant La Torre ☞ PANAMANIAN/COLOMBIAN   Known for their "cheeseburgers in paradise," this friendly, Colombian-owned roadside restaurant serves sandwiches and fresh seafood, and is open principally for breakfast and lunch. Jumbo shrimp, sea bass, and a mixed seafood platter (octopus and clams) can be prepared with lemon and basil, creole-style, or battered and fried. There is also fried chicken as well as snack platters with empanadas and fried *patacones.* Wash it all down with a fresh natural juice or a *pipa,* meaning a hacked-open coconut with a straw.

Just before Portobelo, on right-hand side. ℭ 448-2039. Reservations not accepted. Main courses $6.25–$10; burgers $3. MC, V. Mon–Fri 9:30am–7pm; Sat–Sun 8am–7:30pm.

5 Isla Grande

20km (13 miles) from Portobelo; 105km (65 miles) from Panama City

Isla Grande is a Caribbean island getaway frequented by residents of Panama City because it's close enough to get to without flying. A tiny village stretches along the western shore, and there are no roads—residents get around by foot or water taxi. During high season and some weekends Isla Grande can get very festive, with drinking and loud reggae music; weekdays are often dead. The largest beach is in front of the Hotel Isla Grande, which has a day-use fee of $3 per person; otherwise you'll need to walk along the shoreline trail or hire a water taxi for a couple of bucks to take you to the beach on the north shore of the island. A short boat ride to Isla Mamey will put you on an uninhabited beach, and there are other boat tours, too, but mostly people come here just to unplug for a day or two. Altogether, Isla Grande is an idyllic place, though it's best for travelers who'd like a taste of the Caribbean but are not planning to visit other island destinations in Panama.

ESSENTIALS

GETTING THERE & DEPARTING By Car or Taxi   To get to Isla Grande, you'll want to continue past Portobelo along a pockmarked road for about 20km (13 miles) to **La Guaira,** an impoverished fishing village with two piers: one with boats to the Bananas Resort and, 2km (1¼ miles) beyond it, the pier for boats to Isla Grande. You can park at either dock, but the Isla Grande dock charges a $2-per-day fee. And upon your return, you can count on some slacker hanging around and asking for a $1 or $2 for additional "security" when you leave—and they're not nice if you decide not to pay.

There are few taxis in Portobelo to get you here, but if you find one, expect to pay around $5.

By Bus   For buses from Colón or Panama City to La Guaira, you'll need to follow the same procedure you would for Portobelo (see "Getting There & Departing" in "Portobelo," above), but catch a bus to La Guaira instead of Portobelo when transferring in Sabanitas.

By Water Taxi   The Bananas Resort includes water-taxi service to their resort for guests staying there, or for those visiting on a day pass. Boat taxis at the public pier charge $1.50 one-way to Isla Grande, or $3 per person to Bananas. (They'll sometimes charge a $10 minimum if there aren't enough people.) When the sea is rough, you might get a little wet.

FUN IN THE WATER
SCUBA DIVING & SNORKELING

Panama Divers (p. 154), based out of Portobelo, can put together a day excursion from Isla Grande (reservations required). On Isla Grande, there is the certified and locally run **Isla Grande Dive Center** (© **6501-4374;** www.buceoenpanama.com) that offers scuba diving and snorkeling, with lodging on the island or round-trip transportation from Panama City. All hotels and cabins on Isla Grande contract this company for diving and snorkeling. The Dive Center has snorkel rental, too, for $6.

BEACHES & BOATING

There is no "day tour" center with a roster of excursions and set prices; instead, you'll need to hire a local boatman and negotiate a price. If you're staying on the island, your hotel can organize a boat tour for you with a local, or in a pinch you can find a boat and driver at the main dock near Cabañas Jackson, or at the pier in La Guaira. It's best to plan ahead and reserve a time with a local boat, but on slow days you shouldn't have a problem finding a willing captain. Also, check the pier at the Hotel Isla Grande, or check with the staff there to see if they have boat trips planned.

Day boat tours usually include a zip through a mangrove swamp and a visit to one of the offshore islands such as **Mamey Island,** a private island up for sale but still open to day visitors. There is a fine white-sand beach here with good snorkeling opportunities, but you'll need to bring your own gear. This trip can range between $35 and $50, depending on the amount of time you'd like to stay on the beach (in the event that they drop you off and pick you up later).

WHERE TO STAY & DINE

Hotels and cabins on Isla Grande fill during weekends and the high season, from late November to early April. Outside of these dates, it is difficult to find a restaurant that is open, so stick with the hotels mentioned below, or try **Villa Ensueño** (© **448-2964**), or the reggae bar **Club Punta Proa** (no phone) in the village, both of which serve midrange Panamanian fare (seafood or chicken) with coconut rice, beans, and plantains. The **Candy Rose** (© 448-2947) has simple meals and dining on a seafront deck.

Bananas Resort 🐾🐾 *Kids*   Located on a secluded shore of Isla Grande, this "boutique" resort is not luxurious, but it is the nicest place on the island. Bananas is a pint-size resort backed by steep jungle, with a thin strip of beach and rooms that have oceanfront balconies. There are enough activities (even if it's just lounging by the pool) for the place to be equally appealing to families and couples. The resort recently added two cabinlike stand-alone units near the water; each cabin houses two attractive suites that have a kitchenette. The rest of the guest rooms at the resort are within cheery, lemon-yellow A-frame units set slightly above the pool and activities area. Each has three spacious rooms with two double beds, and the two on the ground floor interconnect, if necessary. If you're a couple, choose the top floor, which provides the most privacy. The resort opened in 1998, but they haven't been scrupulous about upkeep on these guest rooms: they're comfortable, but a tad worn. The grounds, however, are meticulously groomed, and there are a nice pool, open-air restaurant and bar, volleyball court, sports gear, and day excursions (the latter for an additional cost). Swimming conditions at the narrow beach are less than ideal owing to lots of rock and coral, and sometimes the sea here can be too choppy. If you're traveling with a group, consider renting their private villa 5 minutes away, with its own pool, kitchen, terrace and outdoor dining area, and four rooms. The nightly price is $300 for one to six guests, less if you stay 2 or more nights. All rates include boat transportation, lodging, and breakfast, with meals and excursions ordered a la carte. Transportation from Panama City is once a day in the morning, for $20 per person, with a minimum of four passengers. There is a heliport here if you feel like jetting in VIP-style. A single steep trail leads to the village on the other side of the island; otherwise, you'll need a $3 water taxi.

Bananas offers a **day pass** to visit the resort and use their pool and facilities; the cost is $35 per person, and includes round-trip boat transportation, lunch, and a cocktail. This also means that weekends are busier here, so think about visiting on a weekday. In general, service is friendly but lackadaisical, and the food is hit-or-miss (usually depending on what's in season), but it's still the best on the island. Their collection of small bird cages with ratty macaws and toucans is a little unsettling to eco-conscious travelers.

Isla Grande. © 263-9510. www.bananasresort.com. 28 units. $99 double; $119 on Saturday; $129 suite. AE, MC, V. **Amenities:** Restaurant; bar; outdoor pool; volleyball court; kayaks; free snorkeling gear; kids' games; excursions. *In room:* A/C, TV, hair dryer, safe, no phone.

Hotel Isla Grande *Kids*   The only thing you can really say about the Hotel Isla Grande is that it fronts a perfect half-moon beach with golden sand and a calm-water swimming area that's ideal for kids. The rest of the property looks as if the owners had ideas that were bigger than their funding. There is a drab, motel-like unit with guest rooms adorned with mismatched wallpaper and dingy bathrooms, and a second such building that appears to be stalled in the middle of construction—with no end date in sight. Your best bet here is one of the candy-colored cabins on the beach that cost

$50 per night for four guests from Monday to Thursday, and $60 Friday through Sunday. They're nothing special, but they're clean, and open straight onto the sand. Given the swimming area here, and the kids' playground, the hotel receives a lot of Panamanian families, but really the place seems better suited for a bunch of guys who aren't too picky and just want to kick back with a cooler of beer. Also, if you're looking for anonymity, this is your spot because no one on the staff will ever pay you any attention. An open-air, cantina-style restaurant here serves simple meals.

Isla Grande. Ⓒ 448-2019 (hotel) or 225-2798 (Panama City). 55 units. $35 double Sun–Thurs; $50 double Fri–Sat. MC, V. **Amenities:** Restaurant; kayaks; kids' playground; excursions. *In room:* A/C, no phone.

Sister Moon Hotel ⓖ   Perched on a hilly slope and surrounded by arching palms, the Sister Moon is on a more secluded area of the island, about a 20-minute walk from the village. It's a funky, castaway-style place ideal for easygoing travelers who don't need much more than a bed, a hammock, and the sound of the crashing sea. Guest rooms are divided into cabin units. The quality of guest rooms here varies, but all are stripped-down, with stone floors, a basic bed, and a private bathroom. There are also bunk-bed units for backpackers who don't mind sharing. Their Rum Bar is popular, drawing surfers in occasionally after they've finished riding the waves that front the hotel—keep in mind that the surf is pretty loud here most of the time. The property has places to just lounge around: on a terrace over the sea or beside their compact pool. There are never a lot of people here to share the place with so you have a sense of freedom. The boat ride here is $2.50 per person, doubled in the evening. Snorkeling gear is not for rent, so you'll need to bring your own. The hotel is a 2- to 3-minute walk from the pier.

Isla Grande. Ⓒ 226-9861. www.hotelsistermoon.com. 14 units. $55 double; $74 high season (high-season price includes dinner). MC, V. **Amenities:** Restaurant; bar; outdoor swimming pool; sun deck; pool table; tour desk. *In room:* No phone.

A LUXURY ECOLODGE EAST OF ISLA GRANDE

Coral Lodge ⓖⓖⓖ *Moments*   Elegant yet relaxed, remote yet close to a wealth of outdoor activities, this brand-new player on the boutique eco-resort scene gets it right. The lodge sits midway between Isla Grande and the San Blas Archipelago, spread around a tiny, dreamy inlet ringed with white sand and backed by coconut palms and thick jungle. The American-Peruvian owner, who sold his previous lodge in Costa Rica to build his dream lodge here, has built a model of resort development, protecting the environment and working with local people while providing guests with all the creature comforts and an unforgettable experience. Call it "sustainable luxury." The units are handsome, individual thatched-hut *casitas* (little houses) strung over turquoise water and a coral bed, meaning you can snorkel just outside your door. Like the rest of the buildings here, they are painted in neutral tones of chocolate and ecru, and decorated with Indonesian furnishings and art. The rooms feature fine bedding, walk-in showers, and a large, in-bedroom whirlpool tub. Glass sliding doors open onto a small deck with a hammock and chaise longue. This is one of the few ecolodges with air-conditioning, which is greatly appreciated in the Caribbean heat. On the other side of the inlet, about a 5-minute walk from the cabins, is an indoor fine-dining restaurant fronted by an outdoor infinity pool; there is also an over-the-water, open-air dining area for lunch or afternoon cocktails. The cuisine here is to die for, and the staff truly makes you feel at home.

Of course, it's not cheap, and getting here is part of the adventure. You must fly by small plane into Porvenir, in the San Blas Islands, then take a powerboat for 45 minutes to the lodge. Alternatively, there is a 40-minute boat ride east from the lodge to the village Miramar, where you can return to (or arrive from) Panama City, 2½ hours away. Rates include all meals and use of their kayaks and snorkeling equipment; however, transportation to the lodge (an additional $360 for two, round-trip) and diving excursions—provided by the highly reputable Panama Divers—are an additional cost.

Incidentally, this is a diver's paradise; just 4.8km (3 miles) away is a relatively unexplored reef called Baja Escribano, with pristine coral, sponges, and marine life such as manta rays and nurse sharks. Considering that diving is prohibited in nearby San Blas, the Coral Lodge (located within the Colón Province) holds an edge over that destination—but they'll take you snorkeling in the San Blas if you want. Note that the Coral Lodge does not accept children under 12.

Colón Province, 45 min. by boat from Miramar. ℂ 317-6754. www.corallodge.com. 6 units. $215 per person, based on double occupancy. AE, MC, V. **Amenities:** 2 restaurants; bar; outdoor pool; diving excursions; cultural excursions in San Blas; kayaks; free snorkeling gear. *In room:* A/C, whirlpool tub, no phone.

6 Isla Taboga ★★

19km (12 miles) from Panama City, in the Bay of Panama

Isla Taboga, known as the "Island of Flowers" for its lush bougainvillea, hibiscus, and jasmine, isn't a destination with adventurous offerings; instead, it's a place to escape the streets of Panama City, enjoy the fresh sea breeze, get a little beach time in, and enjoy a lazy lunch. The island is only 19km (12 miles) off the coast, and the ferry ride here provides passengers with a dazzling view of Panama City and ships waiting to transit the canal. The drowsy, charming village here is a nice place to stroll; you'll find a couple of restaurants and hotels, but really this is a very low-key excursion and most visitors only stay for the day. If your Panama travel plans include a beach destination such as Bocas or the San Blas Peninsula, skip Isla Taboga. But if you've got a lot of time in Panama City and are looking for a quick excursion, this is a do-it-yourself trip that doesn't require a tour operator or a lot of advance planning—just show up at the ferry dock and head over.

Isla Taboga is one of the most important historical sites in Panama. The village was founded in 1524, and later conquistador Francisco Pizarro pushed off from here on his way to conquer Peru. During the 17th century, the island became the haunt of pirates in search of treasure, and in the 19th century it was a port for the Pacific Steamship Navigation Company, which brought over hundreds of Irish, whose Anglo-Saxon names can be seen on gravestones here. The United States even used Isla Taboga as training ground for military practice during World War II. Today the village is home to about 1,000 residents.

ESSENTIALS

GETTING THERE & AROUND   Ferry service to Isla Taboga is provided by **Barcos Calypso Queen** (ℂ 314-1730), which leaves from the Isla Naos pier on the Amador Causeway, next to the Smithsonian's Centro de Exhibiciones. From Panama City to Isla Taboga, the ferry goes Monday, Wednesday, and Friday at 8:30am and 3:30pm; Tuesday and Thursday at 8:30am only; and Saturday, Sunday, and holidays at 8am, 10:30am, and 4pm. Service from Isla Taboga to Panama City is Monday, Wednesday, and Friday at 9:30am and 4:30pm; Tuesday and Thursday at 4:30pm;

and Saturday, Sunday, and holidays at 9am, 3pm, and 5pm. The cost is $10 adults, $7 children 12 and under, and $7 seniors. Arrive about 30 minutes to 1 hour before departure. There is a cafe at the dock.

You'll get around Isla Taboga primarily on walking paths. There are also a few roads for the three service vehicles on the island. (They occasionally double as taxis.) Nearly everyone here walks, but a few residents get around by golf cart.

WHAT TO SEE & DO

There's not much to do here other than amble around the little village and snap photos. When you arrive, head left from the pier into the village—the streets are hilly so you'll do a lot of walking up and down. At the town center is **Iglesia San Pedro,** the second-oldest Spanish colonial church in the Western Hemisphere. In the plaza, locals meet to chat and play games. If you're okay with walking, continue southeast toward Cerro de las Cruces, and continue up a moderate path to a lookout point that offers a sweeping view of the sea and other islands in the area. The west side of the island is the **Taboga Wildlife Refuge** that protects nesting brown pelicans, but it's mostly off-limits.

Beaches here aren't secluded and can get a little busy on weekends, but they offer soft sand and blue water. The best beach here is **Playa Restinga,** in front of the old Hotel Taboga (closed), going past the pier after the end of town. Like all beaches on the island, this beach is free; the hotels mentioned below will either rent snorkel gear or put you in touch with someone who does. Playa Honda is the beach that fronts the village.

WHERE TO STAY & DINE

The best food in town is at **Vereda Tropical Hotel**'s restaurant (see below), and there is a cafeteria at **Hotel Taboga.** For inexpensive but good Panamanian-style fare in an open-air setting, try **Donde Pope Si Hay** (no phone), open Thursday to Sunday. Expect to find seafood and meats served with rice and *patacones* for about $3.50 to $8. **Restaurante Chu** serves greasy Chinese food for about $4 to $8 a dish.

Cerrito Tropical ⟨ Opened in 2005, the Cerrito Tropical has delightful apartments with kitchenettes for independent travelers or for long-term stays. Like the Vereda (below), the property sits up on a hillside, offering sea views from two of the apartments, the Palma and the Mango (two-bedroom and three-bedroom units, respectively). The other apartments have views of the forest and mango trees, and all rooms open onto a balcony with a hammock. Accommodations are very clean and tidy, and the owners of the Cerrito Tropical, a couple from Canada and the Dutch Caribbean, are warm and friendly. The garden features an open-air patio. Four of the Cerrito's units are apartments, although they're run more like a B&B, with breakfast and maid service. These are usually rented weekly, but you can ask about shorter stays. A one-bedroom unit can be rented by the day. Depending on the season, rates can drop to $55 per night.

Isla Taboga. ⟨ **6489-0074.** www.cerritotropicalpanama.com. 5 units. $385 (1-bedroom apt, weekly rate); $78 double (nightly). MC, V. *In room:* A/C, free Wi-Fi, no phone.

Kool Hostel If you just need a cheap place to stay and aren't too fussy, try this spot. The Kool Hostel has three rooms that are shared accommodations, with shared bathrooms (divided by sexes), and it's run by "Che" the Argentine. If you are here during a slow period, you might not have to share with many travelers, or share at all. There's a communal kitchen, book exchange, and bicycle and snorkel-gear rental. You'll find this place by heading left from the pier—but Che is usually waiting at the pier.

Isla Taboga. ✆ **690-2545.** luisveron@hotmail.com. 3 units. $10 per person. No credit cards. **Amenities:** Communal kitchen; snorkeling gear rental; bike rental. *In room:* No phone.

Vereda Tropical Hotel ✯✯✯ *(Finds)*   This gorgeous hotel is one of the newest on the island, and it is the best lodging on Taboga. Perched high on a hill and overlooking Playa Honda near the pier, the Vereda Tropical has stunning views of the sea. (You can even make out Panama City from here.) The decor leans toward Mexican-style, with bold colors, ceramic tile floors, arched doorways, and swirling iron balustrades; an atrium lights the interior patio and its fountain. Rooms are decorated differently; some open onto balconies. They all are comfy and have good beds. The antiquity of the building means rooms have wonderful, high ceilings. The **Pelicanos Bar** is here, and has a touch of marine kitsch, but the big bonus is the **restaurant**—one of the best in the Panama Province. The view from their open-air veranda is dynamite. They serve tasty, fusion-style cuisine and wonderfully refreshing fruit drinks. Try their Vereda Tropical cocktail with passion fruit juice and *seco*. The menu has pastas, pizzas, and fresh seafood, though you might want to just come here to sip a drink and enjoy the view.

Isla Taboga. ✆ **250-2154.** www.veredatropicalhotel.com. 12 units. $75 double with sea view; $65 double with town view. MC, V. **Amenities:** Restaurant; bar; laundry; Internet desk. *In room:* TV, no phone.

7 Archipiélago de las Perlas

64km (40 miles) S of Panama City, in the Pacific Ocean

Historically famous for its pearls and more recently as the island Shangri-La for television's *Survivor* series in 2003 and 2006, the Archipiélago de las Perlas (Pearl Islands) is nevertheless an unsung beach destination that has taken a back seat to places such as Bocas del Toro. Perhaps residents have done a bad job promoting the Pearl Islands as a getaway destination—or perhaps keeping the masses at bay has always been the goal. Whatever the reason, the archipelago deserves a look. It's surprisingly close to Panama City, just 20 minutes by small plane. The rich aquatic life here offers world-class snorkeling, and even manta rays and schools of tropical fish can be seen by just popping on a mask and walking out from the beach. The cerulean sea laps at picture-postcard white- and golden-sand beaches backed by a forest canopy. And the big-game sport fishing around the islands is revered by fishers around the world. Need I say more?

The archipelago is composed of more than 200 islands and islets, the majority of which are unnamed and uninhabited. The most developed of the islands is Isla Contadora, with a full range of amenities including hotels and B&Bs, restaurants, tour companies, and daily flights. Isla San José is privately owned and home to one luxury resort, the Hacienda del Mar, but that's it. There are plans for a hotel on Isla del Rey, the largest island in the archipelago and the site of a forthcoming residential development. Beyond these islands there is nowhere else to stay in the archipelago, though small islands and islets can be visited as part of a day trip.

Tip: Here in the Pearl Islands, the weather is drier than in the rest of Panama, meaning that low season (May–Dec) can be quite enjoyable and cooler, with showers lasting an hour or so rather than an all-day downpour. Lodging rates drop during this time, and there are so few people on Isla Contadora it almost feels deserted.

ISLA CONTADORA

Isla Contadora is a relatively tiny island with a dozen white-sand beaches including Panama's only nude beach, Playa Suecas. The island harbors a reputation as the exclusive playground for the Panamanian elite and international figures such as Christian Dior, Julio Iglesias, and the deposed Shah of Iran, all of whom constructed palatial mansions here during the past 50 years. Isla Contadora once offered only a couple of funky hotels, but now several attractive and affordable B&Bs have opened their doors, providing comfortable lodging and services to more demanding travelers. Still, those seeking five-star luxury will want to head straight to **Hacienda del Mar** (see "Isla San José," below).

Isla Contadora is so-named because of its historical role as the "counting house," a colonial-era distribution center that recorded and classified pearls before they were shipped to Spain. African slaves were brought to Isla Contadora to harvest pearls, and their descendants still work here, although most cannot afford to live on Isla Contadora and instead live on neighboring Isla Saboga, a 10-minute ferry ride away.

The island's center of activity is at the end of the airport runway on the northeastern side of the island; here you'll find public telephones, a few restaurants and bars, grocery stores, and a basic medical clinic (© **250-4209**). Walk around to the back if no one answers the door. At press time, an Internet cafe was in the works, with plans to open next to the dive center across from the airstrip; there's also Internet service inside Restaurant Sagitario. The island doesn't have a post office, and although credit cards are accepted at hotels, there are no ATMs—so you'll want to bring enough cash to cover expenses. No need to pack your snazziest outfits, as the look here is beach casual.

ESSENTIALS

GETTING THERE & DEPARTING   By Plane   Aeroperlas (© **351-7500;** www.aeroperlas.com) has two daily flights (Mon–Sat) to Isla Contadora leaving Panama City at 8:45am and 5:10pm; return flights leave at 9:15am and 5:40pm. On Sundays, Aeroperlas offers four flights from Isla Contadora to Panama City, at 9:15am, 3:40pm, 4:40pm, and 5:40pm; from Panama City flights are at 8:45am, 3:10pm, 4:10pm, and 5:10pm. **Air Panama** (© **316-9000;** www.flyairpanama.com) offers flights Monday through Saturday departing at 9:30am, and an additional flight on Friday and one flight on Sunday at 4:30pm; their return flights are Monday through Saturday at 10am, and an additional flight on Friday and one on Sunday at 5pm. Both airlines charge $30 one-way.

GETTING AROUND   Isla Contadora is a compact island, and though most roads are paved there are few vehicles—and no taxis—on the island. People get around by walking, by bicycle or, more popularly, by ATV or golf cart. Motorized transportation is expensive, more than $40 a day. Ask your hotel about a multiple-day discount for a golf cart, or if they provide drop-off and pickup service around town. Most visitors get a kick out of coasting the island on a cart, searching out the perfect beach or ogling the stately vacation homes that line the streets. If your hotel doesn't have a vehicle for rent, **Bill Carney** (© **6513-9064;** bill@perlareal.com) at the Perla Real Inn has a fleet of **golf carts** he rents out for $52 for 24 hours. **Waterland Adventures** (© **6673-3020;** mozartlee@cableonda.net) has 4WD **ATVs** for rent for about $30 a day.

WHAT TO SEE & DO

BEACHES   The principal activity on Isla Contadora is spending sun-drenched days lounging on the beach, reading a book, and cooling off with a dip in the turquoise sea.

There are no strong riptides and powerful waves here so swimming is safe, even for kids. Surfers, however, should look elsewhere. There are 13 beaches on the island, all perfectly lovely and virtually empty every day except for weekends and holidays. Panama's sole nude beach, **Playa Suecas (Swedish Beach)**, is located on Isla Contadora and can be reached by taking the dirt road at the end of **Playa Larga (Long Beach)**, the strip of beach that fronts the Hotel Contadora Resort. This beach, like its neighbor, **Playa Galeón,** is convenient for its proximity to restaurants and shops. Both beaches are also recommended for snorkeling, and there are outfitters here that rent snorkel equipment, jet skis, and other marine toys. There are also a couple of beachfront bars. **Playa Ejecutiva** is a pretty beach on a tiny cove on the north side of the island, and **Playa Cacique** (often referred to as "Playa Hawaii") is another good option for solitude and beautiful tropical surroundings. During the high season, you'll find the fewest people on Playa Suecas.

Beyond the beaches at Isla Contadora, the region is replete with uninhabited islands with isolated and heavenly beaches—those seeking to really get away from other people will find this a tantalizing option. You can visit other islands either by hiring a local boatman or taking part in a half-day or full-day excursion. **Isla Chapera** has a couple of empty beaches that are surrounded with a rich variety and abundance of marine life that provides for some of the best snorkeling in the area, and it's located straight across from Playa Cacique, about a 10-minute boat ride away. A local boatman can take you here in a wooden *cayuco* for about $20 per hour (if he waits for you), or about $40 if you want drop-off and pickup; the cost depends on the fluctuating price of gas. Bring a picnic lunch and beverages because there are no stores or restaurants here. Local boatmen can be found at the beach at Punta Galeón. For organized excursions and charter-boat rentals, see "Snorkeling," below. Also, check out the Hotel Contadora Resort (see below) and their "day pass."

DIVING   **Coral Dreams (© 6603-2944;** www.coral-dreams.com), at the airport runway, is Isla Contadora's only full-fledged scuba operation, run by a friendly young Argentine couple. Dives take place around the island and never exceed 18m (60 ft.), with visibilities of 4.5 to 9.1m (15–30 ft.) of mostly sponges, some brain and fan coral, and an abundance of marine life. Two-tank dives cost $75 for certified divers. Coral Dreams also offers course instruction, including their intensive Discover Scuba course ($100), which lasts 1½ days and is for beginners who are short on time or who just want a taste of the diving experience; there's also a 4- to 5-day course for full scuba certification ($300). Coral Dreams recently purchased a more luxurious 15-passenger pleasure boat for excursions; the cost is $800 total and includes food and equipment. They also offer half-day snorkeling excursions around the area for $20 per person, and snorkel-equipment rental for $10 per day.

FISHING   The Pearl Islands are legendary for deep-sea fishing. **Panama Yacht Tours** offers fishing trips to the Pearl Islands (p. 73), or there is a local outfit called **Las Perlas Fishing & Snorkeling** (see "Snorkeling," below). They have an 11m (36-ft.) Bowl-Bimini Top fishing boat with a twin 200-horsepower engine and capacity for up to 14 anglers; all necessary gear (rods and spears) to reel in monster fish such as marlin, tuna, amberjack, and barracuda is included. The cost varies depending on the season and the escalating price of gas, but expect to pay from $125 to $140 per hour (minimum 2 hr.). Their 7.9m (26-ft.) boat with 115 horsepower is good for 3 to 10 anglers, and costs $50 to $65 per hour (minimum 2 hr.; reservations required). To get to the good stuff, you'll need at least a half-day outing that can get you farther south and into deep waters. If you just want to get out and cast a line for an hour or so, negotiate with local boatmen at Punta Galeón beach; they often have a few beat-up poles lying around and charge lower rates. *Tip:* If you've caught fish but don't have a kitchen, the restaurants at Villa Romántica and El Suizo will prepare your fish for you and your friends at a negotiated price.

ATVs & JET SKIS   The Argentine/Panamanian-run concession **Waterland Adventures** (© **6673-3020** or 6671-9000—ask for Mozart or Juan; mozartlee@cableonda. net) operates on Playa Larga in front of the Hotel Contadora, with jet skis, boat rentals, and ATV rentals for exploring the island. Again, the soaring cost of gas determines the price, but generally, prices are: jet skis $85 for 1 hour, $45 for a half-hour, $25 for 15 minutes; 4WD ATVs cost $30 an hour—negotiate a price if renting for several hours.

GLASSBOTTOM BOAT   Coral Dreams (see above) has a glass-bottom boat excursion for $15 per person (minimum four people). The trip lasts 2 to 3 hours and circumnavigates the island, passing over reefs and schools of fish, and stopping for a quick snorkeling session. This is an ideal option for travelers who don't want to spend much, if any, time in the water. The cost is $15 per person, and includes snorkel equipment.

SHOPPING FOR PEARLS   **Casaya Island** is home to a very humble village with no electricity, and residents collect and sell pearls to visitors from their homes. There are no "stores" here; typically, when residents see a tourist walking by, they'll pop out with their glass jars and matchboxes that they use to store loose pearls, which are teeny tiny, irregularly shaped, and varying in luster, costing from $5 to $25. On Sundays, residents pour into the streets, drink a lot of warm beer (there's no electricity, remember), and hold cock fights that usually either repel or fascinate visitors. Otherwise, this is a low-key excursion, recommended more as a pleasant 1-hour boat ride to get to the Casaya, and the contact with the locals. The average cost is $40 round-trip for a maximum of four people; ask your hotel to hook you up with a boatman, or find one at the Punta Galeón dock.

SNORKELING   Isla Contadora offers outstanding snorkeling opportunities, with five coral fields encircling the island, which attract a wealth of marine life, including schools of tropical fish, white-tipped reef sharks, manta rays, and turtles. At Playa Larga, the Hotel Contadora rents snorkel gear for about $5; from here you can reach one of the best snorkeling spots on the island at Punta Verde, located at the southeastern end of Playa Larga. Other prime spots include Playa Ejecutiva and Punta Galeón.

If you're serious about snorkeling, I recommend you take part in an organized excursion offered by **Las Perlas Fishing & Snorkeling** (© **6689-4916** or 6605-5057; teremarco 2004@yahoo.it), run by an Italian couple, Teresa and Marco, who visit neighboring islands aboard their 7.9m (26-ft.) fiberglass boat. Charter-boat rentals that include snorkeling gear cost $50 to $60 per hour (maximum eight people). Scheduled excursions from 9:30am to 1pm cost $35 for adults, $15 for kids under 12 (minimum 2 persons, maximum 12; price includes gear). The snorkeling excursion visits the idyllic islands Chapera, Mogo Mogo, and Boyarena, the latter of which is a white-sand atoll with superb snorkeling opportunities. The couple also offer a 2-hour marine **bird-watching** tour (2–4pm; cost is $25 adults, $12 kids 6–12, free for kids under 6) to the islands of Bartolomé, Pacheca, and Pachequilla, with snorkeling included. Coral

Dreams rents quality snorkel gear for $10 a day, and they offer similar snorkeling and bird-watching trips around the area for $20 per person (see "Diving," above).

WHERE TO STAY & DINE

A slow-moving (some would say stagnant) tourism economy means many hotel owners are willing to drop their prices on weekdays and during the low season. The price for a weeklong stay or longer can also be negotiated. Restaurants on the island are expensive, and most do not serve memorable meals. If you want something cheap, try Restaurante Sagitario (see below); or try the little joint that adjoins the **minimarket Duty Free**—their simple *comida corriente* costs about $2 to $3.

Casa del Sol �   This attractive B&B is located in the home of a young German-British couple who opened their doors in 2004 with just one guest room. However, by the time this book is published, they will have finished building a new wing with four rooms, two of which will have kitchenettes and living areas. The B&B is located in a quiet residential neighborhood on the western side of the island, next to the Perla Inn and the Contadora Island Inn, and about a 20-minute walk from the airfield. The guest room within their house is a comfortable spare room with a private bathroom, and guests have access to the common living area and back patio. Best of all is the low price. The couple are on-site to cater to all guests' needs, including arranging tours and providing information about the area. There are a couple of ATVs, a golf cart ($50 per day), and bicycles ($3 per hour) for getting around. Casa del Sol is the only lodging option in the area with Wi-Fi. They'll let you use their laptop if you don't have one. Price includes a full breakfast.

Located on the western side of the island. ⓒ 250-4212. www.panama-isla-contadora.com. $50–$60 double. AE, MC, V. **Amenities:** ATV and mountain-bike rentals; Wi-Fi. *In room:* No phone.

Contadora Island Inn 🌟🌟   This delightful inn is more aptly called a B&B since it is located within a converted, low-slung home without a full-time "front desk" staff—but the charming American owners live down the road and are on call 24 hours a day, and they pop in frequently. The setting is blissfully tranquil, especially if you're staying in one of the rooms that open onto the back patio, and there are plenty of common areas that give guests enough breathing room to relax and do their own thing. The B&B is located just up the street from the Casa del Sol. Nights are so quiet that the only sound is the soft chirping of crickets. If you need absolute privacy, a hotel is a better bet for you, but most travelers enjoy the light camaraderie that can develop between guests over a delicious breakfast, which includes freshly baked bread. Because the B&B has been totally renovated, rooms are modern, with contemporary decor, ample closet space, and spotlessly clean bathrooms. Many visitors choose to spend days, sometimes weeks, here, especially if booking the Frigata Magnífico room, which is spacious and has a kitchenette and French doors that open onto a back patio. Their Guayacama room has private access. They'll rent out the entire house for $600 per night from December to April and $500 per night May to November.

Located on the western side of the island. ⓒ 6593-4509. www.contadoraislandinn.com. 5 units. $55–$60 double; $80 deluxe room with kitchenette. MC, V. **Amenities:** Full kitchen (in common area). *In room:* A/C, safe, no phone.

El Suizo (formerly Restaurante Geralds) 🌟🌟 EUROPEAN/PANAMANIAN
It's the best restaurant on Isla Contadora, but you'll pay top dollar to enjoy it. Named for its Swiss owner, El Suizo's fare is mostly European with dashes of Panamanian flavor. The restaurant is open-air and tastefully designed, with wood tables and a bar, and

is located on a sloping hill near the airport. There isn't a view, but the ambience is pleasant and refined. You can have the fresh catch of the day with a choice of sauces such as hollandaise or white wine; jumbo prawns fried in beer batter or served with pineapple juice and cucumber ragout; filet mignon with green pepper sauce; or beef stroganoff. Their fish stew is a delicious starter or light meal. During busy weekends, it's best to make dinner reservations.

Near the airport. ✆ **6560-3824.** elsuizorestaurant@gmail.com. Reservations accepted. Main courses $14–$23. MC, V. Mon–Fri 11am–3pm and 6pm–midnight; Sat–Sun 11am–midnight.

Hotel Contadora Resort 🐾 *(Kids)*   Isla Contadora's oldest hotel (built in 1974) is in dire need of a total overhaul to bring it back to its grandeur of yesteryear. As it stands, the Hotel Contadora's best assets are its lovely location fronting a white-sand beach, its proximity to the airstrip and services, two large outdoor pools, and oddball attractions such as a minizoo with spider monkeys, ocelots, and prancing peacocks—but the animals look as fatigued as the hotel's exteriors, which could use a lot of TLC. The Contadora operates as a full-service resort with all-inclusive packages that include lodging, meals, and activities. There are 354 rooms, but only 200 or so are used (presumably because the staff finds upkeep overwhelming), the best of which are closer to the southern end of Playa Larga, with direct access to the beach. There are kids' activities, snorkel and kayak rentals, tennis courts, and an open-air disco. Avoid rooms by the pool during high season, which can be loud. The best rooms here in terms of upkeep and space are the suites, which have kitchenettes and dining areas—but the weird addition of a spare double bed is an incongruous amenity to the dining area. Drab decor, chipped and peeling paint, and clean but slightly battered bathrooms are consistent in every room, as is the small patio with a hammock outside. During low season, the hotel opens just one restaurant but rotates restaurants every day. The one perk here is the **"day pass"** for visitors to Playa Larga who are not staying at the hotel, which for $15 during lunch, or $25 during dinner (until midnight), includes an all-you-can-eat-and-drink buffet and use of their swimming pools.

Playa Larga. ✆ **264-1510.** www.hotelcontadora.com. 354 units. $58 per person, based on double occupancy (includes 3 meals and activities). AE, MC, V. **Amenities:** 3 restaurants; 3 bars; outdoor disco; nightly shows (during high season); 2 outdoor pools; sports equipment; kayak rental; bicycle rental; minizoo; kids' activities; 24-hr. room service; laundry service. *In room:* A/C, TV, minibar, safe.

Perla Real Inn 🌟🌟🌟 *(Value)*   Built with great attention to detail and style, the Perla Real is a gem of a B&B. The young owners hail from California, and the style of their new inn is heavily influenced by the Spanish missions of that state. The rose-colored building has two stories that center around a small patio courtyard with a bubbling fountain. Rooms have cool white stucco walls accented with stencil art, Mexican ceramic floors and countertops, and handmade furniture and heavy wood doors held in place by hand-forged nails. There are just four doubles, and their two suites have a full kitchen for independent travelers or extended stays (room rates are discounted for stays of 7 nights or more). Each room has a comfy queen-size bed with crisp sheets, French doors, and a private entrance. The Perla Real is located next to the Casa del Sol and Contadora Island Inn in a whisper-quiet residential area, about a 20-minute walk to the air strip. Continental breakfast is included. Guests can rent golf carts for $45 per day, or $35 for 2 hours. What is surprising is the value the Perla Inn offers, with rates for a double (outside of the Christmas holiday season) ranging from $65 to $75—less than half the price of the Punta Galeón. That hotel has a sea view and a pool, but the rooms and the premises here are more tastefully appointed.

Located on the western side of the island. ℭ **250-4095** or 6513-9064. www.perlareal.com. 6 units. $65–$95 double; $90–$145 suite. MC, V. **Amenities:** Tour desk; gift shop; golf cart rental. *In room:* A/C, minibar, beach towels.

Punta Galeón Resort & Restaurant 🐚🐚   This is the best full-service hotel on the island, and one of the better options for dining on Isla Contadora. They call themselves a resort, but really Punta Galeón is just a midsize hotel that offers a lot of amenities. It's located across the street from the airstrip, which isn't as bad as it sounds; in fact, it's quite convenient and there are only a couple of small planes that land here each day. The Punta Galeón is Colombian-run, and the owners also operate the Hotel Contadora—however, because this resort opened in 2001, the grounds and facilities are still in good shape. What I like best about the Punta Galeón is that all rooms are in a one-story building spread across a bluff, and all have direct ocean views, sliding glass doors that open onto individual patios, and an elevated wooden boardwalk with benches that hug the cliff and wrap the property. There's also a cool breeze on this side of the island. Guest rooms are a little kooky, look slightly 1970s, and have the feel of a submarine with cantilevered bed platforms, whitewashed walls, and okay mattresses. Rooms are also on the small side, but the connecting patio adds space. Breakfast is included.

The hotel has two mediocre restaurants, the year-round outdoor **La Popa,** open from 7am to 11:30pm, which offers simple meals, salads, and pastas for about $6 to $14. Their weekend and high-season restaurant, **Pelicano's,** is open for dinner only from 3 to 11:30pm, and serves fish and meat with creative sauces for $10 to $16. It's the only restaurant on the island with air-conditioning.

Isla Contadora. ℭ **250-4220.** www.puntagaleon.com. 48 units. $165 double. AE, MC, V. **Amenities:** Restaurant; outdoor pool; sauna; Turkish bath; sports equipment; concierge; business center; 24-hr. room service. *In room:* A/C, TV, minibar.

Restaurante Sagitario 🐚 PANAMANIAN   Where the locals go for home cooking and cheap prices, Sagitario, sometimes called "Matilde's" after the owner, often serves fresh jumbo prawns for as low as $6. There's also sea bass, ceviche, chicken, and stewed pork. All dishes come with rice and beans. The special of the day costs $2.50.

Paseo Urraca, near the health clinic. ℭ **250-4091.** Reservations not accepted. Main courses $2–$7. No credit cards. Daily 7am–9pm (Fri–Sat until 10pm).

Villa Romántica   Seaside kitsch, 1970s love-motel renaissance, or a tribute to cheesy *telenovelas?* It's difficult to fathom what the Austrian owner of Villa Romántica envisioned when he converted his holiday home into a full-service hotel. Certainly there is no other hotel in Panama like it. Perched above Playa Cacique, a secluded beach with soft golden sand, the hotel also has a popular, breezy restaurant with sea views—it could be said that the hotel and restaurant's location is the best on the island. But it all runs downhill from there. Rooms are spacious enough, but the decor is busy and tragically mismatched—depending on your perspective, the utter tackiness of the rooms can either be fun or a little unsettling. The price is high, too, for what you get, so make sure you have an ocean view because really that's what you're paying for. The owner, a gregarious expat who is colorful enough to be known all over the islands, recently landscaped the front of the hotel with a funky little miniature golf course that undoubtedly will appeal to kids, and he offers boat rides in the area and day excursions. Service is erratic and could use some polishing.

Restaurante Romántico 🐚 serves mostly seafood with a choice of sauces such as curry pineapple or garlic, as well as meat dishes and salads. The food quality depends on who's cooking and what's brought in that day, but the view here is lovely. The restaurant is open daily from 7am to 3pm and 6 to 10pm; main courses run $10 to $20.

Playa Cacique. ℭ **250-4067**. www.villa-romantica.com. High season doubles $84–$96, $200 suite; low season doubles $96–$114, $250 suite. MC, V. **Amenities:** Restaurant; tour desk; sports equipment; miniature golf course. *In room:* A/C, TV, no phone.

ISLA SAN JOSE

This private island is quite large at 44 sq. km (17 sq. miles). It is almost totally covered with forest, save for a luxury lodge, an airstrip, and more than 97km (60 miles) of roads built by the U.S military when it held training operations and weapons testing from World War II and onward here. Today the owner of the island is the Panamanian George Novey, who is also the owner of Air Panama. The Hacienda del Mar (see below) arranges flights here for visitors on Air Panama.

WHERE TO STAY & DINE

Hacienda del Mar ✸✸✸   This is one of the most special first-class beach lodges in Panama, both because of its pristine, gorgeous surroundings and white-sand beaches, and because of its service. "Hacienda" is somewhat of a misnomer for such an intimate place; the island is private, and there are no town or other buildings in sight. Despite its remoteness, though, it's surprisingly easy to get here via a short plane ride from Panama City—making it an upscale beach resort for discriminating travelers who aren't looking to journey far from the capital. From the minute you arrive, you'll be taken care of by an attentive and welcoming staff—they'll even be there for your arrival with a rum cocktail to get your relaxation started. There is a main "clubhouse" with their restaurant, bar, spring-fed swimming pool, and games area, and 14 separate-unit bungalows that are spread around a promontory. The bungalows are best described as rustically elegant, built predominantly out of the handsome bamboolike *caña blanca*. Each bungalow has ocean views, and a balcony/deck with chaise-longue chairs to kick back on and enjoy the unsurpassed beauty of the island's surroundings. The front door opens onto flowering hibiscus and jasmine. For the price, it's best said that the rooms are not so much luxurious as they are ultra-comfortable, and like most eco-oriented lodges, there is no TV or Internet in the rooms, encouraging guests to unplug from the modern world. Junior-suite bungalows have an additional couch and a little more room, and their VIP suites have a separate living room. Each bungalow is sold as a unit, not per person. Breakfast is included, with other meals a la carte.

If you're into sport fishing, this is your place. The Hacienda has five boats that can take you shore or deep-sea fishing (they'll cook up whatever you catch back at the lodge) for wahoo, amberjack, sailfish, and tuna. This, as with most excursions here that involve a boat or guide, costs extra. There are also wildlife and bird-watching tours, ATV tours across the island, canoeing and kayaking, scuba diving and snorkeling, jet-ski tours, and mountain bike riding. Because this is a private island, wildlife has been allowed to flourish, so don't be surprised to see a collared peccary or brocket deer during your stay. The meals here are absolutely delicious—made using fresh seafood and organic fruits and vegetables—and are served on an open-air deck infused with sunset colors and candlelight. Prices below do not include airfare (an extra $125 round-trip), and reflect low to high season rates. Check their website, as they often lower prices by $50 or more if booking between Sunday and Wednesday.

Isla San Jose. ℭ **269-6634**, or 866/433-5627 in the U.S. www.haciendadelmar.com. 14 units. $235–$330 standard; $280–$393 junior suite; $318–$475 VIP suite. AE, MC, V. **Amenities:** Restaurant; 2 bars; outdoor pool; fitness center; sauna; game room; fishing excursions; sports equipment; nature excursions; rental snorkeling gear. *In room:* A/C, minibar (in some rooms), coffeemaker, no phone.

8 East of Panama City

East of Panama City, the Pan-American Highway travels toward the renowned Darién region, but not before passing the turnoff to the only road that connects the Comarca Kuna Yala and the eastern Caribbean coast with central Panama. The 37km (23-mile) road begins just past the town of El Llano, and ends at Cartí Suitupo, passing through hilly country cloaked in thick rainforest, much of it unexplored and replete with wildlife. This is one of Panama's best bird-watching spots, and sightings of monkeys are common, too. Additionally, at intervening points sweeping views provide a chance to see both the Pacific Ocean and the Caribbean Sea. There is no bus service along this route, and though the road is in good shape, it still requires a 4WD vehicle. The lodge below can provide transportation to the Kuna coast, where it is possible to hire a *cayuco* boat to go to one of the islands in the Comarca.

A NATURE LODGE IN THE WILDERNESS

Burbayar Lodge *☆☆*   Rated as one of Panama's top bird-watching lodges for both its location and its quality of guides, the Burbayar is a pared-down lodge that envelops travelers in wild, natural surroundings. The Burbayar is best described as rustic adventure—there's no electricity, for example, and showers produce only tepid water—but the accommodations and the property are so well designed that rusticity feels 100% appropriate in such lush jungle surroundings. At night, kerosene lamps add an air of romance to the lodge. The Burbayar is a good bet for travelers seeking to delve into the rainforest without having to travel far from Panama City, and the price here is cheaper than that of its counterparts near the canal. Also, this is a relatively untrammeled area of Panama where the only other people you'll see are local Kuna Indians. The lodge comprises five thatched-roof, stylish cabins built of recycled local woods and palms (each cabin has a private bathroom) and a main dining/lounge area, strung along the ridge of a hill. Neatly manicured gardens, a tiny chapel, and a mini orchid farm add to the lodge's beauty. The Burbayar is frequented by bird-watching enthusiasts, yet it is ideal for any traveler who seeks to spend his days hiking through rainforest and relaxing in the afternoon in a hammock, listing to the sounds of nature. The lodge offers treks to the Caribbean coast, and to Lake Bayano for a boat ride to an Emberá Indian community. Meals are hearty and served family-style. The service at the Burbayar is a highlight; the Spanish owner, Iñaki, is enthusiastic and friendly and he's exceptionally attentive to his guests. The staff, as well as the lodge's guides, are warm and friendly, too, making guests feel like part of a family.

El Llano. *☎* **264-1679.** www.burbayar.com. 5 units. $135 per person, all-inclusive. No credit cards. **Amenities:** Restaurant; guided tours. *In room:* No phone.

7

Central Panama

Central Panama in this guide is defined by the Panamá and Coclé provinces west of Panama City, and the Herrera and Los Santos provinces that make up what's known as the Azuero Peninsula. The Central region includes **El Valle de Antón,** a lovely mountain village located in the center of a volcanic crater; **Pacific Beaches,** with an array of lodging accommodations from rustic cabins to all-inclusive destination resorts; and the charm of Panama's cultural "heartland," the **Azuero Peninsula,** dotted with colonial villages and home to the liveliest festivals in Panama. What these destinations all have in common is that they are reached by vehicle (or bus) from Panama City, not by plane—unless of course you charter a plane to fly to Pedasí, at the tip of the peninsula. This region begs to be explored by car, so consider renting a vehicle, which will give you the freedom to plan your own itinerary and wander at your own pace, stopping off at villages and attractions that interest you and buying gastronomic treats from vendors that line the highway.

The Interamerican Highway (Pan-American Highway) and the Carretera Nacional are modern roads that are easy to drive and do not require any kind of special considerations or a 4WD. Distance is measured by markers that show the kilometers from Panama City—this is how locals give directions, for instance: "Turn at kilometer 54." The markers are white and look like oversize dominoes.

El Valle de Antón is characterized by year-round spring weather conditions, and a cooler cloud forest in higher areas; the Pacific Beaches are driest from January to March; and, because of mass deforestation, the Azuero Peninsula is very dry in comparison to the rest of Panama.

1 Pacific Beaches

Every weekend, hordes of residents from Panama City and the interior head out to the Pacific Coast to frolic on the beaches of the Panamá and Coclé provinces. Until a decade ago, this long stretch of beach backed by dusty cliffs was the home of fishermen and humble people who moved here after their villages were flooded with the building of the Panama Canal. But the beaches' proximity to Panama City (just 30 min. to 2 hr. from downtown) has proved tempting to well-heeled Panamanians and foreign retirees, and now the coast is the haunt of extravagant homes, manicured residential communities, and a few splashy megaresorts. There are three exclusive seaside golf courses—Playa Coronado, Tucan Country Club, and the new Mantaray course near the Decameron—and a couple of surf schools with packages or day lessons if you're short on time. And Panama's only RV park is located here, close to Santa Clara. Most coastal destinations in this section see few people outside of weekends, and at some beaches during low season, weekends can be relatively free of crowds. The modern, four-lane Interamericana (also called Panamericana) Highway connects the city

Roadside Gastronomy

If you're like me and relish sampling local delicacies, especially those found at cheap road stops and hole-in-the-walls that usually go unnoticed by tourists, try these culinary gems. **Bollos Chorreranos** (no phone; Fri–Sat 8am–8pm, Sun–Thurs 8am–6pm) is an open-air dive recognizable by the dozens of parked cars of Panamanians out front. It's on the highway outside Chorrera, 35km (22 miles) west of Panama City. Every Panama City resident, it seems, stops here for local specialties that include *tasajo,* an out-of-this-world gooey smoked beef; *bollos,* tamale-like corn patties filled with chicken or coconut; *chichas,* fresh juices such as passion fruit and the exotic guanabana; and the regionally famous *chicheme,* a thick, sweet beverage made with corn and cinnamon, and said to "put hair on your chest" and "pump you up." Farther down the road, at kilometer 57, next to the defunct Texaco station, is **Queso Chela** (no phone; daily 7am–8pm) with heavenly light fresh cheeses, fresh yogurt (even *chicheme* yogurt), soft egg bread, warm beef and chicken empanadas, and *chichas* to wash it all down. Don't miss the fresh roasted cashews sold at the front door—this is what cashews were meant to taste like. The town Chorrera is known for its juicy pineapple. If pineapple is in season, road vendors often sell three for $1; a little farther past Chorrera, vendors sell mango and papaya. At Antón, vendors sell sweet treats such as candies and coconut cakes.

with the coast's beaches, which are listed in this section in descending southwest order: Playa Bonita, Gorgona, Coronado, Santa Clara, and Farallón (Playa Blanca). The farther you drive from Panama City, the whiter the sand turns and the bluer the sea. The sands of some of the beaches have a lot of iron and are blackish.

GETTING THERE & DEPARTING

There are two exit routes from the city: the Puente de las Américas (Bridge of the Americas) that spans the mouth of the canal; and the new cable-stayed span bridge Puente Centenario, built in 2004, that crosses the canal at the Gaillard (Culebra) Cut, the section of the canal whose excavation cost the most lives during its construction. Both routes are nearly the same in terms of distance, and each has a toll of 50¢. Do not leave Panama City from 3:30 to 6:30pm, or return between 7 and 9am, when heavy traffic jams could add an extra 30 minutes to an hour to your travel time.

By Car   For the Bridge of the Americas, take Avenida de los Mártires along Cerro Ancón, which connects with the Panamericana and the bridge. For the Puente Centenario, head out past the Miraflores Locks until you see the bridge entrance. The four-lane Interamericana Highway is in good shape, and turnoffs are marked by either a municipal sign or promotional billboard.

By Bus or Taxi   Buses leave from the Albrook Terminal. Buses will drop you off at the turnoff for each beach, where cheap taxis (about $3) wait for the quick ride to the beach. Taxis from the city charge an average of $50 for transportation to all beaches listed in this section, less if heading to the Intercontinental Resort in nearby Playa

Central Panama

Caribbean Sea

C.R.

Panama City

Santiago

COL

Area of detail

- - - - Ferry
Diving, Snorkeling
Beach
Park, Reserve

0   50 mi
0   50 km

COLÓN

Lago Gatún   Gamboa   Chilibre
Lagarterita   Panama Canal
La Laguna
Arosemena   PANAMA CITY
Arraiján   Veracruz

Veraguas

Belén

Coclecito

Toabré

PANAMÁ   La Chorrera
Capira   I. Taboga
Punta Chame   Bahía de Panamá
Chame   I. Toque

OMAR TORRIJOS NATIONAL PARK
Cerro Peña Blanca

Cerro Chicú   El Cope

Santa Fé   Huacas del Quije

La Yeguada

91   San Francisco   Calobre

Olá

COCLÉ

Caimito
Churuquita Grande   El Valle de Antón
Penonomé
Antón   Santa Clara
Río Hato   Playa El Palmar
Playa Río Mar
Playa Santa Clara
Playa Farellón

Cerro Gaitál   La Laguna
San Carlos   Playa Gorgona
Playa Coronado

ALTOS DE CAMPANA NAT'L PARK

American Highway

Natá
Pocrí   Aguadulce

VERAGUAS

1   Santiago

Atalaya

Divisa
Pan   Santa María
Parita

Bahía de Parita

Playa Blanca

SARIGUA NAT'L PARK

Golfo de Panamá

Montijo   Ocú   Pesé
Puerto Mutis

HERRERA

Chitré
Los Santos
Guararé

Péñon de la Onda Wildlife Preserve

Las Minas   Los Pozos
El Toro

Anguión   Montuoso Forest Reserve

Mariato

Isla Coiba

Güerita

Península de Azuero LOS SANTOS

Macaracas

Las Tablas
3   71   Pocrí

Los Asientos
Los Destiladeros   Pedasí

Isla Iguana Wildlife Refuge

Playa Pedasí
Playa Punta Mala

Arenas   Cerro Hoya   Jobero
La Tronosa Forest Reserve

Tonosí

Isla Cañas Wildlife Preserve   Playa Venado

Playa Destiladeros

CERRO HOYA NATIONAL PARK

Punta Mariato   Cambutal

0   20 mi
0   20 km

Bonita. Some resorts here provide transportation for guests from both airports or any hotel in Panama City. **Pesantez Tours** (✆ **263-7577;** www.pesantez-tours.com) has round-trip transportation, dropping off and picking up on different dates, for $56 per person to beaches like Santa Clara.

PLAYA KOBBE (BONITA)

The formal name for this area is Playa Kobbe, but with the opening of the Intercontinental the area is also commonly referred to as Playa Bonita. This is the closest beach to Panama City. Take the first exit after the Bridge of the Americas and follow the road 6.5km (4 miles) to get here. A taxi from downtown will cost you about $30 one-way, or $55 from the international airport. Apart from the resort and an upscale residential community with an 18-hole golf course, there is Playa Kobbe—the public beach (with a lifeguard), which charges $7 (price includes a snack), and at which you can rent boats.

A LUXURY RESORT

Intercontinental Playa Bonita Resort & Spa 🐦🐦🐦   The great thing about this brand-new resort, set on a small inlet on the Pacific Coast and backed by lush jungle, is its proximity to Panama City and the canal area; plus it offers plenty of activities if you feel like getting away from the pool for a day. The five-star Intercontinental is also one of the most luxurious and relaxing resorts in Panama, and a tad more exclusive than the Playa Blanca and Decameron resorts in Farallón—those resorts, however, are located on better beaches, with whiter sand and bluer water. Also, there is no evening entertainment, late-night partying, or discos here, and therefore the resort appeals more to romantic couples or families.

The Intercontinental's whitewashed exteriors feel Mediterranean, and the interior decor is tropical Indonesian, with lots of neutral tones like dark chocolate and ecru. A vast lobby with floor-to-ceiling windows looks out onto the heart of the resort, a palm-fringed maze of swimming pools with a swim-up bar, restaurants, a beach volleyball court, Jet Skis, and an activity center that rents snorkeling equipment and kayaks. My only caveat with this resort is that when the tide is low, there is no beach—just a lot of goopy mud. All guest rooms are exquisite, with plush beds and stocked, marble-inlaid bathrooms. Balconies overlook the pool, the beach and, farther beyond, the view of Isla Taboga and ships waiting to enter the canal. Their 28 Club Rooms are larger but are not suites, and they have picture windows and access to a private lounge that serves snacks all day. The staff is bright and enthusiastic—I really emphasize this because I enjoyed some of the most friendly service I've had anywhere in Panama. The elegant spa is also one of the country's best, with a full range of exotic treatments. And the food is delicious, too—but Panama City is so close that you could have a dinner there if you wanted. The owners of the Intercontinental also own the Gamboa Rainforest Resort, and they have excursions there, or you can play a round of golf at the world-class Tucán Golf Course nearby.

Playa Kobbe, Punta Bruja. 📞 **211-8600,** or 800/424-6835 in the U.S. www.ichotelsgroup.com. 330 units. $225 double; $300 Club Room. AE, MC, V. **Amenities:** 3 restaurants; 2 bars; outdoor pool; access to Tucán Golf Course; sports equipment; kayak rental; snorkeling gear; spa and fitness center w/whirlpool, steam, and sauna; business center; salon; gift shop; concierge; tour desk; kids' activities; 24-hr. room service; babysitting; laundry service. In room: A/C, TV, minibar, hair dryer.

PLAYA GORGONA

This is the next stretch of sand on the coast, but it's quite a drive from Playa Bonita—about 79km (49 miles) from the Bridge of the Americas. Gorgona is a small town with three salt-and-pepper sand beaches, including Playa Malibu, a popular surf spot (you'll need a 4WD to get to this beach); Arena Negra, a charcoal-sand beach commonly used by fishermen; and the Gorgona Beach itself. During the winter, strong currents create poor swimming conditions here. These are not the nicest beaches on the coast, and accommodations consist mostly of inexpensive, weathered *cabañas*.

WHERE TO STAY & DINE

Cabañas de Playa Gorgona   These low-cost, self-catering cabins are popular with Panamanian families who pile in with tons of kids and boom boxes on weekends. The complex opened in 1984, and not much has been updated since, especially the spartan cabin interiors. The cabins are made of cement and are perpendicular to the beach, meaning no views. Each has a tiny front patio, a hammock, and a simple kitchenette, but no hot water. There is also a communal barbecue area, beachfront tables with thatched roofs for day visitors, and three swimming pools. Accommodations options consist of a studio with a single room, a one-bedroom cabin, and a two-bedroom cabin. The latter has maid's quarters, but you'd think a family that could afford a maid could afford to stay at a nicer place than this. Weekend rates are for a minimum of 2 nights; linens, towels, soap, and toilet paper cost an additional $2.50. The complex has simple meals at their cafeteria Rancho Sol y Mar.

Playa Gorgona, end of the road. (C) 269-2433 in Panama City, or 240-6160 in Gorgona. 40 units. $40 1-bedroom cabin weekdays; $100 1-bedroom cabin weekends (2 nights required). No credit cards. **Amenities:** Restaurant; outdoor pool; kids' pool; picnic *bohios*. In room: A/C, kitchenette, no phone.

Cabañas Villanita   This bright yellow house has four cinder-block cabins for up to six people, with kitchens, a dining area, and patio with a barbecue and hammock. It's located on the beach, but there is also a small pool for when the current is too strong to swim in the ocean. Each cabin has two bedrooms; one has a springy double bed, the other bunk beds for four guests. They're nothing fancy about this spot, but it is nicer than the cabins at Cabañas de Playa Gorgona (see above).

End of the road at Gorgona beach. (C) 240-5314. 4 units. $65 per cabin. No credit cards. **Amenities:** Outdoor pool; barbecue pits. In room: A/C, TV, no phone.

Hotel Canadian (*Value*)   This hotel is not located on the beach—in fact, it's a couple of blocks off the highway in Chame, just before Gorgona. The hotel acts as a base for travelers taking part in a host of outdoor activities in both El Valle and the surrounding coastal area. As the name states, the hotel is Canadian-owned. The guesthouse is very tranquil and sits atop a knoll, offering views of lush coastal forest, and there is a swimming pool. Of the seven units, five are doubles and two are family-size units. Guest rooms are simple but tidy and well-maintained, with decent beds and lots of closet space. The friendly owners Katie and Ralph can put together one of 21 different tours for guests, or get you to the beach in Gorgona if you'd just like to kick back on the sand. They have an open-air bar and restaurant, and breakfast is included. Prices are nightly, with discounts for extended stays.

Chame. (C) 240-6066. www.hotelcanadianpanama.com. 7 units. $35 double. No credit cards. **Amenities:** Restaurant; bar; outdoor pool; tours. In room: TV, no phone.

Rincón Catracho (*Finds*)   Catracho serves delicious food, and is a real find in such a modest town. The menu features dishes such as filet mignon, veal cutlets, seafood dishes, pastas, and even tacos, which are all very tasty and reasonably priced. The owner, a German, is a retired international chef who sought to open his own place—and good thing he did because this area needed a solid dining option. During the low season, call ahead to let them know you're coming.

Follow paved road, right at grocery store. (C) 240-5807. Reservations recommended for dinner. Main courses $5–$10. No credit cards. Thurs–Sun 7am–9pm.

PLAYA CORONADO

Playa Coronado is the oldest community on the coast, and the most developed, with a sprawling residential area and full range of services such as a 24-hour El Rey supermarket, shops, and restaurants. It's located 83km (51 miles) from Panama City, and 3km (1¾ miles) from the highway. There are quite a lot of residential homes here that have been around long enough to give off that lived-in feel, unlike other beach areas that are mostly modern condo developments. Both Panamanians and expats like Coronado for its services and for its lengthy beach, though this is certainly not the best beach on the coast—the sand here contains a lot of iron and is dark. There is a controlled security gate to keep the crowds at bay—even if you're not registered at a hotel, tell the gate attendant that you are headed to the Coronado Beach Resort so that he'll let you pass.

WHERE TO STAY & DINE

Club Gaviota For pleasant budget accommodations, this is your best bet in Coronado. There are nine guest rooms in a motel-like building close to the beach, but not close enough to offer ocean views. Rooms are modest but clean, with either one or two double beds; ask for a newer room because their two older units are depressing. Prices are nightly, or as a package with meals for $39 per person, but considering that a double costs $66 per night, you're better off opting for the meal package if you're a couple. Their on-site restaurant serves decent, simple meals, with a la carte options priced at $5 to $12. There is an adult and kids' pool with a good view of the sea.

Paseo George Smith. (© **224-9053.** gaviota@turistaintl.com. 9 units. $65 double. MC, V. **Amenities:** Restaurant; adult and kids' outdoor pool. *In room:* A/C, TV, no phone.

Coronado Golf & Beach Resort (Kids)   The Coronado is the oldest and largest resort on the coast, with facilities that include a world-class golf course, equestrian club, spa, tennis courts, kids' activities, and more—but the resort is not on the beach, which is reached by a 10-minute walk or aboard one of their shuttle buses. With the feel of a stuffy country club, the Coronado would more aptly be called a golf resort than a beach resort; their 18-hole golf course was designed by Tom and George Fazio. People who stay here are principally families and older guests. One highlight at the Coronado is the guest rooms, all of which are very spacious and nicely appointed "suites." Garden suites, their standard option, are 53 sq. m (570 sq. ft.) in size, with a master bedroom, sitting area with two sofa beds, and a dining table; their Royal Suites are the same as Garden Suites but have a second story with an extra bedroom, two queen-size beds (for a total of six guests), and a balcony. Residential Suites are for a maximum of six, with the addition of a kitchenette. At the beach, the Coronado has a roofed activities area with a restaurant and sports equipment for guests only. The Equestrian Club offers horseback riding for $20 an hour, but is open on Saturdays only. There is an excellent steakhouse next to the club, but again it's open to guests only. The staff here is friendly for the most part, but the quality of service is lackluster. The resort claims it has all-inclusive packages, though the prices are really for rooms only, and everything is an additional price—so keep tabs of your tab or you'll be left with an expensive surprise when you check out.

Av. Punta Prieta, Coronado. (© **264-3164** or 240-4444. www.coronadoesvida.com. 75 units. $180 Garden Suite for 2, $250 Royal Suite for 2; $300 Residential Suite for 4 (additional guests are $15 per person; children under 12 stay free). AE, DC, MC, V. **Amenities:** 5 restaurants; 2 bars; disco; Olympic-size pool; kids' pool; tennis courts; billiard and game room; bike rental; ATV rental; Ping-Pong tables; equestrian center; spa and fitness center w/sauna, whirlpools, and Jacuzzis; kids' playground; kids' miniclub with activities; business center. *In room:* A/C, TV, minibar, kitchenette (Residential Suites only), hair dryer, safe, Wi-Fi (some suites).

Corowalk Inn I really only recommend this hotel if you're in a pinch because it's located next to the highway behind El Rey supermarket and shopping area and is a 5-minute drive to the beach (much too far to walk, though). Still, the contemporary hotel with country decor is a very clean establishment, with attractive rooms and amicable service. Make sure you book a room with windows, as a few do not have them. A continental breakfast is included in the price.

Av. Roberto Eisenmann, 1 block from highway. © 240-1516. 14 units. $44 double (weekdays); $66 (weekends). MC, V. *In room:* A/C, TV.

Restaurante Don Chacho 🕏 PANAMANIAN   This casual eatery specializes in delicious roast chicken slowly cooked over a wood fire. They also have a lengthy menu with lots of Panamanian dishes such as the yuca-and-beef treat *carimañola* and tamale-like *bollas,* as well as reasonably priced seafood dishes such as lobster thermidor, fried snapper in coconut sauce, and a surf-and-turf platter. The chef here honed his chops working as a cook for the U.S. military at Fort Clayton, and the food, though simple, is hearty and tasty. Note that the restaurant has a limited menu on Mondays and Tuesdays because of reduced supplies after busy weekends. After turning off the highway onto the road to Coronado, the restaurant is just on the right.

Road to Coronado. © 509-8587. Reservations not accepted. Main courses $4–$12. AE, MC, V. Mon–Wed 8am–8pm; Thurs–Sun 8am–11pm.

Rincon del Chef 🕏 CONTEMPORARY PANAMANIAN   Located almost next door to Don Chacho, in a country-style wooden building that's part of a handicrafts market, this restaurant serves excellent meals prepared by a chef who once ran the kitchen at the Coronado Resort. You'll find traditional dishes, but mostly the food here consists of creative takes on locally available ingredients, such as shrimp and green plantains, and curried seafood; grilled meats and lighter fare are available. Also, the prices are very reasonable, and the waitstaff is attentive. The only problem with Rincon is that they often do not adhere to their posted hours during the low season. Once you turn off the highway, you'll see the restaurant on your right-hand side.

Av. Roberto Eisenmann. No phone. Main courses $5–$10. MC, V. Tues 8am–4pm; Wed–Thurs 8am–8pm; Fri–Sun 7am–10pm.

AN ELEGANT RESTAURANT IN VISTA MAR

Restaurant Vista Mar 🕏🕏🕏 MEDITERRANEAN   The Vista Mar Resort is a new, private residential community whose Restaurant Vista Mar I highly recommend. If you're in the coastal area and seeking an upscale dining experience with delicious, gourmet cuisine, this is your place. The dining area is fresh and chic, with a Moroccan decor and whitewashed walls. The outstanding French chef, Pascual Finet, who once ran the kitchens at Las Bóvedas and Casco Viejo restaurants in Panama City, has created a Mediterranean-influenced menu that incorporates French, Spanish, and Italian dishes. Highlights include duck confit, Galician octopus, and calamari stuffed with crabmeat. Everything is fresh, and flavors are well-combined. They have a solid wine list, too. You can dine indoors or outdoors on their terraced patio that overlooks the sea. Vista Mar is located 90km (56 miles) from Panama City, and 2km (1¼ miles) from the highway turnoff.

Road to Vista Mar. © 215-1111 or 6612-0095. Reservations accepted. Main courses $7–$15. AE, MC, V. Thurs–Tues 11am–10pm (to 11pm Fri–Sat).

PLAYA EL PALMAR

The turnoff for Playa El Palmar is 95km (59 miles) from Panama City, just past the town of San Carlos, which has services such as a supermarket. El Palmar is a gray-sand beach popular with surfers and weekenders from the interior. Along the coastal area are oceanfront properties, and there are two midrange places to stay: the Palmar and the Bay View Resort (see below). The water, depending on the tide, can be blue or dark; also, be aware of riptides when the surf is pounding. Day visitors should look into the Bay View's day pass (see below).

WHERE TO STAY & DINE

Bay View Resort 🏖 *Kids*   The Bay View is not the most elegant resort on the coast; in fact, it's not much of a "resort" at all. But it is a good place to bring the kids and let them splash around in the pool while you take surf lessons or lounge on the pleasant beachfront terrace, and its prices are reasonable. The Bay View is simple and somewhat funky, with leafy green vegetation centered around a fish-shaped swimming pool. A wooden bridge connects this area with a promenade-like terrace where you can gaze out at the sea view, dine, or enjoy the sunset with a cocktail. Guest rooms are pretty basic, with thin curtains and bedspreads, two double beds of so-so quality, and tiled floors. Because the rooms were decorated with cheaper furnishings, they have a slightly worn-down look in spite of the fact that the Bay View only opened a few years ago. The grounds, though, are nicely landscaped for the most part. There are campsites for $10 per night. Note that at high tide there is virtually no beach in front of the resort.

Day visitors may use the pool for $6 adults and $3.50 kids. The Bay View Restaurant sits atop a hill and has a sweeping view of the ocean. They serve mostly seafood, including ceviche, lobster, and fresh sea bass and snapper; they also serve barbecued meats, fresh fruit juices, and a kids' menu. Prices below are for accommodations only, but the resort offers packages that include meals.

Playa El Palmar. ⒸⒻ 240-9621. www.bayviewelpalmar.com. 14 units. May–Nov $50 double Sun–Thurs, $60 Fri–Sat; Dec–Apr $80 double. MC, V. **Amenities:** Restaurant; bar; outdoor pool; soft surfboards for rent; games; volleyball. *In room:* A/C, TV, no phone.

Hotel Palmar Surf Beach & School 🏖   If you're eager to learn to surf, or just want a low-cost and agreeable lodging option on the beach, you might want to check out this spruce two-story hotel. Guest rooms accommodate two to five people, and are bright and clean, with a bare-bones decor and a veranda for enjoying the sea breeze. There is one "suite" for six with a full kitchen—this is the best unit here not just because of its size but because it is the most attractive unit on the property. It's about a 30-second walk through a grove of palms to get to the ocean. Surf classes are $25 per person per hour, which includes surfboard rental, and classes are kept to a maximum of two people. If you pay $35 per hour, they'll include action photos. In the afternoon, their barman serves tasty, well-made cocktails.

Playa El Palmar. ⒸⒻ 240-8004 or 6615-5654. www.palmarpoint.com or palmasurfcamp@hotmail.com. 10 units. $50–$60 up to 3, $60–$70 for 4; $90 suite. No credit cards. **Amenities:** Bar; surf classes; surfboard rental. *In room:* A/C, no phone.

SANTA CLARA

Santa Clara and its neighbor down the road, Farallón, are home to the prettiest beaches in this Pacific coastal area, with clean, white sand and good swimming conditions. While travelers seeking an all-inclusive megaresort will want to head to Farallón, there are relatively few people in Santa Clara—the area has a ban on weekend "Coaster" buses that transport rowdy beachgoers to the coastal region. Santa Clara doesn't have much of a town to speak of, and consists mostly of tourist lodgings and residential and weekend homes for urbanites. It's a little farther from Panama City than other beaches mentioned earlier in this chapter, but it's worth the extra effort to get here, especially if you plan on spending the night. The turnoff for Santa Clara is 113km (70 miles) from Panama City; keep your eyes open as it's easy to miss the turnoff. After turning, the road forks—head left for Las Sirenas, right for Las Veraneras and the public beach. **Taxi Santa Clara** can get you around this area; they hang out at the turnoff junction (© **6606-9084**).

OUTDOOR ACTIVITIES

Most visitors come to Santa Clara just to kick back on the beach and relax. Locals rent **horses** on the beach, but there isn't a corral or specific place to head to—rather, horse owners wander the beach looking for potential riders. The lodging options mentioned below or the day area at the Balneario Santa Clara can put you in touch with a horse-renting local; the cost is $3 per hour. **Bicycles** can be rented at the Casino's Hospedaje at the turnoff for Santa Clara (© **993-2115**) for $2 per hour, or $8 for the day.

Kayak Panama (© **993-3096**; www.kayakpanama.com) operates out of XS Memories (see below), offering kayaking trips and lessons on the Class I to II Chame River from about August to November, when the river is full. They can also put together trips on other rivers if you're looking for a multiple-day itinerary. It's not an action-packed white-water ride, but the river provides outstanding opportunities for catching sight of local fauna, including herons, kingfishers, turtles, and caimans. It's great for families traveling with kids (but not for young children). They also rent kayaks.

See "Farallón," below, for information about other activities in the region with **Extreme Tours.**

WHERE TO STAY & DINE

Las Sirenas 𝒢𝒢 Las Sirenas is a top choice for travelers seeking private cottages with a full kitchen rather than an all-inclusive package. Half the cottages are perched on a bluff and offer cool breeze and sea views, and the other half are smack-dab on the beach itself; all are light and fresh and painted white with a splash of yellow and blue in a somewhat nautical decor. They are not luxurious, but they are clean and attractive, and the beach cottages were recently spruced up with a new coat of paint and larger windows. The grounds at Las Sirenas are abloom with pretty bougainvillea, and the sea is decidedly bluer here than at other beaches closer to Panama City. There is no restaurant here, but Los Camisones is close by, and Las Veraneras is within walking distance, though your best bet is to stock up with supplies beforehand. There is a small grocery store nearby if you've forgotten anything. The cottages have a patio with hammocks and a barbecue that they'll fire up for you when you're ready to cook. The charming, English-speaking family that runs Las Sirenas is very accommodating, and can help with any dinner plans and even provide meals to heat up if you give them enough notice. There are one- and two-bedroom cottages on the bluff, and those on the beach have one bedroom with a double bed as well as a loftlike floor with a single. Maid service happens only once every 3 days.

Santa Clara. © **264-1964** in Santa Clara, or 993-3235 in Panama City. www.lasirenas.com. 11 units. $70–$80 1-bedroom; $100–$110 2-bedroom. MC, V. **Amenities:** Kitchen; barbecue; volleyball court; Ping-Pong; beach umbrellas; kids' playground; Wi-Fi (in common area and some cottages). *In room:* A/C (bedrooms only), TV, no phone.

Las Veraneras This place is overpriced for what you get. Las Veraneras is a restaurant/bar/hotel complex with cabins with kitchens, individual rooms, and a few rather dreary houses nestled in tropical jungle. The best units here are the two-story, five-person cabins with kitchenettes set back and above the beach; three are made of wood with thatched roofs and small balconies that have partial views of the sea, and the other four have no views and are made of cement. Altogether, it's a very tight squeeze for five people, and there's no hot water. The spacious, open-air restaurant has five rooms on stilts above the restaurant/dance floor, and although the new management claims that party nights (something the place has been known for) have been toned down, you can still expect to hear a lot of noise on weekend nights and during the summer. Elsewhere on the property, farther back from the beach and nestled in tropical jungle, are houses for up to 10 guests—but I wouldn't recommend them. On the plus side, there is a huge, circular pool, but really, Las Veraneras is for younger, more bohemian travelers. The restaurant here is open daily from 7am to 9pm, and serves seafood and Panamanian dishes.

Santa Clara. ℂ **993-3313.** 15 units. $50 room; $70 cabin for 5; $160 house for 10. MC, V. **Amenities:** Restaurant; bar; outdoor pool. *In room:* A/C (some cabins), TV, no phone.

XS Memories 𝕽 It's an RV park and they serve the best burgers on the Pacific Coast. Sounds a little incongruous in Panama, and as you might have guessed it's American-owned. XS is located on the north side of the Interamericana highway, so there's no direct beach access. They tend to get a lot of day visitors to their restaurant, and a fair number of hardy American RV travelers who drive all the way from the U.S. to the end of the road in the Darién. They have 22 motor-home hookups, with water, electricity, and septic-tank service, for $10 per day. There's also a campground, and three simple, terra-cotta-tiled cabins; one has a kitchenette and is sized for two guests, another has two double beds, and the third has three double beds. Within the walled complex are a pool; a small zoo; and a restaurant and sports bar with a large-screen TV, kitschy decor, and good, American-style cuisine. As noted, the XS burgers are delicious, and there's also seafood and meat dishes. The restaurant is open Sunday to Monday and Wednesday to Thursday 8am to 8pm, and Friday and Saturday 8am to 10pm.

North side of the Interamericana, near Santa Clara. ℂ **993-3096.** www.xsmemories.com. $55 cabin for 2. MC, V. **Amenities:** Restaurant; sports bar; outdoor pool; RV hookup; campground; on-site tour company; bike rental. *In room:* A/C, TV, no phone.

Restaurante Balneario Santa Clara 𝕽 PANAMANIAN If you'd like to visit Santa Clara for the day, this is where you go. This complex has a decent restaurant, a long row of beachfront picnic tables with thatched roofs (called *ranchos*), a campground, public bathrooms, showers and, on busy weekends, a lifeguard. *Ranchos* cost $5 to rent, hammocks $2. The restaurant specializes in fresh seafood, with crayfish, garlicky clams, and octopus as their specialty, but they also have burgers and a kids' menu. The Balneario is next to Las Veraneras.

Santa Clara. No phone. Reservations not accepted. Main courses $6–$14. No credit cards. Mon–Thurs 10am–7pm; Fri 10am–8pm; Sat–Sun 8am–8pm.

Restaurante Los Camisones 𝕽𝕽 PANAMANIAN This is the best restaurant in the area, though it's not directly on the coast but just off the Interamericana Highway at kilometer 104, about a 10-minute drive back toward Panama City from Santa Clara. It's a casual, open-air restaurant housed under a tremendous thatched roof, and the seafood here is straight-from-the-boat fresh. Los Camisones is Spanish-owned, evidenced by dishes such as Galician octopus sautéed with olive oil and red peppers, and Iberian sausage. There's also Angus beef filet, lamb stew, steamed mussels, breaded oysters, and yummy crepes for dessert. The freshest, most delicious jumbo prawns I have ever sampled in Panama were here at Los Camisones. In fact, the food is so good, the U.S. ambassador to Panama often stops in for meal.

Km 104. ℂ **993-3622.** Main courses $7–$18. AE, MC, V. Mon–Thurs 9:30am–9pm; Fri–Sun 9:30am–11pm.

FARALLON

Farallón is often referred to as Playa Blanca, for the lovely white-sand beach that stretches along the coastal area here. It's mostly known for the gigantic Decameron Resort and the Playa Blanca Resort (see below); there is also a poor village whose residents, to be honest, are resentful of their new resort neighbors. It's not common, but those with a rental vehicle might encounter a bit of rankling from locals on the roads here (usually kids throwing trash at passing vehicles). It's anyone's guess how this area will look in a decade, given the fact that it is a hot property for retirement and weekend homes.

OUTDOOR ADVENTURES

Extreme Tours (© **6671-8445,** or 993-2823 at Playa Blanca; www.extremetours panama.com) is the tour outfitter for the Playa Blanca Resort. They offer exciting outdoor adventures to travelers staying there, lodging elsewhere along the coast, or just visiting for the day. Sample excursions include scuba diving, horseback riding, surf lessons, hiking, rappelling, and water-skiing. They even offer full-day sailing trips with lunch included. You'll need to send them an e-mail for prices, as each tour is customized according to where you are staying and what you're looking for.

WHERE TO STAY & DINE

Playa Blanca Resort 🐾🐾   Formerly known as the Barceló, the Playa Blanca is more manageable than the Decameron—yet still offers a bounty of things to see and do (including doing nothing at all). The entire property is painted white, with cerulean-blue awnings and trim, and is centered around trim gardens and the resort's two pool areas, one more of a party scene, the other peaceful and relatively empty. The 220 rooms look out onto the beach, the pools, or gardens; they are not as extravagant as you would expect from a self-billed five-star resort, but they are roomy and well attended. Standards come with two queen-sizes or a king-size, and suites have a living area and luxury bathroom. The Playa Blanca is very popular with Canadians, as well as Panama City residents and Central American couples and families. The evening entertainment and food—even buffet food—are above par, and there are day activities galore, including excursions to areas like El Valle. All-inclusive prices include three daily meals and use of all facilities; the price does not include sport-gear rental, day excursions, tips, or services like massages.

Note that day visitors not lodging at the resort can pay $45 per person on weekends, $35 on weekdays, to use their swimming pools and installations (does not include gear rental), and the price includes lunch and beverages. For transportation for day trips, call **Pesantez Tours** (© **263-7577;** www.pesantez-tours.com), which charges $30 per person round-trip.

Centro Comercial Paitilla, Av. Balboa. © **264-6444.** www.playablancaresort.com. 220 units. Rates per person based on double occupancy: $52 Sun–Thurs Apr–Dec; $84 Fri–Sat Apr–Dec and daily May–Nov. AE, MC, V. **Amenities:** 4 restaurants; bar; disco; nightly entertainment; 9-hole putting range; tennis courts; volleyball; boat rides; watersports equipment; 2 outdoor whirlpools; dance classes; kids' activities; concierge; tours; business center; gift shops; 24-hr. room service; babysitting; laundry service. *In room:* A/C, TV, minibar, hair dryer; safe, beach towels.

Royal Decameron Beach Resort, Golf, Spa & Casino 🐾🐾🐾 (Kids)   Sprawled across Playa Blanca in multilevel tiers that descend down to the beach, this gargantuan, 820-room resort is the largest, and one of the most upscale, in Panama. With seven swimming pools, an 18-hole golf course, casino, spa, marina, and a host of other facilities, the resort is almost like an amusement park you must navigate with a map.

The Colombian-owned Decameron has handsomely designed interiors and immaculately landscaped, lush tropical grounds. All guest rooms are essentially the same, and come with two queen-size beds or a king-size. They are comfortable and bright, but note that a lot of stairs connect the units to facilities, so if you're not able to climb stairs, ask for a room that has shuttle transportation or is in a convenient location. Do not book a room by the pools unless you want to hear thumping Latin music day and night. Also, sometimes there are a lot of kids running around and screaming, another reason to book far away from the hullabaloo. As an all-inclusive resort, meals, all drinks (alcohol included), nonmotorized watersports equipment, entertainment, kids' activities, and tips are included. The most common complaint heard here is that during busy weeks it is a never-ending lineup to book a reservation in a specialty restaurant (as opposed to the buffets), or to book a day excursion, and so on. The Decameron is popular with honeymooners, Central and South Americans, and Canadians and Europeans.

For an additional cost, guests have access to the beautiful and brand-new **Mantaray Golf Course** ✹✹✹, designed by Randall Thompsen and featuring 18 holes spread across rolling hills, with some sea views. There are driving ranges, a practice putting green, and six flood-lit par-3 holes for nighttime playing.

Playa Blanca. ✆ **993-2255** (resort) or 206-5324 (reservations). www.decameron.com. 820 units. Rates per person based on double occupancy: $79 adults, $39 children. AE, MC, V. **Amenities:** 2 buffet restaurants; 6 specialty restaurants; 2 snack bars; 7 bars; casino; disco; nightly entertainment; 7 outdoor pools; 18-hole golf course; tennis courts; fitness center and spa; watersports equipment; volleyball; boat rides; dance classes; kids' activities; concierge; tours; business center; gift shops; 24-hr. room service; babysitting; laundry service. *In room:* A/C, TV, minibar, safe, hair dryer.

Pipa's ✹✹ SEAFOOD   If you're not staying at the aforementioned resorts, or if you are but would like to get out and find a more "local" experience than lining up at a buffet, walk down to Pipa's—it's located between both resorts. You can reach the restaurant by driving to the Decameron, turning right, and continuing on for about 2km (1¼ miles). Pipa's is owned by a laid-back California couple who serve some of the most delicious seafood found along the coast, like fresh jumbo shrimp and lobster. At night they'll sometimes fire up a beach bonfire. Pipa's is normally pretty mellow, but get enough patrons filled with booze and the mood can turn festive.

Farallón. No phone. Main courses $5–$15. No credit cards. Daily noon–8 or 9pm (can be earlier or later depending on night and number of people).

2 Altos de Campana National Park

90km (56 miles) W of Panama City

This is Panama's first national park, established in 1966 and covering about 4,925 hectares (12,170 acres) of mostly igneous terrain created by the extinct El Valle de Antón Volcano. The park is characterized by rugged peaks—almost completely deforested on the Pacific side—and sloping rainforest on the Atlantic side, and there are dramatic cliffs, lava fields, and one of the most extraordinary lookout points in Panama at Chame Peak. From here, travelers can marvel at the sweeping view of the Canal Basin, Chame Bay and its mangrove swamps, and the Chame River—this is the reason to visit this park, as well as bird-watching. Hiking and other adventure activities are in short supply here. Past the turnoff for Altos de Campana, drive about 4km (2½ miles) to an ANAM **ranger station** (✆ **244-0092**). The entrance fee is $3 per person, and the walk up to the lookout is brief. ANAM has developed a mostly uphill hiking trail here called **Sendero La Cruz,** but you'll need a 4WD to reach the trail head. The park station sometimes has copies of a good illustrated guide to the trail. Bird-watchers should know that the park is home to exotic species that can be difficult to view elsewhere, such as violet hummingbirds, white-tipped sicklebills, and orange-bellied trogons. Taking a public bus here is next to impossible; you'll need a rental vehicle or arrangements with your tour company to make a detour here on your way out to other destinations in the area. A campground here charges $5 per night.

3 El Valle de Antón

124km (77 miles) W of Panama City

Nestled in the crater of the world's second-largest extinct volcano, El Valle de Antón—popularly known as El Valle—is a delightful and relaxing destination popular with urbanites escaping the heat and hectic pace of Panama City. It's about 2 hours from the city, and can be easily reached by rental vehicle or by bus. El Valle is ringed by steep, verdant peaks, and its streets are abloom with flowers and lined with stately weekend homes that open onto well-manicured gardens and lawns. Best of all, El Valle enjoys springtime conditions year-round due to its altitude at 762m (2,500 ft.), with temperatures that vary between 68° and 80°F (20°–27°C).

On Sundays, the main street comes alive when vendors come to town to sell handicrafts, vegetables, and ornamental flowers at the town's famous market, but otherwise El Valle moves at a languid pace, offering low-key activities like bird-watching and bike riding through town. Visitors seeking a little more action can hike through rainforest, race through the forest on a zip line at the Canopy Adventure, or horseback-ride high up to a lookout point.

ESSENTIALS
GETTING THERE & DEPARTING

If you are lodging in El Valle, ask your hotel about transportation to and from Panama City, which they can arrange for you for a price (about the same price as a taxi, or less).

By Car   It's easy to drive to El Valle because the road is well-maintained and suitable for any kind of vehicle (unlike many destinations in Panama, you won't need a 4WD). To get here, take the Interamericana Highway west for 98km (60 miles) until you see the turnoff for El Valle. From the Interamericana, it's 28km (17 miles) to El Valle, along a very curvy road. Drive slowly and keep an eye out for people and animals walking on the road, especially at night. The road is quite scenic, and you'll want to stop occasionally to snap a photo or two.

By Bus   Buses leave from the Albrook Terminal near the national airport every 40 minutes to an hour, depending on demand. The trip takes a little less than an hour and costs $3.50 one-way. Buses are surprisingly convenient because drivers will drop you off at your hotel if you let them know ahead of time, otherwise, buses stop at the market on Avenida Principal. Direct buses run from 6am to 6pm, or you can catch a later bus until 9pm and be dropped off at the highway, where you can flag down any bus headed for Panama City.

By Taxi   A taxi from Panama City costs around $80 one-way; a taxi to any one of the beaches from El Valle costs around $30 one-way.

GETTING AROUND

By Taxi There are only a handful of taxis in El Valle, and on weekends the wait can be up to an hour if your hotel calls one for you. If you're lucky, you might be able to flag one down on main street. The cost to travel around El Valle is $1 to $2.

ORIENTATION

There is an IPAT visitors' kiosk ((C) **983-6474;** Tues and Thurs–Sun 7:30am–3:30pm) at the handicrafts market on Avenida Principal, but they speak limited English and usually have few materials to hand out other than brochures about Panama destinations in general. **Don Pepe** (see "Shopping," below) has maps of El Valle for sale.

FAST FACTS

There is a 24-hour **ATM** inside Banco Nacional on Avenida Principal. The **medical clinic** is located directly behind the Iglesia San José, and is open from 7am to 3pm ((C) **983-6112** for 24-hr. emergencies). The **post office** is located adjacent to the police station and fire brigade on Carlos Arosemna Guardia. There is **Internet service** at FSR Technology Services next to the Supercentro NG on Avenida Principal (Mon–Fri 8am–noon and 1:30–6pm; Sat 8am–5pm; Sun 11am–3pm). Right next door is a **laundry** service, open daily from 10am to 6pm.

WHAT TO SEE & DO
OUTDOOR ACTIVITIES

BIKING There's no better way to get around El Valle than by bicycle. The terrain is perfectly flat and mostly paved, with some bumpy side roads that have potholes and rocks. Around the edge of town, a couple of dirt roads head high into the hills, if you're looking for more of a workout. Many hotels rent bicycles to their guests, or you can rent from **Don Pepe** ((C) **983-6425**) or **Residencial El Valle** ((C) **983-6536**) for $2 per hour, or $8 for a full day. Both locations are next to each other on Avenida Principal.

CANOPY ADVENTURE This exhilarating, adrenaline-fueled activity involves zipping from tree to tree while strapped in a harness connected to a pulley on a steel cable. The adventure begins with a 30-minute walk to a high platform that is flush with the canopy (the uppermost branches of the forest). A guide gives instructions and demonstrates how the equipment works and how to put on the brakes using a thick leather glove; from here you let gravity do the work. The full tour includes four "zips," which are connected by platforms that gradually descend from the canopy, allowing you to appreciate tropical vegetation from different vantage points. You also get to ride over the 150-foot Macho Falls. If you don't have much time, you can do a quick zip (15 min.) closer to the Canopy Adventure entrance, for $11 per person. The full tour takes about 1½ hours, although the actual cumulative time you ride is less than 15 minutes. Part of the experience is spending time on the platform to observe wildlife, the reason the canopy opens daily at 6am, when the animal world is most active (they close at 5pm). The full tour costs $42 per person, and children must be at least 6 years old to participate. Canopy Adventure also offers an easy-to-moderate guided hike through the rainforest for $25 per person, or you can pay $2.50 for a 15- minute walk near the waterfall, where you can swim. Wear sneakers or hiking boots, not flip-flops, and long pants or shorts that are long enough not to ride up while you're seated in the harness. It should go without saying that skirts are not the ideal garb. The Canopy Adventure ((C) **264-5720;** www.canopylodge.com) is owned by Canopy Lodge (see

"Where to Stay," below), and it is located at the Chorro El Macho on the west side of town, about 3km (1¾ miles) from the market. It is recommended that you make a reservation on weekends or during the high season, December through February.

HIKING & BIRD-WATCHING More than 350 species of birds have been recorded in El Valle, placing the lush valley on the list as one of the top five spots in Panama for bird-watching. Canopy Tower, a bird-watching lodge, recently built their second property here to offer a place to view birds commonly found in foothills, rainforest, and cloud forest. A prime spot for bird-watching here is at **Cerro Gaital National Monument** 🐾🐾🐾, which covers the northern slope of El Valle. This national monument also offers one of the **best hikes** in the area, a 2½-hour, easy-to-moderate loop trail that reaches a lookout point where, weather permitting, you can see the Pacific and Atlantic oceans, and even as far as the Panama Canal. The trail is pretty straightforward, but it's always better with a guide who can point out wildlife and make sure you don't get lost (see below). Cerro Gaital is administered by the ANAM park service, which charges a $3.50 entrance fee per person.

The second hiking area is a 3-hour, moderate trail at **La India Dormida** 🐾🐾 — which means "Sleeping Indian Woman" and refers to the outline of the western peaks that locals claim resembles a reclining woman. (Have someone point it out to you—it's hard to make out at first.) It is advisable that you walk this trail with a guide as it is not clearly marked. There is a swimming hole along the way, so bring your swimsuit.

HORSEBACK RIDING Riding horseback is one of the best ways to appreciate El Valle's gorgeous mountain views. Rent horses from a woman named **Mitzila** (© 6646-5813); she and her team offer horseback riding for $4 per hour, or they'll send you out with a guide (limited English spoken) on Calle El Hato. Horseback rides lope along for beginners, while advanced riders note that rocky trails for the most part prohibit full-tilt gallops.

HOT SPRINGS **Pozos Termales** 🐾 (no phone) are springs without the hot—that is, there are a couple of muddy, tepid pools with minerals that ostensibly alleviate ailments like arthritis and rheumatism. What Pozos promotes is fangotherapy, or caking yourself in mineral-rich mud, waiting on a metal bench for it to plaster, and washing it off in a shower. The end result is much softer skin, but although the complex is neat as a pin, this is no glamour spa, rather a public concession with picnic tables, a meandering stream, and a couple of tiny pools that can get too close for comfort on weekends when dozens of visitors come to soak their aches away. The complex is open daily from 8am to 5pm, and costs $2 adults, 50¢ children under 12, 75¢ seniors.

ADVENTURE TOUR OPERATORS

Mario Urriola, a biologist who runs the Serpentario (see "Zoos & Museums," below), is an excellent nature guide, and he heads a group of bilingual bird-watching guides and conservationists who can put together hikes and other outdoor activities. Birding tours cost $25 per person for a half-day; hiking tours cost $30 for a half-day for up to five guests (© 6629-3722; chombond1@latinmail.com).

The **Panama Explorer Club** operates out of the Crater Valley Adventure Spa (see below), where they have an "Adventure Center" with a rock-climbing wall and obstacle course, plus bike rental and organized tours available to the general public (© **983-6942** in El Valle, or 213-2330 in Panama City; www.pexclub.com). Their half-day excursions include rappelling down a waterfall ($20), mountain-bike tours

($10–$15), and kayaking and rafting nearby rivers ($48–$75), one of which is Class I and suitable for kids.

ZOOS & MUSEUMS

Aprovaca Orquídeas   The Asociación de Productores de Orquídeas El Valle y Cabuya (APROVACA) is a nonprofit agency that strives to cultivate and conserve endangered local and regional orchids. At their site there are 147 species on display, but the tiny operation is worth a visit only for those who hold a keen interest in orchid cultivation.

Off Av. Principal near the entrance to town, next to the ANAM office. No phone. Free admission. Daily 10am–3pm.

El Nispero Zoo *(Kids)*   The Nispero Zoo never planned to be a zoo, it just happened. The owner, an agronomist who runs a small for-profit nursery here, had a large collection of animals and birds, and over time so many people donated abandoned or sick animals that it just made sense to open a zoo. The 2.8-hectare (7-acre) El Nispero sits at the foot of Cerro Gaital National Monument. There are 55 species of birds, both exotic imports from Asia and Africa such as golden pheasants and white peacocks, as well as a few tropical species not seen in any zoo outside Panama. A good representation of endemic animals includes a white-faced capuchin and spider monkey, an ocelot and trigillo margay, and a couple of tapirs rescued from Manuel Noriega's home after the invasion. Note that there are no protective railings between you and the cages, and children (and adults!) should be careful not to stick their hands through the chain-link fence that guards the animals. El Nispero's bucolic property has shade trees and a botanical garden that offer quiet spots for reading a book or just reflecting on nature.

El Nispero is also home to the brand-new **Centro de Conservación de Anfibios de El Valle (EVACC),** an amphibian study center sponsored by the Houston, San Antonio, and San Diego zoos. The center will study the bacteria that is wiping out the golden frog, among other amphibians, and work to ensure the amphibians' survival (see "End of the Golden Era for the Golden Frog?" below). The center has aquariums, exhibits, and a video and reading center in English and Spanish.

Turn up Carlos Arosemna Guardia street and follow signs to El Nispero. ℂ 983-6142. Admission $2 adults, $1 children 3–12, free for children under 3. Daily 7am–5pm.

Museo del Valle   It's usually closed, and this museum is worth a look only if you've run out of things to do in El Valle or if you're at the market on Sunday. Located behind the church, the museum has a small collection of pre-Columbian ceramics, colonial religious art, petroglyphs, and domestic utensils.

Av. Principal, behind the church. No phone. Admission 25¢. Sun 10am–2pm.

Serpentario *(Kids)*   This modest serpentarium makes for a quick and fun place to learn about snakes. There are 14 different snakes on display, including a boa constrictor that they'll let you hold while you have your picture taken. A local biologist gives interpretive information.

Av. Principal. ℂ 983-6680. Admission $1 adults, 50¢ kids under 13. Daily 8:30am; closes Mon–Thurs at 5pm; Fri–Sat 7pm; Sun 4pm (hours sometimes reduced during low season).

SPAS

Crater Valley Adventure Spa (see below) has a limited-service spa that offers massages, a tiny sauna, and an outdoor whirlpool, and they have an attractive outdoor

End of the Golden Era for the Golden Frog?

Animal extinction is normally a result of habitat loss, but El Valle's amphibians are facing a more insidious enemy: *Batrachochytrium dendrobatidis*. It's a fungus that infects an amphibian and blocks the creature's ability to breathe, and it is spreading so quickly across Panama that conservationists from the U.S. have recently collected and relocated hundreds of amphibians in a Noah's Ark–style evacuation to prevent a mass extinction. Central to this tragedy is the **Golden Frog** (*Atelopus zeteki),* a beloved cultural symbol in Panama not unlike the bald eagle in the U.S. This little frog can be found on T-shirts, posters, and even lottery tickets, and historically it was considered good luck by pre-Columbian cultures. You can see the frog, among other amphibians, at El Nispero Zoo's new amphibian center. (See "What to See & Do," above.)

pool, ringed with hammocks and lounge chairs, that they'll let you use even if you are not lodging at the hotel. (Crater Valley prefers low-key day visitors and no groups). Surely the best spa in town will be at **La Casa de Lourdes,** which was in the planning stages at the time of this book's publication. This elegant hotel intends to have a full spa including massage, whirlpool, Turkish bath, fangotherapy, and a solarium. If you come in the morning, you can lunch at their fabulous restaurant afterward (the pool here is at their restaurant and not private enough to encourage swimming).

SHOPPING

SUNDAY MARKET ✹✹✹

El Valle is regionally famous for its Sunday Market that takes place along the town's main Avenida Principal. It's not a grand bazaar but a colorful and lively event that draws vendors, many of whom are Ngöbe-Buglé and Emberá Indians from around the area who come to hawk traditional clothing, handicrafts, baskets, ceramics, vegetables, orchids, food items, and more. There is a scaled-down version of the market open every day—Saturdays are often quite happening. Hours for the market are 8am to 5pm.

Next to the market is the **Tienda Artesanía Don Pepe** (© 983-6425; daily 8am–6pm), which has an extensive selection of well-made indigenous art and handicrafts from around Panama, plus other trinkets, souvenirs, and maps. Next door to Don Pepe is the Residencial El Valle and its ground-level shop **David's** (© 983-6536; daily 7am–7pm), with a similar, high-quality selection of handicrafts, many of which are made on the premises.

WHERE TO STAY

There is something for every wallet in El Valle, with good budget accommodations, B&Bs, and two upscale hotels. Park Eden, Casa de Lourdes, and Los Capitanes hotels have rooms for those with disabilities, which is not common in Panama. Note that some hotels jack up their prices on weekends, even during low season.

In addition to the lodging options here, a residence owned by an American/Panamanian couple rents out four rooms with kitchenettes. It's called **Los Nances** (© 983-6126; $50–$60 double, cash only). It's located high up at the end of a rutted road, and the view from here is just phenomenal—but only one room has that view, so be sure to ask for it.

EXPENSIVE

Canopy Lodge ✸✸✸ *(Moments)*   Like its sister property, the Canopy Tower, this lodge caters predominately to bird-watchers—though its stylish sensibilities and its prime location in the lush foothills will appeal to any traveler. Unlike the Canopy Tower, there is no early-morning noise to wake up guests who are less-than-enthusiastic about bird-watching. Set on the shore of a meandering stream, Canopy Lodge is fresh and airy, almost minimalist, with most of the property built with river rock, wood, and glass. Guest rooms have whitewashed walls accented with just a dollop of color from Kuna Indian *mola* art. Each room has two queen-size beds with fluffy down comforters, and bathrooms with walk-in showers and drying racks. Sliding-glass doors open wide onto a long balcony, promoting a sense of oneness with the natural surroundings. Canopy Lodge sells bird-watching packages that include airport transfers, guided tours, meals, and accommodations. Contact them for nightly pricing if you'd like lodging only. There is a handsome open-air lounge with couches and an outstanding library; this space is as enjoyable during sunny days as it is during a downpour.

Road to Chorro El Macho. ✆ **264-5720** or 263-2784. www.canopylodge.com. 8 units. Packages are per person, based on 3 nights/4 days: $567–$876. AE, MC, V. **Amenities:** Restaurant; bar; library; bird-watching and other tours. *In room:* Drying racks, no phone.

La Casa de Lourdes ✸✸✸   Perched on a gently sloping hill above one of the best restaurants in Panama, this new boutique hotel has picturesque views and is one of two deluxe lodging options in El Valle (Canopy Lodge is the other). The motif here is Tuscany with a touch of Panama, and all rooms are decorated with heavy wood sleigh beds and thick curtains; spare, pastel-washed walls; and white-tile floors. The bathrooms have beautiful showers tiled with river rock. There are two "villas" with a total of 14 guest rooms; the three-story villa has suites and Superior rooms with French doors that open onto terraces, and these are the best rooms for their accompanying views. Executives are standard doubles with two twins or one king-size bed; the Senior Suite is a junior suite with an adjoining superior room. Guest rooms feature all the creature comforts of an upscale hotel, but the Lourdes is run somewhat like a B&B, with one 24-hour dedicated manager and a light staff, but no front desk. What really shines here are its on-site restaurant (see "Where to Dine," below), its fabulous library replete with well-chosen literature and nonfiction, and its new spa and gym. Note that the outdoor pool is next to the dining area of the restaurant, so you're "on show," as it were. Weekday rates are 10% to 15% cheaper than the weekend rates shown below, and there is a discount for stays of 2 nights or more.

Calle El Ciclo. ✆ **983-6645.** www.lacasadelourdes.com. 14 units. $112 executive, $130 superior, $175 junior suite. AE, MC, V. **Amenities:** Restaurant; outdoor pool; spa and fitness center w/whirlpool and steam room; library; tour desk; limited room service; babysitting; laundry service. *In room:* A/C, TV, minibar, coffeemaker, safe.

MODERATE

Crater Valley Adventure Spa ✸ *(Kids)*   The Crater Valley Adventure Spa is the perfect destination for travelers seeking accommodations, meals, outdoor activities, and spa services all within the same establishment. Still, it's too small to be referred to as a resort—it's more like a hotel with a full complement of amenities. Kids delight in the hotel's climbing wall, obstacle course, and other activities, and adults enjoy the tranquillity of the campestral surroundings, its spa, and its deliciously refreshing pool—really the highlight of the Crater Valley. The pool circumference is elegantly landscaped with chipped rock and Grecian pillars, and flanked with lounge chairs and hammocks for some serious relaxation. There are eight contemporary guest rooms, but each is different from the next, and some are darker than others. For the asking price, management could stand to tighten the screws on service and maintenance, repairing niggling details such as chipped tiles and ripped curtains that hang around the massage salon. Also, the hotel charges extra for every activity and amenity—so know what you're being charged for ahead of time. Their climbing wall, for example, is $5 per five attempts, not per half-hour. The hotel's sister operation, Panama Explorer Tours, organizes outdoor activities. (See "Adventure Tour Operators," above.)

Vía Ranita Dorada. ℂ 983-6167 or 6695-6190. www.crater-valley.com. 8 units. $79–$98 (4 guests); $98–$122 (6 guests). MC, V. **Amenities:** Restaurant; bar; outdoor pool; spa, outdoor whirlpool; sauna; activities center; bike rental; kids' activities; tour desk; laundry service. In room: TV, no phone.

Hotel & Restaurante Los Capitanes ☆ *Kids* Set on an open space with good views of the peaks surrounding El Valle, this hotel has both budget accommodations and spacious "family" suites, as well as manicured gardens and a friendly atmosphere. The German who runs Los Capitanes was once a sea captain himself, hence the name. There are three stucco buildings. One building is divided into polygon rooms that are differently sized and decorated; some buildings are kid-friendly with bunks and cubby-hole type rooms; one building has a loftlike, second-floor sleeping area perfect for kids. Rooms on the second floor have balconies. All rooms here are clean but modest. Around the property are seating areas with outdoor tables, and they have one of the best (and most popular) restaurants in town. (See "Where to Dine," below.) Note that the owner has begun organizing fun, full-day mule rides for guests, which no other hotel offers.

Calle de la Coopertiva. ℂ 983-6080. www.los-capitanes.com. 14 units. $55 double; $77 junior suite. MC, V. **Amenities:** Restaurant; bar; kids' swimming pool; bicycle rental; Internet room; outdoor barbecue; limited room service; laundry service. In room: TV, fridge.

Hotel Rincón Vallero ☆ The Rincón Vallero has some of the best suites and junior suites in El Valle, but it also has kennel-like double rooms that are not much value, probably because the hotel complex has been adding units like patchwork without maintaining quality. It's altogether a funky but friendly place, with a kids' play area, ponds, and tiny streams that meander through the property, and ceramic toadstools and other decor that make the complex feel a little like a fairyland. The low-slung building has ground-floor rooms only, with separate cabinlike units in the back, behind their popular restaurant. The suites are large enough to feel like a spacious one-bedroom apartment, especially room no. 1, which like the other suites has sloping, bamboo-inlaid ceilings and interesting sunken showers tiled entirely in chipped rock and fitted with a skylight. Doubles are cramped, with small bathrooms, and they don't feature the quality craftsmanship found in the suites.

Calle Espave. ℂ 983-6167 or 6695-6190. www.rinconvallero.com. 17 units. $65–$75 standard; $75–$95 junior suite; $95–$125 suite. AE, MC, V. **Amenities:** Restaurant; bar; outdoor pool and kids' pool; billiard table; Ping-Pong table; kids' playground; limited room service; laundry service. In room: A/C, TV, minibar, safe.

Park Eden Bed & Breakfast ☆☆ *Finds* Tucked away on .8 hectares (2 acres) of pleasant, sylvan gardens, the converted home and four *casitas* of the Park Eden offer some of the most comfortable lodging in El Valle. The Park Eden is the true definition of a B&B: lots of charming, country decor; hearty breakfasts; and warm, gracious service provided by Lionel and Monica, the couple who have owned the property for more than 20 years. Every room is different from the next and will appeal to different

kinds of people. There is a two-story, snug house with room for four guests and a full kitchen; other rooms come with refrigerators, microwaves, and coffeemakers. The Limoneros room is more masculine and has a small private patio, while two others are done in pastels and decorated with figurines and lacy curtains. At the time of publication, the B&B was building two more units with kitchens, for two to four people. All units have private entrances. Breakfast is served in guest rooms or in a lovely glass-enclosed porch, and although they do not have a restaurant, if you arrange it in advance, they will happily serve lunch or a romantic candlelit dinner. Park Eden is popular with bird-watchers and receives lots of return visitors.

Calle Espavé. © 983-6167 or 6695-6190. www.parkeden.com. 7 units. $95 double; $125 room w/full kitchen; $195 house for 4. AE, MC, V. **Amenities:** Tour organization; bicycle rentals; self-service laundry. *In room:* A/C, TV, minifridge, microwave, coffeemaker, full kitchen (some rooms), no phone.

INEXPENSIVE

Golden Valley Hotel 🌴 *Value*   Like the Don Pepe (below), this hotel is located on the main street near the market. The Golden Valley is brand-new and scrupulously clean, and is a good value for the price. A friendly beagle named Yoda mans the front foyer, which has a dining area and lounge with a TV. From here, smallish double rooms branch off a main hallway, and many have river-rock walls, standard beds (mostly with two twins), and lots of light. The Golden Valley is owner-run by an amicable couple, and they have a roofed outdoor seating area with limited views of the peaks surrounding El Valle.

Av. Principal. © 983-6097. 10 units. $33 double. MC, V. **Amenities:** Cafe; TV room; laundry service; Internet service. *In room:* No phone.

Hotel Don Pepe 🌴   Located on the second floor above a restaurant and handicrafts store, the Don Pepe is popular with budget travelers for its low price and on-site services. Rooms are immaculately clean but spartan, and each comes with a double and twin bed, accommodating a total of three guests. The building isn't as nice as the Golden Valley, but Don Pepe does have a rooftop seating area with a direct view of the three peaks of Cerro Gaital. Don Pepe is run by a local family, and service is friendly.

Av. Principal. © 983-6425. hoteldonpepe@hotmail.com. 11 units. $25 double. MC, V. **Amenities:** Restaurant; bike rental; Internet center; gift shop; self-service laundry. *In room:* TV, no phone.

WHERE TO DINE

If you're just looking for a snack, a cup of coffee, or even a to-go sandwich or picnic lunch, stop off at **El Valle Gourmet & Coffee Shop** on the main street (© 6715-5785; Fri noon–9pm, Sat 9am–10:30pm, and Sun and holidays 9am–6pm). The shop has juices, coffee, imported cheeses and cold cuts, sandwiches, frozen meals, jams, tinned delicacies, and more. For an ultra-cheap local meal, try **Refresquería Mr. Lary** (no phone; daily 6am–7pm) on Avenida Principal, in front of the church. They offer daily lunch for $2.25, and traditional Panamanian breakfasts.

EXPENSIVE

La Casa de Lourdes 🌴🌴🌴 CONTEMPORARY PANAMANIAN   Some diners drive from Panama City to El Valle (2 hr. each way) just to have lunch at this regionally famous place on Sundays. I adore this restaurant, too—the food is simply out-of-this-world delicious. As the name states, this is Lourdes's house: She's the chef who oversees the kitchen and creates gourmet cuisine that is mostly updated takes on standard Panamanian fare, blended with other Latin American influences. And who is Lourdes Fábrega de Ward? She's a revered chef who studied with Martha Stewart and

Paul Prudhomme, and her well-honed flair and technique is evident in every dish she prepares. What I like best is how she uses so many exotic Panamanian fruits and vegetables in her meals, such as roast pork with guayabera sauce, or Sunday morning mimosas with marayón (a little like passion fruit). Do not miss the yuca croquettes, clam chowder, or any of the seafood dishes, which change weekly but could include sole with trout mousse, or a blackened sea bass in tamarind sauce. The mostly outdoor dining area is under giant arches of a Tuscan-style manor house, next to an outdoor swimming pool. Saturdays and Sundays are absolutely packed, so come with a reservation if you can.

Calle El Ciclo. (C) 983-6450. www.lacasadelourdes.com. Reservations necessary on Sun, and recommended for all other days. Main courses $8–$18. AE, MC, V. Wed–Mon 7:30am–9pm (to 10pm Fri–Sat).

MODERATE
El Rincón Vallero ✿ PERUVIAN/PANAMANIAN   The best thing about Rincón Vallero is that it's usually open when other restaurants are closed. At dinner, low-hanging lamps provide for a cozy, warm ambience, but the dining area is a little oddball with flagstone floors that wrap around three interior fishponds—be careful where you walk or you might fall in. The menu features a lot of dishes that can be prepared multiple ways, including grilled sea bass with nine different preparations, and pastas including ravioli, cannelloni, and spaghetti with a variety of sauces. Their Panamanian classics, such as jumbo shrimp with garlic and spices, are quite good, as are their Peruvian dishes—a carry-over from the days when a Peruvian owned the hotel/restaurant.

Calle Espave. (C) 983-6167. Reservations accepted. Main courses $5–$12. AE, MC, V. Daily 7:30–10:30am, noon–3:30pm, and 6–9pm.

Los Capitanes ✿✿ GERMAN   Part of the Los Capitanes hotel, the restaurant and bar here are quite popular with locals and tourists alike. It's a 10-minute walk from the main street. The restaurant is housed in a stone-and-metal *bohío;* an outdoor dining area is the site of weekend barbecues during the summer. The food is hearty and good, consisting mostly of German dishes such as smoked pork chops with sauerkraut, *leberkäse* (a German meatloaf), and meat or seafood platters for a group (priced per person: $6.75 paella, $12 meat, $13 seafood). There is also a special of the day. Excellent breakfasts include dishes like German pancakes with apples.

Calle de la Coopertiva. (C) 983-6080. Main courses $7.75–$10. MC, V. Daily 8am–9pm.

INEXPENSIVE
Don Pepe ✿ PANAMANIAN   If you're looking for a cheap, simple meal and a lot of dishes to choose from, this is your place. It's a bit like a diner, but the staff is very friendly and the prices are low. Everything from Chinese food to Panamanian dishes to hamburgers is on offer—try their *ropa vieja,* a stewed beef dish, or carrot mousse flan. There are sandwiches, vegetarian items, and fresh fruit juices and shakes. It's a good place for a quick lunch.

Av. Principal. (C) 983-6425. Reservations not accepted. Main courses $3–$8. MC, V. Mon–Thurs 7am–9pm; Fri–Sun 7am–11pm.

Pizzería Pinocchio's PIZZERIA   Thin-crust pizzas baked in a wood oven are the specialty here, and they are the best pizzas in town. There are a dozen varieties to choose from, as well as traditional pastas like lasagna. The ambience is cafeteria-like—if it doesn't suit you, order your pizza to go.

Av. Principal. (C) 983-6715. Reservations not accepted. Pizzas $4–$5.50. No credit cards. Fri 4–9pm; Sat–Sun and holidays noon–9pm.

4 Western Coclé Province & Penonomé

145km (90 miles) W of Panama City

The Coclé Province from Penonomé to Aguadulce is scarcely visited by foreign tourists, and although local municipalities have initiated the first stages of organized tourism, the region is not yet poised to become a hot spot. Historical, cultural, and natural attractions are scattered around in such a fashion that renting a vehicle or booking a custom tour is key to exploring the area, unless you're headed straight for the Trinidad Lodge outside of Penonomé. Travelers normally visit this area on their way to the Azuero Peninsula, or as a side trip from the Pacific Coast. In this section, villages are highlighted only if they have at least one worthwhile attraction.

The capital of the Coclé Province is **Penonomé,** a town that for a few years during the 17th century was the nation's capital after Panama City had been sacked by the pirate Henry Morgan. Little of the town's colonial history is evident today, and really there isn't much to do and see in Penonomé apart from visiting the **Mercado de Arte-sanías** and **Museo de Penonomé** (see below). Heading north out of Penonomé, **La Pintada** village is regionally known for its own handicrafts fair and especially for its locally renowned straw hats and its cigar factory.

GETTING THERE & DEPARTING

By Bus   Buses leave every 20 minutes from Panama City's Albrook Terminal to Penonomé; it takes a little over 2 hours and costs $4. You'll be dropped off on the Interamericana Highway on the opposite side of the Hotel Dos Continentes. From here, there are local buses to La Pintada that leave every 20 minutes and cost $1. You can also grab a taxi to take you to La Pintada for $3.

By Car   The drive to Penonomé takes 2 hours. The exit is clearly signed and is at the Hotel Dos Continentes.

WHAT TO SEE & DO

The **Mercado de Artesanías** (Mon–Fri 9am–5pm) is located on the Interamericana Highway just before the exit for Penonomé. You'll find a limited selection of mostly Ngöbe-Buglé indigenous handicrafts and clothing. If you're driving to the Azuero Peninsula, you might consider a quick stop to see what they have here and continue on your way. Near the plaza is the small yet interesting **Museo de Penonomé** (ℝ (② **997-8490;** Mon–Sat 9am–12:30pm and 1:30–4pm, Sun 9:30am–1pm; $1 adults, 25¢ kids) on Calle San Antonio at Parque Rubén Darío Carles in what's left of the San Antonio colonial neighborhood. The museum occupies four adjoining homes and displays colonial religious art, pre-Columbian artifacts, and artifacts from the town's initial stages.

WHERE TO STAY & DINE

I don't recommend that you lodge in Penonomé—it's better on the Pacific Coast or at the Trinidad Lodge or La Iguana (see below). You'll only find utilitarian lodging in Penonomé, and most of it is located on the not-so-glamorous Interamericana Highway. If you are in a pinch, and really need an inexpensive place to lay your head down, try the **Hotel La Pradera,** which has clean, modern rooms, a restaurant, and a swimming pool (② **991-0106;** $25 Mon–Thurs, $35 Fri–Sun; MasterCard and Visa are accepted). You'll see it near the western entrance to Penonomé.

LA PINTADA

About 20 minutes from Penonomé is the charming village of La Pintada, known for its *sombreros pintados,* or "painted hats," made from intricately hand-woven black and white fibers of the *bellota* plant. It's a long, arduous task to create this traditional hat, and prices for one average $75 to $80, twice that amount if bought in Panama City. You'll find a good selection of *sombreros pintados* at the **Mercado de Artesanías La Pintada** 𝕲 (Tues–Sun 9am–5pm), as well as *montuño* embroidered shirts, woven rugs, dolls dressed in folkloric dresses such as the pollera, and other regional knick-knacks. The market is on the left side of the main road from Penonomé, once you enter La Pintada.

Another unique attraction, one that will pique the interest of cigar smokers, is a factory tour of **Cigarros Joyas de Panamá** 𝕲 (© 6692-2582). These are the only premium cigars in Panama made with Cuban-seed tobacco. Miriam Padilla launched her cigar operation in the early 1980s with Cuban partners who eventually moved on. After a hiatus for many years, Miriam rebuilt the business and now each month produces more than 300,000 fine cigars, handcrafted in the Cuban tradition, for export. A box of 25 of her cigars sells for about $85 in the U.S., but you can buy them wholesale here. You'll see the factory, which is well signed, just before you enter La Pintada.

TWO ECOLODGES OUTSIDE OF PENONOME

Both lodges mentioned here are located on the road to Churuquita Grande and Caimito. To get here, turn into Penonomé at Hotel Dos Continentes on the Interamericana Highway, then turn right (northeast) onto the road to Churuquita and Caimito. La Iguana is 14km (8½ miles) from the turnoff; the Trinidad is about the same distance from La Iguana (28km/17 miles from the turnoff to Caimito). The Trinidad will pick you up in Penonomé; for the La Iguana, take a taxi from Penonomé.

La Iguana Eco-Resort 𝕲 *Kids*   This ecolodge does not offer luxury or a spa, but it does offer pleasant nature trails, a river, a pool for swimming, a minizoo, and other outdoor activities like horseback riding—all in all, it's an ideal place for kids, but with so few people here, couples will feel perfectly comfortable, too. La Iguana is very inexpensive and nothing fancy, but the new administration recently spruced up the property and repainted guest rooms; each has two double beds and three singles in a loftlike second floor, for a total of five people. Bathrooms are private but without hot water. The owners of La Iguana truly love nature, and even the minizoo is part of their effort to repopulate the area with endemic species that have been in decline. The lodge's restaurant specializes in barbecued meats and seafood, and though simple, the meals are quite good. For an additional price, they'll organize tours around the Coclé area.

Churuquita Grande. © 991-0879. www.laiguanaresort.com. 8 units. $25–$35 for 2 people; each additional person is $5. No credit cards. **Amenities:** Restaurant; outdoor pool; minizoo; outdoor sports field; horseback riding; nature trails; kids' playground. *In room:* A/C (in some rooms, and for an additional price), no phone.

Trinidad Spa & Lodge 𝕲𝕲 *Finds*   The drop-dead views and the fact that this place is known to few outside of Panama City make the Trinidad Spa & Lodge a real find. Recently expanded and rebaptized as the Trinidad, it was previously known as the Posada Ecolodge. The undulating landscape that surrounds the lodge is cloaked in thick, green jungle and dominated by a torlike hill called Cerro La Vieja, among other peaks in the distance. For the past 20 years, the owners have been encouraging regrowth of the forest once shorn clean by farmers; today it is lushly landscaped and attracts lots of birds and other fauna. What also makes this lodge such a find is that

Parque Arqueológico El Caño

El Caño Archaeological Park displays the excavated burial grounds and artifacts of indigenous groups that inhabited this region from A.D. 500 to 1500. Considering that it is one of the most important archaeological sites in Panama, it's surprising that there is less to see here than would fill an hour—much of what was found was shipped to the U.S. when an American amateur archaeologist excavated the site in the 1920s. More importantly, it is estimated that many unearthed burial sites still exist here, yet there is little interpretive information about these or other items. Nevertheless, if you're in the area, this 8.1-hectare (20-acre) park makes for an interesting stop. There are burial mounds and a burial pit with skeletons still intact; a small museum with pottery, tools, and other artifacts taken from burial sites; and a reproduction of what the site is imagined to have originally looked like. (Hours are Tues–Sat 9am–noon and 12:30–4pm, Sun 9am–1pm; admission $1 adults, 25¢ kids.) To get here, take the exit for El Caño, about 27km (19 miles) west of Penonomé, and continue for 3km (1¾ miles), always keeping to the left until you reach the site. If you don't have a vehicle, you'll need to take a taxi from Natá.

their spa services are reasonably priced (about $30 for a 50-min. massage, for example), and they provide guests with delicious, organic cuisine, fine wines, and other sybaritic delights. The Trinidad comprises 19 spacious rooms divided into thatched-roof cabins, with four rooms to each cabin. Please note that guest rooms are not ultra-deluxe and the decor is spare—yet they're perfectly comfortable and have quality beds. By far the best rooms are the Turega and Chichibalí units because of the views and balconies; these units are considered "Premier" rooms and are more expensive even though they're the same size as a standard. There are several trails around the property for hiking, and unique mule rides can be organized, among other excursions. Rates are nightly and include breakfast; sample 2-night packages include three daily meals, two spa treatments, and two eco-tours for $183 per person.

Caimito, Coclé Province. (C) 983-8900 in Panama, or 786/206-0219 in the U.S. www.posadaecologica.com. 19 units. $69 double standard; $99 double premier. MC, V. **Amenities:** Restaurant; bar; full-service spa w/massage, facials, and thermal baths; eco-tours; game room. *In room:* A/C, no phone.

NATA

Natá is the oldest village in Panama, founded by the Spanish in 1522 and named after the powerful *cacique* Natá who once ruled this region. Natá is known for its venerable church **Basilica Menor Santiago Apostal de Natá,** which was erected during the same year and is therefore considered to be the oldest surviving church in the Americas. Extensive renovations took place during the 1990s, yet visitors can still appreciate the church's original wooden columns, altars, and artwork. The church is located on the plaza, about a half-mile from the Interamericana Highway. Natá is 180km (112 miles) from Panama City, and 31km (20 miles) from Penonomé.

5 La Península de Azuero

From Panama City: Chitré is 250km (155 miles); Las Tablas is 282km (175 miles), and Pedasí is 324km (201 miles)

Entering the Azuero Peninsula past Divisa, you'll feel as if you turned your watch back a hundred years. The Azuero Peninsula is considered the cradle of Panamanian folklore and rural culture, passed down from Spanish colonists who settled here during the 17th and 18th centuries. The region is dotted with terra-cotta-tile-and-gingerbread representations of early Spanish villas, and everything is very, very slowly paced—except when residents join together for the raucous festivities for which this region is famous. Nowhere in Panama is **Carnaval** celebrated with as much gusto as it is here in the Azuero, especially in towns such as Las Tablas and Chitré; and religious festivals honoring saints are livened with fireworks, music, and costumed folkloric dances that are as pagan as they are Catholic. The Azuero Peninsula is the birthplace of the pollera, widely considered to be one of the most beautiful traditional dresses in the world. *Seco,* the sugar-cane alcohol and national drink, hails from this region, too. But what makes the Azuero Peninsula special are its people. Panamanians are remarkably friendly, but Azuero residents are beguiling in their fondness for greeting strangers, so practice your *"buenos días"* and get ready to smile.

Festivals & Events in the Azuero Peninsula

Residents of the Azuero Peninsula seemingly live for festivals, and here they are more lively than anywhere else in the country. The following are the major festivals, but the list is by no means comprehensive. Check the IPAT tourism board's website at **www.visitpanama.com** for information about all events taking place during your visit.

February: Carnaval kicks off the Friday before Ash Wednesday and continues until the following Tuesday in this nationwide event—and it's at its rowdiest and most colorful here in the Azuero. See "Party On! Carnaval in the Azuero Peninsula" on p. 202.

March/April: Semana Santa's most colorful celebration is in La Villa de Los Santos and Guararé.

Late April: Feria Internacional del Azuero in La Villa de Los Santos. As at a county fair, this features animal displays, food stalls, and drinking.

June: Festival Corpus Christi in La Villa de Los Santos. This village explodes with activity for the 2-week festival known for its elaborate dances led by men in devil masks.

July 20 to 22: Festival Patronales de La Virgen de Santa Librada in Las Tablas. This festival is famous for its **Festival de la Pollera** on July 22, which showcases the region's most beautiful polleras and elects the year's "Queen of the Pollera."

September 24: Festival de la Mejorana in Guararé. This nationally famous folkloric festival sees hundreds of dancers, musicians, and singers converging for a week of events and serious partying.

October 19: Fundación del Distrito de Chitré in Chitré. A large festival with parades celebrates the founding of the city.

November 10: Grito de la Villa, or "Cry of Independence," in Villa de Los Santos. Commemorates this national independence holiday with parades and music.

The Azuero Peninsula protrudes south from the Panamanian isthmus into the Pacific Ocean, separating the Gulf of Panama to the east and the Gulf of Chiriquí to the west; most of the peninsula is within the Herrera and Los Santos provinces. It is about 100km (60km) wide and 90km (55 miles) long and, sadly, most of the terrain has been completely denuded because of the region's large-scale cattle production. Indeed, a visitor who has just come from the green and lush panorama farther north is in for a surprise here in the Azuero. Some areas, such as Sarigua National Park, have been so thoroughly stripped of vegetation that they are now considered a desert. Oddly, most towns sit inland despite the beautiful coastline here—but investors and foreigners are starting to move in, especially near Pedasí and Playa Venado. This pristine coast could see changes during the next few decades.

So where to go and how to best see this region? You'll notice that destinations or towns in this section seem to include only the highlights, but in most cases there is just one museum or one church to see in each village. Also, decent lodging is scarce here, the reason you won't see much listed outside of Chitré and Pedasí. My advice is to rent a car in Panama City or Chitré and take in the sights at your own pace, stopping from town to town and lodging near Pedasí. This picturesque village has the widest range of lodging and dining options, is close to beaches, and has snorkeling, surfing, and diving, too. If you have a car, you'll also be able to stop at roadside stands that dot the Carretera Nacional and sell everything from fresh watermelon to sausages; there are *fondas,* or cheap food stands, too, with fried Panamanian snacks, as well as open-air cantinas that sell three beers for $1. There are no commercial flights to Chitré and Pedasí (though there are charter flights). Bus service is inexpensive, but you'll need a taxi to get around from the station. It takes more than 4 hours to reach Pedasí by vehicle from Panama City; those with enough time might consider breaking up the trip with a stay in El Valle or on the Pacific Coast.

PARITA

About 25km (16 miles) after Divisa is Parita, one of the most charming villages in Panama. It's a very humble place, but the streets are lined with well-preserved examples of Spanish colonial architecture. At the plaza is the **Iglesia de Santo Domingo de Guzmán,** but apart from this there really aren't any attractions here other than city streets to be wandered and photographed. If you're driving along the Azuero Peninsula, make this a quick stop on your itinerary.

CHITRE

Chitré is the capital of Herrera Province, and it is the largest town on the Azuero Peninsula, founded in 1848. Many of the streets here ooze charm, yet on the whole Chitré isn't as picturesque as Pedasí. Many of its colonial buildings have been replaced by more utilitarian structures, and the downtown bustles with shops hawking cheap plastic goods and clothing. Chitré does offer plentiful services, including lodging and car rental, and it can be a convenient base for exploring the region. Visitors during Carnaval will find higher-quality lodging here than in Las Tablas, but this option is better for those with a rental vehicle (don't forget that Chitré is pretty lively, too, during Carnaval). Before arriving at Chitré, you'll pass through the tiny village of La Arena, which is described below in "What to See & Do."

You'll see an **IPAT tourism office** just before you enter La Arena, but the location is not very convenient, on Calle 19 de Octubre—when the road forks in La Arena, head right toward La Villa los Santos (© **974-4532;** daily 8:30am–4:30pm). The tourism office has a helpful staff and a limited amount of printed information about the history of the area and attractions.

FAST FACTS   Banks: There are 24-hour ATMs at HSBC bank on Avenida Herrera, ½ block north from the plaza; and Banco Nacional on Paseo Enrique Greenzier, near the Hotel Versailles. **Internet:** Sanchi (© **996-9040**), at Calle Aminta Burgos de Amado, 1 block west from the plaza, is open daily from 8am to midnight. **Laundry:** Lavandería Express is on Avenida Herrera, ½ block from the plaza. **Police:** © **996-4333.**

GETTING THERE & AWAY

By Plane   Aeropuerto de Chitré is no longer serviced with regular flights; instead, you'll have to book a charter flight with **Air Panama** (© **316-9000;** www.flyair panama.com); the cost is $637 for three passengers, $770 for five, and $900 for eight.

By Bus & Taxi   The **Transportes de Herrera bus terminal,** a $1.15 taxi ride from the center of town, is located on Calle 19 de Octubre (also called Av. Roberto Ramírez de Diego). The turnoff for this street is next to the Hotel Hong Kong. Buses to and from Panama City cost $7 and run every hour between 6am and 6pm; the trip is 3½ hours. Buses to Las Tablas leave every 15 minutes from 6am to 6:30pm and cost $1.25. For buses to Pedasí, you'll need a bus to Las Tablas, and then you must trans-fer to a Pedasí-bound bus. Or you can take a taxi for $25.

By Car   When you arrive at La Arena, just before Chitré, the road forks; take the left road and continue along the Carretera Nacional, which will take you directly into the center of town. If you turn right at the plaza, the road will funnel back into the Car-retera Nacional south to La Villa de los Santos. Chitré is 37km (23 miles) from the start of the Carretera Nacional at Divisa, and 252km (157 miles) from Panama City.

For **rental cars** in Chitré, try **Hertz** (© **996-2256;** www.hertz.com), located in front of the bus terminal; or **Thrifty** (© **996-9565;** www.thrifty.com), which is on Paseo Enrique Geenzier, just west of the Hotel Versalles.

WHAT TO SEE & DO

There really isn't much to do in the town itself, other than pay a quick visit to the **Museo de Herrera** (© **996-0077;** Tues–Sat 9am–5pm; admission $1 adults, 25¢ kids) at Calle Manuel María Correa and Avenida Julio Arjona; you'll recognize the whitewashed colonial building—it sticks out from its more modern neighbors. The museum staff have put a lot of effort into providing visitors with a better understand-ing of the anthropology and ecology of the Herrera Province, but however well-mean-ing the staff are, the museum is clearly under-funded. Still, there are a few gems here, including pottery dating back to 2500 B.C., and folkloric costumes and polleras. There is a small library with research books about the region; signs are in Spanish only, but the staff is working on an English-language informational brochure.

Take a step into the lovely **Catedral de San Juan Bautista** on the plaza, built at the turn of the 20th century with a bold stone exterior and exposed-wood interior with stained glass and chandeliers.

La Arena

This tiny artisans' village is almost entirely dedicated to pottery making, which began during pre-Columbian times. Most of the vendors who hawk their ceramics along the two principal streets here sell gaily painted pots called *tinajas,* which traditionally were used as all-purpose storage vases but are now primarily decorative. There are also wall hangings, flower pots, and animal figurines, but the best buy here: reproductions of terra-cotta-colored pre-Columbian vases and other such storage vessels. You'll have to look around to find these since it seems that the artisans are opting to create more modern styles, most of which are a little gaudy and not particularly attractive. For a good selection, head to the **Mercado de Artesanías** in the large, white building found where the road divides near the center of town (no phone; daily 9am–4:30pm). For traditional, pre-Columbian-influenced pottery, visit **Cerámica Calderón** (© **974-4946;** daily 8am–5pm), whose owner, Angel Calderón, has been handcrafting beautiful, museum-quality pieces for half a century. Angel and his artisans offer to show visitors how the pieces are made, from pottery wheel to the voluminous ovens out back. The workshop is on the right just as you enter town. La Arena is only 2km (1¼ miles) west of Chitré.

Parque Nacional Sarigua (Sarigua National Park)

Ranking as one of the more bizarre national parks in Panama, Sarigua National Park protects nearly 809 hectares (2,000 acres) of lunarlike wasteland caused by the total destruction of native forest by settlers clearing land for cattle. The park protects large mangrove swamps along the coast, but mostly the protected area is something akin to a desert—or so they'd like you to believe, but really, a visit here provides you with a vivid example of the devastation that occurs when indiscriminate deforestation takes place. After settlers cleared the region of its coastal forests, the forces of wind, ebbing tides, and rain eroded the acidic soil here, leaving deep fissures and oddly shaped land formations. The fascinating sight is, more than anything, a good lesson about protection of forests.

The park lies along the coast and is reached by a well-signed road off the Carretera Nacional, about 10km (6 miles) from Chitré; after the turnoff continue following the signs. There is an ANAM park-ranger station with a lookout point over the expanse of Sarigua (© **966-8216;** admission is $3), and that's about it. But if you've got the time, stop for a quick look.

WHERE TO STAY & DINE

Hotel Guayacanes 𝒢 (Kids)   It isn't luxurious, but it is the most upscale hotel in Chitré. The Guayacanes is close to the bus terminal and about a 5-minute drive or taxi ride from the main drag, which is ideal if you're looking for a tucked-away location to repair to after a day on the streets—but not ideal if you want close contact with the local scene. Formerly part of the Barceló chain, the hotel could easily be called a small resort. It is set on a spacious property and has a casino, an outdoor pool (that can get busy on weekends), gardens, and a kids' play area, among other amenities. Guests are allowed access to the Chitré Golf Club, too. The guest rooms are within a couple of cookie-cutter buildings fanned around a pleasant, artificial lagoon with benches, a fountain, and a waterfall. The rooms are average size, with a country decor and ceramic floors, and there are junior suites and regular suites. Farther south are certainly more interesting places to stay, but considering the amenities offered here and the price, this hotel is an excellent value. There are two good, open-air/indoor restaurants that serve international dishes (daily 7am–11pm), and they allow **day visits** to their pool for $5.50 adults, $3.50 kids, which includes a snack.

Vía Circunvalación. © **996-9758** or 996-8093. www.losguayacanes.com. 64 units. $45 double. AE, MC, V. **Amenities:** 2 restaurants; 2 bars; disco; casino; outdoor pool; tennis courts; gym; kids' play area; tour desk; gift shop; laundry service. *In room:* A/C, TV, hair dryer.

Hotel Hong Kong *⊀* Situated on the busy Carretera Nacional, this hotel does not claim the most glamorous of locations, but kids love their on-site aquatic park. Notwithstanding its Chinese-style roof, the hotel exterior looks like any run-of-the-mill U.S. chain; inside, the Hong Kong motif continues with Chinese art and furnishings. Guest rooms are clean and comfortable, with decent, but slightly garish, furniture, and the price is nice. You can't really walk anywhere except to a McDonald's and other strip-mall-style stores. The aquatic park has three swimming pools and a large, tubular water slide. On weekends, this is a popular place for kids celebrating their birthdays, so expect crowds. The restaurant serves Chinese and international dishes, but the food is inconsistent in quality.

Carretera Nacional at Vía Circunvalación. (🕐 996-4483 or 996-9180. www.welcome.to/hotelhongkong. 30 units. $35 double; $90 during festivals. AE, MC, V. **Amenities:** Restaurant; bar; Internet access; aquatic park. *In room:* A/C, TV.

Hotel Rex *⊀* I like this hotel because it is right on the plaza, it has a decent on-site restaurant and mini–business center with Internet access, and it's dirt-cheap. There's nothing fancy about the place; the rooms are spartan and the beds are average, but there is hot water and even cable TV. Try to get a brighter room on one of the top floors, but if you can't, you can use the common terrace to look out onto the plaza. Finicky travelers should go elsewhere, but if you're trying to curb your costs, this is your place.

I also recommend their ground-floor **restaurant El Mesón,** which overlooks the plaza and features a lengthy menu with something for everyone, including seafood, traditional Panamanian and Spanish dishes, tacos, pasta, sandwiches, and a kids' menu. If you're really hungry, order one of their *parrilladas,* a selection of meats served on a mini-barbecue. The restaurant is open daily from 7am to 1pm; prices are about $4.50 to $9.

Central plaza *(parque).* (🕐 996-4310. hotelrexchitre@hotmail.com. 33 units. $20 double; $40 during Carnaval and other festivals. AE, MC, V. **Amenities:** Restaurant; business center. *In room:* A/C, TV.

Hotel Versalles Despite its boxy, bland exterior, the Hotel Versalles has a soothing lobby full of plants and a central patio with a small outdoor pool, giving you the sensation of being in the Tropics and not in the dry city of Chitré. Guest rooms are modern and clean, but a little musty and with run-of-the-mill decor commonly found in midrange chain hotels. Indeed, there's not a lot of charm here, but it's a good value nonetheless. Also, amenities such as assistance with rental vehicles and admission to the local Chitré Golf Club are available. To get to the town center, you'll need to walk about 10 minutes along a busy road. Doubles have either one or two queen-size beds. The **restaurant** is one of the better dining options in town, serving national dishes such as tasty grilled and fried seafood with rice and beans, and international dishes with a little more flair, plus sandwiches and snacks. The restaurant is open daily from 6:30am to 10:30pm.

Paseo Enrique Geenzier. (🕐 996-4422. www.hotelversalles.com. 60 units. $30–$35 double. AE, MC, V. **Amenities:** Restaurant; bar; outdoor pool; access to the Chitré Golf Club; car rental; business center; gift shop; limited room service; laundry. *In room:* A/C, TV.

LA VILLA DE LOS SANTOS

Just 4km (2½ miles) south of Chitré, you'll cross over Río la Villa and into Los Santos Province. A few minutes later, you'll arrive at the colonial town La Villa de Los Santos, often referred to simply as "Los Santos." This is the site of the famous "Cry of Independence," when Panamanians issued the first official request to liberate themselves from Spanish rule. The letter of request was signed on November 10, 1821, inside what is now the **Museo de la Nacionalidad** (🕐 **966-8192;** Tues–Sat 9am–5pm;

admission $1 adults, 75¢ students, 25¢ kids under 12). The most interesting aspect of the museum, located on the northwest side of Parque Simon Bolívar, is the lovely building it is housed in, with lofty ceilings and handmade ceramic floors. The curators have set up the room to show how it would have looked during the signing of the declaration. There is also a display of pre-Columbian ceramics and other odds and ends, but not enough to keep you here more than 15 minutes.

More worthwhile is a visit to the most beautiful church in the Azuero Peninsula, **Iglesia de San Atanacio,** also located on the Bolívar plaza. This baroque, statuesque church was declared a national monument since most of the interior decorative work is intact from the year it opened, 1782. Some features of the church are even older—the church was built in stages beginning with the retablo (the structure forming the back of the altar) in 1721, and the ornamented archway in 1733. The altar and archway are simply gorgeous, intricately carved with cherubs and flowers that are almost completely covered with gold leaf and decorative paint. There is also a wooden, full-scale sculpture of Christ, as well as plaques designating the names of priests who are buried here.

WHERE TO STAY & DINE

Hotel la Villa ⟨ This midsize hotel is laid out in a motel-like fashion, and offers modest yet pleasant accommodations at a good price. The highlight here is the swimming pool, surrounded by palm trees and leafy vegetation, but the rooms are okay, too—if you book in their newer wing (avoid the dingy, older wing). They're nothing fancy, but the beds are decent, and the clean rooms feature a bit of folkloric art and a good air-conditioning system. There's a restaurant on-site. Just before entering Las Villas, you'll see signs for the hotel and the Restaurant Las Palmeras.

La Villa de los Santos. ⓒ **966-8201.** Fax 966-8201. 38 units. $33–$40 double in new wing; $22 double in older units. V. **Amenities:** Restaurant; outdoor pool. *In room:* A/C, TV.

Kiosco El Ciruelo PANAMANIAN This roadside, cantina-style restaurant is the locals' favorite. Food is cooked over a wood fire, so it's definitely rustic. Expect Panamanian specialties: El Ciruelo is known for its spicy, pork-filled tamales, and there are soups and barbecued meats, too.

La Villa de los Santos. 3km (1¾ miles) southeast of town. No phone. Main courses $1.50–$6. No credit cards.

GUARARE

This blink-and-you-miss-it village is nationally famous for its yearly **La Mejorana** festival (see "Festivals & Events in the Azuero Peninsula" on p. 195); you'll notice the

---

Fun Fact **Did You Know?**

The national dress, the pollera, is from the Azuero Peninsula and is considered to be one of the most beautiful traditional dresses in the world. It consists of a full, gathered skirt over several petticoats, and a flounced top, intricately embroidered with floral designs and trimmed with lace. The pollera is worn during special occasions, and would not be complete without *mosquetas* and *tembelques,* or gold and pearl jewelry, as well as hair combs encrusted with pearls. A pollera takes several months to a year to make, and can cost thousands of dollars.

permanent stage set up in the plaza. Guararé has its charms, but the village is so tranquil it feels almost abandoned. If you're driving past, take a quick spin through town and visit the **Museo Manuel F. Zarate** (© 994-5644; Tues–Sat 8am–4pm; admission 75¢ adults, 25¢ kids under 13), on Calle 21, 2 blocks behind the church. Located within the graceful old home of the founder of La Mejorana festival, this quaint folkloric museum, like all the region's museums, strives to do more but is under-funded. Expect to find dusty displays of polleras from the early 1900s, devil masks, and photos of past reigning queens of La Mejorana festival. Guararé is located 26km (16 miles) south of Chitré; turn on the road at the grocery store.

LAS TABLAS

Las Tablas is the provincial capital of Los Santos, known as the "cradle of national folklore" chiefly for its famous **Carnaval** festivities (see "Party on! Carnaval in the Azuero Peninsula," below). The spruce town is made of adobe colonial homes with iron balustrades and terra-cotta roofs, interspersed with more modern, utilitarian architecture and service-oriented businesses. It has more of a city feel to it than even Chitré, but really, it's a quiet place without much to see or do except wander the streets and relax in the plaza with an ice-cream cone. Most tourists visit Las Tablas only for Carnaval, or on their way south to Pedasí.

The town's sole museum, **Museo de Belisario Porras** (© 994-6326; Tues–Sat 8am–4pm, Sun 9am–noon; admission 50¢ adults, 25¢ kids), located on the south side of the plaza, pays homage to Panama's national hero and three-term president Dr. Belisario Porras, who died in 1942. The museum is inside Porras's old home, and features military decorations, stamps with his likeness, and documents pertaining to his time spent as a national leader, but this museum is easily skipped.

GETTING THERE & DEPARTING

By Bus or Taxi The bus terminal is located about 5 blocks north of the plaza, on the Carretera Nacional and Avenida Dr. Emilio Castro. Buses to Las Tablas from Panama City leave every hour from 6am to 7pm. Buses to Panama City generally leave every hour from 6am until about 5:30pm. Hours change frequently, so it's a good idea to pop in and buy your ticket and check schedules; the fare is $8 for buses with air-conditioning. To Pedasí, buses run every 45 minutes from 6am to 7pm, and cost $2. Taxis are plentiful in Las Tablas; there are taxis at the bus terminal and also at the taxi stand at Calle 2 and the Carretera Nacional, next to the Banco Nacional. A taxi to Pedasí costs about $20.

By Car Las Tablas is 282km (175 miles) from Panama City, and 32km (20 miles) from Chitré. The Carretera Nacional funnels into town and passes the main plaza; if continuing on, you'll need to hang a left at the end of the plaza (Calle Belisario Porras) to keep following the Carretera Nacional out of town.

WHERE TO STAY & DINE

Hotel Piamonte This is as good as it gets in Las Tablas, but really this hotel is just a step above backpacker lodging. The Piamonte is clean, with cheery lemon-yellow halls and friendly service, but guest rooms are very spare, with low-quality mattresses, well-worn bedding, and a lack of windows. The best two rooms are called "junior suites"—a misnomer since they are just more spacious doubles with bureaus and better lighting, but they face the road and are noisier. During Carnaval, the Piamonte only sells 5-night packages for $400 to $500, lodging only, which is pretty steep given the basic accommodations. Still, the hotel has a ground-floor restaurant that is one of

Party On! Carnaval in the Azuero Peninsula

Some say the only thing that Panamanians take seriously is Carnaval, and here in the Azuero, especially in **Las Tablas,** it's celebrated with a fervor unseen elsewhere in Panama. For old-timers who lament that Carnaval has marched toward vulgarity in Panama City, the festival in the Azuero has maintained its folkloric traditions. It begins the Saturday before Ash Wednesday and continues for 4 days with dancing, drinking, music, and parades. The atmosphere is enlivened by the famous rivalry between Calle Arriba and Calle Abajo (High Street and Low Street, respectively), whereby the town is divided into two groups that try to outdo each other with the fanciest costumes and floats, and even their own queens, who are specially chosen for the event. Other highlights include the parade of the polleras. Be forewarned that *mojaderos,* guys who spray passersby with water from pistols, garden hoses, buckets, and even fire hoses, are out before noon, so be prepared to get drenched.

Carnaval is a tremendously enjoyable cultural and party event, but keep in mind that in Las Tablas it is also a raucous and sometimes disorderly event that might be too much for some people. For this reason, many tourists opt to lodge elsewhere and visit Las Tablas for the day. Or, for a low-key version of Carnaval, head to a quieter town such as Pedasí or La Villa de los Santos. *Note:* Hotels in Las Tablas and Chitré, and many others around the Azuero, sell 4- and 5-night Carnaval packages at prices that are about double the standard rate. You will need at least a month's notice, and most hotels will expect you to pay 100% upfront.

the better eateries in town, serving everything from tacos to Panamanian-style meats and seafood to Chinese food. The restaurant is open daily from 7am to 11pm. They'll provide room service, but it's hard to imagine wanting to eat in your room.

Av. Belisario Porras. ✆ 994-6372. 10 units. $25 double; $35 junior suite. AE, MC, V. **Amenities:** Restaurant; Internet. *In room:* A/C, TV, no phone.

Residencial Mariela   The Mariela is the kind of hotel that builds character in those who brave its spartan guest rooms—but if you're a budget-minded traveler perhaps you won't mind. Fronting the Piamonte, and located on the second floor above an appliance and kitchen store, the Mariela is dirt-cheap, about the same in quality as the Piamonte, but with brighter rooms. Beds are cots with low-quality mattresses. The owner is very amicable and helpful, and there's satellite TV, a big bonus. The front rooms are the best for their large windows, and they are next to a terrace overlooking the street. Five-night Carnaval packages go for $350 to $450, lodging only.

Av. Belisario Porras. ✆ 994-6473. 13 units. $17–$20 double. No credit cards.

Pizzeria Portofino PIZZERIA   This takeout-style pizzeria does brisk business because of its cheap thin-crust pizzas, burgers, and sandwiches. It's a good spot for a meal on the run (there are a few tables), or you can order to go. There are also good fresh fruit juices and shakes.

Av. Belisario Porras. No phone. Pizzas $3–$5. No credit cards. Mon–Sat 9am–10pm; Sun 11am–10pm.

Restaurant & Pizzería El Caserón 📄 PANAMANIAN/PIZZERIA   Just off the main street, on a tranquil corner surrounded by colonial homes, this restaurant is housed in a hacienda-style building and offers a pleasant ambience that provokes you to linger a little longer than usual after your meal. Another plus is its extensive menu, with typical Panamanian dishes like barbecued meats in homemade sauce. (Most meats are prepared with local ingredients such as chicken with pineapple, prunes, and cherries, or with mushrooms and almonds.) Pastas, such as their tasty lasagna, are served in large portions, and there are simple pizzas, sandwiches, and farm-style breakfasts. The service is attentive and friendly. Note that the restaurant does not serve alcohol.

Calle Agustín Batista at Calle Moisés Espino. Ⓢ 994-6066. Reservations accepted for groups. Main courses $3–$9. No credit cards. Daily 7am–11pm.

Restaurante Los Faroles 📄 *Kids* PANAMANIAN   The newest restaurant in the area is located outside of town on the road to Chitré—just before entering Las Tablas, you'll see an orangey, hacienda-style building on your left side. There is a breezy wraparound terrace, like the one at El Caserón, which offers an enjoyable ambience, but its location is more isolated and it overlooks the National Highway. Still, the food is a notch above El Caserón's. Hearty platters of barbecued meats and seafood are the specialty here, and there are salads and kids' items. There is also a children's playground.

Carretera Nacional. Ⓢ 994-0777. Main courses $4–$12. MC, V. Tues–Sun 10am–11pm.

PEDASI

Arguably the region's prettiest town, this is without a doubt the choice destination in the region, and I hesitate to say that because it is one of those special places you want to remain a secret. Pedasí is the kind of small town where no passing visitor goes ungreeted—usually locals camped out on their front porch give a pleasant wave to any stranger passing by. The autochthonous architecture is well-preserved, and residents have recently painted and spiffed up most of the facades of residential buildings. The town is one long main street called Avenida Central, with a tidy plaza 2 blocks from the main road. The paved and signed streets and other well-tended civic structures exist because the former president Mireya Moscoso is from here—you'll see her bust in the plaza. Note that this is a languid town without many services other than a bank (Banco Nacional, at the town's entrance) and two restaurants.

Within town there is basic lodging, but a little farther south in the village of **Los Destiladores,** you'll find luxury lodging; and to the southwest in **Playa Venado,** there's high-end beachfront lodging. The region is known for its beaches, surfing, fishing, and Isla Laguna Wildlife refuge. There is even a scuba-diving operation.

VISITOR INFORMATION & ORIENTATION

There is a helpful **IPAT visitor center** (Ⓢ **995-2339;** Mon–Fri 8:30am–4:30pm, Sat–Sun and holidays 8:30am–1:30pm) with brochures about regions throughout Panama, and they occasionally have maps. The staff isn't overly occupied, and will eagerly help you with any transportation or logistics problems. The office is at the entrance to town, on the road to Playa Arenal.

GETTING THERE & DEPARTING

By Plane   Pedasí is served by charter flights only; **Air Panama** (Ⓢ **316-9000;** www.flyairpanama.com) flights cost $650 for three passengers, $825 for five, and $1,080 for nine.

By Car   To continue through Las Tablas to Pedasí, follow the Carretera Nacional until it dead-ends at Avenida Belisario Porras, turn left, and drive until the road turns back into the Carretera Nacional. The road from Las Tablas to Pedasí is straightforward. *Warning:* Mind your speed along this road. It is common knowledge that the police set up speed traps and then demand a bribe, usually about $5. If you are a tourist, they will probably let you go with a warning.

By Bus & Taxi   Buses from Panama City or Chitré change in Las Tablas. Buses from Panama City to Las Tablas are $8; from Las Tablas to Pedasí it is $2. A taxi from Chitré to Pedasí costs around $20.

GETTING AROUND

By Taxi   Taxis do not cruise the streets frequently, but if you wait long enough on a corner one will eventually pass by. If not, call © **995-2275**, or have the IPAT office call for you.

FUN IN THE OCEAN
Beaches

There are a lot of fine beaches in this region, but unfortunately, they are receptacles for trash that currents deposit throughout the year. Sometimes it's just a few pieces here and there; other times it's a poor man's beachcomber's paradise. When the tide is low, you won't notice this as much. **Playa Arenal,** about a mile from the main street in Pedasí, is a prime example, and visitors might only want to stop here briefly before carrying on to the Isla Laguna Wildlife Refuge, which is reached by boat from here— take the road past the scuba shop near the IPAT office. **Playa del Toro** has good swimming conditions but its murky waters are not very inviting. The best beach here is in **Los Destiladores,** another 10km (6 miles) south of Pedasí. The waves pound, but the beach is cleaner and altogether more beautiful. Also, see Playa Venado, below.

Isla Laguna Wildlife Refuge

This island refuge is reached by boat from Playa Arenal, and is about 3km (1¾ miles) from shore. Isla Laguna is only about 55 hectares (136 acres), and it is surrounded by an extensive coral reef that attracts thousands of colorful fish—the blue sea here is ideal for snorkeling. Unfortunately, a lot of trash washes up onshore, carried by currents and left by negligent tourists. The island was also used as target practice by the U.S. military, and it's said that unexploded bombs are still occasionally found here, so be careful and stick to main beaches and trails. There is a $3 charge to visit the island, and no services, so pack a picnic lunch.

As the name states, the island is home to green iguanas; and if you're lucky enough to be here from June to November, humpback whales breed in the area and are commonly seen by boat. The refuge can be reached by hiring a local boatman at Playa Arenal, or you can book a trip with Buzos de Azuero—you'll need to rent snorkel gear from them anyway, so you might as well plan your trip here. The cost is $50 for a half-day, and boats run from 8am to 6pm. The boat ride out is smoothest from April to December; if you've come between January and March, you may not be able to reach the island because of strong winds.

Snorkeling, Diving & Fishing

The Canadian-run scuba center **Buzos de Azuero** (© **995-2405;** www.dive-n-fish panama.com) operates out of Pedasí, offering scuba diving to visit shipwrecks, seamounts, and coral reefs; divers usually can view large pelagic fish and turtles. Diving is best from

April to December; from January to March the sea is churned up and dive trips take place only if conditions are calm. A two-tank dive costs $75 per person, and snorkeling is $50 for a maximum of seven people, not including the $10 snorkeling rental cost.

The center also offers deep-sea fishing and spear fishing for tuna, marlin (May–July), and mahimahi, taking visitors out to Isla Frailes, which has a 46m (150-ft.) drop-off with abundant marine life. Fishing trips cost about $150 for the boat (depending on the cost of gas), and an extra $50 for two rods and a pack of lures. Contact the center for 6-night packages that include transportation and lodging.

WHERE TO STAY

Dim's Hostal ⚜ Located in a converted old home at the entrance to town, this is a very popular hostel in Pedasí. Rooms are en suite but simple, and are a big step above the rooms at Residencial Moscoso (see below). The owners are exceptionally friendly and hospitable. They include breakfast with the already low price, which is served in a pleasant back patio. It's often difficult to get a room if you just show up (especially during high season), so try to book in advance. Note that showers do not have hot water.

Av. Central. ✆ 995-2303. mirely@iname.com. 6 units. $15 single; $20 double. No credit cards. **Amenities:** Kitchen; Internet. *In room:* A/C, no phone.

Residencial Moscoso Frequented by surfers on the cheap, Moscoso's rooms are about as spartan as an insane asylum's. To stay here, you have to find your bohemian side or at the very least be an easygoing traveler who doesn't fuss much with accommodations. Really, for the price it's hard to expect much more. Showers are spigots that shoot out from the wall, and do not have hot water.

Av. Central at Calle Ofelia Reliz. ✆ 995-2203. 19 units. $17 double; $25 quadruple. No credit cards. *In room:* A/C, TV (2 local channels).

Residencial Pedasi Despite the name "residencial," accommodations here are hotel rooms laid out in a motel-like building that looks more attractive from the outside than from the inside. The Pedasí offers the highest quality lodging in town, but still, guest rooms have small windows that let in little light, and the basic decor and firm beds put this hotel slightly below the three-star category. The hotel attracts mostly foreign visitors who come here to fish. Service is friendly.

Av. Central. ✆ 995-2322. 15 units. $20 double. No credit cards. **Amenities:** Restaurant; Internet; laundry service. *In room:* A/C, TV, no phone.

WHERE TO DINE

Dulcerías Yely ⚜⚜ *Finds* PASTRIES/SANDWICHES This delightful little bakery is owned by the amiable Mrs. Dalila Vera de Quintero, who is as sweet as her confections. Dalila puts a lot of love and care into her homemade cakes and sandwiches, and every visitor to Pedasí makes at least one stop here to sample her delicacies. The *queques,* or pound cakes, come in a variety of flavors such as almond, coconut, chocolate, or anise, and are not too sugary. She also has a creamy flan made with condensed milk. But Dalila's specialty is *chicheme,* a drink made of mashed corn and milk and infused with vanilla—it's delicious and filling. There are also fresh *chichas,* or juice, made from local fruits such as cashew, a tart *nance,* and *uva,* a cross between a grape and cherry; most of these fruits are taken from her backyard. For lunch, don't miss her $1.25 sandwiches of either ginger chicken, roast pork, or roast beef and cheese.

Calle Ofelia Reluz at Av. Central. ✆ 995-2205. Reservations not accepted. Sandwiches $1.25; cakes 30¢ a slice. No credit cards. Daily 8am–9pm.

El Puntal ✿✿ FRENCH   In 2006 the French owners of Posada los Destiladores met the need for a more upscale eatery in Pedasí, opening the doors of a historic house on the plaza. When I was last in Pedasí, the restaurant was just opening and fine-tuning their menu; also, they were unsure about lunch hours—check to see if they've opened for lunch during the weekdays. The ambience is candlelit and cozy, and the outstanding chef, Joel Chartier, creates unfussy dishes but with impeccable care, taking advantage of the bounty of seafood available in this area. Nightly dishes can include a red snapper carpaccio and fresh catch of the day served with caramelized ginger and fresh tomato—most of the dishes are French-influenced. There is a wine list, and prices hover around $20 to $25 per bottle.

Central plaza. 🕾 **6676-5571.** Reservations recommended. Main courses $7–$12. MC, V. Lunch on weekends noon–3pm; dinner daily 7–10pm.

Isla Iguana ✿✿ SEAFOOD   This unassuming little restaurant charges what surely are the lowest prices for seafood in Panama. Even langostino, that juicy jumbo shrimp, is just $6, compared to Panama City which sells it for $15 or more. The amiable owner dispatches a local boy on bicycle to pick up fresh seafood that arrives daily from fishermen; whatever is freshest is served that evening, and depending on the season it could be tuna, sea bass, dorado, snapper, or even shark. Try a light meal of sea bass steamed in foil, or garlicky conch or jumbo shrimp, tangy ceviche or meats, or mix it up with a surf and turf. It's a simple affair with open-air dining and metal chairs and tables. Isla Iguana fills up quickly, so come early or expect a crowd. Hearty breakfast with tortillas and yummy *hojaldras* (fried bread).

Av. Central (at the town entrance). 🕾 **6620-4073.** Reservations only for groups. Main courses $3.50–$6. No credit cards. Mon–Tues and Thurs–Fri 11am–10pm; Sat–Sun 6am–10pm (open early on weekdays during high season).

LUXURY LODGING IN LOS DESTILADORES

Los Destiladores is a tiny hamlet about a 5-minute drive from Pedasí. Its two fine resorts offer travelers the most upscale accommodations on the Azuero Peninsula. The beach here is also the best in the area—with the exception of Playa Venado, which has its own deluxe B&B (see below). A taxi to town from here costs $5.

Posada los Destiladores ✿✿✿ *Finds*   Perched above the shore of a golden-sand beach, these rustic but ultra-stylish, individual bungalows are one of the most romantic places to stay on Panama's Pacific Coast. The property is owned and run by French expats; Philippe is the former owner of Las Bóvedas restaurant in Panama City, and Jean Francois is a talented furniture maker who has bestowed unique artistic craftsmanship to the bungalows and main building that form the property. Secluded among 8.1 hectares (20 acres) of tropical plants and teak trees, the bungalows feature bamboo, thatched roofs, and intricately carved custom-made furniture using local materials, such as a four-poster bed made of crooked tree branches. Other details include cobblestone floors, palm-thatched walls, and bathrooms with large, walk-in showers and carved wooden sinks (note that water is tepid, not hot). The bungalows are named after Philippe's ex-girlfriends—one supposes that his favorites were Itzania and Ariel, considering that they are the largest and best rooms here, each with two stories under an A-frame roof, and a terrace strung with hammocks. Beds feature comfortable mattresses; some are on a raised Zen-like platform. Two sun decks jut over the beach, perfect for relaxing to the sounds of the sea. The artistically decorated main lodge is where meals are served.

Los Destiladores. 🕾 **6675-9715.** www.panamabambu.net. 7 units. $75–$125 double bungalow. MC, V. **Amenities:** Restaurant; outdoor pool; tour organization. *In room:* A/C (some rooms), no phone.

Villa Camilla ✿✿✿ *(Moments)*   There is perhaps no finer or more exclusive hotel in Panama than the Villa Camilla. It's also a hotel with a vision. Villa Camilla is owned by the celebrated French architect Gilles Saint-Gilles and his wife Camille, both of whom fell in love with this slice of paradise on the Azuero Peninsula and set about buying property with the eventual intent to sell land to other like-minded people who believe in balancing beauty with ecology. The hotel is a hybrid of an hacienda and a Moroccan villa, with a good dose of modernist chic. To build the property, Gilles set about training local craftsmen to construct the hotel's infrastructure and furniture using traditional techniques, even employing wooden nails to hold beam supports together. The idea is to create a local economy producing furniture and providing living means for local residents. All seven rooms are sophisticated, fresh, and individually designed, with handsome hardwood floors, molded half-walls, hand-carved furniture, and wrought-iron door frames, and some bathrooms have sunken tubs and walk-in showers. Apart from locally produced furniture, personal touches of art and furnishings were brought by the owners from China and Morocco. The guest rooms were built with an emphasis on privacy. There is a separate cottage for families with children; children are not accepted in the other guest rooms. The elegant lounge is mostly open-air and faces the sea and an inviting pool, although it is a 15-minute walk to get to the mostly private beach. The grounds are lushly landscaped: Giles has been busy reforesting the area to bring back the natural luster of the area. Delicious meals made with organic ingredients from their garden are included in the price; breakfast and lunch are served at individual tables, and dinner is served family-style at a formal dining table. Villa Camilla is just up the street from the Posada (above).

Los Destiladores. © 232-6721. www.azueros.com. 7 units. $250–$400 per night, based on double occupancy. AE, MC, V. **Amenities:** Restaurant; outdoor pool; tennis courts; free bicycles; tour organization; occasional yoga classes; Wi-Fi in the salon. *In room:* A/C, hair dryer.

PLAYA VENADO

Playa Venado (often called "Venao") is an up-and-coming destination notable for its surfing and half-moon sandy beach. The surf here breaks left and right, great for both pros and beginners. (For information about surf tours here, see chapter 4.) There's no sign to Playa Venado, so keep your eyes open for the turnoff, about 1.5km (1 mile) from the Playita Resort. If you don't have a vehicle, you'll need a taxi, which will charge around $15. Like most of the beaches in this area, currents bring in trash that can be light or heavy—also, during high tide the sand fills with crabs and is unpleasant to swim in. Low tide brings better swimming conditions. The beach at La Playita (see below) is more suitable for swimming, but they charge $3 to use it. There are four very basic cement cabins on the beach, called **Jardin Cabañas y Restaurante Vista Hermosa,** popular with surfers and backpackers (© 995-8107; $14 per night), and camping is free. Their restaurant serves cheap meals of mostly seafood, beans and rice, and cold beer. During surf competitions this area can take on a party atmosphere. Other lodging is listed below.

The coastline of the Azuero Peninsula is rich with marine life and pelagic fish like tuna—so much so that it is often called the "tuna coast." Here at Playa Venado, the Inter-American Tropical Tuna Commission (IATTC), which monitors tuna fishing to prevent its depletion, has a research facility, **Achotines Laboratory** (© 995-8166; www.iattc.org), that offers educational tours. It sounds dry, but it's actually fascinating to see the various stages of tuna reproduction (among other fish like sea bass and snapper), and especially to witness the frenzy that occurs when the staff feed huge broodstock yellowfin tuna. Kids love it. Visiting hours are Monday through Friday from 8:30am to noon and from 1 to 4:30pm. You must make advance arrangements.

About 11km (6½ miles) from Playa Venado is the **Refugio de Vida Silvestre Isla de Cañas,** an island village that receives more nesting turtles than any other location on the Pacific Coast. From April to October, hundreds of thousands of Pacific green, olive ridley, leatherback, loggerhead, and hawksbill turtles arrive here to lay eggs, but there is no surefire date that guarantees you'll see any. The view of Isla de Cañas, a barrier island reached by boat, is expansive and beautiful and worth seeing even if you do not visit the island itself. Getting here is difficult because there is only one local boat that can take you from mainland (it leaves from the end of the road); if you show up, it may or may not be there; the aforementioned Buzos de Azuero offers tours to the island.

WHERE TO STAY & DINE

La Playita (★ (*Kids*   This is one of the funkiest places on the coast, run by a Panamanian/American horse jockey with a serious penchant for kitsch. La Playita is located on a gorgeous blue-water inlet with tan sand and tranquil swimming conditions. The beach is open to the public and on weekends this area is packed with Panamanian families. That, along with their multitude of birds (including a free-roaming ostrich and two very vocal scarlet macaws), give the property a zoolike ambience. The landscaped grounds, however, are well-tended. There are five rooms whose interiors, oddly, have the feel of an Alpine lodge, with chipped-stone-and- fossilized-wood walls and knobby-wood headboards; three of the rooms can fit up to five people. They have an on-site restaurant, but meals are not included in the price; you can also use their kitchen to cook for yourself. There is watersports gear rental here, too.

Playa Venado. (✆ **996-6727** or 6639-2968. www.playitaresort.com. 5 units. $80 double. No credit cards. **Amenities:** Restaurant; bar; surfboard rental; snorkel gear rental; minizoo; tour organization. *In room:* A/C, no phone.

Villa Marina (★★★ (*Finds*   Tucked away at the end of an unsigned road, this colonial-style beachfront B&B is one of my favorites in Panama. It's difficult to imagine a more idyllic location, set on 89 hectares (220 acres) of private coastal land that allows guests to step off the property and onto the beach. The stunning evening sunsets can be enjoyed from a breezy veranda or from a thatched-roof *bohío* strung with hammocks. There are 10 elegantly appointed rooms with antiques, French windows, and fine bedding, but the ambience is easeful, not fussy, and the amicable staff strive to make guests at home. The hacienda-style B&B has a terra-cotta-tiled roof, and is painted white and cerulean blue, which gives it a fresh, airy feel. Because the common area is shared by guests, this place would be ideal if rented by a group of friends or a family, but individuals and couples are welcomed, too. (It's best to book in advance.) What I especially like about Villa Marina is that you can swim, surf, or horseback ride right outside the door, meaning that you don't have to book a tour. The Villa Marina has three putting greens and a shooting range for golf, and can put together a fishing trip. For those not up for the drive from Panama City, they can book a charter plane for you to Pedasí, and provide transportation from there. If camaraderie grows between guests, meals are served family-style; otherwise they are served individually on the veranda. The food is delicious, hearty, and fresh, and they have a full Argentine barbecue.

Playa Venado. (✆ **211-2277,** or 646/383-7486 in the U.S. www.playavenado.com. 7 units. $125 double; $40 per person additional for meals. MC, V. **Amenities:** Meals; putting green; free surfboards and snorkel gear; horseback riding; fishing trips; walking trails. *In room:* A/C, TV.

8

The Western Highlands & the Gulf of Chiriquí

Western Panama is home to the cool highlands of the Chiriquí Province, a tropical mountain paradise brimming with lush rainforest and trout-filled streams, and dotted with storybook villages nestled on the verdant slopes of the region's dominant peak, the 3,478m (11,410-ft.) Barú Volcano. Given the region's fertile soil and ideal year-round temperatures, the Chiriquí area is Panama's agricultural breadbasket, and many of the mountain's valleys and hillsides are blanketed with a colorful patchwork of fruit trees, vegetable fields, and coffee plantations—one of the country's signature products. The air is fresh and sweet here, and the roads that wind through the peaks and valleys overflow with pretty pink and white impatiens and exotic flowers.

The Chiriquí Highlands region is a mecca for adventure, and travelers can participate in activities such as whitewater rafting and kayaking Class II to Class V rivers, canopy rides, or hiking through primeval forest dripping with vines and bromeliads and interlaced with creeks. Laid-back activities include scenic drives and tours of coffee plantations or orchid farms. The Chiriquí region is well-known as a hot spot for **bird-watching,** and hundreds of species have been recorded in the area, including showcase birds such as the resplendent quetzal, blue cotinga, trogons, and toucans. The area is a corridor for migratory species that pass through from November to April.

The eastern side of the Barú Volcano is home to **Boquete,** an enchanting valley town that has received a lot of press lately as a top retirement area. Indeed, it's not uncommon to see a number of foreigners here. On the volcano's western side are picturesque agricultural communities such as **Cerro Punta.** Both towns are linked by the Los Quetzales Trail that winds through the gorgeous forests of **Parque Nacional Volcán Barú.** Additionally, the western side offers access to one of the most important parks in Central America, **Parque Internacional La Amistad,** which Panama shares with Costa Rica.

The Highlands are accessed from the province's capital **David,** a service-oriented city located on the hot and humid lowlands. A little farther south is the Gulf of Chiriquí, Panama's up-and-coming travel destination that offers outstanding scuba diving, snorkeling, and sport fishing in the crystalline waters around such revered sites as **Isla Coiba,** and the islands in and around **Parque Nacional Golfo Marino.** This chapter covers the extensive region that includes the Highlands, the Gulf, and even the remote village Santa Catalina, for its epic surfing and direct access to Isla Coiba.

The Chiriquí Highlands have microclimates that produce cloud forests and phenomena such as the misting rain *bajareque*, so it is important that you bring clothing that is waterproof if you plan to spend time outdoors. Also, temperatures here are decidedly cooler than in the rest of Panama.

1 David

440km (274 miles) W of Panama City; 40km (25 miles) south of Boquete

David, Panama's third-largest city, with a population of 125,000, has an economy based around commercial services and Chiriquí Province's thriving farming industry. At just 45 minutes from the Costa Rica border, the city has the ambience of a frontier town, and there is little here to offer travelers other than a transportation hub and services. Travelers on their way to Costa Rica often stop in David for the night, but with so little to see and do in town they are up and packing early the following day. Also, owing to David's location on a coastal plain, the heat and humidity here can be suffocating—another reason so many residents escape to the beach or the highlands during weekends, and so few tourists base themselves out of the city.

ESSENTIALS

GETTING THERE & DEPARTING   By Plane   The Aeropuerto Enrique Malek (DAV) is about 4.8km (3 miles) from the city center and is serviced by Air Panama (© 316-9000; www.flyairpanama.com), with flights to and from Panama City, Bocas del Toro, and even San José, Costa Rica. There are three daily round-trip flights from **Panama City** Monday through Friday, and two daily flights on Saturday and Sunday; the cost is $50 one-way. There are flights from **Bocas del Toro** to David on Monday, Wednesday, and Friday at 8:35am, with return flights at 1pm. Flights from **San José** are on Monday, Wednesday, and Friday, at 10am, with the return trip from David leaving at 9:30am.

    Aeroperlas (© 315-7500; www.aeroperlas.com) has three daily flights from **Panama City** to David from Monday to Saturday, and two flights on Sunday; the cost is $66 one-way. From **Bocas del Toro,** there is one flight per day from Monday to Friday, leaving Bocas del Toro at 8:25am, and returning from David at 9am.

    There is an **IPAT visitor center** booth at the airport (no phone; daily 7am–3pm), manned by a helpful and friendly representative who has a limited number of brochures and maps. A taxi into town costs $2 per person.

By Bus   The **Terminal de Transportes** is located on Avenida Estudiante. Daily service to and from Panama City is offered by the bus line **Terminal David–Panama** (© 774-2974 or 775-7074), with regular service leaving every hour daily from 6am to 8pm, and express service leaving daily at 10:45pm, midnight, and 3am. **Padafront** (© 775-8913) has regular bus service at 7:30am, 8:45am, 9:45am, 11am, 12:45am, 2pm, 3:15pm, 6pm, and 7:45pm; express buses leave at 10:45 and midnight. Both companies charge $13 for regular service (7 hr.), and $15 for express service (5½ hr.).

    Volcán–Cerro Punta–Guadalupe buses from David leave every 35 minutes from 5am to 7pm ($2–$3); and buses to **Boquete** leave every 15 minutes from 4:15am to 9pm ($1.45). Buses to Costa Rica via the Paso Canoa border are available from **Panaline** (© 314-6383) and **Tica Bus** (© 314-6385); both companies charge the same price from David as from Panama City ($25 one-way); they leave David for Costa Rica around 5:30pm daily. *Note:* Travelers to and from Costa Rica will need to

show proof of onward travel. If you do not posses such proof, you will be required to buy a round-trip ticket.

By Car   David is reached from Panama City via the Interamericana Highway (Pan-American Highway), which skirts the edge of town and continues on to the Paso Canoa border with Costa Rica. If you are heading on to Boquete or Volcán, see "Getting There & Departing," later in this chapter.

GETTING AROUND   By Taxi   Taxis are plentiful in David. The fare for a taxi from the airport to the city center is $2 per person; to Boquete it is $20; to Volcán it is $35; and to Guadalupe it is $40. Around town, fares cost $1 to $2.

By Car   Rental vehicles are available at the David airport, including **Alamo** (© 236-5777; www.alamopanama.com), **Budget** (© 263-8777; www.budgetpanama.com), **Hertz** (© 721-3345; www.hertz.com), **National** (© 721-0974; www.nationalpanama.com), and **Thrifty** (© 721-2477; www.thrifty.com). It is worth noting that Thrifty offers the cheapest 4WD rental with its Daihatsu Terios for $52 a day; in comparison, other agencies rent 4WDs with prices starting at around $75. They only have 10 Daihatsus and sell out quickly, so book ahead.

FAST FACTS   You'll find banks with ATMs on the streets around the plaza; **Banco Nacional** is at Calle B Norte and Avenida 3 Este/Bolívar on the plaza; **Global Bank** is at Calle A Norte and Avenida 1 Este; and **HSBC** is at Avenida 1era Oeste and Calle D Norte. Cybercafes are plentiful in David, and all hotels offer Internet service to their customers. Also try **American Copy** at Calle Este Norte and Avenida 1 Este; or **Naveg@net** at Avenida 2 Este and Calle A Norte. There are two excellent hospitals here, the **Mae Lewis Hospital** (© 775-4159) and the **Hospital Chiriquí** (© 774-0128). For the **police,** dial © 771-4231. The **post office** can be found 1 block northeast of the plaza on Avenida 4 Este and Calle C Norte, and is open Monday through Saturday from 7am to 5:30pm.

There is an **IPAT visitor center** at Avenida Central and Calle B Norte (© **775-4120;** Mon–Fri 8:30am–5:30pm), but it is largely useless except for maps, which are in short supply. The staff here oddly does not provide the public with much tourist information, nor does it seem to know David well enough to give recommendations.

WHAT TO SEE & DO IN & AROUND DAVID

Despite the fact that David is one of Panama's largest cities, it has surprisingly few attractions to keep a tourist occupied for more than an afternoon—which is why most use the city as a jumping-off point. In 2006, the local government began a half-million-dollar renovation of the historic **Parque Miguel de Cervantes** plaza, which should be ready by the time you read this. The plaza is one of the rare areas in David

---

The Feria Internacional de San José de David

The Feria Internacional de San José de David is the largest commercial, industrial, agricultural, ranching, and folkloric festival in Panama, taking place every year around the middle of March. The weeklong event draws 300,000 people, most of whom come to visit the booths of international companies and catch up on the newest technology, but folklore, culture, and handicrafts play a large role, delighting tourists, too. Check the website **www.feriadedavid.com** for exact dates.

that offers shade trees and a respite from the oppressive heat, and vendors sell ice cream, fresh coconut juice, and cold beverages.

Take a stroll down to **Barrio Bolívar** by following Calle A Norte west of the plaza to Avenida 8 Este. This is "old town," with a couple of blocks that boast the last vestiges of colonial architecture from David's early days. On Avenida 8 Este you'll find the **Museo de Historia y de Arte José de Obaldía** (℃ 775-1217; Tues–Sat 9am–5pm; admission $1 adults, 25¢ children), housed within an 1834 building that once belonged to the founder of the Chiriquí Province, José Domingo de Obaldía. It's a humble museum that requires just 15 minutes to see the odds and ends on display, including archaeological artifacts from the Chiriquí area and pieces from the colonial period.

The **Nuevo Centro Artesanal de David** has a good selection of Panamanian handicrafts for sale, and is located on Vía Boquete, in front of the Autoservicios de Chiriquí (no phone; daily 10am–8pm).

Residents of David escape the heat by heading to **Playa Barqueta,** about 30 minutes' drive from town. This long, black-sand beach is often breezy, and the ocean can be too choppy for swimming (beware of riptides here). Also here is the **Refugio de Vida Silvestre,** a nature preserve that is an excellent spot to view wildlife and birds. It is a turtle-nesting site from about August to October. **Las Olas Resort** is here (see "Where to Stay & Dine," below), and although they have a restaurant, the food quality is uneven—I'd recommend bringing a picnic lunch.

NIGHTLIFE & ENTERTAINMENT

The newly expanded, 24-hour **Fiesta Casino** (℃ 775-6534), opposite the Gran Nacional Hotel, has slots and gaming tables, a restaurant, and a bar. There are two cinemas, the **Alhambra** at the Gran Hotel Nacional (see below), and the **Chiriquí Mall** on the Interamericana Highway (℃ 774-5648); both cinemas have six screens and show mostly American movies.

WHERE TO STAY & DINE

Gran Hotel Nacional ⚓ This 55-year-old hotel, with its attractive, mock-colonial facade, has the fanciest accommodations in David. It also offers the most amenities, including a casino, a cinema, an outdoor swimming pool, and three restaurants. The hotel recently underwent a renovation but the updated interiors look oddly reminiscent of the 1970s, with glossy ceramic floors and smoked-glass partitions. Guest rooms are fresh and clean, with tiled floors, orthopedic mattress beds, and run-of-the-mill, chain-hotel decor. The Gran Nacional hosts mostly businessmen and travelers taking a break during the drive to either Costa Rica or Bocas del Toro. David's humid weather makes the swimming pool key, and their on-site restaurants are decent, serving mostly Panamanian dishes, pizzas, and pastas. Given the dearth of decent restaurants in David, consider **dining** at the hotel even if you're not lodging here. Every day from 5:30 to 10:30pm, the hotel's outdoor restaurant has a barbecue special with beef, chicken, and seafood. The front-desk staff is friendly but inattentive, and could use a refresher course in hospitality.

Av. Central. ℃ 775-2221 or 775-2222. www.panamainfo.com/granhotelnacional. 75 units. $56 standard double; $66 superior double; $72 junior suite. AE, MC, V. **Amenities:** 3 restaurants; bar; outdoor pool; cinema; casino; business center; limited room service; laundry service. *In room:* A/C, TV.

Hotel Castilla ⚓ *Value* This modern and squeaky-clean hotel is centrally located and one of the best values I've seen anywhere in Panama. Guest rooms come with comfortable queen-size beds, large closets, and bathrooms with walk-in showers.

There are spacious standard doubles, most of which are interior rooms with windows that face an air shaft, and suites that face the street and come with two queen-size beds and a small balcony. "Suite" is a misnomer here—they are just huge doubles with a lot of unused space, and are not worth the extra money. Some standard rooms have loud air-conditioners, so ask to see another room if the noise is too much. Also, the showers have lukewarm water, but with the hot weather it's not much of an issue. Their on-site restaurant serves decent Panamanian food and other international dishes. Another perk here is the hotel's 2pm checkout time. Breakfast is not included.

Calle A Norte and Av. 3 Este. ℭ **774-5236** or 774-5260. inmisa@cwp.net/pa. 68 units. $37 double; $60 suite. AE, MC, V. **Amenities:** Restaurant; bar; mini–business center; limited room service. *In room:* A/C, TV.

Purple House Hostel ℛ   This is one of the best budget hostels in the country. The American/Panamanian owners have done quite their share of traveling and understand the need for a homey lodging atmosphere when on the road. The hostel, painted purple as the name indicates, has two private rooms with optional air-conditioning, and shared rooms for four to six guests; all rooms have shared bathrooms. (If it's a slow night, they'll give you a shared room all to yourself.) There is also a communal kitchen and living area with a TV and games, as well as an outdoor area strung with hammocks. The hostel is located in a safe residential area about 10 blocks from the plaza. The owners are very accommodating, and will store luggage and organize excursions for guests.

Av. 6 Oeste and Calle C Sur. ℭ **774-4059.** www.purplehousehostal.com. 5 units. $18 private double; $22 private double with A/C; $6.60–$8.80 per person shared rooms. No credit cards. **Amenities:** Communal kitchen; tour desk; travel information; book exchange; Internet service; laundry service. *In room:* A/C (some rooms), no phone.

Panama Bill's AMERICAN   It's predominately an establishment for gringos, and no wonder, considering the owner is an American who owns another Panama Bill's in Florida. The restaurant is *way* laid-back, with an open-air dining and bar area and a slightly more refined indoor dining area—the outdoor bar draws lots of guys in Hawaiian shirts who come for their dirt-cheap cocktails. The menu features mostly American staples such as Buffalo wings, Caesar salad, barbecue ribs, Texas chili, and burgers, and there's fried and grilled fish and black-bean soup. Service is fast and bilingual.

Av. 1 Oeste and Calle D Norte. ℭ **774-4684.** panamavill@cwpanama.net. Reservations not accepted. Main courses $6–$10. MC, V. Daily 10am–11pm.

Restaurante El Palacio Oriental ℛ ⓥ*alue* CHINESE   The menu at this Chinese restaurant is as thick as a book, and with so many options it is difficult to decide what you'd like. The menu features traditional dishes such as chop suey and chow mein, but given the amount of fresh fish available on the Pacific Coast you might want to opt for a seafood meal. The fare is delicious, and the portions are hearty—two could easily order an appetizer and split a main course if they weren't absolutely starving. The restaurant is often busy and the ambience is lively.

Calle E Norte and Av. Central. ℭ **777-2410.** Reservations not accepted. Main courses $3–$7. MC, V. Daily 10am–11pm.

A BEACH RESORT OUTSIDE OF DAVID

Las Olas Resort ℛ   A full-service resort, this is the only moderately upscale lodging option along this stretch of the Pacific Coast. Las Olas is primarily a beach getaway for residents and honeymooners from the Chiriquí area, and not a "destination" resort for travelers with a short amount of time in Panama. The best thing about Las

Olas is Playa Barqueta, the lengthy, undeveloped black-sand beach that it fronts, and the dreamy tangerine-and-saffron sunsets seen here nightly. If you do not need luxury—and if you just want to spend a night or two on the coast and take long strolls along the beach, join a yoga class, go on a horseback ride, or maybe take a boat ride to an uninhabited island—this is your place. (All excursions and classes are an additional price.) There is a nature reserve nearby, ideal for birding and seeing wildlife. The resort sells all-inclusive packages that include lodging, meals, drinks, and use of the facilities, or you can book for the night and order meals a la carte, but the latter is more expensive. The guest rooms and common areas are tidy and well-kept, though starting to show slight signs of wear and tear. Standard rooms come with a king-size or two queen-size beds, and feature ocean-view terraces, but the rooms are on the small side. If you're here during the rainy season, when you might spend a few hours indoors, a junior suite can be the best option. The resort is largely a cheery place but never seems to be full, or even busy—guests either love the peace and quiet or dislike the empty feeling and less-than-lively ambience. Also, the food is just okay—not bad but not memorable, either. A small spa offers massages and facials.

Playa Barqueta. (C) 800/535-2513 in the U.S., or 772-3000. www.lasolasresort.com. 48 units. $81 per person all-inclusive, $61 per person room only, based on double occupancy. AE, MC, V. **Amenities:** Restaurant; bar; outdoor swimming pool; gym; sauna; massage; facials; bicycles; excursions; horseback riding; yoga classes; Internet access; limited room service; laundry service; games; book exchange. *In room:* A/C, TV, minifridge, coffeemaker, hair dryer, safe.

A SIDE TRIP TO LAS LAJAS

Las Lajas is popular for its long, 10km (6-mile) stretch of tan-sand beach. The current here is not strong, so swimming conditions are better than at many other Pacific Coast beaches. The beach is 70km (44 miles) east of David, along a potholed but paved road from the Interamericana Highway. Along the beach you'll find cabins, thatched *bohio* picnic sites, and a couple of cheap restaurants but it's all a bit weather-beaten and half-open unless it is a summer weekend. The only real place to stay here is **Las 3 Palmeras** ((C) 727-0010; www.las3palmas.com), and even this option is pretty barebones. Some plain wood cabins stand on stilts above the sand; others are huts with parachute fabric roofs. You get just a mattress with a sheet and a pillow, yet the whole establishment is young-spirited and stylish, and attracts a lot of backpackers who come for occasional DJ parties and to chill on the beach. Las 3 Palmeras also has a campground, a restaurant (Dec–May), and excursions. Prices are $20 for two for a cabin, and $9 for two to camp.

To get to Las Lajas beach, head east from David on the Interamericana Highway and turn at the signed road at Las Cruces. Continue for 13km (8 miles), passing through the village Las Lajas, until you reach the beach. The cabins are to the right, but the road peters out and you need to drive across a stretch of sand.

A REMOTE SURF CAMP

Morro Negrito Surf Camp (Finds) Located on an Isla Ensenada 3.2km (2 miles) off the coast of the Chiriquí Gulf, about halfway between Santiago and David, this surf camp limits its guests to 25 to keep waves uncrowded. The accommodations are just a step above camping, with rustic cabins that overlook the Pacific Ocean and neighbor a small community—the focus here is on surfing, not luxury lodging. Transportation from Panama City (5 hr. by bus; 30 min. by jeep or boat), meals, lessons, and other activities are included. The camp sells weeklong packages only, but they are reasonably priced at $550 per person. For surfing, 10 different breaks average between

1.2 and 2.4m (4–8 ft.). Sand breaks with small waves are good for beginners learning how to ride. You can also fish, ride horses, or just chill out in a hammock.

Isla Ensenada. ℂ 760/632-8014 in the U.S. www.surferparadise.com. 10 units. $550 all-inclusive weeklong package. No credit cards accepted at camp. **Amenities:** Restaurant; bar; surf lessons; surf guides; surfboard rental; boat rides; fishing; horseback riding; TV rooms for video playback. *In room:* No phone.

2 Volcán

33km (21 miles) N of David

The road from La Concepción to Volcán slowly winds 34km (21 miles) up from the humid lowlands and into a cooler climate and a landscape characterized by a patchwork of *fincas,* dairy and cattle ranching farms. Eventually, the road opens up to a wide plateau and the village of Volcán, the highlands center for services such as banks, pharmacies, grocery stores, and just about everything else. While Volcán isn't as picturesque as Cerro Punta or Guadalupe, the fresh mountain air and open views of rugged landscape give Volcán a decidedly alpine atmosphere, part of the reason so many European immigrants chose to settle around here in the early 1900s. The town sits at the skirt of the Barú Volcano and offers grand views of that peak, although it is commonly shrouded with a layer of clouds and hidden from view. Considering Volcán's location at the axis of the roads to Guadalupe and Río Sereno, near the Costa Rica–Panama border, the town is a convenient base from which to explore the western highlands area. Volcán is centered around a main street, Avenida Central, which forks in the center. Head right to continue on to Guadalupe and Cerro Punta, and straight ahead for the road to Río Sereno and the Costa Rica.

A B&B ON THE WAY TO VOLCAN

Casa Loma ☆ This little B&B is located in the delightful home of a retired Canadian couple, Dorothy and Claus Claassen, in the blink-and-you-miss-it community of Buena Vista, located 16km (10 miles) from Concepción. The spellbinding views of verdant fields sloping down to the Pacific Ocean are what make this B&B special, and on clear days you can see all the way into Costa Rica. The Casa Loma is in a pastoral setting studded with fruit trees and filled with birds and fluttering butterflies, which makes this place ideal for travelers seeking a quiet, peaceful ambience. Because of its location, the B&B is more suited to travelers with a rental vehicle. Casa Loma has two attractive, bright rooms: a suite with a full kitchen and a double with a kitchenette; both have soothing neutral tones and are adorned with freshly cut flowers. The bathrooms are spacious and showers are fitted with handrails for elderly guests. Outside, you'll find a couple of breezy terraces with tables and a swing chair, and a stand-alone swimming pool. The wonderfully amicable Claassens relocated to this area from Bocas in 2000—they have tons of information about the highlands. From June to October, when they head to Canada, the Claassens only rent their property to long-term guests, most of whom lodge here while searching for property to buy. Otherwise, rooms can be rented for the night—although many guests end up staying longer, having become enraptured with the B&B's lovely surroundings. Stays of a week receive 1 night free, and both rooms can be rented by a family for a discounted price.

Buena Vista. ℂ **770-5605** or 6697-5024. claassendc@email.com. 2 units. $40 double; $45 suite. No credit cards. **Amenities:** Small outdoor pool; Wi-Fi. *In room:* Ceiling fan, TV, kitchenette, no phone.

Blackberry Wine: ¡Salud!

For more than 10 years, Abelardo Coba has been producing delicious organic blackberry wine, which he claims acts as a treatment for and prevention against circulatory problems. His wine is also rich in vitamin C and antioxidants, so you can feel good about drinking it. The blackberries are fermented for 20 days and matured in a barrel for 3 months. Coba has recently been testing out other fruit wines, such as *guayaba* (soursop), mango, and similar exotic fruits. Pick up a bottle at his small facility, just before Volcán, located on the right side of the road. (You'll see a sign for VIÑA DON COBA). There are no regular hours.

ESSENTIALS

GETTING THERE & AWAY   By Bus & Taxi   Buses to **Volcán, Cerro Punta,** and **Guadalupe** leave from the Terminal de Transportes in David every 35 minutes from 5am to 7pm ($2–$3). If traveling from Costa Rica, Panama City, or elsewhere, you'll need to transfer in David. A taxi from David to Volcán is $35; and to Guadalupe it is $40.

By Car   From the David airport, turn left and drive 3.4km (2 miles), then turn left again, onto Calle Miguel Brenes (also called Calle F Sur). Continue for 1.8km (1 mile) until you reach the Interamericana Highway. Turn left and continue to Concepción, 21km (13 miles) after passing the Chiriquí Mall, and turn onto the road to Volcán and Cerro Punta. The turnoff is easy to miss; keep your eyes open for a Shell gas station and turn right after it. The drive from Concepción to Volcán is 34km (21 miles).

FAST FACTS   The only bank with an ATM in the entire western highlands is **Banco Nacional** ((C) 771-4282), located on the main street in front of the police station, after the road forks. **Farmacia Volcán** ((C) 771-4651) is open Sunday through Thursday 7:30am to 10pm; Friday 7:30am to 6pm; and Saturday 6 to 10pm. Fast Internet service is available at **Hotel Don Tavo** ((C) 771-4055) on main street near the church, open from 8am to 11pm daily. The **post office** can be found on the right-hand side of the road to Guadalupe, just after turning on the fork. It's open every day, except Sunday, from 7am to noon and 2 to 6pm.

TOUR OUTFITTERS   **Western Wind Nature** ((C) 771-5049 or 6660-7162; western windnature@yahoo.com), operated by the friendly and knowledgeable birding and naturalist guide Nariño Aizpurua, offers a variety of outdoor excursions including hiking in La Amistad and Volcán Barú parks, canoeing in Lagunas de Volcán, and horseback riding and bird-watching. Nariño's brother, Gonzalo Aizpurua ((C) **6685-1682**) is also a competent nature guide who can customize any outdoor excursion around Volcán. Both speak enough English to be understood. Prices average $40 for a half-day excursion for two, including transportation.

Considering that the renowned Chiriquí Viejo River is on this side of the volcano, travelers can take part in absolutely thrilling white-water rafting offered by the Boquete-based companies **Chiriquí River Rafting** and **Panama Rafters** (see "What to See & Do" under "West of Volcán Barú: Boquete," later in this chapter). Contact these companies directly if possible—hotels in the area have been known to tack on a booking fee.

WHAT TO DO & SEE AROUND VOLCAN

For information about Volcán Barú and La Amistad parks, see "Bambito, Cerro Punta & Guadalupe," p. 221.

SITIO BARRILES ✎   Located 5.5km (3½ miles) southwest of Volcán, Sitio Barriles is an archaeological site on the private land of the Landau family, whose grandfather discovered hundreds of artifacts when excavating to build a coffee plantation. The artifacts are from the Barriles culture, an indigenous population that lived in the area from 600 B.C. to 300 B.C. before being forced to evacuate after the eruption of Volcán Barú. It's a curious attraction because hardly anything is known about the culture, and, accordingly, there's little interpretive information available to visitors. Artifacts include a burial tomb with funeral urns, pottery, and tools made of basalt. One basalt slab, when doused with water, shows ancient etchings. The site is open daily from 7am to 5pm, and can be reached by following the Río Sereno road west out of Volcán; the turnoff is on the left (✆ **575-2121**; there is no charge to visit, but donations are appreciated). The Landau family sells fresh cheese and homemade jams, too.

LAGUNAS DE VOLCAN ✎✎   About a 15-minute drive from Volcán, along a rough, poorly maintained road, sit the highest wetlands in Panama: Lagunas de Volcán. The wetlands comprise two lakes surrounded by exuberant forest, with dramatic views of Volcán Barú rising in the distance. It's a lovely spot to visit, but it especially draws bird-watchers who come to see northern jacanas, tanagers, collared trogons, emerald toucanets, masked ducks, and the rose-throated becard, among others. Western Wind Nature offers canoe trips here, too (see above). To get here you'll need a 4WD vehicle. Turn left off the main road at the sign for Vía Aeropuerto at the Agroquímicas Volcán building, and follow the signs for Lagunas de Volcán. There is no entrance fee. Considering that the Lagunas are close to La Torcaza Estate coffee farm (see below), you might want to tie in a visit to both.

LA TORCAZA ESTATE ✎✎   The Janson Family produces extraordinary coffee, and a visit to their estate gives connoisseurs a chance to learn how coffee is processed (and, of course, to sample and buy coffee at the on-site shop). The splendid views of Volcán Barú and the Janson's lovely farm are worth the visit alone. The Jansons pride themselves on environmental protection, producing shade-grown, organic beans that are handpicked and roasted in small batches, then packed up and shipped overseas to the U.S. and Europe. Their tour is in Spanish and English, and lasts about an hour; tours include a visit to their production facility, followed by coffee tasting. To get here, head west on the main road and turn left at the sign for the Vía Aeropuerto, at the Agroquímicas Volcán building; continue until you see the sign for Janson Family Coffee, turn right, and continue to the airport strip, where you'll turn right and follow the signs. The tour is $10 per person, or you can visit the coffee shop for free (✆ **771-4306**; www.estatecoffee.com; Mon–Fri 8am–4:30pm, Sat 8:30am–1:30pm).

LOS POZOS TERMALES ✎   It's not Baden Baden, but these natural hot springs do offer a place to soak your sore muscles after a day of adventure. The hot springs are located west from Volcán on the road to Río Sereno, 8.5km (5 miles) from the Berard Supermarket. You'll need a 4WD to get through a couple of sticky ruts as you get closer to the hot springs, and because a river crosses the road, it can be impossible to cross after heavy rain.

SHOPPING FOR HANDICRAFTS   Just before entering Volcán, on your left-hand side is **Artesanías Cruz Volcán,** a shop that showcases exquisite woodworking and glasswork crafted by the talented José de la Cruz, who studied his craft in Italy. José has many ready-made items for sale, but given a few days he'll also custom-carve everything from signs to furniture to doors, which can be shipped or picked up later—so stop here on your way into the area rather than on your way out. You can also pick up handicrafts at the gift shop at **San Benito Crafts School** in town, which donates proceeds to the school. The Crafts School holds a market as well every weekend.

A NATURE SANCTUARY & COFFEE FARM WEST OF VOLCAN

Part of the allure of a visit to **Finca Hartmann** ★★★ (© 775-5223; www.fincahartmann. com) is the drive there, which surely ranks among the top-five scenic drives in Panama. The twisting road requires that you take it slowly to avoid oncoming traffic, which whips around hairpin turns; you'll pass through beautiful dense forest that opens periodically for sweeping views. If you have a rental vehicle, this is a highly recommended day trip—or a tour operator can provide transportation.

Finca Hartmann is a boutique coffee farm producing shade-grown, high-quality beans typically sold to small specialty distributors. What's fascinating about their tours is the care that goes into producing such flavorful beans, and the Hartmann family's devotion and passion for the natural environment that surrounds them. More than anything else, the *finca* is known for is its position in the north-south corridor of migrating birds, thus ranking it as one of Panama's **bird-watching hot spots,** and many specialty bird-watching tours include this as part of their itinerary. Finca Hartman sits on the edge of La Amistad Parque Internacional; though they are not "official," hiking trails do exist and can be walked if reservations are made in advance so that a guide can accompany you. The only people you will see around the *finca* and along the trails—if you see anyone at all—are traditional Ngöbe-Buglé Indians.

There is a wooden *rancho* with an attractive coffee-tasting area and a small museum containing extensive bug collections and indigenous artifacts collected in the century that the Hartmanns have lived here. Coffee tours cost $10 per person, but a better bet is to plan a walking-and-coffee tour that includes lunch—contact Finca Hartmann for prices as each full-day tour is organized and priced individually. The Hartmanns have two picturesque but rustic cabins (with no electricity) tucked away in a small cloud forest at the end of a very rough road. The cabins have been used in the past as research centers and for student groups, but at the time of publication, the Hartmanns were considering opening the cabins for tourism, so contact them to see if they are up and running. Finca Hartmann is located in the tiny community of Santa Clara, on the road to Río Sereno. The turnoff is 27km (17 miles) from Volcán. Turn at the signed road and drive 1km (½ mile) until you reach the *finca*.

WHERE TO STAY & DINE

Note: Restaurants close very early in Volcán, usually at 9pm. The Hotel Dos Ríos has a restaurant and pizzeria, and the Hotel Don Tavo has inexpensive meals.

Hotel Dos Ríos ★ *Kids*   Located just on the outskirts west of town, the Hotel Dos Ríos offers the most upscale lodging in Volcán. That's not saying much, but considering the amenities offered and the friendly, helpful service, it's a good base for seeing the sights around the area. The hotel is slathered in colorful, sponged-on paint, and is spaced out in a wide "V," with guest rooms in one wing, and a restaurant and the lively Barriles bar in the other (karaoke noise can be a problem on weekends). The center of the hotel is bisected by a rushing creek. Guest rooms are average size and boast polished wooden floors and artistic, stenciled wall paintings; double rooms have two double beds, and there are triples with a double bed and a bunk bed. The quietest, and largest, rooms are the two suites at the end of the building, which come with a bed and a sofa bed. Kids love the enclosed butterfly garden, and there is a kids' play area and a lot of grassy areas to run around in. The hotel's moderately priced, on-site restaurant, **Estrella Volcanera Restaurant,** serves decent international fare, mostly meats, pasta, and fish, and they have a pizzeria with takeout service, but the dining area is brightly lit at night and does not provide much in the way of ambience (daily 7am–10pm). The staff can put together tours for guests.

Vía Río Sereno, west end of town. © 771-5555. www.dosrios.com.pa. 18 units. $40–$57 double; $60–$78 suite. AE, MC, V. **Amenities:** Restaurant; bar; Internet access; tour desk; kids' play area; gift shop; limited room service; butterfly garden; laundry service. *In room:* TV, hair dryer.

Hotel y Restaurante Don Tavo (Value)   For budget accommodations, you can't beat Hotel Don Tavo. It's located on the main drag and is more attractive than the facade would lead you to believe because it is centered around a pleasant backyard patio garden adorned with a landscape mural and bougainvillea. Rooms are nothing fancy, but simple and clean, with hot-water showers (not typical for budget lodging in Panama). They have an Internet center with fast connections on the premises. The restaurant here, which serves basic Panamanian dishes, is open daily from 7am to 11pm.

Av. Central, near the church. © 771-5144. http://volcanbaru.com/turismo/dontavo. $33 double; $55 quadruple. No credit cards. **Amenities:** Restaurant; Internet center; laundry service. *In room:* TV, no phone.

Acropolis (GG) GREEK   This place is the definition of "no frills," but it serves some of the best food in the area. As a Greek restaurant, the Acropolis is a rather incongruous establishment in the Panamanian highlands, and George, the Greek owner, admits that his cuisine was a tough sell at first to a suspicious local clientele—now he has them coming back as frequent customers. Part of the reason is that George can't find the ingredients he needs, like eggplant, zucchini, and herbs, so he grows his own produce and even raises rabbits to create authentic, and absolutely delicious, Greek dishes. You'll find moussaka (lamb-and-eggplant casserole), dolmades (ground beef wrapped in rice), and souvlaki (roast chicken in pita bread), as well as hummus and tabbouleh. His moussaka is so good that people from as far away as Boquete buy trays of the stuff to bring home. Service is fast, and George, a bit of a character, will engage you in a lengthy conversation if you want to know more about the Volcán area. Knock on the door if the restaurant looks closed.

Av. Central, next to the Accel gas station. © 771-4162 or 6651-4777. Reservations recommended for dinner. Main courses $5–$7. No credit cards. Tues–Sun noon–9pm.

Kitchens (G) SEAFOOD/SANDWICHES   Volcán's newest eatery specializes in fresh trout, served 21 ways. The restaurant is casual and housed in a building that looks like a contemporary wooden wigwam, with chunky wooden chairs and hand-painted tables. Their menu is extensive and a good bet for a group that can't decide what to eat, though trout from a local farm is what most diners order. Trout is served Hawaiian-style, in a tempura batter, grilled with a wedge of lemon, or in myriad other ways, but they serve the fish whole, head and bones included. Ask the waiter if they can debone your trout, as it is tiresome to pick out the tiny spines yourself.

Av. Central, on left-hand side at the entrance to town. © 771-5928. Main courses $5–$13. AE, MC, V. Tues–Sun 11am–8pm.

Restaurante Cerro Brujo ✦✦ *Finds* CONTEMPORARY PANAMANIAN
Tucked away in a residential area about 1km (½ mile) from the main road, this tiny
restaurant, with an arty ambience, serves gourmet food, and is one of the better dining options west of Volcán Barú. The restaurant serves from a fixed-price menu that
changes daily according to what is fresh and available on any given day. When I dined
here, the menu was homemade pea soup, tossed green salad with dill vinaigrette, and
a choice of chicken in coconut and curry, or grilled beef filet. They have a limited wine
list with mostly Chilean varieties. Service is a bit absent-minded, but the owner, Patty,
is a delight and likes to personally greets her customers.

Heading west, turn right at restaurant sign before the road forks. © 6669-9196. Reservations recommended. Fixed-
price menu $11–$13 per person. No credit cards. Daily noon–3pm and 6–9pm. (Call to verify open days during low
season.)

3 Bambito, Cerro Punta & Guadalupe ✦✦✦

Bambito is 18km (11 miles) N of Volcán; Cerro Punta is 7km (4½ miles) from Bambito; Guadalupe is 2.5km (1½ miles)
from Cerro Punta

Bambito, Cerro Punta, and Guadalupe are three of a dozen or so tiny farming communities nestled in a bucolic, alpine paradise. The area is characterized by rugged hills
and peaks cloaked in thick emerald forest that is speckled with flowers and interspersed with a patchwork of colorful fields. Bambito is just a sprinkling of homes and
services along the road. Cerro Punta is located in the crater of an extinct volcano, and
is the epicenter of agricultural production. Cerro Punta sits at 1,800m (5,900 ft.),
looking out over a fertile valley and craggy peaks beyond, and provides for a quick scenic drive past strawberry and flower farms. Guadalupe, too, has flower-filled streets
and is flanked by quiltlike farms that slope up the surrounding hills. From here, the
roads branch out to La Amistad International Park and Volcán Barú National Park.
This is truly the loveliest alpine region in Panama.

WHAT TO SEE & DO IN THE NORTHWESTERN HIGHLANDS

For information about hiking in **Volcán Barú National Park,** see "What to See &
Do," in the Boquete section, later in this chapter. Hikers on this side of the park are
usually headed to Boquete along the stunning **Quetzal Trail.** The trail from this side
of the volcano to Boquete is mostly downhill, and it's recommended that hikers walk
the trail in this direction unless they're looking for a strenuous workout. If you don't
plan on hiking this trail in its entirety, it's worth walking a portion of it and then heading back when you've had enough. The Respingo ranger station can be reached by
walking 45 minutes up a rutted road from the main road near Bajo Grande, or by
driving a 4WD to the station, where you'll find a high-altitude picnic site with views.
For bird-watching and hiking tours here (including walks on the Quetzal Trail), see
"Tour Outfitters," under "Volcán," earlier in this chapter.

Several farms in Cerro Punta are open to the public for visits; there are no regular
hours, so just pop by if you're in the area. Turn at the first left just before Cerro Punta
at the sign for the International Park and continue until you see **Finca Fresas Pariente,** a strawberry farm that will sell their fruit to passersby. Take a left at the road just
past Pariente to **Panaflores,** an extensive flower farm with rows upon rows of flowers
in a rainbow of colors, and an excellent spot for taking photos.

HIKING IN PARQUE INTERNACIONAL LA AMISTAD ₭₭₭

La Amistad Park, popularly known by the Spanish acronym PILA, is "international" in that half the park is located in Costa Rica. La Amistad was formed in 1988 by the Panamanian and Costa Rican governments to protect the virgin forests and fragile ecosystems of the rugged Talamanca Range and its surrounding lowland buffer zones, and to protect one of the most biodiverse areas in the Americas. UNESCO designated the park a World Heritage Site in 1990, but, sadly, this hasn't been 100% effective in staunching encroachment by ranchers and hunters. Still, for the most part the park is totally untouched, creating a home for an extraordinary array of more than 100 mammal species, including endangered tapirs, jaguars, ocelots, pumas, and howler monkeys. There are also more than 400 species of birds like resplendent quetzals, crested eagles, harpy eagles, three-wattled bell birds, and a rare umbrella bird. The Panama side of the park encompasses 207,000 hectares (511,500 acres), the majority of which are part of the Bocas del Toro Province—but it is here at the administration area near Cerro Punta where hikers can access the primeval rainforest that is this park's characteristic feature. This is one of the wettest regions in Panama, so prepare yourself for damp conditions with waterproof clothing and shoes.

What I enjoy about La Amistad is that there are several trails for all levels of ability (and all weather conditions), and there are usually few people here. Also, after a morning of hiking through rainforest, you can have an inexpensive, delicious lunch at a cooperative cafe near the park ranger station, located just past the hamlet of Las Nubes. Three trails leave from the ranger station, and one trail currently under repair (Sendero los Antepasados), which might be open by the time you read this. **Sendero Puma Verde** is the easiest walk here and can be completed in 15 minutes. **Sendero El Retoño** is 2.1km (1.3 miles) and an easy 1-hour loop trail that is mostly flat. The trail is simply gorgeous, taking hikers through a dense jungle and a bamboo tunnel, and across babbling brooks. There are signs along the way identifying trees and other plants. **Sendero La Cascada** is 3.5km (2 miles) and about a 2-hour round-trip hike to a series of lookout points with mountain and valley views, and a crashing 49m (160-ft.) waterfall. Along the way is a detour to a lookout point that, on a very clear day, offers a view that stretches to the Caribbean. Taking this detour will add an extra 1½ hours to your trip; take a left at the fork at the Mirador Barranco. About half of this hike is uphill, and therefore moderately strenuous.

Lastly, **Sendero Cerro Picacho** takes gung-ho hikers along a narrow and poorly marked trail through primary forest up to a peak at 2,937m (9,635 ft.), where you can see from the Pacific to the Caribbean—and you can even spend the night here in a rustic hut. This trail is uphill, about 4km (2.5 miles), and a strenuous slog that should not be attempted without a guide. If you're not already booked with a guide, call the co-op near the ranger station (see below for number) and they can arrange one for you. It takes about 3½ hours each way for this trail.

ANAM charges $3.50 per person to enter the park. Hours are daily from 7:45am to 4pm. There is very rustic lodging in bunks at the station for $5 per person, but you'll need a sleeping bag. They have a grungy kitchen for cooking meals, or you can visit the Asociación Agroecoturística La Amistad (ASAELA) co-op near the station. The small cafe serves daily specials such as stewed chicken, beans, and rice for $2; hot soup for 75¢; and breakfast. They also sell locally produced preserves and other goodies (© **771-2620;** daily 8am–4pm).

FINCA DRACULA ★★

Despite the spooky name, this *finca* is revered as one of the most important orchid farms in Central America, with more than 600 species on display that are cloned to produce 250,000 plants yearly. The farm claims to have the most complete collection of rare American orchid species, some of which no longer exist in their natural habitat. The farm is owned by master orchid horticulturist Andres Maduro, who bought the property in 1969 and has allowed the former cattle ranch to reforest and return to its natural, exuberantly tropical state. The name of the *finca* refers to the Dracula orchid, an elegant purple flower that droops and hides itself during daylight. Tours of the orchid farm are best in April, when there's a higher incidence of blooming orchids, but on any day you're bound to see dozens of orchids in full bloom. Tours are a little pricey at $10 per person, but they include a thorough interpretive tour of the facilities and laboratory to illustrate the delicate process involved in cloning. Tours, in Spanish and English, are daily from 8am to 5pm (© **771-2070;** www.fincadracula.com).

TRUCHAS BAMBITO

This is less of an attraction and more of a place to reel in a fresh trout for dinner, if you have kitchen facilities or if your hotel's restaurant is willing to cook one up for you. Truchas Bambito is part of the Hotel Bambito (see below), but located on the other side of the road. Three pools here are packed with swimming trout; throw a line in and within minutes, or even seconds, you'll be reeling in a fish. Young kids, of course, really get a kick out of this attraction. The cost to rent a pole is $2.50; the cost per pound for a trout is $1.65. It's $3 per pound to have the fish gutted and filleted. Truchas Bambito is open daily from 8am to 3pm; they accept Visa or cash only.

WHERE TO STAY & DINE

In contrast to Volcán, the lodging options below are nestled in forested areas that put travelers closer to natural surroundings (with the exception of Hotel Cerro Punta) and the two parks.

Cabañas Kucikas   These 18 cabins are stand-alone, self-catering units with kitchens stocked with pots and plates. But you'll need to bring your own soap, toilet paper, and any other dispensable items. The two-story, zinc-roofed, A-frame cabins are set in a row on a grassy area and backed by forest. Cabins are for 2 to 10 guests; each is slightly different from the last and ranges in quality, but all show their years and can only be considered a step above budget accommodations. There are several outdoor barbecue areas for guests. You'll find the Cabañas just past the Hotel Bambito, on the left-hand side as you're headed toward Cerro Punta.

Bambito. © **771-4245,** or 512/396-0796 in the U.S. www.cabanaskucikas.com. 18 units. $60 cabin for 2; $70 cabin for 4. No credit cards. **Amenities:** Kids' play area; barbecue area. *In room:* No phone.

Cielito Sur ★★★ *(Finds*   The guest book at the Cielito Sur is filled with visitors' wistful regrets that they couldn't spend another night at this intimate and peaceful B&B—mine included. It's an ideal place for travelers seeking a pretty pastoral setting, snug guest rooms, and easy-to-plan excursions. The Canadian couple who own the Cielito, Janet and Glenn, are former canal employees who opted to retire in Panama after the handover. They couldn't have chosen a lovelier spot to build their B&B, nestled alongside a babbling creek and backed by exuberant foliage interspersed with flowers and tropical fruit trees. There are just four spacious but cozy rooms, each decorated in a country style paired with indigenous artwork. Two rooms are slightly larger and feature kitchenettes, and two have king-size beds that can be divided into two twins. The rooms face the back garden and a long patio terrace where 12 species of hummingbirds whiz about, Disney-like. What I like is the plenitude of common areas so that you don't feel trapped in your room. There's a short trail that winds through the property, a thatched *bohio* hut with hammocks, a cute dining area, a little house with an indoor whirlpool, and a comfy living room with reclining chairs next to a fireplace and a well-stocked library. A hearty breakfast is included. Janet and Glenn can help plan daily excursions, and they seemingly know more about the highlands area than anyone I've met. The Cielito Sur is in Nueva Suiza, 10km (6¼ miles) from Volcán and just before Cerro Punta. Note that the B&B is closed during the month of October, and children must be 12 years or older to stay here.

Nueva Suiza. ⑦ 771-2038. www.cielitosur.com. 4 units. $65–$70 double; $75–$80 double with kitchenette. AE, MC, V. **Amenities:** Coffee shop; whirlpool; tour planning; bicycles for rent; extensive library; gift shop; Wi-Fi. *In room:* Kitchenette (some rooms), hair dryer.

El Manatial Spa & Resort 🦌🦌 *Kids*   This spa/resort, with an exceptionally friendly staff, offers lots of kid-friendly activities yet still feels sophisticated enough to please adults. In 2004, the resort changed hands and was given a face-lift that included the addition of an upscale spa with full services. The resort—about a 5-minute drive past the Hotel Bambito, on the left side—is spread along the foreground of a 121-hectare (300-acre) forested property and surrounded by a large lawn, neatly manicured gardens, and a river backed by forest. It's a beautiful location, and there are walking trails and dirt roads for bicycling. Guest rooms boast handsome teak and pine paneling and polished wood floors; some have wicker furniture (most are quite dark). The junior suite is the best room here, with a small but bright foyer and seating area, and a bedroom with two double beds—but it's a chunk more expensive than a double during high season and not a "value." The Royal Suites have three bedrooms for a total of nine people, and the standard double is really for four: It has two twins and a double bed (not to mention a hammock!) lined in a row in a rectangular room. Clearly, the hotel was originally designed for families with a large brood. The hotel attracts big groups such as the Audubon Society, among others. The reception/bar/spa area is the resort's modern nucleus designed in a vaguely Santa Fe style. The rest of the hotel is traditional, with wood trim and lots of rock walls and flooring. Outside, there is a resort-style pool, an artificial lagoon with novelty trout fishing, a kids' play area, and a zip-line canopy ride for a fast thrill. The **spa** here is very complete, reasonably priced, and open to the public with advance notice. The resort has staff guides, and can put you in touch with a specialty guide if they're booked or a if a guide is unavailable. The **Restaurante Bar La Carreta** serves tasty fare with main courses ranging from $5 to $15.

Bambito. ⑦ 771-5126. www.manantialspa.com. 21 units. $60–$90 double; $90–$150 junior suite; $120–$185 royal suite. AE, MC, V. **Amenities:** Restaurant; bar; outdoor adult and kids' pools; spa w/massage, sauna, Turkish bath, whirlpool, and ski treatments; bicycle rental; trout lagoon; canopy line; walking trails; horseback riding; tours; Ping-Pong; kids' play area; limited room service. *In room:* TV, hair dryer.

Hotel Bambito 🦌   Built in 1981 as a fashionable, full-service mountain hotel, the Bambito has been well maintained over the years but the decor remains the same as the day it opened. The interiors will appeal to fans of a retro-cool aesthetic, though other guests might find it dated and in need of an overhaul. I personally like the style, and find the guest rooms to be comfortable and spaciously appointed with a small sitting area and two double beds. There are also apartment suites with two stories and a

living area. The hotel has fresh white exteriors accented with river rock and A-frame eaves in a vaguely Swiss style, and it is surrounded by handsomely landscaped and tidy grounds that include an artificial lagoon and creek. The restaurant serves decent international food, but they really could stand to spruce up their bar a bit and charge less for drinks. If you catch a fish at their neighboring trout farm (see "What to See & Do," below), they'll prepare it for your evening meal. The hotel is popular with Europeans and Panamanians, and sees its fair share of conventions and weddings. Jimmy Carter stayed at the Bambito when he was negotiating terms for the canal handover; one assumes that he bunked in the presidential suite, the only one in Chiriquí Province. The hotel offers its own tours for an additional price.

Bambito. ⓒ 771-4373 or 771-4374. www.hotelbambito.com. 45 units. $88–$105 double; $120–$154 apt suite (add $20 extra during holidays). AE, MC, V. **Amenities:** Restaurant; bar; heated pool; tennis courts; small gym; whirlpool; sauna; tour desk; limited room service; laundry service; Internet access; trout farm. In room: TV.

Hotel Cerro Punta   It's a little low on style, but Hotel Cerro Punta is clean and inexpensive. The hotel, built in 1983, is on the Cerro Punta's main drag, and has a couple of rooms with mountain views (others are darker and do not have views). Guest rooms have a double bed and a twin that are reasonably comfortable. The Cerro Punta locals who run this hotel are nice people, and the restaurant here serves local dishes that cost between $4 and $9. My only caveat is that the owner is a hunter, and he's decorated his restaurant with the mounted animal heads and skins of native fauna—which might rub nature lovers the wrong way.

Cerro Punta. ⓒ 771-2020. 10 units. $25 double. MC, V. **Amenities:** Restaurant. In room: No phone.

Las Plumas ⓖ (Value   The Dutch owners of Las Plumas offer three homes with full kitchens and living rooms that are truly a bargain. The spacious, stand-alone homes are spread across 2.4 hectares (6 acres) on a grassy clearing surrounded by forest. The homes can be rented nightly (3-night minimum) or long-term. The largest home, Quetzal, is a whopping 223 sq. m (2,400 sq. ft.), and contains three bedrooms, a fireplace, and terrace; the Woodpecker and Tanager houses have less than half the square footage, with two bedrooms each and a gazebo. Sparkling clean and fitted with contemporary furniture and fixtures, the houses contain orthopedic beds and tiled floors.

Paso Ancho. ⓒ 771-5541 or 6527-3848. www.las-plumas.com. 3 units. $60–$75 per night, house for 4 guests. MC, V. **Amenities:** Internet hookup; cellphone rental. In room: TV, kitchen, no phone.

Los Quetzales Lodge & Spa ⓖ   Los Quetzales Lodge & Spa is a destination mountain lodge with guest rooms and backcountry cabins that appeal to hikers, nature lovers, and especially bird-watchers. Los Quetzales leads you to believe that their lodge is tucked away in a national forest, but it is really their handful of rustic wooden cabins that are nestled within the cloud forest of Volcán Barú National Park, about a 25-minute drive away from the lodge and up a brutal road. (They provide transportation to and from the lodge.) The lodge itself sits on the main road of the village of Guadalupe, next to a river and on a grassy property whose landscaping could use a lot of TLC. Los Quetzales offers all-inclusive packages, or you can book a room on a nightly basis (with breakfast included) and order what you want a la carte. Ask for a price list for excursions and do a little math before booking, especially if you have a group and/or are lodging in a cabin—the all-inclusive package is often not much value. All-inclusive prices for cabins, for example, cost $160 per person, but there are kitchen facilities and space for four to six people, so you could save a bundle by bringing your own food. With the all-inclusive plan, they drive guests to the lodge for

meals, which can be a hassle; or send supplies for cooking or ready-made hot meals; or send a chef to cook for you (free for three or more guests; $30 extra for two guests). The main alpine-style lodge has a cozy cedar-wall restaurant and common area next to a brightly lit game space dominated by a Ping-Pong table. Meals, hearty and fairly good, are served buffet-style.

The standard double guest rooms are cramped and dark. The spacious junior and master suites, as well as the stand-alone "duplex," are the best rooms, with wood-paneled walls, kitchenettes, and fireplaces (suites only). The suites can fit four to six people, but be aware that the suites have only one bathroom. There are two cheaper dormitories for up to eight, but they share just one bathroom. Of the six cabins available, I highly recommend only two: units 2 and 3. These rustic cabins are in stunning rainforest swirling with birds, and are attractively designed with patio terraces. They also are near trail heads for hiking. The other cabins are located too far up the road, and are dirty and not well maintained.

The service at Los Quetzales is at best absent-minded (or just absent). Rarely will you find anyone in reception, and when you do, prices are given arbitrarily, reservations are lost, and the staff is grossly unknowledgeable. For example, a guest might make a tour reservation that is not honored the following day, and many of the included trips are led by Spanish-speaking-only guides. The bottom line is that the owner of Los Quetzales cuts too many corners, and nickels-and-dimes guests.

Guadalupe. ⓒ 771-2291. www.losquetzales.com. 22 units, 6 cabins. All-inclusive packages cost, per person, based on double occupancy, $100 double; $120 master suite; $160 cabin. Nightly rates are $60 double, $100 suite, $150 cabin. AE, MC, V. **Amenities:** Restaurant; bar; spa w/massage, sauna, whirlpool, and mud treatments; game room; tours and tour desk; horseback riding; bicycle rental; volleyball; limited library; rubber boots and raingear available; cybercafe. *In room:* Kitchenette and chimney (suites only); no phone.

Parrilla Argentina 🍴 ARGENTINE   This family-run restaurant is known for its grilled Argentine-style steaks and other meats, served in a cozy ambience with checkered tablecloths and candlelight. Start with a creamy trout soup or juicy sausage appetizer, and follow it with a T-bone, New York, or rib-eye steak; or sample trout or sea bass paired with potatoes and a salad. They offer a good selection of Argentine and Chilean wines, and there is a kids' menu.

Bambito. ⓒ 6513-0208. Reservations accepted. Main courses $4.50–$8.50. AE, MC, V. Daily 10am–10pm.

4 West of Volcán Barú: Boquete 🌟🌟🌟

40km (25 miles) from David; 473km (293 miles) from Panama City

Boquete is located in a steep-walled, green, and flower-filled valley on the flank of the Barú Volcano and at the shore of the Caldera River. Despite Boquete's somewhat utilitarian downtown made of cheap, concrete-poured buildings, the town on the whole oozes charm and offers a bounty of activities for travelers. Recently Boquete has climbed the charts to become one of the top-five retirement destinations in the world, and large-scale gated communities have begun their spread on the city's outskirts, much to the chagrin of longtime residents. With so many foreigners living in the area, Boquete has indeed taken on a more international feel than its counterpart Cerro Punta on the other side of the volcano. But, given the bounty of services, tours, attractions, gourmet restaurants, and a wide scale of lodging options, Boquete makes an ideal base for exploring the Chiriquí Highlands. Travelers who are keen to hike the

Boquete

ACCOMMODATIONS ■
Boquete Country Inn **19**
Boquete Garden Inn **2**
The Coffee Estate Inn **7**
Hotel Oasis **15**
Hotel Petit Mozart **11**
Isla Verde Hotel **16**
Kalima Suites **21**
Los Establos **6**
Palo Alto Riverside Hotel **3**
Panamonte Inn &
   Restaurant **9**
Villa Marita **1**

DINING ◆
Boquete Bistro **13**
Delicias del Perú **10**
Hibiscus **14**
La Casona Mexicana **22**
Machu Picchu **20**
Palo Alto Restaurant **4**
Sabrosón **12**

ATTRACTIONS ●
Chiriquí River Rafting **18**
El Explorador **5**
Mi Jardin es Su Jardin **8**
Panama Rafters **17**

C.R.
*Caribbean
Sea*
Colón
★ Panama City
• Boquete
*Golfo de
Panamá*
COL
0   50 mi
0   50 km

ARCO IRIS
Rio Palo Alto
ALTO
LINO
PALO
ALTO
HORQUETA
LOS
NARANJOS
Rio Caldera
← To Sendero
Los Quetzales
BAJO
LINO
← To Volcán
Barú (peak)
Quebrada Grande
LOS
CABEZOS
Quebrada   *La Zumbona*
JARAMILLO
ARRIBA

Volcán Barú
3, 475 m
(11, 400 ft)

See inset map

BOQUETE

VOLCANCITO

JARAMILLO
CENTRO

IPAT
ⓘ Visitor's Center
JARAMILLO
ABAJO
Rio Caldera

Iglesia
San Juan
Bautista ■
*Feria de
las Flores*
Calle Central
Av. A Oeste
Av. Central
Av. A Este
Av. B Este
Calle 1 Sur
Av. B Oeste
Calle 2 Sur
Parque
Médica
Avenida 4
Calle Sur
Calle 5 Sur
Police ■
Rio Caldera
Av. B Porras
Av. A Este
Gas Station ■

ALTO
BOQUETE

(43)

To La Estrella
↓

0   1/2 mi
0   1/2 km

To David
↓

Quetzal Trail would do well to visit Cerro Punta on the western side of the volcano first, and then walk to Boquete, sending their luggage around by vehicle.

ESSENTIALS

GETTING THERE & DEPARTING   Most hotels either provide transportation from the David airport or can arrange for you to be picked up by an independent taxi driver for the 45-mintue drive to Boquete.

By Bus & Taxi   Buses for Boquete leave from the David bus terminal every 25 minutes, take approximately 1 hour, and cost $1.50 one-way. You can catch a bus from Boquete to David from the north side of the main plaza. If you're coming from Bocas del Toro or from Panama City, you'll need to transfer in David. It takes 7 hours by bus from Panama City, and costs $11. A taxi from David to Boquete costs approximately $15 to $20 one-way.

By Car   If you're driving from Panama City, you'll turn right on the signed turnoff for Boquete before entering David, at the intersection next to the Shell gas station.

From the airport in David, turn right onto the main road and drive until you arrive at the intersection with the Shell station, then turn left. Drive until you reach a stop sign at the four-lane highway, turn right, and continue until you see you reach the intersection at the Super Barú supermarket. Turn left and continue onward to Boquete.

The road to Boquete is well-paved; there are two side roads that provide shortcuts if you're driving from the Bocas del Toro area.

GETTING AROUND   If you're a do-it-yourself traveler who likes to explore at your own pace, you'll want to rent a vehicle to get around—but you'll have to do it from the David airport (p. 210); alternatively, some hotels can arrange for a rental car to be delivered to you in Boquete for an additional $30.

Taxis around town cost $1 to $2; unless your hotel is located in the town center, you'll need one to get back and forth. If you're looking for a fluent English-speaking taxi driver for a half- or full-day tour around Boquete, try **Daniel Higgins** (© 6617-0570); he charges $15 per hour.

Local buses cruise Avenida Central and the hilly roads around Boquete, but taxis are so cheap that you'll invariably end up hailing a cab before a bus.

ORIENTATION   Boquete's **CEFATI visitor center** (© 720-4060; daily 9am–6pm) is the large building on your right just before you enter town. With its location high above the Río Caldera, the visitor center provides sweeping views of town. You'll find **Café Kotowa** here, too, with a small shop. On the center's second floor is an interpretive display (in Spanish) of the history and anthropology of the region. Ask for a representative here to give you a quick tour and translate the displays. The center isn't within walking distance from downtown, so you'll need to take a cab ($1) or a local bus (25¢).

Fun Fact   Bajareque

The *bajareque* is a unique weather phenomenon that occurs from December to March, when a fine misting rain is pushed over from the Atlantic and into the highlands. The mist is so soft it "caresses the face," as locals like to say. The combination of sun, wind, and *bajareque* provides endless rainbows.

Boquete sits in a fertile valley below the Barú Volcano, and is bisected by the Caldera River. The main street, Avenida Central, runs the length of town from north to south, and businesses and transportation services are clustered around the main plaza on streets that run east-west. From downtown, a series of paved and gravel roads climb the hilly terrain surrounding Boquete.

FAST FACTS   For the **police,** dial ✆ 104; for the **fire department,** dial ✆ 720-1224. The **Centro Médico San Juan Bautista,** located on Avenida Central, 2 blocks up the road past the Hotel Panamonte, has English-speaking doctors (✆ 720-1881); for serious health problems, you'll need to head to the hospital in David. The **post office** is located on the plaza, and is open Monday to Friday 8am to 5:45pm, and Saturday 8am to 4:45pm; for fast service go to **Mailboxes Etc** (✆ 720-2684) on Avenida Central, in front of the Almacén Reina.

Twenty-four-hour ATMs can be found at **Banco Nacional** and **Global Bank,** which lie across from each other on Avenida Central and Calle 5 Sur (regular hours: Mon–Fri 8am–3pm, Sat 9am–noon). Most hotels have a computer with Internet access for their guests, or try **Java Juice** on Avenida Central.

WHAT TO SEE & DO

There's no shortage of things to see and do in Boquete: adrenaline-pumping outdoor adventures, quiet forays in the rainforest seeking the elusive quetzal, and walks among perfume-scented flowers at public gardens; you can learn how to make a good cup of joe and about the local Ngobe-Buglé tribe . . . and the list goes on. As mentioned throughout this chapter, a lot of visitors opt to rent a car—the area offers so many beautiful scenic drives. Here are a few:

The **Bajo Mono Loop** takes you high above the town along a newly asphalted road for panoramic vistas and beautiful forest scenery. This is a good drive from which to get your bearings and see why everyone's gone wild about living in Boquete. To get here, follow the main road past the church and head left at the fork, passing Café Ruiz and staying left until you see the sign for BAJO MONO. Just as pretty is the **Volcancito Loop**—to get here, follow the main road out of town and when you see the CEFATI visitor center, turn right and follow the loop until you arrive back at town. You can bike these loops as well. (See "Biking," below.)

One of the most beautiful drives in Panama heads to **Finca Suiza** (p. 244) on the main road to the Atlantic Coast, in the Bocas del Toro Province. The scenic drive winds through mountain forests and open fields with sweeping views, and farther down to the lush lowlands and rainforest of Bocas Province. Take the left turn to Caldera 16km (10 miles) south of Boquete and continue along paved/gravel road, until you hit the major road to Bocas. You can also take a completely paved, easier-to-follow road by heading toward David and turning left toward Gualaca.

HIKING & BIRD-WATCHING OUTFITTERS/GUIDES

The following tour outfitters and local guides offer hiking, bird-watching, and other general excursions to destinations and attractions listed below in this section. With their new office in Boquete, the reputable Panama City–based adventure company **Ecocircuitos,** on Avenida Central next to Chiriquí Rafting Company (✆ **720-1506;** www.ecocircuitos.com) is a one-stop shop for short adventures in the Chiriquí area. This book went to publication as they were opening, so you'll need to call or visit them to see what they have in store. Another company, **Coffee Adventures** (see "Coffee Tours," below), offers guided excursions around Boquete even though they are more commonly called upon for their popular tours of the Kotowa coffee estate. Coffee Adventures offers cultural excursions to a Ngöbe-Buglé community near the Caribbean coast, guided hikes on Los Quetzales Trail from Boquete to Cerro Punta (or vice versa), and low-key excursions like bird-watching and trips to the Caldera Hot Springs. **Feliciano González** is a local guide with more than 20 years' experience in the Boquete area (© **6632-8645** or 6624-9940; www.geocities.com/boquete_tours). He has a 4WD vehicle, speaks basic English, and can customize tours of Boquete as well as day hikes on the Quetzales Trail, the Pianista Trail, and the full-day hike to the summit of Volcano Barú ($100 for up to four people). Based in Volcán, **Nariño Aizpurua** (© **6704-4251;** westernwindnature@yahoo.com) is a fun and friendly guide who specializes in bird-watching; he is a recommended guide for Los Quetzales Trail if you plan to start on that side. (See "Volcán," earlier in this chapter, for more information about his other trips.)

For birding, you can't beat local guide **Santiago "Chago" Caballero** (© **6626-2200;** santiagochagotours@hotmail.com) or one of his protégés. Want to see a quetzal? If you're here from December to May, Santiago can guarantee you will—the reason he is such a valued guide in the region. Santiago typically takes birders to Finca Lérida but can customize tours, including searches for wild orchids in the rainforest.

EXPLORING EL PARQUE NACIONAL VOLCAN BARU

As the name states, this national park is centered around the 3,475m (11,500-ft.) extinct **Barú Volcano,** the highest point in the country and the beloved center of adventurous outdoor pursuits for bird-watchers, hikers, rafters, and nature lovers. The park is situated on the Pacific-facing side of the Talamanca Mountain Range, and encompasses 14,000 hectares (34,600 acres) of rugged topography cloaked in primary and secondary rainforest. This rainforest provides a home to nearly 250 species of birds, the most notable of which is the **resplendent quetzal,** whose extraordinary beauty puts the bird in the number-one spot on many a bird-watching list. Other rare birds here include the silky flycatcher, the three-wattled bellbird, and the hairy woodpecker. Owing to the volcano's height and isolation, this area is considered a "bioclimatic island." Its forest is home to unique species of orchids and uncommon flora such as magnolia and giant oak trees, some of which are between 600 and 900 years old. You'll also see wild bamboo gardens and gigantic, gnarled trees dripping with vines and sprouting prehistoric-looking bromeliads from their trunks. In higher reaches, an intermittent cloud forest provokes an eerie ambience. All said, it's a wonderful place to hike and immerse yourself in wild beauty, but come prepared with waterproof outerwear and shoes and a dry change of clothes just in case. In this national park, temperatures average 50° to 60°F (10°–16°C).

Natural beauty aside, the park is economically important because it protects the headwaters that provide irrigation to the country's prime agricultural region, concentrated in the fertile areas of the volcano's skirt. These rivers are also revered by rafters and kayakers for their Class III to Class V rapids, which provide thrills and a sense of remote solitude—a sure recipe for adventure. For more information about rafting, see below.

Volcán Barú National Park is administered by ANAM, which has ranger stations at the Los Quetzales trail heads in both Boquete (Alto Chiquero) and Cerro Punta (El Respingo), and charges a $3-per-person entrance fee. Both ranger stations have a handful of truly rustic bunks with shared bathrooms, which cost $5 per bed. There's not much ambience at the Boquete station to encourage even the hardiest of nature lovers to lodge there, however. A taxi to the ranger station, about 8km (5 miles) from Boquete, costs $3.

HIKING   By any measure, the most popular trail is **Sendero Los Quetzales,** a superb, short-haul day hike—regarded as the best in Panama by most visitors to the country. The rainforest here is thick and lush and dazzling with its array of colorful birds, panoramic lookout points, and crystalline streams rushing across velvety moss-covered rocks. Most important, and most unique, is the fact that the trail connects Cerro Punta (and Guadalupe) with Boquete, allowing hikers to have their baggage sent from one town to the other, and to arrive by foot at their next destination. If you're physically up to it, I recommend the entire trek as one of the region's highlights—but there are *a few things to consider* before setting out. First, Cerro Punta's altitude is 1,981m (6,500 ft.), while Boquete's is 975m (3,200 ft.)—so the trail is mostly down-hill from Cerro Punta. Now, a lot of Boquete residents and tour guides will pooh-pooh the level of difficulty and stamina needed to complete the uphill trail from Boquete to Cerro Punta, but every hiker I saw doing the trail uphill looked just fraz-zled. In other words, if you're fit and looking for a workout, walk Boquete to Cerro Punta; if not, either plan your trip so that you visit the western region of the volcano first and then Boquete or, if you only plan to walk the trail for the day, leave early and drive to Cerro Punta. For those who want to just get out and hike around a little, you'll be okay because the first couple of kilometers from the Boquete ranger station are relatively flat, offer outstanding opportunities to see birds (especially the quetzal), and put you in the middle of a stream-lined forest. You can walk as little or as much as you like and then turn around and head back.

The Quetzales Trail from Boquete begins with a 45-minute walk from the ranger station on a semi-paved road. After the sign for the trail head, the trail continues for about 2 hours before heading up into a steep ascent. Midway up the ascent is a picnic area with tables. Farther up, about halfway along the trail, is a sweeping lookout point, with a roofed eating area and a couple of campsites.

From the Cerro Punta ranger station, a rutted road requiring a 4WD heads down-hill for almost 3km (2 miles) until it reaches the paved road to Cerro Punta. Tour operators and taxis with 4WD traction can make it up and down this road, but few seem willing—so prepare yourself to walk this portion. The total number of trail miles is anyone's guess, as park signs, rangers, and tour guides all disagree on the distance; it's estimated that the trail is about 9.7km (6 miles). From station to station, plan on 6 to 7 hours if walking uphill, and 4½ hours if walking downhill, plus another 45 min-utes to 1 hour for the last leg of the Cerro Punta ranger station to the road.

Keen adventurers might be interested in the trail to the **volcano's summit,** a very arduous climb that puts visitors at the highest point in Panama and offers electrifying views from the Caribbean Sea to the Pacific Ocean. Although this trail can be reached from the Cerro Punta side, the trail from the Boquete side is far easier and better marked. You don't want to get lost on the volcano and spend the night freezing in the wet rainforest. This is but one of the serious considerations you must make when attempting to summit the volcano. The trail, an old service road, is ragged and rough, and even the most agile hikers often slip and fall on the slick downhill trip. Second, the trail is confusing in some areas, so it's highly recommended that you hire a guide. Lastly, the peak is shrouded in thick clouds with such frequency that the chances of seeing the view are not particularly good; but even on good-weather days you'll want to begin the hike at the crack of dawn to increase your chances of clear skies. The trail takes between 5 to 6 hours to climb, and about 4 to 5 hours to descend.

Or you can call Will Holiday at © 6613-5444 (wh@pocketmail.com), an American bush pilot and adventurer, and have him drive you to the top of the summit in his sturdy 4WD. The trail is so steep and treacherous at times that Will must use a winch to pull the jeep up.

RIVER RAFTING & KAYAKING

The translucent rivers that pour down the Talamanca Mountain Range in the Chiriquí Highlands provide for thrilling Class III to V white-water kayaking and rafting, and gentler floats for the whole family. What's special about the Chiriquí area is that relatively few paddlers have discovered it, so rafters and kayakers have the crystalline river and pristine, tropical mountain scenery—replete with birds and wild animals—all to themselves. Also, the variety and number of rivers in this area provide fanatics with enough white-water options to fill a week with rafting or kayaking.

Technical rides that are 2 to 5 hours in duration with Class III to Class V conditions are principally on the **Chiriquí River** east of Volcán Barú and close to Boquete, and the **Chiriquí Viejo River** west of the volcano, near the Costa Rica border. The Chiriquí Viejo River is revered by rafters for its challenging rapids and exuberant scenery, but it is a full-day trip that requires a scenic drive to the other side of the volcano. (Visitors to Volcán or Cerro Punta are closer to the put-in site for this river.) Unfortunately, the Chiriquí Viejo is being threatened by a series of dams for a hydroelectric project—but for now it's pristine and a lot of fun to ride. There are tamer floats, too, such as the **Esti River,** a Class II that is perfect for young rafters, families, and beginners; and there's the **Gariche River,** with Class II and III rapids that are suitable for beginners but a bit more technical and adrenaline-charged than an easy float. Many rivers can be rafted year-round, but others, like the Chiriquí and the Gariche, are rafted from July to November when the rivers are full.

Two reputable rafting companies in Boquete have years of experience and expert knowledge of the region. **Chiriquí River Rafting,** on Avenida Central (© **720-1505** or 6618-0846; www.panama-rafting.com), is run by Héctor Sanchez, a rafting pioneer in the Chiriquí Highlands, with more than 2 decades of experience and an excellent safety record. Héctor and his guides are fluent in English. Depending on the river and logistics, rafting trips cost between $85 and $150, and require a minimum of four guests (a few trips require only three guests); trips include all gear, transportation, and lunch. Héctor can also plan multiple-day packages that include rafting, hiking, fishing, and more. Note that Chiriquí River Rafting offers accommodations at **El Bajareque Lodge,** a hostel-like spot with dynamite views, simple bunks, and communal meals; Héctor also offers more upscale rooms in his private home.

Panama Rafters (© **720-2712;** www.panamarafters.com), with offices next to Java Juice on Avenida Central, is a young, American-owned company run by Kevin Mellinger. In addition to rafting, Panama Rafters also offers kayaking on the many rivers of the Chiriquí Highlands, and they offer beginning and intermediate kayaking instruction. Panama Rafters employs highly qualified guides that adhere to strict Canadian standards. Rafting trips cost an average of $75 for a half-day trip, $90 for a full-day trip—which includes transportation, gear, and lunch. Check out their website or contact them for multiple-day rafting packages with outdoors camping.

OTHER OUTDOOR ACTIVITIES IN THE AREA

BIKING   Boquete provides visitors with kilometer upon kilometer of picturesque, winding roads; moderate terrain; and pastoral views. Bicyclists on main paved roads will need to keep an eye open for speeding motorists, as there are virtually no shoulders and lots of blind curves. For bike rental, check out Panama Rafters on Avenida Central (see above) or Boquete Tree Trek (see "Canopy Tours," below). The cost to rent is $3 per hour. A new half-day bike tour around Boquete is now being offered by **Aventurist** (℃ 720-1635; www.aventurist.com). Tours begin by traveling by vehicle to the scenic heights at Alto Quiel, where bicyclists and their guide descend for 2 hours for a total of 26km (16 miles) until they reach town. Tours leave at 7am and 1pm, and cost $25 per person.

CANOPY TOURS   Canopy tours, the new adventure fad of zipping through the treetops suspended by a harness attached to a cable, are available through **Boquete Tree Trek** at Avenida Central (℃ 720-1635; www.canopypanama.com). This exhilarating ride is appropriate for kids as young as 3, and the weight limit for each rider is 113 kilograms (250 lb.) for men, and 91 kilograms (200 lb.) for women. The zip line is 3km (1¾ miles) long, with a drop of 351m (1,150 ft.), and is located in the upper reaches of the Palo Alto valley, about 45 minutes from town. Women should avoid wearing skirts because of the harness seat. The best attire is long pants or shorts that do not ride up too high, and closed-toe shoes like sneakers or hiking boots.

HOT SPRINGS   The **Caldera Hot Springs** comprises four undeveloped pools in natural surroundings, with mineral water in varying temperature grades. It's worth a stop if you're a huge fan of hot springs, are already in the area, or are looking for a pretty low-key activity—otherwise, I can't figure out what the big to-do about Caldera is, especially considering that it's a good half-hour drive from Boquete. The hot springs are next to the Caldera River, which you can bathe in as well. To get here, you'll need to be part of a tour, or have a 4WD (you might make it in a regular car, but just barely). Head south from Boquete, and 11km (7 miles) later, turn left at the sign for Caldera; once you arrive in Caldera keep driving until you see a sign for the hot springs. Follow a rather brutal dirt road to the end and then walk about 10 minutes to the hot springs.

HORSEBACK RIDING   Eduardo Caño (℃ 720-1750 or 6629-0814), a local guide from Boquete, is the man to go to for horseback riding tours of 2 to 5 hours, loping along trails on the outskirts of Boquete in areas such as Volcancito and Jaramillo. The views of Boquete and the surrounding area are simply splendid, but Eduardo speaks limited English, so unless you know Spanish, you'll need your hotel to call and make arrangements. Sample prices for two are $40 for 2 hours, $60 for 3 hours. Also, contact **Ecocircuitos** (see "Hiking & Bird-Watching Outfitters/Guides," above) for horseback riding or to hire an English-speaking nature guide to accompany you and Eduardo on your ride.

COFFEE TOURS

Did you know that Panama produces some of the most flavorful coffee in the world? A relatively new player on the gourmet-coffee market, the country produces traditional shade-grown-coffee varieties that are generally considered to be more complex and distinctive than those produced by its more famous neighbor, Costa Rica. Most coffee plantations in Panama are centered around Boquete because of the high altitude required for prime coffee growing, and because of the region's fertile volcanic soil.

Coffee tours are available and highly recommended—really, you'll never look at your morning cup of joe the same once you've taken a tour with one of the companies below. Even coffee snobs will glean insight not only into the meticulous growing process but into the economics of the local Ngöbe-Buglé indigenous labor and culture, the "shade-grown" theory to protect the environment and to grow a better bean, the effect coffee has on the world, and what coffee producers really think about Starbucks. Tours are capped off with a "cupping," which, much like a wine-tasting (and *almost* as fun), gives you a chance to sample different flavors, strengths, and roasts. In addition to the following companies, see Finca Lérida's tours below.

Café Ruiz 🦀🦀 is one of the oldest and most respected coffee producers in the country. A tour entails a three-stop visit to the plantation, the processing plant, and the roasting-and-packaging facility (transportation is provided). This is an ideal tour for those interested in seeing large-scale production as opposed to a boutique operation. Tours, led by a jovial and bilingual Ngöbe-Buglé Indian guide, are offered Monday through Saturday from 9am to noon, or from 1 to 4pm; the cost is $14 per person. Alternatively, you can visit the roasting facility for a 1-hour informational session and cupping. Café Ruiz, by the way, sells to Peet's Coffee.

Café Kotowa 🦀🦀 is a boutique coffee farm founded nearly a century ago by a Scottish immigrant, and it's still run by the same family. Kotowa, the indigenous word for "mountain," has earned a reputation for producing award-winning coffee beans, and though they've since moved on to modern production means, the farm's antique, water-powered mill still exists and is part of their fascinating tour. Visits to Kotowa are one-stop—first you amble through the coffee plantation behind the mill, then you tour the production-and-roasting facility, and finally you have a cupping in the old mill. The tour is led by Hans, of **Coffee Adventures** (© 720-3852; www.coffee adventures.net), who pioneered coffee tours in Boquete, and who is animated and amusing. Tours are Monday to Saturday at 9am and cost $20 per person, which includes transportation from Boquete to their farm in Palo Alto. Children must be 10 or older, unless they're part of a private tour. Private tours cost $30 per person but can be scheduled at any time, including Sundays.

SPANISH-LANGUAGE PROGRAMS

Habla Ya Language Center, located on Avenida Central above the Global Bank (© 720-1294; www.hablayapanama.com), offers intensive "survival" Spanish courses, as well as more advanced conversational and fluency courses. Beginner survival courses are ideal for the traveling monolinguals with little time in Boquete but who'd love to speak enough to get around; weekly group classes cost $46 for 5 hours, $170 for 20 hours; weekly private courses cost $75 for 5 hours and $260 for 20 hours. If you plan to spend a lot of time in Boquete, note that the institute offers dance classes and other activities.

ATTRACTIONS IN & AROUND TOWN

Finca Lérida 🦀🦀🦀 (© 720-2285; www.fincalerida.com; open daily sunrise–sunset) is a lovely 324-hectare (800-acre) coffee plantation and nature reserve located 10 minutes from Boquete in the lofty alpine setting of Alto Quiel. The *finca* is widely regarded as one of the most important bird-watching sites in Panama, not only because of the sheer numbers of species on view here but because it is a hot spot for seeing the resplendent quetzal, among other rare birds. The Finca Lérida has stepped up operations lately, building a cozy **B&B** on their property and a new exhibit showcasing their highly rated

Stop & Smell the Flowers: Festivals in Boquete

Boquete's largest annual festival is the **Feria de las Flores y del Café (Flowers and Coffee Festival)**, which coincides with the coffee-harvesting season and takes place at the local fairgrounds in mid-January. The festival is one of the grandest celebrations of flowers in the world, drawing thousands of people to Boquete, clogging roads, and filling up hotels (book well ahead of time). During the 10-day festival, the fairgrounds fill with lushly landscaped and intricately designed flower displays that stretch the length of the facilities. Local residents follow suit and spruce up their gardens, too, giving Boquete the feel of a horticultural Xanadu. Coffee plays a big role, with tastings of local java and sales of coffee by the bag and by the cup. There are other festival-oriented attractions like food stands, live music, amusement rides, handicrafts booths, and more—these activities take place only during the festival, but from January to April the flower exhibits are on display daily; entrance fee is $1.

Later, in mid-April, Boquete holds the same kind of festival but on a reduced scale, the 4-day **Feria de Orquídeas (Orchid Festival)**, when local orchid growers showcase thousands of varieties of these delicate flowers for public viewing (many orchids bloom in Apr). Other large-scale festivals in Boquete are celebrated nationally; however, considering Boquete's charm and desirable ambience, many Panamanians head here for a few days of respite. Book your hotel well ahead of time during these dates: Carnaval (Feb), Semana Santa (Holy Week before Easter), Independence celebrations (weekends of Nov 3, 10, and 28).

coffee and growing process, and giving information about the biodiversity of their property and the surrounding region.

They've also standardized their tours. Finca Lérida has three nature trails (one easy, two moderate) that offer a chance to put yourself in the middle of pristine primary and secondary forest. Independent visitors are charged $10 per person for access to the trails, and though they're marked, there are no maps or interpretive information available. The *finca* works with the best local birding and naturalist guides, if you need one (it's highly recommended if you come to bird-watch); the cost is an additional $25. Or you can book a 2-hour coffee tour for $16 per person, and take to the trails following the tour. For the complete (and somewhat pricey) package, a full-day tour includes a guide, bird-watching, coffee tour, gourmet lunch, transportation to and from Boquete, and access to trails for $310 for two guests.

Mi Jardín es Su Jardín *ƙƙ*, or "My Garden is Your Garden," refers to the lavish private gardens of the González family, who live on the property but have opened their grounds to the public. These gardens are some of the most exquisite in Panama, with hundreds of varieties of flowers expertly tended and cared for. But, weirdly, the whole spread is chockablock with nutty figurines and statues of windmills, dinosaurs, a blue cow, wee little castles, cutouts of frolicking children, and other oddball decorative items. There is a children's playground on the property, too. Admission is free, and the garden is open daily during daylight hours. To get here, head up the main street past the church, and stay left at the fork and continue until you see the gardens on your right-hand side.

One of the more curious attractions in Boquete is **El Explorador** gardens (☏ 720-1989), which provide visitors with splendid panoramic views enhanced by classical background music. But what's really the attraction here are the eccentric gardens sprinkled with vernacular, artlike recycled items: old television sets, a sewing machine, boots used as planters, shopping carts, old bottles, and more. For example, there is a bush clipped to resemble a cartoonish animal, and in its mouth is a plastic doll—but what this means is anyone's guess. The main purpose of the gardens is to offer a place for quiet reflection and "spiritual renewal." To this end, the gardens feature signs (in Spanish only) with uplifting quotes to boost a visitor's self-esteem. As hokey as it seems, you do leave El Explorador feeling a little better. The garden park is owned by the Miranda family, who bought this property and began decorating it according to whim until it grew into a public venue. There is a cafe here with snacks, fresh fruit juices, and coffee. El Explorador costs $1 per person, and is open daily from 9am to 6pm. To get here, stay right at the fork on the main road and follow the signs.

SHOPPING

Coffee is the local product you won't want to leave Boquete without, and bagged beans are sold all around town in cafes and grocery stores. **Café Kotowam,** at the visitor center just before town, sells top-rated blends and souvenir and gift packs. No stores in the Tocuman International airport sell coffee, so don't put off until the last minute buying a few bags of Panama's best. The **Harmony Gift Shop** on Avenida Central, in front of the Boquete Country Inn, has arts and crafts, jewelry, and other gift items for sale. **Souvenir El Cacique,** on Avenida Central at the plaza, has indigenous handicrafts made by the Ngöbe-Buglé, Kuna, and Emberá indigenous groups, plus handicrafts from indigenous groups around Central America.

WHERE TO STAY

Travelers can opt to stay in town and be close to services and restaurants, or outside of the town center in a more forested setting. No hotel mentioned here is farther than a 10-minute drive from town. Air-conditioning is available at some hotels but is really not necessary given the elevation of Boquete. Breakfast is included in the price unless otherwise specified. Note that some hotels sell out for the Flower and Coffee Festival in January, so you'll need to plan ahead.

One unique lodging option is **Tinamou Cottage** (© 720-3852; http://coffee adventures.net/tinamou.html), which is nestled in a coffee plantation and owned by Hans and Terry of Coffee Adventures. The cozy cottage is perfect for a couple seeking a romantic hideaway, or for birders who want a private sanctuary. With a sitting area, a small kitchen, and a queen-size bed, the cottage is a steal at $55 a night.

At the time of writing, **Finca Lérida** (see "Attractions in & Around Town," above) was slated to open what is expected to be one of the best B&Bs in town, located smack dab in the middle of their farm—one of the richest bird-watching areas in Boquete. Contact them for prices and other information.

VERY EXPENSIVE

Palo Alto Riverside Hotel 🐵🐵   Opened in 2006, this boutique hotel is sophisticated and gives discriminating travelers the highest level of accommodations available in Boquete—but you wouldn't know it from the hotel's exterior, which looks a little like a country-style inn. Located on the shore of the Palo Alto River, the hotel is next to its namesake gourmet restaurant. There are only six guest rooms, the best of which are in back, overlooking the river. All are decked out in neutral shades of gray, ecru, and chocolate, and have tiled floors. Each room's design is slightly different from the next, both in shape and adornment, but the standard decor consists of exposed wooden beams, stark walls, Indonesian teak furniture, arching windows, and luxurious bathrooms. The Getzemani suite and Bonsai junior suite have a balcony and a panoramic view; the Guayacan junior suite has a bedroom plus a loftlike sleeping area with additional beds. All rooms have king-size beds with Egyptian cotton sheets. Guest rooms feature lots of amenities, even whirlpool tubs, and the hotel has a "mini" spa with massage and sauna. There are plenty of common areas in which to sit and read or converse—my favorite is the glass-enclosed balcony, with cozy chairs and a large-screen TV, that looks out into the forested greenery. I can't vouch for service at the hotel because it was just opening during my last visit to Boquete, but judging by the high caliber of service provided at the Palo Alto restaurant (see later in this chapter), I'd imagine that similar service can be expected here as well.

Palo Alto. ✆ 720-1076. www.paloaltoriverside.com. 6 units. $165 double; $225 suite. AE, MC, V. **Amenities:** Restaurant; bar; sauna; tour organization; car rental assistance; massage; laundry service; Wi-Fi. *In room:* A/C, TV, DVD player, minibar, safe, whirlpool tubs.

EXPENSIVE

The Coffee Estate Inn ★★★ *(Finds*   If you're an independent traveler but are loathe to work out the details involved in independent travel, this place is your best bet. The Coffee Estate Inn is owned by a friendly Canadian couple, Jane and Barry, who built their inn to satisfy themselves as travelers—a simple concept but one that rarely occurs to so many budding hotel owners. Cozy yet spacious accommodations with all the trimmings, gorgeous views of Volcán Barú, and truly personalized service are the hallmarks of The Coffee Estate Inn, which is located 2.5km (1½ miles) from downtown Boquete, on a very steep slope overlooking the lush valley below. Three contemporary and cheery cabins contain a bedroom for two to three guests, a living area, a fully stocked kitchen, and an outdoor terrace. The cabins are enveloped in native forest, fruit trees, and flowers that attract a myriad of birds. I particularly like the "Jewel" cabin for its secluded, romantic location and for its stunning views of the volcano. At the time of my last visit, the owners were constructing two new "suites" attached to the main building (but with private entrances; contact the inn for details).

When you make a reservation here, they'll send you a 30-page information packet with tips and advice about Boquete and traveling in Panama. The owners recommend that guests rent a vehicle (they'll set this up for you), and they'll provide maps, directions, contacts for the best guides in the area, and anything else you need for a day of adventure. Cook your own meals in the kitchen or indulge yourself in the inn's restaurant with a candlelit, gourmet dinner (they also offer cooking classes). The owners grow and roast their own coffee; guests of 2 nights or more receive a free tour of the property to learn about coffee production and native flora. Note that children must be at least 9 years old to stay here.

Jaramillo Arriba. ✆ 720-2211. www.coffeeestateinn.com. 5 units. $110 double, $30 for an additional guest. MC, V. **Amenities:** Restaurant; tour desk and car rental services; library; cooking classes; gift shop; Wi-Fi. *In room:* TV (in 2 cabins only), fully stocked kitchen, dehumidifier, hair dryer.

Los Establos ★★   Los Establos bills itself as a boutique hotel, but it's more ranchstyle, situated high above Boquete on a spacious, grassy property with splendid views of the valley and Volcán Barú. The accommodations are deluxe, but only the suites come with a view—though a wide patio and plenty of common areas give all guests a place from which to take in the vista. The decor is elegant yet reminiscent of rural

Spain, with a terra-cotta-tiled roof, heavy iron chandeliers, and cowhide rugs; guest rooms have a country decor and fine bedding. The two suites, Luna and Sol, each contain a glass-enclosed seating area with expansive views and four-poster beds; the Sol unit has a masculine decor while Luna is lighter and more feminine. The standard rooms are comfortable, but are on the ground floor and open onto the main foyer. What I really enjoy about this hotel are the open common areas. When this book went to publication, Los Establos was building new guest rooms, a restaurant, and a small spa; this will certainly add to the amenities offered, but it might come with the sacrifice of intimacy. Service is personable and accommodating. The price range below reflects the range from low season to high season (low season is Apr 16–Oct 31). Kids must be at least 14 years old to stay here.

Jaramillo Arriba. ⓒ 720-2685. www.losestablos.net. 6 units. $110–$130 double; $175–$230 suite. AE, MC, V. **Amenities:** Bar; outdoor barbecue area; pool table; games; tour assistance; Internet access; laundry service. *In room:* TV, safe, no phone.

Panamonte Inn & Spa ⚜ Boquete's landmark hotel, built in 1914 and the first lodging here in town, offers storybook charm and beautifully tended gardens. It's a country-style inn, painted sky blue and surrounded by a white picket fence, and decorated with chintz and country-manor furnishings. As delightful as this place is, there's one caveat: guest rooms are cramped, antiquated, and a little musty, though they do have comfy beds. The larger *cabañas,* which have private patio terraces, are double the price and not much value. They've opened a newer wing of guest rooms across the street, but even these rooms have a slightly musty feel. Still, there are several reasons to consider staying here: The location is in town and convenient for travelers without a car; the finest restaurant in Boquete is part of the hotel and they have a terrific open-air bar with a roaring fireplace; and there is a full-service spa on the premises. All that, plus the service is impeccable. If you don't plan on spending a lot of time in your room, book a cheaper unit and take advantage of the hotel's common areas and amenities. The Panamonte has been in the Elliot-Collins family since the 1940s, and Charlie is an award-winning chef here (see "Where to Dine," below).

Av. Central (take a right at the fork). ⓒ 720-1324 or 720-1327. www.panamonteinnandspa.com. 19 units. $65 standard double; $132 cabin. AE, MC, V. **Amenities:** Restaurant; bar; full-service spa with sauna and steam room; tour desk; laundry services; Wi-Fi. *In room:* A/C, TV.

MODERATE

Boquete Country Inn ⚜ This turn-of-the-20th-century residential estate near the town plaza was lovingly restored in 2005 and converted into a New England–style B&B. The best thing about the place? The people who own and run it. Ron and his wife, Yalty, are old Boquete hands, and they are wonderfully personable and warm people. They know this area better than anyone, and they offer a homey environment and personalized service. The Boquete Country Inn sits behind a high wall that separates the B&B and its surrounding .8 hectares (2 acres) of grassy gardens from the main street; a trickling stream also runs along the property. The historic home has five rooms that are individually decorated in varying color schemes, but all have the same style of flowery chintz and country antiques (originals, mind you). At the time of publication, the owners were busy converting another building on their property into five new guest rooms that overlook the stream; check with them for prices. In the main house, the honeymoon suite is the best and largest room, but I also like the blue room because it opens onto the back patio. A perk of this hotel is that the owners have a yacht and can take guests on a full-day trip around the Golfo Marino National Park and out to Isla Coiba. Plus Yalty hosts locally famous Sunday-evening rib barbecues.

Av. Central. ℭ **720-2470.** www.boquetecountryinn.com. 5 units. $50 double; $85 suite. MC, V. **Amenities:** Cafe; private tours; games; Wi-Fi. *In room:* TV, no phone.

Boquete Garden Inn ★★ (value)

This irresistible inn is one of my favorites in Boquete, although it's actually not an inn but five cabin bungalows, a central reception building, and a gazebo lounge scattered around a lovely, well-tended garden on the shore of the Palo Alto River. Formerly known as the Vía Láctea cabins, the Boquete Garden Inn has a brand-new look to go with its new American owners, who are one of the nicest couples you could meet; they really strive to make you feel at home and see that you enjoy the best that Boquete has to offer. The octagon-shaped, ocher-colored cabins, most of which are framed with a riot of bougainvillea, are connected by narrow paths that wind through lushly landscaped grounds. Each cabin has two stories, with a separate guest room on each floor for up to three guests; I personally prefer the second floor for the additional light, but both units are very cozy, offer plenty of space, and come with kitchenettes, a dining table, and a fold-out futon couch. The beds, it should be noted, are feather soft and fitted with fine linens and duvets. It's quite a deal for the price, which includes a hearty, delicious breakfast. The inn is located in the forested Palo Alto section of Boquete, just under 3km (2 miles) from downtown, so you'll need a taxi or a rental vehicle to get back and forth.

Palo Alto. ℭ **720-2376.** www.boquetegardeninn.com. 10 units. $65 double; $80 "suite"; $13 additional person. AE, MC, V. **Amenities:** Cafe; bar; Internet service; tour desk; games; small library; cellphone rental; laundry services. *In room:* Kitchenette; no phone.

Isla Verde Hotel ★★ (Kids)

This is an excellent choice for travelers who seek a peaceful setting and leafy surroundings, but within walking distance of town. Located in a residential area about a 3-minute walk from Boquete, the German-owned Isla Verde features six cheery cabins, called "roundhouses." Half the cabins are for four guests, and half are quite spacious with a capacity for up to six guests (though they're ideal for a group of just four). There is a queen-size bed on the ground floor (but not separate from the living area), and a loft with a double bed; the additional "beds" for the six-person units are two fold-out futon chairs, which look uncomfortable even for young kids. Brand-new at the Isla Verde are four contemporary and fetching suites for couples, each with a terrific outdoor patio that offers forest views, especially from the second-floor units, which are more expensive. The suites have a bedroom and independent living area, and kitchenettes; the cabins have full kitchens. European travelers make up the bulk of guests here, which is apropos because the decor is simple and decidedly European, especially their open-air geodesic dome eating area; there is also an on-site, New Age spa.

Calle 5a Sur and Av. B Oeste. ℭ **720-2533** or 6677-4009. www.islaverdehotel.com. 8 units. Prices based on double occupancy: $80 big roundhouse; $60 small roundhouse; $60–$90 suites. Children under 5 free in parent's room; children 5–18 $5; extra adult $10. MC, V. **Amenities:** Bar; limited spa services (massage and facials); Internet service; tour desk; small library; laundry service; games. *In room:* TV (some rooms), kitchenette; no phone.

Momentum Hotel ★

Located 7km (4½ miles) from town (the farthest lodging option from Boquete reviewed here), and reached by following a left-hand turnoff before arriving in Boquete, this hotel is for independent travelers who desire a lot of open outdoor areas and trails on which to walk or jog. This is also the only hotel in Boquete that has a heated swimming pool and a gym. There are five free-standing cabins spread across a neatly trimmed grassy area with views of the distant Volcán Barú, and two guest rooms within a main building. Though very clean and roomy, the cabins have contemporary furniture but are starkly decorated. Travelers with a rental vehicle will be happiest here, although the Momentum will organize transfers and tours. This is a gay- and lesbian-friendly establishment.

Bajo Boquete. © 720-4385. www.momentum-panama.com. 7 units. $70 cabin for 2; $55 double guest room. MC, V. **Amenities:** Outdoor pool; gym; volleyball; laundry service; Wi-Fi. *In room:* Kitchen (in cabins), no phone.

Villa Marita ✹   Perched high on a plateau above a twisting road 3.5km (2 miles) from town, this hotel is strong in panoramic views of Volcán Barú and the river valley below. It's too far to walk to town, so if you don't mind taking a taxi or driving, the reasonably priced cabins here are an attractive lodging option. There are six mustard-colored cabins, for up to four guests (one bedroom and a sofa bed), which are outfitted with hardwood finishings and a country decor (and a refrigerator). French doors open onto a patio with the dynamite view. There are also three newer and comfortable hotel rooms in the main building, which is a converted home with a lived-in and homey ambience. Families might be interested in their "Big House" unit that sleeps six to eight guests and has a huge kitchen, but no view. There are a grill and deck for your own outdoor barbecue. The friendly, knowledgeable host and his wife will gladly serve you a home-cooked meal with ingredients from their on-site organic greenhouse. There are a lot of common areas here; it's especially fun to enjoy their abundant breakfast buffet under the watchful eye of their pet parrot and toucan. The owners have lived in this area for 40 years, and can help with tours and information about the area.

Alto Lino. © 720-2165. www.villamarita.com. 10 units. $40 double hotel room; $60 cabin; $110 family house. AE, MC, V. **Amenities:** Restaurant; outdoor grill; tour organization; small library; games; Wi-Fi. *In room:* TV, fridge (except in hotel rooms); no phone.

INEXPENSIVE

Hotel Oasis ✹   This simple, low-cost hotel run by a local family has a riverfront location close to the Boquete fairgrounds, offering more scenic accommodations than most budget hotels. It is also brand-new and therefore everything is in working order. You want to book either room no. 1, 2, 4, 5, 11, or 12—they all offer views of the volcano and the river; room no. 4 is the only one with a king-size bed (the others have doubles and twins). Breakfast, which is included, is served on an outdoor patio, and there's a common area with a coffeemaker and microwave. Service is very friendly and helpful, and Hotel Oasis is close to the Flower Festival (when it's going on, in mid-Jan).

Av. Buenos Aires, across the bridge. © 720-1586. www.boquetenet.net. 11 units. $35–$45 double. MC, V. **Amenities:** Laundry service; Internet. *In room:* TV, no phone.

Hotel Petit Mozart ✹   Located on the outskirts of town in a tranquil and forested residential neighborhood, the Petit Mozart offers rooms with a view that stretches out to the Pacific Ocean. There are freshly painted, folksy cabins and guest rooms, a couple of which have a kitchenette for longer-term visitors and can be rented by the week or month. One unit has two bedrooms and a full kitchen, and guest rooms for two are a deal at $35 a night. The Petit Mozart is German-owned and operated by an artist who uses much of the main building as a painting and jewelry-making studio. The 2.5-hectare (4.9-acre) property has a small coffee plantation and fruit trees, and a lawn that slopes out from a pleasant patio terrace. This is a good lodging option for travelers seeking private and tranquil accommodations away from town, but it's a good idea to have your own vehicle; otherwise you'll need to depend on taxis. Breakfast is not included.

Volcancito. ☎ 720-3764 or 6646-1577. coyaldps@hotmail.com. 5 units. $27–$35 double; $110 2-bedroom suite. No credit cards. **Amenities:** Laundry service. *In room:* TV, kitchenette (some rooms), no phone.

Kalima Suites   Just need a central location and a clean place to put your head down for the night? Kalima Suites, located in a modern one-story building near downtown, offers a lot of bang for the buck. There are six "suites," which mean roomy units with a bedroom and separate living area, and they come with a kitchenette. The decor here is pretty bland, but four of the suites have a terrace with mountain views. Also, beds are okay, with cheap linens, and the walls are stark, but the premises are tidy. Breakfast is not included.

Calle 6 Sur and Av. A Este. ☎ 720-2884. www.kalimasuites.net. 6 units. $40 double. MC, V. **Amenities:** Internet access. *In room:* TV, kitchenette.

WHERE TO DINE

Given that many of Boquete's residents are retired folks who tend to dine in or not stay out too late, the restaurants mentioned below can unexpectedly close early or for the night during the low season, from May to November. Also, in addition to these options, several kiosks and cafes offer quick meals and are worth considering.

Worth a stop is the locally famous **Fresas Mary** (☎ 720-3394; daily 9:30am–7pm), which you'll find on the left side of the road to Volcancito, reached by turning onto the road opposite the CEFATI visitor center. The specialties here are *batidos,* or fresh fruit drinks, made with strawberries and local fruits such as *guanábana* (soursop); they also make fresh yogurt and *duros,* or frozen fruit sherbet. Sandwiches and hamburgers go for $1.50. Another spot popular with locals is the German-style bakery and pastry shop **Café Alemana,** located south past the CEFATI building (no phone; Thurs–Mon 11am–8pm), which serves delicious apple and pineapple pies, and other sweets.

The **Deli Barú** (☎ 720-2619; Tues–Sun 9am–8pm) is a gourmet deli with sandwiches, soups, and salads, and a market with an excellent selection of cheeses, cold cuts, wine, fresh bread, and specialty goodies. For fresh fruit juices and cheap sandwiches in town, try **Java Juice** on Avenida Central, next to Panama Rafters (☎ 720-2502; daily 10am–10pm). A mango smoothie and hamburger here cost less than $2. **Café Punto de Encuentro** (☎ 720-2123; daily 7am–noon), located on Calle 6A S, near Avenida Belisario Porras, and often referred to as "Olga's Place," is *the* spot for breakfast. Have your omelets, fruit pancakes, and fresh coffee on their pleasant outdoor patio.

Lastly, if you're in town on a Sunday, do not miss **Yalty's** at the Boquete Country Inn, on Avenida Central (☎ 720-2470). Yalty makes the best ribs in town—probably in the entire Chiriquí Province—and every Sunday she hosts an all-you-can-eat night from 6 to 10pm for $17 per person. (She donates $1 per person to a needy-children's fund.) Apart from her tasty ribs, she serves pasta, fish, and salads, and often puts on folkloric dance performances. Yalty's is BYOB. Call during the low season (mid-Apr to Nov) to verify that her Sunday nights are happening.

MODERATE

Boquete Bistro 🐾🐾 NORTH AMERICAN   Located in an antique, high-ceilinged building, this delightful bistro is owned by Lauretta, who hails from Aspen, which is why the somewhat incongruous, artsy establishment looks as if it were airlifted from

Colorado and dropped here on Boquete's main street. This is where you go when you're hungry for delicious and hearty gringo-style fare in a relaxed ambience that encourages you to linger long after your meal. Lauretta utilizes the freshest produce and ingredients, utilizing her location in the agricultural breadbasket of Panama. Expect well-prepared American dishes and bar appetizers such as barbecue wings, artichoke dip, and quesadillas; plus huge salads and burgers, and main courses such as filet mignon and grilled fish. I especially like their sandwiches, such as pastrami and Swiss, tuna melt, and BLT—they are all so hefty you can feel gravity working against you as you try to lift one.

Av. Central. 𝒞 720-1017. Main courses $8–$10. MC, V. Tues–Sun 11am–11pm; Mon 4–11pm.

Delicias del Perú 𝒻 PERUVIAN   This is a good bet for seafood in town. While oddly there are no strictly Panamanian restaurants in Boquete (besides cheap diners), there are two Peruvian eateries, the Machu Picchu (below) and this pleasant restaurant. The food at Machu Picchu is just a notch more flavorful than at Delicias del Perú, but what I love about this place are its fresh ceviches—there's an entire page devoted to this appetizer alone (try the spicy ceviche with *ají chombo,* or yellow habanero peppers). Other tasty items on the menu are *chupe,* a stewlike dish with shellfish, and sea bass stuffed with shrimp, but there are meat items, too, such as *ají de gallina,* a chicken stew over rice. Do like the Peruvians and order a frosty pisco sour aperitif to start. Delicias has a pleasant outdoor seating area with a forest view.

Av. Central. 𝒞 720-1966. Reservations accepted. Main courses $6–$12. MC, V. Daily noon–11pm.

Hibiscus 𝒻𝒻 FRENCH/PANAMANIAN   When you first glance at Hibiscus's menu, you'll know it's time to "splurge"—even though you really won't have to spend too much money to do so. The Parisian-trained chef, who married a Panamanian and settled here in Boquete, opened this pleasant little restaurant to serve dishes that pay tribute to his homeland, with a few classic dishes such as chicken *cordon bleu,* escargot, and rabbit in mustard sauce. But just as good are the bacon-infused clam chowder, pork terrine with a spicy yogurt and garlic sauce, and *dorado* fish with jalapeño cream sauce. Hibiscus offers a fixed-price menu for $38 for two, which includes an appetizer, main course, dessert, and bottle of wine. One thing that Hibiscus didn't bring from France was a fast waitstaff, so don't come here if you're in a hurry. There are only eight tables, which means you need to make a reservation during high season.

Calle A Este. 𝒞 720-2652. Reservations accepted. Main courses $8–$12. MC, DC, V. Wed–Mon 5–10pm (until 9pm during winter).

Machu Picchu 𝒻𝒻 PERUVIAN   Boquete's newest restaurant is the second Peruvian restaurant to open in a year (Delicias del Perú, above, is the other). The Peruvian chef, Aristóteles, first achieved fame for his tantalizing cuisine at his restaurant in Panama City, also called Machu Picchu, and decided to test his luck on the Boquete dining scene. The restaurant specializes in fare that combines fresh local products with traditional recipes. There are more than 25 appetizers (and double that in entrees); you might want to start with the stuffed potatoes or a "Piqueo Especial Inti Raymi" platter with a diverse sample of seafood delicacies. For a main course, the sea bass with black butter and capers is top-notch, as are the creamy jumbo prawns gratin. There are meat and chicken dishes, too. During weekdays, a fixed-price lunch costs $5.50. The ambience is warm—the restaurant is painted yellow and blue and accented with

Peruvian art. The chef often visits each table to chat with diners. Don't miss the sugary-sweet Suspiro Limeño, a classic caramel-like Peruvian dessert.

Av. Belisario Porras. ✆ 264-9308. Reservations recommended for groups. Main courses $6.50–$12. MC, V. Daily 11am—3pm and 6–11pm.

Palo Alto Restaurante 🕊🕊 INTERNATIONAL   If you're looking for a refined yet tranquil atmosphere where you can dine on fresh trout, a juicy rib-eye or New York steak, barbecue baby back ribs, or a light pasta primavera, this is your place. Located in a stand-alone building on the shore of a scenic river, about a 3-minute drive from town, the Palo Alto is a handsome, upscale eatery serving some of the best cuisine in Boquete. The dining area is Mediterranean-style, and fresh and airy, with brick floors, glass walls, a zinc roof strung with iron chandeliers, and local art. The menu features mostly North American cuisine and pasta, though there are also delicious appetizers such as Thai spring rolls with a fish sauce, kabobs, and Greek *ladopsomo* (pita bread with feta). For lunch there are salads and sandwiches. Service is attentive but not overwhelming. Their wine list is mostly Spanish, with a few Chilean varieties.

Road to Palo Alto. ✆ 720-1076. paloalto@cwpanama.net. Reservations recommended. Main courses $6.50–$14. AE, MC, V. Daily noon–9:30pm.

Panamonte Inn Restaurant 🕊🕊🕊 INTERNATIONAL   This sanctuary of gourmet cuisine is hands-down the best restaurant in Boquete. The food is inventive and consistently good, and service is attentive and courteous. Diners are given the option of dining in the 1940s-style, formal dining area, with its floral motif, but I like to order from their main menu and sit at a table in the ultra-cozy bar/lounge next to a roaring fire. The chef, Charlie Collins, is one of Panama's best. His dishes adapt local products with Scandinavian and New American cooking styles, and he utilizes the freshest and highest-quality ingredients available, such as local Black Angus beef and trout caught from the Caldera River. Trout, it could be said, is the restaurant's trademark dish, served in a variety of ways such as with a garlic and herb sauce. Order a trio of appetizers (such as a raw tuna cocktail) if you're feeling peckish, or dive into a wild-mushroom polenta, pork chops with onion ragout and veal stock and wine sauce, or seafood stew. Polish it off with pie made with a lemon-orange hybrid from the Panamonte's gardens. The bar menu has lighter fare and casual meals like burgers, empanadas, and chicken brochettes, as well as an excellent wine list.

Av. Central. ✆ 720-1324 or 720-1327. Reservations recommended for main dining area. Main courses $9–$12. AE, MC, V. Daily 7–9:30am, 12:30–3pm, and 6–10pm; bar open 8am–11:30pm.

INEXPENSIVE
La Casona Mexicana 🕊 MEXICAN   This restaurant has a good selection of authentic Mexican dishes in addition to Tex-Mex fare. Hearty and well-prepared, the food consists of tasty roasted pork *carnitas,* and a sour cream and chile-based Michoacán chicken, as well as burritos, fajitas, and chimichangas paired with rice and black beans. What they don't have is guacamole, but then you rarely see avocado anywhere in Panama. The dining area is very casual, with the usual Mexican motif: fiery red and orange walls festooned with sombreros.

Av. Central. ✆ 720-1274. Main courses $3.75–$7. MC, V. Daily noon–10:30pm.

Sabrosón PANAMANIAN   For cheap, local fare, you can't beat this cafeteria-style restaurant. The ambience is no-frills, and the food is simply prepared but filling and tasty. Just pop in, stand in line, and when you get to the buffet point at what you'd like behind the glass—they'll heap it on your plate. I like the stewed chicken with rice and a bean salad, but their fresh trout, served fried or sautéed, is okay, too.

Av. Central, near the church. (© 720-2147. Main courses $2–$4. No credit cards. Mon–Thurs 6:30am–10pm; Fri–Sun 6:30am–11pm.

BOQUETE AFTER DARK
Most Boquete residents are tucked into bed by 11pm, but there are a couple of places for a nightcap or a night out. **Zanzíbar,** located on Avenida Central on the right side past the church, is a bar attractively decorated with African odds and ends. It's a cozy place for a cocktail (open Tues–Sun nights until midnight). **Snoopy's** is reached by crossing the yellow bridge over the river at Calle 4 Sur, which has a casual restaurant serving hearty food like sandwiches, burgers, and a couple of meat and fish main courses; there's a barn-size, open-air bar here and a dance floor that is best on Friday and Saturday nights, when it fills with revelers dancing to DJ music. Open until 1am.

A NATURE LODGE WITH HIKING TRAILS
The simple, Swiss-owned **Finca Suiza** 🐾🐾 is one of the best lodges in Panama to spend the night or visit for the day if you're an avid hiker, because the trails are so well-maintained and marked (probably better than any others in the country), and because the scenery and views along the trails are dazzling. Also, you don't need a guide. Finca Suiza is truly a find, located on 81 hectares (200 acres) of land about 56km (35 miles) north of David, on the road to Chiriquí Grande. From the lodge there are three loop trails through dense, emerald tropical forest to lookout points, waterfalls, and through cloud forest. If you're in Boquete for a lengthy period and looking for a day-hiking trip, or if you're traveling from Bocas del Toro and want to stop for the day before heading to David, you'll have to arrive and start hiking between 7am and 10am, and be out of the finca by 4pm during the dry season (mid-Apr to Nov), by 2pm during the rainy season. Admission is $8 per person, paid to the Ngöbe-Buglé woman at the entrance to the finca; you'll need to park your vehicle here and walk up the road until you reach the trail head. If you're staying in the lodge and have a 4WD that can make it up their dirt road, advise them of when you're coming because they let their guard dogs out at night. All trails are moderate, with easy portions, but there's a lot of uphill walking during the first stretch. The **Small Circuit** takes 3½ hours; or you can continue on and complete the **Large Circuit** for a total of 6½ hours, with the option of walking an extra hour to the Mirador Alta Vista lookout point. This lookout point is breathtaking, stretching as far as the mountains of Costa Rica and the Pacific Ocean. Those with a full day can tack on the 3-hour hike through the cloud forest. It is common to hear howler monkeys here, and hikers report having seen white-faced capuchin monkeys and coatimundis. The forest provides nesting sites for many species of birds, but the Finca is not specifically known as a hot bird-watching spot—the focus here is on hiking. Hikers walking the Large Circuit and the cloud-forest circuit must be in good physical shape, and children under 12 are not allowed on the trails. July and August, when everything is green, are the best months to come; March and April are drier months with less foliage.

The **Finca Suiza Lodge** (© 6615-3774; www.panama.net.tc), with its clapboard walls and wooden shutters, looks out toward the Pacific with sweeping, sunset-facing views framed by blooming bougainvillea. There are two spotless guest rooms, each with two twin beds and a private bathroom. The rooms lean more toward comfort than rusticity, but this lodge will appeal more to easygoing nature lovers. There is a cozy living/dining area with a fireplace where meals are served (breakfast $4; dinner $11). Meals are tasty and healthy, made with organic ingredients from the *finca*'s garden. Bring snacks and picnic lunch items with you, and alcohol, as none of these items are available. Rates for a minimum of 2 nights are $44 for the first night, $35 for the second, and credit cards are not accepted. The Swiss owners, Monika and Herbert, answer their phone only from 7 to 9pm, and check e-mails once a week only. Note that the lodge and the trails are closed during June, September, and October.

5 Parque Nacional Marino Golfo de Chiriquí & Islas Secas ⋆⋆⋆

The Chiriquí Gulf National Marine Park is one of Panama's best-kept secrets—but it won't be for long, given its proximity to Boquete and the wave of retirees and expats moving to that area every year. At Boca Chica, the closest town to the park, there are no high-rises, golf courses, or gated communities, just a couple of lodges and a tiny fishing community—and a lot of thick vegetation and crystalline water. The Marine Park was founded in 1994 to protect 14,730 hectares (36,400 acres) of extensive coral reef, mangrove swamps, and marine meadows—the park's most salient characteristics. Another significant feature of this park is its dozens of picturesque rocky outcrops sprinkled across the gulf, as well as its idyllic islands carpeted in forest and lined with slender coconut palms. Several of these islands boast tropical-paradise white-sand beaches lapped by turquoise waters (unlike the Pacific Coast beaches on the mainland), especially **Isla Gámez** and **Isla Bolaños.** While out in the gulf, you can see the purple silhouette of Volcán Barú rising high in the background. The air is fresh and balmy, unlike the interior humid lowlands.

The sea is rich in marine life, providing **scuba divers** and **snorkelers** with the opportunity to see huge schools of colorful tropical fish, as well as large pelagic fish like white-tipped sharks. Scuba divers and snorkelers will need to book a boat tour to get to the offshore islands, where visibility is better than it is near shore (expect up to 15m/50 ft. off shore). The shore near Boca Chica and the pier is shrouded in mangrove and the water is cloudy, not suitable for underwater sports.

As with Coiba, the **sport fishing** in the Chiriquí Gulf beyond the national park is legendary, especially around Islas Ladrones, Islas Secas, and Islas Contreras. Islas Secas is a cluster of 16 private islands that are part of a luxury ecolodge (p. 248), one of the most gorgeous in all of Panama.

Boca Chica fronts a large island called Boca Brava; here two lodges and a restaurant share space with howler monkeys, agoutis, raccoons, and other wildlife, and there are walking trails through the forest. You can reach the island via a $1 water-taxi ride from shore.

ESSENTIALS

GETTING THERE & DEPARTING   By Plane   The closest airport to Boca Chica is in David (see "Getting There & Departing" under "David," earlier in this chapter).

By Bus   There is frequent bus service from David to the town of Horconcitos, but bus service from there to Boca Chica is spotty. Considering that Boca Chica is the jumping-off point for the gulf, nearly every traveler here has arranged accommodations in the area or a day or multiple-day excursion that includes transportation to Boca Chica.

By Car   Heading east from David, drive 38km (24 miles) and turn right on the turnoff for Horconcitos. Drive about 4.8km (3 miles) to Horconcitos, when the road forks; stay right and turn at the sign for Boca Chica. The road continues from here for 16km (10 miles) to Boca Chica. This portion of the road is slated to be paved during 2007, though it is being groomed and does not require a 4WD unless it's raining.

FUN IN & ON THE WATER
FISHING, SNORKELING & SCUBA DIVING

Private overnight fishing and scuba-diving charters that operate around Isla Coiba are described below (under "Isla Coiba"); these charters normally leave from the Pedregal pier near David, or from Puerto Mutis southwest of Santiago. What's new in this area is that Exploration Panama is now offering **day trips to Isla Coiba** from Boca Chica, whereas previously the only day trips to Coiba departed from Santa Catalina. For lodges in Boca Chica that specialize in fishing, see below.

Exploration Panama (© 720-2470; www.explorationpanama.com) is the area's top fishing, boating, scuba-diving, and snorkeling operation. Their offices are in the Boquete Country Inn in Boquete, but they keep their boat docked at Boca Chica. Exploration Panama operates the M/V *Little Ship*, a sturdy and comfortable refurbished U.S. Coast Guard boat with a capacity for 22 day passengers, 6 overnighters. The boat is certified to sail through even the choppiest storm conditions.

The company offers all-inclusive sport-fishing excursions around the Gulf of Chiriquí, including to Coiba, Secas, Contreras, and Hannibal islands, or they get you out to prime fishing spots like Isla Ladrones for the day. They also specialize in day and multiday scuba diving, snorkeling, and pleasure trips around the Marine National Park. More importantly, they've begun to operate day trips in addition to their multiday trips to Isla Coiba from here, which is a real plus because now travelers in Boquete or Cerro Punta need not drive first to Santa Catalina to visit Isla Coiba—however, they will need to spend the night in Boca Chica to get a very early start in the day. Exploration Panama also owns Wahoo Willy's, and can put together a package including meals and lodging for the 1-night/2-day tour. Also, it is a lot more reassuring to visit Isla Coiba aboard the *Little Ship* than aboard a fiberglass *panga* from Santa Catalina.

It's worth mentioning that the American/Panamanian owners of Exploration Panama, Ron and Yalty, are two of the nicest people you'll ever meet, and having been around the Chiriquí area on and off for decades, they offer a wealth of information and loads of amusing anecdotes.

Boca Brava Divers (© 775-3185 or 6600-6191; www.scubadiving-panama.com) is a locally based scuba-diving operation run by a friendly English-speaking Colombian named Carlos, who is a PADI dive master and has lived and dived in the Marine Park region for years. Boca Brava offers a full-day diving trip that can go as far as Islas Secas or Isla Ladrones, leaving at 7am and returning at 4pm; the cost is $150 per person. Boca Brava's boat, a 14m (46-ft.) converted commercial-fishing vessel, has liveaboard accommodations for five guests for multiday scuba-diving trips around the Gulf of Chiriquí, including to Isla Coiba.

WHERE TO STAY & DINE

Gone Fishing 𝕲   During my last visit to Boca Chica, construction was nearly done on this fishing lodge. From the look of it, the lodge promises to offer a "smart-casual" ambience with comfortable, ranch-style accommodations on the shore of Boca Chica. The lodge's focus is on fishing around the Gulf of Chiriquí, both inshore and offshore, aboard one of their two 9.4m (31-ft.) custom open fishing vessels. However, the lodge is for non-fishers, too, who want to come and hang out in natural surroundings and snorkel or dive the region. Considering this, and the fact that they have a swimming pool and a small strip of beach, this is an ideal lodge for fishers traveling with non-fishing spouses. There are two stand-alone cabins and two hotel rooms that are not luxurious—but they aren't basic either, sporting artfully painted walls with colorful marine and jungle murals. The lodge's **restaurant and bar,** which serves American and Panamanian food, is open to the public; they have a breezy terrace with sunset views. Guests pay a nightly fee and order meals and excursions a la carte; daily fishing trips are $1,400 for two anglers, $1,800 for four anglers. Inshore tours to island beaches cost $100 per hour, with a minimum of 3 hours. Children must be at least 10 years old. You'll see the entrance to Gone Fishing on your left side, just before entering Boca Chica.

Boca Chica. ✆ 6573-0151. www.gonefishingpanama.com. 4 units. $100 double. MC, V. **Amenities:** Restaurant; bar; fishing excursions; boat trips; outdoor pool. In room: A/C, no phone.

Panama Big Game Sportfishing Club ★★   When I hear the words "fishing club," I don't think of an upscale lodge with panoramic views, fine cuisine, and first-class fishing expeditions—but that is exactly what you get here at the Big Game Sportfishing Club. Perched high on a hilltop on Boca Brava Island, a couple of minutes from Boca Chica by boat, and accessed by a long flight of stairs or a funicular-style people-mover, Big Game boasts sweeping views of the area and is backed by wooded surroundings teeming with wildlife. The resort is owned by two retired charter-boat skippers and restaurateurs from Miami (one has 30 years of experience as a chef). The lodge gets a lot of American guests, especially groups of buddies who head down together for a week of deepwater fishing and fun. The Sportfishing Club consists of a main building with a bar/dining area centered around a large, curved teak bar, and four attractive cabins. The cabins are surprisingly roomy (56 sq. m/600 sq. ft.) and thoroughly contemporary, accented with colorful cushions and tiled with locally produced ceramics; these units can sleep up to six. The lodge has four fishing boats to accommodate all guests. From the moment you arrive, they'll have their boats stocked with coolers and be ready to take you out to sea. Prices include transportation from the David airport, lodging, fishing, meals and beverages. Three-day packages start on Mondays and Thursdays, and 5-day packages start on Mondays. From June 1 to November 30, guests pay for 3 days of fishing and get four.

Boca Brava Island. ✆ 866/281-1225 in the U.S. www.panama-sportfishing.com. 4 units. 3-day packages $3,481 per person, based on 2 anglers; $2,461 per person, based on 4 anglers; 5-day packages $5,040 per-person, based on 2 anglers, and $3,364 per person, based on 4 anglers. MC, V. **Amenities:** Restaurant; bar; fishing excursions. In room: A/C, no phone.

Wahoo Willy's ★   This casual yet comfortable hotel is on the shore of Boca Chica near a pier and tiny gas station that bustles (but just lightly) throughout the day. Wahoo Willy's is also the only restaurant in Boca Chica that is open to the public, so if you're here for the day and hungry for lunch, stop in—the fish is fresh and just delicious. The hotel has five cheery guest rooms with lots of porthole-style windows and floor-to-ceiling glass walls, allowing light to pour in. Room nos. 2, 3, and 4 have terraces, and all have private bathrooms. Wahoo Willy's is an informal sort of place, but with enough style to put it a notch above budget accommodations. It also gives a "local experience" to guests, who can watch fishermen pulling in their catch of the day, kids playing in the street, and other residents going about their business. The hotel and restaurant are owned by two Americans who also own Exploration Panama and

Wild Orchid Coffee. Exploration Panama can organize any kind of boating, diving, or fishing trips for guests as part of a package.

The **restaurant** serves jumbo shrimp, tuna, sea bass, scallops, and whatever else is in season, with beans and rice; there are snacks, sandwiches, and breakfast. The restaurant has outdoor seating overlooking the water. They're open every day, all day.

Boca Chica. No phone. wahoowillys@hotmail.com. 5 units. $35 single; $49 double. No credit cards. **Amenities:** Restaurant; tours. *In room:* A/C, no phone.

A LUXURY ECOLODGE ON A REMOTE, PRIVATE ISLAND

Islas Secas ✯✯✯ *(Moments)*   Gloriously unfettered by crowds, and encompassed by deep-blue and cerulean waters teeming with marine life, the rustic yet luxurious Islas Secas ecolodge is the best in Panama. Islas Secas comprises 16 remote and private islands off the Pacific Coast; the largest island is home base, with six bungalows *(casitas)* spread about two coves and linked by coral pathways to a palm-fringed central dining area, outdoor lounge, and spa. The *casitas* are 6.1 by 6.1m (20- by 20-ft.) yurts that have a low impact on the environment and boast an aesthetic that is both spare and very stylish, appealing equally to the eco-conscious jet-set and to honeymooners (who receive 2 nights free if they book for 8 nights). There is no air-conditioning, though yurts have an insulation layer that keeps the heat out, and there is also a ceiling fan. The American owner of Islas Secas is a tech wizard with a healthy appetite for the outdoors; when he's not around, his deluxe *casita* with a full kitchen, satellite Internet hookup, and a full deck, can be rented. The *casitas* are elegantly appointed and feature ultra-comfortable beds draped in mosquito netting, deluxe bathrooms, and a small sitting area.

It is difficult to describe Islas Secas without lapsing into superlatives, so here it goes. The service and the cuisine are the best of any resort in Panama. Upon arrival, the staff gathers to welcome guests with a Fantasy Island–style, but heartfelt, greeting with waves and smiles. The staff provides impeccable service and anticipates your needs to the point where you wonder if they are reading your mind. The gourmet cuisine is out-of-this-world delicious, even down to the picnic lunches served on day excursions. Whatever your whim on any given day, the staff can fulfill your desire: sport fishing, surfing, scuba diving, snorkeling, walking through pristine forest, kayaking, or just having the boat captain drop you off on an uninhabited island to play castaway for a day. With tropical views this idyllic and a scattering of wooden *rancho* outdoor lounges, stretching out with a good book can be an enticing activity, too. Upon return to home base, you can pamper yourself with a massage, or have cocktails and watch the sunset. To get here, you'll need to fly by small plane from Panama City, which costs an additional $400 round-trip. Everything else is included, except spa services and fishing charters. Islas Secas is open from mid-December to April only, and children must be 10 or older.

Islas Secas. © **805/729-2737** in the U.S. www.islassecas.com. 6 units. All-inclusive packages based on double occupancy are $495 per person, per night; the large *casita* is $695 per person, per night. AE, MC, V. **Amenities:** Restaurant; bar; spa with massage, facials, and body treatments; day excursions and activities; Internet service; kayaks. *In room:* Ceiling fan, minibar, no phone.

6 Isla Coiba ✯✯✯

SE Gulf of Chiriquí

Once the haunt of pirates, and in recent times an island feared by convicted criminals who were sent there, Isla Coiba is now a treasured national park, UNESCO World Heritage Site, and nature lover's, fisherman's, and scuba-diver's dream destination.

Given Isla Coiba's astounding natural diversity, rich sea life, and rare species, it is frequently referred to as the Galápagos of Central America. Isla Coiba is the largest island in Panama, but the national park spreads beyond the main island, encompassing 38 islands and islets and marine waters for a total of 270,128 hectares (667,500 acres). The area is home to the second-largest coral reef in the eastern Pacific, at **Bahía Damas,** and its waters teem with huge schools of colorful fish, hammerhead and nurse sharks, dolphins, manta rays, tuna, turtles, whales, and other gigantic marine species. Onshore, there are 36 species of mammals and 39 species of reptiles, including saltwater crocodiles. Beyond these impressive numbers, Coiba is one of the last places on earth where it is possible to see a scarlet macaw in the wild. Indeed, few places in the Americas are as wild, remote, and full of life as Isla Coiba National Park.

The island and its surrounding waters owe their pristine state to a notorious penal colony that existed on the island from 1919 to 2004, which kept tourists and developers at bay. Panama sent its most hardened criminals to the island, who considered the isolated penal colony the most punishing sentence the government could hand down. There's talk that the government might reopen the prison for Alcatraz-style tours. Having only recently opened itself to tourism, the island takes a little work to get to for the day, or an expensive all-inclusive package to spend a few nights in the area. The majority of visitors to the island are "temporary" travelers who descend en masse from small to midsize cruise ships to spend a couple of hours snorkeling around **Granito de Oro,** or for a quick walk through the island's jungle trails (70% of the visitors to Coiba in 2006 were American). Granito de Oro is a tiny island whose waters offer outstanding snorkeling and a picture-postcard white-sand beach, but the waters surrounding Coiba are still virgin territory, and snorkeling and diving outfits have yet to discover all of Coiba's treasures. Expect new "hot spots" to come to the public's attention soon.

The park is administered by ANAM, which has a ranger station and basic air-conditioned lodging on a glorious white-sand and turquoise-water beach. The cost to visit Coiba National Park is $10 per person. The cabins are used by fishing, diving, and snorkeling tour outfitters (or by those with a private boat). Day visits to Coiba go through operators in Santa Catalina (see below). There is a landing strip on Coiba, but for charter flights only.

OUTDOOR ADVENTURES IN COIBA
HIKING
There are two short trails at the ANAM station that lead to lookout points, but each is less than .4km (.25-mile) long. **Sendero de los Monos (Trail of the Monkeys)** is located on the shore in front of Granito de Oro island. You must walk this trail very early to see monkeys; otherwise it's just an easy, 45-minute walk through dense forest that starts and ends at different points—you need a boat to get there and be picked up. If you've only got a day here, you might want to skip it.

FISHING
The fishing around Coiba and the Gulf of Chiriquí is legendary, but keep in mind that ANAM only allows catch-and-release fishing within 1.6km (1 mile) of the boundary of the national park–protected area. ANAM only recently began enforcing fishing laws, and after a few misunderstandings, charter boat captains are now aware of restrictions and adhere by them. Fishermen consider this area special due to the size and variety of fish, and the sheer number of fishing sites that could not be covered

even in a week. By far the most renowned sport-fishing areas near Coiba are Hannibal Bank, which is something like an underwater mountain, and Isla Montuosa, but there are plenty of other sites with underwater mountains and deep ledges that attract black marlin, roosterfish, cubera snapper, bluefin trevally, and other very big fish. In addition to the following tour operators, **Exploration Panama** and two lodge-based outfitters operate out of Boca Chica (see "Fishing, Snorkeling & Scuba Diving" under "Parque Nacional Marino Golfo de Chiriquí & Islas Secas," above).

Coiba Adventure (�C 999-8108, or 800/800-0907 in the U.S.; www.coibadventure. com) is operated by American Tom Yust, who has been sport fishing the Coiba area for more than a decade. Coiba Adventure has two boats, the *Joker,* a 9.4m (31-ft.) Bertram, and a 6.4m (21-ft.) Mako. Guests are flown to the Coiba landing strip on a chartered plane from Panama City, and lodging is on the island in the ANAM air-conditioned cabins (a generator is used for backup). Five-night all-inclusive packages cost $3,000 per person.

The **M/V** *Coral Star* (�C 866/924-2837 in the U.S.; www.coralstar.com) is a deluxe, air-conditioned, 35m (115-ft.) mother ship with mahogany and teak interiors and so many amenities that it feels like a floating fishing lodge. The *Coral Star* can accommodate 16 guests, and they also have seven sport-fishing boats for daily excursions. Beyond fishing, the Coral Star offers scuba diving, snorkeling, kayaking, and ecotours, and they can put together a custom canal transit for groups. Itineraries run from Saturday to Thursday and leave from the Pedregal marina in David. All-inclusive packages, based on four anglers, are $4,000 per person from January to April, and $3,200 per person the rest of the year; rates include hotel stay in Panama City and round-trip flights to David. Occasionally, Coral Star has "specialty weeks," during which they invite a fishing "celebrity" along to teach the tricks of the trade.

Pesca Panama (�C 800/946-3474 in the U.S.; www.pescapanama.com) is a U.S.-based company that offers inshore and offshore sport fishing in the Gulf of Chiriquí, around Coiba and Hannibal Bank. Pesca guests stay aboard their "floating lodge," a 21-by-9.1m (70-by-30-ft.) barge with a maximum capacity of 12 guests (four beds per room), and take day fishing trips aboard 8.2m (27-ft.) Ocean Master boats. Rates range from $2,795 to $3,895 per person for 5 nights, and itineraries are set, but they do offer charter trips. They also offer day fishing trips from Pedregal, near David.

SCUBA DIVING & SNORKELING

For overnight and day scuba-diving trips to Coiba, also see **Exploration Panama** in "Scuba Diving" under "Parque Nacional Marino Golfo"; the *Coral Star* ship (above) also offers scuba diving on its fishing expeditions. Alternatively, you can organize day scuba and snorkeling excursions to Isla Coiba with an outfitter in Santa Catalina (see "Scuba Diving," below, under "Santa Catalina").

Panama Divers (℃ 314-0817 or 6613-4405; www.panamadivers.com) is the country's foremost scuba-diving company based out of Panama City and Portobelo. Panama Divers is fully insured and has decades of experience; their 5-night/6-day diving trips include 2 nights in Panama City, and 3 nights of lodging in the cabins at the ANAM ranger station, with ground transportation to their 7.9m (26-ft.) boat at Puerto Mutis. As part of the trip, they also offer fishing, whale-watching, snorkeling, and kayaking. The cost is $1,275 per person, with a maximum of eight divers.

7 Santa Catalina ⟨★⟩

300km (186 miles) SE of David; 360km (223 miles) from Panama City; 110km (68 miles) from Santiago

Santa Catalina is a surfing mecca and humble fishing village in the Veraguas Province, located at the end of a pressed-dirt road south of Santiago and southeast of David. The waves here are epic, with a couple of perfect and easy-to-line-up point breaks that average 1.5 to 6.1m (5–20 ft.). Most of the waves are for advanced surfers only, but a sandy break has waves suitable for beginners and intermediates surfing with a local guide. Offshore islands such as Isla Cebaco also have excellent surfing conditions. Beyond surfing, Santa Catalina has accommodations and services and is close enough to Isla Coiba to reach on a day excursion for scuba diving, snorkeling, or eco-adventures. Local boatmen in *pangas,* or fiberglass boats with 70-horsepower outboard engines, hang around the shore waiting for customers, but it's better to go with one of the two scuba-diving outfits here (see "Scuba Diving," below), which put together day trips and packages with an overnight on Isla Coiba.

Santa Catalina is a scruffy and remote community whose residents generally earn less than $10 a day and live in cinder-block homes. The recent introduction of plastic bottles and packaged products and no garbage service means that the streets are sprinkled with trash. A lot of locals pass the day hanging around the shoreline and waiting for work, or playing soccer. Given that the village sits across from Isla Coiba, and has some of the best waves in Central America, Santa Catalina has that up-and-coming feeling, with the first young adventurers from the U.S. and Europe anchoring themselves here with a hostel or cafe, and grudgingly watching the region slowly develop for tourism. At the moment, Santa Catalina's accommodations are budget-oriented, and some are downright rustic, but you'll find a couple of surprisingly good restaurants here.

The main road from Soná funnels into what is considered "downtown"; heading left will take you along a dirt road to an open coastal area, and to restaurants, hotels, and hostels in a more natural setting. There is a decent, palm-lined beach near the Oasis Hotel, but it is certainly not the prettiest in Panama. Note that there is no public phone in Santa Catalina, and no local public transportation, so you'll need to walk if you don't have a rental vehicle.

ESSENTIALS

GETTING THERE & AWAY   By Bus   Santa Catalina can be reached by public bus from David or Santiago (if coming from Panama City). From Panama City, take the San Isidro bus line to Soná (5 hr; $6 one-way); from David, take a bus to Soná ($6; about 5 hr.). Buses from Soná to Santa Catalina leave at 5:15am, noon, and 4pm, and cost $3.75 one-way; or you can take a taxi for $25.

By Car   The best way to arrive is by rental car so that you can stop and take photos with some truly beautiful surroundings. But getting here by car from David and following the logical shortcut through Las Palmas to Soná is not easy—there is an absolute lack of road signs. From Panama City, it is a little more straightforward. Drive the Interamericana Highway west to Santiago, about 3 hours. Drive through town and past the cathedral, and 2 blocks later turn left. Drive 45km (28 miles), almost to Soná, turning left at a well-signed exit for Santa Catalina. Drive another 45km (28 miles) and turn left at the sign for Santa Catalina at El Tigre Amarillo, continuing for 20km (12 miles) more until you reach Santa Catalina.

Tips **Guayamí Indian Handicrafts**

Ngöbe-Buglé (Guayamí) Indians sell copies of their traditional, flouncy dresses, beaded jewelry, and other handicrafts at stalls along the roadside in **Tolé.** If you're driving from David, stop 97km (60 miles) east of David.

From David, the right-hand turnoff to Soná is just past El Piro. (If you pass the left-hand turnoff for El Prado, you've gone too far.) The road is tiresomely potholed, and though it is supposedly a straight line to Soná, there are many paved and semipaved roads that branch off and can be confusing before you reach Soná—but then again, the countryside is lovely, with tiny villages dotting the road. If you don't want to hassle with getting lost or dealing with unpaved roads, drive the extra 56km (35 miles) toward Santiago, turning right at the sign for Soná and La Peña, and continue following the directions from Panama City.

FUN IN THE OCEAN
SCUBA DIVING

Isla Coiba is not only the best place to scuba dive and snorkel in the area; it's the best place to dive and snorkel in all of Panama. Day excursions to this island and its surrounding waters are available only from local operations based out of Santa Catalina. It's not cheap, and it takes nearly 1½ hours to get there—which is why you might want to check into spending the night on the island at the park-ranger station. (Both outfitters mentioned below can organize this.) Local boat operators will do the round-trip to Isla Coiba for about $250 to $300, but that's without rental equipment, and drivers are not schooled in even rudimentary first aid, nor do they carry radios or much safety equipment. It's a long, bumpy ride over open water, so it pays to play it safe. Closer to Santa Catalina is **Isla Cebaco,** which offers excellent diving and snorkeling around an extensive coral reef; it only takes about a half-hour to get here, and the fare is less.

Scuba Charters (no phone; www.scuba-charters.com) is owned and operated by two Americans who are fully certified and boast years of diving experience (they hail from Florida). The company offers day trips to Coiba aboard their rigid inflatable tunnel hull, including two-tank dives for $95 per person, and snorkeling for $75 per person. Local diving trips near Santa Catalina cost $60 per person, and $40 per person for snorkeling. They'll put together an eco-tour combined with scuba diving at Coiba, too. They're also dive instructors and offer PADI-certified instruction courses for travelers spending 4 or 5 days in the area. You can buy snorkel gear, underwater camera cases, and other marine-related goodies from Scuba Charters.

Scuba Coiba (no phone; www.scubacoiba.com) is a local operation run by an Austrian expat named Herbie Sunk (yes, it's true), with scuba diving, snorkeling, and eco-tours to Isla Coiba. Using local *panga* boats to get to the island gives Scuba Coiba a by-the-seat-of-your-pants feel to the operation, and though Herbie is *way* laid-back to the point of being unenthusiastic, he is fully certified and he offers 2- and 3-night-stay packages on Isla Coiba that include eco-tours to the interior of the island. Two-dive trips to Coiba cost $95 per person; 2-day all-inclusive packages with stays on Coiba (six dives total) are $390 per person.

SURFING

Two companies can plan multiple-day tours to a variety of surf spots, including Santa Catalina, with transportation included: **Panama Surf Tours** (𝒞 6671-7777; www.panamasurftours.com), a respected company with flexible 5- to 8-day tours that range from economical to luxury; and **Panama Surf Expeditions** (𝒞 6582-0402; www.panamasurfexpeditions.com), run by a group of Santa Catalina locals who build custom surf tours for travelers.

Otherwise, if you're interested in surfing with a guide or need lessons, you'll want to book with a surf camp such as **Punta Brava** or **Oasis** (see below).

WHERE TO STAY

Oasis Surf Camp 𝒦 I like this surf camp/hostel because it is the only lodging option that actually sits on the Playa Estero beach, and it's fronted by a row of palms strung with hammocks. It's nice to be able to walk outside to the ocean's edge and feel the sea breeze in the afternoons. The rooms are nothing special, with double and triple units that are basically a cement cabin with beds, but for the price it's hard to ask for more. When I was last at Oasis, they were constructing a couple of larger guest-room units for groups or families of six that were to have thatched roofs and presumably a little more style. The surf camp rents boards and gives lessons for $20 an hour, and they offer day surfing trips around the area for experienced surfers. The owners are a young Italian couple, and they serve excellent meals—Panamanian lunches and Italian dinners—under a thatched *bohio;* it's $5 per meal. The ambience is casual; don't expect to wear anything else here but a swimsuit and shorts. To get here, take the only turnoff road east of the village, follow it to the end, then drive across a creek, on the other side of which is Oasis.

Playa Estero, Santa Catalina. No phone. surfoasis@hotmail.com. 6 units. $25 double; $30 triple. No credit cards. **Amenities:** Restaurant; surf classes; trips; surfboard rental. *In room:* No phone.

Punta Brava Surf Lodge 𝒦 Argentine-owned and -operated, and the only lodging option that offers satellite Internet and phone service, the Punta Brava overlooks a rocky bluff and plateau—not to mention the Santa Catalina surf break. There is no beach here, but the sea views are impressive and the property on the whole is clean and attractive; this combined with the amenities offered here make this the best bet for lodging in Santa Catalina. What's also a plus with the Punta Brava is the fact that the owners have their own 7.6m (25-ft.) and 8.2m (27-ft.) boats, surfboard rentals and classes, and private transfers from the David airport—all of which can be put together in a package. Packages include airport transportation, 7 nights of accommodations, 3 meals per day, beverages, surf guides, one boat trip to Isla Coiba and two boat trips to mainland surf breaks; the cost is $1,000 single occupancy, $600 per person double occupancy, and $500 per person triple occupancy. The owners recently remodeled their five existing units and added six more in their main house, plus a bar and restaurant with outdoor seating. This isn't the lap of luxury, but the pastel-painted rooms do offer standard comfort with mattress beds, air-conditioning, and refrigerators. The new rooms in the main house are brighter and have queen-size beds; the five rooms in the motel-like building have twin beds.

Santa Catalina. 𝒞 6614-3868. www.puntabrava.com. 11 units. $60 double. V. **Amenities:** Restaurant; bar; airport transfers; surf tours; diving tours; satellite Internet and phone connection; surfboard rental. *In room:* A/C, TV (new rooms), minifridge, no phone.

Sol y Mar 𝒜   The Sol y Mar, owned by a young Portuguese surfer and his Pana-manian girlfriend, offers what passes for deluxe accommodations in Santa Catalina, with clean, surfer-stylish guest rooms and French doors that open on a narrow terrace with a hammock. It's located high on a steep slope and set back from the shore, about a 5-minute walk to the beach. Rooms are surrounded by exotic fruit trees, and views from here are of the tops of tropical trees and foliage, and of the ocean in the distance. There is a small but complete outdoor kitchen and eating area, and minifridges in each room to store food. Rooms have two double beds and two foam futon chairs, which supposedly sleep two extra people, in a compact living area. The walls are thin, so expect to listen to your neighbors or whatever they're watching on TV.

Santa Catalina. ✆ 6487-1377. catalinaluis@hotmail.com. 4 units. $40 double. No credit cards. **Amenities:** Com-mon kitchen. *In room:* A/C, TV, minifridge.

WHERE TO DINE

There are a couple of solid dining options in Santa Catalina, and all are located east of town along the road that dead-ends at the Oasis. Otherwise, hotels and hostels here include meals with their packages, or have kitchens for independent cooking. None of the restaurants has a telephone or accepts credit cards; hours are only guidelines, never firmly adhered to during slower weeks; and though restaurants are open daily, they sometimes close on Mondays. **Blanca's** is a local joint and the first that you'll pass on the road. They serve delicious breakfasts and are open all day, from 8am to 10pm (later on weekends). Lunch and dinner dishes are the usual Panamanian-style meat or fish with rice and beans. **Jamming** is an Italian-owned pizzeria, with a dozen or so combinations of mouthwatering thin-crust pizzas baked in a clay oven. The vibe here is reggae-and-rum, and there are a bar and a couple of tables in an open-air thatched-hut *rancho*—this restaurant is a meeting point and what passes for nightlife in town. Jamming is open from around 6:30 to 10 or 10:30pm. There is a **Parrilla Argentina,** owned by two Argentine surfers, with delicious grilled meats and fish paired with salad and potatoes. When I was last there, they did not yet have an alcohol license, so it could still be BYOB. Open from 7 to 10pm.

9

Bocas del Toro Archipelago

The Bocas del Toro Archipelago is a scattering of seven islands and more than 200 islets off the northwestern coast of Panama, near the border with Costa Rica. The region has all the trappings of a Caribbean fantasy: dreamy beaches, thatched-roofed huts, aquamarine sea, thick rainforest, and soft ocean breeze. Add to that a funky, carefree ambience and a large English-speaking population, and it's easy to see why Bocas del Toro is quickly emerging as an eco-tourism hot spot faster than any other part of Panama.

But scratch the surface and you will find an island destination that is as much a paradox as it is paradise. Backpackers and surfers first discovered Bocas, lured by big waves, an underwater playground, and cheap accommodations. Midrange hotels and restaurants moved in, and retirees and expats with disposable income followed, snapping up beachfront properties and building their own tropical Xanadu. Considering that Bocas consists mostly of Ngöbe-Buglé and Teribe Indians plying the waters in dugout canoes, as well as Afro-Caribbeans who go about living much as they have for nearly a century, the contrast between the mix of ethnicities and nationalities here is striking.

The principal island in the region is Isla Colón, 62 sq. km (24 sq. miles) and home to **Bocas Town,** the regional capital and the center of activity in the archipelago. A smaller island called Isla Carenero neighbors Isla Colón, and is a quieter location with a few hotels and restaurants just a minute or two away from Bocas Town by water taxi. Isla Bastimentos and Isla Cristóbal offer accommodations and amenities, and are better choices for travelers seeking a more intimate, castaway-like experience in wild, natural surroundings. Visitors to island lodges also benefit from in-house tours planned by proprietors with local knowledge, but there are plenty of tour operators in Bocas Town to fill your days if you choose to stay closer to shopping, restaurants, and nightlife.

Bocas can hold its own against nearby Costa Rica when it comes to adventure travel in the Caribbean. The diving and snorkeling are outstanding in this region—Bocas is home to some of the best-preserved hard and soft coral on the planet—but make sure your tour operator is willing to take you to the finest examples instead of bleached-out coral in "typical" tourist spots. There are sailing tours, boat tours to deserted islands and visits to Indian communities, hiking through luxuriant rainforest in Isla Bastimentos Park, and riding waves in what is largely considered the surfing epicenter of the southwest Caribbean.

Historically there has always been a rough, end-of-the-line feel to Bocas del Toro, which is perceptible even today. Weathered, plantation-style homes—many of which look as if a good sneeze would level them—line dirt streets, Jimmy Buffett types hold court at waterfront dive bars, and residents and foreign visitors languidly stroll from one point to

(Tips) A Word about Water

The major drawback to Bocas del Toro as a destination is its climate. While the rest of Panama enjoys a generally predictable dry season from December to April, Bocas can experience cloudy skies and **downpours** any time of the year. The most trustworthy months for sunshine are late August to mid-October, and February and March.

Tourists with sensitive digestive tracts should stick to **bottled water** when in Bocas Town. Tap water is treated but not to the same standards as it is in the rest of Panama. Hotels on outlying islands use filtered rainwater that is okay to drink—but you still might want to play it safe and drink bottled water only.

Visitors should be extremely careful when swimming in the ocean because of strong **riptides**—I can attest to this, having been caught in a riptide at Red Frog Beach. It can be the scariest moment of your life, and can affect anyone regardless of his or her abilities as a swimmer. At a beach, find a section of the water that isn't being churned up by looking for clear, not sandy, waves. If you're caught in a riptide, don't panic, no matter how much the waves are tossing you around. Swim parallel to the shore until you feel yourself released from the current, then head back to shore.

another, or kill entire afternoons on a park bench in the town's central plaza, which is choked with overgrown tropical foliage. But underneath this are the rumblings of an upcoming boom in tourism, with multimillion-dollar hotels, gated residential communities, and waterfront condominiums either in the works or already breaking ground. Still, the laid-back friendliness that characterizes Bocas del Toro endures.

1 Isla Colón: Bocas Town (★)

30 min. by boat from Almirante; 1 hr. by boat from Changuinola; 1 hr. by plane from Panama City

Christopher Columbus arrived at what is now known as Bocas del Toro in October 1502, on his fourth and final voyage to the New World. It is said that he repaired his ships at Isla Carenero (thus the moniker "Careening Cay") before continuing on to present-day Portobelo and back to the Veraguas coast in the never-ending quest for gold and riches for the Spanish crown. Columbus never found the fabled gold mines of the highlands backing Bocas del Toro, and the area therefore piqued little interest in the region for the Spanish. By the 17th century the archipelago became the haunt of renegade pirates and buccaneers.

The United Fruit Company first settled Isla Colón in the early 1900s for large-scale banana production, designating **Bocas Town** as headquarters and regional capital. A wave of immigrants from Jamaica, as well as from San Andrés and Providencia, Colombia, followed, so that by the 1920s, Bocas Town had more than 20,000 residents. It ranked as one of the most prosperous regions in Panama, but when a banana blight forced the company to shut down in the 1930s and move operations to the mainland, Bocas Town retreated into a state of relative anonymity.

Fast-forward to the 21st century, and really there hasn't been much change in Bocas Town. But not for long: Tourism, though nascent, is alive on Main Street, and developers have their eye on the waterfront. Yet, at the time of this publication, there is little in the way of upscale accommodations and services here. Finicky travelers will be happiest visiting Bocas Town only as a jumping-off point to a lodge away from the hustle and bustle.

ESSENTIALS

GETTING THERE & DEPARTING   There are two ways to get to Bocas del Toro: via a land/sea combination, or by air. Considering the cheap price of air travel in Panama and the short flight (1 hr. from Panama City), most travelers opt to fly. If crossing into Bocas del Toro from Costa Rica by land, travelers head to Changuinola, where they can grab a boat shuttle to Bocas (1 hr.) or hop over on a small plane from Changuinola (10 min.). *Tip:* If traveling from Costa Rica, remember that Costa Rica is **1 hour ahead** of Panama.

By Plane   The basic but spruce **Bocas International Airport** (© 757-9208) is serviced by daily flights from Panama City, David, Changuinola, and Costa Rica.

Air Panama (© 315-0439; www.flyairpanama.com) has service to Bocas del Toro from Panama City, David, and San José, Costa Rica (for Costa Rica flights, see "From Costa Rica by Plane," below). From **Panama City,** there are two or three daily flights leaving at 6:45am (Mon–Sat); 8am (Sun); 7:15am (Mon, Wed, Fri); and 3:15pm (daily). Return flights from Bocas to Panama City leave 8am (Mon–Sat); 9:15am (Sun); 1:45pm (Mon, Wed, Fri); and 4:30pm (daily). From **David,** there is one flight on Mondays, Wednesdays, and Fridays only, leaving at 1pm; the flight from Bocas to David leaves at 8:35am.

Aeroperlas (© 315-7500; www.aeroperlas.com) offers two daily flights from **Panama City** to Bocas, weekdays at 6:25am and 3pm; Saturdays at 8:05am and 3:05pm; and Sundays at 6:30am and 3:05pm. The return trip to Panama City leaves weekdays 10:30am and 5pm; Saturday 10:15am and 5:15pm; and Sunday at 8:40am and 5:15pm. There are three daily flights from **Changuinola** to Bocas, Monday through Friday at 8:05am, 10am, and 4:40pm; the two daily return flights leave Bocas at 7:50am and 4:20pm; Saturday flights from Changuinola are at 9:50am and 4:50pm; Sundays at 8:15am and 4:50pm. From **David,** flights leave once daily, weekdays only, at 9am; the flight from Bocas is at 8:25am.

By Boat   Bocas Marine & Tours (© 757-9033 in Bocas, 758-4085 in Almirante, or 758-9859 in Changuinola; www.bocasmarinetours.com) has daily boat service between Almirante and Bocas every 30 to 40 minutes, from 6am to 6:30pm (6:30am–6:30pm from Bocas to Almirante). They also offer service from Changuinola (see "From Costa Rica by Road," below).

Taxi 25 (© 757-9028) also operates between Almirante and Bocas, leaving every half-hour from 6am to 6:30pm. Both companies charge $3 per person, one-way, and leave from the Almirante dock; Bocas Marine & Tours is on Main Street in Bocas, and Taxi 25 can be found next to the IPAT office. If you have a vehicle, there is parking for $3 a day at the lot at the Almirante boat dock. To get to the Almirante bus station for the 4-hour bus ride to David, take a $1 taxi that waits at the port.

From Costa Rica by Plane   Air Panama (see above) has service from San José, Costa Rica, on Monday, Wednesday, and Friday at 10am; service from Bocas del Toro to San José leaves at 8:35am. The cost is $140 one-way for adults, $104 one-way for children, and takes about 1 hour. **Nature Air,** a Costa Rican airline that is represented in Panama by **Bocas Air Adventures** (© 656-0460 in Panama, 506/299-6000 in Costa Rica, or 800/235-9272 in the U.S. and Canada; www.natureair.com) has one flight to Bocas from San José (with connections from Quepos, Liberia, and Puerto

---

⌐Tips Being Grounded

Air Panama and Aeroperlas occasionally **cancel flights** when there are not enough passengers to make the flight profitable, or for any other unforeseen problem. It is a frustrating aspect of local air travel in Panama, especially when flights are canceled with short notice. If traveling to Boquete or David from Bocas, your second option is to take a boat to Almirante, and negotiate a fee with a local taxi driver at the dock (around $80 one-way). It is about the same price as a one-way flight for two, and takes around 3 hours. Don't hesitate to negotiate the price and be certain to settle on a fee beforehand.

Bocas Town

To Playa Bluff & Boca del Drago

Cemetery

Hospital

Sandfly Bay

Handicraft Market

Municipal Building

ANAM

Taxi 25 (To Carenero)

Police

IPAT

Airport

ATM

Av. Central

Parque Simon Bolivar

Caribbean Sea
Bocas del Toro Colón ★ Panama City
Golfo de Panamá
C.R. COL.
0   50 mi
0   50 km

0   100 meters
0   100 yards

Magic Bay

ACCOMMODATIONS ■

Bocas Inn/
   Ancon Expeditions **5**
Cocomo-on-the-Sea **1**
Hotel Bocas del Toro **15**
Hotel Casa Max **3**
Hotel El Limbo
   on the Sea **16**
Hotel Laguna **11**
La Veranda **2**
Lula's Bed & Breakfast **4**
Suite Hotel Costes **10**
Swan's Cay Hotel **9**
Tropical Suites **12**

DINING ◆

Buena Vista Grill **14**
Da Claudio **11**
El Pecado de Sabor **24**
La Ballena **7**
Lemongrass **13**
Om Café **8**
Pargo Rojo **6**
Reef **22**

ATTRACTIONS ●

Bocas Marine
   & Tours **18**
Bocas Water Sports **21**
Catamaran Sailing
   Adventures **19**
J & J Transparente
   Boat Tours **17**
Pachamana/
   Starfish Coffee **20**
Shelley's BBQ **25**
Spa Flora Bella **26**
Starfleet Scuba **13**
Super Gourmet **23**

Jiménez) on Tuesday, Thursday, and Saturday, leaving at 8am and returning from Bocas at 10:30am; the flight costs $113 one-way, $226 round-trip. Note that Nature Air is known to increase prices during the high season (Dec 1–Apr 20).

From Costa Rica by Road   Travelers entering Panama from Costa Rica by road at the Sixaola–Guabito border can take a taxi (about $15) to **Changuinola,** then a boat to Bocas del Toro with **Bocas Marine & Tours** (see above). Have your taxi driver take you to the dock at Finca 60, just outside of Changuinola. The boat journey passes through the San San Pond Sak wetlands and an old banana plantation canal, and is so scenic it could be considered a low-price tour. From Changuinola, boats leave daily at 8am, 9:30am, 11am, 12:30pm, 2pm, 3:30pm, and 5pm. From Bocas Town to Changuinola, boats leave at 7am, 8am, 9:30am, 11am, 12:30pm, 2pm, 3:30pm, and 4:30pm. The cost is $5 per person one-way. *Note:* Owing to the increase in fuel cost, Bocas Marine & Tours operates with a minimum of six passengers; this means that when business is slow they might not leave promptly on schedule.

VISITOR INFORMATION   There is an **IPAT visitor center** (© 757-9642; Mon– Fri 8:30am–4:30pm) in a barn-size yellow building on the waterfront at Calle 1, near the police station. It appears that IPAT blew its budget on this sparkling new office, because English-speaking, trained information officers, maps, and brochures are all in

> *Tips* **Money**
>
> Many hotels and restaurants in Bocas del Toro do not accept credit cards, and of those that do, it's **Visa** and **Mastercard only.** Some hotels will request that you pay your deposit via PayPal or a bank deposit in your home country, then pay cash or traveler's checks for the remaining balance. There is a 24-hour ATM at Banco Nacional de Panamá, located at the corner of Calle 4 and Avenida E, and an ATM in the Expreso Taxi 25 building—but bring extra cash in case both are down, which can happen here, especially during high season.

short supply. Around lunchtime, you'll be lucky to find anyone staffing the desk, though on the second floor you'll find a display on the natural history of Bocas, and there are public bathrooms here, too. For additional information about Bocas, try the Web portal **www.bocas.com,** which has links to hotels, tourism services, transportation information, and more.

GETTING AROUND   Everything in Bocas Town is within walking distance, but collective taxis are plentiful if you need one. Most hotels arrange pickup and drop-off for guests arriving by air, but there are also taxis waiting for every arrival at the airport. If arriving by boat, find out where your hotel is in relation to the dock—you may already be close enough to walk. Taxis cost between 50¢ and $1. There are two principal roads on the island: One runs along the coast and ends at Playa Bluff; the other crosses the island to Boca del Drago.

There are **bicycle** rentals on Main Street across from the plaza; all charge $1 an hour, or $5 to $8 a day. Informal **water taxis** are available at the dock next to the IPAT office, with service to neighboring Isla Carenero ($1 one-way) and Isla Bastimentos ($7 one-way to Red Frog Beach). Hours are irregular, with service generally running from 7am to 9pm. Most people visit Isla Bastimentos as part of a day tour; resorts on that island include round-trip transportation in the price and an extra charge for additional trips.

For beaches outside of Bocas Town, see "What to See & Do," below.

ORIENTATION   Bocas is the only town on Isla Colón, centered around a bustling Main Street (Calle 3) and Simon Bolívar Plaza. There are fewer than two dozen streets in Bocas, and most are unpaved. The airport is just a couple of blocks away from the main plaza, meaning you could walk to your hotel if you felt like it. Calles 1 through 10 run west-east and Avenidas A to H run north-south. There is no "downtown," but most hotels and restaurants are concentrated on the south end where Calle 1 meets Main Street. Internet cafes and shops are along Main Street between Avenidas E and D.

FAST FACTS: Bocas Town

Banks See "Money," above.

Courier Services You'll find FedEx and DHL services at Bravo Center on Main Street between Avenidas 2 and 3 (© **757-9229;** bravocenter@bocasmail.com).

Emergency Numbers For an ambulance, call © **757-9814;** for fire, dial © **103;** police, dial © **104** or 757-9217.

Hospital There is a basic hospital clinic in Bocas, located at Calle 10 and Avenida G (© **757-9201**), with a 24-hour emergency room. However, service is limited and those with more serious health problems will need to seek medical care in Panama City.

Internet Access **Bravo Center** on Main Street has Wi-Fi service (daily 10am–7pm); or there's **Internet Bocas Café** (daily 8am–10pm) and **Don Chicho's** (daily 8am–9pm), both on Main Street. All cybercafes charge around $2 per hour.

Laundry There are coin-operated machines and drop-off laundry services including pickup and delivery at **Bubbles** on Avenida C at Main St. (© **6591-3814**; Mon–Sat 8am–6pm).

Post Office The post office is located at Calle A and Avenida 2; no phone. It's run by a no-nonsense woman who maintains hours Monday through Friday from 8am to noon and 2 to 4pm (some days 3–4pm "when I feel like taking a long lunch"), and Saturday 8am to noon.

WHAT TO SEE & DO

The Bocas del Toro Archipelago, despite its location in the warm, cerulean Caribbean Sea, is not a quintessential beach destination. That's not to say that there are no beaches here; in fact, there are a handful of idyllic beaches straight from the pages of a travel magazine—it just takes a little effort to reach them. Also, most beaches in Bocas offer poor swimming conditions because of strong riptides. (See "A Word About Water," above.) The closest decent beach to Bocas Town (Bluff Beach) is an 8km (5-mile) bike- or taxi ride away, and the beaches on Isla Bastimentos can only be reached by boat, followed by a short to medium-long walk. During the calm-water months (early Sept to early Nov), it's possible to arrive directly by boat at the beaches of Isla Bastimentos.

If you don't have an all-inclusive package with your hotel, or if your hotel simply does not offer trips, there are plenty of tour agencies to fulfill your excursion needs. Bocas is a good base for exploring the archipelago—nearly every kind of excursion and destination can be reached from here, including spots for watersports and cultural visits. Trips to Isla Bastimentos and the Zapatilla Cays are better with fast boats that offer flexible itineraries. If you have a group or can afford a private-boat rental, do so because it offers you the freedom to plan your own itinerary.

Tip: The old cliché "You get what you pay for" rings true in Bocas. There are plenty of agencies pitching the same day tour to the masses, usually for dirt-cheap prices. These companies cut corners by hiring semi-qualified guides with little concern for the environment; others try to save on gas by not taking clients far enough to the best snorkeling and diving sites—providing less-than-memorable experiences and the dreaded cattle-herd sensation. To avoid disappointments, when booking, ask detailed questions about destinations, snorkeling and diving sites, safety precautions, and schedules.

BEACHES & OTHER NATURAL ATTRACTIONS
Boca del Drago Beach & Swan's Cay ★★

Boca del Drago is the best beach on Isla Colón for swimming, and when the sea is calm visitors can snorkel from the shore. However, often there isn't much beach to speak of—just a couple of feet or so for throwing down a towel or beach chair, but it's a lovely spot. The beach is on the north shore of Isla Colón. Tour companies include Boca del Drago as part of their standard day tour, including a visit to nearby **Swan's Cay,** a picturesque rocky outcrop and bird sanctuary that attracts nesting boobies, frigates, and the magnificent red-billed tropic bird. There is no coral reef at Swan's Cay, but the sea-battered rocks are still an interesting place to snorkel. Do not disturb nesting birds by going ashore. You can also get to Boca del Drago from Bocas Town by road in a taxi, which costs $25 round-trip and takes 30 minutes. There is an excellent restaurant here called **Restaurant Yasinori** (see "Where to Stay & Dine around Isla Colón," later in this chapter) that also rents snorkel gear, but I recommend renting gear in Bocas and taking it with you.

Bluff Beach ☞

This gorgeous, golden-sand beach would be perfect if it weren't for a light sprinkling of trash. It's still the prettiest beach close to town for catching some rays—but don't plan on getting more than your feet wet here because the ocean is fraught with riptides. The beach is about 8km (5 miles) from the city center and can be reached by taxi for $10 one-way. Some drivers are willing to hang around if you plan on staying an hour or two; if not, you'll need to arrange for pickup later. In this case, negotiate to pay when the driver returns (to make sure that he comes back). You can also rent a bicycle and pedal there, which is quite a pleasant ride if you're up to it. Rain can wreak havoc on the road, so be prepared for lots of puddles. (Incidentally, taxi drivers often inflate their price when the road calls for a 4WD.) On the way out of town you'll pass by the less-scenic **Punch Beach,** which is popular with surfers. Punch is known for its right and left breaks, reef bottom, and swells that average 1.5 to 1.6m (5–6 ft.).

San San Pond Sak Wetlands ☞☞☞

The San San Pond Sak Wetlands, covering nearly 16,187 hectares (40,000 acres), are located on the coast about 4.8km (3 miles) north of Changuinola. The wetlands are home to sloths, white-faced capuchin monkeys, and caimans, but more importantly, San San is the natural habitat of the manatee, an aquatic, elephant-like mammal that weighs between 363 and 544 kilograms (800 and 1,200 lb.). Previously it was difficult to visit San San, but **Starfleet Scuba** (see "Scuba Diving & Snorkeling," below) now offers a full-day excursion (7am–5pm) that provides for an out-of-the-ordinary experience. Because there is so little human traffic in this region, your chances of spotting a manatee are very good, but please note that manatees are protected animals. Do not chase, pet, or harass these magnificent creatures—and report anyone who does. The Starfleet tour takes visitors to the coast, where they are transported by minibus to the put-in site for the *cayuco* (dug-out canoe) to paddle quietly through the wetlands. There is also an easy nature trail for getting out and stretching your legs. The cost includes a full lunch, park entrance fees, guides, and transportation; contact Starfleet for prices.

FUN IN THE WATER
Scuba Diving & Snorkeling

Scuba diving and snorkeling are among the most popular activities in Bocas del Toro, owing to well-preserved displays of hard and soft coral, mangrove swamps, volcanic-rock walls, underwater caves—and balmy water temperatures that average around 86°F (30°C). Beyond tropical reef fish, divers are privy to larger species such as nurse sharks, spotted eagle rays and southern rays, turtles, and more unusual species such as batfish and toadfish. You might also see colorful sponges, and there is even an underwater landing craft that was sunk to create an artificial reef. Snorkeling and diving sites that are recommended are **Crawl Cay** (or Coral Cay), with shallow waters and some of the best coral formations in the area; **Hospital Point,** just a 10-minute boat ride from Bocas and easy to reach by water taxi; **Polo Beach,** a shallow system of caves suitable for snorkelers but reachable only 6 months of the year; **Swan's Cay,** with interesting rock formations created by battering waves and also a migratory-bird site; and **Cayos Zapatillas,** two delicate islands with white-sand beaches surrounded by an extensive reef system that attracts lots of tropical fish. Cayos Zapatillas, it should be noted, has currents and is for strong swimmers only. Divers also head to **Buoy Line** near Isla Solarte, which is a deep-water channel where pelagic and larger marine species can be seen; the same is true of **Tiger Rock,** an offshore site and rocky outcrop whose long distance from Bocas Town keeps the crowds away. Adventurous divers and snorkelers really looking to get away from other travelers might consider visiting **Isla Escudo de Veraguas,** which is a full-day trip and a fairly large undertaking (available usually only Sept–Oct). The beaches here are generally considered to be the loveliest in the entire region.

The principal shortcoming of Bocas del Toro as a diving and snorkeling destination is the **unpredictability of the weather,** with spontaneous downpours and wind gusts that can churn up the sea and cloud visibility. If the focus of your trip is diving and snorkeling, come from September to early November, when the sea is tranquil and flat. Other months with better visibility are March and April, but rain and wind can occur at any time during these months. Dive sites with deeper water and larger species (mostly offshore sites such as Tiger Rock) can be visited only during these more tranquil months.

There are two top notch scuba diving operations in Bocas, both of which are PADI Gold Palm Instructor Development centers, and thus qualified for scuba certification courses and diver-instructor courses (see "Next Vacation: Pick Up a Skill," below). **Bocas Water Sports** on Main Street (© **757-9541;** www.bocaswatersports.com) is the oldest operation in town, run by an amicable Colombian named Jaime. Dive trips include all gear; a two-dive trip is $50 per person, a one-dive trip $40 per person. Trips last 3 hours and must be taken before 2pm. Dives to Tiger Rock and Cayos Zapatillas are $75 per person and only available during calm months. Night dives from 6:30pm to 8:30pm are $50 per person. Snorkeling tours are $17 to $20 for a full day, not including lunch.

Starfleet Scuba, at Calle 1A (© **757-9630;** www.starfleetscuba.com), has a spotless record and a brand-new British owner who last ran diving operations in Indonesia. Starfleet has three boats plus a new, 50-mph inflatable Zodiac boat that gives the company the edge in terms of more quickly getting to remote destinations like Tiger Rock ($90 for minimum of four people; lunch included). Two-tank dives cost $50, a one-tank dive $35; snorkeling tours are $20 per person. Starfleet works in conjunction with the U.K.-based **Ocean Pulse,** a marine-research group that offers 2-week "eco-ventures" to travelers with advanced diving experience. Participants accompany marine biologists exploring new dive sites to monitor for conservation, and are treated to lectures and presentations about species and habitats throughout the day. Packages vary depending on accommodations requirements, so it's best to contact them for prices (© **0175/220-2101** in the U.K.; www.oceanpulse.co.uk).

Next Vacation: Pick Up a Skill

Take advantage of your trip to Bocas del Toro to learn a new skill. Scuba courses taught in swimming pools may earn you the basic dive certification you need, but it doesn't give you much practical experience in open water. Starfleet Scuba and Bocas Water Sports (see "Scuba Diving & Snorkeling," above) offer well-respected **scuba training academies** for everyone from absolute beginners to divers seeking to brush up—and even for those who want to be certified as instructors. The **Discover Scuba** course is a half-day introduction to scuba diving for $65 to $85 per person; the **Scuba Diver** course is 1½ to 2 days for a partial certification program that allows you to dive up to 12m (39 ft.) with a certified dive master, and costs $185 per person; the **Open Water Course** that is the standard certification program for worldwide independent diving takes 3 to 4 days and costs $210 to $235 per person. Contact the companies for more information about Rescue Diver and Instructor programs.

Stop blaming your rusty Spanish for misunderstandings with locals, and start doing something about it. **Spanish-by-the-Sea language classes,** Calle 4, behind Hotel Bahía (© 757-9518; www.spanishbythesea.com), has inexpensive classes that are as long or intensive as you want them to be. Monolinguists can dive into a Traveler's Spanish crash course that lasts 6 hours and is spread over 2 or 3 days ($40 per person). Weekly programs (5 days only) include private courses at $130 for 2 hours a day, at $250 for 4 hours a day. Minigroup courses cost $85 for 2 hours per day, and $160 for 4 hours per day. Spanish-by-the-Sea also has packages that include lodging in a rustic backpacker hostel that caters to younger adults.

Several companies offer snorkeling trips in addition to the two companies mentioned above. Day trips include equipment; lunch is extra so bring cash for a local restaurant, or bring your own food. **J & J Transparente Boat Tours** offers trips to all the islands, but they're garden-variety. Tours cost $17 to $22 per person, and suffer from a get-em-in and get-em-out mentality. However, J & J is the company to call for charter-boat rentals, which cost $200 for a full day, not including lunch.

Catamaran Sailing Adventures at Main Street (© 757-9710 or 6625-8610; www.bocassailing.com) has a 12m (40-ft.) catamaran for laid-back and enjoyable full-day snorkeling trips to Bocas del Drago or around Isla Bastimentos for $30 per person (4-person minimum, 18 maximum), including a sack lunch. Charter rentals cost $250 a day. The catamaran has little protection from the sun, so bring sunscreen and a hat.

Tip: Ask a lot of questions before embarking on the standard, full-day snorkeling tour that starts in Dolphin Bay and ends at Hospital Point. Boat drivers and guides on these tours practice poor environmental management by racing around a dolphin breeding site, and then they dump guests at an expensive restaurant where they are left to "snorkel" around dead coral and bits of trash. See "What to See & Do" in "Isla Bastimentos," later in this chapter.

Watersports

Bocas Water Sports (see above) offers water-skiing for $45 for 1 hour, gear included, using their 7.6m (25-ft.) tour boat (maximum four people). There are many mangrove-fringed canals in the area that provide for glassy water year-round. Full-day water-skiing trips can be arranged; contact the company for price information. Bocas Water Sports also rents one-person kayaks that cost $3 per hour, or $10 half-day. During bad-weather days, you'll only be able to navigate around mangrove swamps and the coast, but on calm days experienced kayakers can make it all the way to Hospital Point.

Boating & Sailing

For catamaran tours, see **Catamaran Sailing Adventures,** under "Scuba Diving and Snorkeling," above. **Boteros Bocatoreños** (℃ 757-9760; boterosbocas@yahoo.com) is a group of local boatmen who have banded together in the face of encroaching competition—they can provide custom tours at slightly lower prices than outfitters. Most speak at least some English, and have local knowledge. Another good source for local boatmen is **Ancon Expeditions** (see Bocas Inn under "Where to Stay in Bocas Town," below). **Sailing Explore** has a 9.1m (30-ft.) sloop for day-sailing excursions and overnight trips to Boca del Drago, Crawl Cay, and as far as Isla Escudo de Veraguas (Sept–Oct). For overnight trips, the sailboat fits four people (it can fit up to six if you're really willing to squeeze in, or if you have kids), and costs $150 per person for 1 night; $240 per person for 2 nights, including meals, kayaks and snorkeling gear. Day excursions leave at 9am and return at 6pm, costing $30 per person (four-person minimum), which includes lunch, soft drinks, and snorkel and kayak equipment.

Surfing

Bocas experiences the largest and most consistent swells from December to March, and during June and July, with reef point breaks, beach breaks, and huge, challenging waves recommended only for experienced surfers. The waves in Bocas are more suitable for shortboarding and bodyboarding; if you're bringing your own board, check with your airline about requirements because some smaller planes may not accept a long board. **Del Toro Surf** (℃ 6570-8277; deltorosurf@yahoo.com.ar) offers surf lessons and board rentals to clients participating in lessons. **Rancho Paraíso** (℃ 757-9415; www.ranchoparaiso.biz) offers lessons, board rentals, and multiple-day packages with transportation to various surf sites; they also offer all-inclusive packages with stays at their pleasant surf hostel located on the road to Bluff Beach. To rent a surfboard, try **Tropix** (℃ 757-9415), located on Main Street across from the plaza, or **Flow** surf shop (no phone) on Avenida H below the Om Restaurant. All offer tips and maps to the best surf spots in the area, as well as information on how to get there.

OTHER ACTIVITIES IN BOCAS TOWN
Scientific Visits

The **Smithsonian Tropical Research Institute** has a base in Bocas del Toro, and is open to the public every Friday from 3 to 5pm. If you're lucky, you'll be around for one of their monthly chats led by a scientist who highlights the center's work and discoveries in the region. Contact the institute at ℃ 212-8000, or visit their site, www.stri.org, for information about upcoming lectures.

Local Events

The **Fería Internacional del Mar (International Festival of the Sea),** which takes place around the second week of September, is a 5-day event featuring handicrafts booths, food stands serving local cuisine, and exhibits by the Smithsonian Institute and ANAM (the park service), with displays of animals and natural history information. Nightly events include folkloric presentations and dances, all culminating with the crowning of the Sea Fair Queen. Contact the IPAT office for exact dates. The **Fundación de la Provincia de Bocas del Toro (Founding Day of Bocas del Toro)** takes place on November 16, and is celebrated with parades and other events; on November 23, residents of Isla Bastimentos celebrate **Bastimentos Day,** with parades and live music. There is a maypole dance in Bocas and on Isla Bastimentos for **Palo de Mayo,** which takes place on May 1. Lastly, on July 16 is the **Día de la Virgen del Carmen,** which honors the patron saint of Bocas with a parade; the following Sunday hundreds make the pilgrimage across the island to visit the shrine of the virgin at La Gruta.

Spa

If you're winding down from a day of activity (and a hammock isn't doing the trick), try **Spa Flora Bella** (© 6591-3814; www.spaflorabella.com), which offers deep tissue massages, reflexology, and hot-stone treatments, as well as an assortment of beauty services such as hair cuts and facials. The spa is located behind Bubbles Laundry at Calle 4 and Avenida Central. Several massage therapists provide in-hotel services; try **Therapueutic Body Work** at © 6632-6269; **Bocas Delight Massage** at © 6577-9915; or **Holistic Alternative Therapy** at © 6686-0235, which has Zen-Shiatsu massage and Thai foot massages.

WHERE TO STAY IN BOCAS TOWN

You still won't find five-star luxury in Bocas Town. There are several very comfortable, midrange lodging options. However, travelers seeking high-end accommodations will be happier at a lodge such as Tranquilo Bay on Isla Bastimentos (see later in this chapter). Easygoing travelers enjoy the laid-back Caribbean vibe in Bocas Town, and its proximity to restaurants, bars, and shopping, not to mention people-watching and cultural encounters. But loud music and other street noise is a factor, and travelers seeking peaceful isolation will do better lodging elsewhere. Neighboring Isla Carenero is close enough that you can occasionally hear music on particularly loud party nights in Bocas, but it still gives travelers an option for being near Bocas without actually staying in it. Nearly every hotel sits over the water, so try to get a view if you can. The north shore of town is usually breezier, which is a definite plus in the Bocas heat. If a price range is shown, it indicates that a hotel applies high- and low-season rates. Low season is generally mid-April to December.

EXPENSIVE

Hotel El Limbo on the Sea ⊛ This oceanfront hotel, centrally located and near restaurants, tour operators, and water taxis, is virtually identical to the neighboring Hotel Bocas del Toro (see below). Hotel Limbo has the edge, with brighter rooms, but the service here can run from inattentive to unfriendly. Guest rooms are not luxurious, but they are neat as a pin and attractively decorated in nautical style, with cooling blues and whites, polished wood floors, and wood paneling. This is one of the only hotels in town with a bathtub. The best rooms are the two with balconies that overlook the water; they provide particularly relaxing places to have drinks or order meals in, but if you can't get one, take advantage of the Limbo's good restaurant and bar on the first floor.

Calle 1 at Main St. © **757-9062.** www.ellimbo.com. 15 units. $73 double standard; $90 double with balcony and street view; $114 double balcony with sea view. AE, MC, V. **Amenities:** Restaurant; bar; waterfront deck; tour desk; limited room service. *In room:* A/C, TV w/DVD player, minibar, safe.

Tropical Suites *Kids* This newer, condo-style hotel lacks charm but makes up for it with spacious guest rooms with kitchenettes. Considering that Tropical Suites rents by the night, week, and month, this is an ideal place for long-term visitors searching the area for property to buy. Half the guest rooms have sparkling waterfront views and terraces, and are absolutely worth the $35 extra per night, especially considering that other rooms face the street. Guest rooms are like studio apartments in that the kitchenette and bed are in the same room. The kitchenettes are spotless and stocked with all the utensils you'll need for cooking. There is a little less hullabaloo here than down the street, and the waterfront terraces feel more private than at other hotels. A fully stocked dock with a water slide, kayaks, and jet skis is available for guest use, and there's a small bar. The setup is perfect for families, although the fold-out couch is large enough for one child only. Rate discounts are usually offered from June to August, and there are discounts for weekly and monthly rentals. The hotel allows guests to tie their boats at their dock.

Calle 1. © **757-9081**. www.tropical-suites.com. 16 units. $125 island view; $160 sea view. AE, MC, V. **Amenities:** Coin-operated laundry; watersports equipment; dock. *In room:* A/C, TV, kitchenettes. whirlpool. hair dryer.

MODERATE

Bocas Inn I recommend this hotel for its location, accommodating staff, and convenience. Owned and managed by Ancon Expeditions, the hotel operates as a base for the their "Bocas del Toro Adventure," a 2-night, 3-day package including boating to Bocas del Drago, hiking through the tropical forest of Isla Bastimentos National Park, and snorkeling around Hospital Point, but independent travelers can stay a night or two and book excursions a la carte. Bocas Inn is in a Caribbean-style wood building on the waterfront, a short walk from Main Street, and the breeze on this side of town keeps things cool. Rooms are comfortable but very basic—travelers seeking plusher accommodations might consider another hotel. The two best rooms face the water and have ocean views as well as a private veranda with hammocks. Fronting the hotel is a lovely, well-maintained tropical garden, and there is a waterfront deck. The staff here run a tight ship. In general, Ancon conducts responsible, high-quality tours and can tailor excursions to group interest. Rates include a delicious breakfast and the 10% hotel tax.

Av. H at Calle 3. © **757-9600**. www.anconexpeditions.com. $77 double sea view; $66 double garden view. AE, MC, V. **Amenities:** Restaurant; bar; waterfront deck; tours. *In room:* A/C, no phone.

Cocomo-on-the-Sea The Cocomo is a pleasant little hotel tucked away behind a white picket fence and a lush garden, about a 5-minute walk to the central part of town. The hotel sits on the waterfront, and feels cool and fresh even on a muggy day. There are only four rooms, all pretty close to each other but bright and airy; each comes with a double bed and a twin. The bathrooms are clean but small. There is a spacious deck, with hammocks and lounge chairs, which is partially covered in case of rain. The hotel staff are friendly, and the American owner can help you plan any tour in the area—although he's not around very much, so try to grab him when you can. Rate includes a good, hearty breakfast, and they have kayaks for guest use.

Av. Norte at 6A St. ©/fax **757-9259**. www.panamainfo.com/cocomo. 4 units. $70 double. MC, V. **Amenities:** Bar; waterfront deck; kayaks; laundry. *In room:* A/C, no phone.

Hotel Bahía This is Bocas's most historic hotel, located in the old United Fruit Company headquarters. It's a lovely example of Caribbean architecture, with breeze-swept verandas, built in 1905. Vestiges of the building's original purpose remain, such as the front desk's barred windows and an enormous steel safe; and the long hall with polished pine floors is antique splendor. Superior doubles are better than standards because they have been recently renovated. Standard rooms are frumpy and need new paint, but even the renovated rooms could have been designed with a little more eye for style, and in keeping with the history of the building. Nevertheless, the superiors are comfortable and have a lot of amenities. The Hotel Bahía has very friendly service, it should be noted, and a good Italian restaurant. Hotel Bahía is not located on the waterfront, nor does it have ocean views.

South end of Main St. © **757-9626**. www.hotelbahia.biz. 18 units. $60–$66 superior double; $55–$44 standard double. MC, V. **Amenities:** Restaurant. *In room:* A/C, TV, minibar (in superior rooms), safe.

Hotel Bocas del Toro ☙   With its full-service restaurant and dock furnished with lounge chairs, this place is virtually identical to Hotel El Limbo on the Sea. Hotel Bocas del Toro features beautiful wood craftsmanship and a fresh, nautical decor, but some of the standard doubles that do not face the water or the street are dark and small; "premium" rooms have balconies. The third-floor "Luxury Room" is a misnomer, but it is one of the best rooms in town for its ample size, long balcony, and water view; and it has a queen-size and a double bed for up to three guests. If you have a laptop, you'll enjoy the free Wi-Fi service in their restaurant. Like the Limbo, this is not a particularly loud hotel, but a lot of action in the area means it's not whisper-quiet, either.

Calle 1 at Main St. © **757-9018** or 757-9771. www.hotelbocasdeltoro.com. 11 units. $56–$70 double standard; $68–$85 double with street view; $88–$110 room with sea view; $108–$135 luxury room. AE, MC, V. **Amenities:** Restaurant; bar; tour desk; massage; Wi-Fi; dock. *In room:* A/C, TV, safe.

Hotel Laguna ☙   None of the rooms come with views, but this hotel does have comfortable rooms in a pretty white building with gingerbread-carved details and wide awnings. The hotel is centrally located just steps from the plaza, and is the only hotel in Bocas Town with purified tap water, if that matters to you. Guest rooms, paneled entirely in wood and decorated with simple furniture, have orthopedic beds. There is one deluxe suite and one slightly larger apartment with a kitchenette and private balcony for those seeking independence; these units can sleep up to six. The hotel has a popular first-floor restaurant, Da Claudio (see "Where to Dine in Bocas Town," below), which serves one of the best breakfasts in town (not included).

Main St. at Av. D. © 757-9091. www.hotellaguna.net. 15 units. $53–$63 double; $132–$152 suite with kitchenette. AE, MC, V. **Amenities:** Restaurant; bar. *In room:* A/C, TV, kitchenette (2 units only).

Suite Hotel Costes ☙ *Value*   Housed in a converted home on busy Main Street, the newer, Italian/Spanish-owned Suite Hotel Costes has simple rooms with balconies and an interior patio with a surfer-style decor. For the price, the hotel is a good value, mainly because of its in-room amenities. My only caveat is that during busy holidays like Carnaval, when prices jump more than $30 per night, the location is less-than-ideal. Try to get a room in the back or on the second floor, as the bottom floor might put you a little too close for comfort with Main Street; also, ground-level rooms have cement floors while upstairs rooms have lovely wood floors. Guest rooms have been decorated in pastel, folksy paintings rendered by a local artist.

Main St. at the plaza. © **757-9848**. www.suitehotelcostes.com. 7 units. $50 double; $80 double during holidays. MC, V. **Amenities:** Cafeteria. *In room:* A/C, TV, minifridge, safe, no phone.

Swan's Cay Hotel   The Swan's Cay Hotel has a convenient location next to the plaza, a waterfront swimming pool, and a lovingly restored antique lobby decorated

with lots of dark mahogany wood, Persian rugs, and intricate Italian furnishings. The elegance of the common areas, which include a handsome, manicured outdoor patio and carved-wood balconies, certainly gives a promising first impression. But the hotel seems to have run out of steam when it got to the guest rooms. Standard doubles are terribly small and dark, with fluorescent bulbs for lighting. There are junior and regular suites, but in these the decor is worn and fussy, and there's no view. The hotel staff have an offhand way of making you feel more like a nuisance than a welcome guest, lending a certain Fawlty Towers feel to the establishment. Perhaps that is why the hotel never seems full. The aboveground, kid-friendly swimming pool is 2 blocks away from the shore. They also have a full-service restaurant with good local and international dishes.

Calle 3 at Av. E. ℂ 757-9090. www.swanscayhotel.com. 46 units. $77 double standard; $200 suite. AE, MC, V. **Amenities:** Restaurant. *In room:* A/C, TV, minibar (in superior rooms), safe.

INEXPENSIVE

Hotel Casa Max   This Dutch-owned hostel is housed in a Caribbean-style, two-story turquoise wooden building, with a barlike common area spread across the ground floor. On the whole, Casa Max offers good value for low-budget travelers, with tasteful but small rooms that are kept very clean. The service is accommodating and friendly, and they include continental breakfast. The hotel is located on a residential street, close to Main Street, but my only caveat is that Casa Max is in front of the surf bar Mondo Taitu, and light sleepers may be awoken by late-night music.

Av. G. ℂ 757-9120. casamax1@hotmail.com. 11 units. $25 double; $35 triple. No credit cards. *In room:* No phone.

La Veranda ☆   Housed in a lovely, converted home built in 1910, this is one of the best economy hotels in Bocas. It's about a 5-minute walk on a paved road to the main strip, but there's an open-air, communal kitchen if you'd like to cook and dine in. The rooms are simple, with mosquito nets, pastel-colored walls, and polished floors. Rooms with a private bathroom cost $20 more, but they are well worth the investment because they are larger and brighter than room nos. 4 and 5, which share a grubby bathroom. The perk at this hotel is its spacious, pleasant veranda, for which the hotel is named. It's a very relaxing place, giving travelers on a shoestring a place to just sleep, while they do their unwinding elsewhere.

Calle G. ℂ 757-9211. www.laverandapanama.tripod.com. 7 units. $29 double with shared bathroom; $49 double with private bathroom; $10 per extra person. No credit cards. **Amenities:** Communal kitchen. *In room:* A/C (at an additional price), no phone.

Lula's Bed & Breakfast ☆   This American-run B&B fronts the Cocomo-on-the-Sea and is across a dirt street from the waterfront, about a 5-minute walk to town. The B&B offers simple, squeaky-clean guest rooms notable for their polished wood floors and wall paneling. The most appealing aspect of Lula's is its "Turtle Deck" balcony, which receives cool breezes—try to get a room that opens onto the balcony (both triples do). In general, guest rooms are on the small side, but not so small as to seem cramped, and the friendly service here makes guests feel at home. The owner grew up in Bocas and can provide in-depth information and excursion-planning information about the area. A continental breakfast is included in the price.

Av. H at Calle 6. ℂ 757-9057. www.lulabb.com. 6 units. $42 double; $47 triple. No credit cards. *In room:* A/C, no phone.

WHERE TO DINE IN BOCAS TOWN

Believe it or not, tiny Bocas is home to one of the few gourmet supermarkets in the country, **Super Gourmet** (ℂ 757-9357; Mon–Sat 9am–7pm), with imported foods, vegetarian and organic products, and very expensive produce. Super Gourmet, which has a full-service delicatessen, is located next to the Hotel Bahía on the south end of Main Street. You'll find good coffee drinks and lots of reading material at **Starfish Coffee** on Main Street next to El Encanto bar, and good breakfasts on a waterfront dock at the **Coffee Bar** inside Hotel El Limbo on the Sea (see "Where to Stay in Bocas Town," above). For cheap, gringo-style fast food, try **McDouglas' Golden Grill** (daily 7:30am–11pm) on Main Street across from the plaza. For pizzas, you can't beat **Alberto's Pizzas** (© 756-9066; Mon–Sat 11am–3pm and 5–11pm), made fresh to order by an Italian who knows his stuff. It's located on Calle 5 at Avenida F, but the building was for sale at press time.

EXPENSIVE

La Ballena 🕵🕵 (Finds) ITALIAN   This cozy little Italian bistro is also western Panama's only wine bar, and an anomaly considering its rum-and-beer Caribbean surroundings. Where else can you eat homemade Italian food, drink Bulgarian wine, listen to Serge Gainsbourg, and chat with a Panamanian waiter? Inside the dining area, hundreds of bottles of imported wines are for sale and on display, lining the walls and stacked on shelves and barrels. Considering the dearth of good wine in Bocas, stepping into La Ballena is much like stepping into a pirate's cache of stolen loot. The ambience is warm, with wooden tables, soft light, and decor that is tastefully kitschy. The Italian owners dote over their cuisine, using only the freshest ingredients and homemade pastas—but prices are high here. For a light meal, try a Gorgonzola thin-crust pizza or bruschetta, or their delicious shellfish pasta.

Av. E (in front of the Municipal Building). © 757-9089. Reservations not accepted. Main courses $12–$25; pastas $6–$22. AE, MC, V. Mon–Sat noon–2pm and 6pm–midnight; Sun 6pm–midnight.

MODERATE

El Pecado de Sabor 🕵 INTERNATIONAL   Occupying the second floor of a somewhat run-down, converted house, El Pecado de Sabor serves Thai, Mexican, Lebanese, and Panamanian food. It is a favorite with locals and travelers with a more sophisticated palate. It sounds like fusion-confusion, but the food comes together well despite its wide-ranging influences. Main courses are mostly seafood such as grilled tuna, snapper, sea bass, and jumbo shrimp served in sauces such as coconut-curry or spicy garlic, and their Thai soup is highly recommended. Light reggae music sets a funky mood, and the staff couldn't be friendlier. But most dining takes place on a balcony that sags so dramatically it feels ready to collapse. It's a little unsettling, and the extra-strength cocktails don't help much.

Main St. (at the plaza). © 6597-0296. Reservations accepted. Main courses $9–$17. MC, V. Tues–Sat 5–10pm.

Lemongrass 🕵🕵🕵 ASIAN   A welcome new addition to the Bocas scene, Lemongrass fills the bill both in terms of innovative, delicious cuisine and waterfront view. Located above the Starfleet Scuba shop, Lemongrass is the brainchild of expat Mike Thompson, who earned his stripes working in restaurants in Thailand and Indonesia. The menu focuses on Asian cuisine using local ingredients as inspiration. Spicy crab cakes, Thai tacos with red-curry chicken, and fresh trout glazed in chile and ginger are a few mouthwatering items on the menu. Lemongrass is the only restaurant with an elevated waterfront view—really the best view of any restaurant in town—and there is a comfy lounge area, occasional live music, and very friendly service.

Calle 1 at Calle 2. © 757-9630. Reservations accepted. Main courses $5–$12 lunch, $10–$17 dinner. MC, V. Fri–Wed noon–midnight for drinks, noon–3pm for lunch, and 6–10pm for dinner.

Om Café 🐟🐟 INDIAN   The welcoming feeling of this eatery, coupled with the mellow vibe that runs throughout, is pure Bocas. The restaurant is located on the second floor, with an open-air dining area and street-facing balcony for watching the world go by. Om Café serves delicious and healthy Indian cuisine such as tandoori chicken, and a host of vegetarian dishes. The restaurant is closed for lunch, but not for breakfast—and this is where the restaurant really shines, serving strong coffee, waffles, fruit pancakes, and Indian-style dishes like eggs Vindaloo. They also serve refreshing fruit juices and yogurt shakes. If you're looking for something a little stronger, Om Café has a nightly martini bar and a "ladies' night" every Tuesday with reduced drink prices for women.

Av. E at Calle 2. © 6587-6757. Main courses $5–$9. No credit cards. Thurs–Tues 8am–noon and 5:30–10pm.

INEXPENSIVE

Buena Vista Grill 🐟 AMERICAN   For more than 10 years Buena Vista has been serving casual, North American fare to homesick expats and travelers seeking food with which they are familiar. On the lengthy menu you'll find Philly cheese steaks, hot Reuben and BLT sandwiches, and arguably the best hamburger in town. Heartier appetites can dig into a surf-and-turf platter of filet mignon and garlic shrimp, or snack on a variety of appetizers such as nachos or fried calamari. With a happy hour from 5 to 7pm, some come to "waste away in Margaritaville." Food is served throughout the day, but dinner only after 5pm.

Calle 1 at Calle 2. © 757-9035. Main courses $8–$14; sandwiches $5–$6. MC, V. Wed–Mon noon–9:30pm.

Da Claudio 🐟 ITALIAN   This restaurant offers mostly Italian fare such as thin-crust pizzas and hearty pastas, with tempting Bocas-style specials like grilled seafood and meats, and a few German dishes. The location of the eatery on the terrace patio of the first floor of the Laguna Hotel, about a half-block from the main plaza, makes this restaurant the best spot for people-watching. Da Claudio also offers excellent, hearty breakfasts and an occasional all-you-can-eat brunch for about $5.

Main St. at Av. D. © 757-9091. Main courses $5–$15. AE, MC, V. Daily 7am–noon and 1:30–10:30pm.

Pargo Rojo 🐟 GREEK/INTERNATIONAL   You can't do better for sit-down lunch or breakfast than Pargo Rojo. It's where you go when you feel like kicking back rather than rushing off on another excursion. The restaurant is in an antique wooden building with an open-air dining room, lofty ceilings, and a soothing north-shore breeze. It's casual, with plastic furniture and colorfully painted walls. Bernard, the Iranian immigrant who owns Pargo Rojo, serves up mostly American, Greek, and Thai food that is hearty yet not heavy. The menu features chicken wraps, blue-cheese burgers, pizzas, and salads, and creative takes on meats and seafood for hungrier diners; breakfast, too, is very good. The staff here are very amicable, but service is slower than on Monday.

Corner of Calle 3 and Av. H. © 757-9035. Reservations not accepted. Main courses $7–$13. No credit cards. Daily 7am–10pm.

Reef   PANAMANIAN   The Reef is a local dive serving ultra-fresh Panamanian seafood in a rough-and-tumble, saltwater ambience. You can't get any closer to the waterfront than at a table at the Reef—one false move and you'll tumble into the sea. The Reef serves home-style cooking, mostly seafood with the usual choice of garlic, creole-style, or fried, with rice, beans, and *patacones*. These dishes are simple yet pleasing, but stay away from their bland sandwiches. I like the Reef for its seafaring Panamanian flavor; here in Bocas, it just feels right.

Main St. on the south end of town. No phone. Main courses $4–$10. No credit cards. Daily 7am–11pm.

Shelley's BBQ ⚓ MEXICAN ROTISSERIE   This is definitely a hole in the wall, but a delicious one at that. Shelley's serves slow-cooked barbecue beef, chicken, and baby back ribs by the pound ($8), or as a meal with rice, beans, and salad. More popular are Shelley's outstanding tacos and quesadillas; at dinner they offer Mexican specialties such as chicken mole and *enchiladas verdes*. There isn't much to this place, just a walk-up ordering counter and a few bar-stool tables, making this the best spot for a quick but filling meal. Shelley's also sells food to go.

Corner of Calle 4 and Av. D. ☏ 757-9779. Main courses $8–$10; taco meals $4–$7. No credit cards. Mon–Sat 10am–10pm.

WHERE TO STAY & DINE AROUND ISLA COLON
EXPENSIVE
Punta Caracol ⚓   Playa Caracol is a string of stylish, thatched-roofed bungalows that gently curve across a sky-blue Caribbean Sea. Travel magazines wax poetic about Punta Caracol as the resort that vacation dreams are made of, and one look at their website and you'll hardly disagree. But really, the resort doesn't live up to its potential, especially when you consider the price. The owner should be applauded for his eco-friendly concept of architecture that treads lightly on the environment (using solar panels for light, for example). The nine tropical-chic bungalows are painted in cheery lime and yellow, and fitted with elegant furnishings and French doors that open onto a veranda overlooking the blue sea. The big perk, then, is that you can swim and snorkel just outside your door. During sunny, calm days, there's no better hangout spot than the chaise longue or hammock on the veranda, where the water laps at your feet. A walkway leads to an enormous, open-air restaurant where guests dine, by candlelight, on white linen tablecloths. But where Playa Caracol fails is with its staff, who are poorly trained and unenthusiastic. The tour desk is disorganized and not able to clearly describe excursions, which come at an additional cost (meals are included, however). Considering that there is no beach here and nowhere else to walk to, a sense of claustrophobia can set in, so good day excursions are a must. A 15-minute water taxi to Bocas is $20, meaning guests are stuck dining on truly mediocre cuisine at the lodge. It can get stuffy in the cabins on steamy hot nights, and in inclement weather, rain and heavy winds can batter the bungalows and make the walk to the restaurant a slippery adventure for older, less-agile guests.

Punta Caracol is a romantic getaway that is best-suited for honeymooners or any couple that wants to be cooped up in their own bungalow paradise—for about 2 days. That said, this is the most upscale lodging on Isla Colón. Five of the cabins are the same size, while one cabin is twice the size of the others and suitable for families (although the resort doesn't accept children under 14). There are also two Luna Suites that are more expensive only because of their additional front terrace. Rates include lodging, breakfast, dinner, and round-trip transportation from Bocas.

15 min. by boat from town. ☏ 6612-1088 or 6676-7186. www.puntacaracol.com.pa. 9 units. $265–$325 per person, double occupancy. AE, MC, V. **Amenities:** Restaurant; bar; tour desk. *In room:* Snorkeling equipment, ceiling fan, raincoats, umbrellas, 12-volt electrical power, no phone.

INEXPENSIVE
Punta Manglar ⚓   Located around the bend of a mangrove forest about a 5-minute boat ride south from town, Punta Manglar is suitable for those who want to be close to Bocas but spend the night in peaceful isolation. The hotel is a series of *cabaña*-style units perched on stilts that are linked together by a wooden walkway,

meaning you can swim and snorkel just outside your door. Beyond this, there is really nowhere to walk to except their restaurant, which serves simple but good meals. There are three stand-alone cabins and two adjoined by a thin wall; all are rustic, and only one unit has air-conditioning—the rest have ceiling fans. Bugs love mangroves, so bring repellent. Also, you must pay for a water taxi for service outside their scheduled hours. Snorkeling equipment is included in the price. Punta Manglar is owned by Bocas Water Sports, and they use this property in conjunction with their scuba and excursions packages.

5-min. boat ride from Bocas Town. ℂ 757-9541. www.puntamanglar.com. 5 units. $45 double; $10 per extra person. MC, V. **Amenities:** Restaurant; snorkeling equipment; tours. *In room:* A/C (in 1 unit), no phone.

Restaurant Yasinori 🎄🎄 PANAMANIAN   This thatched-roof restaurant serves some of the best Panamanian and creole cuisine on the island, as well as fresh-from-the-boat seafood. Choose from red snapper, dorado, jumbo shrimp, octopus, and crab, and have it your way either grilled or with a garlicky sauce, slightly sweet oyster sauce, or onions and tomatoes. They also serve grilled chicken, vegetarian plates, and sandwiches. All meals come with coconut rice, coleslaw, and fried plantains. Don't miss the passion fruit *(maracuyá)* juice, or any of their fresh fruit juices. The open-air ambience goes well with the Caribbean Sea setting.

Bocas del Drago. No phone. Main courses $5–$16. No credit cards. Daily 8am–7pm.

NIGHTLIFE

Bocas Town is Party Central for the archipelago, but there are plenty of low-key venues for a quiet drink, and the town's laid-back, friendly atmosphere creates an environment that encourages meeting fellow travelers and locals. Nearly every bar and restaurant offers happy hour for 2 hours, generally sometime between 4 and 8pm, with beer priced as low as 50¢. **Iguana Bar and Surf Club,** on Calle 1, is the best all-around bar, with a cool surfer theme and a wood-hewn, comfy ambience that's good for conversation and suitable for all ages, though late in the evening the party can pick up. **Buena Vista** is the old-school expat hangout, with a long wooden bar, lapping seafront and decent cocktails. (See "Where to Dine in Bocas Town," above.) The open-air waterfront bar **Barco Hundido (Shipwreck Bar),** on Calle 1, is the all-out party zone with late nights and dancing that culminate with one or two drunk guys jumping into the water on a dare. The bar often has live DJs or bands with a cover charge. **Mondo Taitu,** on Avenida G, caters to 20-something surfers and backpackers, and has cheap drinks and good music late into the night. The awful-sounding **Blue Nasty Mermaid,** on Main Street at Avenida A, has a happy hour from 4 to 6pm and, to keep you going, another from 10 to 11pm; they also have open-mic nights and a sand-floor seating area over the water.

SHOPPING

High-quality handicrafts and fashionable beachwear can be found at **Pachamana,** located on Main Street on the waterfront next to Starfish Coffee at Avenida B (Tues–Sat 9am–12:30pm and 3–6pm). **Artesanía Bri-Bri Emanuel,** at Main Street and Avenida B (Mon–Sat 10am–8pm), specializes in indigenous handicrafts from around Panama. A varied and ultra-cool selection of beachwear, flip-flops, and surf gear can be found at **Flow** (daily 10am–5pm) at Avenue H, below the Om restaurant. You'll find a good selection of handicrafts, including Kuna Indian-made *molas,* at the compact **open-air market** at the end of Main Street and Avenida H.

2 Isla Carenero (Careening Cay)

Isla Carenero practically adjoins Isla Colón, and is about a 2-minute water-taxi ride away. It is a more tranquil location to spend the night than Bocas, meaning you can be close to the action, but get away from it when you choose. Water-taxi service only runs until about 9pm, unless you arrange transportation ahead of time (and even then, taxis aren't enthusiastic about providing service past 10:30pm or so). There are no roads on the island, and it is technically possible to walk around Isla Carenero, though the narrow beach disappears at points and a meandering stroll can become more of a hike across rocks and up and down a few muddy slopes. There are a few hotels and restaurants here, but most of the structures are the very modest homes of local Bocatorinos. Everything on the island is located on the waterfront, but only the hotels on the island's east side face a strip of beach (that, little by little, is disappearing). *Chitras,* those no-see-ums that bite like mad, are common on the island, so come armed with repellent.

WHERE TO STAY & DINE

Careening Cay *&&*   The friendly, welcoming American owners who purchased this small complex in 2005 have put an extraordinary amount of thought into building their vision of a "magical botanical paradise," offering bountiful amenities, personalized service, and cabins surrounded by lush, orchid-studded landscaping and whizzing hummingbirds. Butterflies are the theme here: There are ceramic butterflies inlaid in the walkways, the shop sells mostly butterfly jewelry and crafts, and there's even a butterfly farm in the works. Careening Cay has four fully equipped wood cabins with stocked kitchens, and two bedrooms with a double bed and bunks. The property's centerpiece is a massive, thatched-hut common area that serves snacks and drinks to guests. There's also Careening Cay's new **Cosmic Crab Café,** which you'll want to try even if you don't stay here; set on the waterfront, the Cosmic Crab serves tasty, gringo-style food—snapper with papaya salsa, savory pork meatloaf, and tequila lime shrimp—as well as froufrou cocktails like a frozen red passion. The resort can arrange a private water taxi for groups who feel like lingering a little late after dinner, when normal taxi service comes to a halt. The cabins feel tucked away, but the traffic coming in and out of the restaurant wakes the resort up from its sleepy pace. This is one of the few resorts in Bocas with a sunset view.

Isla Carenero. ⓒ 757-9157. www.careeningcay.com. $100 small cabin (1-room cabin for 2 guests); $125 large cabin for up to 6. MC, V. **Amenities:** Restaurant; bar; sports equipment; gift shop; Wi-Fi; laundry service. *In room:* A/C, kitchen, no phone.

Casa Acuario *&* *Value*   This four-room, baby-blue-colored hotel features "suites over the sea," and in fact the entire property is propped on stilts over water. This is not a secluded hideaway—the oceanfront location feels more exposed than it does at most hotels—but, on the flip side, the guest rooms are huge, like small apartments without a kitchen. (They'll let you use their kitchen.) One step outside your door and you're on a wooden veranda where you can sway in a hammock as you look out at the ocean (and Isla Colón). The owners are American, but the architectural style of the building is pure Caribbean—clapboard walls and carved wooden details. There's no store around, so you'll need to stock up on supplies or take a water taxi in to Bocas for meals.

Isla Carenero. ⓒ 757-9565. www.bocas.com/casa-acuario.htm. $65 double Apr–Aug; $75 double rest of year. No credit cards. **Amenities:** Communal kitchen; waterfront deck. *In room:* A/C, TV, no phone.

Hotel Doña Mara ✐   There's nothing fancy about this Panamanian-owned hotel, but it does front a small beach fringed with palms, and there are lounge chairs and an old dock for sunbathing. The motel-like rooms, centered around a tiny courtyard, are spartan, with tile floors, a bed, a minifridge, and not much more. You might be able to look beyond the lack of amenities, though, considering the great location of the hotel. **Doña Mara Restaurant,** open to the public, specializes in local Panamanian dishes; they also serve tacos and hamburgers, plus a few vegetarian items. On Sundays they hold a special barbecue that draws hungry diners over from Isla Colón. The restaurant is a simple little place, but I recommend it because it has a Caribbean flavor lacking in most Bocas restaurants, and it's a good change to look out over a beach rather than a dock with a string of boats whizzing by. Main courses and sandwiches cost $5.50 to $12. Hotel rates include a continental breakfast and the 10% tax.

Isla Carenero. ✆ 757-9551. www.bocas.com/donamara. 6 units. $55 double. MC, V. **Amenities:** Restaurant; bar; Internet access; Ping-Pong table; beach and dock. *In room:* A/C, TV, minifridge, no phone.

Tierra Verde ✐   Tucked away behind a stand of tall palms on the eastern side of the island, Tierra Verde is owned by two Panamanian surfers, Cookie and Ivan, who can organize surf expeditions for guests. It's a tremendously pleasant location, and there is a small beach fronting the property, but Tierra Verde is more guesthouse than hotel, and nothing is close enough that it doesn't require a water taxi—so bring supplies. The hotel interior is attractively paneled in tropical woods, but guest rooms are tiny and dark, and offer no views, except for the suite, which has a wraparound terrace. The room size, coupled with the isolation of the hotel, means that the quality of your stay could be influenced by other guests lodging at the same time. There is a cheery lobby with an Internet desk, a communal television, and a beverage bar. Service is very informal but friendly, and they can put together any kind of tour. Rates include a light breakfast.

Isla Carenero. ✆ 757-9903. www.hoteltierraverde.com. 7 units. $50–$65 double; $150 suite. No credit cards. **Amenities:** Beverage bar; shared TV room; Internet; tour planning. *In room:* A/C, no phone.

3 Isla Bastimentos

Isla Bastimentos is the second-largest island in the archipelago, and it is one of the region's most popular destinations for its outstanding snorkeling and diving. It is also home to **Isla Bastimentos National Marine Park,** a boomerang-shaped park that protects a species-rich tropical jungle, pristine coral formations, and two tiny Robinson Crusoe–style islands ringed with powdery white sand. There are also a few highly recommended lodges here that put travelers far away from the hustle and bustle of Bocas Town, and closer to the aforementioned attractions.

Taking the island as a whole, Isla Bastimentos is a curious microcosm of ethnicities and income levels, of pristine landscapes and overdeveloped hamlets. There is one town here, the second largest in the Bocas Archipelago, called **Bastimentos Town.** Locals often refer to the town as Old Bank, and it can be found on the western tip of the island, about a 15-minute boat ride from Bocas Town. The community of 200 is principally Afro-Caribbean (many prefer to be called *creole*) descendants from the banana plantation days. It's a little like Jamaica in the 1950s, and the poverty here can be equally heartbreaking and frightening: a collapsed pier, piles of garbage, women playing cards, men drinking beer or lurking about. The official industry here is tourism, but you'd have to be an adventurous soul to brave spending a night here, or even visiting the town's restaurant **Roots** (✆ 6662-1442) for its popular "Blue Mondays" night with cold beer and reggae music. Still, Bocas residents consider Roots *the* local restaurant in the area, for its Caribbean vibe and inexpensive creole food, arguably the best creole food in the Bocas area. **Wizard Beach,** also called First Beach, is a popular surf spot for beginners for its smaller waves and absence of rocks; it can be reached by landing in Bastimentos Town and following a short path, but beware of youths who skulk at the path's entrance, demanding bribes to pass. The beach can also be reached by walking west from **Playa Segunda,** or Second Beach. A little farther east from Bastimentos Town is the shortcut to the popular and gorgeous **Red Frog Beach,** home of the controversial new Red Frog Beach Club, a luxury resort development whose two-bedroom homes sell for more than half a million dollars. The development is slated for completion in 2007, and promises to forever alter what ranks as Bocas's most beautiful beach (see below). Both Playa Segunda and Wizard Beach can be reached by walking from Red Frog Beach.

Beyond Afro-Caribbeans and wealthy foreigners, the island is also home to the Ngöbe-Buglé indigenous group, who live in two tiny communities in **Bahía Honda** and **Salt Creek Village,** the latter located on the southeastern shore and consisting of a cluster of thatched-roof huts, a small school, and a store.

WHAT TO SEE & DO
PARQUE NACIONAL MARINO ISLA BASTIMENTOS
A do-not-miss highlight in Bocas del Toro, this national park is an irregularly shaped swath of virgin tropical forest, pristine coral reef, and two white-sand islands called **Cayos Zapatillas,** or "Little Shoes Cays" (so-named for their resemblance to two footprints). There is no development here save a small park-service hut and a ranger who may or may not charge the $10 per-person entry fee to walk on the islands. The more westerly island has an easy nature path called the "forest behind the reef," and is a worthwhile short jaunt.

The national park covers 12,950 hectares (32,000 acres), more than ¾ of which is marine park with a complex and diverse array of underwater life that makes an outstanding site for snorkeling and diving. Expect to see healthy brain, lettuce, and Elkhorn coral; tropical reef fish such as parrotfish and angelfish; and, in deeper water, spotted eagle rays. The wealth of coral species, fish, and marine invertebrates makes this one of the most extraordinary national parks in Panama. The park is also home to the largest concentration of mangrove swamp on the Caribbean coast. *Note:* When the sea is choppy, swimming and snorkeling here require extra work, and visibility is poor.

On land, the national park protects a portion of the island's dense tropical rainforest and endangered and threatened reptile species such as the Jurassic-era leatherback turtles and hawksbill turtles, which nest along with three other turtle species on **Playa Larga** *ᏔᏔ*, a 5.6km-long (3½-mile) beach on the northern shore. The trail to this beach is one of the unsung excursions in Bocas del Toro, starting in the indigenous village **Salt Creek,** at Old Point, continuing through thick steamy jungle, and ending on a beach with (usually) no one else around. Along the way you might see sloths or white-faced capuchin monkeys, and view many of the island's 68 species of birds. The trail is moderate, with undulations that can be difficult in some areas, requiring hands and shoes sturdier than sandals. Most tour operators offer this trek in conjunction with a visit to Salt Creek; or the village can be visited in conjunction with Zapatilla Cays; also contact **Ancon Expeditions** (p. 62).

Quebrada de Sal, or Salt Creek, is a village community of Ngöbe-Buglé Indians who no longer practice many of their traditions—even the women here no longer wear the billowy, colorful dresses they are known for. Apart from a few cement build-ings, a collection of thatched-roof huts, and a tiny souvenir shop, there isn't much to see here—but combined with the enjoyable boat ride and hike to Playa Larga, this is a pleasant full-day trip if coming from Bocas Town. Visitors are charged $1 to enter.

BEACHES

The loveliest beaches in Bocas del Toro can be found here at Isla Bastimentos and at the Cayos Zapatillas on the eastern tip (part of the national park; see above). Island beaches here play a critical role as the nesting sites for four of Panama's five kinds of marine turtles. From late August to October, when calmer weather prevails, visitors can get to Isla Bastimentos's beaches by taking a boat directly at the shore; the rest of the year you'll have to walk. The easiest beach to reach is **Red Frog Beach,** a heavenly stretch of white sand, arching palms, and turquoise water—but be aware that riptides are treacherous here. The beach gets its name from a strawberry-colored poison frog that inhabits the surrounding forest. The frog is the size of a fingernail and can be dif-ficult to spot; focus your search near trees and around loose leaves, and you'll find one. Standard tours include Red Frog Beach as part of their day tour, but a water taxi can get you here for about $8 (20 min. from Bocas Town). Visitors get off in Magic Bay, pay a $1 entrance fee, and continue along an easy path for 5 minutes. There is a rus-tic bar with soft drinks, beer, and snacks. Continue west along the shore (if you can) to arrive at **Wizard Beach,** sometimes referred to as First Beach. A trail leads from Wizard Beach to Bastimentos Town.

CRAWL CAY

Crawl Cay, alternatively called Coral Cay, is located on the southern tip of Isla Basti-mentos, about 30 minutes from Bocas Town. The area is known for shallow, translu-cent waters and an enormous garden of soft and hard coral, offering excellent snorkeling and diving. The **Crawl Cay Restaurant** is here too, making this one of the most pop-ular excursions in Bocas del Toro. The restaurant, a collection of thatched huts over water, serves Panamanian-style seafood including crab, snapper, and shrimp ($8–$15 for a main course). Orders must be placed a full 1 to 2 hours ahead of time, so don't come hungry, or at least bring a snack to tide you over. Some unscrupulous tour com-panies save on gas by dumping guests here to snorkel around the restaurant—insist that they take you out to the actual reef and then back for lunch.

BAHIA HONDA COMMUNITY & NIVIDA BAT CAVES 🐾🐾

A visit to the Nivida Bat Cave in the Bahía Honda ranks as one of the most enjoyable, even spooky (but in a fun way) half-day tours in Bocas. After a 20-minute ride to Bahía Honda, visitors travel by motorized boat up a jungle-shrouded channel that provides excellent opportunities to see sloths hanging from tree branches and the occa-sional caiman silently resting in shallow water. Visitors walk through an old cacao farm, then don hard hats and rubber boots and enter a subterranean river cave that is home to hundreds of tiny fruit bats. The journey is an impressive, Indiana Jones–style adventure, though not for the ultra-squeamish; tours normally end with a visit to the Bahía Honda Ngöbe-Buglé indigenous community for a typical—and quite deli-cious—lunch. The community comprises 20 indigenous families living in homesteads around the bay, with a small "village" center located on the lee side of Bastimentos Island. Here Ngöbe-Buglé women demonstrate their process of weaving traditional bags, and have many on hand for sale. These tours are run by local operators; contact

The Jungle Lodge (see "Where to Stay and Dine," below), which can plan a trip. Spanish-speaking **Rutilio Milton** (© **6669-6269**) offers tours, or try **Oscar's Bat Cave Tours** (© **6515-9276**). Tours cost about $25 per person, and you'll need to make a reservation at least a day or more in advance for lunch at the community.

WHERE TO STAY & DINE

If you're the kind of traveler who'd rather get away from it all, consider basing yourself out of Isla Bastimentos. The region's best lodges are concentrated here, and a few (Casa Cayuco, El Limbo on the Beach, and Au Natural) front the tranquil waters of the island's eastern shores, providing good swimming conditions year-round and a safe place for families with kids. Because of the distance from Bocas Town, meals are included as part of a package. It can take from 45 minutes to an hour by boat to reach lodges here on Bastimentos. There are no stores here, so bring any necessities with you.

Al Natural ☞ This laid-back resort lives up to its name with open-air, thatched-roof bungalows that blend into the surrounding jungle, while providing beach-level views of the sparkling Caribbean Sea. The setting is lovely and remote, and the concept is well-conceived; however, the price is a little steep for a such rustic accommodations, all of which could use a new coat of shellac. This is not to say that the rooms are uncomfortable—on the contrary, there are hot showers, comfortable mattresses on platforms, and mosquito nets, as well as custom-made furniture and woodwork. Showers are inside each room, and flush toilets are just outside. The owners, who hail from Belgium, are also the hosts, and are very amicable and really charming. But service can be a little lackadaisical. The resort fronts a beach with a tranquil sea year-round, and there is a short trail leading through the jungle and to another beach. There is a dock, game room, and probably the only Ping-Pong table on Isla Bastimentos. The food is mostly seafood, and usually the owners receive kudos for their innovative cuisine. Honeymooners, young adults who are just past their backpacking prime, and easygoing travelers will be happiest here. The difference between the Natural House and the Natural House Deluxe is an additional bed and a ceiling fan; the deluxe is by far the nicest of the bungalows here. Note that Al Natural is closed from May until July 15.

The Al Natural Package includes three meals per day (and wine with dinner), lodging, round-trip transportation, and use of sports equipment; or book their "All Inclusive" package that includes one full-day excursion per day to Zapatilla Cay, fishing, snorkeling, and more. If you stay 7 nights, the final night is free. High-season rates (Dec 1–Apr 30) are shown below; for low-season rates subtract $10 per person for the Deluxe bungalow, and $5 for the Al Natural. Bring beach towels and a flashlight, and any other goodies you can't live without.

Isla Bastimentos. © **757-9004** or 6576-8605. www.bocas.com/alnatura.htm. 5 units. Packages are per person, based on double occupancy: Al Natural Package $95–$120 first night, $70–$95 thereafter; All-Inclusive Package $120 Al Natural, and $145 Deluxe. No credit cards. **Amenities:** Meals; sports equipment; tours; Ping-Pong; games. *In room:* Ceiling fan (deluxe only), no phone.

Casa Cayuco ☞☞ *Kids* This is the newest lodge on Isla Bastimentos, and it is the most kid-friendly due to its tranquil beach, its fun jungle-style lodge, and other features such as a forest trail that meanders past a small lagoon with a "pet" caiman. The lodge is geared toward groups and retreats, but they'll accept independent travelers booking on their own. Their two-story lodge feels very "Swiss Family Robinson," with high ceilings supported by log beams and not much else. The entire lodge is open-air, including the showers, but there are canvas drapes for shutting out the rain, and they also offer three cabins that are entirely enclosed (each fits a total of four people). This is best called an "adventure lodge," not a luxury villa, yet special courses such as yoga retreats and elegant craftsmanship render the lodge a step above "rustic." A trail leads from the lodge to the other side of the peninsula and another beach, but the waves are stronger there, and better swimming can be found right in front of the lodge. The American owners of Casa Cayuco are outdoor enthusiasts and certified guides (owner Tom is a certified scuba instructor and former Outward Bound instructor), and they plan unique excursions in the area such as white-water kayaking and trips to beaches on Isla Escudo de Veraguas. Rates are all-inclusive, with meals, transportation, lodging, excursions, and even transportation and a night's lodging in Panama City. The resort typically books 7-night stays, but if they have space they'll accept a minimum 3-night stay.

Isla Bastimentos. ℂ 509-996-4178. www.casacayuco.com. Packages based on double occupancy cost, per person, $1,195 for 7 nights, $895 for children 5–10; $375 for 3 nights. AE, MC, V (but cash only on premises). **Amenities:** Restaurant; bar; dock; special yoga retreats; tours; sports equipment; Wi-Fi. *In room:* No phone.

Hotel El Limbo on the Beach
This lodge has the best beach on Isla Bastimentos, with clear water (not much sea grass), and a bit of reef for swimming and snorkeling. There's plenty of space to stretch out on a lounge chair and soak up the Caribbean sun. And the free kayaks provided by the hotel are the perfect way to explore the surrounding area. But El Limbo on the Beach suffers from serious mismanagement and overpricing. It's a two-story yellow-and-blue wood building on the shore—not cabins like most properties on Bastimentos. There are six rooms, but only four have ocean views, terraces, and a hammock—and all are the same price. If you reserve a front room, it's a crapshoot as to whether or not your reservation will be honored. The rooms are simply too plain and walls too thin to charge $140 a night for two. (Meals are included but round-trip transportation is $30, and tours are additional.) Extras such as beverages are priced sky-high, so bring your own, and consider booking your own tour independently through another company. Rates are cheaper here if you book through the Internet.

Isla Bastimentos. ℂ 757-9062. www.ellimbo.com. $69 per person, meals included; $30 round-trip transportation to Bocas. AE, MC, V. **Amenities:** Restaurant; sports equipment; beach; tours. *In room:* No phone.

The Jungle Lodge ℜℜℜ *(Finds*
The Jungle Lodge. an idyllic hideaway nestled in thick, tropical forest, is an intimate retreat for travelers who love and are comfortable with nature. It is hands-down one of my favorite lodges in Panama—but I must stress that it is not for everyone. The Jungle Lodge is located on the shore of Bahía Honda, and a short boat ride from the closest beach. The aesthetic is spare yet very stylish, and their 23-hectare (57-acre) property has a screened-in butterfly farm and a creek with natural bathing pools. From the shore, a slatted walkway fringed with aromatic plants leads to an airy pavilion that acts as the lodge's nucleus, with a kitchen, dining area, and library. There are just three thatched-roof *ranchos* (cabins) for two guests each, with hammocks and beds draped in voluminous mosquito nets. The open-air *ranchos* provide a sense of harmony and oneness with the surrounding jungle. At sunset and sunrise, the primal, animated chorus of wildlife that emanates from the jungle canopy is exciting to hear, and if you're lucky you might catch sight of a group of monkeys swinging through the trees. Cabin nos. 2 and 3 are higher up the slope, providing gorgeous, sweeping views, but it's a vigorous hike to reach both. The Jungle Lodge is not

for fussier travelers, or for those who are uncomfortable with the idea of a bird swooping through their bedroom. Two cabins have no electricity. The young hosts, Henry and Margaret, provide a friendly, relaxed environment and are well-versed in the flora, fauna, and culture of Bocas. Their motto is sustainable tourism: buying products from Ngöbe-Buglé Indians and employing them as local guides, and growing their own ingredients on an organic farm for their delicious, gourmet meals (included in the price). There are free activities, but most excursions are an additional cost.

Isla Bastimentos. © **6592-5162** or 6631-5290. www.thejunglelodge.com. $80 per person based on double occupancy. MC, V. **Amenities:** Restaurant; tours; butterfly farm; dugout canoe; surfboard rentals. *In room:* No phone.

Tranquilo Bay ★★★ *(Finds)*   Tranquilo Bay, an elegant and peaceful small resort, is the best option for travelers seeking upscale accommodations on the Bocas Archipelago. Embraced by lush, vibrant jungle and fronted by a thicket of mangrove, this resort is a haven for adventurers who don't believe in giving up creature comforts for a chance to mingle with natural surroundings. The two young couples who own Tranquilo Bay searched Central America before finding their little slice of paradise here, and their satisfaction with Isla Bastimentos shows through their love of discovery and their welcoming spirit. Guests arrive at a dock that pokes through the mangroves, from which a slatted walkway leads to a large principal lodge that houses the dining area, bar, lounge, and library. There are six cabins, two of which are near the lodge and surrounded by vegetation; four can be reached by following a winding path through thick jungle to a clearing high enough to look out onto the sea. The cabin exteriors are pared-down, but inside are very comfortable accommodations in a handsome tropical decor, with orthopedic beds and large bathrooms with ample counter space and hot showers. There are only a few staff members here—Tranquilo Bay is principally run by its owners, who accompany guests on excursions and work like dervishes to make you feel at home. As for excursions, the mantra here is to go where no one else goes, and the owners busy themselves exploring new areas to take guests in the region, including river kayaking on the mainland, snorkeling at remote areas, jungle hikes, and visits to isolated beaches. There is no beach here on the property, but beaches at Zapatillas Cays are a short hop away, and guests can kayak around the mangroves near the resort. Packages include all transportation (in Bocas and in Panama City), meals, drinks, and use of their equipment. The "Close to the Shore" package includes snorkeling, bird-watching, hiking, and kayaking; the "Within the Reef" package includes the aforementioned activities plus activities farther away from the lodge, such as fishing, surfing, and diving.

Isla Bastimentos. © **620-4179**. www.tranquilobay.com. Packages are, per person, based on double occupancy: $1,400–$1,900 7 nights; $930–$1,200 4 nights; $750–$950 3 nights. MC, V. **Amenities:** Restaurant; bar; lounge; library; video and TV room; Wi-Fi; sports equipment; tours. *In room:* A/C, coffeemaker, hair dryer, snack basket, no phone.

4 Isla Solarte

2km (1¼ miles) E of Isla Colón

Isla Solarte, also known as **Nancy's Cay,** is an 1.3-sq.-km (½-sq.-mile) island known for Hospital Point, one of the best areas for snorkeling and close to Isla Colón. Hospital Point is named for an old hospital built by the United Fruit Company to treat plantation workers suffering from yellow fever and malaria. The hospital has since closed, and in its place is a home owned by a local historian named Clyde Stephens, who has written several books about the region and the banana plantation days. Currently an upscale residential community is spreading across the island, attracting foreigners seeking to buy a slice of tropical paradise that is protected by a gate and security services.

5 Isla Cristóbal & Laguna Bocatorito

10km (6¼ miles) S of Isla Colón

Isla Cristóbal is a 37-sq.-km (14-sq.-mile), mostly deforested island south of Isla Colón. The island and a peninsula that juts from the mainland form a nearly enclosed bay called **Laguna Bocatorito,** or Dolphin Bay—so-called for the bottlenose dolphin breeding site found here. It is one of the region's most enjoyable attractions because dolphins swim up close to visiting boats and prance about, much to the delight of visiting travelers. The best time to come is from June to September, when dozens upon dozens of dolphins meet in the bay—creating a wild version of Sea World. For the rest of the year, here's a tip: Try to visit the bay after the morning tour boats do their thing (which amounts to disturbing the dolphins by speeding around in circles in an effort to stir things up and draw the dolphins to the surface), and find a tour or book a custom trip going at a quieter pace. More dolphins show themselves when the bay isn't being churned up. Or better yet, arrange to head out on a kayak rented from the island's only lodge, Hacienda del Toro, which can even provide you with hydrophones to hear what's going on underwater. For tours, see "What to See & Do" under "Isla Colón: Bocas Town," earlier in this chapter.

WHERE TO STAY & DINE

Hacienda del Toro ✹✹ (Kids)   Situated on an old cattle ranch on the verdant shore of Laguna Bocatorito, this newer lodge is a self-styled "Caribbean Dude Ranch," and the only lodge to offer horseback riding among other unique activities. There are three delightful, breezy cabins (containing a total of five rooms) perched high on a couple of plump, grassy hills overlooking the bay. The American owners, Laurie and Neil, are horse trainers from Arizona who settled here in 2004, bringing with them eight quarter horses that they, unbelievably, floated over from the mainland on dugout canoes. You couldn't meet a nicer couple, and they strive to really make their guests feel at home. The cabins are spacious and fresh, in pastel-colored hues and decorated with local art, and they come with feather-soft beds. Each room has a deck that overlooks the bay, and comes with a wide hammock; one cabin has a full kitchen. The main building is an open-air, thatched-roof building used as a dining room and lounge, with a parrot and a toucan usually hopping about on the rafters. Another perk here is this lodge's proximity to the bay and the option to paddle out on a kayak and see bottlenose dolphins—this plus horseback rides make the lodge a kid-pleasing place to stay. (Kids under 10 stay free, too.) Much of the neighboring land is pockmarked with areas of deforestation; however, the owners are letting the area revert to forest, and encouraging their neighbors to do so as well. On a half-day horseback ride, guests will still be able to lope through thick secondary jungle. Rates include breakfast, round-trip transportation from Bocas, and use of kayaks. Excursions, meals, and horseback riding are an additional price. The owners will take guests into town for shopping or a meal for an additional $40, or at no charge if they happen to be heading into town that day.

Isla Cristóbal. ✆ **757-9158** or 6612-9159. www.haciendadeltoro.com. $120 double; extra person $30; free for kids under 10. Deposit required via PayPal, cash only at lodge. **Amenities:** Restaurant; bar; horseback riding tours and lessons; kayaks; tour desk. *In room:* No phone.

10

Comarca Kuna Yala

The Comarca Kuna Yala is a fascinating and primitive region that fulfills every tourist's, yachter's, and cruiser's island fantasy. There are more than 350 picture-postcard islands and islets ringed by powdery white sand, a coral reef, and piercing turquoise water—and most islands are populated with no more than a cluster of coconut palms. Given the pristine beauty of the region, it is *the* premier beach destination in Panama, but what really sets it apart is that it provides you with the opportunity to spend time with the Kuna indigenous group that lives here. The region is formerly known as the San Blas Archipelago, and although many Panamanians continue to use this moniker, it is now officially the Comarca Kuna Yala. The "Kuna Yala" means "Land of the Kuna," and a *comarca* is a semiautonomous province that is governed by three tribal chiefs, or *caciques,* with the input of dozens of regional representatives. As a semiautonomous province, the Kuna have maintained their cultural identity and integrity, and have complete control of economic matters such as tourism. (See "Special Considerations in the San Blas," below.) For example, it is considered improper to travel with an "outside" tour company that has not requested permission from tribal chiefs. Since the colonial period, the Kuna have successfully resisted invasions by pirates, colonists, missionaries, and adventurers—even scientists from the Smithsonian based in the *comarca* were given the boot after the Kuna couldn't establish what their purpose was.

There are an estimated 50,000 Kuna spread across 49 communities in the region, and scattered in areas as far away as Panama City and farther east in the Darién. Of the seven indigenous tribes in Panama, the Kuna Yala are the most visible, not only for their ubiquity but for the kaleidoscopic-colored costumes worn by the women in the tribe. Men wear western clothing, but Kuna women wear skirts and *mola*-appliquéd shirts in yellows and reds, head scarves, a gold ring in their septum, and usually a single black line drawn down the crest of their nose; their arms and legs are bound with tiny beads. The Kuna's livelihood depends on coconut harvesting, fishing, and subsistence farming, and on a very small scale, tourism.

The *comarca* extends well beyond the island region, incorporating the coastal forest on the northern slope of the San Blas Mountain Range. Because it has been allowed to remain untouched, the virgin forest is home to a species diversity not found anywhere else in Panama; if visiting the mainland jungle interests you, you'll need a local guide (your lodge can provide you with one), or you can book a trip with a company such as Xtrop. (See "Adventure-Tour Outfitters & Activities," below.)

LODGING IN THE SAN BLAS ARCHIPELAGO Do not expect to find satellite TV, Internet, widespread telephone service, 24-hour electricity, or even laundry service at lodges and hostels here. This is Panama "unplugged," although

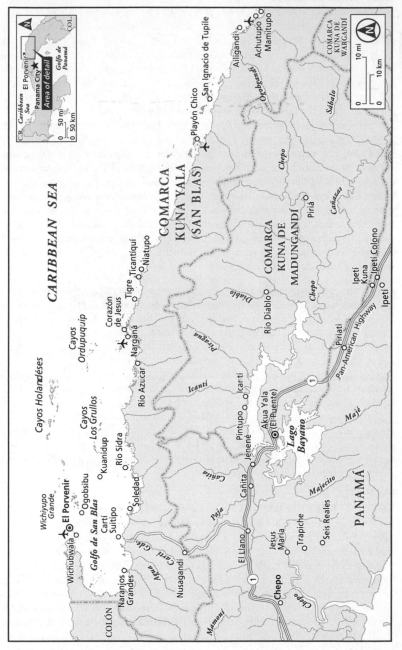

there are two lodges in the eastern side of the *comarca* that provide a few creature comforts to satisfy travelers who do not relish "roughing it." If you're a particularly fussy traveler, you'll want to book with San Blas Sailing Adventures, which has luxury sailboats, or you might want to consider a different beach destination in Panama. Just outside the *comarca's* border, in the Colón Province, is the newly opened **Coral Lodge,** an elegant resort that uses El Porvenir as an arrival base and provides tours to islands within the *comarca.* Some hostels and lodges mentioned in this chapter now have an e-mail address, and some even have websites. E-mails are checked within 2 days; however, you might find it far more convenient to have a travel agency or tour operator book your stay, as

most lodge owners speak little or no English. (See "Adventure-Tour Outfitters & Activities," below.) Also, because credit cards are not accepted in the region, you can charge your stay if booking with a tour operator or agency. It is highly recommended that you book ahead of time to secure a room or *cabaña,* and also to verify that a boat will be waiting at the airport dock to get you there. Spontaneous travelers who just show up will have better luck finding lodging in the El Porvenir area. All prices shown are per person, per night, and are **all-inclusive,** meaning three meals a day and local tours and transportation. Most hostels have Spanish-only guides, or you can go with a tour operator who will provide a bilingual guide during your trip.

1 El Porvenir & Western Comarca Kuna Yala

El Porvenir is the governmental seat of the Comarca Kuna Yala and the principal gateway for most travelers. There isn't much marine life in the immediate area for snorkeling; what you come for here is to swing in a hammock, swim, and get some sun. With this in mind, 2 or 3 nights is about the maximum travelers stay here. There is one hotel on El Porvenir island, but most travelers head straight to the dock for the short boat ride to hostels on the islands of Wichubwala, Nalunega, Ukutupu, and Ogobsibudsup. The cheapest lodging in San Blas can be found in this area, making it a popular destination with backpackers. Porvenir is a service-based island—but that isn't saying much, as all you'll find is an administrative center for governmental offices, a police station, a tiny museum that's usually closed, and public telephones. For a **map** of the region, stop at the police station to get the *Mapa de Comunidades, Recursos Turísticos y Servicios del Golfo de Kuna Yala* (cost $5).

ESSENTIALS

GETTING THERE & DEPARTING   By Plane   Both **Aeroperlas** (© 351-7500; www.aeroperlas.com) and **Air Panama** (© 316-9000; www.flyairpanama.com) have daily flights to El Porvenir, Río Sidra, and Cartí (destinations within the western side of the Comarca) for $75 round-trip. The worst aspect of traveling to the *comarca* is that flights leave at the crack of dawn (6am), although large groups may charter a flight at a later hour. Return flights leave at 7am. *Tip:* If you do not have a return ticket or are unsure of your departure date, Mrs. Oti at the Hotel El Porvenir sells plane tickets for Air Panama. If there is space on Aeroperlas flights, you may simply pay when you arrive at the Albrook Airport. For **charter flights,** contact Air Panama at (© 315-0439; charter@flyairpanama.com).

BY ROAD & BOAT   The only road in the Comarca Kuna Yala is a rough dirt road from El Llano, east of Panama City, to the coast near Cartí Suitupo; from there, *cayuco*

Tips   Special Considerations in the San Blas

All islands here are owned by Kuna families, no matter how isolated or even if they're totally uninhabited. It is not, therefore, permitted to **camp** overnight on an uninhabited island without an owner's permission. Though you will not receive anything as serious as jail time or a fine, it is considered by the Kuna to be a tremendous breach of respect. The **cost to visit an island** is $1 per person; you'll be expected to pay for every island you visit, no matter how close they are to each other. Of course, if an island is uninhabited, the owner might or might not show up to charge you.

Scuba diving is prohibited within the Comarca Kuna Yala, but snorkeling is not. Snorkeling is better in the eastern part of the region, not near El Porvenir. If you are interested in diving just outside the San Blas, you'll need to stay at the nearby **Coral Lodge** in the Colón Province, or contact **Panama Divers.** (See p. 159 and p. 154 for information about both.)

Keep in mind that the main activities here are swinging in a hammock, soaking up the sun, and swimming in crystal-clear water, which is why most travelers stay in the Kuna Yala for only 2 to 3 nights.

Kuna people are extremely sensitive to having their pictures taken. *Always* ask permission before taking a photo of a Kuna Indian, especially if it is a Kuna chief (recognizable by a felt hat and short jacket). Most Kunas, especially those in areas frequented by tourists, will charge $1 to have their photo taken.

At press time, Movistar cellular phones do not have coverage in the *comarca,* but Cable & Wireless does. There are **public telephones** on the islands of El Porvenir, Wichubwala, and Gardi Sugdup, and there are telephones at the Sapibenega Kuna Lodge. Most hostels and lodges on islands have cellphones for emergencies. There are basic **medical facilities** in Gardi Sugdup and Río Sidra; for more serious medical issues you'll need to fly to Panama City.

There are no banks in the entire region, so come with enough cash plus a little extra just in case. Also, bring enough small bills for purchases.

The **food** served in the Comarca is almost always fish and shellfish—usually cooked the same way every day. If you are allergic to fish, are a vegetarian, or simply do not fancy dining on seafood day in and day out, advise your hosts well ahead of time so that they can be prepared when you arrive. Bring snacks and sunscreen because there are no stores.

boats transport travelers to the islands in the insular region. At the time of publication, this road was slated to be paved, but for now it requires a 4WD, and there is no public-bus transportation, meaning almost all travelers arrive at the Comarca by boat or plane.

BY CRUISE SHIP   The Comarca Kuna Yala is a popular cruise-ship destination for its shimmering white-sand beaches. Ships dock and tender guests usually to Ikodue, which has bathrooms. Depending on the circumstances, it can, unfortunately, be an uncomfortable experience as some cruises are approached by poor Kuna women in *cayucos* begging for coins. Kuna women also cart over their handicrafts to sell to visiting cruisers.

GETTING AROUND

Transportation to and from islands is by motorboat (sometimes called a *panga*), or a *cayuco,* which is a large dugout canoe with an outboard motor. All lodging options listed in this chapter provide boat transportation as part of their all-inclusive price; day excursions by boat are included except for faraway destinations such as the Cayos Hollandeses. Travel to and from the western Comarca's gulf to the east (to The Dolphin Lodge or the Sapibenega Lodge) by boat is nearly impossible, due to choppy sea conditions, time (up to 4 hr.), and reluctance by boat owners to undergo the distance. The only air service between the two regions is a thrice-weekly flight from El Porvenir to Corazón de Jesús.

WHAT TO SEE & DO

BEACHES & SNORKELING   Local tours are included in the price of lodging, but to neighboring islands and attractions only. The beaches at **Isla Hierba** are the closest to El Porvenir, and visitors to lodges near that island normally head here when they want to loll in the sun. A popular snorkeling site nearby is **Isla Perro** 𝕲𝕲, which has a sunken ship just off the coast. A stone's throw away is the **Isla Pelicano** 𝕲, with fine white-sand beaches. For the best snorkeling, you'll need to head out to **Cayos Holandéses** 𝕲𝕲𝕲, a chain of utterly perfect islands ringed with blue water and coral, and home to more marine life than you'd find closer to the heavily fished area around El Porvenir. There is also a wreck reef that has sunk many drug-running boats from Colombia. There are no tourism facilities. Private sailboats and yachts like to hang out around the Cayos; Getting here requires extra time (2–3 hours round-trip by boat from El Porvenir), and extra money ($100–$150 depending on the price of gas and number of people). The Cayos are roughly equidistant from El Porvenir and Río Sidra, about 20km (13 miles).

KUNA VILLAGES   Visits to Kuna communities can be custom-arranged with your lodge. Arranging visits is not complicated; however, there are a few villages that are more conservative and have not embraced the idea of tourism. Check your options with your tour/boat guide. The most common village, and really worth a visit because it seems like a metropolis when compared with surrounding island villages, is **Gardi Sugdup.** This island is part of the community **Cartí,** which consists of several island villages and a stretch of coastline. It's a heavily populated island and a warren of passageways that fan out spiderlike around squashed-together wooden huts and cement public buildings and stores. There's a lot of trash floating around the place, but once you get past the dock, you'll find that putting yourself in this middle of this thriving Kuna community is a truly fascinating experience. In terms of tourism, this is probably the most visited Kuna village in the *comarca,* and there are a landing strip here, a store, and a **museum** (daily 8am–4pm; admission $2). It's a humble museum, located in a thatched-roof hut, but there's enough here to keep a visitor's interest. You'll see displays of Kuna culture and rituals, and often a "docent" is available who speaks enough English to convey the meaning behind the artifacts on display.

Adventure-Tour Outfitters & Activities

KAYAKING There is no outfitter with more experience operating in the *comarca,* or one that is more dedicated to preserving the Kuna Yala culture than **Xtrop** ★★★ (© 317-1279; www.xtrop.com), which is short for Expediciones Tropicales. The Panama City–based company is highly respected, specializing in sea-kayak tours with an emphasis on nature and culture, and employing only local Kuna guides. Xtrop, which works with companies like Mountain Travel Sobek in the U.S., has received permission from Kuna chiefs to operate in one the areas that is richest in marine life (they call them "aquatic trails"), and they have access to areas no one else can go, including forested coastal areas. Best of all, Xtrop is very active in developing programs in the region for sustainable tourism, so you can feel good about how your money is spent. Trips are from 3 nights to a week long, and lodging is in tents or huts. Xtrop can also book just lodging for you, if that's the only service you need.

HIKING & GENERAL TOURS Ecocircuitos ★★ (© 314-1586; www.ecocircuitos.com) has guided walks through PEMASKY (Project for the Study and Management of Wilderness Areas of Kuna Yala), a protected coastal jungle in the *comarca* around the road to Cartí Suitupo, that is ranked as one of the best trails in the world for spotting birds and diverse flora. Ecocircuitos also offers multiday trips around Panama that include a couple of days visiting islands in the *comarca.* **Adventures in Panama** (© 877/726-6222 in the U.S.; www.adventuresinpanama.com) can also book lodges for travelers having a hard time doing it on their own.

SAILING San Blas Sailing ★★★ 32-7350, www.sanblassailing.com) is a French-owned company that has a fleet of monohull and multihull sailboats for up to eight passengers. They've been based in the *comarca* since 1997, and know the area intimately. Trips, which run from 4 to 14 nights and include meals, tours, and on-board accommodations, involve sailing around the islands, snorkeling, kayaking, and visiting Kuna villages. If you are looking for fine accommodations in the *comarca,* this is your best bet, but of course you'll spend all your nights on board.

WHERE TO STAY & DINE
AROUND EL PORVENIR

Cabañas Coco Blanco ★ This tiny teardrop-shaped island named Ogobsibu is home to just four cabins. Like most lodging in San Blas, the cabins are ultra-simple, cane-and-bamboo shelters with thatched roofs over sand, but the advantage here is that fewer cabins means fewer people and therefore more privacy. Plus, each cabin has its own bathroom (there is a septic system here). Walk out your front door and you're immediately on the beach. One cabin has a double bed, two have twins, and one has four beds. Because hotels here can only be owned and operated by Kunas, an Italian who would like to be owner instead brings groups to Coco Blanco and oversees operations, and accordingly the Kuna family here cooks a lot of Italian food such as pasta, in addition to seafood and vegetables. The island is about 15 minutes by boat from Porvenir and is more isolated; there is a grassy area and a fine white beach, hammocks, and tables and benches. Occasionally from May to December they'll drop the price to $50 a person; prices include trips to nearby Isla Perro and tours of Gardi Sugdup and its museum.

Isla Ogobsibu. © **6706-7316** or 6700-9427. cabanascocoblanco@yahoo.it. 4 units. $75. No credit cards. **Amenities:** Restaurant. *In room:* Private bathroom, no electricity.

Cabañas Ukuptupu   There are two sand-floor *cabañas* here, but the majority of lodging consists of connecting guest rooms on stilts over water, so you'll hear the sound of the lapping sea. There is a speck of a beach with hammocks and lounge chairs, a cement-floor dining area, and a holding tank for the fresh jumbo shrimp and lobster that are often on the menu; the food here is simple, but very good. The Smithsonian Research Institute built these wooden structures before moving operations in 1998. Thankfully, flush toilets have replaced the outhouse-over-the-sea bathrooms, and though this is the best hostel option in the Porvenir area, the complex is still very rustic. There are electrical outlets and power for a total of 8 hours a day. The best accommodations here, the Casablanc rooms, are spacious and have good views. The Kuna family who run Ukuptupu are very service-oriented, and have an extensive selection of jewelry and crafts on sale. The *cabañas* are located on Ukuptupu Island, about 5 minutes from El Porvenir.

Isla Ukuptupu. © **293-8709** or 6587-4758. www.ukuptupu.com. 11 units. $40. No credit cards. **Amenities:** Restaurant; gifts for sale; pool table; electricity 10am–2pm and 6–10pm.

Cabañas Wailidup ☞   Theses cabins were going up during my last visit to the *comarca,* and they are owned by the friendly and knowledgeable Juan Antonio, who also owns the Kuna Niskua (above). The island is dotted with slender palms and requires all of 10 minutes to circumnavigate; what I like is that it's fronted by a mangrove-lined island and an uninhabited island, which make it feel protected, and according to Juan Antonio, sit-on-top kayaks will be available to explore the area. The simple restaurant and bar here is popular with yachters who stop off for a cocktail. These are the only cabins in the area that are over sand but on stilts, with wooden floors, and they have private bathrooms.

Isla Wailidup. © **259-3471.** kuna-niskua@hotmail.com. 6 units. $75 (estimated price at time of publication). No credit cards. **Amenities:** Restaurant; bar. *In room:* Private bathrooms, no electricity.

Hotel El Porvenir   This hotel is smack-dab next to the airstrip—but flight activity is limited to the early morning, and perhaps some travelers find it convenient to catch a few extra minutes of sleep before boarding their flight out of San Blas. The rooms are very drab, with hardwood floors and sagging beds, but the owner, Mrs. Oti, couldn't be sweeter. There are public telephones on the island, and the hotel has electrical outlets with power from 6 to 10pm. There is also a strip of beach with lounge chairs. The restaurant serves decent—but mostly fried—food with rice.

Isla El Porvenir. © **221-1397** or 6508-6694. hotelelporvenir@hotmail.com. 14 units. $33 (1st night), $30 (thereafter). No credit cards. **Amenities:** Restaurant; public telephone; electricity 6–10pm.

Hotel San Blas   Fronting the sea and offering sand-floor cabins as well as wood-floor hotel rooms, the Hotel San Blas is popular with backpackers. The major drawback here is the beach, which is anchored on both sides with outhouses with open holes directly into the sea—yes, this means you swim through whatever comes out. Understandably, guests head directly out to one of the local beaches on neighboring islands. Showers are in communal bathrooms. There is a large dining area, and the food served here is generally better than many hostels' in San Blas. The elderly owner, Luís Burgos, is replacing the thatched roofs and sprucing up the property. Guest rooms have walls that do not reach the ceiling, so sound carries—ask to see a few rooms because you might be able to place yourself farther away from other guests, and bed quality varies from room to room as well. The island, Nalunega, has a midsize and

The Kuna Society

The Kuna are a tightly knit indigenous group who live much as they have for centuries. Although three male *caciques* reign as policy deciders, it is a matriarchal society in which inheritance is passed down through women. Women are also primary breadwinners, considering the income they earn from selling *mola* panels and other handicrafts to tourists. Still, such modern delving into economics is new for the Kuna, who not very long ago had no word for money, and used coconuts as a "monetary" unit. (As proof of the effects of tourism on society, Kunas use the word "money" instead of *dinero*.)

When a Kuna girl is born, she is given a nickname but does not receive her official Kuna name until she reaches puberty. Of course, the nickname is what everyone goes back to calling her soon after her traditional puberty ceremony. During this ceremony, a girl is expected to cut her hair short and keep it this way her entire adult life. Kuna women, with their colorful dress, gold jewelry, and *mola*-making talent, are guardians of Kuna culture. Men, on the other hand, wear western clothing and rely on coconut-collecting and fishing to make a living. Kunas are monogamous, and consider adultery a crime.

Squat with broad shoulders and disproportionately large heads, the Kuna are the second-smallest people in the world (African pygmies are the smallest). Although scientists still have no idea why, the rate of albinism here is the highest in the world. Albinos are called "Moon Children" and are considered to hold special powers and possess a high intelligence.

Molas are brightly colored reverse-appliqué panels and the principal artistic expression of the Kuna. Molas are made by sewing together layers of fabric and cutting down through the layers to form imaginative designs and figures. Kuna women wear *molas* sewn onto their blouses. *Molas* average $20 per panel, but often the price can be negotiated, especially when buying several.

reasonably clean village with a little under 400 residents, all of whom live in homes packed tightly together, providing travelers with personal contact with local Kunas.

Isla Nalunega. ✆ 257-3310 or 6639-8331. hotelsanblas@hotmail.com. 31 units. $35 adults, $15 kids under 10. No credit cards. **Amenities:** Restaurant; electricity 6–10pm.

Kuna Niskua Lodge ✦   This friendly hostel sits back from the water and does not have sea views or a beach. The rooms are clean and attractive, with stylishly thatched walls, comfortable beds, and private bathrooms. The best thing about the Kuna Niskua is its owner, Juan Antonio, who is Kuna and surely the most informative and hospitable guide in the region. The food served here is the same every night—fish and rice. There is a breezy covered area with hammocks for relaxing. The island here has about 200 people, but it seems more like 50 or so, with narrow passageways and a village center, allowing you to interact with local Kunas, most of whom are more than keen to sell you their handicrafts. Juan Antonio can put together specialized full-day cultural tours for an additional $50; otherwise local tours are included.

Isla Wichubwala. ✆ 259-3471 or 6686-1086. www.kunaniskua.com. 9 units. $40. No credit cards. **Amenities:** Restaurant. *In room:* Private bathroom, electricity 6–10pm.

AROUND RIO SIDRA

Cabañas Kuanidup ✦✦ *Moments*   For those who really want to get away from it all, this remote island is the best in the western *comarca*. It's utterly rustic, but it's such a utopian, castaway-style isle that most visitors actually prefer the Robinson Crusoe–type lodging. To get here, it is better to fly into Río Sidra for a 25-minute boat ride to the island as compared to a 45-minute boat ride from Porvenir. About as large as a soccer field, Isla Kuanidup is fringed with palms strung with hammocks that look picture-perfect in their symmetry. The island is ringed in coral here but there also is a deeper, sandy spot by their dock that makes for an ideal swimming area (many islands have shallow-water beaches). Cabins are small, with a little foyer, sand floors, and an okay foam mattress. Choose a south-facing cabin—the north-facing ones take the brunt of the wind. Miguel, the owner, and his motley crew each morning rake the white sand in Zen-like perfection, and they have a well-stocked supply of beverages and booze. Kuanidup serves seafood only. (Pre-arrange meat or vegetarian dishes beforehand.) Cabins are lined in a row, and do not provide maximum privacy; however the owner has an uninhabited island if you want to get away from your neighbors for the day. There are also a volleyball net, a spacious eating area, and a set of covered picnic tables. Bathrooms (both showers and toilets) are shared, and there is no electricity here; at night guests must use kerosene lamps.

Isla Kuanidup. ✆ 6635-6737. kuani9@hotmail.com. 10 units. $60 Dec–Apr; $50 May–Nov. No credit cards. **Amenities:** Restaurant; bar; volleyball. *In room:* Shared bathrooms, no electricity.

Cabañas Verónica   Formerly known as Robinson's Cabañas, this spot is about a 15-minute boat ride from Río Sidra, the closest airport. It is slightly larger than Kuanidup and darker due to lots of coconut palms and darker sand; also, the rustic cabins are spaced farther apart here than at Kuanidup. When I last visited, the owners were renovating the property by installing a septic system and growing grass on empty patches of dirt, and though it won't be quite as idyllic as Kuanidup, it should come close. Veronica's guide, who speaks a bit of English, can take visitors on a special tour of the coast to visit the owner's inland village and to hike through jungle. The island is home to about 20 iguanas, and there is a good bathing and sunning beach.

Isla Dup Asunikad. ✆ 6679-0489. 8 units. $50. No credit cards. **Amenities:** Restaurant. *In room:* Shared bathrooms, no electricity.

2 Eastern Comarca Kuna Yala

The eastern region of the *comarca* is visited less frequently by tourists than the El Porvenir area. Travelers can expect to find here a higher level of biodiversity and wilder natural surroundings; according to Smithsonian scientists, the islands that dot the coast feature the highest diversity of coral species in Panama, yet this region, too, has suffered from overfishing. If you're lucky, however, you might see dolphins, manta rays, and manatees. Kuna villages in this region, especially **Corazón de Jesús,** are significantly more westernized, and the people who live here don less traditional clothing, live in modern buildings, and participate in modern pastimes like watching TV. If you'd like to visit a traditional village in this region, the tidy island **Isla Tigre** was also the site of the violent overthrow of Panamanian forces in 1925, when the Kuna first asserted their independent authority over the region. Isla Tigre is a little less than 5km (3 miles) east of Corazón de Jesús. This village, along with Playón Chico and Mamitupo, has landing strips with flights from Panama City; Aeroperlas has flights from El Porvenir to Corazón de Jesús three times a week. Otherwise, it is difficult to access this region from the western side of the *comarca*.

You'll find the Comarca Kuna Yala's most **deluxe lodging** in this region, at The Dolphin Lodge and the Sapibenega Lodge, or you can tour the region in kayaks with the outfitter Xtrop (p. 287), which has a special license to visit the area's pristine regions. Lodges mentioned in this section include, in the price, tours in the immediate area; note that there is nowhere to stay on Corazón de Jesús. At the time of publication, a new, upscale lodge called the Tad Ibe Lodge was being constructed there. Check with a travel agent about this lodge's status.

ESSENTIALS

GETTING HERE & DEPARTING   By Plane   Both **Aeroperlas** (© 351-7500; www.aeroperlas.com) and **Air Panama** (© 316-9000; www.flyairpanama.com) have daily flights from Panama City to Corazón de Jesús, Playón Chico, and Mamitupo, all leaving at 6am. The cost is $80 round-trip for Corazón de Jesús, $87 round-trip for Playón Chico, and $97 for Mamitupo.

WHERE TO STAY

The Dolphin Lodge 🏵🏵   If staying in a hut with sand floors is a little too much like roughing it for you, but you'd still like the sensation of sleeping under a traditional Kuna thatched roof, you might want to check out this lodge. Also known as the Uaguinega Ecoresort, this "lodge" (and I use that term loosely) is run by a friendly Kuna family who have outfitted their property with a couple of extra amenities and a roster of tours that take visitors to beaches, on snorkeling trips, on bird-watching tours on the mainland, and on visits to Kuna villages such as the overpopulated, handicrafts-heavy Ustupu; they'll also take you to watch traditional dances on the island of Ogobsucun. Dolphin Lodge comprises 11 cabins, 3 of which are "junior suites"—these units have hardwood floors, ocean views, stylish bamboo-thatched walls, and terraces. Standard cabins have cement floors, some have ocean views, and interior walls are made of wood, not bamboo. Another difference is that standard units have electricity from 6 to 11pm only, while junior suites have 24-hour solar-powered electricity. All cabins are comfortable and clean, with quality mattresses and private bathrooms. This is the only lodge in the Comarca with Internet service. The island of Uaguitupu has no village, and there is only a limited, thin strip of beach; to get here you'll need to fly into Mamitupo. There is also a pleasant, open-air dining area with simple but decent cuisine. They'll usually light a bonfire at night.

Isla Uaguitupu. (℘ **263-7780** or 263-1500. www.dolphinlodge.com. 11 units. Rates are per person, based on double occupancy. $112–$120 1st night double, $105–$110 2nd night double; $125–$145 1st night junior suite, $115–$130 2nd night junior suite. MC, V. **Amenities:** Restaurant; bar; volleyball; Internet. *In room:* Private bathroom, electricity.

Sapibenega Kuna Lodge 🌤🌤 *(Moments*   The Sapibenega is not luxurious, but it does offer the highest quality accommodations in the entire *comarca*—a stay at this lodge was part of the prize for the winner of the *Survivor* TV series. The lodge is located on the gorgeous island of Iskardup, near a group of uninhabited islands; to get here you'll need to fly into Playón Chico and take a 5-minute motorboat ride to the island. Iskardup is ringed with lodging units, including ground-level individual cabins and two new cabins propped up on stilts over the water. These newer units have two rooms per cabin (note that walls are thin and you can hear you neighbors), are more spacious and comfortable, and come with balconies. All cabins have private bathrooms with tiled showers, hardwood floors, cane walls, thatched roofs, and 24-hour electricity. There's not much on the island except an open-air *bohio* bar/restaurant on stilts over the water, hammocks, and that's about it—clearly the main activity at Sapibenega is hanging out and just contemplating nature and life. Daily tours take guests to uninhabited nearby islands, which are great for snorkeling, and cultural tours to Playón Chico and Kolebir, the latter of which is a traditional mainland Kuna village. The lodge can also arrange sailing, bird-watching, and jungle hikes to a waterfall.

Isla Iskardup. (℘ **215-3724** or 6676-5548. www.spaibenega.com. 13 units. Rates are per person, based on double occupancy. Land cabins: $110 low season (June 2–Nov 30), $115 high season 1st night, $103 2nd night. Sea cabins: $125 low season, $140 1st night high season, $126 2nd night. Kids under 2 free, kids ages 2–5 35% discount, kids ages 6–10 25% discount. MC, V. **Amenities:** 2 restaurants; bar. *In room:* Fan, private bathroom, 24-hr. electricity.

11

The Darién Province

The Darién Province, a remote, sparsely populated expanse of tropical rainforest and swampland along Panama's eastern boundary with Colombia, is considered Central America's last grand, untamed wilderness. Home to nearly .8 million hectares (2 million acres) of protected land, the Darién includes **La Reserva Natural Privada Punta Patiño** and the **Parque Nacional del Darién,** the largest national park in Central America and a UNESCO Biosphere Reserve. All of this wilderness is commonly called the "Darién Gap," which refers to the roadless swath of forest that is the "missing link" in the Pan-American Highway from Alaska to Chile. Colombia would like to extend the road, but Panamanians fear widespread environmental destruction and an increase in drug trafficking. For now at least, a road seems unlikely.

Given the Darién's inaccessibility, there are few places a traveler can actually visit within the boundaries of the province. The national park measures a staggering 15,000 hectares (1.5 million acres), yet only the **Pirre** and **Cana** stations offer trails and basic services. On the southern coast at Piñas Bay is the famous Tropic Star Lodge, and there are trails and dugout canoe trips on rivers around Punta Patiño.

Travelers can drive to the end of the Pan-American Highway to Yaviza, but it's unlikely that you'd want to. The road is flanked by mostly deforested land with nothing of interest except for a few blink-and-you-miss-it hamlets providing truly grim lodging and mediocre services. The road is mostly unpaved and requires a 4WD during the rainy season. Some tours use the Pan-American Highway to reach their final destination in the Darién.

The Darién is just not developed for do-it-yourself travelers, and tales abound of travelers getting lost for days in the jungle or having run-ins with terrorist groups along the northern Colombia border. Therefore, it's better to let someone else do the planning for you. Destinations such as the Cana Field Station actually require booking a tour that includes a charter flight to get there. Considering the lack of roads and the inexpensive flights aboard small planes that exist, most travelers fly here anyway, which can be an adventure in itself, soaring above the treetops, viewing Emberá villages below, and holding on tight for a landing on a dirt or grassy landing strip. If booking a tour, you will be put on a charter flight organized by your outfitter, or at the very least they will be able to book you on a regularly scheduled flight.

Tips A Word of Caution for Visitors to the Darién

Travelers to the Darién should not be cavalier. The jungle is dense and can easily disorient hikers, and any kind of walking trip here should always be undertaken with a guide. In the Darién, you'll find a lot more creepy-crawlies than you will in the rest of Panama; snakes, for example, like to slither under fallen leaves and will surprise you if you're not scanning the trail ahead. Hikers should also protect themselves from ticks prevalent in some areas, and from invisible, skin-burrowing chiggers. Tuck your pants into your socks and bring lots of repellent with DEET. There are two seasons here, dry and wet. The May-to-December rainy season is wetter than in most parts of Panama, shrouding your vision and turning trails and roads into slick and gloppy mud. Unless you're fishing at the Tropic Star Lodge, it is not recommended that you visit the Darién during the rainy season. Also, if you're heading to higher altitudes like the Cerro Pirre, bring a jacket because the temperature is much cooler here than in the lowlands.

The border with Colombia near the Caribbean Sea is unsafe due to narco-terrorist activity that spills over into Panama. The destinations mentioned in this chapter, however, are perfectly safe.

1 Western Darién *

The Pan-American Highway from Panama City is a relatively featureless road that is paved until Lago Bayano; from here it's a rocky ride to the endpoint at Yaviza. Given the poor condition of the road, it can take nearly a full day to drive this stretch—and when you're done, the only thing to do is turn around and head back. The exception is the turnoff to Metetí, which leads to Puerto Quimbo and to boats to La Palma, near the Punta Patiño reserve.

It's interesting to note, however, that a new **Chucanti Field Station** (© 6676-2466; www.advantagepanama.com), in the western Darién, was opened recently by Advantage Tours. The biological research station for visiting scientists is also open to nature enthusiasts. Chucanti is a good spot for budget bird-watchers and hikers seeking to visit the Darién. The lodge provides access to the lower primary forests and cloud forests of the region, and visits are accompanied by a guide who provides information about flora and fauna, with additional input from whichever scientist is staying at the station that week. The station is just 135km (85 miles) from Panama City via the Pan-American Highway. At the turnoff near the Cerro Chucanti hill, guides load gear onto mules and guests travel to the station by horse or by walking trail for 3 hours. The station is a simple wood-and-zinc-roof structure surrounded by leafy green forest. There are four guest rooms with private bathrooms, and though they are comfortable, this is a research station with simple amenities. Meals are hearty and typically Panamanian. Prices are $350 for 3 nights/4 days, and include round-trip transportation from Panama City, bilingual guide, lodging, and meals.

Map of Darién region showing Caribbean Sea, Pacific Ocean, Panamá, and Colombia with towns, parks, and reserves.

2 Punta Patiño (★)(★)(★)

Punta Patiño was the first private nature preserve to be established in Panama, and at 30,351 hectares (75,000 acres) it is the country's largest. The preserve is bordered by the Gulf of San Miguel and is characterized by a coastal web of mangrove swamps and the mighty Tiura River, which ribbons through undulating and endangered dry tropical forest. The preserve is also home to Emberá Indian communities and a concentration of harpy eagles, Panama's national bird. Owned and managed by the nonprofit Asociación Nacional Para la Conservación de la Naturaleza (ANCON), the preserve is tangible proof of the ability of nature to recover from human intervention, considering that a large swath of land here was once a cattle ranch and small farming community and now is a thriving forest. It's all here thanks to the hard work and perseverance of ANCON and Panama City mayor Juan Carlos Navarro, an environmentalist who was leading director when the preserve was created. Punta Patiño can be reached by road and boat, or by small plane and boat.

There are several reasons to visit the preserve. The region gives visitors a chance not only to explore dense primary and secondary forest that's home to peccaries, coatimundis, and the world's largest rodent capybaras that feed near the shore; it also provides for an adventurous ride aboard a *piragua*, or motorized dugout canoe, up the Tirua River. Along this river's shores, three species of ancient mangroves thrive and provide refuge for bottlenose dolphins and marine birds such as kingfishers, herons, spoonbills, and ibises. For bird-watchers, the prize sighting here is the harpy eagle, one of the largest predators in the world. Harpy eagles like this region for its concentration of trees like the Quipo, whose chubby trunk and height make for ideal nesting conditions. Another reason to visit Punta Patiño is the **Mogue Emberá Indian community,** which gives travelers a cultural introduction to native peoples and their traditional arts like tagua carvings and basket-making. Through tourism, the Emberá tribes in this area have found a way to make a living that is based on protecting wildlife—instead of killing it—to draw more tourism dollars.

ADVENTURE TOURS & WHERE TO STAY

Visits to the Punta Patiño preserve must be planned as part of an expedition. Two companies currently offer trips to Punta Patiño, which can be as short as 2 nights, that are part of a longer itinerary covering other destinations in the Darién.

Ancon Expeditions (© 269-9415; www.anconexpeditions.com), once the for-profit wing of ANCON but now an independent company, is the Darién's foremost tour operator, offering three options for travelers. The company also owns **Punta Patiño Lodge;** it sits high on a bluff overlooking the Pacific Ocean, and is a simple, two-story building with air-conditioned rooms with private bathrooms. Ancon uses this lodge as a base for all three of their expeditions to Punta Patiño. The quick, in-and-out tour is the 2-night/3-day "Coastal Darién Explorer," which includes light hiking through forest and a day visit by canoe to an Emberá village. Their "Realm of the Harpy Eagle" is 1 day longer, and involves 1 night of tent camping in the Emberá village, with a visit to a harpy-eagle nest.

Worth highlighting is Ancon's "Darién Explorer Trek," the company's signature Darién expedition. This 13-night/14-day adventure begins with an overnight in their Punta Patiño Lodge, followed by a night in an Emberá village. But rather than return to Punta Patiño, the trip continues upstream until reaching El Real, the jumping-off point for the Darién National Park and the trail head to the Pirre ranger station. There is a 2-day hike through virgin rainforest until you reach Cana (see below), eventually returning to Panama City via small plane. This is an adventure for travelers really seeking to experience remote wilderness far off the beaten track from most tours. Ancon's Punta Patiño tours begin with a flight aboard a small plane that touches down on a dirt landing strip at La Palma. The "Realm of the Harpy Eagle" costs $695 per person and includes round-trip airfare.

Ecocircuitos (© 314-1586; www.ecocircuitos.com) is another excellent tour operator offering a Punta Patiño expedition. The major difference between this tour and Ancon's is that Punta Patiño is reached by road along the Pan-American Highway to Puerto Quimba, where travelers board a dugout canoe to go to the Mogue Emberá Indian community. Base camp is set up in the community, with lodging in tents, giving visitors more exposure to the Emberá (the reason why they've dubbed their tour the "Darién Ethnic Expedition"). The trip lasts 2 days/3 nights or 3 nights/4 days, and includes transportation, guided excursions, meals, and lodging. Prices for a 3 night/4 day trip are (approximately) $795 per person, based on two travelers; and $655 per person, based on four travelers.

3 Darién National Park & Cana Field Station ★★★

The .6-million-hectare (1.5-million-acre) Darién National Park is not only the largest park in Panama, it is the largest in Central America. The park extends along 90% of the entire length of the border with Colombia, incorporating a dazzling rainforest rich in biodiversity, coastal lagoons and mangrove swamps, serrated peaks, and toffee-colored rivers that snake down to the Pacific Ocean. The vast size and pristine state of the park mean that populations of endemic and endangered species—jaguars, tapirs, ocelots, and pumas—are allowed to flourish. But what visitors see most, and with surprising frequency, are spider, howler, and white-faced capuchin monkeys, as well as sloths. The Darién is considered one of the last pristine wildernesses in the Americas, and it therefore has been designated a UNESCO Biosphere Site. It is an extraordinary, *Jurassic Park*–like wilderness, ideal for adventurous travelers who seek absolutely primeval surroundings and the sense of being far from civilization and the modern world.

What visitors also come to see here are **birds,** and indeed the Darién forest has been rated as one of the top 10 bird-watching sites in the *world.* Even non-birders can't help getting caught up in the excitement of so many colorful "showcase" species like macaws and toucans fluttering about. Dozens of tanager species in a kaleidoscopic range of colors are here, too, not to mention rare and endemic species such as red-throated caracaras, peregrine falcons, golden-headed quetzals, and the Pirre warbler. There are so many birds and in such abundance that sighting them doesn't take much effort—while swinging in a hammock, for example, you can eye parrots and macaws zipping through the air.

But as vast as the Darién National Park is, the majority of it is largely inaccessible. The only two access points are the ANAM park ranger's **Pirre Station** on the north side of the Cerro Pirre peak, and Ancon Expedition's **Cana Field Station** on the southeast side of the peak (reached by small plane). Cana is owned and operated by **Ancon Expeditions** (© 269-9415; www.anconexpeditions), and trips here must be booked as a tour through that company, unless you are traveling with a tour operator such as Field Guides, Wildland Adventures, or Victor Emanuel Nature Tours (see chapter 4), which subcontract the lodge. Check out Ancon's "Darién Explorer Trek" (under "Punta Patiño," above) for a 14-day tour that arrives at Cana via Punta Patiño and the Pirre Station.

The Darién is one of the few places in Panama where it is recommended that you **do not travel independently and without a guide.** The reasons are plentiful: Hardly a soul here speaks English, there exists a considerable risk of becoming lost on any trail, and you're exposing yourself to a variety of potential pitfalls such as a twisted ankle or snakebites—the nearest medical clinic is hundreds of miles away. Also, with such a diversity of flora and fauna, it pays to have a guide to enhance your experience with interpretive information, cultural information about the Emberá and Wounaan communities, and history of the area.

The ranger station at Pirre (© 299-6965) offers basic shelter with bunk-style beds, a kitchen, and shared bathrooms. There is no electricity, and you must bring all supplies with you like food, water (or a water purifier), flashlights, towels, and so forth. The cost to spend the night is $10, with a park entrance fee of $3. There are several trails from easy to difficult that lead from the ranger station, but as stated earlier, it is unwise to walk these trails without a guide.

The Pirre Station is about a 3-hour walk during the dry season from the village of El Real; or you can get there in 2 hours in a dugout canoe from El Real, followed by a 1-hour hike to the station. There are regularly scheduled flights to El Real from Panama City on **Aeroperlas** (© **315-7500;** www.aeroperlas.com), which has flights every Monday, Wednesday, and Friday for $97 round-trip.

CANA FIELD STATION ★★★

Most travelers to Darién National Park are bird-watchers who visit the Cana Field Station on Ancon's 4-night, 5-day "Ultimate Darién Experience" expedition. Of course, you don't need to be a bird-watcher to visit, but it certainly helps, considering that the only other activities are hiking nature trails and just soaking up the fabulous jungle ambience. The lodge is located a short walk from the old Cana mines, one of the most productive gold mines in the history of the Americas, founded in the early 17th century by the Spaniards. In the late 1600s, the mines drew nearly 20,000 people here, an incredible figure given how empty and remote the area now is. The mine closed in the 18th century, but reopened in the late 1800s complete with train service to Boca de Cupe to ship gold, people, and equipment from Cana. Antique mining machinery and remnants of the train remain, and part of the fascination is seeing how thoroughly they've been swallowed up by jungle.

With the Cana Field Station, it's all about location, location, location—this is surely one of the most stunning sites in Panama, framed by verdant jungle whose trees drip with vines and sprout spiky bromeliads, and are interspersed with a riot of flowering trees. Because the lodge faces an open expanse, it provides a spectacular amphitheater for bird-watching, allowing guests to spy many species from a reclining chair or hammock on the front porch. The lodge is research-station rustic, but with comfortable beds with a sheet, shared bathrooms with hot water, a separate dining hall, and a roofed area strung with hammocks for hanging out. It's the kind of place where easygoing nature lovers will be happiest, those who do not mind queuing up for a shower, getting dressed by flashlight, or sharing simply prepared communal meals. Days begin at the crack of dawn, usually around 6:30am, to take advantage of early birding activity. Expeditions are led by Ancon's bilingual guides, who are some of the best in their field, and the staff are a convivial group of local Dariénites. From the lodge, there are several short trails around the property, and a longer, half-day hike up through thick, species-rich jungle to the top of Cerro Pierre peak, where guests sleep overnight at Ancon's tent-camping site. From here there is a sweeping view of the Darién National Park, and the option to walk higher into the cloud forest in search of the elusive golden-headed quetzal.

Trips to Cana include guides, excursions, meals, and a round-trip charter flight. Itineraries are for set dates but have some flexibility, or can be undertaken with a minimum of four travelers. Price per person for the 4-night trip, based on at least four travelers, is $995.

4 Bahía Piñas & the Tropic Star Lodge ★★★

Visitors to Bahía Piñas come for the legendary sport fishing. Beyond the Tropic Star Lodge, there are two villages near Bahía Piñas, but both hold little interest to travelers. If the cost of the Tropic Star is too rich for your blood, you'd be better off setting up a fishing trip elsewhere along the Pacific Coast rather than eking out a local tour in Jacqué. **Aeroperlas** (© 315-7500; www.aeroperlas.com) and **Air Panama** (© 315-0439; www.flyairpanama.com) have three weekly flights to Bahía Piña from Panama City for $100 round-trip.

WHERE TO STAY & DINE

Tropic Star Lodge ☆☆☆   Panama's premiere wilderness fishing lodge is revered in sport-fishing circles around the world for record-breaking sailfish and black marlin, among other monster billfish species. It's one of Panama's earliest ecolodge success stories, founded in 1961 by a Texan oil tycoon as a private getaway but later developed into a full-scale fishing lodge in 1968. The American Kittredge family has owned the lodge since 1976. Tropic Star enjoys a gorgeous location fronting Piñas Bay and backed by a road-less tangle of wild jungle that stretches for a hundred miles. It's the kind of place that attracts international VIPs, sports stars, and other celebrities, but the lodge's exclusivity owes more to its remoteness and access to renowned fishing spots than to its luxuriousness. Any sport-fishing fanatic will feel comfortable here, and the owners are family-friendly in order to turn future generations on to sport fishing. The lodge's secret asset is the **Zane Grey Reef,** an underwater seamount that attracts a rich supply of baitfish and the giant billfish that come here to feed. Most of the fishing is done within 9.7 to 19km (6–12 miles) of the shore aboard one of their dozen 9.4m (31-ft.) Bertram boats. Since the lodge's inception, fishermen here have broken more than 200 world records, 40 of which are still valid today. Given this, the lodge can book a full 1 to 2 years ahead of time during high season.

The lodge has a maximum capacity of 36 guests who are personally attended to by 80 employees wearing Hawaiian shirts and big smiles. Guest rooms are individual air-conditioned cabins spread across a hilly slope, and feature outdoor decks that look out onto scenic Piñas Bay. Rooms come with two twins or a king-size bed, and are spacious and comfortably appointed but not as plush as those of a five-star hotel. The lodge has been impeccably maintained and updated throughout the years without forfeiting its original, retro-1960s design. There is also the "palacio" for a group of six, which used to be the original owner's home and is reached by cable car or 122 steps up the hill. The palacio has three bedrooms and a sunken living room.

The four-course meals are excellent; everything is baked, homemade, and fresh, especially the fish, of course. Rates include fishing excursions, lodging, meals, and all drinks except cocktails. Beyond fishing, there are plenty of other activities available such as scuba diving, kayaking the Río Piñas, hiking the lodge's wilderness trail that connects the white-sand Playa Blanca beach, or taking a cruise upriver to visit a Wounaan village. Packages below show price range from low season (Apr–Sept) and high season (Dec–Mar); the lodge shuts October to November. To get here, you take a regularly scheduled flight or a small charter plane from Panama City (see above) to Piñas Bay, where they'll pick you up for the 10-minute boat ride to the lodge.

Piñas Bay. © **800/682-3424.** www.tropicstar.com. 16 units. Packages per person, based on double occupancy: 7 nights $4,850–$5,495; 4 nights $2,895–$3,250. AE, MC, V. **Amenities:** Restaurant; bar; outdoor pool; sport-fishing excursions; kayaks; cultural excursions. *In room:* A/C, no phone.

Appendix A:
Panama in Depth

Perhaps the most curious thing about Panama is that, given the country's natural beauty and accessibility, as well as its stable and friendly environment, it has existed off the radar of international travelers and investors for so long. Panama is poised to be the next big thing in travel, yet it is still largely undeveloped for tourism and blissfully empty of people, unlike its neighbor Costa Rica. Also unlike that country, Panama claims a history rich with Spanish conquistadores and colonists, pirates, goldminers and adventurers, canal engineering, international trade, and mass immigration from countries as close as Jamaica and as far away as China. The pastiche of European and African cultures blended with the country's seven indigenous groups has had a tangible effect on Panama's architecture, cuisine, language, and folklore.

Given Panama's compact size and diversity, visitors here can take part in wildly different experiences without having to travel very far. And now that the dust has long settled after the infamous Noriega era, political stability has taken hold and offered hope for the country's future. This chapter will help you understand a little more about Panama's history, people, and culture.

1 Panama Today

Panama has 3.2 million residents, and collectively more than a third live in Panama City, Colón, and David, the country's three largest cities. The remaining population is concentrated mostly in small towns and villages in central Panama and the Azuero Peninsula. Roughly 70% of the population are *mestizo*, or a mix of Amerindians and Caucasians; 14% are African descent, 10% are white and other immigrant races, and 6% Amerindian. About 30% of the population are under the age of 14.

There are seven indigenous groups in Panama who, despite foreign influences and modern advancements, have, to differing degrees, held onto their culture and languages. Ethnic tribes such as the **Kuna,** who live along the central Caribbean coast, are a semiautonomous and insular society that has hardly changed over the last century. However,

the eastern Kuna community, near the Darién, has adapted to modern society, wears Western clothing, and practices few native traditions. The **Ngöbe-Buglé** are two tribes that are culturally similar and collectively referred to as Guaymí. Ngöbe-Buglés live in the highlands of western Panama and eastern Costa Rica, and are the country's largest indigenous group; many travel nomadically and make their living in coffee production. Eastern Panama is home to two indigenous groups, the **Emberá** and the **Wounaan**—several Emberá communities are close enough to Panama City to be visited for the day. Tiny populations of **Teribe** (also called Naso) and **Bri Bri** live scattered around mainland Bocas del Toro.

People of African descent first came to Panama as slaves of the Spanish during the 16th century, and many escaped into

Darién Province where they settled and became known as *cimarrones*. In and around Portobelo and the eastern Caribbean coast, they call themselves **Congos**. During the 19th century, jobs in canal building and banana plantations lured immigrants from Jamaica, Barbados, and Colombia, who settled along the western Caribbean coast and are commonly referred to as **Afro-Caribbeans** or *creoles*.

One thing you'll find about Panamanians is that they are warm and outgoing people who are eager to help strangers. Panamanians no longer indulge in afternoon siestas, but you will notice that things move at a languid pace. Given this and the country's nascent tourism infrastructure, even well-respected tour companies and other tourism establishments can't always be relied upon for punctuality. If you are an impatient person, or in a hurry, you will not fare well in Panama—so *relax*. You're on vacation, right?

Panama has a dollarized economy whose major natural resources are its rainforests, beaches, and oceans, making this country an irresistible draw for tourism—though it hasn't really taken off yet. Panama's principal source of income is derived from the services sector, including the Panama Canal, the Colón Free Trade Zone, banking, and flagship registry among other "export" services, all of which total about three-quarters of the country's GDP. The withdrawal of U.S. canal workers and military personnel in 2000 had a devastating effect on Panama City's local economy, but a growth explosion in the construction sector is currently underway thanks to juicy tax incentives, and glitzy skyscrapers seemingly shoot up overnight like mushrooms along the city's shoreline. Panama has very effectively sold itself as a retirement haven, with its low cost of living, inexpensive land,

and dollar-based economy, and many of those who were just passing through are now putting down stakes in gated communities or taking on new roles as hotel or restaurant owners. Foreign investors lured by get-rich-quick schemes are snapping up property in a real-estate boom that has many locals grumbling about the soaring value of land. On the legislative side, the Panamanian government has reformed its tax structure, opened its borders to free trade with key nations like the U.S., and implemented a social security overhaul. Yet money laundering, political corruption, and cocaine transshipment continue to be problems, as is widespread unemployment, with indigenous groups and Colón residents faring the worst. As the nation grows economically, the split between the rich and the poor widens. Today, about 40% of the population is under the poverty level and lacks adequate housing, access to medical care, and proper nutrition.

The current president of Panama is Martín Torrijos, a member of the center-left Democratic Revolutionary Party and son of the late populist dictator Omar Torrijos. Torrijos maintains a political balance between free-trade economic incentives and fiscal responsibility on the one hand, and, on the other, embracing his father's populist past and reaching out to the poor. One week he's shaking hands with Fidel Castro, the next he's fishing with former U.S. president George H. W. Bush.

The current hot-button topic in Panama is the $5 billion projected expansion of the Panama Canal. Worldwide tankers have grown too big to fit in the canal, and those ships that can fit must line up for hours to cross. Congress has already approved the expansion, and even though the canal is privately owned, there will be a referendum in late 2006 to placate a wary public.

2 History 101

EARLY HISTORY Little is known about the ancient cultures that inhabited Panama before the arrival of the Spanish. The pre-Columbian cultures in this region did not build large cities or develop an advanced culture like the Mayans or the Incas did, and much of what was left behind has been stolen by looters or engulfed in jungle. We know that the most advanced cultures came from Central Panama, such as the Monagrillo (2500–1700 B.C.), who were one of the first pre-Columbian societies in the Americas to produce ceramics. Excavation of sites such as Conte, near Natá, have unearthed elaborate burial pits with *huacas* (ceremonial figurines) and jewelry, which demonstrates an early introduction to metallurgy during the first century, as well as trade with Colombia and even Mexico. What little remains of Panama's prized artifacts can be viewed at the Museo Antropológico Reina Torres de Araúz in Panama City.

SPAIN CONQUERS PANAMA The first of many Spanish explorers to reach Panama was Rodrigo de Bastidas, who sailed from Venezuela along Panama's Caribbean coast in 1501 in search of gold. His first mate was Vasco Nuñez de Balboa, who would return later and seal his fate as one of Panama's most important

historical figures. A year later, Christopher Columbus, on his fourth and final voyage to the New World, sailed into Bocas del Toro and stopped at various points along the isthmus, one of which he named Puerto Bello, now known as Portobelo. Estimates vary, but historians believe that between 1 and 2 million indigenous people were in Panama at that time. Groups such as the Kuna, the Chocó, and the Guaymí lived in small communities and were highly skilled in pottery making, stonecutting, and metallurgy. Because they frequently wore gold ornaments, Spanish explorers during the following years would be further convinced of the existence of fabled El Dorado, the city of gold. Columbus attempted to establish a colony, Santa María de Belen, near Río Belen, but was forced out after a raid by local Indians.

Meanwhile, Balboa had settled in the Dominican Republic but had racked up huge debts. In 1510, he escaped his creditors by hiding out as a stowaway on a boat bound for Panama. In the years since Columbus's failed attempt, many other Spaniards had tried to colonize the coast, but were thwarted by disease and indigenous raids. Balboa suggested settling at Antigua de Darién, where he became a tough but successful administrator who

Dateline

- **12,000 B.C.** Earliest record of human inhabitants in Panama.
- **100 B.C.–0** Pre-Columbian groups set up a trade network with neighbors and practice metallurgy.
- **1501** The Spanish explorer Rodrigo de Bastidas sails past the Panamanian coast.
- **1513** Vasco Núñez de Balboa is the first European to see the Pacific Ocean from the New World.

- **1519** Panama City is founded by Pedro Arias de Avila on a muddy swamp on the Pacific Coast.
- **Mid-1500s to late 1800s** Portobelo's trade fairs are among the largest and most opulent in the world.
- **1671** Welsh buccaneer Henry Morgan sacks and burns Panama City.
- **1821** On September 15, Panama, along with the rest

of Central America, gains independence from Spain.
- **1855** A U.S. group of investors builds the Panama Railway; from 1848 to 1869 tens of thousands of forty-niners cross the isthmus.
- **1893** The French canal attempt collapses in disgrace.
- **1903** Panama wins independence from Colombia, with U.S. backing.

both subjugated Indians as well as befriended conquered tribes. Having listened to stories by Indians about another sea, Balboa set out in 1513 with Francisco Pizarro and a band of Indian slaves, and hacked his way through perilous jungle for 25 days until he arrived at the Pacific Coast, where he claimed the sea and all the its shores for the king of Spain. Balboa was later beheaded by a jealous new governor, Pedro Arias de Avila (Pedrarias the Cruel), on a trumped-up charge of treason.

In 1519, Pedrarias settled a fishing village called Panama, which meant "plenty of fish" in the local language, and resettled Nombre de Dios on the Atlantic to create a passageway for transporting Peruvian gold and riches from the Pacific to Spanish galleons in the Caribbean Sea. The trail was called the Camino Real, or Royal Trail, but later a faster and easier route was established, called the Camino de las Cruces. The land portion of this trail was two-thirds shorter, and met with the Chagres River, which could be sailed out to the Caribbean Sea. This trail can be walked today, and portions of the stone-inlaid path still exist.

With Incan gold nearly exhausted, the Spanish turned their interests to the immense supply of silver found in Peruvian mines, and in 1537 they held their first trading fair, which would grow into one of the most important fairs in the world. With so much wealth changing hands on the isthmus, pirate attacks became increasingly common, and ports like Nombre de Dios declined in importance after having been raided by the English pirate Sir Francis Drake twice in 1572 and 1573. Portobelo was refortified and became the main port of trade. Panama City, on the other side of the isthmus, flourished with trade profits, and was considered one of the wealthiest cities in the Americas.

By the mid–17th century, dwindling supplies of silver and gold from the Peruvian mines and ongoing pirate attacks precipitated a severe decline in the amount of precious metals being transported to Spain. In 1671, the notorious Welsh buccaneer Henry Morgan sailed up the Chagres River, crossed the isthmus, and overpowered Panama City, sacking the city and leaving it in flames. Those who escaped the attack rebuilt Panama City, 2 years later, at what is now known as Casco Viejo.

Spain finally abandoned the isthmus crossing and Portobelo after the city was attacked by the British Admiral Edward Vernon, and returned to sailing around Cape Horn to reach Peru.

INDEPENDENCE FROM SPAIN & THE GOLD RUSH Spain granted independence to its Central America colonies in 1821, and Panama was

---

- **1914** The Panama Canal, one of the engineering wonders of the world, is completed.
- **1941** Women are given the right to vote.
- **1964** Anti-U.S. sentiment reaches a high point with student protests ("Los Mártires") that end with two dozen dead.
- **1966** Altos de Campana becomes Panama's first national park.
- **1968** National Guard General Omar Torrijos overthrows

Arnulfo Arias, a three-time presidential winner who'd served only 11 days of his term.
- **1977** Torrijos and Jimmy Carter sign a treaty to hand over the Panama Canal on December 31, 1999.
- **1981** Omar Torrijos dies in a plane crash, and National Guard Colonel Manuel Noriega begins reign of terror and drug-running in Panama.
- **1989** The U.S. invades Panama, known in the States

as Operation Just Cause. Noriega is captured and flown to the U.S., where he is tried and convicted on drug charges.
- **1999** The U.S. hands over the canal to Panama and shuts down its military bases. Mireya Moscoso is the first female elected president.
- **2004** Martín Torrijos, the son of Omar Torrijos, becomes Panama's youngest president ever.

absorbed into "Gran Colombia," a union led by liberator Simón Bolívar that included Colombia, Venezuela, and Ecuador. Panama attempted to split from Colombia three times during the 19th century, but wouldn't be successful until the U.S.-backed attempt in 1903.

Having been a colonial backwater since the pullout of the Spanish in the late 17th century, Panama was restored to prosperity from 1848 to 1869 during the height of the California Gold Rush. Given that crossing from the Atlantic to the Pacific of the U.S. was a long, arduous journey by wagon and prone to Indian attacks and other pitfalls, gold-seekers chose to sail to Panama, cross the Las Cruces trail, and sail on to California. In 1855, an American group of financiers built the Panama Railroad, greatly reducing the travel time between coasts. In 20 years, a total of 600,000 people crossed the isthmus, and both Colón and Panama City benefited enormously from the business earned in hotels, restaurants, and other services.

THE PANAMA CANAL The history of the canal dates back to 1539, when King Charles I of Spain dispatched a survey team to study the feasibility of a canal, but the team deemed such a pursuit impossible. The first real attempt at construction of a canal was begun in 1880 by the French, led by Ferdinand de Lesseps, the charismatic architect of the Suez Canal. De Lesseps had been convinced that a sea-level canal was the only option. Once workers broke ground, however, engineers soon saw the impracticality of a sea-level canal but were unable to convince the stubborn de Lesseps, and for years rumors flew, financial debts mounted, and nearly 20,000 workers perished before the endeavor collapsed. Few had anticipated the enormous challenge presented by the Panamanian jungle, with its mucky swamps, torrential downpours, landslides, floods, and, most debilitating of all, mosquito-borne diseases such as malaria and yellow fever.

Meanwhile, Panama was embroiled in political strife and a nonstop pursuit to separate itself from Colombia. Following the French failure with the canal, the U.S. expressed interest in taking over construction but was rebuffed by the Colombian government. In response, the U.S. backed a growing independence movement in Panama that declared its separation from Colombia on November 3, 1903. The U.S. officially recognized Panama, and sent its battleships to protect the new nation from Colombian troops, who turned back home after a few days.

A French canal engineer on the de Lesseps project, Philippe Bunau-Varilla, a major shareholder of the abandoned canal project, had been grudgingly given negotiating-envoy status by the Panamanian government for the new U.S.-built canal. His controversial Hay-Bunau-Varilla Treaty gave the U.S. overly generous rights that included the use, occupation, and sovereign control of a 16km-wide (10-mile) swath of land across the isthmus, and was entitled to annex more land if necessary to operate the canal. The U.S. would also be allowed to intervene in Panama's affairs.

The French had excavated ⅔ of the canal, built hospitals, and left behind machinery and the operating railway, as well as a sizeable workforce of Afro-Caribbeans. For the next 10 years, the U.S., having essentially eradicated tropical disease, pulled off what seemed impossible in terms of engineering: carving out a path through the Continental Divide, constructing an elevated canal system, and making the largest man-made lake in the world.

THE 20TH CENTURY TO THE PRESENT A stormy political climate ensued in Panama for the following decades, with frequent changes of administration. Presidents and other political figures were typically *rabiblancos*, or wealthy, white elites loathed by the generally poor and dark-skinned public. One especially controversial character in the political scene was Arnulfo Arias, a racist yet populist, one-time sympathizer of the fascist movement who would be voted into and thrown out of the presidency three times. Increasingly, Panamanians were discontented with the U.S. presence and, in particular, its control of the canal. In 1964, several U.S. high-school students in the Canal Zone raised the American flag at their school and ignited protests by Panamanian college students. The protests culminated in the deaths of more than two dozen Panamanians, an event that is now called "Día de los Mártires," or Martyrs Day.

By 1974, the U.S. had begun to consider transferring the canal to Panama. Arias was once again voted into power and after strong-arming the National Guard, he was deposed in a military coup led by Omar Torrijos Herrera, a colonel of the National Guard. Torrijos was an authoritarian leader but a champion of the poor who espoused land redistribution and social programs—a "dictatorship with a heart," as he called it. His most popular achievement came in 1977, with the signing of a treaty with then-president Jimmy Carter that relinquished control of the canal to Panama on December 31, 1999. Also part of the treaty was the closing of U.S. military bases and the U.S. right to intervene only if it perceived a threat against the security of the canal. On July 31, 1981, Torrijos died in a plane accident.

By 1983, the National Guard, now renamed the Panamanian Defense Forces (PDF), was firmly controlled by Colonel Manuel Antonio Noriega, and continued to dominate political and everyday life in Panama. Noriega created the so-called Dignity Battalions that aimed to stifle citizen dissent through force, and terrorize anyone who opposed the PDF. For the next 6 years, Noriega kept the Panamanian public in a state of virtual fear, running the country through presidents he had placed in power via rigged elections, killing and torturing his opponents, and involving himself in drug trafficking.

The U.S. imposed tough economic sanctions on Panama that included freezing government assets in U.S. banks, and withholding canal fees, spurning widespread protests against Noriega across Panama City. In 1989, a fresh set of presidential elections pitted the Noriega-picked candidate against Guillermo Endara. When Endara won, Noriega annulled the election amid widespread claims by foreign observers of fraud on the part of the Noriega regime.

With Panama veering out of control, the U.S. began sending troops to bases in the Canal Zone. On December 20, 1989, the U.S. launched Operation Just Cause, led by 25,000 soldiers who pounded the city for 6 days, leaving anywhere from 500 to 7,000 dead, depending on whom you asked. Noriega fled and hid in the offices of the Vatican *nuncio,* where he asked for asylum. He later surrendered and was flown to the U.S., where he was tried, charged, and sentenced to 40 years in prison. The sentence was later reduced and Noriega is now expected to be released in 2007. Though Noriega will serve jail time in Panama if he returns, Panamanians are justifiably nervous about his release.

In the wake of Noriega's extradition, Guillermo Endara was sworn in as president where he presided over a country racked by instability. In 1994, a former Torrijos associate, Ernesto Pérez Balladares, was sworn in as president and instituted sweeping economic reforms and worked to rebuild Panama's relationship with the U.S., which still had control of the canal. The same year, the constitution was changed to ban the military in Panama. Balladares was followed

A Feast of Languages

Spanish is the official language, but other languages are spoken in pockets around Panama. The country's seven indigenous groups speak a variety of dialects of Wounaan, Teribe, Emberá, Kuna, and Ngöbe-Buglé (Guayamí), the latter two being the most common given that they are the largest indigenous communities in Panama. In the Bocas del Toro region, descendants of Jamaican immigrants who came to work on banana plantations speak what's known as "Guari Guari," alternatively spelled "Wari Wari." It is also sometimes referred to as creole English, but really the language is patois English blended with Spanish and Guayamí (Ngöbe-Buglé) words. Native English speakers have a difficult time understanding Guari Guari. A good place to hear Guari Guari is at Old Bank on Isla Bastimentos.

San Miguel creole French, spoken by immigrants from Santa Lucía during the 19th century, is a dying language in Panama that's rarely heard any longer. On the other hand, Chinese immigrants, many of whom work as merchants running corner stores and small markets called *chinitos*, continue to speak their native tongue. Adding to this mélange is Arabic, spoken by immigrants from the Middle East.

by Mireya Moscoso in 1999, the ex-wife of Arias and Panama's first female president. During her 5 years in power, however, her approval ratings dropped to less than 30%; she was generally viewed as grossly incompetent and prone to cronyism and corruption. Moscoso oversaw the much-anticipated handover of the canal. Despite decades of protest against the U.S. presence, many Panamanians in the end expressed ambivalence about the pullout when faced with the economic impact on businesses and the loss of jobs. Still, the handover has defied everyone's expectations, and the canal is run today as well, if not better, than before. Panama's current president is Martín Torrijos, the son of the late Omar Torrijos, voted into office in 2004. The country's youngest president, he has a platform to increase jobs and security, and to fight against corruption.

3 Panamanian Food & Drink

Panama is a melting pot of ethnicities, and its cuisine is accordingly influenced by its diverse population. Within Panama City, travelers will find something from every corner of the world, including French, Japanese, Italian, Thai, Middle Eastern, and Chinese food—all of it very good and true to its roots. In regional areas, traditional Panamanian cuisine is an overlapping mix of Afro-Caribbean, indigenous, and Spanish cooking influences incorporating a variety of tropical fruits, vegetables, and herbs. Most Panamanian restaurants are casual—diners, beachfront cafes, and roadside *fondas* (food stands). A large U.S. population has spawned North American cafes and bistros serving burgers and the like, and fast-food chains are plentiful in Panama City.

MEALS & DINING CUSTOMS

Panamanian cuisine is tasty but can be repetitive given that every meal is based around coconut rice and beans, and fried green plantains called *patacones*. A lot of Panamanian food is fried—just stop at a *fonda* and see for yourself. Even breakfast is a selection of fried meats and breads.

Dining hours generally follow North American customs, with restaurants opening early around 7 or 8am for breakfast, serving lunch from noon to 2pm, and dinner from 7 to 10pm. In smaller towns, you'll find that restaurants close as early as 9 or sometimes even 8pm. Upscale restaurants in Panama City serve until 11pm.

BREAKFAST   Start your day with a cup of fresh-brewed Panamanian joe. Breakfast menus around the country feature standbys like scrambled eggs, toast, and fruit, but Panamanians like their tortillas, too. These are not Mexican-style tortillas but deep-fried corn batter topped with eggs and cheese, something akin to huevos rancheros. *Hojaldras,* deep-fried bread sprinkled with powdered sugar like a Panamanian doughnut, are another common breakfast staple. Afro-Caribbeans eat greasy meats like pork with their breakfast; if your cholesterol level is low, give it a try. A hearty breakfast of "Caribbean porridge," made of rice, beans, and pork, is called *gallo pinto,* or "spotted rooster," and can be found in local joints.

APPETIZERS & SNACKS   Ceviche, raw cubes of fish and onion marinated in lemon juice, is a popular dish throughout Latin America. It's usually made with sea bass or with shrimp or octopus. Crunchy cornmeal pastries stuffed with meat are called empanadas—greasy but good when they're fresh and hot. The yuca root, a Panamanian staple, when fried, substitutes for french fries. Yuca is also used for a *carimañola;* the yuca is mashed and formed into a roll stuffed with meat and boiled eggs, then deep-fried. Plantains are served in two varieties: *patacones,*

or green plantains, cut in rounds, pounded and deep-fried, and salted; or *plátanos maduros,* ripe plantains, broiled or sautéed in oil. Ripe plantains are also called *plátanos en tentación* when they are slightly caramelized with sugar and cinnamon. Plantains and *patacones,* along with coconut rice *(arroz con coco)* and beans *(frijoles),* are the standard accompaniment to traditional Panamanian dishes. Another popular snack is a tamale; much like the Mexican version, tamales are cornmeal patties stuffed with meat and steamed in a banana leaf. Sandwiches in Panama are called *emparedados.*

MEAT & POULTRY   There is perhaps no dish more emblematic of Panama than the *sancocho,* a chicken stew made with a starchy root called *ñame* and seasoned with a cilantro-like herb called culantro. Sancocho is said to put strength back into your body after a late night out. Meat is commonplace, served as a *bistec* (steak), or in a popular dish called *ropa vieja,* meaning "old clothes" and consisting of shredded beef with a spicy tomato sauce served over rice. Chicken is a staple, too, as is pork. In the Caribbean, some locals still eat turtle soup and turtle eggs, although it is usually kept under wraps due to vocal conservation efforts to protect turtles—these are endangered creatures, so refuse turtle if ever given the chance.

SEAFOOD   Panama, which means "abundance of fish," lives up to its name with lots of fresh delicacies from the sea, including *pargo* (red snapper), *corvina* (sea bass), *langostino* (jumbo shrimp), *langosta* (lobster), calamari, *cangrejo* (crab), and *pulpo* (octopus). Traditional Panamanian seafood dishes come four ways: fried, grilled, *al ajillo* (with a spicy garlic sauce), or *a la española* (sautéed with tomatoes and onions). Lobster and jumbo shrimp are expensive because of overfishing and dwindling supplies.

VEGETABLES   Panama's agricultural breadbasket is around the flank of Volcán Barú in the western Highlands; here the volcanic soil and high altitudes encourage year-round growing conditions, and vegetables are readily available. Elsewhere, the hot, humid weather is not conducive to growing vegetables, which is why you'll see so few served with meals. Salads are not hard to come by, but traditional Panamanian fare is typically only served with just a small cabbage salad topped with a slice of tomato. Sometimes you'll see corn, or the exotic root vegetables such as the aforementioned yuca and *ñamé.*

FRUITS   Panama has a wealth of tropical fruits, but the most common you'll see (especially at breakfast) are pineapple, papaya, banana, and melon. Other fruits are the *maracuyá,* or passion fruit, which is better as a juice than off the tree; *guanabana,* or soursop; and *guayaba,* or guava.

DESSERTS   *Pastel tres leches,* or "three-milk cake," is made with just that: evaporated, condensed, and regular milk, cooked into a rich, puddinglike cake. Flan is as popular here as it is all over Latin America. Street vendors in Panama City (especially on Av. Balboa or in Casco Viejo) sell *raspados,* or fruit-juice-flavored snow cones. Panamanians like to top the cone off with a dollop of condensed milk.

BEVERAGES   Major brands of soft drinks are available in Panama. You can't find a more fresh-off-the-tree beverage than a *pipa,* the sweet, clear liquid of an unripe coconut. Roadside vendors hack a hole in the crown of the coconut, pop in a straw, and for about 25¢ you have what some refer to as the "nectar of the gods." It is also said to aid digestion. *Chicha* is the common name for juice, and the variety of fresh fruit juices in Panama is a tasty and refreshing elixir on a hot day. *Chichas* come in a variety of common flavors such as watermelon and pineapple, but there are more exotic *chichas* such as

chicha con arroz y piña, a beverage made from rice and boiled pineapple skins; *naranjilla,* a tropical fruit whose juice has the taste of apple cider; or *chicha de marañón,* a beverage made from the fruit of a cashew tree. A local favorite in the outskirts of Panama City (mostly sold at roadside stands) is *chicheme,* a corn-based beverage mixed with water, sugar, and cinnamon. Panamanians tout the drink for its nutritional properties.

Panama is known for its high-quality coffee, with Café Durán being the most common brand. Kotowa, the Jansen Family, and Café Ruiz are all excellent, too. *Café con leche* is coffee with milk (usually condensed) or cream.

BEER, WINE & LIQUOR   When in Panama, do as the locals do and down an icy cold local beer. Beer is Panama's most popular alcoholic drink, and there is a wide variety of national brands to sample, such as Balboa, Atlas, Panamá, Soberana, and Cristal—all light pale lagers, none of which are particularly outstanding, but all taste divine in a hot, sticky climate. International brands such as Heineken, Corona, and Guinness can be found even in small-town markets.

Panama's most famous drink is *seco,* a sugar-cane-distilled alcohol produced in Herrera and commonly served with milk and ice. You won't find *seco* in trendy bars or high-end restaurants; it's consumed mostly in rural communities and cantinas. Also popular in Panama are rum, vodka, and scotch.

You'll find Chilean, U.S., and Spanish wines on most menus, but the selection is limited, and restaurants serve red wines cold (must have something to do with the climate). But wine consumption is increasing in Panama, evidenced by the growing number of upscale restaurants that put time and thought into their wine lists, and there are a few wine-specialty stores popping up here and there.

Appendix B:
Glossary of Spanish
Terms & Phrases

The official language of Panama is Spanish. However, with so many new hotel owners hailing from the U.S. and Canada, English is widely spoken in the tour industry. But this doesn't get you off the hook—taxi drivers, waiters, local tour guides, and everyday Panamanians speak little or no English. Arm yourself with basic words and phrases in Spanish and your trip won't be a constant battle to make yourself understood. Panamanians appreciate the effort, and really, part of the fun of traveling is learning the local lingo. Due to the long U.S. presence in Panama, you'll hear a few expressions that have been adapted from English, such as "parkear," meaning to park, or "watchiman," for security guard (watchman).

Panamanians speak at a relatively relaxed speed, and they have a more neutral accent when compared with their Latin American neighbors. Panamanians speaking in a slangy manner have a tendency to drop the "d" from words that end in *–ido* or *–ado*, as in *pelao,* instead of *pelado.* Like most Latin Americans, Panamanians are more conscious of salutations. Before launching into conversation or asking a question, do not forget a greeting such as "Buenos días" or "Buenas tardes," or like most Panamanians say, simply "Buenas."

1 Basic Words & Phrases

English	Spanish	Pronunciation
Hello	**Buenos días**	*bweh*-nohss *dee*-ahss
How are you?	**¿Cómo está usted?**	*koh*-moh ehss-*tah* oo-*stehd*
Very well	**Muy bien**	mwee byehn
Thank you	**Gracias**	*grah*-syahss
Good-bye	**Adiós**	ad-*dyohss*
Please	**Por favor**	pohr fah-*vohr*
Yes	**Sí**	see
No	**No**	noh
Excuse me (to get by someone)	**Perdóneme**	pehr-*doh*-neh-meh
Excuse me (to begin a question)	**Disculpe**	dees-*kool*-peh
Give me	**Deme**	*deh*-meh
Where is . . . ?	**¿Dónde está . . . ?**	*dohn*-deh ehss-*tah*
the station	**la estación**	la ehss-*tah*-syohn
the bus stop	**la parada**	la pah-*rah*-dah

English	Spanish	Pronunciation
a hotel	**un hotel**	oon oh-*tehl*
a restaurant	**un restaurante**	oon res-tow-*rahn*-teh
the toilet	**el baño**	el *bah*-nyo
To the right	**A la derecha**	ah lah deh-*reh*-chah
To the left	**A la izquierda**	ah lah ees-*kyehr*-dah
Straight ahead	**Adelante**	ah-deh-*lahn*-teh
I would like . . .	**Quiero . . .**	*kyeh*-roh
to eat	**comer**	ko-*mehr*
a room	**una habitación**	oo-nah ah-bee-tah-*syohn*
How much is it?	**¿Cuánto?**	*kwahn*-toh
The check	**La cuenta**	la *kwen*-tah
When?	**¿Cuándo?**	*kwan*-doh
What?	**¿Qué?**	keh
Yesterday	**Ayer**	ah-*yehr*
Today	**Hoy**	oy
Tomorrow	**Mañana**	mah-*nyah*-nah
Breakfast	**Desayuno**	deh-sah-*yoo*-noh
Lunch	**Comida**	coh-*mee*-dah
Dinner	**Cena**	*seh*-nah
Do you speak English?	**¿Habla usted inglés?**	*ah*-blah oo-*stehd* een-*glehss*
I don't understand Spanish very well.	**No (lo) entiendo muy bien el español.**	noh (loh) ehn-*tyehn*-do mwee byehn el ehss-pah-*nyohl*

NUMBERS

1 **Uno** (*oo*-noh)
2 **Dos** (dohss)
3 **Tres** (trehss)
4 **Cuatro** (*kwah*-troh)
5 **Cinco** (*seen*-koh)

6 **Seis** (sayss)
7 **Siete** (*syeh*-teh)
8 **Ocho** (*oh*-choh)
9 **Nueve** (*nweh*-beh)
10 **Diez** (dyehss)

DAYS OF THE WEEK

Monday	**Lunes**	(*loo*-nehss)
Tuesday	**Martes**	(*mahr*-tehss)
Wednesday	**Miércoles**	(*myehr*-koh-lehss)
Thursday	**Jueves**	(*wheh*-behss)
Friday	**Viernes**	(*byehr*-nehss)
Saturday	**Sábado**	(*sah*-bah-doh)
Sunday	**Domingo**	(doh-*meen*-goh)

2 Some Typical Panamanian Words & Phrases

A la orden   You're welcome.

Bien cuidado   A homeless person or beggar. Means "well taken care of," and refers to what such a person says when seeking a tip for having watched a parked car.

Blanco   Cigarette.

Bomba   Gas station.

Buay   Boy, adapted from English.

Buco   A lot, from the French "beaucoup."

Buenón/buenote   A handsome man.

Casa bruja   Cheap home made of scraps and usually built illegally on taken land.

Chinito   Corner store or small market, so-called because they are usually owned by Chinese descendants.

Cholo   Villager or country bumpkin.

¡Chuleta!   Interjection, akin to "Oh my God!" or "Shoot!"

Con mucho gusto   With pleasure.

Diablo Rojo   Red Devil, name for the old school buses used for public transportation.

Fría   Slang for beer.

Fulo/a   Blonde.

Gallo   Distasteful, tacky, awful.

Goma   Hangover.

Guaro   Hard alcohol.

Guial   Girl, adapted from English.

Ir por fuera   To leave. "*Voy por fuera*" means "I'm leaving."

La "U"   University.

Maleante   Gang member or low-class male.

Mami/Papi   Commonly used to address a stranger with friendly affection, or used to describe an attractive woman or man.

Palo   One dollar or one balboa, as in "It costs 10 *palos*."

Pebre   Food.

Pelado   Young boy, usually pronounced *pelao*.

Policia muerto   Speed bump, means "dead policeman."

Push button   A pay-by-the-hour motel, adapted from motels that attracted U.S. military personnel and had signs saying "push the button to shut the door."

Priti   Pretty, but can also be used to describe something nice.

Racataca   A low-class, tacky woman.

Rabiblanco/a   Term for a member of the elite, usually Caucasian. Translated, the term means "white tailed."

Refresco   Soft drink.

Tongo   Slang for police officer.

Vaina   Thing or object.

Washington   A dollar.

Yeye   Wealthy show-off.

3 Menu Terms

FISH

Almejas   Clams
Atún   Tuna
Bacalao   Cod
Calamares   Squid
Camarones   Shrimp
Cangrejo   Crab
Ceviche   Marinated seafood salad
Corvina   Sea bass

Dorado   Dolphin or mahimahi
Langosta   Lobster
Langostina   Jumbo shrimp
Lenguado   Sole
Ostras   Oysters
Pargo   Red Snapper
Pulpo   Octopus
Trucha   Trout

MEATS

Bistec   Beefsteak
Cordero   Lamb
Costillas   Ribs
Jamón   Ham

Pavo   Turkey
Pollo   Chicken
Puerco   Pork
Tasajo   Gooey smoked beef

VEGETABLES

Aceitunas   Olives
Ensalada   Salad
Lechuga   Lettuce
Ñamé   Starchy root vegetable

Papa   Potato
Tomate   Tomato
Yuca   Cassava or manioc

FRUITS

Fresa   Strawberry
Guayaba   Guava
Manzana   Apple
Maracuyá   Passion fruit
Marañyón   Cashew nut fruit

Naranja   Orange
Piña   Pineapple
Plátano   Plantain
Sandía   Watermelon

BASICS

Aceite   Oil
Ajo   Garlic
Azúcar   Sugar
Bollos   Corn patties filled with chicken or coconut
Chicha   Fruit juice
Chicheme   Sweet and hearty corn drink
Empanada   Crunchy cornmeal pastry filled with meat
Emparedado   Sandwich
Frito   Fried
Gallo   Corn tortilla topped with meat or chicken
Gallo pinto   Rice and bean soup

Hielo   Ice
Limón   Lemon
Mantequilla   Butter
Miel   Honey
Mostaza   Mustard
Pan   Bread
Patacones   Pounded and fried green plantains
Pimienta   Pepper
Queso   Cheese
Sal   Salt
Sancocho   Chicken stew
Tamale   Filled cornmeal pastry
Tortilla   Flat corn pancake

Appendix C:
Panamanian Wildlife

with assistance from E. Z. Weaver

For such a tiny country, Panama is incredibly rich in biodiversity—some scientists call the country "hyperdiverse" given that flora and fauna from both North and South America meet here on this land bridge. Panama is home to a greater number of bird species than found in the U.S. and Canada combined, and there are more species of plants in the Canal Basin than found in all of Europe. Whether you come to Panama to check 100 or so species off your birding list, or just to check out of the rat race for a week or so, you'll be surrounded by a rich and varied collection of flora and fauna. The information below is meant to be a selective introduction to some of what you might see.

In many instances, the prime viewing recommendations should be taken with a firm dose of reality. Most casual visitors and even many dedicated naturalists will never see a jaguar or kinkajou. However, anyone traveling with a sharp, knowledgeable guide should be able to see a broad selection of Panama's impressive flora and fauna.

1 Fauna

MAMMALS

Panama is home to more than 225 species of mammals. While it is very unlikely that you will spot a puma, you have good odds of catching a glimpse of a monkey, coatimundi, agouti, or sloth.

SCIENTIFIC NAME *Panthera onca*

WORTH NOTING This cat measures from 1 to 1.8m (3½–6 ft.) plus tail and is distinguished by its tan/yellowish fur with black spots. The name comes from *yaguar,* a Guaraní (indigenous group from Paraguay) word.

PRIME VIEWING **Jaguars** exist in major tracts of primary and secondary forest in Panama, as well as savannahs and swamps. Jaguars are endangered and it is extremely difficult to see in the wild. The largest concentrations of jaguars can be found in La Amistad International Park and Darién National Park.

Jaguar

SCIENTIFIC NAME   *Leopardus pardalis*

WORTH NOTING   Commonly mistaken for a margay, **ocelots** are larger and were once highly valued for their fur. Known for their fierce territorial disputes, ocelots are mostly nocturnal and sleep in trees.

PRIME VIEWING   Ocelots are found in forests throughout Panama, especially in La Amistad and Darién parks, and they are occasionally spotted on walks in Soberanía National Park.

Ocelot

SCIENTIFIC NAME   *Tapirus bairdii*

WORTH NOTING   Also known as the *danta* or *macho de monte,* **Baird's tapir** is the largest land mammal in Panama, growing to 2m (6½ ft.) in length and 1.2m (4 ft.) in height. Tapirs are active both day and night, foraging along riverbanks, streams, and forest clearings.

PRIME VIEWING   An endangered species, tapirs can be found in wet forested areas, particularly on the Caribbean and south Pacific slopes. They are occasionally seen in the Darién wilderness.

Baird's Tapir

Kinkajou

SCIENTIFIC NAME   *Potos flavus*

WORTH NOTING   The nocturnal, tree-dwelling **kinkajou** has large eyes that give it a childlike appearance.

PRIME VIEWING   Kinkajous are found in forests throughout Panama, but you really need to do a night trip to see one.

SCIENTIFIC NAME   *Mazama americana*

WORTH NOTING   These small animals measure 1 to 1.4m (3½–4½ ft.). Their size allows them to slip through dense vegetation. Small, straight antlers distinguish the male.

PRIME VIEWING   The **red brocket deer** is easily spotted on Isla Contadora, but is also found in Soberanía National Park and on Isla Coiba.

Red Brocket Deer

SCIENTIFIC NAME   *Leopardus wiedii*

WORTH NOTING   An endangered species, the **margay** is one of the smaller wild cats of the region, and is often found in trees like its cousin, the ocelot.

PRIME VIEWING   Forests in all regions of Panama.

Margay

Puma

SCIENTIFIC NAME   *Puma concolor*

WORTH NOTING   Nearly 1.5m (5 ft.) long when fully grown, these feline predators are the largest unspotted cats in the region. Also known as a mountain lion, the **puma** is brownish, reddish-brown, or tawny in color with a white throat.

PRIME VIEWING   Puma prowl in lowland forests, and semi-open areas.

SCIENTIFIC NAME   *Nasua narica*

WORTH NOTING   Known as *gato solo* in Panama, the raccoonlike **coatimundi** can adapt to habitat disturbances and is often spotted near hotels and nature lodges. Active both day and night, it is equally comfortable on the ground and in trees.

PRIME VIEWING   Found throughout Panama in lowland rainforest and cloud forests. They are social animals, and are sometimes found in groups of 10 to 20.

Coatimundi

SCIENTIFIC NAME   *Dasyprocta*

WORTH NOTING   The **agouti paca** is a rabbit-size rodent with glossy orange-brown fur that is easy to see, but they flee in panic when they realize they have been spotted. Agoutis live in rainforest and savanna areas. The agouti is sometimes confused with its larger cousin, the paca. In Panama, they're commonly referred to as *ñeque,* or *conejo pintado:* "painted rabbit."

PRIME VIEWING   Agoutis like river valleys, swamps, and dense tropical forest, and they are commonly seen in the Metropolitan Park, on Cerro Ancon, in the Canal Zone, and on Isla Coiba.

Agouti Paca

Collared Peccary

SCIENTIFIC NAME   *Tayassu tajacu*

WORTH NOTING   Called *saino* in Panama, the **collared peccary** is a black or brown piglike animal that travels in small groups (larger where populations are still numerous) and has a strong musk odor.

PRIME VIEWING   Tropical dry and rainforest in most of Panama. Note that peccaries can be aggressive and it's best to keep your distance if you see one.

SCIENTIFIC NAME   *Cyclopes didactylus*

WORTH NOTING   Also known as the pygmy or silky **anteater,** this nocturnal creature grows up to 18 centimeters (7 in.), not counting its thick tail (which is as long or longer than its body).

PRIME VIEWING   The anteater lives in wet tropical forests in all regions of Panama, but can be difficult to spot because it is nocturnal and lives high in trees.

Anteater

SCIENTIFIC NAME   *Dasypus novemcinctus*

WORTH NOTING   The prehistoric-looking **armadillo** is nocturnal and terrestrial.

PRIME VIEWING   Armadillos are found throughout Panama usually poking around leafy understory.

Armadillo

Three-Toed Sloth

SCIENTIFIC NAME   *Bradypus variegatus*

WORTH NOTING   The larger and more commonly sighted of Panama's two sloth species, the **three-toed sloth** has long, coarse brown to gray fur and a distinctive eye band. They have three long and sharp claws on each foreleg. Except for brief periods used for defecation, these slow-moving creatures are entirely arboreal.

PRIME VIEWING   Low- and middle-elevation forests in all of Panama. This is one of the most commonly seen animals; look for them hanging on to tree branches.

SCIENTIFIC NAME   *Alouatta palliata*

WORTH NOTING   The highly social **mantled howler monkey** grows to 56 centimeters (22 in.) in size and often travels in groups of 10 to 30. The characteristic loud roar of the male can be heard as far as 1.6km (1 mile) away.

PRIME VIEWING   Wet and dry forests across Panama. Almost entirely arboreal, they tend to favor the higher reaches of the canopy.

Mantled Howler Monkey

Spider Monkey

SCIENTIFIC NAME   *Ateles geoffroyi*

WORTH NOTING   **Spider monkeys** are extremely agile in trees, rarely touching down on the forest floor. They are large monkeys (64 centimeters/25 in.) with brown or silvery fur, and they often sport a worried look.

PRIME VIEWING   Throughout the Canal Basin and in the Darién forest.

Hairy-Legged Bat

SCIENTIFIC NAME   *Myotis keaysi*

WORTH NOTING   The **hairy-legged bat** grows to a whopping 5.1 centimeters (2 in.) in length, not including the length of its tail.

PRIME VIEWING   In caves, forests, rock crevices, gardens, and buildings throughout Panama.

BIRDS

Panama has more than 940 identified species of resident and migrant birds. The variety of habitats and compact nature of the country make it a major bird-watching destination.

SCIENTIFIC NAME   *Ramphastos sulfuratus*

WORTH NOTING   The rainbow-colored canoe-shape bill and brightly colored feathers make the **keel-billed toucan** a favorite of bird-watching tours. The toucan can grow to about 51 centimeters (20 in.) in length. It's similar in size and shape to the chestnut mandibled toucan. Panama also is home to several smaller toucanet and aracari species.

PRIME VIEWING   Lowland forests on the Caribbean and north Pacific slopes. The keel-billed toucan is often spotted around the Canal Zone and in the Darién.

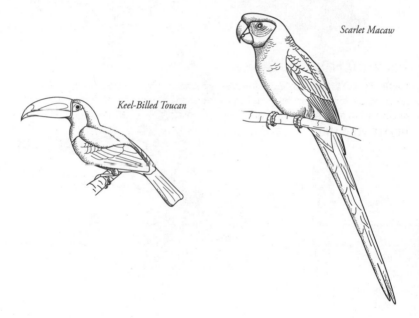

Scarlet Macaw

Keel-Billed Toucan

SCIENTIFIC NAME   *Ara macao*

WORTH NOTING   Known as *guacamaya* in Panama, the **scarlet macaw** is a long-tailed member of the parrot family. It can reach 89 centimeters (35 in.) in length. The bird is endangered over most of its range, particularly because it is so coveted as a pet. Its loud squawk and rainbow-colored feathers are quite distinctive.

PRIME VIEWING   Given the declining numbers of scarlet macaws in the wild, Isla Coiba National Park is the only region where these magnificent birds exist in numbers.

SCIENTIFIC NAME   *Pharomchrus mocinno*

WORTH NOTING   Perhaps the most distinctive and spectacular bird in Central America, the **resplendent quetzal,** of the trogon family, can grow to 37 centimeters (14½ in.). The males are distinctive, with bright red chests, iridescent blue-green coats, a yellow bill, and tail feathers that can reach another 76 centimeters (30 in.) in length. The females lack the long tail feathers and have duller beak and less pronounced red chest.

PRIME VIEWING   High-elevation wet and cloud forests, particularly in Volcán Barú National Park and the Finca Lérida estate near Boquete.

Replendent Quetzal

Magnificent Frigate Bird

SCIENTIFIC NAME   *Fregata magnificens*

WORTH NOTING   The **magnificent frigate bird** is a naturally agile flier and it swoops (unlike other seabirds, it doesn't dive or swim) to pluck food from the water's surface or—more commonly—it steals catch from the mouths of other birds.

PRIME VIEWING   Along the shores and coastal islands of both coasts. Often seen soaring high overhead.

SCIENTIFIC NAME   *Psarocolius montezuma*

WORTH NOTING   **Montezuma's oropendola** has a black head, brown body, a yellow-edged tail, a large black bill with an orange tip, and a blue patch under the eye. These birds build long, teardrop-shape hanging nests, often found in large groups. They have several distinct loud calls, including one that they make while briefly hanging upside down.

PRIME VIEWING   Low and middle elevations along the Caribbean slope, especially around Bocas del Toro. The black oropendola lives east of the Canal Zone.

Montezuma's Oropendola

Red-Eyed Tree Frog

AMPHIBIANS

Frogs, toads, and salamanders are actually some of the most beguiling, beautiful, and easy-to-spot residents of tropical forests.

SCIENTIFIC NAME   *Agalychnis callidryas*

WORTH NOTING   The colorful 7.6-centimeter (3-in.) **red-eyed tree frog** usually has a pale or dark green back, sometimes with white or yellow spots, with blue-purple patches and vertical bars on the body, orange hands and feet, and deep red eyes. Also known as the gaudy leaf frog. Nocturnal.

PRIME VIEWING   Low- and middle-elevation wet forests throughout Panama. This is a very beautiful and distinctive-looking frog that you will often see on T-shirts and postcards if not in the wild.

REPTILES

Panama's reptile species range from the frightening and justly feared fer-de-lance pit viper and massive American crocodile to a wide variety of turtles and lizards. ***Note:*** Sea turtles are included in "Sea Life," below.

SCIENTIFIC NAME   *Boa constrictor*

WORTH NOTING   Adult **boa constrictors** average about 1.8 to 3m (6–10 ft.) in length and weigh over 27 kilograms (60 lb.). Their coloration camouflages them, but look for patterns of cream, brown, gray, and black ovals and diamonds.

PRIME VIEWING   Low- and middle-elevation wet and dry forests, countrywide. They often live in rafters and eaves of homes in rural areas.

Boa Constrictor

SCIENTIFIC NAME   *Bothrops atrox*

WORTH NOTING   The aggressive **fer-de-lance** is a pit viper that can grow to 2.4m (8 ft.) in length, and it is considered the most dangerous snake of Central and South America. Beige, brown, or black triangles flank either side of the head, while the area under the head is a vivid yellow. These snakes begin life as arboreal but become increasingly terrestrial as they grow older and larger.

PRIME VIEWING   All regions, but especially the Darién.

Fer-de-Lance

Green Iguana

SCIENTIFIC NAME   *Iguana iguana*

WORTH NOTING   **Green iguanas** can vary in shades ranging from bright green to a dull grayish-green, with quite a bit of orange mixed in. The iguana will often perch on a branch overhanging a river and plunge into the water when threatened.

PRIME VIEWING   All lowland regions of the country, living near rivers and streams, along both coasts.

Basilisk

SCIENTIFIC NAME   *Basiliscus vittatus*

WORTH NOTING   The **basilisk** can run across the surface of water for short distances by using its hind legs and holding its body almost upright; thus, the reptile is also known as "the Jesus Christ lizard."

PRIME VIEWING   In trees and on rocks located near water in wet forests throughout the country.

American Crocodile

SCIENTIFIC NAME   *Crocodylus acutus*

WORTH NOTING   Although an endangered species, environmental awareness and protection policies have allowed the massive **American crocodile** to mount an impressive comeback in recent years. While these reptiles can reach lengths of 6.4m (21 ft.), most are much smaller, usually less than 4m (13 ft.).

PRIME VIEWING Near swamps, mangrove swamps, estuaries, large rivers, and coastal lowlands, countrywide. You'll see these beasts in the canal and the Chagres River.

SEA LIFE

With 2,490km (1,547 miles) of shoreline on both the Pacific and Caribbean coasts, Panama has a rich diversity of underwater flora and fauna.

SCIENTIFIC NAME *Rhincodon typus*

WORTH NOTING Although the **whale shark** grows to lengths of 14m (45 ft.) or more, its gentle nature makes swimming with them a special treat for divers and snorkelers.

PRIME VIEWING Whale sharks can be seen in the Pacific, off Coiba Island and around the Pearl Islands.

Whale Shark

SCIENTIFIC NAME *Dermochelys coriacea*

WORTH NOTING The world's largest sea turtle (reaching nearly 2.4m/8 ft. in length and weighing more than 544 kilograms/1,200 lb.), the **leatherback sea turtle** is now an endangered species.

PRIME VIEWING These large reptiles nest in the Caribbean around Bocas del Toro on beaches on Isla Bastimentos and in the San San Pond Sak Wetlands; in the Pacific, they are known to nest on Isla Cañas.

Leatherback Sea Turtle

Olive Ridley Sea Turtle

SCIENTIFIC NAME *Lepidochelys olivacea*

WORTH NOTING Also known as tortuga mulata, the **olive ridley sea turtle** is the smallest of the turtles that visit Panama, and they are famous for their massive group nestings, or *arribadas*.

PRIME VIEWING There is no guaranteed date for viewing an *arribada,* but you definitely won't see one during the dry season from December to March. The best site to view these turtles is at Isla Cañas.

SCIENTIFIC NAME   *Trichechus manatus*

WORTH NOTING   Manatees in Panama are Antillean manatees, a subspecies of the West Indian manatee. These "sea cows" can reach lengths of 3 to 4m (10–13 ft.) and weigh 499 to 1,588 kilograms (1,100–3,500 lb.).

PRIME VIEWING   Coastal mangroves, especially in the San San Pond Sak Wetlands, and along the coast of the Comarca Kuna Yala.

Manatee

SCIENTIFIC NAME   *Manta birostris*

WORTH NOTING   Manta rays are the largest type of rays, with a wingspan that can reach 6m (20 ft.) and a body weight known to exceed 1,361 kilograms (3,000 lb.). Despite their daunting appearance, manta rays are quite gentle. If you are snorkeling or diving, watch for one of these extraordinary and graceful creatures.

PRIME VIEWING   In mangrove swamps and coral reef, especially alongside steep walls and drop-offs, in the Caribbean and Pacific.

Manta Ray

Stingray

SCIENTIFIC NAME   *Dasyatis americana*

WORTH NOTING   True to their name, **stingrays** can give you a painful shock if you touch the venomous spine at the base of their tails. Be careful when wading in sandy areas, where they prefer to bury themselves.

PRIME VIEWING   Along both coasts and around islands, especially in shallow sand or grassy areas.

Nurse Shark

SCIENTIFIC NAME *Ginglymostoma cirratum*

WORTH NOTING The most frequently spotted shark in Panamanian waters, the **nurse shark** spends most of its time resting on the ocean floor. Reaching lengths of 4.3m (14 ft.), their heads are larger than those of most sharks, and they appear to be missing the bottom half of their tail.

PRIME VIEWING Along the coast and especially around offshore islands.

Barracuda

SCIENTIFIC NAME *Sphyraena barracuda*

WORTH NOTING The **barracuda** is a slender fish with two dorsal fins and a large mouth. Juvenile barracudas often swim near the shore, so exercise caution, as attacks on humans occasionally occur.

PRIME VIEWING Found in both the Caribbean and Pacific oceans.

Moray Eel

SCIENTIFIC NAME *Gymnothorax mordax*

WORTH NOTING Distinguished by a swaying serpent-head and teeth-filled jaw that continually opens and closes, the **moray eel** is most commonly seen with only its head appearing from behind rocks. At night, however, it leaves its home along the reef to hunt for small fish, crustaceans, shrimp, and octopus.

PRIME VIEWING Rocky areas and reefs off both coasts.

SCIENTIFIC NAME   *Megaptera novaeangliae*

WORTH NOTING   The migratory **humpbacked whale** spends the winters in the Southern Hemisphere and migrates north along Pacific Coast from June to September. These mammals have black backs and whitish throat and chest areas. Whales breed when spending time off the coast of Panama.

PRIME VIEWING   Humpback whales can be spotted off the shore of the Pacific Coast, around Coiba Island, the Pearl Islands, and the Azuero Peninsula.

Humpbacked Whale

SCIENTIFIC NAME   *Tursiops truncates*

WORTH NOTING   Their wide tail fin, dark gray back, and light gray sides identify **bottle-nosed dolphins.** Dolphins grow to lengths of 3.7m (12 ft.) and weigh up to 635 kilograms (1,400 lb.).

PRIME VIEWING   Along both coasts, especially in Dolphin Bay in Bocas del Toro, the Gulf of Chiriquí, and around Punta Patiño.

Bottle-Nosed Dolphin

SCIENTIFIC NAME   *Diploria strigosa*

WORTH NOTING   The distinctive **brain coral** is named for its striking physical similarity to a human brain.

PRIME VIEWING   Reefs off both coasts.

Brain Coral

INVERTEBRATES

Creepy crawlies, biting bugs, spiders, and the like give most folks chills. But this group, which includes moths, butterflies, ants, beetles, and even crabs, includes some of the most fascinating and easily viewed fauna in Panama.

SCIENTIFIC NAME   *Morpho peleides*

WORTH NOTING   The large **blue morpho** butterfly, with a wingspan of up to 15 centimeters (6 in.), has brilliantly iridescent blue wings when opened. Fast and erratic fliers, they are often glimpsed flitting across your peripheral vision in dense forest.

PRIME VIEWING   Countrywide, particularly in moist environments.

Blue Morpho

Leafcutter Ants

SCIENTIFIC NAME   *Atta cephalotes*

WORTH NOTING   You can't miss the miniature rainforest highways formed by these industrious little red **leafcutter ants** carrying their freshly cut payload. The ants do not actually eat the leaves, but instead feed off a fungus that grows on the decomposing leaves in their massive underground nests.

PRIME VIEWING   Can be found in most forests countrywide.

SCIENTIFIC NAME   *Nephila clavipes*

WORTH NOTING   The common neotropical **golden silk spider** weaves meticulous webs that can be as much as .5m (2 ft.) across. The adult female of this species can reach 7.6 centimeters (3 in.) in length, including the legs, although the males are tiny. The silk of this spider is extremely strong and is being studied for industrial purposes.

PRIME VIEWING   Lowland forests on both coasts.

SCIENTIFIC NAME   *Gecarcinus quadratus*

Golden Silk Spider

Mouthless Crab

WORTH NOTING   The nocturnal **mouthless crab** is a distinctively colored land crab with bright orange legs, purple claws, and a deep black shell or carapace.

PRIME VIEWING   All along the Pacific Coast.

2 Flora

TREES

It's often a good thing to be able to identify specific trees within a forest. We've included illustrations to get you started.

SCIENTIFIC NAME   *Ceiba pentandra*

WORTH NOTING   Also known as the kapok tree, **ceiba** trees are typically emergent (their large umbrella-shape canopies emerge above the forest canopy), making the species among the tallest trees in the tropical forest. Reaching as high as 60m (197 ft.), their thick columnar trunks often have large buttresses. Ceiba trees may flower as little as once every 5 years, especially in wetter forests.

PRIME VIEWING   Countrywide.

Ceiba

SCIENTIFIC NAME   *Enterolobium cyclocarpum*

WORTH NOTING   The **guanacaste** tree is one of the largest trees found in Central America, and is called *corotu* in Panama. It can reach a total elevation of over 39m (130 ft.); its straight trunk composes 9 to 12m (30–40 ft.) of the height (the trunk's diameter measures more than 1.8m/6 ft.).

PRIME VIEWING   Countrywide.

Guanacaste

SCIENTIFIC NAME   *Ficus aurea*

WORTH NOTING   This parasitic tree gets its name from the fact that it envelops and eventually strangles its host tree. The *matapalo,* or **strangler fig,** begins as an epiphyte, whose seeds are deposited high in a tree's canopy by bats, birds, or monkeys. The young strangler then sends long roots down to the earth. The sap is used to relieve burns.

PRIME VIEWING   Primary and secondary forests countrywide.

Strangler Fig

SCIENTIFIC NAME   *Cecropia obtusifolia*

WORTH NOTING   Several **cecropia** (trumpet tree) species are found in Panama. Most are characterized by large, handlike clusters of broad leaves, and a hollow, bamboolike trunk. They are "gap specialists," fast-growing opportunists that can fill in a gap caused by a tree fall or landslide. Their trunks are usually home to Aztec ants.

PRIME VIEWING   Primary and secondary forests, rivers, and roadsides, countrywide.

Cecropia

Gumbo Limbo

SCIENTIFIC NAME   *Bursera simaruba*

WORTH NOTING   The bark of the **gumbo limbo** is its most distinguishing feature: A paper-thin red outer layer, when peeled off the tree, reveals a bright green bark. In Panama the tree is called *carate,* and the peeling bark is a defense against invasive vegetation like the strangler fig. The bark is used as a remedy for gum disease; gumbo-limbo–bark tea allegedly alleviates hypertension. Another remarkable property is the tree's ability to root from its cut branches, which when planted right end up, develop roots and leaves, forming a new tree within a few years.

PRIME VIEWING   Primary and secondary forests, countrywide.

FLOWERS & OTHER PLANTS

Panama's biodiversity is exemplified by its 10,000 species of plants.

SCIENTIFIC NAME   *Heliconia collinsiana*

WORTH NOTING   **Heliconias** are closely related to bananas and birds-of-paradise, and their beautiful, crab claw–shaped pink flowers are commonly used as ornamental decoration.

PRIME VIEWING   Low to middle elevations countrywide, usually found along streams and lakes.

Heliconia

Hotlips

SCIENTIFIC NAME   *Psychotria poeppigiana*

WORTH NOTING   Related to coffee, **hotlips** is a forest flower with thick red "lips" that resemble the Rolling Stones logo. The small white flowers (found inside the red "lips") attract a variety of butterflies and hummingbirds.

PRIME VIEWING   In the undergrowth of dense forests countrywide.

Poor Man's Umbrella

SCIENTIFIC NAME   *Gunnera insignis*

WORTH NOTING   The **poor man's umbrella,** a broad-leafed rainforest ground plant, is a member of the rhubarb family. The massive leaves are often used, as the colloquial name suggests, for protection during rainstorms.

PRIME VIEWING   Low- to middle-elevation moist forests countrywide. Commonly seen in the Chiriquí Highlands.

Index

See also Accommodations and Restaurant indexes, below.

FROMMER'S® COMPLETE TRAVEL GUIDES

Alaska	Florida	Portugal
Amalfi Coast	France	Prague & the Best of the Czech Republic
American Southwest	Germany	Provence & the Riviera
Amsterdam	Greece	Puerto Rico
Argentina & Chile	Greek Islands	Rome
Arizona	Hawaii	San Antonio & Austin
Atlanta	Hong Kong	San Diego
Australia	Honolulu, Waikiki & Oahu	San Francisco
Austria	India	Santa Fe, Taos & Albuquerque
Bahamas	Ireland	Scandinavia
Barcelona	Israel	Scotland
Beijing	Italy	Seattle
Belgium, Holland & Luxembourg	Jamaica	Seville, Granada & the Best of Andalusia
Belize	Japan	Shanghai
Bermuda	Kauai	Sicily
Boston	Las Vegas	Singapore & Malaysia
Brazil	London	South Africa
British Columbia & the Canadian Rockies	Los Angeles	South America
Brussels & Bruges	Los Cabos & Baja	South Florida
Budapest & the Best of Hungary	Madrid	South Pacific
Buenos Aires	Maine Coast	Southeast Asia
Calgary	Maryland & Delaware	Spain
California	Maui	Sweden
Canada	Mexico	Switzerland
Cancún, Cozumel & the Yucatán	Montana & Wyoming	Tahiti & French Polynesia
Cape Cod, Nantucket & Martha's Vineyard	Montréal & Québec City	Texas
Caribbean	Moscow & St. Petersburg	Thailand
Caribbean Ports of Call	Munich & the Bavarian Alps	Tokyo
Carolinas & Georgia	Nashville & Memphis	Toronto
Chicago	New England	Turkey
China	Newfoundland & Labrador	USA
Colorado	New Mexico	Utah
Costa Rica	New Orleans	Vancouver & Victoria
Croatia	New York City	Vermont, New Hampshire & Maine
Cuba	New York State	Vienna & the Danube Valley
Denmark	New Zealand	Vietnam
Denver, Boulder & Colorado Springs	Northern Italy	Virgin Islands
Edinburgh & Glasgow	Norway	Virginia
England	Nova Scotia, New Brunswick & Prince Edward Island	Walt Disney World® & Orlando
Europe	Oregon	Washington, D.C.
Europe by Rail	Paris	Washington State
Florence, Tuscany & Umbria	Peru	
	Philadelphia & the Amish Country	

FROMMER'S® DAY BY DAY GUIDES

Amsterdam	London	Rome
Chicago	New York City	San Francisco
Florence & Tuscany	Paris	Venice

PAULINE FROMMER'S GUIDES! SEE MORE. SPEND LESS.

Hawaii	Italy	New York City

FROMMER'S® PORTABLE GUIDES

Acapulco, Ixtapa & Zihuatanejo	Dublin	Rio de Janeiro
Amsterdam	Florence	San Diego
Aruba	Las Vegas	San Francisco
Australia's Great Barrier Reef	Las Vegas for Non-Gamblers	Savannah
Bahamas	London	St. Martin, Sint Maarten, Anguila & St. Bart's
Big Island of Hawaii	Maui	Turks & Caicos
Boston	Nantucket & Martha's Vineyard	Vancouver
California Wine Country	New Orleans	Venice
Cancún	New York City	Virgin Islands
Cayman Islands	Paris	Washington, D.C.
Charleston	Portland	Whistler
Chicago	Puerto Rico	
Dominican Republic	Puerto Vallarta, Manzanillo & Guadalajara	

FROMMER'S® CRUISE GUIDES

Alaska Cruises & Ports of Call

Cruises & Ports of Call

European Cruises & Ports of Call

FROMMER'S® NATIONAL PARK GUIDES

Algonquin Provincial Park
Banff & Jasper
Grand Canyon

National Parks of the American West
Rocky Mountain
Yellowstone & Grand Teton

Yosemite and Sequoia & Kings
 Canyon
Zion & Bryce Canyon

FROMMER'S® MEMORABLE WALKS

London
New York

Paris
Rome

San Francisco

FROMMER'S® WITH KIDS GUIDES

Chicago
Hawaii
Las Vegas
London

National Parks
New York City
San Francisco

Toronto
Walt Disney World® & Orlando
Washington, D.C.

SUZY GERSHMAN'S BORN TO SHOP GUIDES

France
Hong Kong, Shanghai & Beijing
Italy

London
New York

Paris
San Francisco

FROMMER'S® IRREVERENT GUIDES

Amsterdam
Boston
Chicago
Las Vegas

London
Los Angeles
Manhattan
Paris

Rome
San Francisco
Walt Disney World®
Washington, D.C.

FROMMER'S® BEST-LOVED DRIVING TOURS

Austria
Britain
California
France

Germany
Ireland
Italy
New England

Northern Italy
Scotland
Spain
Tuscany & Umbria

THE UNOFFICIAL GUIDES®

Adventure Travel in Alaska
Beyond Disney
California with Kids
Central Italy
Chicago
Cruises
Disneyland®
England
Florida
Florida with Kids

Hawaii
Ireland
Las Vegas
London
Maui
Mexico's Best Beach Resorts
Mini Mickey
New Orleans
New York City

Paris
San Francisco
South Florida including Miami &
 the Keys
Walt Disney World®
Walt Disney World® for
 Grown-ups
Walt Disney World® with Kids
Washington, D.C.

SPECIAL-INTEREST TITLES

Athens Past & Present
Best Places to Raise Your Family
Cities Ranked & Rated
500 Places to Take Your Kids Before They Grow Up
Frommer's Best Day Trips from London
Frommer's Best RV & Tent Campgrounds
 in the U.S.A.

Frommer's Exploring America by RV
Frommer's NYC Free & Dirt Cheap
Frommer's Road Atlas Europe
Frommer's Road Atlas Ireland
Great Escapes From NYC Without Wheels
Retirement Places Rated

FROMMER'S® PHRASEFINDER DICTIONARY GUIDES

French

Italian

Spanish

THE NEW TRAVELOCITY GUARANTEE

EVERYTHING YOU BOOK WILL BE RIGHT, OR WE'LL WORK WITH OUR TRAVEL PARTNERS TO MAKE IT RIGHT, RIGHT AWAY.

*To drive home the point,
we're going to use the word "right" in every single sentence.*

Let's get right to it. Right to the meat! Only Travelocity guarantees everything about your booking will be right, or we'll work with our travel partners to make it right, right away. Right on!

Here's a picture taken smack dab right in the middle of Antigua, where the guarantee also covers you.

The guarantee covers all but one of the items pictured to the right.

For example, what if the ocean view you booked actually looks out at a downright ugly parking lot? You'd be right to call – we're there for you. And no one in their right mind would be pleased to learn the rental car place has closed and left them stranded. Call Travelocity and we'll help get you back on the right track.

Now, you may be thinking, "Yeah, right, I'm so sure." That's OK; you have the right to remain skeptical. That is until we mention help is always right around the corner. Call us right off the bat, knowing that our customer service reps are there for you 24/7. Righting wrongs. Left and right.

Now if you're guessing there are some things we can't control, like the weather, well you're right. But we can help you with most things – to get all the details in righting,* visit **travelocity.com/guarantee.**

*Sorry, spelling things right is one of the few things not covered under the guarantee.

I'd give my right arm for a guarantee like this, although I'm glad I don't have to.

travelocity
You'll never roam alone.